Data Structures and the
Standard Template Library

Data Structures and the Standard Template Library

William J. Collins
Lafayette College

Boston   Burr Ridge, IL   Dubuque, IA   Madison, WI   New York   San Francisco   St. Louis
Bangkok   Bogotá   Caracas   Kuala Lumpur   Lisbon   London   Madrid   Mexico City
Milan   Montreal   New Delhi   Santiago   Seoul   Singapore   Sydney   Taipei   Toronto

McGraw-Hill Higher Education

A Division of The **McGraw-Hill** Companies

DATA STRUCTURES AND THE STANDARD TEMPLATE LIBRARY

Published by McGraw-Hill, a business unit of The McGraw-Hill Companies, Inc., 1221 Avenue of the Americas, New York, NY 10020. Copyright © 2003 by The McGraw-Hill Companies, Inc. All rights reserved. No part of this publication may be reproduced or distributed in any form or by any means, or stored in a database or retrieval system, without the prior written consent of The McGraw-Hill Companies, Inc., including, but not limited to, in any network or other electronic storage or transmission, or broadcast for distance learning.

Some ancillaries, including electronic and print components, may not be available to customers outside the United States.

This book is printed on acid-free paper.

International   1 2 3 4 5 6 7 8 9 0 QPD/QPD 0 9 8 7 6 5 4 3 2 1
Domestic   2 3 4 5 6 7 8 9 0 QPD/QPD 0 9 8 7 6 5 4 3

ISBN 0–07–236965–5
ISBN 0–07–115097–8 (ISE)

General manager: *Thomas E. Casson*
Publisher: *Elizabeth A. Jones*
Developmental editor: *Emily J. Lupash*
Executive marketing manager: *John Wannemacher*
Project manager: *Jane Mohr*
Senior production supervisor: *Sandy Ludovissy*
Coordinator of freelance design: *David W. Hash*
Cover designer: *Rokusek Design*
Senior supplement producer: *Stacy A. Patch*
Media technology senior producer: *Phillip Meek*
Compositor: *Lachina Publishing Services*
Typeface: *10/12.5 Times Roman*
Printer: *Quebecor World Fairfield, PA*

Library of Congress Cataloging-in-Publication Data

Collins, William J.
    Data structures and the standard template library / William J. Collins. — 1st ed.
        p.   cm.
    ISBN 0–07–236965–5
    1. Data structures (Computer science).   2. Standard template library.   I. Title.

    QA76.9.D35 C65   2003
    005.7′3—dc21   2001052187
                                                                             CIP

INTERNATIONAL EDITION ISBN 0–07–115097–8
Copyright © 2003. Exclusive rights by The McGraw-Hill Companies, Inc., for manufacture and export. This book cannot be re-exported from the country to which it is sold by McGraw-Hill. The International Edition is not available in North America.

www.mhhe.com

BRIEF CONTENTS

CONTENTS

A P P E N D I X 1
Mathematical Background 619

A P P E N D I X 2
The string Class 633

A P P E N D I X 3
Polymorphism 647

PREFACE

This book is intended for a course in data structures and algorithms. The implementation language is C++, and it is assumed that students have taken an introductory course in which that language was used. That course need not have been object-oriented, but it should have covered the fundamental statements and data types, as well as arrays and the basics of file processing.

THE STANDARD TEMPLATE LIBRARY

One of the distinctive features of this text is its reliance on the Standard Template Library—specifically, the implementation of that library provided by the Hewlett-Packard Company. There are several advantages to this approach. First, students will be working with code that has been extensively tested; they need not depend on modules created by the instructor or textbook author. Second, students will have the opportunity to study professionals' code, which is substantially more efficient—and succinct—than what students have seen before. Third, the library is available for later courses in the curriculum, and beyond!

For the most part, the library does not prescribe an implementation of these data structures. This has the advantage that we can initially focus on the services provided to users rather than on implementation details. For the definitions of these classes, we turn to the original implementation by Stepanov and others (see Stepanov and Lee, 1994) at Hewlett-Packard Research Labs. This Hewlett-Packard implementation is the basis for all implementations the author is aware of.

OTHER IMPLEMENTATIONS CONSIDERED

As important as the Hewlett-Packard implementation of the Standard Template Library is, it cannot be the exclusive focus of such a fundamental course in data structures and algorithms. Approaches that differ from those in the Hewlett-Packard implementation also deserve consideration. For example, the implementation of the list class utilizes a doubly linked list with a header node, so there is a separate section on singly linked lists and doubly linked lists with head and tail fields. There is also a discussion of the trade-offs of one design over the other. Also, there is coverage of data structures (such as graphs) and algorithms (such as backtracking) that are not yet included in the Standard Template Library.

This text also satisfies another essential need of a data structures and algorithms course: Students practice developing their own data structures. There are programming projects in which data structures are either created "from the ground up" or extended from examples in the chapters. And there are other projects to develop or extend applications that *use* the Standard Template Library.

STANDARD C++

All the code presented is based on ANSI/ISO Standard C++ and has been tested both on a Windows platform (C++Builder and Visual C++) and on a Unix platform (G++). The Standard Template Library specifications—but no particular implementation—are part of ANSI/ISO C++.

PEDAGOGICAL FEATURES

This text offers several features that may improve the teaching environment for instructors and the learning environment for students. Each chapter starts with a list of objectives and concludes with at least one major programming assignment. Each data structure is carefully described, with a precondition and postcondition for each method. In addition, most of the methods include examples of how to call the method, and the results of that call.

The details, especially of the Hewlett-Packard implementation of the Standard Template Library, are carefully investigated in the text and reinforced in a suite of 29 labs. See the "Organization of the Labs" section of this preface for more information about these labs. Each chapter has a variety of exercises, and the answers to all the exercises are available to the instructor.

SUPPORT MATERIAL

The website for all the support material is

www.mhhe.com/collins

That website has links to the following information for students:

- An overview of the labs and how to access them
- The source code for all projects developed in the text
- Applets for projects that have a strong visual component

Additionally, instructors can obtain the following from the website:

- Instructors' options with regard to the labs
- PowerPoint slides for each chapter (approximately 1500 slides)
- Answers to every chapter exercise, PowerPoint-presentation exercise, and lab experiment

SYNOPSES OF THE CHAPTERS

Chapter 1 presents those features of C++ that serve as the foundation for subsequent chapters. Most of the material reflects an object orientation: classes, inheritance, constructors, destructors, and operator overloading. There are lab experiments to review classes, as well as on inheritance and operator overloading.

Chapter 2 introduces container classes and issues related to the storage of containers. Pointers are needed both for contiguous and linked storage. As an illustration of linked storage, a singly-linked-list class is created. This oversimplified

Linked class provides a backdrop for presenting several key features of the Standard Template Library, such as templates, iterators, and generic algorithms. The associated lab experiments are on pointers, iterators, operator overloading, and generic algorithms.

Chapter 3, an introduction to software engineering, outlines the four stages of the software-development life cycle: analysis, design, implementation, and maintenance. The Unified Modeling Language is introduced as a design tool to depict inheritance, composition, and aggregation. Big-O notation, which pervades subsequent chapters, allows environment-independent estimates of the time requirements for methods. Both run-time validation, with drivers, and timing are discussed, and for each of those topics there is a follow-up lab.

Chapter 4, on recursion, represents a temporary shift in emphasis from data structures to algorithms. Backtracking is introduced, as a general technique for problem solving. And the same BackTrack class is used for searching a maze; placing eight queens on a chessboard, where none is under attack by another queen; and illustrating that a knight can traverse every square in a chessboard without landing on any square more than once. Other applications of recursion, such as for the Towers of Hanoi game and generating permutations, further highlight the elegance of recursion, especially when compared to the corresponding iterative methods. Recursion is also encountered in later chapters, notably in the implementation of Quick Sort and in the definition of binary trees. Moreover, recursion is an indispensable— even if seldom used—tool for every computing professional.

In Chapter 5, we begin our study of the Standard Template Library with the vector and deque classes. A vector is a smart array: automatically resizable, and with methods to handle insertions and deletions at any index. Furthermore, vectors are templated, so the method to insert an **int** item into a vector of **int** items is the same method used to insert a **string** item into a vector of string items. The design starts with the *method interface*—precondition, postcondition, and method heading—of the most widely used methods in the vector class. There follows an outline of the Hewlett-Packard implementation, and further details are available in a lab. The application of the vector class, high-precision arithmetic, is essential for public-key cryptography. This application is extended in a lab and in a programming project. A deque is similar to a vector, at least from a data structures perspective. But the implementation details are considerably different, and some of these details are investigated in a lab.

Chapter 6 presents the list data structure and class, characterized by linear-time methods for inserting, removing, or retrieving at an arbitrary position. This property makes a compelling case for the use of *list iterators:* objects that traverse a list object and have constant-time methods for inserting, removing, or retrieving at the "current" iterator position. The doubly linked, circular implementation is introduced in this chapter, and additional details are covered in a lab. The application is a small line editor, for which list iterators are well suited. This application is extended in a programming project. There is a lab experiment on iterator categories, and another to perform a run-time comparison of vectors, deques, and lists.

The queue and stack classes are the subjects of Chapter 7. Both of these classes are ***container adaptors:*** They adapt the method interfaces of some other class. For both the queue and stack classes, the default "other" class is the deque class. The resulting method definitions for the stack and queue classes are one-liners. The specific application of queues—calculating the average waiting time at a car wash— falls into the general category of *computer simulation.* There are two applications of the stack class: the implementation of recursion, and the conversion from infix to postfix. This latter application is expanded in a lab, and forms the basis for a project on evaluating a condition.

Chapter 8 focuses on binary trees in general, and binary search trees in particular. The essential features of binary trees are presented; these are important for understanding later material on AVL trees, red-black trees, heaps, Huffman trees, and decision trees. The binary-search-tree class is a monochromatic version of the Hewlett-Packard implementation of red-black trees.

In Chapter 9, we look at AVL trees. Rotations are introduced as the mechanism by which rebalancing is accomplished. With the help of Fibonacci trees, we establish that the height of an AVL tree is always logarithmic in the number of items in the tree. The AVLTree class is not part of the Standard Template Library, but includes several important features, such as function objects; there is a follow-up lab on this difficult topic. The entire class is implemented, except for the erase method (Project 9.1). The application of AVL trees is a simple spell-checker.

Red-black trees are investigated in Chapter 10. The algorithms for inserting and deleting in a red-black tree are carefully studied, and there are associated lab experiments. Red-black trees are not in the Standard Template Library, but they are the basis for most implementations of four associative-container classes that *are* in the Standard Template Library: the set, map, multiset, and multimap classes. In a set, each item consists of a key only, and duplicate keys are not allowed. A multiset allows duplicate keys. In a map, each item has a unique key part and also another part. A multimap allows duplicate keys. There is an application to count the frequency of each word in a file, and lab experiments on the four associative-container classes.

Chapter 11 introduces the priority_queue class, which is another container adaptor. The default is the vector class, but behind the scenes there is a heap, allowing insertions in constant average time, and removal of the highest-priority element in logarithmic time, even in the worst case. Implementations that are list-based and set-based are also considered. The application is in the area of data compression, specifically, Huffman encodings: Given a text file, generate a minimal, prefix-free encoding. The project assignment is to convert the encoding back to the original text file. The lab experiment incorporates fairness into a priority queue, so that ties for the highest-priority item are always resolved in favor of the item that was on the priority queue for the longest time.

Sorting is the topic of Chapter 12. Estimates of the minimum lower bounds for comparison-based sorts are developed. Four "fast" sorts are investigated: Tree Sort (for multisets), Heap Sort (for random-access containers), Merge Sort (for lists), and

Quick Sort (for random-access containers). The chapter's lab experiment compares these sorts on randomly generated values. The project assignment is to sort a file of names and social security numbers.

Chapter 13 starts with a review of sequential and binary searching, and then investigates hashing. Currently there are no hash classes supported by either Standard C++ or the Hewlett-Packard implementation of the Standard Template Library. A hash_map class is developed. This class has method interfaces that are identical to those in the map class, except that the average time for inserting, deleting, or searching is constant instead of logarithmic! Applications include the creation and maintenance of a symbol table, and a revision of the spell-checker application from Chapter 9. There is also a comparison of chained hashing and open-address hashing; this comparison is further explored in a programming project. The speed of the hash_map class is the subject of a lab experiment.

The most general data structures—graphs, trees, and networks—are presented in Chapter 14. There are outlines of the essential algorithms: breadth-first iteration, depth-first iteration, connectedness, finding a minimum spanning tree, and finding the shortest path between two vertices. The only class developed is the (directed) network class, with an adjacency-list implementation. Other classes, such as undirected_graph and undirected_network, can be straightforwardly defined as subclasses of the network class. The Traveling Salesperson problem is investigated in a lab, and there is a programming project to complete an adjacency-matrix version of the network class. Another backtracking application is presented, with the same BackTrack class that was introduced in Chapter 4.

With each chapter, there is an associated web page that includes all programs developed in the chapter, and applets, where appropriate, to animate the concepts presented.

APPENDICES

Appendix 1 contains the background that will allow students to comprehend the mathematical aspects of the chapters. Summation notation and the rudimentary properties of logarithms are essential, and the material on mathematical induction will lead to a deeper appreciation of the analysis of binary trees and open-address hashing.

The string class is the subject of Appendix 2. This powerful class is an important part of the Standard Template Library and allows students to avoid the drudgery of character arrays.

Polymorphism, the ability of a pointer to refer to different objects in an object hierarchy, is introduced in Appendix 3. Polymorphism is an essential feature of object-oriented programming, but has been relegated to appendix status because it is not a necessary topic in an introduction to data structures and algorithms.

ORGANIZATION OF THE LABS

There are 29 website labs associated with this text. For both students and instructors, the Uniform Resource Locator (URL) is

www.mhhe.com/collins

The labs do not contain essential material, but provide reinforcement of the text material. For example, after the vector, deque, and list classes have been investigated, there is a lab to perform some timing experiments on those three classes.

    The labs are self-contained, so the instructor has considerable flexibility in assigning the labs. They can be assigned as

1. Closed labs
2. Open labs
3. Ungraded homework

    In addition to the obvious benefit of promoting active learning, these labs also encourage use of the scientific method. Basically, each lab is set up as an experiment. Students *observe* some phenomenon, such as the organization of the Standard Template Library's list class. They then formulate and submit a *hypothesis*—with their own code—about the phenomenon. After *testing* and, perhaps, revising their hypothesis, they submit the *conclusions* they drew from the experiment.

ACKNOWLEDGMENTS

Chun Wai Liew initiated the study of the Standard Template Library at Lafayette College, and also contributed his general expertise in C++. The following reviewers made many helpful suggestions:

    Moe Bidgoli, *Saginaw Valley State University*
    Scott Cannon, *Utah State University*
    Jiang-Hsing Chu, *Southern Illinois University, Carbondale*
    Karen C. Davis, *University of Cincinnati*
    Matthew Evett, *Florida Atlantic University*
    Eduardo B. Fernandez, *Florida Atlantic State University*
    Sheila Foster, *California State University, Long Beach*
    Mahmood Haghighi, *Bradley University*
    Jack Hodges, *San Francisco State University*
    Robert A. Hogue, *Youngstown State University*
    Christopher Lacher, *Florida State University*
    Gopal Lakhani, *Texas Tech University*
    Tracy Bradley Maples, *California State University, Long Beach*

Nancy E. Miller, *Mississippi State University*
G. M. Prabhu, *Iowa State University*
Zhi-Li Zhang, *University of Minnesota*

It was a pleasure to work with the McGraw-Hill team: Emily Lupash, Betsy Jones, Jane Mohr, Lucy Mullins, and Philip Meek.

Several students from Lafayette College made important contributions. Eric Panchenko created all the applets and many of the driver programs. And Eric, along with Yi Sun and Xenia Taoubina, developed the overall format of the labs. Finally, I am indebted to all the students at Lafayette College who participated in the class testing of the book and endured earlier versions of the labs.

Bill Collins

1

Classes in C++

This is a book about programming: specifically, about understanding and using data structures and algorithms. The C++ Standard Template Library has a rich collection of both data structures and algorithms. Chapters 2 through 12 will focus on what the library is and how to use the library to simplify your programming efforts. For this information to make sense to you, you will need to be familiar with certain aspects of classes that are presented in this chapter. Some of what follows may be a review for you; some may be brand new. All the material is needed, either for the library itself or to enable you to use the library in your programming projects. ■

CHAPTER OBJECTIVES

1. Understand the fundamentals of classes, objects, and messages.

2. Compare a developer's view of a class with a user's view of that class.

3. Be able to apply the Principle of Data Abstraction, the Open-Closed Principle, and the Subclass Substitution Rule.

1.1 | CLASSES

A class combines variables with functions that act on those variables.

A *class* is a user-defined type consisting of a collection of variables—called *fields*—together with a collection of functions—called *methods*—that operate on those fields.[1] A class encapsulates the passive components (fields) and active components (methods) into a single entity. This encapsulation improves program modularity: by isolating a class from the rest of the program, we make the program easier to understand and to modify.

Suppose that in trying to solve some problem, we decide that we need to work with calendar dates. Let's assume that no such class is already available to us, so we will create a class called Date. The class Date will consist of one or more fields to hold a date, and methods that act on those fields. Initially, we need not worry about choosing the fields that will represent a date, nor the methods that will act on those fields. Since we, and maybe others after us, will be using Date, we first need to determine the *responsibilities* of the Date class. That is, what is the class expected to provide to its users? Assume the responsibilities are to

1. Construct a date, given a month, day, and year
2. Read in the month, day, and year of a date
3. Determine if a given date is valid
4. Return the next date after a given date
5. Return the date previous to a given date
6. Return the day of the week (such as Tuesday) on which a given date occurs
7. Determine if a given date is prior to some other date
8. Write out a date in the form *month-name, day, year*, such as May 10, 2004

1.1.1   Method Interfaces

A method interface provides everything a user needs to know about a method.

A class's responsibilities are refined into *method interfaces:* the explicit information a user will need in order to invoke the methods. Each method interface will have three parts: a precondition, a postcondition, and a method heading followed by a semicolon. A *precondition* is an assumption about the state of the program just prior to the execution of the method. A *postcondition* is a claim about the state of the program just after the execution of the method, provided the precondition was true beforehand.

For example, here is the method interface for the isValid method:

```
// Postcondition: true has been returned if this Date is legal: the year must be
//                an integer between 1800 and 2200, inclusive; the month
//                must be an integer between 1 and 12, inclusive; the day
//                must be an integer between 1 and the maximum number of
```

---

[1]"Fields" are also referred to as data members, member variables, instance variables, or attributes. "Methods" are also known as member functions, services, or operations.

```
//                  days for the given month and year, inclusive. Otherwise,
//                  false has been returned.
bool isValid( );
```

There is no precondition given because nothing special is assumed about the state of the program prior to a call to the method. Technically, the precondition is simply **true**. But we will omit writing the precondition when that occurs. Every method should accomplish something, so the postcondition will always be given explicitly. In order to clarify the phrase "this Date" in the postcondition, we need to define the term "object," the basis for object-oriented programming.

1.1.2   Objects

Given a class, an *object*—sometimes called an *instance* of the class—is a variable that has the fields of and can call the methods of that class. For example, if we define

```
Date myDate;
```

then myDate is an object of type Date. If we later write

```
if (myDate.isValid( ))
        cout << "The date is valid.";
else
        cout << "The date is not valid.";
```

then the object myDate is invoking its isValid method. For that reason, myDate is referred to as the *calling object:* the object that calls the method.

Within the postcondition of the isValid method, the phrase "this Date" refers to the calling object. So the **bool** value returned depends on the current value of the calling object. For example, suppose for the object myDate, the values of the fields represent March 17, 2003. Then the invocation

```
myDate.isValid( )
```

will return the value **true**. But if myDate's fields represent April 31, 2003, the invocation

```
myDate.isValid( )
```

will return **false**.

In general, the syntax for a method invocation consists of an object followed by a dot followed by the method identifier followed by a parenthesized argument list. In object-oriented parlance, a *message* is the invocation of a method by an object. For example, myDate.next( ) returns the date that immediately follows the calling object's date. In this message, the object myDate is invoking the next method in the Date class. The term "message" is meant to suggest that a communication is being sent from one part of a program to another part. For example, the message this Date.next( ) may be sent from a method in some class other than the Date class.

When we refine the responsibilities for Date's methods, we get the following method interfaces:

```
// Postcondition: this Date has been constructed from month, day,
//                and year.
Date (int month, int day, int year);
```

> *Note*   An explanation of this method and a sample message are given in Section 1.1.4.

```
// Postcondition: this Date's date has been set from the month, day, and year
//                read in.
void readInto( );
```

> *Example*   Suppose we have the following:
>
> Date lastDate;
>
> lastDate.readInto( );
>
> If the input line contains
>
> 12 1 2003
>
> then the value of lastDate's fields will represent the date December 1, 2003.

```
// Postcondition: true has been returned if this Date is legal: the year must be
//                an integer between 1800 and 2200, inclusive; the month
//                must be an integer between 1 and 12, inclusive; the day
//                must be an integer between 1 and the maximum number of
//                days for the given month and year, inclusive. Otherwise,
//                false has been returned.
bool isValid( );
```

> *Example*   Suppose currentDate is an object in the class Date. If the values of the fields in that object represent February 29, 2004, then currentDate.isValid( ) would return the value true. But if the values of the fields in currentDate represent February 29, 2005, then current Date.isValid( ) would return **false**.

```
// Precondition: this Date is valid.
// Postcondition: the Date just after this Date has been returned.
Date next( );
```

Example Suppose date is an object in the class Date. If the values of that object's fields represent February 29, 2000, then the message date.next( ) would return a value representing March 1, 2000. What would happen if date had an invalid value and date.next( ) were called? Because an invalid date would not satisfy the precondition, the result would be undefined. That is, there may be no date returned, a nonsense date returned, a program crash, etc. The user of a class has the responsibility of making sure a method's precondition is satisfied before calling the method. For example, a user could proceed as follows:

```
if (date.isValid( ))
        . . . date.next( ) . . .
else
        cout << "Invalid date" << endl;
```

```
// Precondition: this Date is valid.
// Postcondition: the Date just before this Date has been returned.
Date previous( );
```

```
// Precondition: this Date is valid.
// Postcondition: the day of the week—"Sunday", "Monday", and so on—on
//                which this Date falls has been returned.
string dayOfWeek( );
```

Example Suppose meetingDate is an object in the Date class, and meetingDate has been constructed so that its fields represent the date June 12, 2003. Then the message

```
meetingDate.dayOfWeek( )
```

will return "Thursday".

Note The string class is part of ANSI Standard C++, so we will use it freely throughout the text and labs. Appendix 2 explains this class in detail; please read that appendix now if you are unfamiliar with this very important class.

```
// Precondition: this Date and otherDate are valid dates.
// Postcondition: true has been returned if this Date precedes otherDate.
//                Otherwise, false has been returned.
bool isPriorTo (Date otherDate);
```

Example   Suppose that currentDate is a Date object whose field values represent March 27, 2003, and that startDate is a Date object whose fields represent January 1, 2004. Then

currentDate.isPriorTo (startDate)

will return **true**.

```
// Precondition: this Date is valid.
// Postcondition: this Date has been written out in the form month-name day,
//                year.
void print( );
```

Example   Suppose newDate is an object in the Date class, and the values of newDate's fields represent the date January 28, 2003. If we have

newDate.print( );

the output will be

January 28, 2003

This view of a class has been from the user's perspective, focusing on information needed by users of the class. In Section 1.1.3, we will look at the developer's perspective and compare the two perspectives.

1.1.3   Data Abstraction

Data abstraction is the separation of what a class provides to users from how the class is defined.

So far, we have concentrated on method interfaces, that is, *what* the class provides to programmers, rather than on the class's fields and method definitions, that is, *how* the class is defined. This separation—called ***data abstraction***—of *what* from *how* is an essential feature of object-oriented programming. Programmers who use the Date class will not care about how a date is represented or how the methods are defined. The fields—that is, the representation of the date—may take one of the following forms, or may be something entirely different:

> **int** *fields* month, day, *and* year: with values such as "2" for month, "28" for day, and "2002" for year
>
> *A seven-digit or eight digit* **long** *field* theDate: with values such as "1042005" (for January 4, 2005) and "10042005" (for October 4, 2005)
>
> *An eight-character string field* theDate: with values such as "02282002"
>
> *A ten-character string field* theDate: with values such as "02-28-2002"

What would be wrong with a six-character string field theDate—with values such as "022802"?

Similarly, there may be a choice of method definitions for some of the methods. For example, the definition of the isValid( ) method may use a **switch** statement or a sequence of **else-if** statements:

```
if (month == 4 || month == 6 || month == 9 || month == 11)
        return 30; // 30 days hath September, April, June and November
else if (month == 1 || month == 3 || month == 5 || month == 7 ||
        month == 8 || month == 10 || month == 12)
        return 31; // January, March, May, July, August, October, December
else if (year % 4 != 0 || (year % 100 == 0 && year % 400 != 0))
        return  28; // one year is slightly less than 365.25 days
    return 29;
```

A complete Date-class oriented project, including a specific implementation of the Date class, is available from the Source Code link on the book's website.

Such details as the field and method definitions would be a distraction when you are trying to develop a class that *uses* the Date class. It may be that someone else has already completed the definition of the Date class. Then you should use that Date class, rather than creating extra work for yourself. But even if you must define the Date class yourself, you can postpone that work until after you have completed the development of the classes that use the Date class. By working with Date's method interfaces, you increase the independence of those other classes: their effectiveness will not be affected by any changes to the Date class that do not affect the method interfaces.

When programmers focus on what the class provides rather than on the implementation details of that class, they are applying the Principle of Data Abstraction:

Principle of Data Abstraction

A user's code should not access the implementation details of the class used.

One important aspect of the Principle of Data Abstraction is that if class A uses class B, then class A's methods should not access class B's fields. In fact, class B's fields should be accessed only in class B's methods. For example, suppose the following definition is made *outside* of the Date class:

```
Date currentDate;
```

Then an expression such as

```
currentDate.month
```

would be a violation of the Principle of Data Abstraction because whether or not the Date class has a month field is an implementation detail. Even if the Date class has a month field, the developer is free to make any changes to the Date class that do not affect the method interfaces. For example, the developer could modify the Date class to have a single field:

```
string theDate;
```

The Principle of Data Abstraction is a benefit to users of a class because they are freed from reliance on implementation details of that class. This assumes, of course, that the class's method interfaces provide all the information that a user of that class needs. The developer of a class should create methods with sufficient functionality that users need not rely on any implementation details. That functionality should be clearly spelled out in the method interfaces.

The precondition and postcondition of a method are part of an implicit *contract* between the developer and the user. The terms of the contract are as follows:

> If the user of the method ensures that the precondition is true before the method is invoked, the developer guarantees that the postcondition will be true at the end of the execution of the method.

We can summarize our discussion of classes so far by saying that from the *developer's* perspective, a class consists of fields and the definitions of methods that act on those fields. A *user's* view is an abstraction of this: A class consists of method interfaces.

The Standard Template Library is, basically, a collection of thoroughly tested classes that are useful in a variety of applications. The applications and most of the assigned projects will *use* the Standard Template Library, so they will rely only on the method interfaces, not on the definitions of that library's methods.

1.1.4   Constructors

C++ allows the definition of an object to include the initialization of the object. This relieves the programmer of the burden of remembering to initialize the object. The mechanism for defining-plus-initializing is the ***constructor:*** a special method in a class that has the same name as the class. Each time an object in a class is defined, a constructor for that class is invoked automatically. For example, we can construct a Date object as follows:

```
Date startDate (7, 1, 2003);
```

The syntax is a bit unusual: the class identifier followed by the object identifier followed by a parenthesized argument list. The fields in the object startDate now represent the date July 1, 2003. The definition of this constructor method depends on the fields in the Date class. For example, if the Date class has **int** fields month, day, and year, we could have the following definition:

```
Date (int monthIn, int dayIn, int yearIn)
{
     month = monthIn;
     day = dayIn;
     year = yearIn;
} // 3-parameter constructor
```

Alternatively, if the Date class has a single field;

    long theDate;

the definition of the constructor could then have a single (obscure) assignment statement:

```
Date (int monthIn, int dayIn, int yearIn)
{
        theDate = ((monthIn * 100) + dayIn) * 10000 + yearIn;
} // 3-parameter constructor
```

This discussion raises a question: What happens if an object is defined without this constructor? Then the Date class must also define a zero-parameter constuctor. For example, suppose we have the following:

    Date today; // note: no parentheses after today

    today.readInto( );

In this case, a zero-parameter constructor is called—even though there are no parentheses in the definition of today. For example, if the Date class has **int** fields month, day, and year, we might have the following definition:

```
// Postcondition: This Date object has been initialized to January 1, 1800.
Date( ) // note that parentheses are required here
{
        month = 1;
        day = 1;
        year = 1800;
} // zero-parameter constructor
```

That is, this constructor will initialize today's date to January 1, 1800. This initial value will then be overwritten when the readInto method is invoked.

What if a class does not explicitly define any constructor? Then a zero-parameter constructor is automatically generated by the compiler. For this reason, a zero-parameter constructor is called a ***default constructor.*** But if a class defines *any* constructors, the compiler will not generate a default constructor. In that case, unless one of the constructors is the default constructor, every instance of that class must be defined using a constructor that has at least one parameter. To be on the safe side, when you define a class that has any constructors, you should explicitly define a default constructor. Section 1.1.9 provides another reason for this precaution.

A default constructor is a constructor with no parameters.

A constructor, with or without parameters, does not automatically initialize the fields in the class, so explicit code must be written to initialize an **int** field, for example. An exception is made for each ***object field,*** that is, a field whose type is itself a class. Object fields are initialized according to the appropriate constructor for that class. For example, suppose a Calendar class has two fields:

    Date startDate,
        endDate (12, 31, 2200);

If we declare

    Calendar calendar;

the default constructor for the Calendar class is invoked. At the beginning of the execution of that constructor, the startDate field of the Calendar object calendar will be initialized to represent January 1, 1800, and the endDate field will be initialized to represent December 31, 2200.

Section 1.1.5 continues our discussion of method interfaces, method definitions, and constructors with another example.

1.1.5   An Employee **Class**

For another example of a class, let's create a class called Employee for the employees in a company. The information available on each employee consists of the employee's name and gross pay. The responsibilities of the Employee class are to

1.   Initialize an employee's name to an empty string and gross pay to 0.00
2.   Read in an employee's name and gross pay
3.   Determine if the input sentinel has been reached (name of "*", gross pay of −1.00)
4.   Determine if an employee's gross pay is greater than some other employee's gross pay
5.   Get a copy of an employee's name and gross pay
6.   Write out an employee's name and gross pay

From these responsibilities, we develop the method interfaces:

```
// Postcondition: this Employee's name has been set to the empty string and
//                this Employee's gross pay has been set to 0.00.
Employee( );

// Postcondition: this Employee's name and gross pay have been read in.
void readInto( );

// Postcondition: true has been returned if this Employee contains the
//                sentinels. Otherwise, false has been returned.
bool isSentinel( ) const;

// Postcondition: true has been returned if this Employee's gross pay is
//                greater than that of otherEmployee. Otherwise, false has
//                been returned.
bool makesMoreThan (const Employee& otherEmployee) const;

// Postcondition: this Employee contains a copy of otherEmployee.
void getCopyOf (const Employee& otherEmployee);
```

Note What is returned is a distinct copy of otherEmployee. For example, suppose the input contains

Smith,John 100000.00
Siddiqi,Amena 120000.00

and we have the following statements:

Employee oldEmployee,
        newEmployee;

newEmployee.readInto( );
oldEmployee.getCopyOf (newEmployee);
newEmployee.readInto( );

Then after the first call to readInto, we have

newEmployee

Smith,John	100000.00

oldEmployee

	0.00

After the getCopyOf method is invoked, we have

newEmployee

Smith,John	100000.00

oldEmployee

Smith,John	100000.00

Finally, the second invocation of readInto gives us

newEmployee

Siddiqi,Amena	120000.00

oldEmployee

Smith,John	100000.00

// Postcondition: this Employee's name and gross pay have been
//   written out.
void printOut( ) **const**;

The Employee class's method interfaces are all that will be needed by programmers who use the Employee class. A developer of the class, on the other hand, must decide what fields to have and then define the methods. For example, the developer may well decide to have two fields: the employee's name (a string) and grossPay (a **double**). The method headings and fields (with their types) constitute a *class declaration.*

The file that contains a class declaration is referred to as a ***header file.*** Here is the header file, employee1.h, that includes the class declaration of the Employee class:

```
#ifndef EMPLOYEE
#define EMPLOYEE

#include <string>

using namespace std;

class Employee
{
    public:

        // Postcondition: this Employee's name has been set to the empty
        //                string and this Employee's gross pay has been
        //                set to 0.00.
        Employee( );

        // Postcondition: this Employee's name and gross pay have been
        //                read in.
        void readInto( );

        // Postcondition: The value true has been returned if this
        //                Employee is the sentinel. Otherwise, false has
        //                been returned.
        bool isSentinel( ) const;

        // Postcondition: this Employee's name and gross pay have been
        //                written out.
        void printOut( ) const;

        // Postcondition: this Employee has a copy of otherEmployee.
        void getCopyOf (const Employee& otherEmployee);

        // Postcondition: The value true has been returned if this
        //                Employee's gross pay is greater than
        //                otherEmployee's gross pay. Otherwise, false has
        //                been returned.
        bool makesMoreThan (const Employee& otherEmployee) const;
```

```
    private:

            string name;
            double grossPay;

            const static string EMPTY_STRING;
            const static string NAME_SENTINEL;
            const static double GROSS_PAY_SENTINEL;
}; // Employee
#endif
```

Let's look at this file in detail. Every line that starts with the symbol "#" contains a ***compiler directive:*** a message to the compiler. The first two lines,

```
#ifndef EMPLOYEE
#define EMPLOYEE
```

inform the compiler that if the identifier EMPLOYEE has not yet been defined (**if n**ot **def**ined) in this project, then EMPLOYEE is hereby defined. The reason for these directives is to avoid any attempts to redeclare an identifier—redeclaring an identifier is an error. So if this file—specifically the identifier EMPLOYEE—has not yet been encountered by the compiler, then the file will be compiled. Otherwise, the entire file, all the way down to

```
#endif
```

will be ignored by the compiler. So no redeclaration will occur even if several files in the project have

```
#include "employee1.h"
```

The next compiler directive,

```
#include <string>
```

informs the compiler to include the Standard Template Library's string class in this project. Appendix 2 covers that class in detail. For now, all you need to know is that you can define a string object, and then use that object for reading, writing, assigning, and comparing. For example,

```
string s;

cin >> s;
cout << s;
s = "yes";
if (s < "wow")
while (s != "end")
if (s [0] > 'm') // if the character at index 0 of s is > 'm'
. . .
```

There is one more preliminary feature we need to discuss before we can get to the Employee class itself. The identifiers—such as string—in the Standard Template Library are grouped together into what is called the std namespace. The ***using*** *directive* consists of the keywords **using** and **namespace** followed by a given namespace. In particular,

   using namespace std;

informs the compiler that the std namespace is being used, so string refers to the class defined in the Standard Template Library, even if another file in this project defined its own string identifier.

   Now we can focus on the Employee class. Employee has been declared to be a class—**class** is a keyword—with six methods, two fields, and three constant identifiers. Note that the closing of a **class** (or **struct**) declaration *must* be followed by a semicolon.

   Methods are distinguished from fields (and other identifiers) by the presence of parentheses, so the parentheses are required even for a method that has no formal parameters.

   There are some other noteworthy features of this class declaration:

■ The constructor

   Employee( );

   As we saw in Section 1.1.4, a constructor relieves a user of a class of the burden of performing explicit initializations of objects. The initialization is automatically performed when the object is defined, such as

   Employee bestPaid;

   A constructor has the same name as the class, and no return type. A constructor without parameters is referred to as a *default constructor* because if you do not define any constructors, the C++ compiler will automatically supply a zero-parameter constructor (just to legalize definitions such as the one given for bestPaid).

A constant reference parameter provides both efficiency and security.

■ In the getCopyOf method, otherEmployee is a ***constant reference parameter.*** As a reference parameter—indicated by the ampersand—only the address of the corresponding argument is sent when the method is called, so no copy of that argument is made. This saves both time and space. Also, because of the keyword **const**, it would be illegal to modify otherEmployee within the getCopyOf method. This provides security that the corresponding argument will not be modified.

■ The keyword **const** also appears at the end of the heading for the isSentinel, printOut, and makesMoreThan methods. This guarantees that those methods will not modify the calling object. In the makesMoreThan method, the parameter otherEmployee is, again, a constant reference parameter.

■ Note the keyword **public** followed by a colon in the declaration of Employee. In C++, different members (that is, fields, constants, and methods) of a class can have different levels of protection that specify which kinds of code can access that particular member. Another level of protection is indicated by using **private**: (don't forget the colon!). This level of protection allows only methods of that class to access the member. The default protection level if you do not specify one is **private**.

■ The name and grossPay fields are **private**, so these fields cannot be accessed outside of the Employee class's methods.

■ EMPTY_STRING, NAME_SENTINEL, and GROSS_PAY_SENTINEL are *class-constant* identifiers: they apply to all instances of the Employee class rather than to an individual instance. It makes sense that there should be just one copy of GROSS_PAY_SENTINEL, for example, rather than a copy for each instance of the Employee class. To specify that these are class-related, not object-related, the keyword **static** is part of the declaration. The constant values are supplied in the class definition, which is described in Section 1.1.6.

1.1.6   Definition of the Employee **Class**

The file that contains a class definition is referred to as a *source file.* To define a class, we must provide definitions for its methods and class constants. A method definition is a complete function: heading plus body. Here is the source file, employee1. cpp, which contains the class definition for Employee:

```
#include <iostream>

#include <iomanip> // declares output formatting objects

#include "employee1.h" // declares Employee class

Employee::Employee( )
{
      name = EMPTY_STRING;
      grossPay = 0.00;
} // default constructor

void Employee::readInto( )
{
      const string NAME_AND_PAY_PROMPT =
            "Please enter a name and gross pay, to quit, enter ";

      cout << NAME_AND_PAY_PROMPT << NAME_SENTINEL << " "
            < GROSS_PAY_SENTINEL;
      cin > > name > > grossPay;
} // readInto

bool Employee::isSentinel( ) const
{
      if (name == NAME_SENTINEL && grossPay ==
```

```
                          GROSS_PAY_SENTINEL)
            return true;
        return false;
    } // isSentinel

    void Employee::printOut( ) const
    {
        cout << name << " $" << setiosflags (ios::fixed) << setprecision (2)
                    << grossPay << endl;
    } // printOut

    void Employee::getCopyOf (const Employee& otherEmployee)
    {
        name = otherEmployee.name;
        grossPay = otherEmployee.grossPay;
    } // getCopyOf

    bool Employee::makesMoreThan (const Employee& otherEmployee) const
    {
        return grossPay > otherEmployee.grossPay;
    } // makesMoreThan

    const string Employee::EMPTY_STRING = ""; // static not used here
    const string Employee::NAME_SENTINEL = "*";
    const double Employee::GROSS_PAY_SENTINEL = −1.0;
```

The **public** level of protection allows access by any piece of code. The methods of a class are usually made **public**, since they are what we want other pieces of code to call when using the class. For Employee objects, any piece of code can call the constructor and the other methods: isSentinel, readInto, writeOut, getCopyOf, and makesMoreThan.

To distinguish a class's methods from other functions, a qualifier is required. The qualifier consists of the class name followed by, not one, but two colons. So the method definition for readInto, for example, starts out with

```
    void Employee::readInto( )
```

This heading designates that readInto is a method in the Employee class. The two consecutive colons are known as the *scope-resolution operator:* the left operand is the class and the right operand is the member of that class. The scope-resolution operator removes any possibility of ambiguity about the readInto identifier, even if there were a nonmethod function called readInto or even another class in that file with a readInto identifier.

Notice that the definition of a class-constant identifier provides its value. The scope-resolution operator must be included, but the keyword static is omitted.

Within a method definition, the fields and methods of the calling object are accessed without the class identifier. So when you see a field all by itself in a method definition, that field is assumed to be a field in the object that called the method. Of course, class constants also appear without a calling object, but that is because they are associated with the class itself, not an instance of the class.

None of these implementation details would be of interest to a *user* of the Employee class. For example, suppose we want to find the best-paid employee in a company. For this application, we will develop a Company class that uses the Employee class. The responsibilities of the Company class are to construct a company and to find and print out the name and gross pay of that company's best-paid employee, that is, of the employee with the largest gross pay. We refine these responsibilities into method interfaces for a default constructor, findBestPaid and printBest Paid methods:

```
// Postcondition: this Company has been initialized.
Company( );

// Postcondition: this Company's best-paid employee has been determined.
void findBestPaid( );

// Postcondition: this Company's best-paid employee has been printed out.
void printBestPaid( ) const;
```

The details of these Company methods, and the main function that starts everything, are in Lab 1.

LAB   **Lab 1: The** Company **project.**

(All Labs Are Optional.)   **LAB**

As noted in Section 1.1.3, we should use existing classes whenever possible. What if a class has most, but not all, of the methods needed for an application? We could simply scrap the existing class and develop our own, but that would be time-consuming and inefficient. Another option is to copy the needed parts of the class and incorporate those parts into a new class that we develop. The danger with that option is that those parts may be incorrect or inefficient. If the developer of the original class replaces the incorrect or inefficient code, our class would still be erroneous or inefficient. A better alternative is to use inheritance, which is explained in Section 1.1.7.

1.1.7 Inheritance

We should strive to write program components that are reusable. For example, instead of defining a function that calculates the mean of 10 values, it would be better to define a function that calculates the mean of any number of values. By writing reusable code, we not only save time, but we also avoid the risk of incorrectly modifying the existing code.

*Inheritance is the
ability to define a new
class that includes all
the fields and some or
all of the methods of
an existing class.*

One way that reusability can be applied to classes is through a special and powerful property of classes: inheritance. ***Inheritance*** is the ability to define a new class that includes all the fields and some or all of the methods of an existing class. The previously existing class is called the ***superclass, base class,*** or ***ancestor class.*** The new class, which may declare new fields and methods, is called the ***subclass***, ***derived class,*** or ***descendant class.*** A subclass may also ***override*** existing methods by giving them method definitions that differ from those in the superclass.

As an example of how inheritance works, let's start with the class Employee. Suppose that several applications use Employee. A new application involves finding the best-paid *hourly* employee. For this application, the input consists of the employee's name, hours worked (an **int**), and pay rate (a **double**). The gross pay is the hours worked times the pay rate.

We could alter Employee by adding hoursWorked and payRate fields and modifying the readInto and isSentinel methods. But it is risky to modify, for the sake of a new application, a class that is being used successfully in existing applications. The underlying concept is known as the Open-Closed Principle:

> **The Open-Closed Principle**
> Every class should be open—that is, able to be extended through inheritance—and closed—that is, stable for existing applications.

In particular, the Employee class should not be altered for the sake of the new application. Instead of rewriting Employee, we will develop HourlyEmployee, a subclass of Employee. Each object in HourlyEmployee will have the information from Employee—name and gross pay—as well as hours worked and pay rate. The makes MoreThan, getCopyOf, and printOut methods need not be changed, because an object in the HourlyEmployee class can invoke those methods just as an Employee object did. After all, an hourly employee *is* an employee! Here are the interfaces for the new HourlyEmployee versions of the readInto and isSentinel methods.

```
// Postcondition: this HourlyEmployee's name, hours worked and pay rate
//                have been read in, and the gross pay has been calculated.
void readInto( );
```

```
// Postcondition: true has been returned if this HourlyEmployee contains the
//                sentinels. Otherwise, false has been returned.
bool isSentinel( ) const;
```

Before we can get to the complete declaration and definition of the HourlyEmployee class, we need to see how subclass methods are able to access superclass members.

1.1.8   Protected Access

Recall that the default protection level in a class declaration is **private** and that the only code that can access any **private** fields or methods is the code of the class methods themselves. In particular, this implies that methods of any subclasses cannot access these **private** fields or methods. We could make these fields and methods **public**, but then any code—even from another class—would have access, which is not what we want either. To handle the case of subclass code access, the **protected** level of protection is used.

Here's how **protected** works. Suppose x is a member—that is, a field, constant, or method—of class A. If we write

protected:

before the declaration of x, then any of A's methods can access x, and *any method of any subclass of* A *can access* x, but no other code can access x.

Since we would like to promote reusability in the form of subclassing, usually the fields and class constants of a class are given **protected**, rather than **private**, access. For this reason, we have revised the Employee class declaration to give the fields and class constants **protected** rather than **private** status:

```cpp
#ifndef EMPLOYEE
#define EMPLOYEE

#include <string>

using namespace std;

class Employee
{
    public:
    // Postcondition: this Employee's name has been set to "" and gross
    //                pay to 0.00.
    Employee( );

    // Postcondition: the value true has been returned if this Employee is
    //                the sentinel. Otherwise, false has been returned.
    bool isSentinel( ) const;

    // Postcondition: the name and gross pay of this Employee have been
    //                read in.
    void readInto( );

    // Postcondition: this Employee's name and gross pay have been
    //                written out.
    void printOut( ) const;

    // Postcondition: this Employee contains a copy of otherEmployee.
    void getCopyOf (const Employee& otherEmployee);

    // Postcondition: the value true has been returned if this Employee's
    //                gross pay is greater than otherEmployee's gross pay.
```

```
        //             Otherwise, false has been returned.
        bool makesMoreThan (const Employee& otherEmployee) const;

    protected:

        string name;
        double grossPay;

        const static string EMPTY_STRING;
        const static string NAME_SENTINEL;
        const static double GROSS_PAY_SENTINEL;

    }; // Employee
    #endif
```

Incidentally, this change to the Employee class not only does not violate the Open-Closed Principle, the change is mandated by that principle, so that the Employee class can be legitimately subclassed.

To summarize, the most restrictive level of protection is private: accessible only to methods of the class. A somewhat less restrictive level of protection is protected: accessible only to methods of the class and its subclasses. The least restrictive level of protection is public: accessible to any code.

*A **protected** member of a class is accessible only within the methods of that class and its subclasses.*

We can now return to the development of a class for hourly employees.

1.1.9   The HourlyEmployee **Class**

In general, the declaration of a subclass begins as follows:

```
    class <subclass identifier> : public <superclass identifier>
```

Here the reserved word **public** means that the protection level of each superclass member determines its accessibility within the subclass's methods. That is, **public** and **protected** members of the superclass can be accessed by any subclass method, and **private** members of the superclass are inaccessible in the subclass methods.

Except for this feature, the rest of the HourlyEmployee class declaration has the same format as a normal class declaration, and declares or defines only the new fields and new or overriding methods of the subclass. The fields and class constants are given **protected**—instead of **private**—status for the sake of potential subclasses of HourlyEmployee. Here is the declaration of HourlyEmployee:

```
    #ifndef HOURLY_EMPLOYEE
    #define HOURLY_EMPLOYEE

    #include "employee1.h"

    class HourlyEmployee : public Employee
    {
        public:

        // Postcondition: this HourlyEmployee has been initialized.
```

```
HourlyEmployee( );

// Postcondition: this HourlyEmployee's name, hours worked and
//      pay rate have been read in.
void readInto( );

// Postcondition: true has been returned if the sentinels were read in.
//                  Otherwise, false has been returned.
bool isSentinel( ) const;

protected:
        int hoursWorked;
        double payRate;

        const static int HOURS_WORKED_SENTINEL;
        const static double PAY_RATE_SENTINEL;
}; // HourlyEmployee

#endif
```

What about the name and grossPay fields from the Employee class? They will be initialized by the Employee class's default constructor. Whenever any subclass constructor is called, the superclass's default constructor is automatically called.[2] This ensures that, at least, all the superclass's object fields will be properly initialized.

Here is the source file, hourlyEmployee2.cpp:

```
#include <iostream>

#include "hourlyEmployee2.h"

HourlyEmployee::HourlyEmployee( ) { }

void HourlyEmployee::readInto( )
{
        const string NAME_HOURS_RATE_PROMPT =
                "Please enter a name, hours worked and pay rate. The sentinels
                        are ";

        cout << NAME_HOURS_RATE_PROMPT << NAME_SENTINEL <<
                " "
                << HOURS_WORKED_SENTINEL << " " <<
                        PAY_RATE_SENTINEL << ": ";

        cin > > name > > hoursWorked > > payRate;

        grossPay = hoursWorked * payRate;
```

---

[2]A compile-time error message is generated if the superclass has defined at least one constructor but no default constructor.

```
} // readInto

bool HourlyEmployee::isSentinel( ) const
{
    if (name == NAME_SENTINEL
            && hoursWorked == HOURS_WORKED_SENTINEL
            && payRate == PAY_RATE_SENTINEL)
        return true;
        return false;
} // isSentinel

const int HourlyEmployee::HOURS_WORKED_SENTINEL = −1;
const double HourlyEmployee::PAY_RATE_SENTINEL = −1.00;
```

We want to find and print out the name of the best-paid hourly employee in a company. Just as we have created HourlyEmployee, a subclass of Employee, we need to create Company2, a subclass of Company. Why? Because the Company class makes no mention of an HourlyEmployee. We can easily remedy that problem in Company2, a user of HourlyEmployee. To Company2, all that matter are Hourly Employee's method interfaces. Company2 differs from Company in only one respect: the findBestPaid method is overridden because the employee object in that method is defined as

```
HourlyEmployee employee;
```

instead of

```
Employee employee;
```

Here is the declaration of Company2:

```
#ifndef COMPANY2
#define COMPANY2

#include "company1.h"

class Company2 : public Company
{
    public:
        // Postcondition: The hourly employee with the highest gross pay
        //                has been determined. Ties have been ignored.
        void findBestPaid( );
}; // Company2

#endif
```

And here is the definition of Company2:

```
#include "company2.h"
#include "hourlyEmployee2.h"
```

```
void Company2::findBestPaid( )
{
        HourlyEmployee employee;

        employee.readInto( );
        if (!employee.isSentinel( ))
        {
                atLeastOneEmployee = true;
                while (!employee.isSentinel( ))
                {
                        if (employee.makesMoreThan (bestPaid))
                                bestPaid.getCopyOf (employee);
                        employee.readInto( );
                } // while
        } // input does not start with sentinel
} // findBestPaid
```

One curiosity of this method is in the line

        bestPaid.getCopyOf (employee);

The Employee class's getCopyOf method, which is not overridden, specifies that the formal parameter is of type Employee. But when getCopyOf is called in the definition of findBestPaid in Company2, the argument employee is of type HourlyEmployee, not of type Employee. Because HourlyEmployee is a subclass of Employee, wherever an Employee object is called for in an expression, an HourlyEmployee object can be substituted. This is an application of the Subclass Substitution Rule:

Subclass Substitution Rule

Wherever a superclass object is called for in an expression, a subclass object may be substituted.

The Subclass Substitution Rule makes sense if you keep in mind that a subclass object is also a superclass object. For example, an HourlyEmployee is also an Employee. But the following would be illegal:

        employee = bestPaid; // illegal

This assignment is illegal because an Employee is not necessarily an HourlyEmployee. The Subclass Substitution Rule does not apply because the left-hand side of an assignment statement must be a variable, not an arbitrary expression.

Lab 2 has more of the details of inheritance.

LAB **Lab 2: More details of inheritance.**

(All Labs Are Optional.) **LAB**

In the example used, the superclass Employee has only one subclass, Hourly Employee, and Company's only subclass is Company2. In some situations there may be an entire hierarchy of classes. For example, a ***stream*** is a sequence of information traveling from a source to a destination. Here is part of the C++ hierarchy of stream classes:

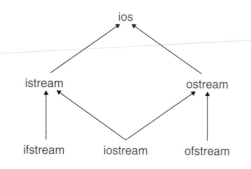

Briefly, the ios class handles low-level input-output, such as status bits and associated methods: eof( ), clear( ), and so on. The istream class adds to ios the extraction operator, **operator>>**, and ostream adds the insertion operator, **operator<<**. The ifstream class extends istream by adding open and close methods. The iostream class extends both istream and ostream by additing a special constructor. What is most noteworthy here is that iostream is an example of ***multiple inheritance:*** iostream is a subclass with two base classes, istream and ostream.

You will often encounter the following situation. You are developing a class B, and you realize that the methods of some other class, A, will be helpful. One possibility is for B to inherit from A; that is, B will be a subclass of A. Then all of A's methods are available to B. An alternative is to define, in class B, a field whose class is A. Then the methods of A can be invoked by that field. It is important to grasp the distinction between these two ways to access class A.

Inheritance describes an ***is-a*** relationship. An HourlyEmployee *is an* Employee. An iostream *is an* istream. It is also true that an istream *is an* ios, so an iostream *is an* ios. To put it mathematically, the relation *is-a* is transitive.

On the other hand, the fields in a class constitute a ***has-a*** relationship to the class. For example, the name field in the Employee class is of type string, so we can say an Employee *has a* string. Also, the bestPaid field in the Company class is of type Employee, so we can say a Company *has an* Employee.

Typically, if class B shares the overall functionality of A, then inheritance of A by B is preferable. But if there is only one component of B that will benefit from A's methods, the better alternative will be to define a class A object as a field in class B. That object can invoke the relevant methods from class A. Often, the choice is not clear-cut, so experience is your best guide.

With an object-oriented approach, the emphasis is not so much on developing the program as a whole but on developing modular program-parts, namely, classes.

These classes not only make the program easier to understand and to maintain, but they are reusable for other programs as well. A further advantage to this approach is that decisions about a class can easily be modified. We first decide what classes will be needed. And because each class interacts with other classes through its method interfaces, we can change the class's fields and method definitions as desired as long as the method interfaces remain intact.

In Section 1.1.10, we explore one of the convenient features of C++: the ability to define easily remembered operators instead of easily forgotten or misspelled method identifiers.

1.1.10   Operator Overloading

One minor annoyance with some method identifiers is that they are special names for common operators. For example, in the Employee class, we used the method identifier readInto instead of the insertion operator, operator>>. C++ allows us to use the operator instead of the method identifier, that is, to extend the meaning of the operator to a method in a class. The technical term is *operator overloading:* giving an additional meaning to an existing operator. Actually, you have already seen examples of operator overloading. For example, operator+ means integer addition if both operands are of type **int**, floating-point addition if both operands are of type **float**, and concatenation if both operands are string objects.

To see how to overload an operator within a class, let's start with an easy example. Here is the declaration of **operator>** as overloaded for the Employee class:

```
// Postcondition: The value true has been returned if this Employee's gross
//                pay is greater than otherEmployee's gross pay. Otherwise,
//                false has been returned.
bool operator> (const Employee& otherEmployee) const;
```

This declaration is identical to the declaration in Section 1.1.5 of the method makesMoreThan, except that the method identifier makesMoreThan has been replaced with

```
operator>
```

Note that **operator** is a keyword.

From this declaration, you could probably infer that the definition is as follows:

```
bool Employee::operator> (const Employee& otherEmployee) const
{
      return grossPay > otherEmployee.grossPay;
} // overloading >
```

Now **operator>** replaces the makesMoreThan method, so an expression such as

```
employee.makesMoreThan (bestPaid)
```

would be replaced with

employee > bestPaid

In general, when a method is replaced by an operator, the calling object—such as employee—becomes the operand to the left of the operator. The method's argument—such as bestPaid—becomes the operand to the right of the operator. The overloading of operator= is similar to the overloading of operator>. The details are in Lab 3.

1.1.11   Friends

Now we tackle the overloading of operator<<. But that operator is defined for the ostream class, not for the Employee class. So the hangup is that we need to allow operator<< to access the fields in the Employee class. One way to accomplish this objective would be to make those fields **public** instead of **protected**. But then every user would be able to access those fields, and that could tie users too closely to the implementation details of Employee.

What we want is a compromise so that the fields of Employee will still have **protected** status but will also be accessible to objects—such as cout—in the ostream class. C++ provides a solution[3] with the friend declaration. In the declaration of Employee, the keyword **friend** specifies that **operator**<< is a "friend" of Employee. Given two classes A and B, a method m of class A is a *friend* of class B if method m is allowed access to all members—**public**, **private**, or **protected**—of class B. For this to work, class B must declare as a friend the method m from class A. Here, from the file employee3.h, is the declaration of **operator**<< as a friend of the Employee class:

```
friend ostream& operator<< (ostream& stream,
                            const Employee& employee);
```

This overloaded version of operator<< returns a reference to an ostream—that is, output stream—object, so the definition of operator<< in employee3.cpp is

```
ostream& operator<< (ostream& stream, const Employee& employee)
{
    cout << employee.name << " $" << setiosflags(ios::fixed)
         << setprecision (2) << employee.grossPay << endl;

    return stream;
} // overloading <<
```

Because operator<< has been declared to be a friend of the Employee class, the definition of that operator is allowed to access the name and grossPay fields of Employee.

---

[3]It can be said that the main problem with C++ is that it provides a solution to every problem! This approach leads to a powerful but hard-to-master language.

Now that **operator**<< has been overloaded, we can rewrite findBestPaid( ) by replacing

    bestPaid.printOut( );

with

    cout << bestPaid;

Note that it would be illegal, in findBestPaid( ), to write

    cout << bestPaid.name << " $" << bestPaid.grossPay;

because findBestPaid( ) is not allowed to access the fields of Employee. In other words, findBestPaid( ) is *not* a friend of Employee. If we had wanted to, we could have made findBestPaid( ) a friend of Employee. In fact, we could have made the entire Company class a friend of Employee by declaring, in employee.h,

    friend class Company; // the keyword "class" is required for a class that is a
                              // friend

Then the findBestPaid( ) and printBestPaid( ) methods of the Company class would be able to access all the members of the Employee class. Note that friendship is not a symmetric relationship: the declaration makes Company a friend of Employee, but does *not* make Employee a friend of Company. So the Employee class cannot access the nonpublic members of the Company class.

In addition to befriending, there is another interesting aspect of the declaration of operator<<: the returned value is a reference to an ostream object. This is noteworthy because cout is itself an ostream object. So we can apply operator<< more than once in the same statement. For example, we can write

    cout << BEST_PAID_MESSAGE << bestPaid;

The first part of this statement, cout << BEST_PAID_MESSAGE, returns a reference to an ostream object, and this object applies its **operator**<< to bestPaid. In general, when an operator returns a reference to the same type as the object that calls the operator, several invocations of that operator can be chained together.

Lab 3 explores the overloading of **operator**=, which is similar to the overloading of **operator**>, and the overloading of **operator**>>, which is similar to the overloading of **operator**<<.

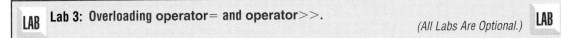

LAB   **Lab 3: Overloading operator= and operator>>.**
                                                    (All Labs Are Optional.)   LAB

In Section 1.1.3, we introduced the Principle of Data Abstraction, whereby code that uses a given class *should* not access the implementation details of that class. Does this place all the burden on the user? Where does the **protected** modifier fit in? And what about **friend**? Section 1.1.12 describes the extent to which C++ can prohibit user's code from accessing implementation details of the class used.

1.1.12 Information Hiding

The Principle of Data Abstraction states that a user's code should not access the implementation details of the class used. By following that principle, the user's code is protected from changes to those implementation details, such as a change in fields. Protection is further enhanced if a user's code *cannot* access the implementation details of the class used. We state this prohibition in a principle:

Principle of Information Hiding

A language should allow the developer of a class to prevent a user's code from accessing the implementation details of the class.

The burden of obeying the Principle of Data Abstraction falls on users, whereas the Principle of Information Hiding relates to a language feature in support of class developers. The goal of both principles is the same: to protect users of a class from any internal changes to the class. An internal change is one that affects the definition of the class but does not affect the class's public-method interfaces.

We have seen that C++ supports information hiding through the use of the **private** and **protected** modifiers for methods and fields. The **private** modifier attains complete hiding: only the class's methods can access nonlocal variables and methods that are **private**. The **protected** modifier provides complete hiding from users in general but does allow access to any subclass of the class.

The visibility modifier **public** allows access to any class. Finally, C++ provides a loophole to avoid information hiding: the **friend** modifier. As we saw in Section 1.1.11, if class A declares class B (or a method in class B) with the **friend** modifier, then all of class A's members, even the **private** members, are accessible in class B (or in the befriended method in class B).

SUMMARY

This chapter, and Labs 1 to 3, introduced a collection of C++ topics that will better prepare you to understand and use the Standard Template Library. Most of the chapter investigated the object-oriented features of C++. For example, C++ supports these essential features of an object-oriented language:

> *Encapsulation:* with classes, header and source files, and the scope-resolution operator
>
> *Inheritance:* with subclasses and **protected** members

The third essential feature of an object-oriented language, polymorphism, is explained in Appendix 3.

We also saw three principles associated with object-oriented programming:

> *Principle of Data Abstraction:* A user's code should not access the implementation details of the class used.

Open-Closed Principle: Every class should be open—that is, able to be extended through inheritance—and closed—that is, stable for existing applications.

Principle of Information Hiding: A language should allow the developer of a class to prevent a user's code from accessing the implementation details of the class.

EXERCISES

1.1   Reimplement the Date class's isValid method in the dateMain project—available from the Source Code link on the book's website—on the assumption that the Date class has a single field:

long theDate;

The format of the date will be *(m)mddyyyy,* that is, one or two digits for the month, two digits for the day of the month, and four digits for the year. For example, the value 1042005 would represent January 4, 2005; the value 10042005 would represent October 4, 2005.

1.2   a.   In the Date class, develop a method interface for a daysLeftInMonth method. If, for example, myDate is a Date object whose date is February 13, 2003, then

    myDate.daysLeftInMonth( )

will return 15.

    b.   Define the daysLeftInMonth( ) method from the method interface developed in Exercise 1.2a. Assume the Date class has **int** fields day, month, and year.

    Hint   Use the daysInMonth method.

1.3   In the Employee class, here is the method interface for an equalTo method:

// Postcondition: **true** has been returned if this Employee has the same gross
//   pay as otherEmployee. Otherwise, **false** has been returned.
bool equalTo (**const** Employee& otherEmployee) **const**;

    a.   Define this method.

    b.   Replace the equalTo method with an overloaded version of the operator ==.

    Hint   All you need to change is the heading.

1.4   Here is the header file for a simple class:

```
#ifndef AGE
#define AGE

class Age
{
    public:
        // Postcondition: this Age has been initialized to 0.
        Age( );

        // Postcondition: this Age has been initialized to newAge.
        Age (int newAge);

        // Postcondition: this Age has been returned.
        int getAge( );

        // Postcondition: this Age has been set to newAge;
        void setAge (int newAge);
    protected:
        int age;
}; // class Age

#endif
```

a. Create the source file (Age.cpp) for the Age class.

b. Create a file with a main function that defines Age objects and invokes each method at least twice.

1.5   With the Age class in Exercise 1.4a as a guide, develop a Salary class to read in salaries from the input until the sentinel (−1.00) is reached, and to print out how many of those salaries are above average. The average salary is the total of the salaries divided by the number of salaries. In addition to a default constructor, there will be two methods, whose interfaces are as follows:

```
// Postcondition: The average of all salaries in the input (sentinel = −1.0) has
//                been determined.
void findAverageSalary( );

// Precondition: There was at least one salary (before the sentinel) in the input.
// Postcondition: The above-average salaries in the input have been printed.
void printAboveAverageSalaries( );
```

Assume that each line of input, except the last line, contains a legitimate salary, and that there is at least 1 and at most 100 such salaries in the input. Test your Salary class with a main function.

1.6   Here is the header file, SimpleClass.h, for a simple class:

```
#ifndef SIMPLE_CLASS
#define SIMPLE_CLASS
```

```
class SimpleClass
{
    public:

        // Postcondition: This SimpleClass object has been
        //                initialized to the minimum GPA and printed.
        SimpleClass( );

        // Postcondition: This SimpleClass's minimum GPA has been
        //                initialized to gpa_in and printed.
        SimpleClass (float gpa_in);

    protected:
        const static float MIN_GPA;
        float gpa;
}; // SimpleClass

#endif
```

Develop the corresponding source file, SimpleClass.cpp. Here is a main function to test the SimpleClass class:

```
#include <iostream>
#include <string>
#include "SimpleClass.h"

using namespace std;

int main( )
{
    const string CLOSE_WINDOW_PROMPT =
        "Please press the Enter key to close this output window.";

    SimpleClass sc1;

    SimpleClass sc2 (3.2);

    cout << endl << endl << CLOSE_WINDOW_PROMPT;
    cin.get( );

    return 0;
} // main
```

The output should be

```
2
3.2
```

Please press the Enter key to close this output window.

1.7   In SimpleClass.h of Exercise 1.6, replace the line

float gpa;

with the line

float gpa = MIN_GPA;

What happened when you tried to remake and rerun the project?

1.8   In SimpleClass.cpp from Exercise 1.6, comment out the default constructor in the header file, but not in the source file. What happened when you tried to remake and rerun the project? What if you comment out the default constructor in the source file but not in the header file? What if you comment out the default constructor from both the header file and the source file?

1.9   In SimpleClass.cpp from Exercise 1.6, use the following for the definition of the default constructor:

SimpleClass::SimpleClass( ) { }

What happens when you tried to remake and rerun the project?

1.10 It is legal to include method definitions in a header file. What efficiency is gained by putting method definitions in a source file separate from the header file?

PROGRAMMING PROJECT 1.1

A Sequence **Class**

In this project, you will get to be a developer of a class, and then become a user of that class. To start with, here are method interfaces for a Sequence class that holds a sequence of items of type string.

```
// Postcondition: this is an empty Sequence.
Sequence( );

// Postcondition: true has been returned if this Sequence cannot store any more
//                items. Otherwise, false has been returned.
bool full( ) const;

// Postcondition: the number of items currently in this Sequence has been returned.
int size( ) const;

// Precondition: this Sequence will hold at least one more item.
// Postcondition: s has been appended (inserted at the end of) this Sequence.
void push_back (const string& s);

// Precondition: this Sequence has at least k items.
// Postcondition: a reference to the item at position k in this Sequence has been
//                returned.
string& operator[ ] (int k);
```

Part 1

Define the methods in the Sequence class.

> *Hint*   Use the following fields:
>
> ```
> string data [MAX_SIZE]    // an array to store the items
> int count;                // the number of items currently in the Sequence
> ```
>
> with
>
> ```
> const static int MAX_SIZE = 10; // legal for constants of type int
> ```

Part 2

Create a main function to test your Sequence class. Read in words one per line. When the sentinel (you pick the sentinel) is reached, determine the alphabetically smallest and largest words in the Sequence, replace each word that has the value "no" with "yes", and then determine how many words in the Sequence are between "aardvark" and "panda".

Storage Structures for Container Classes

This chapter continues your preparation for the study of data structures in general and the Standard Template Library in particular. We start with what many people consider the most difficult and error-prone feature of C++: the concept of pointers. But pointers are also powerful and very widely used, so you will have to come to grips with them sooner or later. This chapter also introduces container classes: the object-oriented version of data structures. A ***container class*** is a class in which each instance has a collection of items. Of particular interest are the choices of a storage structure for a container class. The main alternatives are an array and a linked structure. Finally, we look at an important component of the Standard Template Library, generic algorithms: predefined, template functions that augment the collection of methods in a container class. ■

CHAPTER OBJECTIVES

1. Understand pointers and dynamic variables.

2. Explore the advantages and disadvantages of contiguous structures and linked structures.

3. Study the fields and methods in the Linked class.

4. Be able to create and use a template class.

5. Define and use an iterator.

6. Learn where to find—and how to use—generic algorithms.

2.1 | POINTERS

Modern programming languages allow the programmer to explicitly create and destroy variables during the execution of a program. The storage areas for these variables, called *dynamic variables,* are allocated when needed and deallocated when no longer needed. A large section of memory—the *heap*—is reserved for dynamic variables.

Unlike ordinary variables, dynamic variables are never accessed directly. In fact, a dynamic variable does not even have an identifier. Instead, dynamic variables are always accessed indirectly, by means of a pointer variable. A *pointer variable* is a variable that contains the address of another variable, usually a dynamic variable. A pointer type consists of a type followed by an asterisk. For a simple example, we can declare

A pointer variable contains the address of another variable.

    int* scorePtr;

This declares the variable scorePtr to be a pointer variable. Eventually, scorePtr will contain the address of an **int** variable. To create a dynamic variable pointed to by scorePtr, the **new** operator is used:

*The **new** operator allocates space for a dynamic variable.*

    scorePtr = **new int**;

The operand for the **new** operator is the type—in this example, **int**—for which storage is to be allocated, and the operator returns a pointer to the storage allocated. In other words, when the assignment statement scorePtr = **new int**; is executed, a dynamic variable of type **int** will be created, and the address of that dynamic variable will be stored in scorePtr. Pictorially, we draw an arrow from the pointer variable to the dynamic variable:

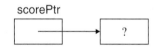

The question mark indicates that the dynamic variable has not yet been given a value. If we want to access or modify the dynamic variable, we must do so through a pointer variable, in this case, scorePtr. This is done by placing an asterisk *in front of* scorePtr, for example,

    *scorePtr = 7; // stores 7 in the dynamic variable

    cin >> *scorePtr; // reads from the input into the dynamic variable

    if (*scorePtr == 0) // tests to see if the dynamic variable contains 0

In our example the dynamic variable was of type **int**. In many applications, the types of dynamic variables will be classes. Here is an example in which we create a dynamic object, that is, a dynamic variable whose type is a class. Recall the Employee class from Chapter 1. We first declare a pointer variable:

    Employee* employeePtr;

As we did with scorePtr, we create the dynamic Employee variable with a call to the **new** operator:

>   employeePtr = **new** Employee;

To access a member (that is, a field or method) of the dynamic object of type Employee, we apply the ***dereference*** operator, the asterisk:

>   (*employeePtr).readInto( );

The extra parentheses are necessary because the ***member selection*** operator—the dot—has higher precedence than the dereference operator. But dereferencing a pointer that points to a dynamic object and then selecting a member of that object is such a common operation that C++ has a special symbol for that purpose. The ***dereference-and-select*** operator, $->$, is used as follows:

>   employeePtr $->$ readInto( );

Care must be taken in defining pointer variables because the C++ compiler implicitly associates the * with the variable, not with the type. For example, consider the following:

>   Employee* emp1Ptr,
>   emp2Ptr;

We have declared one pointer variable, emp1Ptr. The variable emp2Ptr is—in spite of its pointer-sounding name—just a regular Employee object. When you want to declare more than one pointer variable of the same type, you can precede the declaration with a **typedef** to give a name to the pointer type. For example,

>   **typedef** Employee* EmployeePtr;

makes EmployeePtr another name for the type Employee*. The name declared in a **typedef** can then be used to declare a variable. For example,

>   EmployeePtr emp1Ptr,
>   emp2Ptr;

declares two variables that are pointers to Employee objects. Note that the * is not used in this case. A **typedef** merely declares another name for a type.

Another way to declare two pointer variables of the same type is to use two declarations:

>   Employee* emp1Ptr;
>   Employee* emp2Ptr;

2.1.1   The Heap versus the Stack

You may wonder why we declare variables that point to employees instead of declaring employees directly. One reason is to save space on the ***stack***—the part of memory where local variables are stored. Assume the declarations of emp1Ptr and emp2Ptr are made in the findBestPaid( ) method of the Company class. Since emp1Ptr and emp2Ptr are local, the only stack space allocated would be for the pointers themselves, whereas significantly more stack space would be required to hold two employees. Of course, with dynamic variables, space for the two employees would be on the heap, but the heap is much more spacious than the stack. If each object in a class consists of a collection of items, the advantage of the heap over the stack is compelling.

2.1.2   Reference Parameters

Reference parameters represent a subtle use of pointers. A *reference parameter* is an unmodifiable pointer that is automatically dereferenced. When the function is called, the pointer gets the address of the corresponding argument; throughout the execution of that function, the pointer maintains that same address. During the execution of the function, the pointer is automatically dereferenced; that is, if x is a reference parameter, each occurrence of x in the function is interpreted as

   *x

For example, suppose we have the following program fragment:

```
void sample (int& i)
{
     i = 3;
}// sample

int main( )
{
     int j = 5;

     sample (j);
     cout << j;
     return 0;
} // main
```

As its definition indicates, j is an **int** variable with an initial value of 5. The type of the parameter i is not **int**, but rather pointer-to-**int**. When the function sample is called from main, the *address* of the argument j is copied into i. The following picture shows the contents of the relevant portion of memory when the call is made:

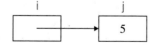

Because reference parameters are automatically dereferenced, the assignment

   i = 3;

is interpreted as

   *i = 3;

When this statement is executed, there is a change in the value of *i, that is, a change in the value of j:

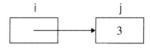

So the output from the program will be 3, not 5.

2.1.3 Pointer Fields

A class can contain fields of a pointer type, including a pointer to its own type, for example,

```
class Student
{
    public:
        . . . // method declarations

    protected:
        string name;
        float gpa;
        Student* next;
}; // Student
```

Then one of the fields in a Student object is a pointer to another Student object, and one of *its* fields is a pointer to yet another Student object, and so on. Such a class can be used to "link" together any number of student records. This very important application of pointers is explored in Section 2.3.2 and is the basis for the most common implementation of several classes in the Standard Template Library: list, map, and set.

Another application of pointers is in support of polymorphism, the subject of Appendix 3.

2.1.4 Arrays and Pointers

Pointers to arrays are special. A pointer to an array of items has the type pointer-to-item. For example, a pointer to an array of ints could be declared as

```
int* scores;
```

Note that there is no indication of the size of the array, and in fact, scores can be used to point to a single int or to an array of ints.

To allocate an array on the heap, the number of items needed is enclosed in brackets. For example,

```
cin >> n;

scores = new int [n];
```

allocates space for an array of n **int**s and stores in scores the address of the first item of the array. Notice that the size of the array is the value stored in n, and this value is not known until run-time. In general, when the space for an array is allocated from the heap, the size of that array need not be known at compile-time; it can be determined at run-time!

How are array items accessed? The index operator, **operator**[ ], automatically dereferences a pointer to an array and accesses the corresponding memory location. As you have undoubtedly noticed from your previous work in C++, the first item of an array has an index of 0. For example, scores [0] will access the first item of the array, and scores [2] will access the third item of the array. Note that there is no asterisk in this expression. This is because an array variable is considered to be an automatically dereferenced pointer to the first item of the array it names.

Universal Array-Pointer Law

In general, for any array **a** and nonnegative integer i, a [i] is the same as *(a + i).

For example, with scores as we have defined it,

> scores [3]

accesses the same item as

> *(scores + 3)

If you simply declare

> **float** a [100];

within a function, then the space for the array is allocated, not from the heap, but from the stack. The size of any stored-on-the-stack array must be given by a constant. Even then, the Array-Pointer Law holds.

Lab 4 reinforces the distinction between pointer-variable assignments and dynamic-variable assignments.

LAB   **Lab 4:** **Pointer-variable assignments versus dynamic-variable assignments.**   *(All Labs Are Optional.)*   **LAB**

2.1.5   Deallocation of Dynamic Variables

The memory for dynamic variables is allocated when the **new** operator is invoked, but what about deallocation? A dynamic variable that is no longer accessible is referred to as *garbage* or a *memory leak.* If your program generates too much garbage, you will run out of memory, which is an error condition. Are you responsible for garbage collection, that is, for deallocating inaccessible dynamic variables?

The **delete** *operator deallocates the space occupied by a dynamic variable.*

Unfortunately, you must handle your own garbage. C++ provides a **delete** operator to deallocate the space for a dynamic variable. This operator has one operand: a pointer to the dynamic variable whose space is to be deallocated. So we can write the following:

```
Node* nodePtr;

nodePtr = new Node;

// work with *nodePtr

    . . .

delete nodePtr;
```

This last statement deallocates the space for the dynamic variable pointed to by nodePtr; it would now be illegal to attempt to dereference nodePtr. And, whether or not the **delete** operator has been called, we can specify that a pointer variable is not pointing anywhere by assigning the constant identifier NULL to that pointer variable:

```
nodePtr = NULL;
```

To deallocate the space for a dynamic array, use an empty index after the keyword **delete**, for example,

```
string* names;

names = new string [500];

// work with the array names

    . . .

delete[ ] names;
```

In Section 2.3.5, we will revisit the **delete** operator in the context of deallocating a large number of dynamic variables.

2.2 | ARRAYS

Recall from Section 2.1.4 that an array variable is actually a pointer variable that contains the address of the first entry in the array. For example, we can do the following:

```
string* names;          // declares names to be of type pointer-to-string

names = new string [5]; // defines names to be (a pointer to) an actual array
                        // of 5 strings

names [0] = "Cromer";   // stores "Cromer" at the first entry in the array names
names [3] = "Panchenko"; // stores "Panchenko" at 4th entry in the array
                        // names
```

By the Array-Pointer Law, the above assignment of "Cromer" to names [0] is equivalent to

```
*names = "Cromer";
```

The assignment of "Panchenko" to names [3] is equivalent to

```
*(names + 3) = "Panchenko";
```

The size of an array is fixed once the array has been created, but a new array—pointed to by the same pointer variable—can later be created. For example, we can write

```
string* names;
int n;

cin >> n;
names = new string [n];
. . .
delete [ ] names; // to avoid a memory leak
names = new string [2 * n];
```

Consecutive items in an array are stored ***contiguously,*** that is, in adjoining locations. An important consequence of contiguity is that an individual element in an array can be accessed without first accessing any of the other individual elements. For example, names [2] can be accessed immediately—we need not access names [0] and names [1] first in order to reach names [2]. This ***random-access*** property of arrays will come in handy in Chapters 5, 11, and 13. In each case we will need a storage structure in which an item can be accessed quickly given its relative position, so an array will be appropriate in each case.

There are several drawbacks to arrays. First, because the items are contiguous, the size of an array is fixed. Space for the entire array must be allocated before any items can be stored in the array. If that size is too large, the extra space will be unused. If too small, a larger array must be allocated and the contents of the smaller array moved to the larger array.

Another drawback to arrays is that inserting and deleting in an array may require that many items be moved. For example, suppose an array's indices go from 0 to 999, and there are items stored in order at the locations with indices 0 to 755. If a new item belongs at index 300, we must first move the items at indices 300 to 755 into the locations at indices 301 to 756 before the new item can be inserted. Figure 2.1 shows the effect of such an insertion.

Up until now in your programming career, you may not have appreciated the random-access feature of arrays. That's because you have probably not yet seen an alternative to arrays for storing a collection of items in main memory. In Section 2.3 we introduce such an alternative, which also happens to be a very common use for dynamic objects.

2.3 | CONTAINER CLASSES

*A **container class** is a class in which each instance consists of a collection of items.*

A ***container*** is a variable that consists of a collection of items. The only container we have seen so far is the array, but almost all our work from here on will be devoted to other containers, namely, to instances of container classes. A ***container class*** is a class whose objects are containers. In Chapters 5 through 14 we will study a number of container classes that have wide applicability. Often, these container classes

Figure 2.1 | Insertion in an array: to insert "Kalena" at index 300 in the array on the left, the elements at indices 300, 301, . . . , 756 must first be moved, respectively, to indices 301, 302, . . . , 757.

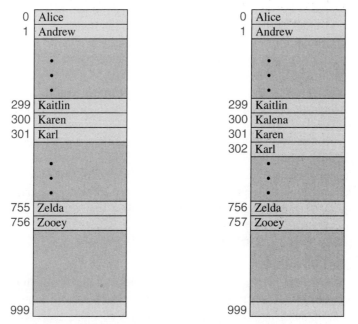

have similar method interfaces. For example, each container class has an empty method whose interface is

```
// Postcondition: true has been returned if the container has no items.
//                 Otherwise, false has been returned.
bool empty( ) const;
```

Suppose myList is an object in the container class list, and myList has four items. The execution of

```
cout << myList.empty( );
```

will produce output of

```
0
```

because in C++, the constants 0 and **false** are synonyms (and both are synonymous with NULL).

Of course, a method interface does not indicate *how* the method's task will be accomplished. In Chapters 5 through 14, we will investigate the details for each container class studied. But we can now introduce a simple classification of container classes according to the way the items are stored.

2.3.1 Storage Structures for Container Classes

Container objects, that is, objects that are instances of a container class, usually consume memory in proportion to the number of items in the container. So the way such a container is stored in memory can have a substantial impact on the efficiency of a program. One straightforward way to store a container object in memory is to store the individual items contiguously: in an array. The container class will provide methods and overloaded operators for creating and maintaining the underlying array. From the user's point of view, such a class has the advantages of an array (such as the familiar index operator, **operator** [ ], and random-access) without the drawbacks (maintaining the size of the array, and writing the code to insert or delete items). This approach is realized in Chapter 5, where we study the Standard Template Library's vector class.

Another approach to storing a container object in memory is to adopt a pointer-based linked structure, the subject of Section 2.3.2. As you will see in the remaining chapters, projects, and labs, both approaches have wide applicability.

2.3.2 Linked Structures

We can store a container in main memory without using an array. The basic idea is to associate with each item a **link**—that is, a pointer—to the next item in the container. So the entire container of items is linked together like a chain necklace. We now create a simple example of a container class: Linked. The Linked class is not part of the Standard Template Library. In fact, with only three methods (initially), it is a "toy" class, whose only practical value is to give you an idea of some of the issues in implementing container classes. Labs 5, 6, and 7 give you the opportunity to experiment with this class.

As usual, we start with a user's view. What must this class provide to users? The first concern we need to address is what the type of the items will be. Do we want a Linked container of **int**s, of Employee objects, or objects of some other type? Whichever choice we make will drastically limit the usefulness of the container class. The best choice is to let the user choose! That is, we will let the user of the Linked class decide the item type when the Linked container object is defined. Creating this flexible Linked class relies on a powerful feature of C++: templates.

We will not define a single container class. Instead, we will define a **template,** or mold, that will allow the creation, at compile-time, of a container class of some fixed type. The fixed type is treated as if it were an "argument type" of the container class. Here the name of the template class is Linked, and a user follows the class identifier with a **template argument**[1] in angle brackets after the class name. For example, here are the definitions for a Linked container of **int**s and a Linked container of Employee objects:

When a container class is templated, each instantiation of the class includes a template argument: the type of the individual items.

---

[1]For simplicity, we assume that there is a single template argument. Later, we will encounter classes with several template arguments.

Linked<**int**> intList;

Linked<Employee> employeeList;

From that point on, it would be illegal to insert anything but an **int** into intList, and illegal to insert anything but an Employee object into employeeList. We will get to some examples after we have supplied the method interfaces for the Linked class.

Now let's look at how templates are handled in the definition of the class Linked. We start with the keyword **template** followed, in angle brackets, by the keyword **class** and an identifier: the ***template parameter.*** That identifier will be replaced by the type—such as **int** or Employee—supplied by the user when the class is instantiated at compile-time. Here is the beginning of the definition:

```
template<class T>
class Linked
{
```

As will be seen in the next paragraph, whenever we need to provide an item type in the definition of the Linked class, we simply use T. You might think it strange that such a powerful feature requires so little work. The hard part, which you can safely ignore, is for the compiler to implement templates correctly and efficiently.

For now, the Linked class will have only three responsibilities: to create an empty Linked object, to return the number of items in a Linked object, and to insert a new item at the front of a Linked object. Here are the method interfaces:

When a template class is instantiated, the template argument replaces each occurrence of the template parameter in the class's definition.

```
// Postcondition: this Linked object is empty, that is, it contains no items.
Linked( );

// Postcondition: the number of items in this Linked object has been returned.
long size( ) const;

// Postcondition: newItem has been inserted at the front of this Linked object.
void push_front (const T& newItem);
```

Notice that the parameter of push_front is of type T, the template parameter.

We can now update the two Linked objects, intList and employeeList:

```
intList.push_front (27);
intList.push_front (51);
intList.push_front (12);

Employee employee;

employee.readInto( );
while (!employee.isSentinel( ))
{
    employeeList.push_front (employee);
    employee.readInto( );
} // while
```

Each item is inserted at the front of its container, so, for example, intList now contains

12, 51, 27

in that order.

There is nothing more to be said about the Linked class from the user's perspective, so let's turn our attention to the fields and implementation of this class. One possibility is to have an array field and store the items in the array. This option is explored in Exercise 2.3.

Another strategy is to store each item in the container in a **struct**[2] called Node. Node will have two fields: an item field of type T, and a next field of type Node*, that is, pointer-to-Node:

```
struct Node
{
    T item;
    Node* next;
}; // struct Node
```

Node will be a **protected** class in Linked. Because all the members of Node are **public**, any method in Linked will be able to access the item and next fields of Node. The only fields in Linked are

```
Node* head; // points to first node
long length; // number of items in the container
```

The definition of the default constructor is straightforward:

```
Linked( )
{
    head = NULL;
    length = 0;
} // default constructor
```

You may have noticed that the scope-resolution operator

```
::
```

is not part of the definition. That's because the definition is included in the header file, linked.h. Up until now, each class has had a header file, with declarations, and a source file, with method definitions. In general, nothing that allocates storage should be in a header file; then the header can be precompiled rather than compiled anew for each project. But with templates, no storage is allocated until an object in the class is defined. *So, for the sake of simplicity, we will put both the declarations and method definitions in the header file linked.h.*

---

[2]A **struct** is a class in which each member is **public**. It is legal to have methods in a **struct**, but usually, a **struct** object has fields only.

The definition of the size( ) method is even simpler than the definition of the default constructor:

```
long size( ) const
{
        return length;
} // method size
```

Before we get to the definition of the push_front method, let's see what happens when that method is called. Suppose we have defined a Linked object—in the main function, for example:

Linked<string> sneakerList;

The default constructor is invoked at this point, so we have

sneakerList.head   sneakerList.length

NULL		0

Now we add an item to the front of sneakerList:

sneakerList.push_front ("Nike");

The effect of this message will be to create a Node object pointed to by sneaker List.head. The item field in that node will have the value "Nike". The next field in that node should not point anywhere, so its value will be NULL. And, of course, sneakerList.length must be incremented. That gives us

sneakerList.head   sneakerList.length

| Nike | NULL | | 1 |
|------|------| |---|

Again, all a user can do is to add an item to the front of sneakerList:

sneakerList.push_front ("Adidas");

First, a new Node object will be created. We don't want sneakerList.head to point to the new node yet because then the node with "Nike" would be inaccessible. Instead, when the new Node object is created, it will be pointed to by newHead, a Node pointer. The new node's item field gets the value "Adidas". The new node's next field points to the initial node (the one with "Nike" in its item field). We now have

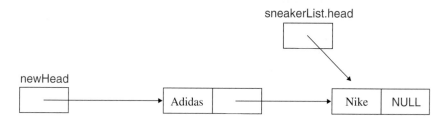

Finally, we store in sneakerList.head the address that is in newHead:

sneakerList.head

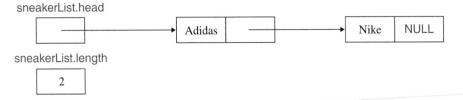

sneakerList.length

2

From what you have seen so far, you can probably figure out how to store an entire container of items: each item gets put into a Node object that is inserted at the front of the Linked object. Here is the complete definition of push_front:

```
void push_front (const T& newItem)
{
        Node* newHead = new Node;
        newHead −> item = newItem;
        newHead −> next = head;
        head = newHead;
        length++;
} // method push_front
```

This example is oversimplified in that the Linked class has very little functionality. In a realistic application, we might want a method that removes the front item from a Linked object. And we may want a user to be able to access each item in the list. But would we need one method to print out the items, another method to find the largest item, and so on? As we will see in Section 2.3.3 on iterators, there is an elegant solution to the problem of looping through all the items in a container.

The important point of the implementation of Linked is that a linked structure for storing a container of items is different from an array in several key respects:

1. The size of the container need not be known in advance. We simply add items at will. So we do not have to worry, as we would with an array, about allocating too much space or too little space. But it should be noted that in each Node object, the next field itself takes up extra space because it contains program information rather than problem information.

2. Random access is not available. To create a method to reach an item we would have to start by accessing the head item (that is, the item field in the Node object pointed to by head), and then accessing the next item after the head item, and so on.

2.3.3   Iterators

In Section 2.3.2, we noted that in order for the Linked class to have any practical value, we would want users to be able to loop through a Linked container. How can this be accomplished without violating the Principle of Data Abstraction, that is, without allowing user's code to access the implementation details of the Linked class? The solution is in the use of iterators. An ***iterator*** is an object that allows the user of a container to loop through the container without violating the Principle of Data Abstraction.

Embedded in almost every container class, there is an iterator class that allows a user to access each item in a container. The container class has begin( ) and end( ) methods. The begin( ) method returns an iterator positioned at the first item in the container object, and the end( ) method returns an iterator that is positioned *beyond* the last item in the container object.

What other methods must an iterator class provide to permit looping through a container? One iterator operator needed, **operator++**, advances the calling iterator object to the next item in the container. If the iterator is positioned at the last item, **operator++** will position that iterator just past the last item. Also, there should be an iterator **operator*** that dereferences the item where the iterator is currently positioned. Finally, we will have **operator==** and **operator!=** operator methods to test iterators for equality and for inequality.

The following main function illustrates the use of iterators on a Linked container of salaries. The program reads in a list of salaries and then prints out each salary that is above the average salary. The salaries are stored in the Linked container with the push_front method, and then an iterator loops through the Linked container and prints each salary greater than the average salary.

Here is the main function:

An iterator allows a user's code to loop through a container without accessing the implementation details of the container class.

```
int main( )
{
      const string PROMPT =
          "Please enter a salary; the sentinel is ";

      const string RESULTS =
          "Here are the above-average salaries:";

      const string CLOSE_WINDOW_PROMPT =
          "Please press the Enter key to close this output window.";

      const float SENTINEL = −1.00;

      Linked<float> salaryList;

      float salary,
          total = 0.00;

      cout << PROMPT << SENTINEL << ": ";
      cin >> salary;
      while (salary != SENTINEL)
      {
          salaryList.push_front (salary);
          total += salary;
          cout << PROMPT << SENTINEL << ": ";
```

```
                    cin >> salary;
           } // reading in and adding up salaries

           float average;
           if (salaryList.size( ) > 0)
                   average = total/salaryList.size( );

           Linked<float>::Iterator itr;

           cout << RESULTS << endl;
           for (itr = salaryList.begin( ); itr != salaryList.end( ); itr++)
                   if (*itr > average)
                           cout << *itr << endl;

           cout << endl << endl << CLOSE_WINDOW_PROMPT;
           cin.get( );
           cin.get( );

                   return 0;
       } // main
```

Pay special attention to the declaration of itr:

```
   Linked<float>::Iterator itr;
```

In general, for each container class, its iterator class is embedded in the container class; that's why the scope-resolution operator is needed. The iterator class provides the methods for traversing that container class. In other words, iterators are the behind-the-scenes workhorses that enable users of a container class to loop through a container.

2.3.4   Design and Implementation of the Iterator Class

We now develop the Iterator class that supports the Linked class. Because of C++'s obsession with efficiency, the **struct** Node object and the class Iterator are embedded in the class Linked. So Linked methods will be able to access any field in Node or Iterator simply by specifying the field. As we are creating the Iterator class, we will also need to expand the Linked class (for example, with begin( ) and end( ) methods).

Here is an outline of the Linked class:

```
   template<class T>
   class Linked {

       protected:
           struct Node
           {
                   T item;
                   Node* next;
           }; // struct Node
```

```
        Node* head;
        long length;

    public:
        class Iterator {

            // public, private and protected members of Iterator
            . . .
        } // class Iterator

        // definitions of Linked-class methods
        . . .
    } // class Linked
```

Our simplified Iterator class will have one field:

```
    Node* nodePtr;
```

There is an Iterator constructor to initialize nodePtr:

```
    // Postcondition: The iterator has been initialized through newPtr.
    Iterator (Node* newPtr)
    {
        nodePtr = newPtr;
    } // constructor
```

This constructor should not be **public** because users should not have access to the Node class. But as we noted in Chapter 1, if a class has any constructor, there is no automatically defined default constructor. So we will explicitly define a **public** default constructor so a user can construct an Iterator object. Part of the definition of the Iterator class is

```
    public:

        // Postcondition: This Iterator object has been constructed.
        Iterator( ) { } // default constructor
```

The definition of the postincrement operator, **operator++(int)**, has three steps. First, a temporary Iterator object, temp, is assigned the value of the calling object. Then nodePtr is incremented. Finally, temp is returned. The assignment of the calling object illustrates a neat feature of C++, the **this** pointer. Within a method, the keyword **this** points to the calling object, so ***this** refers to the calling object itself.

How can we "increment" the pointer nodePtr? By making the nodePtr point to the next Node object, that is, by assigning

```
    nodePtr = (*nodePtr).next;
```

Here is the code:

```
    // Precondition: this Iterator object is positioned at an item.
    // Postcondition: this Iterator object has advanced in
```

```
//                    the Linked object and the item this Iterator was positioned at
//                    (before this call) has been returned.
Iterator operator++ (int)
{
       Iterator temp = *this;
       nodePtr = (*nodePtr).next;
       return temp;
} // post-increment ++
```

The dummy parameter type, **int**, is used to signify the postincrement version of the operator ++. Lab 5 includes the definition of the preincrement operator and several other operators in the Iterator class.

LAB   **Lab 5: Defining the other iterator operators.**

(All Labs Are Optional.)   **LAB**

2.3.5 The pop_front **Method**

Another useful method in the Linked class is pop_front, which deletes the front item from the container. Here is the method interface:

```
// Precondition: this Linked container is not empty.
// Postcondition: the front item has been deleted from this Linked container.
void pop_front( );
```

A possible definition of pop_front is the following:

```
void pop_front( )
{
       head = (*head).next;
       --length;
} // method pop_front
```

This definition has a subtle but dangerous flaw: what had been the front node before this call is now garbage—still taking up memory but no longer accessible. This garbage can pile up and eventually cause your program to run out of memory. The solution is to deallocate the unused space by calling the **delete** operator. Here is the revised version of pop_front:

```
void pop_front( )
{
       Node* oldHead = head;
       head = (*head).next;
       delete oldHead; // deallocates *oldHead
       --length;
} // pop_front
```

The oldHead pointer allows us to ensure that the space head points to at the beginning of the call is not deallocated until after head has been adjusted. And the space for oldHead itself is automatically deallocated at the end of the execution of the call to pop_front.

2.3.6   Destructors

What if we want to delete every item in a Linked container? One possibility is for the user to do this directly, by iterating through the container and calling pop_front during each iteration. A better idea is to define a destroy method that iterates through the container and calls pop_front during each iteration. The trouble with this idea is that a user might forget to call destroy, especially for containers that can no longer be accessed. For example, if you define a Linked object within some method, at the end of the execution of that method, the object is *out-of-scope,* that is, the object can no longer be accessed.

Recall that for initializing an object, the possibility of user forgetfulness prompted the C++ developers to provide constructors: initialization methods that are automatically invoked when an object is defined. For destroying an out-of-scope object, the possibility of user forgetfulness prompted C++ developers to provide a ***destructor:*** a method, deallocating the object's space, that is automatically invoked when the object goes out of scope.

A destructor method is automatically called when an instance of a class goes out of scope, that is, is no longer accessible.

A destructor heading starts with a tilde (~) followed by the class identifier followed by parentheses. For example, here is the method interface for the Linked destructor:

```
// Postcondition: The space allocated for this Linked object has been
//                deallocated.
~Linked( )
```

Note that *a destructor has no return type and no parameters*!

Here is the complete definition:

```
~Linked( )
{
     while (head != NULL)
          pop_front( );
} // destructor
```

Recall that if you do not create a constructor for a class, the compiler will generate one for you. This default constructor has no parameters and simply invokes the default constructor for each object field in the class. But be careful! If you create any constructor, the compiler will not create a default constructor for you; then you must explicitly define a default constructor if you need one. And you will need one if you create a subclass of the given class, because subclass constructors automatically start by calling their superclass's default constructor.

Similarly, if you do not create a destructor for a class, the compiler will generate one for you. This default destructor simply invokes the default destructor for each object field in the class. But there are no object fields in the Linked class, so such a destructor would not have accomplished anything. That is why we had to define our own.

Finally, we need to say a few words about constant identifiers. For example, suppose we declared the following in the Linked class's declaration/definition:

```
protected:
        const static string HEADING ;
```

The definition of this identifier would occur after the end of the class declaration and before the #endif. The definition must be templated because Linked is a templated class:

```
template<class T>
const string Linked<T>::HEADING = "This is a linked list.";
```

HEADING may be accessed only in the methods of the Linked class or in the methods of a subclass of the Linked class.

Lab 6 deals with another extension to the Linked class: overloading **operator**=.

LAB   **Lab 6: Overloading operator**=.

(All Labs Are Optional.)   **LAB**

Section 2.3.7 indicates that for many container classes, there are a large number of predefined functions to accomplish some common tasks.

2.3.7   Generic Algorithms

Just as we should not reinvent the wheel by creating a class that already exists, we should not define a method that has already been defined. The Standard Template Library provides not only a large number of useful container classes, but also a large number of functions—for sorting, searching, copying, accumulating, and so on—that can be applied to container objects. As a bonus, these functions, called *generic algorithms,* can be applied to arrays! And for further flexibility, all the generic algorithms are template functions.

The idea behind template functions is the same as for template classes. A template for a function is a framework for the function definition; the template includes an unspecified type (or types). When the function is called, that type is specified so the compiler can generate the appropriate code for the function. For example, the template function swap can be called to swap the values of two variables of an unspecified type; that type may be a container (with an overloaded **operator**=) or even **int**. Here—straight from the file algorith.h of the Hewlett-Packard implementation of the Standard Template Library—is the function definition:

```
template <class T>
inline void swap (T& a, T& b)
{
      T tmp = a;
      a = b;
      b = tmp;
}
```

Recall that **template** is a keyword and is always followed by <**class** . . . >. The type identifier T following the keyword **class** will be undefined at this time. When the function call is translated into machine language by the compiler, the type of the argument replaces the unspecified type. The type identifier may be a class, such as string, Employee, or Linked. Or the type may be a simple type, such as **int** or **double**. The keyword **inline** tells the compiler to generate machine code directly—not a function call—whenever this function is invoked. For example, suppose we had

```
float x,
      y;
. . .
swap (x, y);
```

the machine code generated would be the same as if we had written

```
float x,
      y;

. . .
float tmp = x;
x = y;
y = tmp;
```

In-line functions are handled more efficiently than function calls because there is no need to pass arguments to parameters, transfer control to the function called, and return control once the call is complete. In-line functions must not contain loops and must be nonrecursive (recursion is introduced in Chapter 4).

The following program, swap.cpp, swaps the values of two strings and then swaps the values of two **int**s:

```
#include <iostream>

#include <algorithm> // defines most of the generic algorithms

#include <string>

using namespace std;

int main( )
{
      const string CLOSE_WINDOW_PROMPT =
```

```
                              "Please press the Enter key to close this output window.";
                        string s1 = "yes",
                               s2 = "no";
                        swap (s1, s2);
                        cout << s1 << " " << s2 << endl; // output:: no yes

                        int i1 = 58,
                            i2 = 902;
                        swap (i1, i2);
                        cout << i1 << " " << i2 << endl; // output: 902 58

                        cout << endl << endl << CLOSE_WINDOW_PROMPT;
                        cin.get( );
                        return 0;
                } // main
```

For another example of a template function, here is one to add up the items in an array. In this program the function add_up is defined and then called twice, once to add up an array of **double**s and once to add up an array of **int**s.

```
#include <iostream>

#include <string> // declares string class

using namespace std;

// Postcondition: The value returned is the sum of the items in a [0 . . . n − 1].
template <class T >
T add_up (T a[ ], int n)
{
      T sum = 0;

      for (int i = 0; i < n; i++)

            sum = sum + a [i];
      return sum;
} // add_up

int main( )
{
      const string DOUBLE_MESSAGE =
            "The sum of the doubles is";
      const string INT_MESSAGE =
            "The sum of the ints is ";
      const string CLOSE_WINDOW_PROMPT =
            "Please press the Enter key to close this output window.";

      const int SIZE1 = 5;
```

```
const int SIZE2 = 20;

double weight [SIZE1] = { 3.2, 3.1, 2.9, 3.1, 3.0 };
int count [SIZE2];

cout << DOUBLE_MESSAGE << add_up (weight, SIZE1) << endl
          << endl;
     // output:: The sum of the doubles is 15.3
for (int i = 0; i < SIZE2; i++)
     count [i] = i;
cout << INT_MESSAGE << add_up (count, SIZE2) << endl
          << endl;
     // output:: The sum of the ints is 190

cout << endl << CLOSE_WINDOW_PROMPT;
cin.get( );
return 0;
} // main
```

There is a drawback to the template function add_up: it works only on arrays. Even though we have seen only one container class so far (the Linked class), we will soon be spending a lot of time with container classes. So it would be preferable to have a template function that would add up the items, not only in an array, but also in a container object.

Such a function does exist. It is the accumulate function, defined in the file numeric.h. Here is the complete definition:

```
// Postcondition: the value returned is the sum of init and all of the items in
//                 the container from position first (inclusive) to last (exclusive)
template <class InputIterator, class T>;
T accumulate (InputIterator first, InputIterator last, T init)
{
     while (first != last)
          init = init + *first++;
     return init;
} // accumulate
```

This function has two template types: InputIterator and T. T is the as-yet-unspecified type of the initial value, the return value, and the values that iterators first and last are positioned at. The type of the parameters first and last is InputIterator, but what capabilities must an input iterator have? An input iterator must be able to

Access—not necessarily to modify—each item in the container

Advance to the next item in a container

Determine when the end of the container has been reached

Input iterators are so named because they reflect the activity in reading an input stream. The only operators that an input iterator must support are

Iterator dereferencing, that is, **operator***

Iterator incrementing, that is, **operator**++

Iterator-equality tests, that is, **operator**== and **operator**!=

Note that those are exactly the operators accumulate uses for the iterators first and last! Since the Iterator class embedded in the Linked class has these operators, that Iterator class falls into the just defined broad category of InputIterators. That is, we can use accumulate to add up the items in a Linked container. Recall that the Linked methods begin( ) and end( ) return Iterators, which, as we have just seen, qualify as input iterators. Here is the code:

```
Linked<int> list;

. . .

int sum = accumulate (list.begin( ), list.end( ), 0);
```

*A **generic algorithm**
is a template function
that applies to
container objects,
through iterators,
and to arrays,
through pointers.*

The template function accumulate is an example of a generic algorithm. A **generic algorithm** is a template function that applies to container objects and to arrays. To accumulate the items in an array, all we need for arguments are pointers to the beginning and one past the end of where we want to accumulate in the array, and an initial value. Recall that an array variable itself is actually a pointer to the beginning of the array. So the array variable plus the size of the array is a pointer to one past the end of the array. We can rewrite the program to add an array of **double**s and an array of **int**s by omitting the definition of add_up and replacing the two calls to add_up with

```
cout << DOUBLE_MESSAGE << accumulate (weight, weight + SIZE1,
        0.0) << endl << endl;
```

and

```
cout << INT_MESSAGE << accumulate (count, count + SIZE2, 0) << endl
        << endl;
```

Lab 7 further investigates the versatility of generic algorithms in general and the accumulate function in particular.

LAB   **Lab 7: More on generic algorithms.**

(All Labs Are Optional.)   **LAB**

We end this chapter with a brief look at a user's view of containers.

2.3.8   Data Structures and the Standard Template Library

*A **data structure**
is a container as
viewed by a user.*

A **data structure** is a container as viewed by a user. Except for the array, all containers in C++ are instances of some container class, so our interest in data structures is restricted to container classes. Specifically, a user of a container class can

1. Create an instance of that class

2. Invoke the **public** methods of that class

A developer completes that picture by providing fields and method definitions. We then say that a developer has ***implemented*** the data structure. For example, if we focus on the method interfaces of the Linked class, we are treating that class as a data structure. But when we look at a specific choice of fields and method definitions, we are considering an implementation of that data structure.

The Standard Template Library includes data structures that have a wide variety of applications. In Standard C++, of which the Standard Template Library is a part, *the implementation details of the data structures are not specified.* Compiler writers are free to provide any implementation that satisfies the method interfaces of the given container class. Starting in Chapter 5, we will look at the data structures in the Standard Template Library and study possible implementations of each. Incidentally, almost all the container classes are templated and have an associated iterator class, so those topics will prove useful in those chapters.

SUMMARY

The concepts of pointers and dynamic variables are vital to an in-depth understanding of C++. One of the relevant concepts is the Universal Array-Pointer Law.

> **Universal Array-Pointer Law**
> For any array **a** and nonnegative integer i, a [i] is the same as *(a + i).

A *container class* is one in which each object that is an instance of that class consists of a collection of items. A *container* object—an instance of a container class—can be stored contiguously, in an array, or in a linked structure. In a linked structure each item is stored in a **struct** called a *node,* which also contains a pointer to another node.

Associated with almost every container class is an iterator class. *Iterators* are objects that allow a user to loop through a container object without violating the Principle of Data Abstraction. Most iterator classes have the following operators:

operator!=	// to compare an iterator to another iterator
operator++	// to advance the iterator to the next position in the container
operator*	// to return the item the iterator is positioned at

And most container classes have a begin( ) method that returns an iterator positioned at the beginning of the container, and an end( ) method that returns an iterator positioned *just after* the last position in the container.

The Linked class is a very simple example of a container class. Not surprisingly, the Linked class has a linked structure.

Much of the Standard Template Library consists of the method interfaces for various container classes. Compiler writers are allowed to implement those container classes as desired as long as the method interfaces are satisfied.

EXERCISES

2.1 a. Create a Linked container, intList, of **int**s. Insert five integers into intList.

b. Create itr, to iterate through a Linked container of **int**s.

c. Print out intList.

d. Create two Linked containers, oddList and evenList, of **int**s.

e. For each item in intList, insert a copy of that item into either oddList or evenList, depending on whether the item is an odd or even integer.

f. Print out oddList and evenList.

2.2 a. Create employeeList, a Linked container of Employee objects.

b. Read in five employees from the input and insert each employee onto the front of employeeList. Read in a sixth employee whose name is "**ZZZ**" and whose gross pay is $100,000.00.

c. From employeeList, print out the name and gross pay of each employee whose gross pay exceeds that of the sixth employee.

> *Hint*   Use an iterator.

2.3 Implement the original (three-method) Linked class with an array. Start with a default capacity of 100 for the array, and double the capacity whenever the current capacity is exceeded.

> *Hint*   In addition to an array field, include a front field that holds the index of the front item. Increment front whenever an item is inserted. In what sense is this "better" than inserting each new item at index 0?

2.4 Explain why the following definition of the push_front method would be incorrect:

```
void push_front (const T& newItem)
{
      head = new Node;
      head −> item = newItem;
      head −> next = head;
      length++;
} // method push_front
```

2.5 Give two examples, from this chapter or Labs 4 to 6, of Linked-class methods that loop through the container without using an Iterator object.

2.6 In the Linked class, the embedded Iterator class has no decrement operator, **operator--(int)**. In fact, with the current design and implementation of the Iterator class, it would be impossible to define such an operator. Explain. Propose a modification to the Iterator class so that a postdecrement operator could be defined.

PROGRAMMING PROJECT 2.1

Extending the Linked Class

In Lab 6, you extended the Linked class by declaring and defining **operator**=. Here are method interfaces for some additional methods:

```
// Postcondition: true has been returned if this Linked object contains no items.
//                Otherwise, false has been returned.
bool empty( ) const;
```

```
// Postcondition: true has been returned if this Linked object and otherLinked contain
//                the same items in the same order. Otherwise, false has been
//                returned.
bool operator== (const Linked& otherLinked) const;
```

```
// Postcondition: true has been returned if this Linked object and otherLinked do not
//                contain the same items in the same order. Otherwise, false has
//                been returned.
bool operator!= (const Linked& otherLinked) const;
```

1. Define those methods.

2. Test your definitions with a main function that defines and manipulates two Linked objects of **int**s:

```
Linked<int> intList1,
            intList2;
```

Include several invocations of each method you defined in part 1, and for each method that returns a **bool** value, include one invocation for which **true** is returned and one invocation for which **false** is returned. Include enough output to indicate that your methods are correct.

3. Retest your definitions with a main function that defines and manipulates two Linked objects of Employees objects (you will need to overload **operator**== for the Employee class):

```
Linked<Employee> empList1,
                 empList2;
```

Create both Linked objects by reading from the keyboard until the sentinel is reached. Include several invocations of each method you defined in part 1.

CHAPTER 3

Introduction to Software Engineering

The computers of today are much more powerful than those in use when you were born. If we take the number of transistors on a chip as a crude measure of computing power, then computing power has doubled approximately every 18 months since 1967. This amazing statistic is known as Moore's Law, first formulated in 1965 by Gordon Moore, chairperson of Intel, Inc. Because of this steady advance in hardware capability, it is feasible for computers to solve very complex problems in a relatively short time. But the development of the correspondingly large programs requires a systematic approach. Typically, developing a 10,000-line program is *much* more than twice as difficult as developing a 5000-line program. ■

CHAPTER OBJECTIVES

1. Understand the four stages in the software development life cycle.

2. Develop dependency diagrams using the Unified Modeling Language.

3. Create test cases for methods, classes, and projects.

4. Perform both Big-O analysis and run-time analysis of methods.

3.1 | THE SOFTWARE DEVELOPMENT LIFE CYCLE

To enable programmers to manage the complexity associated with large programs, the discipline of software engineering has emerged. ***Software engineering*** is the application of principles, techniques, and tools to the production of software. Some of the relevant concepts originate in mathematics (formalism, Big-O analysis), some in the physical sciences (the scientific method), and some in engineering (project life cycle). Most of these concepts will be introduced in this chapter and then illustrated in the labs and in the remaining chapters.

The model we will study is referred to as the ***software development life cycle,*** a sequence of four stages that comprise a programming project. Some of those stages will have several substages, and so, to give you the big picture, here is a list of the stages in their chronological order:

1. *Problem analysis:* to carefully formulate the problem to be solved
2. *Program design:* to determine the classes needed to solve the problem, how they are related, and, for each class not already available, to determine the method interfaces and fields for that class
3. *Program implementation:* to define the methods for those classes not already available, and to validate, analyze, and integrate those classes
4. *Program maintenance:* to produce modifications to the earlier stages

The life cycle is seldom a sequential process. Rather, it is ***iterative:*** while working on a later stage, you often find that you need to redo some or all of your work from earlier stages.

3.2 | PROBLEM ANALYSIS

We assume we have been given a description of a problem. This description will probably be brief and may even contain ambiguities. But we need to have a clear understanding of the problem before we can build a program to solve the problem. The goal in the problem-analysis stage is to develop a clear understanding of *what* is to be done. We intentionally omit any indication of *how* the problem will be solved. In so doing we are practicing a generalization of the Principle of Data Abstraction. This generalization is known as the ***Principle of Abstraction:***

> **Principle of Abstraction**
> When trying to solve a problem, separate *what* is to be done from *how* it will be done.

In abstracting what needs to be done from how it will be done, we avoid getting bogged down in details that should be addressed at later stages, and possibly by other people.

Most of the work in the problem-analysis stage consists in providing *functional specifications:* detailed, unambiguous statements that describe what the program should do in terms of the input and output. The specifications should answer such questions as

1. What is the format of the input? What are the types and ranges of input values?
2. What is to be the format of the output? What are the types and ranges of output values?
3. What tasks are to be performed?
4. Will the program be interactive, that is, will the input be entered in response to the output? Or will the input files be created before the program is run? If the program is to be interactive, what will signal the end of the input?
5. How will input errors be handled, that is, how much input editing is to be performed? One advantage of interactive programs is that when incorrect input is entered, an error message can be printed, so the user can correct the error immediately. For example, the following specifications may apply to a year that is to be input:

    The year should be an integer between 1800 and 2200, inclusive. The year should be entered in response to the prompt "Please enter the year:".

    a. If the value entered is not a four-digit integer, the error message to be printed is "Error—the year entered is not a four-digit integer."
    b. If the value entered is a four-digit integer but is not in the range 1800–2200, the error message to be printed is "Error—the year entered is not in the range 1800–2200."
    c. Each time an incorrect value is entered for the year the corresponding error message and the prompt should be printed.

Should the specifications disallow all input errors? From the point of view of the developer of the program, the safe answer is "yes." If the program fails, either by terminating unexpectedly or by producing incorrect output, the programmer will be the prime suspect anyway. Programmers prefer to construct programs that are able to withstand the slings and arrows of outrageous inputs. That is, programmers would rather construct *robust* programs: those that do not terminate unexpectedly from invalid input. A robust program allows a user to recover from input errors: when an input error occurs, the user is notified—usually by a printed message—of the error and prompted for correct input.

But the final decision on input editing rests with the client, the one who is paying for the program. In some cases, such as national defense and patient monitoring, the cost of an unexpected termination or incorrect output can be catastrophic. In a business environment, decisions based on incorrect output can also have disastrous results. Often, however, some kinds of input errors can safely be ignored. For example, suppose the application is to produce a bill for a hospital patient. The client—the hospital administrator—may decide that it would be too costly, in terms of programmer time, to check each field in the patient's hospital record for correctness.

3.2.1   System Tests

In accordance with the specifications given, sample input values are created and the corresponding output is produced by hand. At this stage, the sample inputs and sample outputs serve mainly to confirm our understanding of the problem and the input-output formats. Later, after the program has been written, they serve as test cases to increase our confidence that the program performs according to the specifications. It is preferable to generate these system tests before, rather than after, the program has been written because otherwise, the way the program is written may unconsciously bias how it is tested.

As a simple example, we might have the following system test for a program that calculates the mean of a list of test scores. The sample input is shown in bold-face to distinguish the input from the output.

System Test   This program calculates the mean of a list of test scores. Each score must be an integer between 0 and 100, inclusive. A value of −1 is used as the sentinel.

> Please enter a test score: **80**
>
> Please enter a test score: **90**
>
> Please enter a test score: **700**
>
> Error: The score must be an integer between 0 and 100, inclusive.
>
> Please enter a test score: **7o**
>
> Error: The score must be an integer between 0 and 100, inclusive.
>
> Please enter a test score: **70**
>
> Please enter a test score: **−1**
>
> The mean is 80.0.

The development of comprehensive system tests is a formidable, time-consuming task. If a critical test is omitted, the program may contain an error that, by Murphy's Law, shows up at the least opportune, most costly moment.

The person who develops the specifications and system tests is a *systems analyst.* A systems analyst has several responsibilities. First, the systems analyst must understand the needs of the end-users—those who will, ultimately, run the program. Second, the systems analyst and the client must agree on the problem to be solved. Finally, the systems analyst must be able to provide an explicit and detailed description of that problem to the programmers.

All of this communication is greatly facilitated by documentation. Explicit documents such as the functional specifications tend to preclude later disagreements as to what was said and who agreed to what. Documentation provides the only visible evidence of the project other than the program's source code. We will note other kinds of documentation as we discuss later stages in the problem-solving process.

After the specifications and system tests have been created, the next stage is to design the program needed to solve the problem.

3.3 | PROGRAM DESIGN

In this stage we decide what classes will be needed to solve the problem, and how those classes are related. It is no exaggeration to say that the effort programmers invest in this stage has the greatest impact on the overall success of the project. A company may well have thousands of classes available. If one of those classes is appropriate for your project but you are unaware of that class, you could waste hundreds of hours re-creating the class. By browsing the software library for a few hours, you can make the difference between an on-time, underbudget project and one that is late and overbudget. Do not reinvent the wheel!

3.3.1   Method Interfaces and Fields

We will simply (and gladly) use those classes that are already available. For most of the projects we will encounter in the remaining chapters, the Standard Template Library supplies some of the needed classes. For virtually all projects, there will be at least one class that we need to create. For each such class, we start by enumerating the class's responsibilities; that is, the services the class must provide to users. We refine these responsibilities into method interfaces. We also determine the fields for the class, but postpone the method definitions until the program implementation stage. In other words, we develop the header file during design, and the source file in the implementation stage.

For example, in the best-paid-employee problem from Chapter 1, we identified the following responsibilities of the **Employee** class:

> To initialize an employee's name to a blank and gross pay to 0.00
>
> To read in an employee's name and gross pay
>
> To determine if the input sentinel has been reached
>
> To determine if an employee's gross pay is greater than some other employee's gross pay
>
> To get a copy of an employee's name and gross pay
>
> To write out an employee's name and gross pay

These responsibilities were then refined into method interfaces:

```
// Postcondition: this Employee's name has been set to an empty string and
//                gross pay has been set to 0.00.
Employee( );


// Postcondition: this Employee's name and gross pay have been read in.
void readInto( );


// Postcondition: true has been returned if this Employee was the sentinel.
//                Otherwise, false has been returned.
bool isSentinel( ) const;
```

```
// Postcondition: true has been returned if this Employee's gross pay is
//                 greater than that of otherEmployee. Otherwise, false has
//                 been returned.
bool makesMoreThan (const Employee& otherEmployee) const;


// Postcondition:  this Employee contains a copy of otherEmployee.
void getCopyOf (const Employee& otherEmployee);


// Postcondition: this Employee's name and gross pay have been written out.
void printOut( ) const;
```

The precondition and postcondition of a method interface constitute a **contract** between the developer of a method and a programmer who uses that method. If the user ascertains that the precondition is met before the method is called, then the developer guarantees that the method will eventually terminate and, when it does, the postcondition will be true. If the precondition happens to be false and the user invokes the method anyway, the developer accepts no responsibility for the result: incorrect answers, program crash, bankruptcy, ...

The Employee class has two fields:

```
string name;

double grossPay;
```

Another needed class is Company, whose responsibilities are to find the best-paid employee and to print the name and gross pay of the best-paid employee. The method interfaces are

```
// Postcondition: The best-paid employee in this Company has been
//                 determined.
void findBestPaid( );


// Postcondition: The name and gross pay of the best-paid employee in this
//                 Company have been printed out.
void printBestPaid( );
```

In the Company class, the only field is

```
Employee bestPaid;
```

A method interface is a method-level tool for documenting design decisions. Section 3.3.2 deals with a class-level documentation tool.

3.3.2   Dependency Diagrams

An important tool for documentation of the relationship between classes is the dependency diagram. A **dependency diagram** is a chart that shows the dependencies between classes and between fields and calling objects in the project. The symbols used to indicate these relationships are from the ***Unified Modeling Language*** (UML)—an industry-standardized language that incorporates current software-engineering practices that deal with the modeling of systems. For example, if class A is a subclass of class B, an arrow with a solid head is drawn from A to B. Figure 3.1 has part of a dependency diagram for the design of the best-paid-hourly-employee problem.

The dependency relationship between an object field in a class and a calling object of that class is more complicated. Suppose that we have the following:

```
class X
{
      Y y;

      . . .
}; // class X
 ;
```

There are two cases to consider:

1. *Composition.* When the space for an object of type X is deallocated, the space for object y is also deallocated. In other words, the existence of y *is dependent on* X's object.

2. *Aggregation.* When the space for an object of type X is deallocated, the space for the object y is not deallocated. In other words, the existence of y *is independent of* X's object.

For example, in the Employee class, the name object exists only as long as the calling Employee object exists. Recall, from Chapter 2, that if a class has no explicit destructor, it is given an implicit destructor by the compiler. This implicit destructor simply calls the destructor (explicit or implicit) for each field in the class. So when an Employee object goes out of scope, the space for its name field is deallocated. That is, the name object is dependent on the calling Employee object, and we have an example of composition.

Figure 3.1 I Part of a dependency diagram for the design of the best-paid-hourly-employee problem.

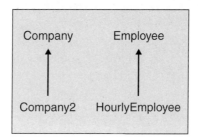

To depict composition in the Unified Modeling Language, an arrow is drawn from the enclosing class to the field; the arrow begins with a filled diamond. Figure 3.2 illustrates the dependency of the name object to the Employee class and of the bestPaid object to the Company class (also composition).

Aggregation occurs when a pointer to the field object is returned by one of the methods in the enclosing class. For example, we could have the following:

```
class X
{
        protected:
              Y y;
        public:
              Y* sendIt( )
              {
                    . . .
                    return &y;
              } // method sendIt
      . . .
}; // class X
```

In this case, we do not want the space for y to be deallocated when the space for the calling X object is deallocated because a pointer to y is returned by sendIt. That returned pointer may still be in existence when the calling X object is deallocated, so the y object pointed to should still be accessible at that time. To ensure that the y object is still accessible when the space for the X object is deallocated, the enclosing class must have an explicit destructor which does not deallocate the space for y.

In the Unified Modeling Language, aggregation is depicted by an arrow from the enclosing class to the field object; the arrow begins with a hollow diamond. Figure 3.3 illustrates aggregation for the example just discussed.

Figure 3.2 I The dependency diagram for **composition** in the Unified Modeling Language. The object name is dependent on the calling Employee object, and the object bestPaid is dependent on the calling Company object.

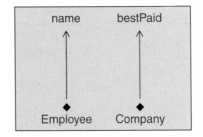

Figure 3.3 I An illustration of ***aggregation*** in the Unified Modeling Language. The space for the object y is not deallocated when the space for the calling X object is deallocated.

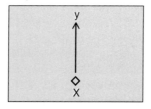

In C++, the decision as to whether composition or aggregation applies is made by the developer (of class X for example). This decision determines whether the class should have an explicit destructor and, if so, its definition.

As soon as the design has been completed, work on the implementation stage can commence. That stage is discussed in Section 3.4. The last part of the program design stage—determining the fields for each class—is sometimes considered to be part of the program implementation stage. This distinction is not practically significant because the same team usually works on both the design and the implementation.

3.4 I PROGRAM IMPLEMENTATION

In this stage, we first complete the definition of each new class by supplying the method definitions. We then try to determine the correctness and efficiency of each of the class's methods. When we are reasonably confident that a method behaves well locally, we consider how well it fits in with the other methods in the class and how well the class fits in with other classes in the project. We consider method correctness first because an incorrect method is worthless, while an inefficient method may still be usable.

Section 3.4.1 deals with techniques to gain confidence that a method is correct.

3.4.1   Method Validation

The most popular technique for increasing confidence in the correctness of a method is to *validate* the method, that is, to test the method with a number of sample values for the fields and parameters (and inputs, if the method includes any input statements). We then compare the actual results with the results expected according to the method's postcondition.

For example, suppose we want to test the next( ) method in the Date class described in Chapter 1. Special care should be given to make sure that the method works properly for *boundary values* such as the last day of a month and the last month of the year. Here are some test data:

Sample value of calling object			Expected result for next( )		
Day	**Month**	**Year**	**Day**	**Month**	**Year**
17	11	2003	18	11	2003
30	11	2003	1	12	2003
31	12	2003	1	1	2004
28	2	2000	29	2	2000
28	2	2003	1	3	2003
28	2	2004	29	2	2004
28	2	2100	1	3	2100

The last four lines in the table reflect the fact that the Earth travels around the sun in approximately 365.2425 days. A *leap year* is a year that is both evenly divisible by 4 and either not evenly divisible by 100 or evenly divisible by 400.

If the next( ) method passes these tests, our confidence in that method's correctness will increase. But we cannot yet be certain of the method's correctness because we have not tried all possible tests. In general, it is rarely feasible to run all possible tests, and so we cannot infer correctness based on testing alone. As E. W. Dijkstra has wisely noted, *testing can reveal the presence of errors but not the absence of errors.*

Another problem with testing is the objectivity of the tester: the person who constructs the test data. Programmers tend to view their work favorably, even glowingly ("a masterpiece," "a thing of beauty and a joy forever," "the eighth wonder of the world"). As such, programmers are ill-suited to test their own methods because the purpose of testing is to uncover errors. Ideally the person who constructs test data should hope that the method will fail the test. In a classroom setting the instructor may appear to satisfy this criterion!

If a class has a single method, we can set up a test regimen that deals with that method in isolation. More often, a class will have several methods, and we will need to test them in concert. For example, we may need to test method m1( ) followed by method m2( ), and also test method m2( ) followed by method m1( ). A *driver* is a program created specifically to test the methods in a class. A production-strength driver that permits methods to be tested extensively is more complex than an ad hoc driver for a single method. The topic of drivers is pursued in Lab 8.

LAB   **Lab 8: Drivers.**

(All Labs Are Optional.)   **LAB**

Just as it is unusual for a class to have a single method, it is unlikely that a project will have a single class. For a multiclass project, which class should be tested first? In an object-oriented environment, bottom-up testing is the norm. With *bottom-up testing,* a project's low-level classes—those that are used by but do not use other classes—are tested and then integrated with higher-level classes and so on. After each of the component classes has satisfied its tests, we can perform *system testing,* that is, testing the project as a whole. Inputs for the first few system tests are provided as part of the problem analysis stage. If the project passes those tests, we conduct additional tests until we are convinced the project is correct, that is, that it meets the specifications.

The purpose of testing is to detect errors in a program (or to increase confidence that no errors exist in the program). When testing reveals that there is an error in your program, you must then determine what brought about the error. This may entail some serious detective work. And the purpose of detection is correction. The entire validation phase—testing, detection, and correction—is iterative. Once an error has been corrected, the testing should start over, because the "correction" may have created new errors.

3.4.2   Is Correctness Feasible?

As we noted at the start of this chapter, the trend in recent years has been toward increasingly powerful software. (One recent advertisement defined a *large* program as one "with more than one million lines of code.") But there is a continuing shortage of qualified systems analysts and programmers, and management's view of projects has been traditionally characterized by impatience. As a result, errors are now considered an inevitable feature of "completed" systems.

From the perspective of software professionals, this situation is intolerable. What can be done? First, and this is a major change, management must take a long-term view of software. The classes being developed for the current project can be reused indefinitely, either directly or through inheritance. So the extra time spent on ensuring the correctness of those classes is really an investment in the future. Furthermore, there has to be an obsession with quality by every member of the software team. Systems analysts must work harder to specify exactly what is to be done. Programmers need to intensify their efforts to establish correctness. The overall goal is to create an environment hostile to errors, so that some day software warranties will be as common as hardware warranties.

From management's point of view, an obsession with perfection is hostile to profitability. If the development team has 99 percent confidence in the correctness of a system, that system will probably be shipped, so that profits can start rolling in. To delay shipping until there is 100 percent confidence might take so much extra time that the profitability of the project would decline sharply. Of course, shipping a system that still has *lots* of errors will undermine the company's credibility, so a balance must be struck. In an object-oriented environment, the conflict is not so much between correctness and profitability as between short-term profitability and long-term profitability.

Now that we have looked at the validation of methods, classes, and projects, we turn our attention to assessing their efficiency.

3.4.3   Estimating the Efficiency of Methods

The correctness of a method depends only on whether the method does *what* it is supposed to do. But the efficiency of a method depends to a great extent on *how* that method is defined. How can efficiency be measured? We could compile and execute the method repeatedly in a program specifically created for that task. But then the analysis would depend on the compiler, operating system, and computer used. At this stage, we prefer a more abstract analysis that can be performed by directly investigating the method's definition. The question, then, is how can we estimate the execution-time requirements of a method from the method's definition?

We take the number of statements executed in a trace of a method as a measure of the execution-time requirements of that method. This measure will be represented as a function of the "size" of the problem. For example, the size of a sorting problem is the number of values to be sorted. Typically, a problem with *n* input records is said to be "of size *n*."

Given a method for a problem of size *n*, let **worstTime(n)** be the maximum (over all possible parameters and input values) number of statements executed in a trace of the method. Sometimes we will also be interested in the average-case performance of a method. We define **averageTime(n)** to be the average number of statements executed in a trace of the method. This average is taken over all invocations of the method, and we assume that each possible arrangement of the *n* problem values is equally likely. For some applications, this last assumption is unrealistic, so the averageTime(*n*) may not be relevant.

Occasionally, especially in Chapters 4 and 12, we will also be interested in estimating the space requirements of a method. To that end, we define **worst Space(n)** to be the maximum number of variables accessed in a trace of the method, and **averageSpace(n)** to be the average number of variables accessed in a trace of the method.

3.4.4   Big-O Notation

We need not calculate worstTime(*n*) and averageTime(*n*)—or worstSpace(*n*) and averageSpace(*n*)—exactly since they are only crude approximations of the time requirements of the corresponding method. Instead, we approximate those functions by means of **Big-O** notation. Because we are looking at the method by itself, this "approximation of an approximation" is quite satisfactory for giving us an idea of how fast the method will be.

The basic idea behind Big-O notation is that we often want to determine an **upper bound** for the behavior of a function, that is, to determine how bad the function can get. For example, suppose we are given a function *f*. If some function *g* is, loosely speaking, an upper bound for *f*, then we say that *f* is Big O of *g*. When we replace "loosely speaking" with specifics, we get the following definition:

Let g be a function that has nonnegative integer arguments and returns a nonnegative value for all arguments. We define $O(g)$ to be the set of functions f such that for some pair of nonnegative constants C and K,

$$f(n) \leq Cg(n) \quad \text{for all } n \geq K$$

If f is in $O(g)$, we say that f is "O of g," or "f is of order g."

The idea behind Big-O notation is that if f is $O(g)$ then eventually f is bounded above by some constant times g, so we can use $O(g)$ as a crude upper-bound estimate of the function f.

By a standard abuse of notation, we often associate a function with the value it calculates. For example, let g be the function defined by

$$g(n) = n^3 \quad \text{for } n = 0, 1, 2, \ldots$$

Instead of writing $O(g)$ we write $O(n^3)$.

EXAMPLE 3.1

Let f be the function defined as follows:

$$f(n) = n(n + 3) + 4 \qquad \text{for } n = 0, 1, 2, \ldots$$

Show that f is $O(n^2)$.

■ **Solution**

We need to find nonnegative constants C and K such that $f(n) \leq Cn^2$ for all $n \geq K$. We first rewrite the function definition:

$$f(n) = n^2 + 3n + 4 \qquad \text{for } n = 0, 1, 2, \ldots$$

We then show that each term in that definition is less than or equal to some constant times n^2 for $n \geq$ some nonnegative integer. Right away, we get

$$n^2 \leq 1n^2 \qquad \text{for } n \geq 0$$
$$3n \leq 3n^2 \qquad \text{for } n \geq 0$$
$$4 \leq 4n^2 \qquad \text{for } n \geq 1$$

So for any $n \geq 1$,

$$f(n) \leq n^2 + 3n^2 + 4n^2 = 8n^2$$

That is, for $C = 8$ and $K = 1$, $f(n) \leq Cn^2$ for all $n \geq K$. This shows that f is $O(n^2)$.

In general, if f is a polynomial of the form

$$a_k n^k + a_{k-1} n^{k-1} + \ldots + a_1 n + a_0$$

then we can establish that f is $O(n^k)$ by choosing $K = 1$, $C = |a_k| + |a_{k-1}| + \ldots + |a_1| + |a_0|$, and proceeding as in Example 3.1.

Example 3.2 shows that we can ignore the base of a logarithm when determining the order of a function.

EXAMPLE 3.2

Let a and b be positive constants. Show that if f is $O(\log_a n)$, then f is also $O(\log_b n)$.

■ **Solution**

Assume that f is $O(\log_a n)$. Then there are nonnegative constants C and K such that for all $n \geq K$,

$$f(n) \leq C \log_a n$$

By a fundamental property of logarithms (see Appendix 1),

$$\log_a n = (\log_a b)(\log_b n) \text{ for any } n > 0$$

Let $C_1 = C \log_a b$.
Then for all $n \geq K$, we have

$$f(n) \leq C \log_a n = C \log_a b \log_b n = C_1 \log_b n,$$

and so f is $O(\log_b n)$.

Note that Big-O notation merely gives an upper bound for a function. For example, if f is $O(n^2)$, then f is also $O(n^2 + 5n + 2)$, $O(n^3)$, and $O(n^{10} + 3)$. Whenever possible, we choose the smallest element from the hierarchy of orders, of which the most commonly used are shown in Figure 3.4. To say that $O(g)$ is the **smallest upper bound** of f means that f is $O(g)$ and for any function h, if f is $O(h)$, then $O(g) \subset O(h)$.

For example, if $f(n) = n + 7$ for $n = 0, 1, 2, \ldots$, it is most appropriate to say that f is $O(n)$—even though f is also $O(n \log n)$ and $O(n^3)$. Figure 3.5 shows some more examples of functions and where they fit in the order hierarchy.

For a concrete example of the differences between different orders, suppose $n = 1$ million. Then

$$\log_2 n \approx 20$$
$$n = 1 \text{ million}$$
$$n \log_2 n \approx 20 \text{ million}$$
$$n^2 = 1 \text{ trillion}$$

Notice the huge difference between $\log_2 n$ and n, and between $n \log_2 n$ and n^2. In Chapter 8, we will study a data structure—the binary search tree—for which average Time(n) is $O(\log n)$ for inserting, removing and searching but worstTime(n) is $O(n)$ for those methods. Similarly, in Chapter 12, the contrast between $n \log_2 n$ and n^2 gives tangible evidence of the difference between simple sorts, whose averageTime(n) is $O(n^2)$, and fast sorts, whose averageTime(n) is $O(n \log n)$.

Figure 3.4 I Some elements in the hierarchy of orders. The symbol "⊂" means "is contained in." For example, every function that is in $O(1)$ is also in $O(\log n)$.

$$O(1) \subset O(\log n) \subset O(n^{1/2}) \subset O(n) \subset O(n \log n) \subset O(n^2) \subset O(n^3) \subset \cdots \subset O(2^n) \cdots$$

Figure 3.5 I Some sample functions in the order hierarchy.

Order	Sample function
$O(1)$	$f(n) = 3000$
$O(\log n)$	$f(n) = [n \log_2(n + 1) + 2]/(n + 1)$
$O(n)$	$f(n) = 5 \log_2 n + n$
$O(n \log n)$	$f(n) = \log_2 n^n$ (See Appendix 1)
$O(n^2)$	$f(n) = n(n + 1)/2$

Section 3.4.5 illustrates how easy it can be to approximate worstTime(n)—or averageTime(n)—with the help of Big-O notation.

3.4.5 Getting Big-O Estimates Quickly

By estimating the number of loop iterations in a method, we can often determine at a glance the smallest upper bound in the order hierarchy for worstTime(n). Let S represent any sequence of statements whose execution does not include a loop statement for which the number of iterations depends on n. The following method skeletons provide paradigms for determining the smallest upper bound for worstTime(n) in the hierarchy of orders.

Use Big-O notation to obtain a quick but crude estimate of the smallest upper bound for worstTime(n) and averageTime(n).

1. worstTime(n) is $O(1)$:

    S

    Note that the execution of S may entail the execution of millions of statements! For example:

    ```
    double sum = 0;
    for (int i = 0; i < 10000000; i++)
        sum += sqrt (i);
    ```

    The reason that worstTime(n) is $O(1)$ is that the number of loop iterations is constant and therefore independent of n. In fact, we often bypass Big-O notation in this case and say that worstTime(n) is "constant."
2. worstTime(n) is $O(\log n)$:

    ```
    while (n > 1)
    {
        n = n / 2;
        S
    ```

} // while

Let $t(n)$ be the number of times that S is executed. Then $t(n)$ is equal to the number of times that n can be divided by 2 until n is 1. By Example A1.3, $t(n)$ is the largest integer $\leq \log_2 n$. That is, $t(n) = \text{floor}(\log_2 n)$.[1] Therefore $t(n)$ is $O(\log n)$, and so worstTime(n) is also $O(\log n)$.

The phenomenon of repeatedly splitting a container in two will reappear time and again in Chapters 4 and 8 through 12. Be on the lookout for the splitting: it signals that worstTime(n) will be $O(\log n)$.

The Rule of Splitting

If during each loop iteration, *n* is divided by some constant greater than 1, the number of iterations will be $O(\log n)$.

When $O(\log n)$ is the smallest upper bound of worstTime(n), we say that worstTime(n) is "logarithmic in n."

3. worstTime(n) is $O(n)$:

```
S
for (i = 0; i < n; i++)
{
        S
} // for
S
```

The reason that worstTime(n) is $O(n)$ is simply that the **for** loop is executed n times. It does not matter how many statements are executed during each iteration of the **for** loop.

When n is the smallest upper bound for worstTime(n), we say that worstTime(n) is "linear in n."

4. worstTime(n) is $O(n \log n)$:

```
for (i = 0; i < n; i++)
{
        m = n;
        while (m > 1)
        {
                m = m / 2;
                S
        } // while
} // for
```

---

[1] floor(x) returns the largest integer that is less than or equal to x.

The **for** loop is executed n times. For each iteration of the **for** loop, the **while** loop is executed floor($\log_2 n$) times—see example 2 in this list. Therefore worstTime(n) is $O(n \log n)$.

5. worstTime(n) is $O(n^2)$:

    a.   **for** (i = 0; i < n; i++)

            for (j = 0; j < n; j++)

            {

                S

            } // for j

The number of times that S is executed is n^2.

    b.   **for** (i = 0; i < n; i++)

            for (j = i; j < n; j++)

            {

                S

            } // for j

The number of times that S is executed is

$$n + (n - 1) + (n - 2) + \cdots + 3 + 2 + 1 = \sum_{k=1}^{n} k$$

As shown in Example A1.1, this sum is equal to

$$n(n + 1) / 2$$

which is $O(n^2)$. That is, worstTime(n) is $O(n^2)$.

    c.   **for** (i = 0; i < n; i++)

        {

            S

        } // for i

        for (i = 0; i < n; i++)

            for (j = 0; j < n; j++)

            {

                S

            } // for j

For the first segment, worstTime(n) is $O(n)$, and for the second segment, worstTime(n) is $O(n^2)$, so for both segments together, worstTime(n) is $O(n^2)$. In general, for the sequence

A

B

if worstTime(n) is $O(f)$ for A and worstTime(n) is $O(g)$ for B, then worstTime(n) is $O(f + g)$ for the sequence A, B.

When n^2 is the smallest upper bound of worstTime(n), we say that worstTime(n) is "quadratic in n."

We prefer to use plain English ("constant," "logarithmic," "linear,","quadratic") whenever possible. But as we will see in Section 3.4.6 on trade-offs, there will still be many occasions when all we can specify is a Big-O estimate of some upper bound, not necessarily the lowest upper bound in the hierarchy of orders.

Suppose we have a method whose worstTime(n) is linear in n. Then we can write

$$\text{worstTime}(n) \approx Cn \quad \text{for some constant } C$$

What will be the effect of doubling the size of the problem, that is, of doubling n?

$$\begin{aligned}
\text{worstTime}(2n) &\approx C\,2\,n \\
&= 2\,Cn \\
&\approx 2\,\text{worstTime}(n)
\end{aligned}$$

In other words, if we double n, we double the estimate of worst time.

Similarly, if a method has worstTime(n) that is quadratic in n, we can write

$$\text{worstTime}(n) \approx Cn^2 \quad \text{for some constant } C$$

Then

$$\begin{aligned}
\text{worstTime}(2n) &\approx C(2n)^2 \\
&= C4n^2 \\
&= 4Cn^2 \\
&\approx 4\,\text{worstTime}(n)
\end{aligned}$$

In other words, if we double n, we quadruple the estimate of worst time. Other examples of this kind of relationship are explored in Exercise 3.7, Exercise 12.5, and in Labs 16 and 27.

Figure 3.6 shows the relative growth rates of six orders in the order hierarchy. That figure indicates why Big-O differences eventually dominate other factors in estimating the behavior of a function. For example, if n is sufficiently large, $T_1(n) = n^2 / 100$ is much greater than $T_2(n) = 100n \log_2 n$ even though T_1 is smaller than T_2 for arguments less than 100,000.

A *polynomial-time* method is one for which worstTime(n) is $O(n^k)$ for some positive integer k. For example, a method whose worstTime(n) is $O(n^2)$ is a polynomial-time method. Similarly, a method whose worstTime(n) is $O(n \log n)$ is a polynomial-time method because $O(n \log n) \subset O(n^2)$. When we try to develop a method to solve a given problem, we prefer polynomial-time methods whenever possible; otherwise, it will be infeasible to run the method for large values of n. As you can see from Figure 3.6, a method whose worstTime(n) is $O(2^n)$ grows too rapidly to be useful for large values of n. Such methods, because they are not polynomial-time, are called *exponential-time* methods. An *intractable problem* is one for which any method to solve the problem is an exponential-time method. For example, a problem that

Figure 3.6 | The graphs of worstTime(*n*) for several orders of functions.

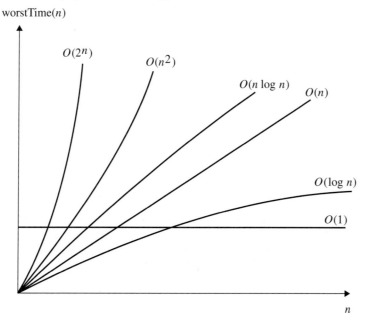

requires 2^n values to be printed is intractable. We will see two examples of intractable problems in Chapter 4. Lab 29 investigates the traveling salesperson problem, for which the only known methods to solve the problem are exponential-time methods. It is an open question whether the traveling salesperson problem is intractable, because there may be a polynomial-time method to solve that problem.

If we are working on a single method only, it may be feasible to optimize that method's averageTime(*n*) and worstTime(*n*), with the intent of optimizing execution time. But for the management of an entire project, it is usually necessary to strike a balance. Section 3.4.6 explores the relevance of other factors, such as memory utilization and project deadlines.

3.4.6 Trade-Offs

In Section 3.4.5 we saw how to analyze a method with respect to its execution-time requirements. The same Big-O notation allows us to estimate a method's memory requirements. Ideally, we will be able to develop methods that are both fast enough *and* small enough. But in the real world, we seldom attain the ideal. More likely, we will encounter one or more of the following obstacles during programming:

1. The program's estimated execution time may be longer than acceptable according to the performance specifications. *Performance specifications,* when given, state the upper bounds for time and space for all or part of a program.

2. The program's estimated memory requirements may be larger than acceptable according to the performance specifications.

3. The program may require understanding a technique about which the programmer is only vaguely familiar. This may create an unacceptable delay of the entire project.

Often, a trade-off must be made: a program that reduces one of the three obstacles may intensify the other two. The point is that real-life programming involves hard decisions. It is not nearly enough that you can develop programs that run. Adapting to constraints such as these will make you a better programmer by increasing your flexibility.

Up until now, we have separated concerns about correctness from concerns about efficiency. According to the Principle of Data Abstraction, the correctness of code that uses a class should be independent of that class's implementation details. But the efficiency of that code may well depend on those details. In other words, the developer of a class is free—for the sake of efficiency—to choose any combination of fields and method definitions, provided the correctness of the class's methods do not rely on those choices. For example, suppose a class developer can create three different versions of a class:

A. Correct, inefficient, does not allow users to access fields

B. Correct, somewhat efficient, does not allow users to access fields

C. Correct, highly efficient, allows users to access fields

In most cases, the appropriate choice is B. Choosing C would violate the Principle of Data Abstraction because the correctness of a program that uses C could depend on C's fields.

We can incorporate efficiency estimates into the correctness of a method by including performance specifications in the method's postcondition. For example, part of the postcondition for the generic algorithm sort in Chapter 12 is

worstTime(n) is $O(n^2)$

Then for a definition of that method to be correct, its worst time would have to be no worse than quadratic in n. Recall that the Big-O estimates provide **upper bounds** only. But the method developer is free to improve on the upper bound for worst time without violating the contract. For example, the developer may provide a different definition of the sort method for which worstTime(n) is $O(n \log n)$.

Here are three conventions regarding the specification of Big-O estimates in the postconditions of methods:

1. The variable n refers to the number of items in the container.

2. For many methods, worstTime(n) is $O(1)$. If no estimate of worstTime(n) is given, you may assume that worstTime(n) is $O(1)$.

3. Often, averageTime(n) has the same Big-O estimate as worstTime(n). When they are different, we will specify both.

It is worth emphasizing that all the work done during all the stages has a documentable component, for example, the specifications of the problem analysis stage, the method interfaces and dependency diagrams of the program design stage, and the Big-O analysis of the program implementation stage. In general, formal documentation at each stage tends to reduce ambiguity and focus responsibility.

Big-O analysis provides a cross-platform estimate of the efficiency of a method. Section 3.4.7 explores the execution-time tools for dealing with efficiency.

3.4.7 Run-Time Analysis

We have seen that Big-O notation allows us to estimate the efficiency of methods independently of any particular computing environment. For practical reasons, we may also want to estimate efficiency within some fixed environment. Why settle for estimates? For one thing, *in multiprogramming environments such as Windows, it is very difficult to determine how long a single task takes.* Why? Because there is so much going on behind the scenes, such as maintaining the desktop clock, executing a wait-loop until a mouse click occurs, and updating information from your mailer and browser. At any given time, there might be dozens of such processes under control of the Windows manager. And each process will get a time slice of several milliseconds. The bottom line is that the elapsed time for a task is seldom an accurate measure of how long the task took.

Estimating run-time with elapsed time can be grossly inaccurate.

Another problem with seeking an exact measure of efficiency is that it might take a very long time: O(forever). For example, suppose we are comparing two sorting methods, and we want to determine the average time each one takes to sort some container. The time may depend heavily on the particular ordering of the items chosen. Because the number of different orderings of n items is $n!$, it is not feasible to generate every possible ordering, run the method for each ordering, and calculate the average time.

Instead, we would probably generate a sample ordering that is in "no particular order." The statistical concept corresponding to "no particular order" is randomness. We will use the time to sort a random sample as an estimate of the average sorting time.

To assist with our needs in the areas of timing, C++ supplies the time and rand functions.

The time **Function**   C++'s time function takes as an argument a pointer to a **struct** object that holds information about the current time (such as the hour, day, and year). When called with a NULL argument, the value returned is of type **long** representing the time elapsed, in seconds, since midnight of January 1, 1970, coordinated universal time.

To determine the elapsed time for a task, we calculate the elapsed time immediately before and immediately after the code for the task and then subtract the "before" time from the "after" time. For example, a program to perform timing tests will often include the following program skeleton:

```
// Determine the time a task consumes.

#include <iostream>
#include <string>
#include <time.h> // declares time function

int main ( )
{
        const string TIME_MESSAGE_1 = "The elapsed time was ";

        const string TIME_MESSAGE_2 = " seconds.";

        const string CLOSE_WINDOW _PROMPT =
                "Please press the Enter key to close this output window:";

        long start_time,
                finish_time,
                elapsed_time;

        start_time = time (NULL);

        // Perform the task:

        . . .

        // Calculate elapsed time for the task:
        finish_time = time (NULL);
        elapsed_time = finish_time − start_time;
        cout << TIME_MESSAGE_1 << elapsed_time <<
                        TIME_MESSAGE_2
                << endl;

        cout << endl << endl << CLOSE_WINDOW_PROMPT;
        cin.get( );
        return 0;
} // main
```

You might balk at the imprecision of measuring time in whole seconds. But as has been noted, it is difficult to isolate the execution time of a task in a multiprogramming environment. The "noise" from other factors, such as the utilization of the cache memory and the existence of disk buffers from previous executions, can result in widely varying times even for consecutive executions of the same task. So you should view any elapsed-time results for a task only as a crude estimate of the actual execution time—even cruder than the Big-O analysis.

Timing is the main topic of Lab 9. That lab also reinforces material on randomness, introduced in Section 3.4.8.

3.4.8 **Randomness**

Given a collection of numbers, a number is selected *randomly* from the collection if each number has an equal chance of being selected. A number so selected is called a *random number,* and a function that returns a random number is called a *random-*

number generator. C++ has a system function rand that provides a random number generator. Strictly speaking, the rand function is a pseudo-random number generator since the numbers calculated are not random at all—they are determined by the function. They appear to be random if we do not see how they are calculated. The function rand is declared in the system header file stdlib.h.

The rand function takes no parameters and returns a pseudo-random number in the range from 0 to RAND_MAX (the constant identifier RAND_MAX is defined in stdlib.h as the value 0x7fff, which is hexadecimal for 32,767).

The value calculated by the rand function depends on the seed it is given. The seed is a predeclared **unsigned int** whose initial value is set using the srand function. The srand function takes one **unsigned int** argument and sets the seed to that number. Calling rand before any call to srand generates the same sequence as calling srand with 1 passed as the seed. Each time the function rand is called, the current value of the seed is used to determine the next value of the seed. This new value for the seed determines the value returned by rand.

For example, suppose that two programs have

```
#include <stdlib.h> // declares srand and rand functions

srand (100);
for (int i = 0; i < 5; i++)
        cout << rand ( ) << endl;
```

The output from both programs would be exactly the same:[2]

```
1862
11548
3973
4846
9095
```

This repeatability can be helpful when we want to compare the behavior of programs, as we often will in subsequent labs and in Chapters 4 through 14. In general, repeatability is an essential feature of the scientific method.

If we do not want repeatability, we start by calling the function srand with time (NULL) as an argument. This implies that unless you run the program twice within the same second (which is barely possible), you will never get the same sequence of pseudo-random numbers.

For example, we can write

```
#include <stdlib.h> // declares srand and rand functions

srand (time (NULL));
for (int i = 0; i < 5; i++)
        cout << rand ( ) << endl;
```

---

[2]The actual sequence produced depends on the computing platform.

Each time the program is run, we would get a different sequence of five random integers between 0 and RAND_MAX.

The functions time and rand, and their use in timing experiments, are emphasized in Lab 9.

LAB   **Lab 9: Timing and randomness.**

(All Labs Are Optional.)   **LAB**

We conclude this introduction to program implementation with the topic of casting. The basic idea with casting is that, to alter the evaluation of an expression, the type of the expression is temporarily interpreted as a different type.

3.4.9   Casting

To explicitly change the type of an expression, C++ provides type casting. A *cast* consists of a type—in parentheses—followed by the expression whose value is to be cast. For example, we can convert an expression from **long** to **float** as follows:

```
long i = 3,
     j = 5;

cout << i / j << endl; // output will be 0

cout << (float) i / j << endl; // output will be .6
```

The casting operator—the parentheses—has a higher priority than the division operator, so i is floated before the division by j is performed. An alternate notation puts the expression to be cast in parentheses:

```
cout << float (i) / j << endl;
```

A type consisting of more than an identifier must be parenthesized, and an expression consisting of more than an identifier or literal must be parenthesized. Occasionally, both the type and the expression need parentheses. For example, we could have:

```
(Node*)(head->next)
```

Generally, when using a cast, the size of the value of the expression, in bytes, should be the same size as the size of the type. This is because usually a cast does not change the actual bits of the value, just the interpretation of those bits. However, for numbers, C++ defines conversions between the different types of numbers, so you can cast between them even if they are not the same size. For example, we can cast **short** to **float**. For another example, we can cast an **int** to a **char**:

```
int i = 65;

cout << (char) i << endl;
```

will convert the type of i in the output statement to **char**, so the output will be

A

since the sixty-fifth character in the ASCII collating sequence is 'A'.

We can also cast a **char** to an **int**. For example, suppose we have

    char new_char = 'D';

    cout << (int) new_char;

The output will be 68 because 'D' is the sixty-eighth character in the ASCII collating sequence.

All pointers are the same size—typically, 4 bytes—so casting between them is legal. We will use this fact to good effect in Chapter 4, when we explore the mystical topic of **void** pointers. But be careful with casting! If you cast an expression whose value has a certain size to an expression whose value has a smaller size, important information may be lost. For example, a loss of precision can occur if you cast a **long** to an **int**, or a **double** to a **float**.

The final stage in the program development life cycle is program maintenance.

3.5 | PROGRAM MAINTENANCE

After the program implementation stage has been completed, the program is ready for end-users. Some programs, called *production* programs, are run periodically for several years. As time goes by, it is almost inevitable that such a program will undergo some alterations. *Program maintenance* refers to modifications to a program that has been deployed. This maintenance can be performed by the same team of analysts, designers, and programmers who developed the program originally. More often, a new team—with a fresh perspective—is assembled.

Software maintenance is fundamentally different from hardware maintenance because code does not deteriorate. Disk drives have a mean time to failure, but **switch** statements do not start to lose cases after prolonged use. So what does software maintenance entail? The maintenance team is responsible for correcting discovered errors and for preventing errors from creating program failures in the future. But most of the effort of the maintenance team is devoted to making enhancements to the original system.

Enhancing an existing program can be a challenging task. Maintenance is easier if the original project was developed with a view toward maintainability, such as if the system tests were comprehensive, and the classes were highly modular.

For example, consider tax-calculation software. The tax tables change yearly, so they should be in a separate class. Also, taxpayer identification might be expanded to allow a digital signature, in addition to the usual data: name, address, social security number, and so on. Then the class with those fields will have to be expanded to include additional functionality. Because the tax code gets increasingly complex from year to year (maybe it only seems that way), the need for modularity increases correspondingly.

Program maintenance is by no means a minor activity. At some companies, over 50 percent of programmer time, on average, is spent on program maintenance. This underscores the need for documentation during all stages of the software development life cycle. Without documentation, maintaining even your own programs is a frustrating and time-consuming task.

SUMMARY

This chapter introduced the basic concepts of *software engineering:* the application of principles, techniques, and tools to the production of programs. The chronology of program production, the software-development life cycle, consists of four stages. Each stage has a documentable component, and the entire process is usually iterative, not linear.

In the problem analysis stage, detailed specifications and systems tests are developed.

During the program design stage, new classes are created as needed. For each such class, method interfaces and fields are determined. Dependency diagrams illustrate the inheritance relationships between the classes and the dependence or independence of object fields on calling objects.

In the program implementation stage, methods are defined for the classes introduced in the program design stage. Big-O notation allows us to quickly estimate the time-space efficiency of methods. Project validation proceeds from the bottom up. Low-level classes are tested—with a driver—and then used in the testing of higher-level classes. Ultimately, the project is validated, with systems tests developed during the problem analysis stage, as well as with additional tests. Run-time analysis often uses the time and random functions.

After the program has been validated, alterations to the problem or program can be made during the program maintenance stage.

EXERCISES

3.1   Create a method,

   void sample (**int** n);

   for which worstTime(n) is $O(n)$ but worstTime(n) is not linear in n.

   Hint $O(n)$ provides an upper bound, but "linear in n" indicates the smallest upper bound.

3.2   Study the following:

```
// Make i the smallest index in 0 . . . n − 1 such that a [i]= item.
i = 0;
while (a [i] != item)
     i++;
```

Assume that a is an array of n items and that there is at least one index k in $0 \ldots n - 1$ such that a [k] = item. Find a function g such that worstTime(n) is $O(g)$, and $O(g)$ is the smallest upper bound of worstTime(n).

3.3   Study the following code for an array a of strings:

```
// Make a [0 . . . n −1] sorted (in increasing order):
for (i = 0; i < n−1; i++)
{
        // Make a [0 . . . i] sorted and <= a [i + 1 . . . n−1]:
        position = i;
        for (j = i+1; j < n; j++)
            if (a [j] < a [position])
                position = j;

        string temp = a [i];
        a [i] = a [position];
        a [position] = temp;

} // outer for
```

a.   When $i = 0$, there are $n - 1$ iterations of the inner **for** loop. How many iterations are there when $i = 1$? When $i = 2$?

b.   Determine as a function of n, the total number of iterations of the inner **for** loop as i takes on values from 0 to $n - 2$.

c.   Find a function g such that worstTime(n)—for the outer **for** statement— is $O(g)$, and $O(g)$ is the smallest upper bound of worstTime(n).

3.4   For each of the following functions f, where $n = 0, 1, 2, 3, \ldots$, find a function g such that $O(g)$ is the smallest upper bound of f:

a. $f(n) = (2 + n)(3 + \log_2 n)$

b. $f(n) = 11 \log_2 n + n / 2 - 3452$

c. $f(n) = 1 + 2 + 3 + \ldots + n$

d. $f(n) = n(3 + n) - 7n$

e. $f(n) = 7n + (n - 1) \log_{10}(n - 4)$

f. $f(n) = \log_2(n^2) + n$

g. $f(n) = \dfrac{(n + 1) \log_2(n + 1) - (n + 1) + 1}{n}$

h. $f(n) = n + n/2 + n/4 + n/8 + n/16 + \ldots$

3.5   In the order hierarchy, we have $\ldots, O(\log n) \subset O(n^{1/2}), \ldots$. Show that, for any integer $n > 16$, $\log_2 n < n^{1/2}$.

Hint from calculus   Show that for all real numbers $x > 16$, the slope of the function $\log_2 x$ is less than the slope of the function $x^{1/2}$. Since $\log_2(16) = 16^{1/2}$, we conclude that for all real numbers $x > 16$, $\log_2 x < x^{1/2}$.

3.6   For each of the following code segments, find a function g such that $O(g)$ is the smallest upper bound of worstTime(n). In each segment, S represents a sequence of statements in which there are no n-dependent loops.

a.   for (i = 0; i * i < n; i++)

   S

b.   **for** (i = 0; sqrt (i) < n; i++)

   S

c.   k = 1;
   for (i = 0; i < n; i++)
      k *= 2;
   for (i = 0; i < k; i++)
      S

Hint   In each case, 2 is part of the answer.

3.7   a.   Suppose we have a method whose worstTime(n) is linear in n. Determine the effect of tripling n on the estimate of worst time. That is, estimate worstTime(3n) in terms of worstTime(n).

   b.   Suppose we have a method whose worstTime(n) is quadratic in n. Determine the effect of tripling n on the estimate of worst time. That is, estimate worstTime(3n) in terms of worstTime(n).

   c.   Suppose we have a method whose worstTime(n) is constant. Determine the effect of tripling n on the estimate of worst time. That is, estimate worstTime(3n) in terms of worstTime(n).

3.8   Develop functional specifications for the following problem: Given a list of test scores, determine how many are below the average score.

3.9   Create system tests for the problem described in Exercise 3.8.

3.10 Design and implement, with a Linked object, the program for the problem described in Exercises 3.8 and 3.9.

3.11 Show that $O(n) = O(n + 7)$.

Hint   Use the definition of Big-O.

3.12 Which one of the following expressions has a random integer value in the range from 1 to 6, inclusive?

a.   rand( ) % 6

b.   rand( ) % 5 + 1

c.   rand( ) % 7

d.   rand( ) % 6 + 1

PROGRAMMING PROJECT 3.1

Further Expansion of the Linked Class

1. Expand the Linked class from Lab 8 by adding a pop_back method. Here is the method interface:

    ```
    // Precondition: This Linked object is not empty.
    // Postcondition: The item that was at the back of this Linked object before this call
    //                has been deleted from this Linked object. The worstTime(n) is O(n).
    void pop_back( );
    ```

2. Expand the LinkedDriver class from Lab 8 to validate the pop_back method.

3. Suppose we start with an empty Linked container of **int**s:

    ```
    Linked <int> intList;
    ```

    Compare the time for n push_fronts followed by n pop_fronts to the time for n push_backs followed by n pop_backs. Choose n large enough so that the difference is at least 2 seconds. Are these times consistent with your Big-O analysis?

CHAPTER 4

Recursion

One of the skills that distinguishes a novice programmer from an experienced one is an understanding of recursion. The goal of this chapter is to give you a feel for situations in which a recursive function is appropriate. Along the way you may start to see the power and elegance of recursion, as well as its potential for misuse.

Recursion plays a role in the most common implementation of the Standard Template Library: the copy function in the (red-black) tree class and the algorithm sort. But the value of recursion extends far beyond these two instances. For example, one of the applications of the stack class in Chapter 7 is the translation of recursive functions into machine code. And in Chapter 8, most of the definitions relating to binary trees are, or can be, recursive. The sooner you are exposed to recursion, the more likely you will be able to spot situations where it is appropriate—and to use it! ■

CHAPTER OBJECTIVES

1. Recognize the characteristics of those problems for which recursive solutions may be appropriate.

2. Compare recursive and iterative functions with respect to time, space, and ease of development.

3. Trace the execution of a recursive function with the help of execution frames.

4. Understand the backtracking strategy for solving problems.

4.1 | INTRODUCTION

Roughly, a function is ***recursive*** if it contains a call to itself.[1] From this description, you may initially fear that the execution of a recursive function will lead to an infinite sequence of recursive calls. But under normal circumstances, this calamity does not occur, and the sequence of calls eventually stops. To show you how this works, here is the skeleton of a typical recursive function:

```
if (simplest case)
            solve directly
else
            make a recursive call to a simpler case
```

This outline suggests that recursion should be considered whenever the problem to be solved has these two characteristics:

1.   Complex cases of the problem can be reduced to simpler cases that have the same form as the original problem.
2.   The simplest case(s) can be solved directly.

Incidentally, if you are familiar with the Principle of Mathematical Induction (see Appendix 1), you may have observed that these two characteristics correspond to the inductive case and base case, respectively.

As we work through the examples, do not be inhibited by old ways of thinking. As each problem is stated, try to frame a solution in terms of a simpler problem of the same form. Think recursively!

4.2 | FACTORIALS

Given a positive integer n, the ***factorial*** of n, written $n!$, is the product of all integers between n and 1, inclusive. For example,

$$4! = 4 \cdot 3 \cdot 2 \cdot 1 = 24$$

and

$$6! = 6 \cdot 5 \cdot 4 \cdot 3 \cdot 2 \cdot 1 = 720$$

Another way to calculate 4! is as follows:

$$4! = 4 \cdot 3!$$

This formulation is not helpful unless we know what 3! is. But we can continue to calculate factorials in terms of smaller factorials (Aha!):

$$3! = 3 \cdot 2!$$
$$2! = 2 \cdot 1!$$

---

[1]A formal definition of "recursive" is given in Section 4.8.

Observe that 1! can be calculated directly: its value is 1. Now we work backwards to calculate 4!:

$$2! = 2 \cdot 1! = 2 \cdot 1 = \ 2$$
$$3! = 3 \cdot 2! = 3 \cdot 2 = \ 6$$
$$4! = 4 \cdot 3! = 4 \cdot 6 = 24$$

For $n > 1$, we reduce the problem of calculating $n!$ to the problem of calculating $(n - 1)!$ We stop reducing when we get to 1!, which is simply 1. These observations lead to the following function; for the sake of completeness,[2] we define 0! to be 1.

```
// Precondition: n >= 0.
// Postcondition: The value returned is n!, the product of all integers between
//                1 and n, inclusive. The worstTime(n) is O(n).
long factorial (int n)
{
        if (n == 0 || n == 1)
                return 1;
        else
                return n * factorial (n − 1);
} // factorial
```

Within factorial, there is a call to factorial, so factorial is recursive. A driver for this function is available from the Source Code on the book's website.

The following chart traces the execution of factorial with an initial argument of 4:

n	Formula for factorial(n)	Value of factorial(n)

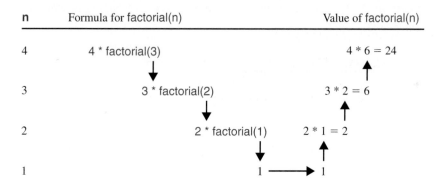

The formal parameter n has its value reduced by 1 with each recursive call. But after the final call with n = 1, the *previous* values of n are needed for the multiplications. For example, when n = 4, the calculation of n * factorial (n − 1) is postponed until the call to factorial (n − 1) is completed. When this finally happens and the value 6 [that is, factorial (3)] is returned, the value of 4 for n must be available.

---

[2]The number of combinations of n things taken k at a time is calculated as $n!/[k! \cdot (n - k)!]$. When $n = k$, we get $n!/(n! \cdot 0!)$, which has the value 1 because $0! = 1$.

Somehow, the value of n must be saved when the call to factorial (n − 1) is made. That value must be restored after the call to factorial (n − 1) is completed so that the value of n * factorial (n − 1) can be calculated. The beauty of recursion is that the programmer does not explicitly handle these savings and restorings; the computer does the work.

The precondition of the factorial function asserts that n is a nonnegative integer. What would happen if a user called factorial (−1)? Since n is neither 0 nor 1, the **else** part would be executed, including a call to factorial (−2). Within that call, n would still be unequal to 0 or 1, so there would be a call to factorial (−3), then to factorial (−4), factorial (−5), and so on. Eventually, saving all those copies of n would overflow an area of memory called the **stack**. This phenomenon is known as *infinite recursion.*

For the above factorial function, infinite recursion is avoided if the value of the argument is greater than or equal to 0, as the precondition asserts. In general, infinite recursion is avoided if each recursive call makes progress toward a "simplest" case. Notice what would happen if we replaced

(n == 0 || n == 1)

with

(n <= 1)

Then infinite recursion would not occur for a negative argument. Instead, 1 would be returned. This version is more dangerous for users because they might not realize when the argument violated the precondition. In general, no answer is better than a wrong answer.

4.2.1   Execution Frames

Execution frames show what happens when a recursive method is executed.

The trace of a recursive function can be illustrated through *execution frames:* boxes that contain information related to each invocation of the function. Each execution frame includes the values of parameters and other local variables. Each frame also has the relevant part of the recursive function's code—especially the recursive calls, with values for the arguments. When a recursive call is made, a new execution frame will be constructed on top of the current one; this new frame is destroyed when the call has been completed. A check mark indicates either the statement being executed in the current frame or the statement, in a previous frame, whose recursive call created the current frame.

For example, here is a step-by-step, execution-frame trace of the factorial function after an initial call of factorial (4):

Step 0:   n = 4
           ✓ **return** 4 * factorial (3);

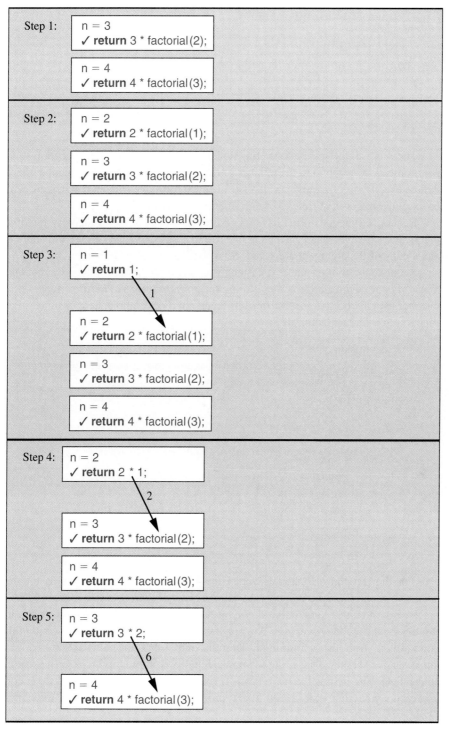

continued

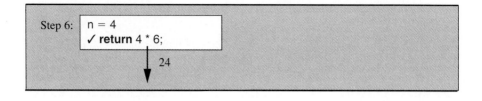

The analysis of the factorial function is fairly clear-cut. The execution-time requirements correspond to the number of recursive calls. For any argument n, there will be exactly n − 1 recursive calls. During each recursive call, an **if** statement will be executed in constant time, so worstTime(*n*) is linear in *n*.

Recursive functions often have an additional cost in terms of memory requirements. For example, when each recursive call to factorial is made, the return address and a copy of the argument are saved. So worstSpace(*n*) is also linear in *n*.

Recursion can often make it easier for us to solve problems, but *any problem that can be solved recursively can also be solved iteratively.* An *iterative* function is one that uses a loop statement instead of recursion. For example, here is an iterative function to calculate factorials:

```
// Precondition: n >= 0.
// Postcondition: The value returned is n!, the product of all integers between
//                1 and n, inclusive. The worstTime(n) is O(n).
long factorial (int n)
{
        int product = n;

        if (n == 0)
                return 1;
        for (int i = n − 1; i > 1; i--)
                product = product * i;

        return product;
} // function factorial
```

For this version of factorial, worstTime(*n*) is linear in *n,* the same as for the recursive version. But no matter what value *n* has, only three variables are used in a trace of the iterative version, so there are no significant memory requirements, in contrast to the recursive version. You may further argue that the iterative version follows directly from the definition of factorials, and in that sense it is also superior to the recursive version. That is a good point. Finally, both functions are fairly easy to understand. The iterative version has two more variables, but the recursive version represents your first exposure to a new problem-solving technique, and that takes some extra effort.

So in this example, the iterative version of the factorial function is better than the recursive version. The whole purpose of the example was to provide a simple situation in which recursion was worth considering, even though we ultimately decided that iteration was better. In the example given in Section 4.3, an iterative alternative is not as appealing.

4.3 | DECIMAL-TO-BINARY

Humans count in base 10, possibly because we were born with 10 fingers. Computers count naturally in base two because of the binary nature of electronics. One of the tasks a computer performs is to convert from decimal (base 10) to binary (base 2). Let's develop a function to solve a simplified version of this problem:

Given a nonnegative integer n, write out its binary equivalent.

For example, if n is 25, its binary equivalent is 11001. There are several approaches to solving this problem. One of them is based on the following observation:

The rightmost bit has the value of $n\%\ 2$; the other bits are the binary equivalent of $n\ /\ 2$. (Aha!)

For example, if n is 25, the rightmost bit in the binary equivalent of n is 25 % 2, namely, 1; the remaining bits are the binary equivalent of 25 / 2, that is, the binary equivalent of 12. So we can obtain all the bits as follows:

```
25 % 2 = 1; 25/2 = 12

12 % 2 = 0; 12/2 = 6

6 % 2 = 0; 6/2 = 3

3 % 2 = 1; 3/2 = 1

1 % 2 = 1; 1/2 = 0
```

We write out the remainder bits from the bottom up, so that the rightmost bit will be written last. The output would then be

11001

Our function to determine the binary equivalent will be called writeBinary. The following table graphically illustrates the effect of calling writeBinary (25):

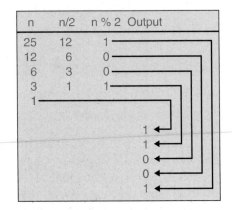

This discussion suggests that in determining the binary equivalent we must perform *all* the calculations before we do any writing. Speaking recursively, we need to
write out the binary equivalent of *n / 2 before* we write out *n* % 2. In other words, in
the writeBinary function we need to put the recursive call before the output statement.
We stop when *n / 2* is 0, that is, when *n* is less than or equal to 1.

The function is

```
// Precondition: n >= 0.
// Postcondition: The binary equivalent of n has been printed. The
//                worstTime(n) is O(log n).
void writeBinary (int n)
{
      if (n == 0 || n == 1)
            cout << n;
      else
      {
            writeBinary (n / 2);
            cout << n % 2;
      } // else
} // writeBinary
```

Here is a step-by-step, execution-frame trace of the writeBinary function after an initial call of writeBinary (12):

Step 0:   n = 12
          ✓ writeBinary (6);
          cout << 0;

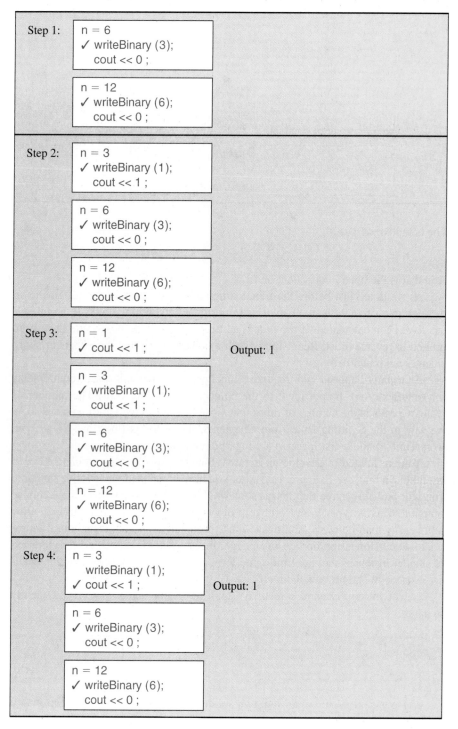

continued

Step 5:
```
n = 6
    writeBinary (3);
  ✓ cout << 0 ;
```
Output: 0

```
n = 12
  ✓ writeBinary (6);
    cout << 0 ;
```

Step 6:
```
n = 12
    writeBinary (6);
  ✓ cout << 0 ;
```
Output: 0

The complete output is

    1100

And that is the binary equivalent of 12.

As we noted just before the function definition, the order of the statements in the **else** part of writeBinary enables us to postpone *any* writing until *all* the bit values have been calculated. If the order had been reversed, the bits would have been printed in reverse order. Recursion is such a powerful tool that the effects of slight changes are magnified.

As usually happens with recursive functions, the time and space requirements for writeBinary are proportional to the number of recursive calls. The number of recursive calls is the number of times that *n* can be divided by 2 until *n* equals 1. As we saw in the Splitting Rule from Chapter 3, this value is floor($\log_2 n$), so both worstTime(n) and worstSpace(n) are logarithmic in *n*.

You are invited to develop an iterative function to solve this problem. (If you would like a hint, see Exercise 4.2.) After you have completed the iterative function, you will probably agree that it was somewhat harder to develop than the recursive function. This is typical, and probably obvious: Recursive solutions usually flow more easily than iterative solutions to those problems for which recursion is appropriate. Recursion is appropriate when larger instances of the problem can be reduced to smaller instances that have the same form as the larger instances, and the smallest instance(s) can be solved directly.

Lab 10 introduces another recursive application, one that occurs very frequently in nature.

LAB   **Lab 10: Fibonacci numbers.**

                                            (All Labs Are Optional.)   **LAB**

For our next problem, an iterative solution is *much* harder to develop than a recursive solution.

4.4 I TOWERS OF HANOI

In the Towers of Hanoi game, there are three poles, labeled *A, B,* and *C,* and several, different-sized, numbered disks, each with a hole in the center. Initially, all the disks are on pole *A,* with the largest disk on the bottom, then the next largest, and so on. Figure 4.1 shows the initial configuration if we started with four disks, numbered from smallest to largest.

The object of the game is to move all the disks from pole *A* to pole *B;* pole *C* is used for temporary storage.[3] The rules of the game are

1. Only one disk may be moved at a time.
2. No disk may ever be placed on top of a smaller disk.
3. Other than the prohibition of rule 2, the top disk on any pole may be moved to either of the other poles.

Let's try to play the game with the initial configuration given in Figure 4.1. We are immediately faced with a dilemma: Do we move disk 1 to pole *B* or to pole *C*? If we make the wrong move, we may end up with the four disks on pole *C* rather than on pole *B*.

Instead of trying to figure out where disk 1 should be moved initially, we will focus our attention on disk 4, the bottom disk. Of course, we can't move disk 4 right away, but eventually, disk 4 will have to be moved from pole *A* to pole *B*. By the rules of the game, the configuration just before moving disk 4 must be as shown in Figure 4.2.

Does this observation help us to figure out how to move four disks from *A* to *B*? Well, sort of. We still need to determine how to move three disks (one at a time) from pole *A* to pole *C*. We can then move disk 4 from *A* to *B*. Finally, we will need to determine how to move three disks (one at a time) from *C* to *B*.

Figure 4.1 I The starting position for the Towers of Hanoi game with four disks.

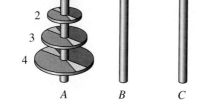

---

[3]Some versions make the object of the game to move the disks from pole *A* to pole *C,* with *B* as a temporary.

Figure 4.2 | The game configuration for the Towers of Hanoi game just before moving disk 4 from Pole *A* to pole *B*.

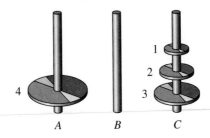

The significance of this strategy is that we have reduced the problem from figuring out how to move four disks to one of figuring out how to move three disks (Aha!). We still need to determine how to move three disks from one pole to another pole.

But the above strategy can be reapplied! To move three disks from, say, pole *A* to pole *C*, we first move two disks (one at a time) from *A* to *B*, then we move disk 3 from *A* to *C*, and finally, we move two disks from *B* to *C*. Continually reducing the problem, we eventually face the trivial task of moving disk 1 from one pole to another.

There is nothing special about the number 4 in this approach. For any positive integer *n* we can describe how to move *n* disks from pole *A* to pole *B*: If *n* = 1, we simply move disk 1 from pole *A* to pole *B*. For *n* > 1,

1. First, move *n* − 1 disks from pole *A* to pole *C*, using pole *B* as a temporary.
2. Then move disk *n* from pole *A* to pole *B*.
3. Finally, move *n* − 1 disks from pole *C* to pole *B*, using pole *A* as a temporary.

This does not quite solve the problem because, for example, we have not described how to move *n* − 1 disks from *A* to *C*. But our strategy is easily generalized by replacing the constants *A, B,* and *C* with variables *Origin, Destination,* and *Temporary.* For example, we will initially have

> Origin = *A*
> Destination = *B*
> Temporary = *C*

Then the general strategy for moving *n* disks from Origin to Destination is as follows. If *n* is 1, move disk 1 from origin to destination. Otherwise,

1. Move *n* − 1 disks (one at a time) from Origin to Temporary.
2. Move disk *n* from Origin to Destination.
3. Move *n* − 1 disks (one at a time) from Temporary to Destination.

The following recursive function incorporates this strategy:

```
// Precondition: n > 0.
// Postcondition: The steps needed to move n disks from pole orig to pole
```

```
//                    dest have been written out. Pole temp is used for temporary
//                    storage. The worstTime(n) is O(2^n).
void move (int n, char orig, char dest, char temp)
{
    if (n == 1)
            cout << "Move disk 1 from " << orig << " to "
                    << dest << endl;
    else
    {
            move (n − 1, orig, temp, dest);
            cout << "Move disk " << n << " from " << orig
                    << " to " << dest << endl;
            move (n − 1, temp, dest, orig);
    } // else
} // move
```

It is difficult to trace the execution of this function because the interrelationship of parameter and argument values makes it difficult to keep track of which pole is currently the origin, which is the destination, and which is the temporary. In the following execution frames, the parameter values are the argument values from the call, and the argument values for subsequent calls come from the function code and the current parameter values. For example, suppose the initial call is

```
move (3, 'A', 'B', 'C');
```

Then the parameter values at step 0 will be those argument values, so we have

```
n = 3
orig = 'A'
dest = 'B'
temp = 'C'
```

Because n is not equal to 1, the **else** part of the move function is executed:

```
move (n − 1, orig, temp, dest);
cout << "Move disk" << n << " from" << orig << "to" << dest << endl;
move (n − 1, temp, dest, orig);
```

The values of those arguments are obtained from the parameters' values, so we have

```
move (2, 'A', 'C', 'B');
cout << "Move disk 3 from A to B" << endl;
move (2, 'C', 'B', 'A');
```

Here is a step-by-step, execution-frame trace of the move function when the initial call is

```
move (3, 'A', 'B', 'C');
```

Make sure you understand how to obtain the parameter values and argument values before you try to follow the trace.

	Output:

Step 0:
```
n = 3
orig = 'A'
dest = 'B'
temp = 'C'
✓ move (2, 'A', 'C', 'B');
  cout << "Move disk 3 from A to B" << endl;
  move (2, 'C', 'B', 'A');
```

Step 1:
```
n = 2
orig = 'A'
dest = 'C'
temp = 'B'
✓ move (1, 'A', 'B', 'C');
  cout << "Move disk 2 from A to C" << endl;
  move (1, 'B', 'C', 'A');
```
```
n = 3
orig = 'A'
dest = 'B'
temp = 'C'
✓ move (2, 'A', 'C', 'B');
  cout << "Move disk 3 from A to B" << endl;
  move (2, 'C', 'B', 'A');
```

Step 2:
```
n = 1
orig = 'A'
dest = 'B'
temp = 'C'
✓ cout << "Move disk 1 from A to B" << endl;
```
Move disk 1 from A to B
```
n = 2
orig = 'A'
dest = 'C'
temp = 'B'
✓ move (1, 'A', 'B', 'C');
  cout << "Move disk 2 from A to C" << endl;
  move (1, 'B', 'C', 'A');
```
```
n = 3
orig = 'A'
dest = 'B'
temp = 'C'
✓ move (2, 'A', 'C', 'B');
  cout << "Move disk 3 from A to B" << endl;
  move (2, 'C', 'B', 'A');
```

Step 3:

```
n = 2
orig = 'A'
dest = 'C'
temp = 'B'
    move (1, 'A', 'B', 'C');
✓   cout << "Move disk 2 from A to C" << endl;
    move (1, 'B', 'C', 'A');
```

Move disk 2 from A to C

```
n = 3
orig = 'A'
dest = 'B'
temp = 'C'
✓   move (2, 'A', 'C', 'B');
    cout << "Move disk 3 from A to B" << endl;
    move (2, 'C', 'B', 'A');
```

Step 4:

```
n = 2
orig = 'A'
dest = 'C'
temp = 'B'
    move (1, 'A', 'B', 'C');
    cout << "Move disk 2 from A to C" << endl;
✓   move (1, 'B', 'C', 'A');
```

```
n = 3
orig = 'A'
dest = 'B'
temp = 'C'
✓   move (2, 'A', 'C', 'B');
    cout << "Move disk 3 from A to B" << endl;
    move (2, 'C', 'B', 'A');
```

Step 5:

```
n = 1
orig = 'B'
dest = 'C'
temp = 'A'
✓   cout << "Move disk 1 from B to C" << endl;
```

Move disk 1 from B to C

```
n = 2
orig = 'A'
dest = 'C'
temp = 'B'
    move (1, 'A', 'B', 'C');
    cout << "Move disk 2 from A to C" << endl;
✓   move (1, 'B', 'C', 'A');
```

continued

```
n = 3
orig = 'A'
dest = 'B'
temp = 'C'
✓ move (2, 'A', 'C', 'B');
  cout << "Move disk 3 from A to B" << endl;
  move (2, 'C', 'B', 'A');
```

Step 6:
```
n = 3
orig = 'A'
dest = 'B'
temp = 'C'
  move (2, 'A', 'C', 'B');
✓ cout << "Move disk 3 from A to B" << endl;     Move disk 3 from A to B
  move (2, 'C', 'B', 'A');
```

Step 7:
```
n = 3
orig = 'A'
dest = 'B'
temp = 'C'
  move (2, 'A', 'C', 'B');
  cout << "Move disk 3 from A to B" << endl;
✓ move (2, 'C', 'B', 'A');
```

Step 8:
```
n = 2
orig = 'C'
dest = 'B'
temp = 'A'
✓ move (1, 'C', 'A', 'B');
  cout << "Move disk 2 from C to B" << endl;
  move (1, 'A', 'B', 'C');
```

```
n = 3
orig = 'A'
dest = 'B'
temp = 'C'
  move (2, 'A', 'C', 'B');
  cout << "Move disk 3 from A to B" << endl;
✓ move (2, 'C', 'B', 'A');
```

Step 9:
```
n = 1
orig = 'C'
dest = 'A'
temp = 'B'
✓ cout << "Move disk 1 from C to A" << endl;     Move disk 1 from C to A
```

```
n = 2
orig = 'C'
dest = 'B'
temp = 'A'
✓  move (1, 'C', 'A', 'B');
   cout << "Move disk 2 from C to B" << endl;
   move (1, 'A', 'B', 'C');
```

```
n = 3
orig = 'A'
dest = 'B'
temp = 'C'
   move (2, 'A', 'C', 'B');
   cout << "Move disk 3 from A to B" << endl;
✓  move (2, 'C', 'B', 'A');
```

Step 10:
```
n = 2
orig = 'C'
dest = 'B'
temp = 'A'
   move (1, 'C', 'A', 'B');
✓  cout << "Move disk 2 from C to B" << endl;      Move disk 2 from C to B
   move (1, 'A', 'B', 'C');
```

```
n = 3
orig = 'A'
dest = 'B'
temp = 'C'
   move (2, 'A', 'C', 'B');
   cout << "Move disk 3 from A to B" << endl;
✓  move (2, 'C', 'B', 'A');
```

Step 11:
```
n = 2
orig = 'C'
dest = 'B'
temp = 'A'
   move (1, 'C', 'A', 'B');
   cout << "Move disk 2 from C to B" << endl;
✓  move (1, 'A', 'B', 'C');
```

```
n = 3
orig = 'A'
dest = 'B'
temp = 'C'
   move (2, 'A', 'C', 'B');
   cout << "Move disk 3 from A to B" << endl;
✓  move (2, 'C', 'B', 'A');
```

continued

Step 12:
```
n = 1
orig = 'A'
dest = 'B'
temp = 'C'
✓ cout << "Move disk 1 from A to B" << endl;        Move disk 1 from A to B

n = 2
orig = 'C'
dest = 'B'
temp = 'A'
    move (1, 'C', 'A', 'B');
    cout << "Move disk 2 from C to B" << endl;
✓  move (1, 'A', 'B', 'C');

n = 3
orig = 'A'
dest = 'B'
temp = 'C'
    move (2, 'A', 'C', 'B');
    cout << "Move disk 3 from A to B" << endl;
✓  move (2, 'C', 'B', 'A');
```

Notice the disparity between the relative ease in developing the recursive function and the relative difficulty in tracing its execution. Imagine what it would be like to trace the execution of move(15, 'A', 'B', 'C')! Fortunately, you need not undergo such torture. Computers handle this type of tedious detail very well. You "merely" develop the correct program and the computer handles the execution. For the move function—as well as for the other recursive functions in this chapter—you can actually *prove* the correctness of the function. See Exercise 4.17.

A recursive function does not explicitly describe the considerable detail involved in its execution. For this reason, recursion is sometimes referred to as "the lazy programmer's problem-solving tool." If you want to appreciate the value of recursion, try to develop an iterative version of the move function. Project 4.1 provides some hints.

4.4.1   A Recurrence Relation

What about worstTime(n), where n is the number of disks? In determining the time requirements of a recursive function, the number of calls to the function is of paramount importance. Let $c(n)$ be the number of calls to the move function for a given value of n. Then worstTime(n) $\approx c(n)$ for any positive integer n, so all we need to do is determine the order of $c(n)$ to get the order of worstTime(n). When $n = 1$, there is a single call to move, so $c(1) = 1$. For $n > 1$, we start with the initial call to move with n as the first argument, and within that call we have two calls to move with $n - 1$ as the first argument. That is, for $n > 1$,

$$c(n) = 1 + 2c(n - 1)$$

This equation is called a ***recurrence relation*** because it defines $c(n)$ in terms of earlier values. For $n > 2$, we can calculate $c(n - 1)$ as follows: We start with the initial call to move, and within that call we have two calls to move with n − 2 as the first argument. That is, for $n > 2$,

$$c(n - 1) = 1 + 2c(n - 1)$$

If we substitute this back into the first equation for c, we get, for $n > 2$,

$$
\begin{aligned}
c(n) &= 1 + 2c(n - 1) \\
&= 1 + 2[1 + 2c(n - 2)] \\
&= 3 + 4c(n - 2)
\end{aligned}
$$

For $n > 3$, we can substitute again to get

$$
\begin{aligned}
c(n) &= 3 + 4c(n - 2) \\
&= 3 + 4[1 + 2c(n - 3)] \\
&= 7 + 8c(n - 3)
\end{aligned}
$$

There seems to be a pattern here. For any positive integers n and k with $n > k$, it appears that

$$c(n) = 2^k - 1 + 2^k c(n - k)$$

When $n - k = 1$, the substituting stops. Since we then have $k = n - 1$,

$$
\begin{aligned}
c(n) &= 2^{n-1} - 1 + 2^{n-1} c(1) \\
&= 2^{n-1} - 1 + 2^{n-1}(1) \\
&= 2^n - 1
\end{aligned}
$$

This can be proved by mathematical induction. We conclude that $c(n)$ is $O(2^n)$ and so worstTime(n) is $O(2^n)$, and this is minimal. That is, if worstTime(n) is also $O(g)$ for some function g, then $O(2^n) \subset O(g)$. Because any function used to solve the Towers of Hanoi problem must make at least 2^n moves, any such function takes exponential time, which means that the Towers of Hanoi problem is intractable.

The memory requirements for move are modest because although space is allocated when move is called, that space is deallocated when the call is completed. So the amount of additional memory needed for move depends, not simply on the number of calls to move, but on the maximum number of started-but-not-completed calls. We can determine this number from the execution frames. Each time a recursive call is made, another frame is constructed, and each time a return is made, that frame is destroyed. For example, if $n = 3$ in the original call to move, then the maximum number of execution frames is 3. In general, the maximum number of execution frames is n. So worstSpace(n) is linear in n.

Section 4.5 deals with a general strategy for solving problems: backtracking, a strategy you have employed whenever you had to retrace your steps on the way to some goal. Of special significance is the abstraction of components needed for all backtracking applications from the components specific to a single application.

4.5 | BACKTRACKING

The basic idea with backtracking is this: from a given starting position, we want to reach a goal position. We repeatedly choose, maybe by guessing, what our next position should be. If a given choice is valid—that is, the new position might be on a path to the goal—we advance to that new position and continue. If a choice leads to a dead end, we back up to the previous position and make another choice. ***Backtracking*** is the strategy of trying to reach a goal by a sequence of chosen positions, with a retracing in reverse order of positions that cannot lead to the goal.

For example, look at the picture in Figure 4.3. We start at position P0 and we want to find a path to the goal position, P16. We are allowed to move in only two directions: north and west. But from any position, we cannot "see" any farther than the next position. Here is the strategy: from any position, we first try to go north; if we are unable to go north, we try to go west; if we are unable to go west, we back up to the most recent position where we chose north and try to choose west instead. After each move, we check to see if we are done, that is, if we have reached the goal position. The positions in Figure 4.3 are numbered in the order they would be tried according to this strategy.

Figure 4.3 casts some light on the phrase "retracing in reverse order." When we are unable to go north or west from position P4, we first back up to position P3, where west is not an option. So we back up to P2. From position P2, going west is an option, and we go west to P5. From P5, north is not an option, but west is an option, and we get to P6. We then go north to P7, a dead end. We then back up to P1, and move west to P8. From P8 we do not go north to P5, because we have already discovered that P5 leads to a dead end. So we move west from P8, and eventually reach the goal position.

The path to the goal should not include any of the dead ends, and this indicates one of the subtleties of backtracking. When a position is visited, it is recorded as

Figure 4.3 | Backtracking to obtain a path to a goal. The solution path is P0, P1, P8, P9, P10, P12, P13, P14, P15, P16.

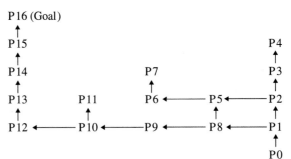

being on the path to the goal, but this recording must be undone if the position leads only to a dead end.

Instead of developing a backtracking method for a particular application, we will utilize a generalized backtracking algorithm from Wirth (1976, p. 138). We then demonstrate that algorithm on a particular application. The BackTrack class we will discuss is based on one in Noonan (2000). The implementation details of the application class will be inaccessible in the BackTrack class, which works through a header file, Application.h. The corresponding source file will be implemented by the particular application.

The user of the BackTrack class supplies

■ A source file to implement Application.h

■ A Position class to define what "position" means for this application

The Application methods are generalizations from the discussion just before and just after Figure 4.3. For example, one method determines if a given position is valid, that is, if the position could be on a path to a goal. Here is the header file, Application.h, which also declares an Iterator class for iterating from a given position:

Any backtracking application uses the same main *function,* BackTrack *class, and* Application *header.*

```
#ifndef APPLICATION
#define APPLICATION

#include <iostream>
#include "Position.h"

using namespace std;

class Application
{
        friend ostream& operator<< (ostream& stream,
                                    Application& app);
    public:

            // Postcondition: the initial state for this Application has been
            //                generated—from input or assignments—and the
            //                start position has been returned.
            Position generateInitialState( );

            // Postcondition: true has been returned if pos can be on the path
            //                to a goal. Otherwise, false has been returned.
            bool valid (const Position& pos);

            // Precondition: pos represents a valid position.
            // Postcondition: pos has been recorded as a valid position.
            void record (const Position& pos);
```

```
                    // Postcondition: true has been returned if pos is the final position
                    //                 for this application. Otherwise, false has been
                    //                 returned.
                    bool done (const Position& pos);

                    // Postcondition: pos has been marked as not being on the path
                    //                 to a goal.
                    void undo (const Position& pos);

            class Iterator
            {
                    public:

                    // Postcondition: This Iterator has been initialized.
                    Iterator ( );

                    // Postcondition: This Iterator has been initialized from pos.
                    Iterator (const Position& pos);

                    // Precondition: This Iterator can advance from this position.
                    // Postcondition: The current position for this Iterator has been
                    //                 returned, and this Iterator has advanced to the
                    //                 next position.
                    Position operator++ (int);

                    //Postcondition: This Iterator cannot advance any further.
                    bool atEnd( );
                    protected:
                    void* fieldPtr;        // explained later
            };//class Iterator
        };// class Application


        #endif
```

The Application class needs no fields because for each problem there will be just one instance of **Application**. Also, any fields could change for each application, that is, for each implementation of that class. Instead, for each implementation, the source file corresponding to Application.h will define variables specific to that implementation.

The embedded Iterator class, on the other hand, will have several instances for a given application. So we need to have fields to distinguish one iterator object from another. But the Iterator class's fields will also vary from one application to the next. By defining a dummy field, fieldPtr, we allow each implementation of the Application class to denote the actual fields for that application. The details of how this is done are given in Section 4.5.1 when we look at a specific application.

The BackTrack class is generic: devoid of any application-specific information. Here is the header file:

```
#ifndef BACKTRACK
#define BACKTRACK

#include "Application.h";
#include "Position.h";

class BackTrack
{
       public:

              // Postcondition: this BackTrack object has been initialized from app.
              BackTrack (const Application& app);

              // Postcondition: a solution going through pos has been
              //                attempted. If that attempt was successful, true
              //                has been returned. Otherwise, false has been
              //                returned.
              bool tryToSolve (Position pos);
       protected:
              Application app;
}; // class BackTrack


#endif
```

Let's focus on the tryToSolve method, the essence of backtracking. For any value of pos, we create an iterator starting at that position, and loop until either we succeed or the iterator can go no farther. During each loop iteration, we consider the next move generated by the iterator. There are three possibilities:

1. One of those choices is a goal position. Then the loop terminates and **true** is returned to indicate success.
2. One of those choices is valid but not a goal position. Then a recursive call to tryToSolve is made, starting at the valid choice.
3. None of the choices is valid. Then the loop terminates and **false** is returned to indicate failure to reach a goal position from the current position.

Here is the source file, BackTrack.cpp:

```
#include "BackTrack.h"

using namespace std;

BackTrack::BackTrack (const Application& app)
{
      this -> app = app;
} // constructor
```

```
bool BackTrack:::tryToSolve (Position pos)
{
        bool success = false;

        Position::Iterator itr = pos.begin( );
        while (!success && itr!= pos.end( ))
        {
                pos = itr++;
                if (app.valid (pos))
                {
                        app.record (pos);
                        if (app.done (pos))
                                success = true;
                        else
                        {
                                success = tryToSolve (pos);
                                if (!success)
                                        app.undo (pos);
                        } // not done
                } // a valid position
        } // while
        return success;
} // method tryToSolve
```

The argument to tryToSolve represents a valid and recorded position. Whenever a return is made from tryToSolve, the precall value of pos is restored, to be undone if it leads to a dead end.

The main function initializes the application and generates the initial state. The generateInitialState method may read in or assign the value for the start position. In either case, the start position is returned by that method and recorded; the start position cannot be backtracked over. The initial call to tryToSolve eventually leads to success or failure: for success, the final state of the application is printed.

Here is BacktrackMain.cpp:

```
#include <iostream>
#include <string>
#include "BackTrack.h"
#include "Application.h"
#include "Position.h"

using namespace std;

int main( )
{
```

```
const string INITIAL_STATE =
        "The initial state is as follows:\n";
const string SUCCESS =
        "\n\nA solution has been found:";
const string FAILURE =
        "\n\nThere is no solution:";
const string CLOSE_WINDOW_PROMPT =
        "Please press the Enter key to close this output window.";

Application app;
BackTrack b (app);

cout << INITIAL_STATE;
Position start = app.generateInitialState( );
cout << app;
if (!app.valid (start))
        cout << FAILURE << endl;
else
{
        app.record (start);
        if (app.done (start) || b.tryToSolve (start))
                cout << SUCCESS << endl << app;
        else
        {
                app.undo (start);
                cout << FAILURE << endl;
        } // failure
} // start is valid

cout << endl << endl << CLOSE_WINDOW_PROMPT;
cin.get( );

return 0;
} // main
```

Now that we have developed a framework for backtracking, it is easy to utilize this framework to solve a variety of problems. One of these problems is presented in Section 4.5.1, two more in Projects 4.2 and 4.3, and another in Chapter 14.

4.5.1   An A-maze-ing Application

For one application of backtracking, let's develop a program to try to find a path through a maze. For example, Figure 4.4 has a 7 × 13 maze, with a 1 representing a corridor and a 0 representing a wall. Only horizontal and vertical moves are allowed;

Figure 4.4 | A maze: 1 represents a corridor and 0 represents a wall. Assume the starting position is in the upper left-hand corner, and the goal position is in the lower right-hand corner.

```
1 1 1 0 1 1 0 0 0 1 1 1 1
1 0 1 1 1 0 1 1 1 1 1 0 1
1 0 0 0 1 0 1 0 1 0 1 0 1
1 0 0 0 1 1 1 0 1 0 1 1 1
1 1 1 1 1 0 0 0 0 1 0 0 0
0 0 0 0 1 0 0 0 0 0 0 0 0
0 0 0 0 1 1 1 1 1 1 1 1 1
```

diagonal moves are prohibited. The starting position, which must have a 1, is in the upper left-hand corner and the goal position is in the lower right-hand corner.

A successful traversal of this maze will show a path leading from the start position to the goal position. We mark each such position with the number 9. Because there are two possible paths through this maze, the actual path chosen will depend on how the iterator class orders the possible choices. For the sake of specificity, assume the choices are ordered north, east, south, and west. For example, from the position at coordinates (5, 8), the first choice would be (4, 8), followed by (5, 9), (6, 8), and (5, 7).

From the initial position at (0, 0), the following positions are recorded as possibly being on a solution path:

(0, 1) // moving east
(0, 2) // moving east
(1, 2) // moving south
(1, 3) // moving east
(1, 4) // moving east
(0, 4) // moving north
(0, 5) // moving east;

This last position is a dead end, so we "undo" (0, 5) and (0, 4), backtrack to (1, 4), and then record

(2, 4) // moving south
(3, 4) // moving south
(3, 5) // moving east;

From here we eventually reach a dead end. After we undo (3, 5) and retrace to (3, 4), we advance—without any further backtracking—to the goal position. Figure 4.5 shows the corresponding path through the maze of Figure 4.4, with path positions marked with 9s and dead-end positions marked with 2s.

For this application, a position is simply a pair: row, column. The Position class is easily developed. Here is Position.h:

Figure 4.5 | A path through the maze of Figure 4.4. The path positions are marked with 9s and the dead-end positions are marked with 2s.

```
9 9 9 0 2 2 0 0 0 2 2 2 2
1 0 9 9 9 0 2 2 2 2 2 0 2
1 0 0 0 9 0 2 0 2 0 2 0 2
1 0 0 0 9 2 2 0 2 0 2 2 2
1 1 1 1 9 0 0 0 0 1 0 0 0
0 0 0 0 9 0 0 0 0 0 0 0 0
0 0 0 0 9 9 9 9 9 9 9 9 9
```

```cpp
#ifndef POSITION
#define POSITION

class Position
{
        protected:
                int row,
                    column;

        public:
                Position( );
                Position (int row, int column);
                void setPosition (int row, int column);
                int getRow( );
                int getColumn( );
}; // class Position

#endif
```

And here is Position.cpp:

```cpp
#include "Position.h"

Position::Position( )
{
        row = 0;
        column = 0;
} // default constructor

Position::Position (int row, int column)
{
        this -> row = row;
        this -> column = column;
} // constructor
```

```
void Position::setPosition (int row, int column)
{
    this -> row = row;
    this -> column = column;
} // method setPosition

int Position::getRow( )
{
    return row;
} // method getRow( )

int Position::getColumn( )
{
    return column;
} // method getColumn( )
```

The header file Application.h is implemented in Maze.cpp. Here, except for the embedded Iterator class, is Maze.cpp:

```
#include <iostream>
#include "Application.h"

const short WALL = 0;

const short CORRIDOR = 1;

const short PATH = 9;

const short TRIED = 2;

const short ROWS = 7;

const short COLUMNS = 13;

short grid[ROWS][COLUMNS] =
{
    {1, 1, 1, 0, 1, 1, 0, 0, 0, 1, 1, 1, 1},
    {1, 0, 1, 1, 1, 0, 1, 1, 1, 1, 1, 0, 1},
    {1, 0, 0, 0, 1, 0, 1, 0, 1, 0, 1, 0, 1},
    {1, 0, 0, 0, 1, 1, 1, 0, 1, 0, 1, 1, 1},
    {1, 1, 1, 1, 1, 0, 0, 0, 0, 0, 0, 0, 0},
    {0, 0, 0, 0, 1, 0, 0, 0, 0, 0, 0, 0, 0},
    {0, 0, 0, 0, 1, 1, 1, 1, 1, 1, 1, 1, 1}
}; // grid

Position start,
         finish;

using namespace std;
```

```
Position Application::generateInitialState( )
{
        const string START_PROMPT =
                "Please enter the start row and start column: ";
        const string FINISH_PROMPT =
                "Please enter the finish row and finish column: ";

        int row,
            column;

        cout << START_PROMPT;
        cin  >> row >> column;
        start.setPosition (row, column);
        cout << FINISH_PROMPT;
        cin >> row >> column;
        cin.get( );
        finish.setPosition (row, column);
        return start;
} // method generateInitialState

bool Application::valid (const Position& pos)
{
        if (pos.getRow( ) >= 0 && pos.getRow( ) < ROWS &&
                pos.getColumn( ) >= 0 && pos.getColumn( ) < COLUMNS &&
                grid [pos.getRow( )][pos.getColumn( )] == CORRIDOR)
                        return true;
        return false;
} // method valid

void Application::record (const Position& pos)
{
        grid [pos.getRow( )][pos.getColumn( )] = PATH;
} // method record

bool Application::done (const Position& pos)
{
        return pos.getRow( ) == finish.getRow( ) &&
                pos.getColumn( ) == finish.getColumn( );
} // method done

void Application::undo (const Position& pos)
{
        grid [pos.getRow( )][pos.getColumn( )] = TRIED;
} // method undo
```

```
ostream& operator<< (ostream& stream, Application& app)
{
    cout << endl;

    for (int row = 0; row < ROWS; row++)
    {
        for (int column = 0; column < COLUMNS; column++)
            cout << grid [row][column] << ' ';
        cout << endl;
    } // outer for
    return stream;
} // operator <<
```

In Maze.cpp, the constant and variable identifiers (such as WALL, CORRIDOR, grid, start, and finish) are not fields because their meaning is restricted to the maze implementation of the Application class.

All that remains of Maze.cpp is the development of the embedded Iterator class. This class has three **int** fields:

row	// this Iterator's current row
column	// this Iterator's current column
direction	// this Iterator's direction: 0 for north, 1 for east, 2 for south, 3 for west

But a class's fields *must* be specified in the header file, not in the source file. We are now in a dilemma: the header file, Application.h, is generic, so it *cannot* contain information specific to the maze application. We get out of this dilemma with the help of a **void** pointer:

```
void* fieldPtr;
```

Your first impression may be that a **void** pointer points to nothing. But in fact, the opposite is true: any kind of pointer can be assigned to a **void** pointer! For example, we can do the following:

```
void* ptr;
int* intPtr = new int;
string* stringPtr = new string;

*intPtr = 50;
ptr = intPtr;
cout << *(int*)ptr << endl;

*stringPtr = "yes";
ptr = stringPtr;
cout << *(string*)ptr << endl;
```

The output will be

50

yes

Notice, in this code, that a **void** pointer must be explicitly cast to a specific pointer type before the **void** pointer can be dereferenced.

The header file, Application.h, defined fieldPtr to be a **void** pointer, and the source file, Maze.cpp, declares a **struct** (a class with all **public** members) with three fields:

```
struct itrFields
{
     int row,
         column,
         direction;
}; // itrFields
```

The Iterator constructor assigns to fieldPtr a variable whose type is this **struct** pointer, and the ++ and atEnd( ) methods utilize—through casting—the resulting value of *fieldPtr. Here is the implementation of the Iterator methods:

```
Application::Iterator::Iterator (Position pos)
{
     itrFields* itrPtr = new itrFields;
     itrPtr -> row = pos.getRow( );
     itrPtr -> column = pos.getColumn( );
     itrPtr -> direction = 0;
     fieldPtr = itrPtr;
} // constructor

Position Application::Iterator::operator++(int)
{
     itrFields* itrPtr = (itrFields*)fieldPtr;
     int nextRow = itrPtr -> row,
         nextColumn = itrPtr -> column;
     switch (itrPtr -> direction++)
     {
          case 0: nextRow = itrPtr -> row -1; // north
               break;
          case 1: nextColumn = itrPtr -> column + 1; // east
               break;
          case 2: nextRow = itrPtr -> row + 1; // south
               break;
          case 3: nextColumn = itrPtr -> column - 1; // west
     } // switch;
     Position next (nextRow, nextColumn);
```

```
        return next;
    } // operator ++
```

```
    bool Application::Iterator::atEnd( )
    {
        return ((itrFields*)fieldPtr) -> direction >= 3;
    } // method atEnd
```

Because fieldPtr is a field in Iterator, there is one copy of fieldPtr for each instance of Iterator. So even when there are distinct iterators created during separate recursive calls to tryToSolve, each iterator has its own fieldPtr. The reason we can avoid a **void** pointer for the grid field is that there is just one grid field for the application, so we needn't worry about the overlapping effects of multiple instances of grid.

Rather than provide a step-by-step trace, we list the first few *valid* choices after the original call of tryToSolve (pos), with pos = (0, 0):

```
(0, 1) // moving east
(0, 2) // moving east
(1, 2) // moving south
(1, 3) // moving east
(1, 4) // moving east
(0, 4) // moving north
(0, 5) // moving east; dead end; retrace to (1, 4) and rechoose
(2, 4) // moving south
(3, 4) // moving south
(3, 5) // moving east; start of a long dead end
    . . .
```

How long does the tryToSolve method take for this application? Suppose the maze has n positions. In the worst case, such as in Figure 4.6, every position would be considered, so worstTime(n) is linear in n. And with more than half of the positions valid, there would be $O(n)$ recursive calls to tryToSolve, so worstSpace(n) is also linear in n.

Figure 4.6 ∣ A worst-case maze: in columns 1, 4, 7, . . . , every row except the last contains a 0; every other position in the maze contains a 1.

```
1 0 1 1 0 1 1 0
1 0 1 1 0 1 1 0
1 0 1 1 0 1 1 0
. . . . . . . .
. . . . . . . .
. . . . . . . .
1 0 1 1 0 1 1 0
1 0 1 1 0 1 1 0
1 1 1 1 1 1 1 1
```

Projects 4.2 and 4.3 contain two more applications of backtracking. Because the example we just discussed separates the backtracking aspects from the maze-traversing aspects, the BackTrack class and the Application header file are unchanged for the new projects, and so is the main function! In fact, for Projects 4.2 and 4.3, the Position class is also unchanged. To complete Project 4.2 and 4.3, all you need to do is supply an implementation of Application.h.

We now turn our attention to a widely known search technique: binary search. We will develop a recursive function to perform a binary search on an array. Lab 11 follows up on this with an iterative binary-search algorithm that has wider applicability.

4.6 | BINARY SEARCH

Suppose you want to search an array for an item. The simplest way to proceed is sequentially: start at the first location, and keep checking successively higher locations until either the item is found or you reach the end of the array. This search strategy, known as a *sequential search,* is the basis for the generic algorithm find in algorith.h:

```
template <class InputIterator, class T>
InputIterator find (InputIterator first,  // positioned at first item in container
                    InputIterator last,  // positioned beyond last item in container
                    const T& value)
{
        while (first != last && *first != value)
                ++first;
        return first;
}
```

That algorithm works on container objects (with iterators) as well as with arrays (with pointers). For example, we can sequentially search a Linked container of employees or an array of 20 salaries:

```
Linked<Employee>::Iterator itr = find (employees.begin( ),
            employees. end( ), newEmployee);
double* salaryPtr = find (salaries, salaries + 20, newSalary);
if (itr != employees.end( ))
        cout << "newEmployee found!" << endl;
if (salaryPtr != salaries + 20)
        cout << "newSalary found at index" << (salaryPtr − salaries);
```

For a sequential search of an array, the worst time occurs if the search is unsuccessful. In that case, the entire array must be scanned, so worstTime(n) is linear in n. In the average case, assuming each location is equally likely to house the item sought, we probe about $n/2$ items, so averageTime(n) is also linear in n.

Can we improve on this? Definitely! In this section we will study an array-search technique for which worstTime(n) and averageTime(n) are only logarithmic in n.

Given an array to be searched and a value to be searched for, we will develop a *binary search,* so called because the region searched is divided by two at each stage until the search is completed. One important restriction is this:

A binary search requires that the array be sorted.

We assume that **operator**< is defined on the items in the array. For the sake of generality, we want to be able to search a sorted array of any item type for which **operator**< is defined: string, **int**, a user-defined class, and so on. So our function will have the item type T as a template:

>   **template**<**class** T>

For the sake of simplicity, our function will return either **true** or **false**, depending on whether the value sought was found. Lab 11 extends this idea to a function that indicates where the value sought belongs in the sorted array; that is, where the value could be inserted without disordering the array. Also, the function developed below is recursive, whereas Lab 11 investigates an iterative version that is in the typical implementation of the Standard Template Library.

Our function will have three parameters:

1. A pointer to the first location in the region being searched
2. A pointer to the first location *beyond* the region being searched
3. The value sought.

Here is the complete method interface:

```
// Precondition: The array, from first to just before last, is sorted according to
//                operator<.
// Postcondition: true has been returned if value occurs in the array from first
//                to just before last. Otherwise, false has been returned. The
//                worstTime(n) is O(log n).
template<class T>
bool binary_search (T* first, T* last, const T& value);
```

Notice that T* is used as a pointer to a location in the array. If myArray is an array of 5 items, then myArray is a pointer to the first location in the array, and myArray + 5 is a pointer to one beyond the fifth location in the array. So the second argument in a call to binary_search points, not to the last location in the region being searched, but to *one location beyond* the region being searched. Your journey through the Standard Template Library will be smoother if you commit this one-step-beyond idea to your long-term memory!

Here is a file with a main function that has a few sample calls to the binary_search function in the Standard Template Library:

```
#include <iostream>
#include <string>
#include <algorithm> // defines binary_search algorithm
```

```
using namespace std;

int main( )
{
    const string CLOSE_WINDOW_PROMPT =
        "Please press the Enter key to close this output window.";

    const string FOUND_MESSAGE = " was found.";

    const string NOT_FOUND_MESSAGE = " was not found.";

    const int INT1 = 111;

    const int INT2 = 702;

    const string STRING1 = "Ken";

    const string STRING2 = "Ed";

    const string STRING3 = "Abe";

    int scores [9] = {7, 22, 84, 106, 117, 200, 494, 555, 702};

    string names [10] = {"Ada", "Ben", "Carol", "Dave", "Ed", "Frank",
                         "Gerri", "Helen", "Iggy", "Joan"};

    if (binary_search (scores, scores + 9, INT1))
        cout << INT1 << FOUND_MESSAGE << endl;
    else
        cout << INT1 << NOT_FOUND_MESSAGE << endl;

    if (binary_search (scores, scores + 9, INT2))
        cout << INT2 << FOUND_MESSAGE << endl;
    else
        cout << INT2 << NOT_FOUND_MESSAGE << endl;

    if (binary_search (names, names + 10, STRING1))
        cout << STRING1 << FOUND_MESSAGE << endl;
    else
        cout << STRING1 << NOT_FOUND_MESSAGE << endl;

    if (binary_search (names, names + 10, STRING2))
        cout << STRING2 << FOUND_MESSAGE << endl;
    else
        cout << STRING2 << NOT_FOUND_MESSAGE << endl;

    if (binary_search (names, names + 10, STRING3))
        cout << STRING3 << FOUND_MESSAGE << endl;
    else
        cout << STRING3 << NOT_FOUND_MESSAGE << endl;
```

```
            cout << endl << endl << CLOSE_WINDOW_PROMPT;
            cin.get( );
            return 0;
        } // main
```

The output from the program is

```
111 was not found.
702 was found.
Ken was not found.
Ed was found.
Abe was not found.
```

Please press the Enter key to close this output window.

The basic strategy for the recursive binary_search algorithm starts by finding the middle item in the region from first to just before last. The middle item has the value of *middle, where middle is defined as

```
T* middle = first + (last − first) / 2;
```

The pointer arithmetic on the right-hand side of this assignment statement is quite unusual: Two pointers can be subtracted to yield the (integer) distance between them, and a pointer can be incremented by a scaler.

If the middle item is less than value (the item sought), perform a binary search on the region from the new value for first, namely, middle + 1, to just before last, that is

```
if (*middle < value)
        binary_search (middle + 1, last, value);
```

Otherwise, if value is less than the middle item, then perform a binary search on the region from first to the new value for last, namely, middle. That is,

```
else if (value < *middle)
        binary_search (first, middle, value);
```

Otherwise, return **true** (because the middle item must be equal to value).

For example, let's follow this strategy in searching for "Ed" in the array names shown in Figure 4.7. This figure shows the state of the program when the binary_search function is called to find "Ed". The assignment

```
middle = first + (last − first) / 2;
```

makes middle point to the item "Frank".

The middle item, "Frank", is not less than "Ed", but "Ed" is less than "Frank", so we perform a binary search of the region from first to just before the middle location. The call is

```
binary_search (first, middle, value);
```

Figure 4.7 | The state of the program at the beginning of the call to binary_search (names, names + 10, "Ed"). The search for "Ed" will be conducted in the region from indices 0 through 9.

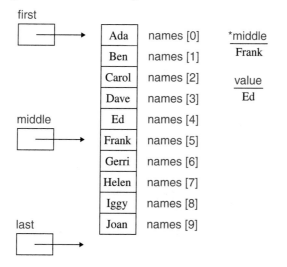

The formal parameter last gets the value of the argument middle. During this execution of binary_search, the assignment

middle = first + (last − first) / 2;

makes middle point to the location with item "Carol". See Figure 4.8.

The middle item, "Carol", is less than "Ed", so a binary search is performed on the region from index 3 (just after "Carol") to just before index 5 (where last is pointing). The call is

binary_search (middle + 1, last, value);

The formal parameter first gets the value of the argument middle + 1. During this execution of binary_search, the assignment

middle = first + (last − first) / 2;

makes middle point to the location with item "Ed". See Figure 4.9. Success! The middle item is equal to value, so **true** is returned.

The only unresolved issue is what happens if the array does not have an item equal to value. In that case, we want to return **false**. It is appropriate to search any region for which first < last, so we stop searching if first >= last.

Here is the complete definition:

```
template<class T>
bool binary_search (T* first, T* last, const T& value)
```

Figure 4.8 | The state of the program at the beginning of the binary search for "Ed" in the region from indices 0 through 4.

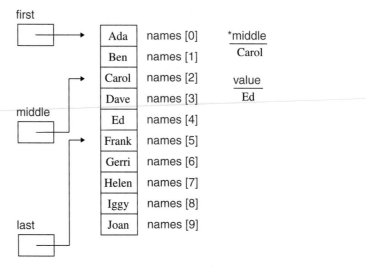

Figure 4.9 | The state of the program at the beginning of the binary search for "Ed" in the region from indices 3 to just before 5.

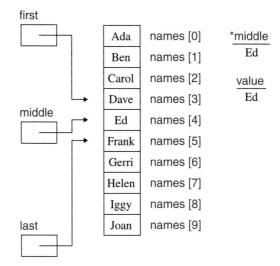

```
    {
        if (first >= last)
            return false;
        T* middle = first + (last - first) / 2;
        if (*middle < value)
            return binary_search (middle + 1, last, value);
        else if (value < *middle)
            return binary_search (first, middle, value);
        return true;
    } // binary_search
```

The following is an execution trace of this function after an initial call of

```
binary_search (names, names + 10, "Dan");
```

where the names array is as has been defined. Note that "Dan" is not in the names array.

Step 0:
```
names = ["Ada", "Ben", "Carol", "Dave", "Ed", "Frank", "Gerri",
         "Helen", "Iggy", "Joan"]

first = names
last = names + 10
value = "Dan"
middle = names + 5
*middle = "Frank"

return binary_search (names, names + 5, "Dan");
```

Step 1:
```
names = ["Ada", "Ben", "Carol", "Dave", "Ed", "Frank", "Gerri",
         "Helen", "Iggy", "Joan"]

first = names
last = names + 5
value = "Dan"
middle = names + 2
*middle = "Carol"

return binary_search (names + 3, names + 5, "Dan");
```

```
names = ["Ada", "Ben", "Carol", "Dave", "Ed", "Frank", "Gerri",
         "Helen", "Iggy", "Joan"]

first = names
last = names + 10
value = "Dan"
middle = names + 5
*middle = "Frank"

return binary_search (names, names + 5, "Dan");
```

continued

Step 2:
```
names = ["Ada", "Ben", "Carol", "Dave", "Ed", "Frank", "Gerri",
         "Helen", "Iggy", "Joan"]

first = names + 3
last = names + 5
value = "Dan"
middle = names + 4
*middle = "Ed"

return binary_search (names + 3, names + 4, "Dan");
```

```
names = ["Ada", "Ben", "Carol", "Dave", "Ed", "Frank", "Gerri",
         "Helen", "Iggy", "Joan"]

first = names
last = names + 5
value = "Dan"
middle = names + 2
*middle = "Carol"

return binary_search (names + 3, names + 5, "Dan");
```

```
names = ["Ada", "Ben", "Carol", "Dave", "Ed", "Frank", "Gerri",
         "Helen", "Iggy", "Joan"]

first = names
last = names + 10
value = "Dan"
middle = names + 5
*middle = "Frank"

return binary_search (names, names + 5, "Dan");
```

Step 3:
```
names = ["Ada", "Ben", "Carol", "Dave", "Ed", "Frank", "Gerri",
         "Helen", "Iggy", "Joan"]

first = names + 3
last = names + 4
value = "Dan"
middle = names + 3
*middle = "Dave"

return binary_search (names + 3, names + 3, "Dan");
```

```
names = ["Ada", "Ben", "Carol", "Dave", "Ed", "Frank", "Gerri",
         "Helen", "Iggy", "Joan"]

first = names + 3
last = names + 5
value = "Dan"
middle = names + 4
*middle = "Ed"

return binary_search (names + 3, names + 4, "Dan");
```

names = ["Ada", "Ben", "Carol", "Dave", "Ed", "Frank", "Gerri",
        "Helen", "Iggy", "Joan"]

first = names
last = names + 5
value = "Dan"
middle = names + 2
*middle = "Carol"

return binary_search (names + 3, names + 5, "Dan");

---

names = ["Ada", "Ben", "Carol", "Dave", "Ed", "Frank", "Gerri",
        "Helen", "Iggy", "Joan"]

first = names
last = names + 10
value = "Dan"
middle = names + 5
*middle = "Frank"

return binary_search (names, names + 5, "Dan");

Step 4:

names = ["Ada", "Ben", "Carol", "Dave", "Ed", "Frank", "Gerri",
        "Helen", "Iggy", "Joan"]
first = names + 3
last = names + 3
value = "Dan"

return false;

↓ **false**

names = ["Ada", "Ben", "Carol", "Dave", "Ed", "Frank", "Gerri",
        "Helen", "Iggy", "Joan"]
first = names + 3
last = names + 4
value = "Dan"
middle = names + 3
*middle = "Dave"

return binary_search (names + 3, names + 3, "Dan");

↓ **false**

names = ["Ada", "Ben", "Carol", "Dave", "Ed", "Frank", "Gerri",
        "Helen", "Iggy", "Joan"]
first = names + 3
last = names + 5
value = "Dan"
middle = names + 4
*middle = "Ed"

return binary_search (names + 3, names + 4, "Dan");

↓ **false**

continued

```
names = ["Ada", "Ben", "Carol", "Dave", "Ed", "Frank", "Gerri",
         "Helen", "Iggy", "Joan"]
first = names
last = names + 5
value = "Dan"
middle = names + 2
*middle = "Carol"

return binary_search (names + 3, names + 5, "Dan");
```

false

```
names = ["Ada", "Ben", "Carol", "Dave", "Ed", "Frank", "Gerri",
         "Helen", "Iggy", "Joan"]
first = names
last = names + 10
value = "Dan"
middle = names + 5
*middle = "Frank"

return binary_search (names, names + 5, "Dan");
```

false

How long does the binary_search function take? We need to make a distinction between an unsuccessful search, in which the item is not found, and a successful search, in which the item is found. We start with an analysis of an unsuccessful search.

During an execution of binary_search, suppose the middle item is not equal to value. Then the size of the region searched during the next execution is, approximately, halved. If the item sought is not in the array, we keep dividing by 2 until the size of the region is 0. The number of times n can be divided by 2 until $n = 0$ is floor($\log_2 n$) + 1 (see Example A1.2). So worstTime(n) is logarithmic in n. The same number of calls to binary_search will be performed in the average case of an unsuccessful search, so averageTime(n) is logarithmic in n.

The worst case for a successful search requires only one more call to binary_search than the worst case (or average case) for an unsuccessful search. So for a successful search, worstTime(n) is logarithmic in n. In the average case for a successful search, the analysis—see Exercise 4.13—is more complicated, but the result is the same: averageTime(n) is logarithmic in n.

During each call, a constant amount of information is saved: the entire array is not saved, only a pointer to the array. So the space requirements are also logarithmic in n, for both successful and unsuccessful searches and for both the worst case and the average case.

In Lab 11, you will get to see an iterative implementation of binary_search, one of the generic algorithms in the Standard Template Library.

LAB **Lab 11:** **Iterative binary search.**

(All Labs Are Optional.) LAB

The next example is from Eric Roberts' delightful book *Thinking Recursively* [see Roberts (1986)].

4.7 | GENERATING PERMUTATIONS

A *permutation* is an arrangement of items in a linear order. For example, if the items are the letters 'A', 'B', 'C' and 'D', we can generate the following 24 permutations:

ABCD	BACD	CABD	DABC
ABDC	BADC	CADB	DACB
ACBD	BCAD	CBAD	DBAC
ACDB	BCDA	CBDA	DBCA
ADBC	BDAC	CDAB	DCAB
ADCB	BDCA	CDBA	DCBA

In general, for n items, there are n choices for the first item in a permutation. After the first item has been chosen, there are $(n - 1)$ choices for the second item. Continuing in this fashion, we see that the total number of permutations of n items is

$$n(n - 1)(n - 2) \ldots (2)(1)$$

That is, there are $n!$ different permutations of n items.

From this example, if the string s = "ABCD", we can print out the permutations of s by printing:

The six permutations that start with 'A'

The six permutations that start with 'B'

The six permutations that start with 'C'

The six permutations that start with 'D'

How can we accomplish the printing of the six permutations that start with 'A'? Look at the list of permutations and try to figure out how to proceed. (Hint: 6 = 3!)

The key observation is that, for those six permutations, each one starts with 'A' and is followed by a different permutation of "BCD." This suggests a recursive solution. For each of the six permutations of "BCD," we write out the entire string of s, and so we get the six permutations of "ABCD" that start with 'A'.

For the next six permutations, we first swap 'A' and 'B', so that s = "BACD". We then repeat this process—this time permuting "ACD" and printing out all of s for each permutation.

For the next six permutations, we start by swapping 'B' and 'C', that is, s [0] and s [2], so that s = "CABD". We then permute "ABD" (that is, s [1 . . . 3]) and print s after each permutation.

For the last six permutations, we start by swapping s [0] and s [3] (that is, 'C' and 'D')—so that s = "DABC"—and then print s after each permutation of s [1 . . . 3] (that is, "ABC").

As we did in Lab 9 with the efficient, recursive Fibonacci function, we make permute a wrapper function. Then the starting position for each level of permuting can be an argument to the recursive function. This implementation detail is hidden in the definition of the wrapper function, which takes a constant reference parameter s, and passes s to the recursive function. Then the original string s will be unchanged by the permute function.

Here is the wrapper function:

```
// Postcondition: all the permutations of s have been printed.
void permute (const string& s)
{
        rec_permute (s, 0);
} // permute
```

The function interface for the recursive function is

```
// Postcondition: s has been printed for each permutation of s [k. . . s.length( )
//                  − 1].
void rec_permute (string s, unsigned k);
```

The parameter k is **unsigned** because it is compared to s.length( ), which returns an **unsigned int**.

The swapping and permuting can be accomplished in a **for** loop:

```
for (unsigned i = k; i < s.length( ); i++)
{
        swap (s [i], s [k]); // swap is a generic algorithm
        rec_permute (s, k + 1);
} // for
```

Notice that, when the loop is executed for the first time, s [i] is swapped with itself. The effect of this is to leave s [i] fixed during the first iteration. For example, in permuting "ABCD", we start by leaving 'A' fixed and permuting "BCD".

The sequence of recursive calls stops when k equals s.length( ) − 1. When this happens, we write out s. The complete function is quite brief:

```
// Postcondition: s has been printed for each permutation of s [k . . . s.length
//                  ( ) − 1].
void rec_permute (string s, unsigned k)
{
        if (k == s.length( ) − 1)
                cout << s << endl;
        else
                for (unsigned i = k; i < s.length( ); i++)
                {
                        swap (s [i], s [k]); // swap is a generic algorithm
                        rec_permute (s, k + 1);
                } // for
} // rec_permute
```

Keep in mind that the value of s is not changed by the recursive calls: s is a value parameter in rec_permute. But the value of s *is* changed by the swaps. For example, when

rec_permute ("BAC", 1);

is called, then during the execution of that call, the value of s changes after each call to swap in the **for** statement. The sequence of values for s is

"BAC"   (before the first iteration of the **for** loop)
"BAC"   (after swapping s [1] and s [1])
"BCA"   (after swapping s [1] and s [2])

Here is an execution trace of rec_permute after an initial call of

permute ("ABC");

invokes a call to

rec_permute ("ABC", 0);

Output:

Step 0:
```
s = "ABC"
k = 0
i = 0
    swap s [0] with s [0]
    s is now "ABC"
✓   rec_permute ("ABC", 1);
```

Step 1:
```
s = "ABC"
k = 1
i = 1
    swap s [1] with s [1]
    s is now "ABC"
✓   rec_permute ("ABC", 2);
```

```
s = "ABC"
k = 0
i = 0
    swap s [0] with s [0]
    s is now "ABC"
✓   rec_permute ("ABC", 1);
```

Step 2:
```
s = "ABC"
k = 2
✓   cout << "ABC" << endl;        ABC
```

continued

```
s = "ABC"
k = 1
i = 1
        swap s [1] with s [1]
        s is now "ABC"
    ✓   rec_permute ("ABC", 2);
```

```
s = "ABC"
k = 0
i = 0
        swap s [0] with s [0]
        s is now "ABC"
    ✓   rec_permute ("ABC", 1);
```

Step 3:
```
s = "ABC"
k = 1
i = 2
        swap s [2] with s [1]
        s is now "ACB"
    ✓   rec_permute ("ACB", 2);
```

```
s = "ABC"
k = 0
i = 0
        swap s [0] with s [0]
        s is now "ABC"
    ✓   rec_permute ("ABC", 1);
```

Step 4:
```
s = "ACB"
k = 2
    ✓   cout << "ACB" << endl;
```
ACB

```
s = "ABC"
k = 1
i = 2
        swap s [2] with s [1]
        s is now "ACB"
    ✓   rec_permute ("ACB", 2);
```

```
s = "ABC"
k = 0
i = 0

    swap s [0] with s [0]
    s is now "ABC"
✓   rec_permute ("ABC", 1);
```

Step 5:
```
s = "ABC"
k = 0
i = 1

    swap s [1] with s [0]
    s is now "BAC"
✓   rec_permute ("BAC", 1);
```

Step 6:
```
s = "BAC"
k = 1
i = 1

    swap s [1] with s [1]
    s is now "BAC"
✓   rec_permute ("BAC", 2);
```

```
s = "ABC"
k = 0
i = 1

    swap s [1] with s [0]
    s is now "BAC"
✓   rec_permute ("BAC", 1);
```

Step 7:
```
s = "BAC"
k = 2

✓   cout << "BAC" << endl;                    BAC
```

```
s = "BAC"
k = 1
i = 1

    swap s [1] with s [1]
    s is now "BAC"
✓   rec_permute ("BAC", 2);
```

continued

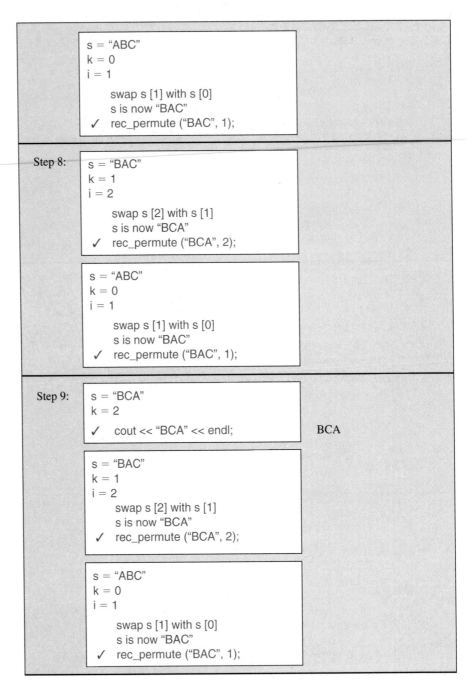

s = "ABC"
k = 0
i = 1

    swap s [1] with s [0]
    s is now "BAC"
✓ rec_permute ("BAC", 1);

Step 8:

s = "BAC"
k = 1
i = 2

    swap s [2] with s [1]
    s is now "BCA"
✓ rec_permute ("BCA", 2);

s = "ABC"
k = 0
i = 1

    swap s [1] with s [0]
    s is now "BAC"
✓ rec_permute ("BAC", 1);

Step 9:

s = "BCA"
k = 2

✓ cout << "BCA" << endl;   BCA

s = "BAC"
k = 1
i = 2

    swap s [2] with s [1]
    s is now "BCA"
✓ rec_permute ("BCA", 2);

s = "ABC"
k = 0
i = 1

    swap s [1] with s [0]
    s is now "BAC"
✓ rec_permute ("BAC", 1);

Step 10:

> s = "BAC"
> k = 0
> i = 2
>
>   swap s [2] with s [0]
>   s is now "CAB"
> ✓   rec_permute ("CAB", 1);

NOTE: This is the third iteration of the original execution of the **for** statement, so s starts with the value it had at the end of the second iteration (the bottom box in step 9), namely, "BAC".

Step 11:

> s = "CAB"
> k = 1
> i = 1
>
>   swap s [1] with s [1]
>   s is now "CAB"
> ✓   rec_permute ("CAB", 2);

> s = "BAC"
> k = 0
> i = 2
>
>   swap s [2] with s [0]
>   s is now "CAB"
> ✓   rec_permute ("CAB", 1);

Step 12:

> s = "CAB"
> k = 2
>
> ✓   cout << "CAB" << endl;   CAB

> s = "CAB"
> k = 1
> i = 1
>
>   swap s [1] with s [1]
>   s is now "CAB"
> ✓   rec_permute ("CAB", 2);

> s = "BAC"
> k = 0
> i = 2
>
>   swap s [2] with s [0]
>   s is now "CAB"
> ✓   rec_permute ("CAB", 1);

continued

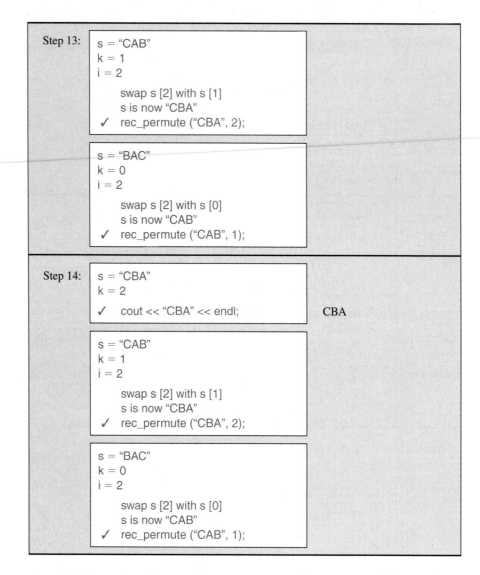

Step 13:
```
s = "CAB"
k = 1
i = 2

        swap s [2] with s [1]
        s is now "CBA"
     ✓  rec_permute ("CBA", 2);
```

```
s = "BAC"
k = 0
i = 2

        swap s [2] with s [0]
        s is now "CAB"
     ✓  rec_permute ("CAB", 1);
```

Step 14:
```
s = "CBA"
k = 2

     ✓  cout << "CBA" << endl;          CBA
```

```
s = "CAB"
k = 1
i = 2

        swap s [2] with s [1]
        s is now "CBA"
     ✓  rec_permute ("CBA", 2);
```

```
s = "BAC"
k = 0
i = 2

        swap s [2] with s [0]
        s is now "CAB"
     ✓  rec_permute ("CAB", 1);
```

4.7.1   Estimating the Time and Space Requirements

For the time requirements, assume that k starts out at 0, and let n represent the length of s. Then the **for** loop is iterated n times, and there are n recursive calls to permute. For each of the n iterations of the **for** loop, rec_permute is called again with $k = 1$, and we get $n - 1$ (additional) recursive calls to rec_permute. The total number of recursive calls so far is then $n + n(n - 1)$.

This process continues until $k = n - 1$, at which time s is printed. The total number of recursive calls is $n + n(n - 1) + n(n - 1)(n - 2) + \ldots + n(n - 1)(n - 2) \ldots 3 + n!$

Since $n \geq 1$, the value of each term in this sum is at most half the value of the next term. Starting at the rightmost and next-to-rightmost two terms in this sum, we get (see Section A1.3 for an explanation of product notation):

$$\prod_{i=3}^{n} i \leq (1/2) n!$$

For the second and third terms from the right,

$$\prod_{i=4}^{n} i \leq (1/2) \prod_{i=3}^{n} i \leq 1/4\, n!$$

So we get

$$\prod_{i=4}^{n} i \leq (1/2^2)\, n!$$

The exponent on the right-hand side is 2 less than the starting index for i on the left-hand side. Continuing in this fashion, we get the following for the leftmost term:

$$n = \prod_{i=n}^{n} i \leq (1/2^{n-2})\, n!$$

Then

$$n + n(n-1) + n(n-1)(n-2) + \cdots + n(n-1)(n-2) \cdots 3 + n! \leq$$
$$(1/2^{n-2})n! + (1/2^{n-3})n! + \cdots + (1/2^2)n! + (1/2^1)n! + n!$$

This last sum is less than $2n!$; that is, the number of recursive calls is less than $2n!$, so worstTime(n) is $O(n!)$, and this is minimal because $n!$ permutations must be output. Because $2^n < n!$ for $n \geq 4$, any function that prints $n!$ values must be an exponential-time function, and we conclude that printing $n!$ values is intractable.

What are the space requirements? At any time, there are at most n activations of rec_permute. Since s is a value parameter, the n characters in s are saved with each activation, so the space requirements are quadratic in n. Practically speaking, the space requirements are small relative to the time requirements. For example, if $n = 13$, n^2 is only 169, whereas $n!$ is more than 6 billion.

The development of this recursive function was not easy. Developing an iterative version would be even harder except for the generic algorithm next_permutation in the $<$algorithm$>$ file of the Standard Template Library. This iterative function returns a **bool** result and takes two parameters: an iterator (or pointer) positioned at the start of the container to be permuted, and an iterator (or pointer) positioned *one past* the last item in that container. If another permutation can be performed—that is, if the container is not yet in reverse lexicographic order—the next higher permutation is performed and **true** is returned. If the container is already in reverse lexicographic order, then it is reversed, to yield the original (forward) lexicographic order and **false** is returned.

Note that string is a container class in the Standard Template Library, so the begin and end methods are defined for string objects. Table 4.1 shows the sequence of calls to next_permutation when s = "123" and the statement is

    while (next_permutation (s.begin( ), s.end( ))

In order for all permutations of s to be printed, s must be in *lexicographic order:* the order imposed by the ASCII collating sequence. Fortunately, the sort generic algorithm comes to the rescue. Here is a version of the permute function that uses next_permutation:

```
// Postcondition: every permutation of s has been printed.
void permute (string s)
{
     sort (s.begin( ), s.end( ));
     cout << endl << s << endl;
     while (next_permutation (s.begin( ), s.end( ))
          cout << s << endl;
} // function permute
```

Each of the $n!$ permutations is printed, so the **while** loop is executed $n! - 1$ times. The next_permutation function has constant worstTime(n), so for this iterative version of permute, worstTime(n) is $O(n!)$, and this is minimal.

In Section 4.1, we informally described a recursive function as a function that called itself. Section 4.8 indicates why that description would not suffice as a definition.

4.8 | INDIRECT RECURSION

C++ allows functions to be indirectly recursive. For example, if function A calls function B and function B calls function A, then both A and B are recursive.

Because indirect recursion is legal, we cannot simply define a function to be recursive if it calls itself. To provide a formal definition of "recursive," we first define "active." A function is *active* if it is being executed or has called an active function. For example, consider a chain of function calls

Table 4.1

Before call	After call	Return value
123	132	true
132	213	true
213	231	true
231	312	true
312	321	true
321	123	false

A ⟶ B ⟶ C ⟶ D

That is, A calls B, B calls C, and C calls D. When D is being executed, the active functions are

>   D, because it is being executed
>   C, because it has called D and D is active
>   B, because it has called C and C is active
>   A, because it has called B and B is active

We can now define "recursive." A function is **recursive** if it can be called while it is active. For example, suppose we had the following sequence of calls:

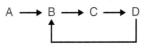

Then B, C, and D are recursive because each can be called while it is active.

When a recursive function is invoked, a certain amount of information must be saved so that information will not be written over during the execution of the recursive call. This information is restored when the execution of the recursive call has been completed. This saving and restoring, and other work related to the support of recursion, carry some cost in terms of execution time and memory space. Section 4.9 estimates the cost of recursion and speculates whether the cost is justified.

*A method is **recursive** if it can be called while it is active.*

4.9 I THE COST OF RECURSION

We have seen that some information is saved every time a function calls itself. The information is collectively referred to as an **activation record** because it pertains to the execution state of the currently active function. In fact, an activation record is created whenever *any* function is called; this relieves the compiler of the burden of determining if a given function is—directly or indirectly—recursive.

Essentially, an activation record is an execution frame without the statements. Each activation record contains

1. The return address, that is, the address of the statement that will be executed when the call has been completed.
2. The value of each value formal parameter: a copy of the corresponding argument is made.
3. The address of each reference formal parameter (Section 7.5 has an example of a recursive function with a reference formal parameter).
4. The values of the function's other local variables.

After the call has been completed, the previous activation record's information is restored and the execution of the calling function is resumed. There is an execution-time cost of saving and restoring these records, and the records themselves take up space. But these costs are negligible relative to the cost of a programmer's time to develop an iterative function when a recursive function would be more appropriate. Recursive methods, such as move and rec_permute, are far simpler and more elegant than their iterative counterparts.

How can you decide whether a recursive function or iterative function is more appropriate? Basically, if you can readily develop an iterative solution, go for it! If not, you need to decide if recursion is appropriate for the problem. That is, if complex cases of the problem can be reduced to simpler cases of the same form as the original, and if the simplest case(s) can be solved directly, you should try to develop a recursive function.

If an iterative function is not easy to develop, and recursion is appropriate, how does recursion compare with iteration? At worst, the recursive version will take about as long (and have similar time and space performance) as the iterative version. At best, developing the recursive function will take far less time than developing the iterative version, and have similar time and space performance. See, for example, the move, tryToSolve, and rec_permute functions in this chapter. Of course, it is possible to design an inefficient recursive function, such as the original version of fib in Lab 9, just as iterative functions can have poor performance.

In this chapter we have focused on what recursion is. We postpone to Chapter 7 a discussion of the mechanism, called a *stack,* by which the compiler implements the saving and restoring of activation records. As we saw in Chapter 3, the separation of what is done from how it is done is a critically important principle in problem solving.

SUMMARY

The purpose of this chapter is to familiarize you with the basic idea of recursion so that you will be able to understand the recursive functions in Chapters 8 and 12 and to design your own recursive functions when the need arises.

A function is *recursive* if it can be called while it is active. An *active* function is one that either is being executed or has called an active function.

Recursion should be considered for any problem that has the following characteristics:

1. Complex cases of the problem can be reduced to simpler cases that have the same form as the original problem.
2. The simplest case(s) can be solved directly.

For such problems, it is often straightforward to develop a recursive function. But it may turn out that an *iterative* function—one that has a loop—may consume less execution time and less memory. For some problems, it is easier to develop an iterative solution than a recursive solution. Occasionally—see the move, tryToSolve, and rec_permute functions—the opposite is true.

Whenever any function (recursive or not) is called, a new activation record is created to provide a frame of reference for the execution of the function. Each activation record contains

1. The return address, that is, the address of the statement that will be executed when the call has been completed.
2. The value of each value formal parameter: a copy of the corresponding argument is made.
3. The address of each reference formal parameter (two memory accesses are required to access the corresponding argument).
4. The values of the function's other local variables.

Activation records make recursion possible because they hold information that might otherwise be destroyed if the function called itself. When the execution of the current function has been completed, a return is made to the address specified in the current activation record.

EXERCISES

4.1 What is wrong with the following function for calculating factorials?

```
// Precondition: n >= 0.
// Postcondition: n! has been returned.
long fact (int n)
{
        if (n == 0 || n == 1)
                return 1;
        else
                return fact (n+1) / (n+1);
} // fact
```

4.2 Develop an iterative version of the writeBinary function. Test that function with a main function that inputs a nonnegative decimal integer and then calls the iterative writeBinary function.

Hint   Use a **while** loop to generate the bit values, an array to hold those values, and a **for** loop with a negative step to write out those values.

4.3 Show the first three steps in an execution-frames trace of the move function for the Towers of Hanoi problem after an initial (incorrect) call of

move (0, 'A', 'B', 'C');

4.4 Perform an execution-frames trace to determine the output from the following *incorrect* version of the rec_permute function after an initial call of rec_permute ("ABC", 0);

```
// Postcondition: s has been printed for each permutation of
//                 s [k . . . s.length( ) − 1].
void rec_permute (string s, unsigned k)
{
    if (k == s.length( ) − 1)
        cout << s << endl;
    else
        for (unsigned i = k; i < s.length( ) ; i++)
        {
            swap (s [i], s [k + 1]);
            rec_permute (s, k + 1);
        } // for
} // rec_permute
```

Check your output by substituting this rec_permute method with the rec_permute method in the permutation project—see the Source Code link on the book's website.

4.5 Perform an execution-frames trace to determine the output from the following *incorrect* version of the rec_permute function after an initial call of

rec_permute ("ABC", 0);

```
// Postcondition: s has been printed for each permutation of
//                 s [k . . . s.length( ) − 1].
void rec_permute (string s, unsigned k)
{
    if (k == s.length( ) − 1)
        cout << s << endl;
    else
        for (unsigned i = k; i < s.length( ) ; i++)
        {
            rec_permute (s, k + 1);
            swap (s [i], s [k]);
        } // for
} // rec_permute
```

Check your output by substituting this rec_permute method with the rec_permute method in the permutation project—see the Source Code link on the book's website.

4.6 Study the generic algorithm next_permutation in <algorithm>. Describe in simple English how that algorithm works if the container contains 7, 1, 4, 6, 5, 3, 2.

4.7 Given two positive integers i and j, the greatest common divisor of i and j, written

$$\gcd(i, j)$$

is the largest integer k such that

$$(i \% k = 0) \quad \text{and} \quad (j \% k = 0)$$

For example, gcd(35, 21) = 7 and gcd(8, 15) = 1. Develop a recursive function that returns the greatest common divisor of i and j. Test your function with a main function that inputs two positive integers and outputs their greatest common divisor. Here is the function interface:

```
// Precondition: i > 0, j > 0.
// Postcondition: the greatest common divisor of i and j has been returned.
int gcd (int i, int j);
```

Big hint   According to Euclid's algorithm, the greatest common divisor of i and j is j if $i \% j = 0$. Otherwise, the greatest common divisor of i and j is the greatest common divisor of j and $(i \% j)$.

4.8   A *palindrome* is a string that is the same from right to left as from left to right. For example, the following are palindromes:

ABADABA

RADAR

OTTO

MADAMIMADAM

EVE

For this exercise, we restrict each string to uppercase letters only. (You are asked to remove this restriction in Exercise 4.9.)

     Develop a recursive function to test for palindromes. The function interface is

```
// Postcondition: true has been returned if s [i...j] is a palindrome.
//                Otherwise, false has been returned.
bool isPalindrome (string s, int i, int j);
```

Test your function with a main function that inputs a string and outputs whether or not the string is a palindrome.

Hint   If i >= j, s [i . . . j] is a (trivial) palindrome. Otherwise, s [i . . . j] is a palindrome if and only if s [i] = s [j] and s [i + 1 . . . j − 1] is a palindrome.

4.9   Extend the recursive function developed in Exercise 4.8 so that, in testing to see whether s is a palindrome, nonletters are ignored and no distinction is made between uppercase and lowercase letters. For example, the following are palindromes:

Madam, I'm Adam.

Able was I'ere I saw Elba.

A man. A plan. A canal. Panama!

Hint   To convert a lowercase letter to uppercase, use the toupper function in ctype.h. This function takes one parameter: a **char** ch. If ch is in the range 'a' . . . 'z', then the ordinal value of the uppercase version of ch is returned. Otherwise, the ordinal value of ch itself is returned. For example, since the ordinal value of 'B' is 66,

```
cout << toupper ('b') << endl
        << (char)toupper ('b') << endl
        << (char)toupper ('D') << endl
        << (char)toupper ('?') << endl;
```

will output

```
66
B
D
?
```

4.10   In the Linked class from Chapter 2, use recursion to develop a reversePrint method that will print out a Linked object in reverse order. For example, if we have

```
Linked<string> myList;

myList.pushFront ("yes");
myList.pushFront ("no");
myList.pushFront ("maybe");
myList.pushFront ("but");
myList.reversePrint( );
```

the output would be

```
yes
no
maybe
but
```

4.11   a.   Develop a recursive function power that returns the result of integer exponentiation. The interface is

```
// Precondition: n >=0.
// Postcondition: iⁿ has been returned.
long power (int i, int n);
```

Hint   We define $0^0 = 1$, so for any integer i, $i^0 = 1$. For any integer i and for any $n > 0$,

$$i^n = i \; (i^{n-1})$$

b.   Develop an iterative version of power.

c.   Develop a recursive version of power for which worstTime(n) is $O(\log n)$.

Hint   If n is even, power(i, n) = power(i * i, n / 2); if n is odd, power (i, n) = i * i^{n-1} = i * power (i * i, n / 2).

In all three cases, test your power function with a main function that reads in values for i and n and outputs i^n.

4.12 Develop a recursive function to determine the number of distinct ways in which a given amount of money in cents could be changed into quarters, dimes, nickels, and pennies. For example, if the amount is 17 cents, then there are six ways to make change:

1 dime, 1 nickel, and 2 pennies

1 dime and 7 pennies

3 nickels and 2 pennies

2 nickels and 7 pennies

1 nickel and 12 pennies

17 pennies

Here is the function interface:

```
// Precondition: denomination = 1 (for penny), 2 (for nickel), 3 (for dime),or 4
//               (for quarter).
// Postcondition: If amount < 0, then 0 has been returned. Otherwise, the
//               value returned is the number of ways that amount can be
//               changed into coins whose denomination is no larger than
//               denomination.
int ways (int amount, int denomination);
```

For the sake of simplifying the ways function, develop a function coins that returns the value of each denomination. Thus, coins(1) returns 1, coins(2) returns 5, coins(3) returns 10, and coins(4) returns 25.

Test your ways and coins functions with a main function that inputs an amount in cents and outputs the number of ways that amount can be changed into quarters, dimes, nickels, and pennies.

Hint   The number of ways you can make change for an amount using coins no larger than a quarter is equal to the number of ways you can make change for amount − 25 using coins no larger than a quarter, plus the number of ways you can make change for amount using coins no larger than a dime.

4.13 Show that, for the recursive binary_search function, averageTime(n) is logarithmic in n for a successful search.

Hint Let n represent the size of the array to be searched. Because the average number of calls is a nondecreasing function of n, it it enough to show that the claim is true for values of n that are one less than a power of 2. So assume that

$$n = 2^{k-1} \quad \text{for some positive integer } k$$

In a successful search,

One call is sufficient if the item sought is halfway through the region to be searched.

Two calls are needed if the item sought is one-fourth or three-fourths of the way through that region.

Three calls are needed if the item sought is one-eighth, three-eighths, five-eighths, or seven-eighths of the way through the region.

and so on.

The total number of calls for all successful searches is

$$(1 \cdot 1) + (2 \cdot 2) + (3 \cdot 4) + (4 \cdot 8) + (5 \cdot 16) + \cdots + (k \cdot 2^{k-1})$$

The average number of calls, and hence an estimate of the averageTime(n), is this sum divided by n. Now use the result from Exercise A1.3 and the fact that

$$k = \log_2(n + 1)$$

4.14 What change would have to be made to the recursive binary_search function to enable that algorithm to make only one comparison of items per call?

Hint See Lab 11.

4.15 What change(s) would be needed in the Maze application in order for the end-user to be able to enter the name of a file that held the maze?

4.16 What change(s) would be needed in the Maze application so that diagonal moves would be valid?

4.17 Use the Principle of Mathematical Induction (Appendix 1) to show that the move function in the Towers of Hanoi example is correct.

Hint For $n = 1, 2, 3, \ldots,$ let S_n be the statement: move (n, orig, dest, temp) prints out the steps to move n disks from any pole orig to any other pole dest.

a. *Base case.* Show that S_1 is true.

b. *Inductive case.* Let n be any integer greater than 1 and assume S_{n-1} is true. Then show that S_n is true. According to the code of the move function, what happens when move (n, orig, dest, temp) is called?

4.18 In an execution trace of the move function in the Towers of Hanoi application, the number of steps is equal to the number of recursive calls to move plus the number of output statements. Because each call to move (including the call when $n = 1$) includes an output statement, the number of recursive calls to move is always one less than the number of output statements, and the number of output statements is $2^n - 1$. For example, in the execution trace shown in the chapter, $n = 3$, so the number of steps is $6 + 7$ (recall that we started at step 0, so the last step is step 12). How many steps would there be for an execution trace with $n = 4$? In general, how many steps are there, as a function of n?

PROGRAMMING PROJECT 4.1

An Iterative Version of Towers of Hanoi

Develop an iterative version of the move method in the Towers of Hanoi game. Test that method with a main function that inputs the number of disks and then calls move.

Hint   We can determine the proper move at each stage provided we can answer the following three questions:

1.   *Which disk is to be moved?* To answer this question, we set up an n-bit counter, where n is the number of disks, and initialize that counter to all zeros. For example, if $n = 5$, we would start with

00000

Each bit position corresponds to a disk: the rightmost bit corresponds to disk 1, the next rightmost bit to disk 2, and so on. At each stage, the rightmost zero bit corresponds to the disk to be moved, so the first disk to be moved is, as you would expect, disk 1.

After a disk has been moved, we increment the counter as follows: starting at the rightmost bit and working to the left, keep flipping bits (0 to 1, 1 to 0) until a zero gets flipped. For example, the first few increments and moves are as follows:

```
00000 // move disk 1
00001 // move disk 2
00010 // move disk 1
00011 // move disk 3
00100 // move disk 1
00101 // move disk 2
```

After 31 moves, the counter will contain all 1s, so no further moves will be needed or possible. In general, $2^n - 1$ moves and increments will be made.

2. *In which direction should that disk be moved?* If n is odd, then odd-numbered disks move clockwise:

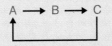

and even-numbered disks move counterclockwise:

A ← B ← C

If n is even, even-numbered disks move clockwise and odd-numbered disks move counterclockwise.

  If we number the poles 0, 1, and 2 instead of A, B, and C, then movements can be accomplished simply with modular arithmetic. Namely, if we are currently at pole k, then

$$k = (k + 1) \% 3$$

achieves a clockwise move, and

$$k = (k + 2) \% 3$$

achieves a counterclockwise move. For output, we cast back to a character:

```
cout << char (k + 'A');
```

3. *Where is that disk now?* Keep track of where disk 1 is. If the counter indicates that disk 1 is to be moved, use the answer to question 2 to move that disk. If the counter indicates that the disk to be moved is not disk 1, then the answer to question 2 tells you where that disk is now. Why? Because that disk cannot be moved on top of disk 1 and cannot be moved from the pole where disk 1 is now.

PROGRAMMING PROJECT 4.2

The Eight Queens Problem

Develop and validate a program to place eight queens on a chessboard in such a way that no queen is under attack from any other queen.

Analysis

A chessboard has eight rows and eight columns. In the game of chess, the queen is the most powerful piece: she can attack any piece in her row, any piece in her column, and any piece in either of her diagonals. See Figure 4.10.

Figure 4.10 | Positions vulnerable to a queen in chess. The arrows indicate the positions that can be attacked by the queen (Q) in the center of the figure.

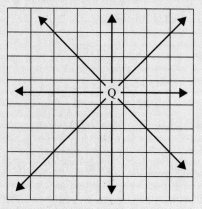

There is no input for this problem. The output should show the chessboard after the placement of the eight queens. For example:

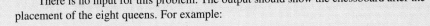

	0	1	2	3	4	5	6	7
0	Q							
1							Q	
2					Q			
3								Q
4		Q						
5				Q				
6						Q		
7			Q					

The lines are not part of the required output.

Hint There must be exactly one queen in each row and exactly one queen in each column. Start with a queen at (0, 0), that is, row 0 and column 0, and place a queen in each column. A valid position is one that is not in the same row, column, or diagonal as any queen placed in a previous column. The QueensIterator constructor should advance to row 0 of the next column. The **operator++ (int)** should advance to the next row in the same column. So the first time tryToSolve is called, the choices are

(0, 1) // invalid: in the same row as the queen at (0, 0)
(1, 1) // invalid: in the same diagonal as the queen at (0, 0)
(2, 1) // valid

When tryToSolve is called again, the choices are

(0, 2) // invalid: in the same row as the queen at (0, 0)
(1, 2) // invalid: in the same diagonal as the queen at (1, 2)
(2, 2) // invalid: in the same row as the queen at (1, 2)
(3, 2) // invalid: in the same diagonal as the queen at (1, 2)
(4, 2) // valid

PROGRAMMING PROJECT 4.3

A Knight's Tour

Develop and validate a program to show the moves of a knight in traversing a chessboard.

Analysis

A chessboard has eight rows and eight columns. From its current position, a knight's next position will be either two rows and one column or one row and two columns from the current position. For example, Figure 4.11 shows the legal moves of a knight at position (5, 3), that is, row 5 and column 3.

Figure 4.11 I For a knight (K) at coordinates (5, 3), the legal moves are to the grid entries labeled K0 through K7.

	0	1	2	3	4	5	6	7
0								
1								
2								
3			K7		K0			
4		K6				K1		
5				K				
6		K5				K2		
7			K4		K3			

For simplicity, suppose the knight starts at position (0, 0). Assume the moves are tried in the order given in Figure 4.11. That is, from position (row, column), the order tried is

$$(row - 2, column + 1)$$
$$(row - 1, column + 2)$$
$$(row + 1, column + 2)$$
$$(row + 2, column + 1)$$
$$(row + 2, column - 1)$$
$$(row + 1, column - 2)$$
$$(row - 1, column - 2)$$
$$(row - 2, column - 1)$$

Figure 4.12 shows the first few moves.

Figure 4.12 | The first few valid moves by a knight that starts at position (0, 0) and iterates according to the order shown in Figure 4.11. The integer at each filled entry indicates the order in which the moves were made.

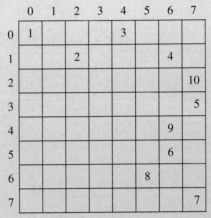

	0	1	2	3	4	5	6	7
0	1				3			
1			2				4	
2								10
3								5
4							9	
5							6	
6						8		
7								7

For the nine moves, starting at (0, 0), in Figure 4.12, no backtracking occurs. In fact, the first 36 moves are never backtracked over. But the total number of backtracks is substantial: over 3 million. The solution obtained by this order of iteration is

	0	1	2	3	4	5	6	7
0	1	38	55	34	3	36	19	22
1	54	47	2	37	20	23	4	17
2	39	56	33	46	35	18	21	10
3	48	53	40	57	24	11	16	5
4	59	32	45	52	41	26	9	12
5	44	49	58	25	62	15	6	27
6	31	60	51	42	29	8	13	64
7	50	43	30	61	14	63	28	7

Notice that the thirty-seventh move, from position (1, 3), does not take the first available choice—to position (3, 2)—nor the second available choice—to position (2, 1). Both of those choices led to dead ends, and backtracking occurred. The third available choice, to (0, 1), eventually led to a solution.

System Test 1   The lines are not part of the required output. Please enter the starting row and column:

                        0   0

(continued on next page)

(continued from previous page)

The solution is

	0	1	2	3	4	5	6	7
0	1	38	55	34	3	36	19	22
1	54	47	2	37	20	23	4	17
2	39	56	33	46	35	18	21	10
3	48	53	40	57	24	11	16	5
4	59	32	45	52	41	26	9	12
5	44	49	58	25	62	15	6	27
6	31	60	51	42	29	8	13	64
7	50	43	30	61	14	63	28	7

System Test 2   Please enter the starting row and column:

3   5

The solution is

	0	1	2	3	4	5	6	7
0	33	42	35	38	31	40	19	10
1	36	57	32	41	20	9	2	17
2	43	34	37	30	39	18	11	8
3	56	51	58	21	28	1	16	3
4	59	44	29	52	47	22	7	12
5	50	55	46	27	62	15	4	23
6	45	60	53	48	25	6	13	64
7	54	49	26	61	14	63	24	5

This solution requires 11 million backtracks. Some starting positions, for example (0,1), require over 600 million backtracks. But for every possible starting position, there is a solution; see

http://www.wealth4freedom.com/WORLDNEWSSTAND/knightstour.htm

Even though the solutions appear almost instantly, that does not imply that the solutions can be obtained without backtracking. For each starting position, the corresponding solution—originally obtained through backtracking—has been saved in a file.

CHAPTER 5

Vectors and Deques

I n this chapter we begin our study of the Standard Template Library's data structures. As noted in Chapter 2, each data structure is provided as a collection of method interfaces for some container class. As befits a user's perspective, the Standard Template Library does not specify any implementation details; we will consider possible implementations in Sections 5.2.5 and 5.4.1.

The container classes introduced here are the vector class and the deque class. These classes, and the list class in Chapter 6, are called *sequential* container classes. In a sequential object, we can think of the items as being stored in succession, from the first to the last. For example, a sequential object pets might have the items arranged as follows: "dog", "cat", "iguana", "gerbil". Here "dog" is the first item and "gerbil" is the last item. In this example, the items are not in alphabetical order.

A vector is the class version of a one-dimensional array. Like an array, the items in a vector are stored contiguously. But unlike an array, a vector's size is automatically increased as needed during the execution of a program. After you have seen how powerful and easy to use a vector is, you will seldom bother with arrays again! A deque—pronounced "deck"—is also array-like, allowing *random access* of any item in constant time. But for inserting or deleting at the front of a deque, averageTime(n) is constant, versus linear in n for an array or a vector. For both vectors and deques, this chapter's application is in the area of public-key cryptography. ■

In a sequential container, the items are stored in succession, from first to last.

CHAPTER OBJECTIVES

1. Understand the relationships among the major components of the Standard Template Library: container classes, iterators, and generic algorithms.

2. Compare the user's view and the developer's view of the vector and deque classes.

3. Be able to decide when use of a vector or deque is preferable to use of an array—and when use of an array is preferable to use of either a vector or deque.

4. Compare the user's view and the developer's view of the VeryLongInt class.

5.1 | THE STANDARD TEMPLATE LIBRARY

One of the major goals of object-oriented programming is code reuse, for example, by inheritance. In general, it is preferable to use already developed classes than to start each project from scratch. In the specific case of container classes, having a library of validated, efficient container classes can significantly reduce project-development time. The Standard Template Library (Stepanov and Lee, 1994) provides such a library. The three major components of the Standard Template Library are

1. A collection of template container classes
2. A collection of generic algorithms, that is, template functions
3. A collection of iterator categories, that is, families of iterator classes

In the Standard Template Library, generic algorithms operate on containers through iterators.

As you saw in Lab 7, the generic algorithms operate on containers through iterators. For example, the generic algorithm find will search a container for a given item. But that search cannot be based on any specific details of the container class itself, because then the use of find would be restricted to that container class only. Rather, in another example of code reuse, any container whose associated iterator class is in the InputIterator category can be searched with the find algorithm. In effect, an iterator abstracts from its container the information needed to access all the items in that container.

There is no prescribed implementation of the Standard Template Library.

The Standard Template Library is part of the official C++ language, as accredited by the American National Standards Institute. But that simply means that the method and function interfaces are prescribed. *There is no prescribed implementation:* developers are free to implement the classes and generic algorithms in any way, as long as the interfaces are satisfied. The original implementation, developed at Hewlett-Packard Research Lab by Stepanov, Lee, and others, is the basis for many of the implementations available today: Microsoft's Visual C++, Inprise's C++Builder, Metroworks' CodeWarrior, to name a few. We will study that original implementation, and also suggest alternatives where feasible.

The first container class we will study in the Standard Template Library is the vector class, which is, basically, the class version of an array. We start by defining what a vector is, look at the interfaces for a few of the many vector methods, and compare vectors to arrays. We then give an overview of the standard implementation of the vector class and finish up with an application that uses vectors. The deque class receives the same treatment.

5.2 | VECTORS

A *vector* is a finite sequence of items such that

1. Given the index of any item in the sequence, the item at that index can be accessed or modified in constant time.
2. An insertion at the back of the sequence takes only constant time, on average, but worstTime(n) is $O(n)$, where n represents the number of items in the sequence.
3. For a deletion at the back of the sequence, worstTime(n) is constant.
4. For arbitrary insertions and deletions, worstTime(n) is $O(n)$, and so is averageTime(n).

The vector class—as with all the classes in the Standard Template Library—is templated. That is, the type of the items may be a primitive type, such as **int** or **double**, or it may be a class, such as the string class or the Employee class introduced in Chapter 1. For example, we can define an empty vector of strings as follows:

    vector<string> fruits;

Duplicate items are allowed in a vector. So if we insert "oranges", "apples", "grapes," and "apples" into fruits, then that vector will have four items. The item "oranges" is at index 0, "apples" at index 1, "grapes" at index 2, and "apples" at index 3. These items are not in alphabetical order. In fact, the items in a vector will not necessarily even be comparable. For example, suppose the vector is a *text,* that is, a sequence of lines. Then it makes no sense to say that one line is "less than" another line. Of course, we can still compare the indices of the lines and say, for example, that the index of the current line is less than the index of some other line.

The vector class has two template parameters:

template <**class** T, **class** Allocator = allocator>

The template parameter T stands for the type of the items. The Allocator parameter relates to the memory-allocation model (for example, whether a pointer to T is defined as T*, the default, or something more exotic, such as T __far*). The flexibility required to handle a variety of allocation models is the root cause of much of the complexity in implementations of the Standard Template Library. For the sake of simplicity, we assume the default allocation model, given by the allocator class and defined in <defalloc>. Following the advice in the standard reference (Musser and Saini, 1996, p. 274), we "omit any further mention of the Allocator parameter." In fact,

> Henceforth, all declarations and definitions will assume the default allocation model.

Section 5.2.1 begins the design of the vector class by providing the user's view, that is, the method interfaces. There are more than 50 methods in the vector class, so we will focus on the ones you are most likely to need in an application. The method interfaces do not mandate any particular collection of fields or method definitions. This separation is the essence of data abstraction.

Each method's time requirements are specified with Big-O notation because we are merely establishing an upper bound: a particular implementation of the method may reduce that upper bound. If no time estimate for a method is given, you may assume that worstTime(n) is constant, where n refers to the number of items in the vector. If a method's average-time estimate is the same as the worst-time estimate, only the worst-time estimate is given.

5.2.1   Method Interfaces for the vector Class

Here are the interfaces—see Table 5.1 for a thumbnail sketch—of the most widely used methods in the vector class.

1.   // Postcondition: this vector is empty; that is, it does not contain any items.
vector( );

Table 5.1 | Brief description of some vector methods (assume the following definition: vector<**double**>::iterator itr;)

Method	Effect
vector<**double**> weights	**weights** is an empty vector
weights.push_back (107.2)	107.2 inserted at the back of vector **weights**
weights.insert (itr, 125.0)	125.0 inserted where **itr** is positioned; items from the insertion point to the back of **weights** are moved one position further back; returns an iterator positioned at the newly inserted item
weights.pop_back( )	The back item in **weights** has been deleted
weights.erase (itr)	The item where **itr** was positioned has been deleted; items at higher positions move lower; invalidates all iterators to all positions past the erasure position
weights.size( )	Returns the number of items in **weights**
weights.empty( )	Returns **true** if **weights** has no items; otherwise, **false**
weights [3] = 110.5	Replaces the item at index 3 of **weights** with 110.5
itr = weights.begin( )	**itr** is positioned at the item at the front of **weights**
itr == weights.end( )	Returns **true** if **itr** is positioned just beyond the back item in **weights**; otherwise, **false**
weights.front( ) = 105.0	105.0 replaces the item at index 0 in **weights**

Example Here are the definitions to create empty vectors of fruits, employees, and test scores:

```
vector<string> fruits;
vector<Employee> employees;
vector<int> scores;
```

Note There is also a constructor—called a ***copy constructor***—that initializes a vector to a copy of some other vector. The heading is

```
vector (const vector<T>& x);
```

For example, if the vector fruits has already been constructed as in our example, we can write:

```
vector<string> newFruits (fruits);
```

Then newFruits is defined and also initialized to a copy of fruits.

2.   `// Postcondition: A copy of x has been inserted at the back of this vector.`
`//                 The averageTime(n) is constant, and worstTime(n) is O(n),`
`//                 but for n consecutive push_backs, worstTime(n) is only O(n).`
`void push_back (const T& x);`

Example Here is the code to create a vector of four items:

```
vector<string> fruits;

fruits.push_back ("oranges");
fruits.push_back ("apples");
fruits.push_back ("grapes");
fruits.push_back ("apples");
```

The vector fruits will now contain the following items in the order indicated:

"oranges", "apples", "grapes", "apples"

Note The interface does not prescribe any implementation details. In a typical implementation, the first call to push_back allocates a block of storage (for example, 1K bytes) for the vector. Subsequent insertions may fill up the block in which the vector is stored. If an insertion cannot be made in the current block because that block is full, a reallocation is performed, and the entire vector is copied to a new block that is twice the size of the current block. Then all the iterators and references to the previous block are no longer valid.

3. // Precondition: The iterator position is positioned at a location between the
// front and one-beyond-the-back of the vector.
// Postcondition: A copy of x is in the location where the iterator position is
// positioned. Each item that was, before the call, in a location
// with index $>=$ position's index has been moved to the
// location at the next higher index. An iterator positioned at the
// newly inserted item has been returned. The worstTime(n) is O(n).
iterator insert (iterator position, **const** T& x);

Example   Suppose that fruits is the vector from the push_back example, with items in the following order:

"oranges", "apples", "grapes", "apples"

If the iterator itr is positioned at the item "grapes" at index 2, then

vector<string>::iterator new_itr = fruits.insert (itr, "kiwi");

will cause fruits to become

"oranges", "apples", "kiwi", "grapes", "apples"

and the iterator new_itr will be positioned at the item "kiwi" at index 2. And itr has been invalidated; that is, you cannot be sure where itr is positioned, or even whether itr is still positioned at an item in fruits.

Note 1   If an insertion causes reallocation (see the note for the push_back method), old iterators and references are invalidated. If no reallocation occurs, only iterators and references at or beyond the insertion point become invalid.

Note 2   The push_back method is a special case of insert.

4. // Precondition: The vector is not empty.
// Postcondition: The item that was, before this call, at the back of the vector
// has been deleted from the vector.
void pop_back( );

Example   Suppose that fruits is the vector from the example of the insert method, with items in the following order:

"oranges", "apples", "kiwi", "grapes", "apples"

If the message is

fruits.pop_back( );

then fruits will have the following items in the following order:

"oranges", "apples", "kiwi", "grapes"

5. // Precondition: The iterator position is positioned at an item in the vector.
// Postcondition: The item that was, before this call, in the location where
//   position is positioned has been deleted from the vector. Each
//   item that was, before the call, in a location with index >
//   position's index has been moved to the location at the next
//   lower index. The worstTime(n) is O(n).
void erase (iterator position);

> *Example* Suppose that fruits is the vector from the example of the
> pop_back method, with items in the following order:
>
> "oranges", "apples", "kiwi", "grapes"
>
> If the iterator itr is positioned at the item "apples" and the following mes-
> sage is sent,
>
> fruits.erase (itr);
>
> then fruits will contain the following items in the following order:
>
> "oranges", "kiwi", "grapes"

> *Note 1* The **erase** method invalidates all iterators and references after
> the point of the erasure.

> *Note 2* The pop_back method is a special case of **erase**.

> *Note 3* There is a version of the **erase** method that has two iterator
> parameters: first and last. All the items between first (inclusive) and last
> (exclusive) will be erased. For example, suppose that fruits is a vector
> with items in the following order:
>
> "oranges", "apples", "kiwi", "grapes"
>
> If the iterator itr1 is positioned at the item "apples" and itr2 is positioned
> at "grapes" and the following message is sent,
>
> fruits.erase (itr1, itr2);
>
> then fruits will contain the following items in the following order:
>
> "oranges", "grapes"

The item "grapes" is not erased because itr2, the second argument in the call to erase, is *one past* the last item to be erased. The time for this erase method is proportional to the number of items in the vector *after* last, because those are the items that have to be moved.

6.   // Postcondition: The number of items in the vector has been returned.
unsigned size ( ) **const;**

> *Example*   Suppose that fruits is a vector with items in the following order:
>
> "oranges", "kiwi", "grapes"
>
> If we have
>
> cout << fruits.size( ) ;
>
> then the output will be
>
> 3
>
> *Note 1*   In ANSI Standard C++, the return type is given as size_type. And in stddef.h, we have
>
> **typedef unsigned** size_t;
>
> Finally, from the default allocator,
>
> **typedef** size_t size_type;
>
> So the return type is **unsigned**.
>
> *Note 2*   To determine how many more items can be inserted before a reallocation will occur, use the size method in conjunction with the capacity method. The capacity method, whose interface is given in Project 5.2, returns the number of items that can be stored in the vector before a reallocation will occur. For example, if vec is a vector object,
>
> cout << vec.capacity( ) − vec.size( );
>
> will output the number of additional items that can be inserted in vec before a reallocation will occur.

7.   // Postcondition: If this vector contains no items, true has been returned;
         //   otherwise, false has been returned.
bool empty( ) **const;**

Example Suppose that fruits is a vector with items in the following order:

"oranges", "kiwi", "grapes"

If we have

while (!fruits.empty( ))
       fruits.pop_back( );

the loop will be executed three times, and then fruits will be empty.

8.   // Precondition: $0 <= n <$ the number of items in the vector.
    // Postcondition: A reference to the item n items from the beginning of the
    //   vector has been returned.
    T& **operator**[ ] (**unsigned** n);

Example 1 Suppose that fruits is a vector with items in the following order:

"oranges", "kiwi", "grapes"

If we have

cout $<<$ fruits [1] ;

then the output will be

kiwi

Example 2 Suppose that fruits is a vector with items in the following order:

"oranges", "kiwi", "grapes"

If we have

fruits [1] = "limes";

then fruits will contain the following items in the following order:

"oranges", "limes", "grapes"

Example 3 We can use this index operator to iterate through a vector. For example, suppose that fruits is a vector with items in the following order:

"oranges", "limes", "grapes"

If we have

```
for (int i = 0; i < fruits.size( ); i++)
        cout << fruits [i] << endl;
```

then the output will be

oranges
limes
grapes

Note 1 The postcondition does not state what might happen if the value of the argument is less than 0 or greater than or equal to the number of items in the vector. It is the responsibility of the *user* of the vector class to ensure that the precondition is true before the method is called.

Note 2 This method returns a *reference,* that is, an address. So the contents of that address can be changed, as was done in example 2 of this method interface.

Note 3 Applying this operator does not change the size of the vector.

9. // Postcondition: An iterator positioned at the front of the vector has been
   //   returned.
   iterator begin( );

   Example Suppose that fruits is a vector with items in the following order:

   "oranges", "kiwi", "grapes"

   If we have

   vector<string>::iterator itr = fruits.begin( );

   then itr is positioned at the item "oranges".

10. // Postcondition: An iterator positioned JUST AFTER the last item in the vector
    //   has been returned.
    iterator end( );

    Example Suppose that fruits is a vector with items in the following order:

    "oranges", "kiwi", "grapes"

If we have

vector<string>::iterator itr = fruits.end( );

then itr is positioned just after the item "grapes". So the message

fruits.insert (itr, "lemons");

will have the same effect on the vector as the message

fruits.push_back ("lemons");

Namely, fruits will contain the following items in the following order:

"oranges", "kiwi", "grapes", "lemons"

Note If the vector is empty, the iterator returned by begin( ) is equal to the iterator returned by end( ).

11. // Precondition: this vector is not empty.
// Postcondition: a reference to the front item in this vector has been returned.
T& front( );

Example Suppose that fruits is a vector with items in the following order:

"oranges", "kiwi", "lemons", "grapes"

If we have

cout << fruits.front( );

the output will be

oranges

Note 1 This method can be used to replace the front item in a vector. For example, suppose we write

fruits.front( ) = "pears";

The front item in fruits will become "pears". This is equivalent to

fruits [0] = "pears";

Note 2 There is a similar method to return a reference to the back item in a vector:

T& back( );

In example 3 of method interface 8, we saw one way to iterate through a vector using the index operator, **operator**[ ]. Section 5.2.2 describes the vector class's iterator class, which provides an alternative—but equivalent—iteration tool.

5.2.2   Vector Iterators

The iterators associated with the vector class are, in fact, pointers, so anything you are able to accomplish on an array with a pointer you will be able to accomplish on a vector with an iterator. In particular, we have the following vector-iterator (that is, pointer) operators: $++$, $+$, $*$, $!=$, and $==$. For example, suppose that fruits is a vector with items in the following order:

"oranges", "kiwi", "grapes", "lemons"

We can print out all the items in fruits as follows:

```
vector<string>::iterator itr;
for (itr = fruits.begin( ); itr != fruits.end( ); itr++)
    cout << *itr << endl;
```

In example 3 of method interface 8, we saw another way to accomplish the same task using the index operator, **operator**[ ]:

```
for (unsigned i = 0; i < fruits.size( ); i++)
    cout << fruits [i] << endl;
```

In general, if itr is a vector iterator positioned at an item in a vector vec, then *itr references the same item as vec [itr − vec.begin( )]. Similarly, if vec is a vector, then we get the Vector-Iterator Corollary of the Array-Pointer Law.

Vector-Iterator Corollary

vec [n] is equivalent to *(vec.begin( ) + n).

Because a vector-iterator can access any item in a vector immediately, vector-iterators are in the category of random-access iterators.

Here is a short program that illustrates several vector methods in concert. A vector of random salaries is generated through calls to push_back, the sum of those salaries is calculated with the generic algorithm accumulate (from Chapter 3), and then the above-average salaries are printed twice, once with an index-based loop and once with an iterator-based loop.

```
#include <vector>
#include <iostream>
#include <string>
#include <stdlib>
#include <numeric>
```

```
using namespace std;

int main( )
{
        const string PROMPT = "Please enter the number of salaries: ";

        const string ERROR_MESSAGE =
            "The number of salaries should be > 0.";

        const double SALARY_FACTOR = 5.00; // to make the salaries realistic

        const string AVERAGE = "The average salary is ";

        const string ABOVE = "The above-average salaries are: ";

        const string CLOSE_WINDOW_PROMPT =
            "Please press the Enter key to close this output window.";

        vector<double> salaries;
        vector<double>::iterator itr;

        int n; // the number of salaries

        cout << PROMPT;
        cin >> n;
        if (n <= 0)
            cout << ERROR_MESSAGE << endl;
        else
        {
            for (int i = 0; i < n; i++)
                salaries.push_back (rand( ) * SALARY_FACTOR);

            double salarySum = accumulate (salaries.begin( ),
                                        salaries.end( ), 0.00);
            double averageSalary = salarySum / n;
            cout << endl << AVERAGE << averageSalary << endl;

            cout << endl << endl << ABOVE << endl;
            for (int i = 0; i < n; i++)
                if (salaries [i] > averageSalary)
                    cout << salaries [i] << endl;

            cout << endl << endl << ABOVE << endl;
            for (itr = salaries.begin( ); itr != salaries.end( ); itr++)
                if (*itr > averageSalary)
                    cout << *itr << endl;
        } // n > 0
```

```
            cout << endl << endl << CLOSE_WINDOW_PROMPT;
            cin.get( );
            cin.get( );

            return 0;
        } // main
```

At this point, you might think that a vector is like an automatically resizable array, with methods. That's about it! In Section 5.2.3, we expand on that idea a bit, and also compare vectors with the Linked class from Chapter 2.

5.2.3   Comparison of Vectors to Other Containers

How does a vector container compare with an array? The main advantage of vectors over arrays is that the vector methods have already been developed, whereas the user of an array must create whatever code is necessary to maintain the array. For example, to insert or erase at an arbitrary location in an array, you must write the code to open up or close up the space. The vector class's insert and erase methods handle this automatically. And the push_back and insert methods automatically resize a vector if the current block the vector resides in is not big enough.

Both vectors and arrays can invoke the generic algorithms in the Standard Template Library. And both vectors and arrays allow items to be accessed or modified with the help of the index operator, **operator**[ ]. The only time that an array is preferable to a vector occurs when you want a quick initialization. For example, we can define an array and initialize it all at once:

```
        string[ ] words = {"yes", "no", "maybe"};
```

The only other container class we have seen so far is the very primitive Linked class from Chapter 2. For an insertion at the front of a Linked container, worstTime(n) is constant, whereas an insertion in a vector takes constant time only on average. In the worst case, when the size is increased, all the items must be copied to a larger vector, but this is an infrequent occurrence. An advantage for vectors is that there are methods for inserting and removing an item at any position in the container. The Linked class has no such methods.

Finally, vector-iterators are random-access iterators; that is, a vector-iterator can access any item in a vector in constant time. Linked iterators are not as powerful; to access any item in a Linked container, worstTime(n) is linear in the distance to the front of the container. The category for linked iterators is *forward-iterator:* an iterator in this category can advance through a Linked container only by increments of one. There is no decrement operator, and scalar addition is not allowed either.

It would be very easy for you to get lost in the details of the original vector class implementation—the one provided by the Hewlett-Packard Company. That implementation is not only efficient, as you would expect, but very concise. It also has a higher level of generality than you need to concern yourself with for now: It is not restricted to a single memory-allocation model. Sections 5.2.4 and 5.2.5 give you a road map for understanding that implementation, for which the following copyright notice applies:

5.2.4 Possible Fields of the vector Class

There is no single implementation of the Standard Template Library. The standard reference, *STL Tutorial and Reference Guide* (Musser and Saini, 1996), supplies method interfaces and notes, and examples of how to *use* the Standard Template Library. As long as the method interfaces are satisfied, implementers have considerable latitude in choosing the fields and method definitions. The outline in this section is based on the first such implementation, from Hewlett-Packard Research Lab.

For the vector class, the first question we need to ask is, "Where will the items be stored?" We need a contiguous storage structure to support random access. An array! So we will have a pointer,

> start, with the address of the first location in the array

We also have a couple of other pointers:

> finish, which points to the location *just after* the item at the back of the vector
>
> end_of_storage, which points to the location *just after* the last location allocated for the array

Your compiler might use different identifiers for these fields, or conceivably, have fields with different meanings.

5.2.5   An Implementation of the vector Class

Now that we have specified the fields we will have, we can immediately knock off a few of the method definitions. The default constructor does not allocate a block of memory for an array. Instead, all three pointer fields are intialized to NULL, that is, 0. Incidentally, the begin( ) method simply returns start, the end( ) method simply returns finish, and the size( ) method returns finish − start. So the following code would produce the expected output of 0:

```
vector<double> weights;
cout << weights.size( );
```

When the first item is inserted into the vector (using the push_back or insert method), a block of memory on the heap is allocated. The size of this block may vary from one compiler to the next. For specificity, we assume that 1024 bytes are allocated and that a **double** occupies 8 bytes. If the first insertion message is

weights.push_back (7.3);

then an array of 128 doubles is allocated, as shown in Figure 5.1.

As illustrated in Figure 5.1, the start and finish fields are pointing to the first and second locations in the array, respectively, and the end_of_storage field is pointing to the location just after the last allocated location in the array. The message

weights.size( )

would return the value 1, namely, finish − start. And the messages

weights.begin( )

and

weights.end( )

would return iterators (that is, pointers) positioned at the locations with indices 0 and 1, respectively.

What role does end_of_storage play in this implementation? Suppose an additional 127 **double**s are inserted into weights. Figure 5.2 shows the effect on memory.

Now suppose the following message is sent:

weights.push_back (15.5);

Figure 5.1 | The vector<**double**> weights after 7.3 is inserted using the push_back method.

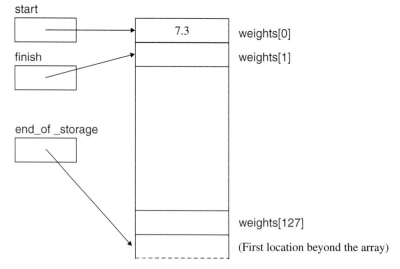

Figure 5.2 | The vector<**double**> weights with 128 items.

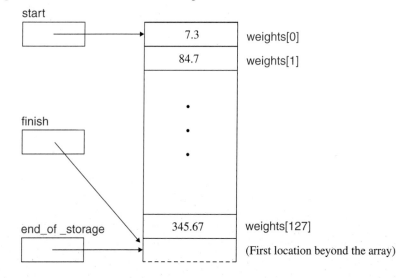

The symptom of a problem is that finish = end_of_storage. The item 15.5 cannot be stored in the current block allocated for weights. Nor can we store that item at the location pointed to by end_of_storage because that location might hold some other program variable (or other important information).

Instead, the size of the underlying array must be increased to accommodate the new item, and that means that a new block of heap storage is allocated. Then the old items are copied to the new array, the old array is deallocated and its items destroyed (more on this shortly), and the new item is inserted into the new array. To avoid frequent recopying, *a block of double the current size is allocated.* Figure 5.3 shows the relevant portion of memory after this new block has been allocated, the old items copied to the new block, the new item inserted, and the old block deallocated.

This resizing strategy indicates why, for the push_back method, averageTime(n) is constant. Suppose the current capacity of the vector is n items, and the vector is full. If we now call push_back n times to insert n additional items, how much data movement will there be? To insert the first new item, a block to hold $2n$ items is allocated, the n old items are moved to this new block, and then the new item is appended. The next $n - 1$ calls to push_back entail only one movement each, so the total number of items moved by the n calls to push_back is $2n$, for an average of only two movements per call to push_back.

The worstTime(n) is linear in n, and this occurs when the vector is resized. But then, as we saw in the previous paragraph, the next $n - 1$ calls to push_back take only constant time. This phenomenon—the same worstTime(n) estimate for one method call as for n method calls—occurs frequently enough that it has spawned a function of its own: ***amortizedTime(n)***. The idea is if we amortize—that is, spread out—the

If a vector object's underlying array is full and an insertion is attempted, the capacity of the underlying array is doubled.

Figure 5.3 | The vector<**double**> weights after after resizing.

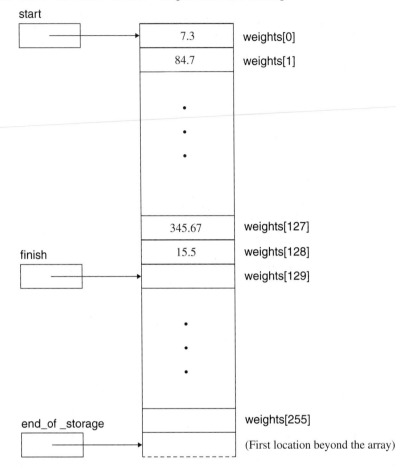

cost of the method calls over a long sequence, the total cost of the method calls divided by the number of method calls may be small. Here, "cost" refers to the number of statements executed. For the push_back method, amortizedTime(n) is constant. When applicable, amortizedTime(n) conveys a more realistic estimate than worstTime(n). And the calculation of amortizedTime(n) does not assume that each call has the same probability as any other call—an assumption we needed to calculate averageTime(n).

An insertion at any location other than the back of the vector requires that each item from the insertion location on be moved to the location at the next-higher index from its current location. For example, suppose we start with the vector shown in Figure 5.3, and the message is

weights.insert (weights.begin( ) + 1, 19.94);

Figure 5.4 I The vector<**double**> weights from Figure 5.3 after 19.94 was inserted at index 1.

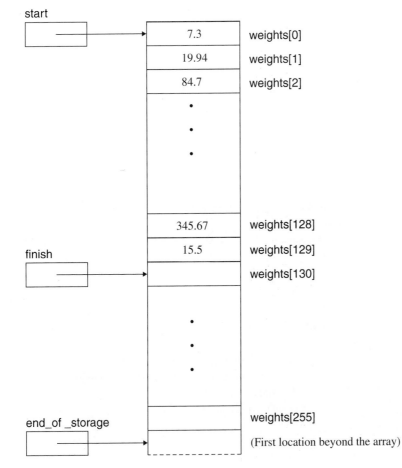

Recall that the begin method returns start, so weights.begin( ) + 1 points to the location at index 1. Each item, from index 128 down to index 1, must be moved to the location at the next higher index. Item 15.5 is moved to the location at index 129, then 345.67 is moved to the location at index 128, . . . , and then 84.7 is moved to the location at index 2. Finally, 19.94 is moved to the location at index 1, as shown in Figure 5.4. Note that finish had to be changed as a result of this insertion, and an insertion requires resizing if the current block is filled to capacity.

To give you the flavor of the data movement, here is the code for the insert method in the simple case, that is, when no resizing is required and position != end( ):

```
if (finish != end_of_storage)
{
```

```
            construct (finish, *(finish − 1));
            copy_backward(position, finish − 1, finish);
            *position = x;
            ++finish;
      }
```

The call to construct copies the last item in the vector (pointed to by finish − 1) to the next higher location. Then the generic algorithm copy_backward copies *(finish − 2) to *(finish − 1), *(finish − 3) to *(finish − 2), . . . , *position to *(position + 1). Finally, x is stored at position and finish is incremented.

Here is the complete definition of insert, with an explanation immediately following:

```
      iterator insert(iterator position, const T& x)
      {
            size_type n = position − begin( );
            if (finish != end_of_storage)
                  if (position == end( ))
                  {
                        construct(finish, x);
                        finish++;
                  }
                  else
                  {
                        construct (finish, *(finish − 1));
                        copy_backward(position, finish − 1, finish);
                        *position = x;
                        ++finish;
                  }
            else
            {
                  size_type len = size( ) ? 2 * size( ): static_allocator.init_page_size( );
                  iterator tmp = static_allocator.allocate(len);
                  uninitialized_copy(begin( ), position, tmp);
                  construct(tmp + (position − begin( )), x);
                  uninitialized_copy(position, end( ), tmp + (position − begin( )) + 1);
                  destroy(begin( ), end( ));
                  static_allocator.deallocate(begin( ));
                  end_of_storage = tmp + len;
                  finish = tmp + size( ) + 1;
                  start = tmp;
            }
            return begin( ) + n;
      }
```

The most puzzling line in this definition is the assignment statement:

size_type len = size( ) ? 2 * size( ) : static_allocator.init_page_size( );

Because we assume the default allocator, size_type means the same as **unsigned int**. The right-hand side of the assignment statement is an application of the *conditional operator.* What is that? The conditional operator provides a shorthand for the usual **if/else** statement. For example, instead of writing

if (first > second)
          big = first;
else
          big = second;

we can simply write

big = (first > second) ? first : second;

The syntax for a conditional expression is

condition ? expression_t : expression_f

The meaning is this: if condition has the value **true**, the value of the conditional expression is the value of expression_t. Otherwise, the value of the conditional expression is the value of expression_f.

But in the puzzling assignment statement, instead of a condition, we simply have a call to the size method:

size( )

In C++, **false** and 0 are synonyms (both are synonymous with NULL). And **true** is equated with any nonzero integer. To say that the condition size( ) is **true** means that size( ) is nonzero. So the meaning of the puzzling statement is this: If this vector's size is not zero, len is assigned twice the size of this vector; otherwise, len is assigned the initial block size.

The rest of the insert method is not too difficult to figure out, but you may wonder why the following call is made:

destroy(begin( ), end( ));

The destructor for each item in the vector is called. This is a precaution in case those items took up more space than just the array locations. For example, each item in a vector could itself be a Linked object. The space that the Linked object takes up in the array would be minimal: the head and length fields. But the nodes in the Linked object would no long be accessible. If that space were not deallocated, the resulting memory leak could cause your program to run out of memory. If the item takes up no more space than the single array location, the destructor does nothing.

By contrast with push_back and insert, the implementation of the pop_back method is a breeze. There is never any resizing, so all that happens is that the pointer finish is decremented and, again as a precaution, the destructor for the popped item is called. The general-purpose erase method is more complicated than pop_back only in that items are moved to close up the space left by the erased item.

Lab 12 covers some more of the implementation details of the vector class.

LAB   **Lab 12:** **More implementation details of the** vector **class.**

(All Labs Are Optional.)   **LAB**

After all this low-level work on the vector class, it may be refreshing to move to a higher level, namely, an application of that class. The application deals with arbitrarily high precision arithmetic, a topic in public-key cryptography.

5.3 | A VECTOR APPLICATON: HIGH-PRECISION ARITHMETIC

APPLICATION

We now introduce high-precision arithmetic as an application of the vector class. We will get to the details shortly, but it is worth recalling that the *use* of a class is independent (except for efficiency) of *how* the class is implemented. So we are not locked in—fortunately—to any particular implementation of the vector class.

In public-key cryptography, information is encoded and decoded using integers more than 100 digits long. The essential facts about these ***very long integers*** are

1. It takes relatively little time—$O(n^3)$—to generate a very long integer with n digits that is prime.[1] For example, suppose we want to generate a prime number that has 500 digits. Then the number of loop iterations required is approximately $500^3 = 125,000,000$.

Public-key cryptography relies on the exponential difficulty of factoring the product of two very large primes given only the product.

2. It takes a very long time—roughly, $10^{n/2}$ loop iterations—to determine the prime factors of a very long integer with n digits that is not prime. For example, suppose we want to factor a nonprime number that has 500 digits. Then the number of loop iterations required is approximately $10^{500/2} = 10^{250}$.

3. Assume that you have generated p and q, two very long integers that are prime. The product $(p - 1)(q - 1)$ can be calculated quickly, and you can supply this product to anyone who wants to send you a message. The sender encodes a message by using this product—see Simmons (1992) for details. The product and the encoded message are ***public,*** that is, transmitted over an insecure channel such as a telephone, postal service, or computer network.

4. But decoding the message requires knowing the values of p and q. Since determining the factors p and q takes prohibitively long, only you can decode the message.

Very long integers require far greater precision than is directly available in programming languages. We will now define, design, and implement a simple version

---

[1] An integer $p > 1$ is ***prime*** if the only positive-integer factors of p are 1 and p itself.

of the very_long_int class. Exercise 5.5 asks you to amplify this version, Lab 13 involves the development of a driver for the amplified version, and Project 5.1 further expands the very_long_int class.

5.3.1 Design of the very_long_int Class

Each object in the very_long_int class will contain a nonnegative integer of indeterminate size. There will be only three methods: A very long integer can have its value read in, written out, or incremented by another very long integer. Here are the method interfaces:

1. // Precondition: The input starts with a sequence of digits followed by an 'X',
    //   with blanks, end-of-line markers, and invalid digit characters
    //   ignored. There are no leading zeroes, except for 0 itself, which
    //   has a single 0.
    // Postcondition: very_long contains the very long integer whose digits came
    //   from instream, and a reference to instream has been
    //   returned.The worstTime(n) is O(n), where n is the number of
    //   digit characters in the input.
    friend istream& **operator**>> (istream& instream, very_long_int& very_long);

    Example Suppose the input contains

    473A53
    81X

    and the input statement is

    cin >> very_long;

    Then very_long will contain the integer 4735381.

2. // Postcondition: The value of very_long has been written to outstream. The
    //   worstTime(n) is O(n), where n is the size of very_long.
    friend ostream& **operator**<< (ostream& outstream,
                              const very_long_int very_long);

3. // Postcondition: The value returned is the sum of the calling object (the
    //   left-hand operand) and other_very_long (the right-hand
    //   operand). The worstTime(n) is O(n), where n is the maximum
    //   of the number of digits in the calling object and
    //   other_very_long.
    very_long_int **operator**+ (**const** very_long_int& other_very_long);

    Example Suppose that new_int and old_int are very long integers with values of 12345678901234567890 and 15, respectively. If the message sent is new_int + old_int

then the value returned will be 123456789012334567905.

What fields will the very_long_int class have? We will need some kind of container, with each digit as an item in that container. But what kind of container will we need: array, a vector object or a Linked object? The automatic resizing feature of vectors makes them more appealing than arrays for this application, and with vectors, we have plenty of already developed methods. As far as choosing between a vector and a Linked structure, the drawback to the Linked class is that its iterators are merely *forward* iterators. That is, we can iterate through a Linked container only from front to back. That might make addition very inefficient, so we choose the vector class for this application.

Which is the appropriate relationship between very_long_int and vector: the is-a (inheritance) or the has-a (composition/aggregation) relationship? That is, should very_long_int be a subclass of vector, or should very_long_int have a field of type vector? The primary purpose of the very_long_int class is to perform arithmetic, so it shares little functionality with the vector class. It makes more sense to say "a very_long_int has a vector" than "a very_long_int is a vector."

So the only field in the very_long_int class will be digits, a vector object. Figure 5.5 has a dependency diagram for the very_long_int class. Composition applies because the destructor for the vector digits is automatically called when very_long_int's implicit destructor is called.

Each item in the vector digits will be a single digit. What integer type should we use for a digit? To save space we choose **char**, because on virtually all compilers, a variable of type **char** takes up only one byte. The field definition is

vector<**char**> digits;

The digits will be stored in the vector digits in the usual order, from front to back. For example, if the value of a very_long_int is 758, the 7 would be stored at index 0, the 5 at index 1, and the 8 at index 2.

Now that we have seen the method interfaces and fields, we turn our attention to the implementation of the class.

Figure 5.5 | The dependency diagram for the very_long_int class.

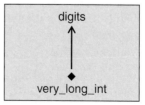

5.3.2 An Implementation of the very_long_int Class

Here are the implementations of the overloaded operators: **operator>>**, **operator<<**, and **operator+**. Keep in mind the strengths (fast random access and back-insertions) and weakness (slow insertions at other-than-the-back locations) of the vector class. Of course, none of what follows depends—except for efficiency—on the implementation details of the vector class itself: All we rely on are the method interfaces.

1. istream& **operator>>** (istream& instream, very_long_int& very_long)

    Start by erasing everything in very_long to get an empty container. Then keep reading in characters until 'X' is reached. For each digit character, the corresponding digit value is appended to digits with a call to push_back.
        Here is the method definition:

    ```
    istream& operator>> (istream& instream, very_long_int& very_long)
    {
         const char LOWEST_DIGIT_CHAR = '0';

         const char HIGHEST_DIGIT_CHAR = '9';

         const char SENTINEL = 'X';

         char digit_char;

         very_long.digits.erase (very_long.digits.begin( ), very_long.digits.end( ));
         do
         {
              // Each digit read in so far has been appended to digits.
              instream >> digit_char;
              if ((LOWEST_DIGIT_CHAR <= digit_char) &&
                       (digit_char <= HIGHEST_DIGIT_CHAR))
                   very_long.digits.push_back (digit_char −
                            LOWEST_DIGIT_CHAR);
         } // do
         while (digit_char != SENTINEL);

         return instream;
    } // overloading >>
    ```

    How long will this operator take? There is one loop iteration for each digit character in the input. The average time for each loop iteration depends on push_back's average time, which is constant. So for **operator>>**, averageTime(n) is linear in n, the number of digit characters in the input.
        What about worstTime(n)? The analysis is related to the analysis of the vector class's push_back method. Recall that the worstTime(n) for n calls to push_back is linear in n. That is, worstTime(n) for **operator>>** is linear in n.

2.   ostream& **operator**<< (ostream& outstream, very_long_int very_long)

Starting at index 0, we traverse the vector digits and write out each digit retrieved. Because the declared type of each digit is **char**, we need to cast to **int**. Otherwise, for example, if the digit value was 7, the output would be the seventh ASCII character; no character would be printed, but a bell would sound!

Here is the code:

```
ostream& operator<< (ostream& outstream, const very_long_int very_long)
{
        for (unsigned i = 0; i < very_long.digits.size( ); i++)
                outstream << (int)very_long.digits [i];
        return outstream;
} // overloading <<
```

For this operator, worstTime(n) is linear in n because the number of iterations of the loop is digits.size, and the index operator takes constant time.

We could rewrite the **for** statement with an iterator instead of an index:

```
vector<char>::iterator itr;
for (itr = very_long.digits.begin( ); itr != very_long.digits.end( ); itr++)
        cout << int (*itr);
```

3.   very_long_int very_long_int::**operator**+ (**const** very_long_int&
                           other_very_long)

We add the calling object and other_very_long object digit by digit, starting with the *least* significant digit in each number. The partial sum, divided by 10, is appended to the very_long_int object sum. The automatically called default constructor for the very_long_int class does nothing—except to call the default constructor for the digits field of sum. That call makes digits an empty *vector*.

If the partial sum is greater than 10, a carry is generated. Because we will be using push_back for the partial sums for the sake of efficiency, we must reverse the vector digits after adding so that the most significant digit will end up at index 0. For example, suppose newInt is a very_long_int object with the value 328 and oldInt is a very_long_int object with the value 47. If the message is

newInt + oldInt

then after adding and pushing back digit by digit, sum will have the value 573. When this is reversed, sum will have the correct value, 375. So we call the generic algorithm reverse before returning sum.

Here is the code for overloading **operator**+:

```
very_long_int very_long_int::operator+ (const very_long_int&
                           other_very_long)
{
        unsigned carry = 0,
```

```
                larger_size,
                partial_sum;

        very_long_int sum;

        if (digits.size( ) > other_very_long.digits.size( ))
                larger_size = digits.size( );
        else
                larger_size = other_very_long.digits.size( );

        for (unsigned i = 0; i < larger_size; i++)
        {
                partial_sum = least (i) + other_very_long.least (i) + carry;
                carry = partial_sum / 10;
                sum.digits.push_back (partial_sum % 10);
        } // for

        if (carry == 1)
                sum.digits.push_back (carry);
        reverse (sum.digits.begin( ), sum.digits.end( ));
        return sum;
} // overloading +
```

The least method is an example of a nonpublic, **helper** method: It is created to simplify the implementation of another method. In this case, least (i) returns the ith least significant digit in the given digit vector. The units (rightmost) digit is considered the zeroth least significant digit, the tens digit is considered the first least significant digit, and so on. For example, suppose the vector digits has the value 3284971, and i is 2. Then the digit returned will be 9 because 9 is the second least significant digit in the vector digits; the zeroth least-significant digit is 1 and the first least-significant digit is 7. The method definition is

```
// Postcondition: If i >= digits.size( ), 0 has been returned; else the ith least
//                    significant digit in digits has been returned. The least
//                    significant digit is the 0th least significant digit.
char very_long_int::least (unsigned i) const
{
        if (i >= digits.size( ))
                return 0;
        else
                return digits [digits.size( ) − i − 1] ;
} // least
```

Assume, for simplicity, that the calling object and the other_very_long object are very long integers of size n. For the least method, averageTime(n) is constant. Appending to a vector takes only constant time, on average, so averageTime(n) for the **for** statement in the definition of **operator**+ is linear in n. For the reverse generic algorithm, averageTime(n) is linear in n, so for **operator+**, averageTime(n) is linear in n. By the same analysis used for **operator<<**, we can show that for **operator+**, worstTime(n) is linear in n.

Note that if we stored the digits in reverse order, the definition of **operator+** would be slightly simpler, and its time estimate would be unchanged. But the time to read in a very long integer would be quadratic in n because each digit would be inserted at the front of the vector digits.

Exercise 5.5 extends the class very_long_int, and Lab 13 deals with the implementation of this extension.

LAB   **Lab 13: Extending the** very_long_int **class.**

(All Labs Are Optional.)   **LAB**

5.4 | DEQUES

The next sequential class we consider is the deque class. "Deque" is an abbreviation for "double ended queue," but is pronounced "deck." A *deque* is a finite sequence of items such that

1.   Given the index of any item in the sequence, the item at that index can be accessed or modified in constant time.
2.   An insertion at the front or back of the sequence takes only constant time, on average, but worstTime(n) is $O(n)$, where n represents the number of items in the sequence.

A deque is fast for insertions or deletions at the front or back, whereas a vector is fast only for insertions or deletions at the back.

3.   For a deletion at the front or back of the sequence, worstTime(n) is constant.
4.   For arbitrary insertions and deletions, worstTime(n) is $O(n)$, and so is averageTime(n).

Conceptually, the only difference between a vector and a deque is this: A deque object can quickly insert or delete at the front or back of itself, whereas a vector object is fast only for insertions or deletions at the back of itself.

The deque class does not have (or need) the capacity and reserve methods that the vector class has. Other than those, the deque class and its associated iterator class have all the method interfaces that the vector class and its iterator class have, and there are two more deque methods:

```
// Postcondition: A copy of x has been inserted at the front of this deque. The
//                averageTime(n) is constant, and worstTime(n) is O(n)—but
//                for n consecutive insertions, worstTime(n) is only O(n). That
//                is, amortizedTime(n) is constant.
void push_front (const T& x);
```

// Postcondition: The item at the front of this deque has been erased.
void pop_front( );

> *Note*   The fact that no time estimates are given in the postcondition for
> pop_front implies that worstTime(n) is constant.

Clearly, for insertions and deletions at the beginning of a container, deques will be
much faster than vectors. Here are some similarities:

1.   For both vectors and deques, any item can be retrieved or replaced given its
     index or iterator, and worstTime(n) is constant for these operations.
2.   For both vectors and deques, to insert an item at the back, averageTime(n) is
     constant, and worstTime(n) is $O(n)$—but for n consecutive back-insertions,
     worstTime(n) is only $O(n)$. That is, amortizedTime(n) is constant.
3.   For both vectors and deques, to delete the back item, worstTime(n) is constant.

From the estimates for push_front and pop_front, you may well get the impression that deques are sometimes faster than vectors, and never slower. In Section
5.4.1, when we look at the typical fields and implementation of the deque class, you
will get some insight into why deques are somewhat slower than vectors except for
insertions and deletions at or near the front. But first, here is a simple program that
illustrates a deque:

```
#include <deque>
#include <iostream>
#include <istring>

using namespace std;

int main( )
{
      const string CLOSE_WINDOW_PROMPT =
            "Please press the Enter key to close this output window.";

      deque<string> words;
      deque<string>::iterator itr;

      words.push_back ("yes");
      words.push_back ("no");
      words.push_front ("maybe");
      words.push_front ("wow");

      cout << endl << "the deque after 4 insertions:" << endl;
      for (unsigned i = 0; i < words.size( ); i++)
            cout << words [i] << endl;
```

```
            words.pop_front( );
            words.pop_back( );

            cout << endl << "the deque after deleting the front and back items"
                  << endl;
            for (itr = words.begin( ); itr != words.end( ); itr++)
                  cout << (*itr) << endl;

            words.front( ) = "now";
            words.back( ) = "but";

            cout << endl << "the deque after replacing \"maybe\" with \"now\" "
                  << "and \"yes\" with \"but\"" << endl << *(words.begin( )) << endl
                  << *(words.end( ) - 1);

            cout << endl << endl << CLOSE_WINDOW_PROMPT;
            cin.get( );

            return 0;
      } // main
```

Notice that the front item in words was accessed in three different ways:

```
      words [0]
      words.front( )
      *words.begin( )
```

Similarly, the back item was accessed in three different ways. The output from the program is

```
      the deque after 4 insertions:
      wow
      maybe
      yes
      no

      the deque after deleting the front and back items
      maybe
      yes

      the deque after replacing "maybe" with "now" and "yes" with "but"
      now
      but

      Please press the Enter key to close this output window.
```

5.4.1   Fields and Implementation of the deque Class

As usual, we will focus on the Hewlett-Packard design and implementation of the deque class. Project 5.2 pursues a simpler (but not as efficient) version. In the Hewlett-Packard design of the deque class, the major field is an array of pointers to contiguous blocks of storage that hold the items. All the blocks have the same size.

The number of items a block can hold is 1K bytes/item-size. The array of pointers, called the *map array,* will initially have unused locations at the beginning and end of the array. The middle locations will point to blocks currently holding the items in the deque. The fields start and finish are iterators that point to the first and one-beyond-the-last items in the deque, respectively.

For a simplified example, suppose each block holds five items, and the deque object pets has these 11 items, in sequence: "dog", "cat", "pig", "gerbil", "canary", "duck", "cow", "horse", "parrot", "fox", "rabbit". Figure 5.6 shows how the deque object pets would be represented, with question marks to indicate unused locations.

A message such as

    pets.pop_front( );

would be handled quite easily: start would now point to "cat". But what effect would the following messages have on the deque?

    pets.push_back ("mouse");

    pets.push_back ("iguana");

Figure 5.6 | A deque with 11 items.

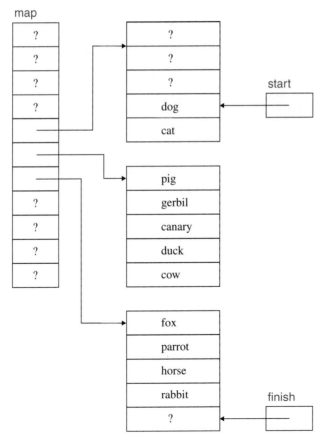

The item "mouse" is added to the end of the third block (block 2), and the iterator finish would point to the location *after* the end of the third block. When an attempt is made to append "iguana", the iterator finish would be pointing beyond the end of the block, so a new block would have to be allocated. Figure 5.7 shows the representation of the deque object pets after the pop_front and two push_backs.

Figure 5.7 I The deque from Figure 5.6 after a pop_front and two push_backs.

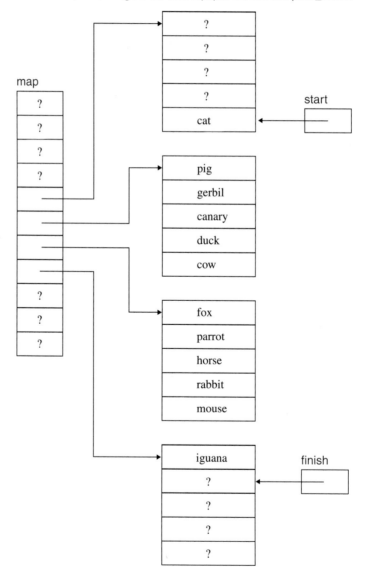

You may wonder how, in the push_back method, the determination could be made that a new block had to be allocated. The answer to these and other mysteries lies in the fields of the iterator class embedded in the deque class. Each iterator has four fields. When we loosely say "an iterator is positioned at item x," here are the four fields and their meanings with respect to item x:

1. first, a pointer to the first item in the block that contains item x
2. current, a pointer to item x
3. last, a pointer to the location *one beyond* the last item in the block that contains item x
4. node, a pointer to the location in map that points to the beginning of the block that contains item x

For example, suppose the deque iterator itr is positioned at the item "duck" in the deque of Figure 5.7. Figure 5.8 shows the field values in the iterators itr, start, and finish. In this figure, a box with back slashes represents the location just after the end of a block. Please take a few minutes to study Figure 5.8 carefully.

These superiterators allow the deque methods to use simple arithmetic to accomplish fast insertions and deletions at either the beginning or the end, and fast retrieval or replacement of any item, given its index. For example, suppose we have

    pets [9] = "goose";

To return a reference to the item at index 9, we must know the block number to look in, and the offset from the beginning of that block. First we need to know where to start, that is, how far into block 0 is the first item? Subtracting start.first from start.current, we get 4, which means that the first item—item 0—in pets is at an offset of 4 from the first block. We then add 4 and the given index, 9, to get 13. This tells us how far from the beginning of the first block—block 0—we need to go. Since the block size is 5, 13/5 gives us the block number, namely 2. Also, the offset in that block is given by 13 % 5, namely 3.

So a reference to the location at an offset of 3 from block 2 is returned. The item "rabbit" at that location is replaced with "goose". And now "goose" is at index 9 in the deque—remember that the first item, "cat", is at index 0.

If another pop_front message were sent to the deque object pets, the first block would be unused, so it would be deallocated, and the iterator start would be adjusted accordingly. Here is the code for pop_front( ):

```
void pop_front( )
{
        destroy(start.current); // calls destructor for item pointed to by start.current
        ++start.current;
        --length;
        if (empty( ) || begin( ).current == begin( ).last)
                deallocate_at_begin( ); // deallocated this block

}
```

Figure 5.8 | The **deque** from Figure 5.7 with iterator details. Note that finish.current is positioned just beyond the last item in the deque.

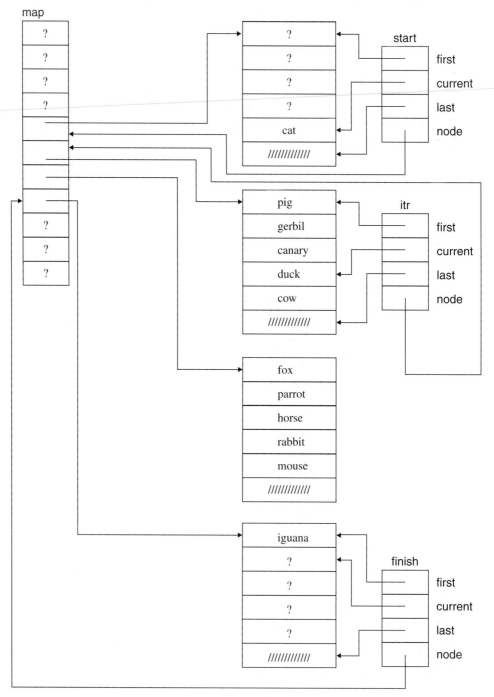

The push_front method first determines if a new block needs to be allocated at the beginning of the deque. Then start.current is decremented to point to the next available location at the front of the new block. Here is the code:

```
void push_front(const T& x)
{
        if (empty( ) || begin( ).current == begin( ).first)
                allocate_at_begin( );
        --start.current;
        construct(start.current, x); // copy x's object into location pointed to by
                                     // start.current
        ++length;
}
```

Is resizing ever needed? Yes. If all the map pointers were pointing to blocks in use and we needed another block, map would be doubled in size, and the old pointers would be centered in the new map array. So the Big-O time estimates for insertion in a deque are the same as for a vector: averageTime(n) is constant, worstTime(n) is linear in n, and amortizedTime(n) is constant.

When there is a resizing, only the map array is affected: none of the blocks in use would be changed in any way! Recall that with the vector class, an increase beyond current capacity entailed copying *all* the vector items to the new array. The only time you have any rearranging of items is when there is an insertion or deletion at a location other than the beginning or end of the deque. For example, in the deque object pets of Figure 5.8 if the message were

```
itr.erase( );
```

then this would entail moving down the four items above "duck" in the deque (and the iterator start would have to be adjusted as well). Moving items can be costly, especially if there are a lot of them or each one is large. But even here, the deque class provides a nice touch. As we have just seen, if the item to be deleted is closer to the front of the deque, the previous items are moved down. If, however, the item to be deleted is closer to the back of the deque, the subsequent items are moved up. So a deletion (or insertion) in the interior of a deque entails moving, on average, only one-fourth of the items.

You have seen some of the behind-the-scenes complexity of the deque class, but little of its power. To what extent is a deque better than a vector? Let's count the ways:

1. There is no movement of items during resizing. When an insertion at the front or back of a deque requires an extra block, no items in the deque need to be moved. On those rare occasions where the map itself is too small, a new double-sized map is created and the old map is copied into the middle of the new map, but no items are moved. With a vector, all the items are moved during a resizing.

2. For the pop_front method in the deque class, worstTime(n) is constant. The vector class does not even have a pop_front method because its worstTime(n) would be linear in n, but some innocent user of the vector class might assume the worstTime(n) is constant, as it is for pop_back. To delete the front item from a vector vec, you would do the following:

   vec.erase (vec.begin( ));

   And worstTime(n) would be linear in n.

3. In a deque, the push_front method takes only constant time, on average. The vector class does not even have a push_front method (see note 2). With a deque, there is a possibility that the map might be resized in response to a push_front, so worstTime(n) is $O(n)$ because the size of the map is proportional to the number of items in the deque. But amortizedTime(n) is constant.

4. In a deque, unused blocks are deallocated. If a deque is shrunk to the point where one of the outer two blocks (positioned at start or finish) is no longer in use, that block is deallocated. Recall that vectors grow but never shrink.

5. For insertions and deletions in the interior, a deque requires fewer data movements than a vector. For example, if the item to be removed is closer to the beginning of the deque, only the items before the deletion point are moved. Otherwise, only the items after the deletion point are moved. On average, only 25 percent of the items will be moved, versus 50 percent for a vector.

The big drawback for a deque is the modular arithmetic needed to convert an index into a block address. In fact, unless most of the operations are at or near the front of a container, a vector will be faster than a deque. Lab 16 has some timing experiments that compare vectors, deques and lists (the list class is introduced in Chapter 6). In the meantime, Lab 14 has more details of the Hewlett-Packard implementation of the deque class.

LAB **Lab 14:** More details of Hewlett-Packard's deque **class** implementation.   *(All Labs Are Optional.)* **LAB**

5.5 | A DEQUE APPLICATION: VERY LONG INTEGERS

APPLICATION

How would the deque class handle very long integers? Basically, we could use the method definitions from the very_long_int class. But now digits would be a deque object instead of a vector object. The only changes—for the sake of efficiency, not correctness—would be in overloading **operator**+. Instead of using push_back for the partial sum and the carry, we would use push_front. Then the digits would not be backwards, so we would avoid the call to reverse. These changes would not affect the Big-O time, but would slightly speed up the actual run-time.

SUMMARY

In this chapter we introduced two sequential container classes: the vector class and the deque class. Vectors are much more powerful than arrays. For example, vectors are automatically resizable. When a vector outgrows the current capacity, an array of twice that size is created, and the vector is copied to that array. This is similar to what a hermit crab does each time it outgrows its shell. A further advantage of vectors over arrays is that, for inserting and deleting, users are relieved of the burden of writing code to make space for the new entry or to close up the space of the deleted entry.

A deque has the same methods as a vector, except that a vector has capacity and reserve methods (see Project 5.2) and a deque has push_front and pop_front methods. The push_front method takes only constant time, on average, and the pop_front method always takes constant time.

The applications of vectors and deques were in high-precision arithmetic, which is important in public-key cryptography.

EXERCISES

5.1   a.   Suppose we make the following definitions:

```
vector<char> letters;
vector<char>::iterator itr;
```

What word would be output from the following sequence of statements?

```
letters.push_back ('f');
letters.push_back ('i');
letters.push_back ('e');
letters.push_back ('r');
letters.push_back ('c');
letters.push_back ('e');

itr = letters.begin( );
cout << *itr;
itr++;
cout << *itr;

cout << letters [3];
itr += 4;
cout << *itr;
```

5.2   Suppose vector_plus is a subclass of the vector class. Assume that vector_plus has no new fields. Define each of the following vector_plus methods:

   a.   // Precondition: There is an item in the calling object that equals item.
         // Postcondition: An item that equals item has been deleted from the
         //   calling object. The worstTime(n) is O(n).
         void erase_item (**const** T& item);

Hint   Start by calling the generic algorithm find. For example, suppose we have

item* ptr = find (fruits.begin( ), fruits.end( ), "bananas");

Then ptr will be positioned at an occurrence of "bananas" in fruits, or just beyond the last item in fruits if "bananas" does not occur in fruits.

b.   // Postcondition: The calling object contains all of its original items
     //   followed by all of the items that were in vec. If an
     //   item appeared once in the original calling object and
     //   once in vec, that item would appear twice in the merged
     //   object.
     void merge (**const** vector_plus<T>& vec);

Hint   This can be accomplished with repeated calls to push_back.

c.   // Postcondition: The value returned is the number of unique items in the
     //   calling object. An item is unique if it occurs exactly once
     //   in the container. The worstTime(n) is O(n * n).
     int unique_count( )**const**;

Hint   Use the generic algorithm count. For example, suppose we have

int n = 0;
count (fruits.begin( ), fruits.end( ), "bananas", n);

Then n will contain the number of occurrences of "bananas" in fruits.

5.3   In designing the very_long_int class, we decided to use (has-a) rather than inherit from (is-a) the vector class. Why?

5.4   Modify the design of the very_long_int class as follows: Each item in digits consists of a five-digit integer. What effect do you think this will have on Big-O time? What about run-time?

5.5   Extend the very_long_int class by adding methods to initialize, to compare, and to calculate Fibonacci numbers. The method interfaces are as follows:

a.   // Postcondition: this very_long_int is empty.
     very_long_int( );

b.   // Precondition: n is a nonnegative integer (not an object in the
     //   very_long_int class).
     // Postcondition: this very_long_int has been initialized to n.
     void initialize (**unsigned** n);

c. // Precondition: n is a nonnegative integer (not an object in the
   //   very_long_int class).
   // Postcondition: this very_long_int has been constructed with the initial
   //   value of n.
   very_long_int (**unsigned** n);

   Example   Suppose the message is

   very_long_int temp_int (1);

   Then the effect will be to give the very_long_int object temp_int the value 1.

   Hint   n % 10 returns the rightmost digit in n.

d. // Postcondition: true has been returned if this very_long_int's value is
   //   less than the value of other_very_long. Otherwise, false
   //   has been returned. The WorstTime(n) is O(n)
   bool operator< (**const** very_long_int& other_very_long) **const**;

   Example   Suppose we define

   very_long_int new_int (154),
           old_int (215);

   If the following message is sent

   new_int < old_int

   then **true** will be returned.

   Hint   If the sizes of the two very_long_ints are different, then the very_long_int with the smaller size is less than the very_long_int with the larger size.[2] If the sizes are equal, start at the most significant digit; compare the two very_long_ints digit by digit until (unless) the corresponding digits in the two numbers differ.

e. // Postcondition: true has been returned if this very_long_int's value is
   //   greater than the value of other_very_long_int.
   //   Otherwise, false has been returned.
   bool operator> (**const** very_long_int& other_very_long) **const**;

[2]Recall that very_long_ints have no leading zeros.

f.   // Postcondition: true has been returned if this very_long_int's value is
     //   equal to the value of other_very_long_int. Otherwise,
     //   false has been returned. The worstTime(n) is O(n).
     bool operator== (**const** very_long_int& other_very_long) **const**;

g.   // Precondition: n is a positive integer (not an object in the very_long_int
     //   class).
     // Postcondition: The value returned is the nth Fibonacci number.
     //   The worstTime(n) is O(n * n).
     very_long_int fibonacci (**int** n) **const**;

Example   Suppose the following message is sent

temp_int.fibonacci (100);

The very_long_int returned will have the value
354224848179261915075—the one-hundredth Fibonacci number.

Hint   Mimic the iterative design of the Fibonacci function in Lab 10.
Both i and n will be ordinary integers, but previous, current, and temp
will be very_long_ints.

5.6   Suppose, in developing the very_long_int class, we decide that the vector
digits will contain the integer in *reverse* order. For example, if the input
contained "386X", when the 3 is read in, it would be stored in position 0.
The 8 would then be read in and stored in position 0, bumping the 3 to
position 1. Finally, the 6 would be read in and stored in position 0, so we
would have 6, 8, 3 in positions 0 through 2, respectively. Redefine the
overloaded operators >>, <<, and + accordingly. Determine the Big-O
time for >>, <<, and +.

5.7   The vector class has neither a push_front method nor a pop_front method. In
your opinion, why were these methods omitted?

PROGRAMMING PROJECT 5.1

Extending the very_long_int Class

In the very_long_int class, develop an overloaded operator for multiplication and a factorial method. Here are the interfaces:

```
// Postcondition: The value returned is the product of this very_long_int and
//                otherVeryLong. The worstTime(n) is O (n * n), where n is the
//                maximum of the number of digits in the pre-call value of the calling
//                object and the number of digits in other_very_long.
very_long_int operator* (const very_long_int& otherVeryLong);


// Precondition: n >= 0.
// Postcondition: The factorial of n has been returned. The worstTime(n) is O (n log
//                (n!)): n multiplications, and each product has fewer digits than log
//                (n!), the number of digits in n!
very_long_int factorial (int n);
```

Validate your methods in the driver program from Lab 13.

PROGRAMMING PROJECT 5.2

An Alternative Implementation of the deque **Class**

Implement the deque class with the vector class. Do not use the deque class in the Hewlett-Packard implementation of the Standard Template Library. Instead, you should develop your own simple implementation as a subclass of the vector class. It will help if you are familiar with a few additional vector methods:

1.   // Postcondition: A vector of size n has been constructed. The value of each item is
   //   given by the default constructor of T.
   vector (**unsigned** n);

2.   // Postcondition: The number of items that can be stored in the vector without
   //   resizing has been returned.
   unsigned capacity( ) **const;**

3.   // Postcondition: If the vector's current capacity, before this call, was less than n, the
   //   vector has been resized to a capacity >= n.
   void reserve (**unsigned** n);

Your implementation of the deque class will have (at least) two fields beyond those in vector:

> **unsigned** front = START_SIZE / 2,
>   back = START_SIZE / 2 − 1;

The front and back fields will be indices of the front and back of the deque, respectively. The constructor initializes the deque to START_SIZE (say, 100) items, each with the value given by T's constructor. Then front starts out at 50 and back at 49. Several methods are overridden. For example, begin( ) returns start + front, and end( ) returns start + back + 1.

Basically, to apply the push_front method to item x, we set

> front ++;
> (*this) [0] = x;

To apply the push_back method to x, we set

> back++;
> (*this) [back − front] = x

At any time, the size of the deque is given by back − front + 1. There is a complication if, prior to a call to push_front, front has the value 0—or if, prior to a call to push_back, back has the value capacity( ) − 1. In either case, we double the size of the vector:

> reserve (2 * capacity( ));

The original contents of the deque are now in the lower half of the resized deque, so we need to recenter by shifting those items to higher indices. If we set

> **unsigned** n = capacity( );

then the item at index $n/2$ will be moved to index $3n/4$, the item at index $n/2 − 1$ will be moved to index $3n/4 − 1$, and so on. The insertion can now be made as has been described.

CHAPTER 6

Lists

In this chapter we continue our study of the Standard Template Library's data structures by introducing another sequential container class: the list class. There are some significant performance differences between lists and vectors (or deques). For example, lists lack the random-access feature of vectors: to access a list's item from an index requires a loop that starts at the beginning or end of the list, whichever is closer to the index. But lists allow constant-time insertions and deletions, once an iterator is positioned where the insertion or deletion should be made. This fact makes iterators essential for almost all list applications, and furthermore, the list class lacks an index operator, **operator**[ ].

After we define what a list is, we enumerate some of the method interfaces for the list class and its associated iterator class. This *user's* view is all that the Standard Template Library specifies. We then provide an outline of the Hewlett-Packard design and implementation, and suggest simpler (but less efficient) designs. The application of lists, a simple line editor, takes advantage of a list's ability to quickly make consecutive insertions and deletions anywhere in the list. ■

CHAPTER OBJECTIVES

1. Understand the list class, both from the user's perspective and from the developer's perspective.

2. Given an application that requires a sequential container class, be able to decide whether a list, vector, or deque would be more appropriate.

3. Compare the Hewlett-Packard design of the list class with a singly linked design and a doubly linked design with head and tail fields.

6.1 | LISTS

In everyday life we construct lists as a way to impose order on reality: grocery lists, sign-up sheets, telephone directories, class rosters, TV schedules, and so on. For this reason, problems are often stated in terms of lists:

> Given a list of test scores, sort them into increasing order.
>
> Print out a list of all club members whose dues are overdue.

A *list,* sometimes called a *linked list,* is a finite sequence of items such that

1. Accessing or modifying an arbitrary item in the sequence takes linear time.
2. Given an iterator at a position in the sequence, inserting or deleting one item at that position takes constant time.

Starting in Section 6.1.1, we will design and implement a list class corresponding to this data structure. How do the two list properties compare with the behavior of vector objects? Recall that to access or modify the item in position k for a vector vec, we apply the index operator

    vec [k]

The index operator is also used with a deque. With a list, we must use an iterator. Suppose lis is an instance of the list class, and we want to access the item k positions from the beginning of lis. We proceed sequentially either from the start of lis up to position k or from the end of lis down to position k, whichever route is shorter:

```
if (k < lis.size( ) / 2)
{
        // loop forward from beginning of lis:
        itr = lis.begin( );
        for (int i = 0; i < k; i++)
                itr++;
} // if
else
{
        // loop backward from end of lis:
        itr = lis.end( );
        for (int i = lis.size( ); i > k; i−−)
                itr−−;
} // else
```

The time for this access is proportional to k. Let n represent the number of items in the list. In the worst case, when k = n, the number of loop iterations is $n/2$, which is linear in n. The average distance from k to the beginning or end of the list is $n/4$, which is also linear in n.

The reason we lose the constant-time access we had for vectors and deques is that list iterators are not random-access iterators, but merely *bidirectional iterators.*

That means from a given position in the list, an iterator can go forward one position or go backward one position. Recall that, in constrast, a random-access iterator could immediately go forward or backward any number of positions.

But once an iterator is correctly positioned, an insertion or deletion at that position in a list takes only constant time, versus linear time for a vector or deque. This provides the major motivation for using a list instead of a vector (or deque): when the application entails a lot of insertions and/or deletions at positions other than the back (for a deque, front or back) of the container.

Lists can be spliced together in only constant time. For an example of what splicing means, suppose list1 contains the items

> "television", "radio", "stereo", "CD player"

and the iterator itr is positioned at "radio". If list2 contains the items

> "camcorder", "VCR", "laser disk player"

we can send the following message:

> list1.splice (itr, list2);

As a result, the items from list2 will be removed from list2 and inserted into list1 in front of the item "radio". So list1 will contain

> "television", "camcorder", "VCR", "laser disk player", "radio", "stereo", "CD player"

and list2 will be empty. You can probably see why splicing vectors or deques requires linear time proportional to the size of the container supplying the items to be spliced.

6.1.1   Method Interfaces for the list Class

The method interfaces for the list class and its associated iterator class are similar to those we saw for vectors and deques. We'll start with interfaces for the most widely used methods in the list class. Table 6.1 has a thumbnail sketch of these methods. The list class is a template class with template-parameter T, representing the type of the items in the list.

1. // Postcondition: this list is empty.
    list( );

> *Note*   This default constructor is usually invoked implicitly, for example,
>
> list<Employee> employees;
>
> makes employees an empty list, whose items will be of type Employee.

2. // Postcondition: this list has been constructed and initialized to a copy of x.
    //   The worstTime(n) is O(n), where n is the size of x.
    list (**const** list<T>& x);

Table 6.1 I Brief description of some list methods (assume the following definition: list<double>::iterator itr;)

Method	Effect
list<**double**> x	x is an empty list
list<**double**> weights (x)	the list object weights contains a copy of the list object x
weights.push_front (8.3)	8.3 is inserted at the front of weights
weights.push_back (107.2)	107.2 is inserted at the back of weights
weights.insert (itr, 125.0)	125.0 is inserted where itr is positioned; items from the insertion point to the back of weights are moved up; returns an iterator positioned at the newly inserted item
weights.pop_front( )	The front item in weights has been deleted
weights.pop_back( )	The back item in weights has been deleted
weights.erase (itr)	The item where itr was positioned has been deleted; the only iterators and references invalidated are those positioned at the deleted item
weights.erase (itr1, itr2)	The items in weights, from where itr1 is positioned (inclusive) to where itr2 is positioned (exclusive) have been deleted
weights.size( )	Returns the number of items in weights
weights.empty( )	Returns **true** if weights has no items; otherwise, **false**
itr = weights.begin( )	itr is positioned at the item at the front of weights
itr == weight.end( )	Returns **true** if itr is positioned just beyond the back item in weights; otherwise, **false**
new_weights = weights	The previously defined list object new_weights contains a copy of weights
weights.splice (itr,old_weights)	All the items in old_weights are now in weights in front of where itr is positioned. The time for this method is constant no matter how many items were originally in weights or old_weights
weights.sort( )	The items in weights are in order according to **operator**<

Example   Suppose that old_words, a list of strings, was defined earlier. If we write

list <string>new_words (old_words);

then new_words has been constructed and contains a copy of old_words.

Note   Recall, from Chapter 5, that this kind of constructor is referred to as a ***copy constructor.***

3. // Postcondition: x has been inserted at the front of this list.
    void push_front (**const** T& x);

>   *Note*   The vector class did not have a push_front method. Such a method might have given the impression that inserting at the front of a vector object was fast.

4. // Postcondition: x has been inserted at the back of this list.
    void push_back (**const** T& x);

5. // Postcondition: x has been inserted in this list in front of the item that position
    //   was positioned at before this call. An iterator positioned at x
    //   has been returned.
    iterator insert (iterator position, **const** T& x);

>   *Note*   The worstTime(n) is constant. For the insert method in the vector class, worstTime(n) is $O(n)$.

6. // Precondition: this list is not empty.
    // Postcondition: the item that was at the front of this list before this call was
    //   made has been deleted from this list.
    void pop_front( );

7. // Precondition: this list is not empty.
    // Postcondition: the item that was at the back of this list before this call was
    //   made has been deleted from this list.
    void pop_back( );

8. // Precondition: position is positioned at an item in this list.
    // Postcondition: the item that position was positioned at before this call was
    //   made has been deleted from this list.
    void erase (iterator position);

>   *Note*   The worstTime(n) is constant. For the erase method in the vector class, worstTime(n) is $O(n)$.

9. // Precondition: first is positioned at some item in this list, and last is positioned
    //   one past some item in this list.

```
// Postcondition: all the items that, before this call was made, were in the range
//                 from first (inclusive) to last (exclusive) have been deleted from
//                 this list.
void erase (iterator first, iterator last);
```

> *Note* The time for this method is proportional to the number of items removed. Recall that for the corresponding **vector** method, the time is proportional to the number of items *after* the last item removed (because those trailing items are moved down to fill up the deleted slots).

10.
```
// Postcondition: the number of items in this list has been returned.
unsigned size( ) const;
```

11.
```
// Postcondition: true has been returned if this list is empty. Otherwise, false
//                 has been returned.
bool empty( ) const;
```

12.
```
// Postcondition: an iterator positioned at the front of this list has been returned.
iterator begin( );
```

13.
```
// Postcondition: an iterator positioned after the last item in this list has been
//                 returned.
iterator end( );
```

> *Note* If the calling object list is empty, the iterator returned by the begin method is equal to the iterator returned by the end method.

14.
```
// Postcondition: this list contains a copy of x, and a reference to this list
//                 has been returned.
list<T>& operator= (const list<T>& x);
```

> *Note* This assignment operator differs from the copy constructor (method number 2) in that the calling object for the copy constructor was being defined as well as being initialized to the parameter x.

15.
```
// Postcondition: The contents of x have been inserted, starting at position, into
//                 this list, and x is empty.
void splice (iterator position, list<T>& x);
```

> *Note* This method takes constant time, no matter how big x is.

16.
```
// Precondition: operator< is defined for type T.
// Postcondition: the items in this list are in ascending order. The worstTime (n)
//                 is O (n log n).
void sort( );
```

> *Note* We will study this method in Chapter 12.

There are also front and back methods, with the same method interfaces as the vector versions.

6.1.2   Iterator Interfaces

The list class supports bidirectional iterators, not random-access iterators. This is clearly seen by the absence of operator+. Here are the interfaces:

1.   // Postcondition: this iterator is now positioned at the next position in this list,
//   and a reference to this iterator has been returned.
iterator& **operator**++( );

> *Note*   This is the *preincrement* operator; that is, the iterator advances and a reference to the newly positioned iterator is returned. For example, suppose that cities is a list object that contains the following list of cities:
>
> "Boston", "College Station", "Lansing", "Pasadena"
>
> If itr is a list iterator positioned at "College Station" and we write
>
> list<string>::iterator new_itr = ++itr;
>
> then both itr and new_itr are positioned at "Lansing".

2.   // Postcondition: this iterator is now positioned at the next position in this list,
//   and a copy of this iterator's previous value has been returned.
iterator **operator**++ (**int**)

> *Note*   This is the *postincrement operator;* that is, the iterator advances, but the iterator's value before advancing is returned. The postincrement operator has an **int** parameter whose only purpose is to distinguish this operator from the preincrement operator. In fact, there is no argument corresponding to the **int** parameter. For example, suppose that cities is a list object that contains the following list of cities:
>
> "Boston", "College Station", "Lansing", "Pasadena"
>
> If itr is a list iterator positioned at "College Station" and we write
>
> list<string>::iterator old_itr = itr++;
>
> then itr is positioned at "Lansing", but old_itr is positioned at "College Station".

3.   // Postcondition: this iterator is now positioned at the previous position in this
//   list, and a reference to this iterator has been returned.
iterator& **operator**--( ); // pre-decrement

4.   // Postcondition: this iterator is now positioned at the previous position in this
//   list, and a copy of this iterator's previous value has been

```
//                returned.
iterator operator−−(int); // post-decrement
```

5.
```
// Precondition: this iterator is positioned at an item in this list.
// Postcondition: a reference to the item this iterator is positioned at has been
//                returned.
T& operator*( );
```

> *Example*   Suppose that itr is positioned at the item "Lansing". If we write

> ```
> cout << (*itr);
> ```

> the output will be

> Lansing

> *Note*   Because a reference is returned, we can use this operator to alter the value of an item in the list. For example,

> ```
> *itr = "Detroit";
> ```

> will change the value of the item itr is positioned at to "Detroit".

6.
```
// Postcondition: true has been returned if this iterator is positioned at the
//                same place in this list x is positioned at. Otherwise, false has
//                been returned.
bool operator== (const iterator& x);
```

> *Note*   There is also **operator!=**.

Here is a small program that illustrates several of the list methods and list-iterator operators:

```
#include <list>
#include <iostream>
#include <string>

using namespace std;

int main( )
{
        list<string> words;
        list<string>::iterator itr;

        words.push_back ("yes");
        words.push_back ("no");
        words.push_front ("maybe");
        words.push_front ("wow");
```

```
cout << "size = " << words.size( ) << endl;

cout << endl << "the list after 4 insertions:" << endl;
for (itr = words.begin( ); itr != words.end( ); itr++)
        cout << (*itr) << endl;

words.pop_front( );
words.pop_back( );

cout << endl << "the list after 2 deletions:" << endl;
for (itr = words.begin( ); itr != words.end( ); itr++)
        cout << (*itr) << endl;
cin.get( );

    return 0;

} // main
```

The output from this program is

```
size = 4

the list after 4 insertions:
wow
maybe
yes
no

the list after 2 deletions:
maybe
yes
```

Before we start looking at possible implementations of the list class, we should compare lists and vectors (or deques) from the user's point of view, that is, as data structures in the Standard Template Library. Section 6.1.3 explores the differences between lists and vectors as data structures.

6.1.3 Differences between List Methods and Vector or Deque Methods

The most significant difference between the list methods and the vector or deque methods is the absence of the index operator, operator[ ], from the list class. The omission is intended as a warning that lists lack the random-access property. We saw in Section 6.1 that we could simulate the effect of the index operator by looping from the front or back of a list, but the time would be linear in the number of items between the front (or back) item and the item at the given index.

Choose a vector (or deque) if the application entails accessing or modifying items at widely varying positions in a sequential container.

So if the application entails a lot of accessing and/or modifying of items at widely varying positions in a sequential container, it will be completed much faster if a vector or deque is used instead of a list.

On the other hand, to insert or erase the item that an iterator is positioned at takes only constant time with a list, versus linear time with a vector or deque.

If a large part of an application consists of iterating through a sequential container and making insertions or erasures during the iterations, the application will be completed much faster if a list is used instead of either a vector or a deque.

Another difference between the list class and the vector or deque class is the extent of iterator invalidation as a result of insertions and deletions. Generally speaking, insertions and deletions in a list invalidate only the obvious iterators. For example, suppose that lis is a list object and itr1 and itr2 are iterators. If itr1 is positioned at item1 and itr2 is positioned at some later item, the message

    lis.erase (itr1);

will invalidate itr1. That is, as you would expect, itr1 should no longer be depended on to point to item1. But itr2 would still be pointing to the same item it was pointing to before the erase message was sent.

Now suppose we had the same scenario for a vector vec and we sent the message

    vec.erase (itr1);

Then itr2 will no longer be positioned at the item it was positioned at before the erase message was sent. The reason is that deletion in a vector causes a relocation of items beyond the point of erasure. A similar problem arises when deleting from a deque. And itr1 would also be invalidated because the erase method calls the destructor for the item itr1 was positioned at.

The status of iterators after inserting is similar. For a list, no items are moved, so iterators are still positioned where they were positioned before the insertion. For vectors, insertions can necessitate moving items, so iterators may be invalidated. Specifically, if the new size is greater than the old capacity, an expansion will occur, and all iterators and references are invalidated. Otherwise, only the iterators and references at or beyond the point of insertion are invalidated. The situation with deques is similar to vectors, except that invalidation applies from the insertion point to the front or back of the deque, whichever is closer to the insertion point.

6.1.4   Fields and Implementation of the list Class

In this section, we present an overview of one implementation of the Standard Template Library's list class, namely, the Hewlett-Packard version. Because of the C++ passion for efficiency, all widely used implementations—including the Hewlett-Packard implementation—are somewhat complex. In Section 6.1.6 we will consider some simpler—and less efficient—designs.

As with all the other template classes in the Hewlett-Packard implementation, the class declaration and method definitions for the list class are in the same file. The essential fields are length and node, defined in the following:

```
template<class T>
class list {
    protected:
        unsigned length;

        struct list_node
        {
            list_node* next;
            list_node* prev;
            T data; // holds one item
        }; // list_node

        list_node* node;
```

Figure 6.1 shows that the list nodes are strung together like beads in a necklace.

It is somewhat weird that a pointer to a node would have the identifier node, rather than node_ptr, for example, but this is common in virtually all implementations (probably because other implementations are based on Hewlett-Packard's).

The list_node pointed to by node is called the **_header node._** In the header node, the data field is unused and, initially, the prev and next fields[1] point back to the header node itself. That is, the default constructor includes the following code:

```
(*node).next = node;
(*node).prev = node;
```

So after the default constructor has been called, we have

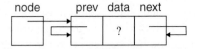

In a nonempty list, the header node's next field points to the first item in the list and the prev field points to the last item in the list. So the list is stored as a circular, doubly linked list. For example, Figure 6.2 has a list container with two string items.

Figure 6.1 I In a list, each item is housed in a node that also includes pointers to the previous and next nodes.

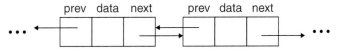

---

[1]In the Hewlett-Packard implementation, the type of prev and next is given as **void*** because list_node* is correct only for the default allocator. But since we are assuming the default allocator, we substitute list_node*.

Figure 6.2 I A list with two items: "cat" and "duck". Each item is stored in a **struct** that also has prev and next fields.

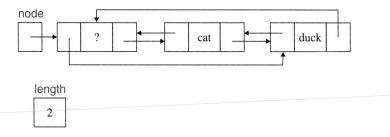

The use of links to connect list nodes was the idea behind the Linked class in Chapter 2, but here each node has a prev pointer as well as a next pointer, and there is a header node.

Before we look at the definitions of some list methods, we need to say a little about the embedded iterator class. That class has two protected members: a field and a constructor:

```
protected:
        list_node* node;
        iterator (list_node* x) : node (x) { }
```

This constructor heading has a ***constructor-initializer section:*** a colon followed by any number of field initializations separated by commas. Each ***field initialization*** consists of the field identifier and, in parentheses, the initial value. The effect here is that the node field is initialized to x. In fact, the same effect could be accomplished without an initialization section by assigning x to node within the constructor definition.[2] Note that this is the node field in the iterator class, not the node field in the list class.

The reason the constructor is **protected** is that ordinary users will know nothing of list_node, so will have no cause to invoke this constructor. There is a default constructor, which is **public**. The definitions of the **public** methods in the iterator class are not unexpected. For example,

---

[2]A constructor-initializer section would be necessary if a constructor for an object field had to be called prior to the execution of the new class's constructor. For example, we might have

```
class D {
public:
        D (int i): v (i) {cout<< v << endl;}
protected:
        very_long_int v;
```

A constructor-initializer section is also needed to intitialize any non-**static** constants that have class scope.

```
public:
    iterator( ) { }

    T& operator*( ) const { return(*node).data;}

    iterator& operator++ ( )
    {
        node = (*node).next; return *this;
    }
    iterator operator++ (int)
    {
        iterator tmp = *this; ++*this; return tmp;
    }
```

Lab 15 has more details on the iterator class.

Now we can get to the list methods. We will define eight methods: begin, end, insert, push_front, push_back, erase (with one parameter), pop_front, and pop_back. As you can see from Figure 6.2, the header node is pointed to by the next field of the last list_node. That is, the header node is *one past* the last list_node in the list. So it makes sense that the end method in the list class returns an iterator positioned at the header node. Here is the definition:

```
    iterator end ( ) { return node; }
```

Something strange is going on here. The value returned is node, that is, a *pointer* to the header node. But the return type of the end method is iterator! An iterator has a pointer field (also called node), but an iterator is an object, not a pointer. In C++, if an expression of an inappropriate type is encountered, the compiler will, if possible, perform an ***automatic type conversion*** to the appropriate type. In this case, the type list_node* needs to be converted to type iterator. And an automatic type conversion can be performed thanks to the protected constructor we saw a little while ago in the iterator class:

```
    iterator (list_node* x) : node(x) { }
```

So what is really returned by the end method is not a copy of the list class's node field but rather an iterator constructed from the list class's node field.

As you can also see from Figure 6.2, the begin method should return an iterator positioned at the same list_node that the header node's next field is pointing to, namely, the list_node that has the first item in the list. The definition of the begin method, also employing automatic type conversion, is

```
    iterator begin( ) { return(*node).next; }
```

Now let's tackle the insert method:

```
    iterator insert (iterator position, const T& x);
```

This method stores an item x in list_node, adjusts some next and prev pointer fields to make that list_node be "in front of" the list_node pointed to by the iterator position, and returns an iterator positioned at the newly inserted node. For example, in Figure 6.3, pets is the list container from Figure 6.2 and the iterator position is positioned at the list_node containing "duck".

Figure 6.4 shows the effect of the message

    pets.insert (itr, "dog");

on the list pets from Figure 6.3.

The key observation for you to make from Figure 6.4 is this:

> When an insertion is made in a **list** container, no items are relocated.

From Figure 6.4, we can infer the following steps to implement the insert method:

    iterator insert (iterator position, **const** T& x);

1. allocate space for a list_node, pointed to by tmp.
2. Store item x in tmp's data field.
3. Assign to tmp's next field (technically, the next field of the link_node pointed to by tmp) the value of position.node.
4. Assign to tmp's prev field the value of the prev field of the link_node pointed to by position.node.

Figure 6.3 | The list from Figure 6.2, with the iterator **position** positioned at the list_node containing "duck".

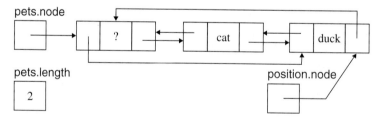

Figure 6.4 | The list from Figure 6.3 after "dog" is inserted.

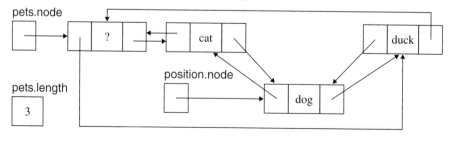

5. Assign the value of tmp to the next field of the link_node pointed to by the prev field of the list_node pointed to by position.node.

6. Assign the value of tmp to the prev field of the link_node pointed to by position.node. This assignment must be made *after* assignments 4 and 5; otherwise, the node that preceded position's node would be inaccessible.

7. Increment length.

8. Return tmp.

At this point, you could fill in most of the definition of the insert method. For example, step 4 would be written as

```
(*tmp).prev = (*position.node).prev;
```

But your definition would probably implement step 1 with

```
list_node *tmp = new list_node;
```

That would be effective but inefficient. For one thing, every list_node has the same size, but the general-purpose heap manager could not take advantage of this uniformity. Also, depending on the computer system, each call to the **new** operator may generate an interrupt, and these repeated interrupts could drastically slow down a project's execution.

The approach taken in the Hewlett-Packard implementation is to have the list class develop its own memory-management routines: get_node for allocating list nodes, and put_node for deallocation. Here is the resulting definition of insert:

```
iterator insert (iterator position, const T& x)
{
        list_node* tmp = get_node( );
        construct(value_allocator.address((*tmp).data), x);
        (*tmp).next = position.node;
        (*tmp).prev = (*position.node).prev;
        (* ((*position.node).prev)).next = tmp;
        (*position.node).prev = tmp;
        ++length;
        return tmp;
}
```

The details of the get_node method are covered in Lab 15, and the basics of list storage are explored in Section 6.1.5. To get a full appreciation of a list class implementation, you should peruse the actual code in your compiler's implementation of the list class. It will probably be quite similar to the implementation shown here.

The definitions of the push_front and push_back methods are one-liners:

```
void push_front(const T& x) { insert(begin( ), x); }
void push_back(const T& x) { insert(end( ), x); }
```

Because of the header node, every list node has a previous list node and a next list node, and this simplifies insertions and removals.

The brevity of these two definitions illustrates the beauty of having a header node: *the* insert *method also handles front insertions and back insertions!* The insert method always inserts the new item (in a list node) between two list nodes. For push_front method, the item is inserted between the header node and what had been the front node. For the push_back method, the item is inserted between what had been the back node and the header node.

We still have three more methods to define: erase, pop_front, and pop_back. But once we have defined the erase method, the definitions of pop_front and pop_back will follow easily (thanks again to having a header node). With the insert method, we attached a new item (in a link_node) to a list. The erase method *detaches* an item from the list. Figure 6.5 shows a three-item list, with an iterator positioned at one of the items.

To erase the item "dog" from pets, there are, essentially, two steps:

1. Change the next field in cat's list_node to point to duck's list_node.
2. Change the prev field in duck's list_node to point to cat's list _node.

The effect of carrying out these two steps is shown in Figure 6.6.

There is still some housekeeping to take care of: the destructor for the string object "dog" must be called, the link_node that had "dog" has to be deallocated, and the length field has to be decremented. Here is the definition:

void erase(iterator position)

Figure 6.5 | A tidied-up version of the three-item list from Figure 6.4.

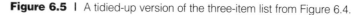
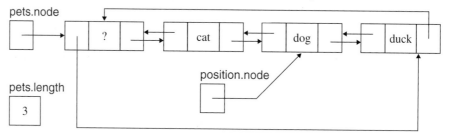

Figure 6.6 | The list from Figure 6.5 after detaching "dog".

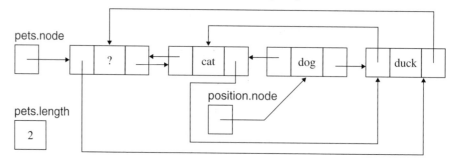

```
    {
        (*((*position.node).prev)).next = (*position.node).next;
        (*((*position.node).next)).prev = (*position.node).prev;
        destroy(value_allocator.address((*position.node).data));
        put_node(position.node);
        −−length;
    }
```

Section 6.1.5 will explain how the put_node method deallocates the space for a deleted node.

The pop_front method erases the item that begin( ) is positioned at, and the pop_back method erases the item just before where end( ) is positioned:

```
void pop_front( ) { erase(begin( )); }

void pop_back( )
{
    iterator tmp = end( );
    erase(−−tmp);
}
```

We finish up this implementation of the list class by studying the allocation and deallocation of list nodes.

6.1.5   Storage of list Nodes

In Section 6.1.4, we saw that the insert method called the get_node method to return a pointer to the node that will hold the item to be inserted. The definition of the get_node method is discussed in Lab 15, but for that discussion to make sense, we need to study how list nodes are stored.

When the first insertion is made in a list, a chunk of memory—typically, 1K bytes—is allocated. This chunk, called a **buffer**, is used for subsequent insertions until the buffer is filled—we'll ignore for now what happens when the buffer is filled and how deletions fit into this representation. To determine when the buffer is filled, the list class has a next_avail field, pointing to the node to be used in the next insertion, and a last field, pointing one past the last node in the buffer:

```
list_node* next_avail;
list_node* last;
```

Figure 6.7 illustrates a list object, pets, with four items: "cat", "dog", "duck", and "lion".

The next_avail field is used whenever a new node is allocated, whether the allocation is for insert, push_front, or push_back. In Figure 6.7, for example, a call to push_back would adjust the prev and next fields of next_avail's list node so that list node's prev field would point to the "lion" list node and that list node's next field would point to the header node. And then next_avail itself would be incremented. For example, Figure 6.8 shows the effect of

Figure 6.7 I A list of four pets, stored in **buffer**.

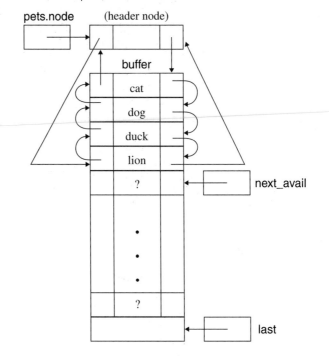

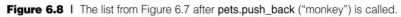

Figure 6.8 I The list from Figure 6.7 after **pets.push_back** ("monkey") is called.

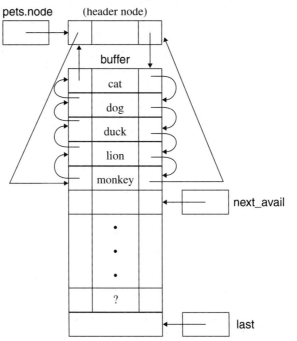

pets.push_back ("monkey");

on the configuration shown in Figure 6.7.

There are two more details we need to consider: What happens when the buffer gets used up, and what happens to deleted nodes? When the buffer is full, that is, when next_avail = last, a new buffer of the same size is allocated. To keep track of all of a list's buffers—so they can later be deallocated when the list is destroyed—the list class has a buffer_list field. This field contains a pointer to a singly linked list whose nodes are of type list_node_buffer. Each list_node_buffer has two fields: a pointer to a buffer, and a pointer to the next list_node_buffer:

```
struct list_node_buffer
{
        list_node_buffer* next_buffer;
        list_node* buffer;
};

list_node_buffer* buffer_list;
```

For example, Figure 6.9 shows a list with three buffers allocated.

Lastly, but not leastly, we need to say something about deletions. It would be wasteful if deleted nodes were just left to rot. Instead, there is a list of nodes that had once been in the list but were subsequently erased. These recycled nodes are organized in a singly linked list. The free_list field in the list class holds a pointer to the most recently deleted node:

```
list_node* free_list;
```

This node's prev field is ignored, and its next field points to the node that had been next most recently erased. That (next most recently erased) node's next field points to the third most recently erased node, and so on as the free list winds its way through all the allocated buffers. A deleted node is appended to the free list in the put_node method:

```
void put_node(link_type p)
{
        p->next = free_list;
        free_list = p;
}
```

For example, if "duck" is deleted from the five-pet list in Figure 6.8, then Figure 6.10 shows how the list is affected.

Whenever an insertion—including push_front or push_back—occurs, the free list is checked. If the free list is not empty, its front node is used for the insertion and deleted from the free list. If the free list is empty, next_avail's node is used unless next_avail = last. In that case, a new buffer is allocated and chained to the beginning of the buffer list, and the first node in that new buffer is allocated.

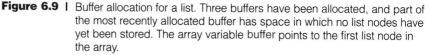

Figure 6.9 I Buffer allocation for a list. Three buffers have been allocated, and part of the most recently allocated buffer has space in which no list nodes have yet been stored. The array variable buffer points to the first list node in the array.

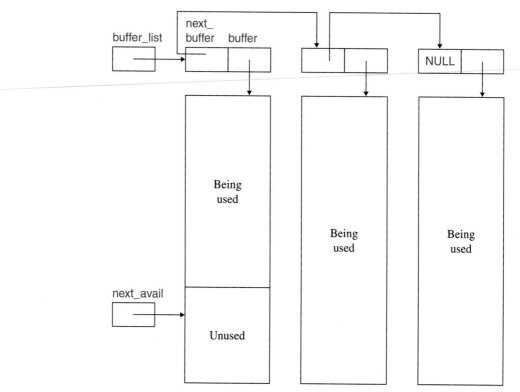

The space for the various buffers and lists is not deallocated until the list is destroyed. So if your application creates a large list and then deletes almost all the items, *all* the list's space will still be allocated.

Lab 15 has still more details of the Hewlett-Packard implementation, and Lab 16 has an experiment comparing vectors, deques, and lists. And now that you have seen several kinds of iterators—random-access and bidirectional—you are ready to study the organization of iterators in the Standard Template Library.

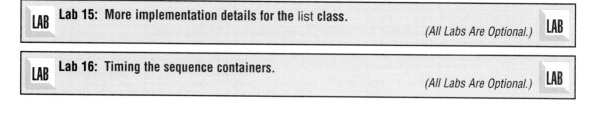

LAB   **Lab 15: More implementation details for the list class.**
                                                                     (All Labs Are Optional.)   **LAB**

LAB   **Lab 16: Timing the sequence containers.**
                                                                     (All Labs Are Optional.)   **LAB**

Figure 6.10 | The list from Figure 6.8 after "duck" is erased. The node with "duck" is now at the head of, in fact the only node in, the free list.

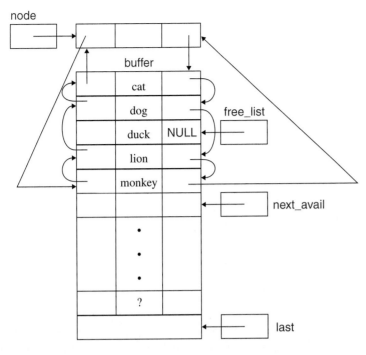

Lab 17: Iterators, part 2.

(All Labs Are Optional.)

As we trumpeted in Section 6.1.4, one of the major, yet subtle features of the Hewlett-Packard implementation is the header node. Because of this node, we did not need a special case for inserting at the front or back, or for removing from the front or back. Each given node always has a node in front of the given node and a node in back of the given node. Specifically, the header node is always located before the first node in a list, and the header node is always located behind the last node in a list.

This advantage of header nodes will become apparent in Section 6.1.6, when we look at alternative implementations of the list class. The implementations are simpler but less efficient than the Hewlett-Packard implementation of the list class. You will get the opportunity, in Project 6.2, to complete one of the implementations outlined in Section 6.1.6.

6.1.6   Alternative Implementations of the list Class

We now explore a few other implementations of the list class. For the sake of simplicity, we will rely on the heap manager's implementation of the new and delete operators for the allocation and deallocation of list nodes. How about the singly linked Linked class from Chapter 2? Here are the fields in the Linked class:

```
protected:
    struct Node
    {
        T item;
        Node* next;
    }; // struct Node

    Node* head;
    Node* tail; // this field was added in Lab 8
    long length;
```

Could we expand the Linked class to satisfy all the method interfaces for the list class? The problem comes with the postconditions—specifically, the time estimates—of some of the list methods.

For example, the postcondition for the pop_back method in the list class does not explicitly include a time estimate. By convention, that means that for any implementation of that method, worstTime(n) must be constant. How would our pop_back method work for the Linked container in Figure 6.11?

The pop_back method would have to make NULL the next field of the node *before* the tail node. And for that task, a loop is needed, so worstTime(n) would be linear in n. That would violate the constant-time requirement of the pop_back method interface in the list class. So we must abandon our attempt at a singly linked implementation of the list class.

What if we modify the Linked class to make it doubly linked? Figure 6.12 shows the corresponding three-item list from Figure 6.11.

Here are the field definitions:

```
protected:
    struct Node
    {
        T item;
        Node* next;
        Node* prev;
    }; // struct Node

    Node* head;
    Node* tail;
    long length;
```

Figure 6.11 I A Linked container with three items. How would a **pop_back** method be defined for this class?

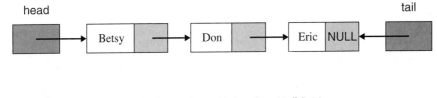

Figure 6.12 I A doubly linked container with **head** and **tail** fields.

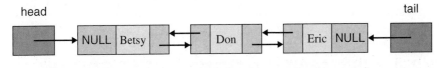

The default constructor would simply set head and tail to NULL and length to 0. But we now have NULL references to watch out for. For example, the push_front method would have a special case for an empty container:

```
void push_front (const T& x)
{
      Node* temp_head = new Node;
      (*temp_head).item = x;
      (*temp_head).next = head;
      (*temp_head).prev = NULL;
      length++;
      if (head == NULL)
      {
            head = temp_head;
            tail = head;
      } // if
      else
      {
            (*head).prev = temp_head;
            head = temp_head;
      } // else

} // method push_front
```

A similar test would be needed for push_back. For pop_front and pop_back, a special case would be needed for removal of the only item in the container. Also, the insert method would first test

```
if (head == NULL || position.node == head)
```

The bottom line for this implementation is that it is encumbered by the special cases for inserting or deleting at the front or back of a list. The Hewlett-Packard implementation avoided special cases by having a dummy node—the header node—that was both in front of the first node in a list *and* in back of the last node.

You will get to flesh out the details of the doubly linked head and tail implementation if you undertake Project 6.2. This version uses the new and delete operators for space management, so it will be somewhat less efficient than the Hewlett-Packard implementation, which has its own memory-management methods (get_node and put_node).

In Section 6.2, we leave behind the nitty-gritty of implementation details and look at an application of the list class: a simple text editor.

APPLICATION 6.2 | LIST APPLICATION: A LINE EDITOR

As an illustration of the list class, let's develop a line editor. A *line editor* is a program that manipulates text, line by line. We assume that each line is at most 75 characters long. The first line of the text is thought of as line 0, and one of the lines is designated the *current line.* Each editing command begins with a dollar sign, and *only* editing commands begin with a dollar sign. There are eight editing commands. Here are four of the commands; the remaining four are specified in Project 6.1.

1. **$Insert**

   Each subsequent line, up to the next editing command, will be inserted in the text *after* the current line. The last line inserted becomes the current line. If the text is empty when $Insert is called, then the insertions become the only lines in the text. For example, suppose the text is empty and we have the following:

   $Insert
   Water, water every where,
   And all the boards did shrink;
   Water, water every where,
   Nor any drop to drink.

   Then after the insertions, the text would be as follows, with ">" to indicate the current line:

   Water, water every where,
   And all the boards did shrink;
   Water, water every where,
   >Nor any drop to drink.

   For another example, suppose the text is

   Now is the
   >time for
   citizens to come to
   the
   aid of their country.

Then the sequence

$Insert
all
good

will cause the text to become

Now is the
time for
all
>good
citizens to come to
the
aid of their country.

2. **$Delete k m**
    Each line in the text between lines *k* and *m*, inclusive, will be deleted. If the
    current line had been in this range, the new current line will be line $k - 1$.
    Otherwise, the current line is the same line that it was before this command.
    For example, suppose the text is

Now is the
time for
all
>good
citizens to come to
the
aid of their country.

The command

$Delete 3 5

will cause the text to become

Now is the
time for
>all
aid of their country.

If *k* has the value 0 and the current line is one of the lines deleted, the interpretation is that, after the deletion, the current line is before any of the lines in
the text. So if the $Insert command follows, the insertions are made *in front of*
the first line of the text. For example, suppose the text is

a
s
>p
a
r
k

and the commands are

$Delete 0 2
$Insert
q
u

then the text becomes

   q
\>u
    a
    r
    k

After the deletion but before the insertion, the current line was before any line in the text. The insertion inserted two lines at the beginning of the text, so the current line is now "u". The following error messages should be printed when appropriate:

*** Error: The first line number > the second.
*** Error: The first line number < 0.
*** Error: The second line number > last line number.
*** Error: The command is not followed by two integers.

3. **$Line m**

   The line whose line number is m becomes the current line. For example, if the text is

     Mairzy doats
      an dozy doats
   \>an liddle lamsy divy.

   then the command

   $Line 0

   will make line 0 the current line:

   \>Mairzy doats
     and dozy doats
     and liddle lamsy divy.

   The command

   $Line −1

   followed by the $Insert command, is used to insert lines at the beginning of the text. An error message should be printed if m is either less than −1 or greater than the last line number in the text. See command 2.

4. **$Done**

   This terminates the execution of the text editor. For convenience, we will print out the final text. An error message should be printed for any illegal command, such as "$End", "$insert", or "?Insert".

System Test 1 The input is in boldface.

Please enter a line:
$Insert

Please enter a line:
This is line zero.

Please enter a line:
This is line one.

Please enter a line:
This is line two.

Please enter a line:
$Line 1

Please enter a line:
$Insert

Please enter a line:
This is line 1.5.

Please enter a line:
This is line 1.6.

Please enter a line:
This is line 1.7.

Please enter a line:
This is line 1.8.

Please enter a line:
$Delete 1 3

Please enter a line:
$Done

Here is the final text:
  This is line zero.
  This is line 1.7.
>This is line 1.8.
  This is line two.

Please press the Enter key to close this output window.

System Test 2 The input is in boldface.

Please enter a line:
Insert
*** Error: Not one of the given commands

Please enter a line:
$Insert

Please enter a line:
a

Please enter a line:

b

Please enter a line:

$line

*** Error: Not one of the given commands

Please enter a line:

$Line 2

*** Error: The line number must be less than the text size.

Please enter a line:

$Done

Here is the final text:

   a

>b

Please press the Enter key to close this output window.

6.2.1 Design of the Editor Class

In order to decide what methods the Editor class should contain, we ask what does an editor have to do? From the editor commands given, some of the responsibilities are apparent:

- To parse the line to see if it is a legal command
- To check the commands for errors
- To manage the text

This is enough to start with. The parse method will interpret a line read in. This method will have the line as its only parameter. What should parse return? For some commands—$Insert, $Delete, and $Line—an error message should be returned if the command cannot be carried out. For some commands—$Done—the entire text should be returned. In Project 6.1, there is a command, $Print, for which either an error message or some text should be returned. How can we distinguish between an error message and text? According to the specifications of the problem, a text line cannot start with a "$", so by prepending that character to any error message, we can tell which is which. The parse method will return a string, representing an error message if the first character is "$", and text for the $Done command (for the $Insert, $Delete, and $Line commands, and for inserting a line, a blank line will be returned if there is no error).

The command_check method will check each command for errors, and for each of the four commands there will be a separate method. Here are the method interfaces:

```
// Postcondition: this Editor is empty.
void Editor( );
```

```
// Postcondition: if line is a legal command, that command has been carried
//                out and the result of carrying out that command has been
//                returned. If line is to be inserted, that has been attempted
//                and the result has been returned. Otherwise, an illegal-
//                command error message has been returned.
string parse (const string& line);


// Postcondition: line has been checked for errors. If no error was found, the
//                command has been processed and the result returned.
//                Otherwise, an error message has been returned.
string command_check (const string& line);


// Postcondition: if line is not too long, it has been inserted into this Editor and
//                a blank line has been returned. Otherwise, an error
//                message has been returned.
string insert _command (const string& line);


// Postcondition: lines k through m of the text have been deleted, if possible,
//                and a blank line has been returned. Otherwise, an
//                error message has been returned.
string delete_command (int k, int m);


// Postcondition: the line at index m has become the current line in the text, if
//                possible, and a blank line has been returned. Otherwise, an
//                error message has been returned.
string line_command (int m);


// Postcondition: the execution of the editor has been completed and the text
//                has been returned.
string done_command( );
```

Before we can start to define these six methods, we have to decide what fields we will have. One of the fields will hold the text, so we'll call it text. The text will be a sequence, and we will often need to make insertions and/or deletions in the interior of the text, so text should be an object in the list class (surprise!).

To keep track of the current line, we could either have an integer field, current LineNumber, or an iterator field, current. Some of the commands—$Delete and $Line—work with line numbers, but list insertions and deletions require iterators, so it is not easy to say which would be better. How about both? We'll try that solution, even though both fields will have to be updated for each insertion and deletion. The **bool** field inserting will determine whether the line entered is to be inserted into the

Editor or is to be treated as a command. All the fields are protected to allow their use by subclasses:

```
protected:
    list<string> text;
    list<string>::iterator current;
    int currentLineNumber;
    bool inserting;
```

Here is the dependency diagram, with two examples of composition:

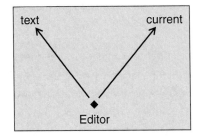

Now that we know the method interfaces and fields, we can implement the Editor class by defining those methods.

6.2.2   **Implementation of the** Editor **Class**

The default constructor explicitly initializes the fields, except text, which is initialized by *its* default constructor.

```
Editor::Editor( )
{
    current = text.begin( );
    currentLineNumber = −1;
    inserting = false;
} // default constructor
```

The parse method determines if the line represents a command or is to be inserted. If neither, the command-start character ('$') is prepended to the error message.

```
string Editor::parse (const string& line)
{
    if (line.substr (0, 1) != COMMAND_START)
        if (inserting)
                return insert_command (line);
        else
                return COMMAND_START +
                    MISSING_COMMAND_ERROR +
                    COMMAND_START;
    return command_check (line);
} // parse
```

The command_check message separates the command from the command arguments and invokes the appropriate command. For the $Delete and $Line commands, we must extract line numbers from the command line. For example, suppose the line contains

$Line 173

The position of the blank is determined with the string method find. The substring "173" starts at the first blank position + 1, and goes until the end of the string. The string method substr returns that substring, which is converted to an array of characters with the string method c_str. Finally, the atoi function converts that array of digit characters into an integer.

```
string Editor::command_check (const string& line)
{
        string command;
        int blank_pos1 = line.find (BLANK),
            blank_pos2;

        if (blank_pos1 >= 0) // line has at least one argument
                command = line.substr (0, blank_pos1);
        else
                command = line;
        if (command == INSERT_COMMAND)
        {
                inserting = true;
                return BLANK;
        } // $Insert
        else
        {
                int k,
                    m;

                inserting = false;

                if (command == DELETE_COMMAND)
                {
                        // find k and m
                        if (blank_pos1 >= 0)
                        {
                                blank_pos2 = line.find (BLANK, blank_pos1 + 1);
                                if (blank_pos2 >= 0)
                                {
                                        k = atoi (line.substr (blank_pos1 + 1,
                                            blank_pos2 - blank_pos1 - 1).c_str( ));
                                        m = atoi (line.substr (blank_pos2 + 1).c_str( ));
                                        return delete_command (k, m);
```

```
                              } // two line numbers given
                              return COMMAND_START +
                                     MISSING_NUMBER_ERROR;
                         } // at least one line number given
                         return COMMAND_START +
                                TWO_NUMBERS_ERROR;
                    } // $Delete
                    else if (command == LINE_COMMAND)
                    {
                         // find m
                         if (blank_pos1 >= 0)
                         {
                              m = atoi (line.substr (blank_pos1 + 1).c_str( ));
                              return line_command (m);
                         } // line number given
                         return COMMAND_START + MISSING_NUMBER_ERROR;
                    } // $Line
                    else if (command == DONE_COMMAND)
                         return done_command( );
                    return COMMAND_START + ILLEGAL_COMMAND_ERROR;
               } // not an insert command
          } // command_check
```

Finally, we get to the real work, managing the list object text. The constant-time insert_command method checks for a line that is too long and, if it is not, inserts line in text *after* the line where current is positioned:

```
     string Editor::insert_command (const string& line)
     {
          if (line.length( ) > MAX_LINE_LENGTH)
               return COMMAND_START + LINE_TOO_LONG_ERROR;
          current = text.insert (++current, line);
          currentLineNumber++;
          return BLANK;
     } // insert
```

The delete_command first checks for errors, such as $k < 0$. Otherwise, we start an iterator first at the beginning of the text and then increment first k times. We then erase the next $m - k$ items in the text. After that loop, we need to update current and currentLineNumber. Notice that deciding whether to update current would be somewhat difficult if we did not have a currentLineNumber field. Here is the definition of the delete_command method:

```
     string Editor::delete_command (int k, int m)
     {
```

```
    if (k < 0)
        return COMMAND_START + FIRST_TOO_SMALL_ERROR;
    if (m >= (int)text.size( ))
        return COMMAND_START + SECOND_TOO_LARGE_ERROR;
    if (k > m)
        return COMMAND_START +
                FIRST_GREATER_THAN_SECOND_ERROR;

    list<string>::iterator first = text.begin( );

    for (int i = 0; i < k; i++)
        first++;

    for (int i = k; i <= m; i++)
        text.erase (first++);

    if (currentLineNumber >= k && currentLineNumber <= m)
    {
        currentLineNumber = k − 1;
        current = −−first;
    } // if
    else if (currentLineNumber > m)
        currentLineNumber −= m + 1 − k ; // current is unchanged
    return BLANK;
    } // delete_command
```

How long does the delete_command method take? Let n represent the number of lines in text. In the worst case, with k = 0 and m = $n − 1$, each line will be erased, and each call to the erase method takes constant time, so worstTime(n) is linear in n. On average, the value of m will be about $n/2$, so the number of iterations—and averageTime(n)—is still linear in n.

The line_command increments or decrements current, depending on where currentLineNumber is in relation to n:

```
    string Editor::line_command (int m)
    {
        if (m < −1)
            return COMMAND_START + FIRST_TOO_SMALL_ERROR;
        if (m >= (int)text.size( ))
            return COMMAND_START + FIRST_TOO_LARGE_ERROR;
        if (currentLineNumber < m)
        {
            for (int i = currentLineNumber; i < m; i++)
                current++;
            currentLineNumber = m;
        } // if
```

```
        else
        {
            for (int i = currentLineNumber; i > m; i--)
                current--;
            currentLineNumber = m;
        } // else
        return BLANK;
} // line_command
```

Let n represent the number of lines of text. In the worst case, when current LineNumber $= -1$ and m $= n - 1$, current will iterate through each line of text, so worstTime(n) is linear in n. On average, the distance between currentLineNumber and m will be about $n/2$, and so the average number of iterations—and average Time(n)—is still linear in n.

For the done_command method, we return the text, including the current line marker:

```
string Editor::done_command( )
{
    const string FINAL_MESSAGE = "Here is the final text: \n"; string
        text_string = FINAL_MESSAGE;

    if (currentLineNumber == -1)
        text_string += " >\n";
    for (list<string>::iterator itr = text.begin( ); itr != text.end( ); itr++)
        if (itr == current)
            text_string += " >" + *itr + "\n";
        else
            text_string += " " + *itr + "\n";
    return text_string;
} // done_command
```

This method iterates through each line of text, so worstTime(n) and averageTime(n) are linear in n.

The main function handles all the input-output for the line-editor application.

The main function defines editor, an Editor object, and then calls editor.parse (line) for each line of input. The result returned is stripped of the leading "$", if there is one, and printed. Inputting a line presents a problem. The extraction operator, operator>>, could be used to read in a command, but we won't know, at that point, whether the line also includes line numbers, as part of the $Delete and $Line commands, for example. That determination is made in the Editor class's methods, which have no input statements. So we will need to read in an entire line, whitespace and all, in the main function. C++ provides the getline function for such occasions. The function interface is

```
// Postcondition: the characters in inStream, stripped of leading whitespace,
//                 from the current character up to '\n', have been stored in line.
istream& getline (istream& inStream, string& line);
```

The Editor methods can then subdivide the line.

Here is the definition, with a do loop to ensure that the result from the $Done command is printed before the loop terminates:

```
int main( )
{
        const string PROMPT = "Please enter a line: ";
        const string CLOSE_WINDOW_PROMPT =
                "Please press the Enter key to close this output window.";

        Editor editor;

        string result;

        string line;

        do
        {
                cout << PROMPT<< endl;
                getline (cin, line);
                result = editor.parse (line);
                if (result.substr (0, 1) != COMMAND_START)
                        cout << result << endl << endl;
                else
                        cout << result.substr (1) << endl << endl;
        } // do
        while (line != DONE_COMMAND);

        cout << CLOSE_WINDOW_PROMPT;
        cin.get( );
        return 0;
} // main
```

There is one iteration of the do loop for each item in the text (there are also other iterations of the loop). So worstTime(n) is at least linear in n. To get a better estimate, we would need to know the sequence of commands.

Without changing the Editor class, the program can be modified to accept file input and send the output to a file. Here is the revised main function.

```
int main( )
{
        const string IN_PROMPT = "Please enter the path for the input file: ";

        const string OUT_PROMPT =
                "Please enter the path for the output file: ";

        const string ECHO = "The line was: ";

        const string CLOSE_WINDOW_PROMPT =
                "Please press the Enter key to close this output window.";
```

```
        Editor editor;

        string result;

        string inFileName,
                outFileName,
                line;

        fstream inFile,
                outFile;

    cout << IN_PROMPT;
    cin >> inFileName;
    cout << OUT_PROMPT;
    cin >> outFileName;
    inFile.open (inFileName.c_str( ), ios::in);
    outFile.open (outFileName.c_str( ), ios::out);

    do
    {
        getline (inFile, line);
        outFile << ECHO << line << endl;
        result = editor.parse (line);
        if (result.substr (0, 1) != COMMAND_START)
            outFile << result << endl << endl;
        else
            outFile << result.substr (1) << endl << endl;
    } // do
    while (line != DONE_COMMAND);
    outFile.close( );

    cout << CLOSE_WINDOW_PROMPT;
    cin.get( );
    return 0;
} // main
```

All the relevant files are available from the Source Code link on the book's website.

SUMMARY

The focus of this chapter is the list class. Lists are sequential containers that lack the random-access ability of vectors and deques. But they take only constant time for insertions and deletions in the interior—versus linear time for vectors and deques. This constant-time aspect holds because the insert and erase methods require as a parameter an iterator that is positioned where the insertion or deletion is to occur.

The application, a simple line editor, took advantage of the list class's ability to quickly make multiple insertions and deletions anywhere in the list.

EXERCISES

6.1   a.   Suppose we define the following:

```
list <char> letters;
list<char>::iterator itr;
```

Show the sequence of letters in the list after each of the following messages is sent:

```
itr = letters.begin( );
letters.insert (itr, 'f');
letters.insert (itr, 'e');
itr++;
letters.insert (itr, 'r');
itr++;
itr++;
letters.insert (itr, 't'); // Hint: we now have e,r,f,t
letters.insert (itr, 'e');
letters.erase (letters.begin( ));
itr--;
itr--;
letters.insert (itr, 'p');
itr++;
letters.insert (itr, 'e');
itr = letters.end( );
itr--;
letters.insert (itr, 'c');
```

b.   Write the code to print out the final contents of letters in part a.

c.   Redo part a, with letters being an array of characters instead of a list of characters.

d.   Redo part a, with letters being a string instead of a list of characters.

e.   Redo part a, with letters being a vector of characters instead of a string.

f.   Redo part a, with letters being a deque of characters instead of a string.

6.2   Compare lists with vectors and deques with respect to the Big-O time for access, insertions, and deletions.

6.3   Show the effect of the following messages on the list in Figure 6.4, repeated here:

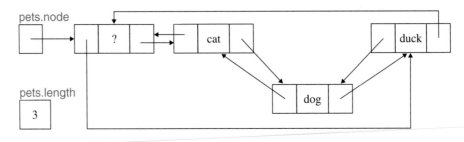

```
list<string>::iterator position = pets.begin( );
pets.push_front('bunny"):
pets.erase (position);
pets.push_back ('frog");
```

6.4   Which do you think would provide a faster implementation of the very_long_int class: a vector, a deque, or a list? Why?

6.5   Suppose that the list class utilized the heap manager—with the new and delete operators—for memory allocation and deallocation. Define the insert method and the one-parameter erase method.

6.6   In the Editor class's delete_command method, the variables k and m are of type **int**. Why would it be a mistake if the type of k were **unsigned**?

6.7   Suppose myList is a list object whose items are of type **double**. Write the code to print out the items in reverse order.

6.8   Figure 6.10 is repeated here:

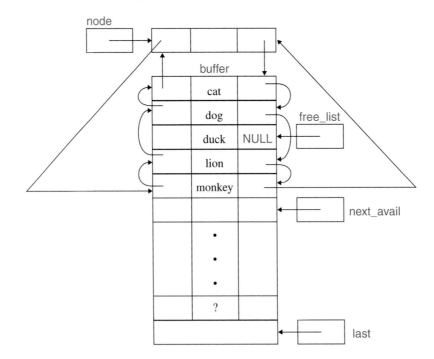

If "lion" is deleted from this list, what will that node's next field point to:

a. The node whose item is "cat"?

b. The node whose item is "dog"?

c. The node whose item is "duck"?

d. The header node?

Hint   The deleted node becomes the front node in the free list.

6.9   If the list class were designed with head and tail fields, we could avoid NULL values for the prev and next fields in each list node by making the list circular. That is—in a nonempty list—the head node's prev field would point to the tail node, and the tail node's next field would point to the head node. What effect would this design have on the implementation of the begin, end, and push_front methods?

PROGRAMMING PROJECT 6.1

Extending the Editor Class

Extend the Editor class to include methods with the following interfaces:

5.   **$Change**
     %X%Y%

In the current line, each occurrence of the string given by X will be replaced by the string given by Y. For example, suppose the current line is

bear ruin'd choirs, wear late the sweet birds sang

Then the command

$Change
%ear%are%

will cause the current line to become

bare ruin'd choirs, ware late the sweet birds sang

If we then issue the command

$Change
%wa%whe%

we would get

bare ruin'd choirs, where late the sweet birds sang

Notes
1.   If either X or Y contains a percent sign, the end-user should select another delimiter. For example,

     $Change
     #0.16#16%#

2.   The string given by Y may be the empty string. For example, if current line is

     aid of their country.

     then the command

     $Change
     %of %%

     will change the current line to

     aid their country.

3.   If the delimiter occurs fewer than three times, the error message to be printed is

     *** Error: Delimiter must occur three times.

6. **$Last**

The line number of the last line in the text will be printed. For example, if the text is

> I heard a bird sing
> \> in the dark of December.
> A magical thing
> and a joy to remember.

then

$Last

will cause **3** to be printed. The text and the designation of the current line are unchanged.

7. **$Print k m**

Each line number and line in the text, from lines *k* through *m*, inclusive, will be printed. For example, if the text is

> Winston Churchill once said that
> \> democracy is the worst
> form of government
> except for all the others.

then command

$Print 0 2

will cause the following to be printed:

0 Winston Churchill once said that
1 democracy is the worst
2 form of government

The text and the designation of the current line are unchanged. As in command 2, an error message should be printed if (1) *k* is greater than *m*, or if (2) *k* is less than 0 or *m* is greater than the last line number in the text.

System Test 1   Sample input is in boldface.

Please enter a line:
$Insert

Please enter a line:
You can fool

Please enter a line:
some of the people

Please enter a line:
some of the times,

(continued on next page)

(continued from previous page)

Please enter a line:
but you cannot foul

Please enter a line:
all of the peeple

Please enter a line:
all of the time.

Please enter a line:
$Line 2

Please enter a line:
$Print 2 1
*** Error: The first line number > the second.

Please enter a line:
$Print 2 2

2 some of the times,

Please enter a line:
$Change %s%%

Please enter a line:
$Print 2 2

2 ome of the time,

Please enter a line:
$Change %o%so
*** Error: Delimiter must occur three times.

Please enter a line:
$Change %o%so%

Please enter a line:
$Print 2 2

2 some sof the time,

Please enter a line:
Change
*** Error: Command must begin with $.

Please enter a line:
$Change %sof%of%

Please enter a line:
$Print 2 2

2 some of the time,

Please enter a line:
$Line -1

Please enter a line:
$Insert

Please enter a line:
Lincoln once said that

Please enter a line:
you can fool

Please enter a line:
some of the people

Please enter a line:
all the time and

Please enter a line:
all of the time and

Please enter a line:
$Last

10

Please enter a line:
$Print 0 10

0 Lincoln once said that
1 you can fool
2 some of the people
3 all the time and
4 all of the time and
5 You can fool
6 some of the people
7 some of the time,
8 but you cannot foul
9 all of the peeple
10 all of the time.

Please enter a line:
$Line 5

(continued on next page)

(continued from previous page)

Please enter a line:
$Change %Y%y%

Please enter a line:
$Print 5 5

5 you can fool

Please enter a line:
$Line 6

Please enter a line:
$Change %some%all%

Please enter a line:
$Print 6 6

6 all of the people

Please enter a line:
$Line 8

Please enter a line:
$Change %ul%ol%

Please enter a line:
$Print 8 8

8 but you cannot fool

Please enter a line:
$Line 9

Please enter a line:
$Change %ee%eo%

Please enter a line:
$Print 9 9

9 all of the people

Please enter a line:
$Delete 3 3

Please enter a line:
$Print 0 10
*** Error: The second line number is greater than the number of lines in the text.

Please enter a line:
$Last

9

Please enter a line:
$Print 0 9

0 Lincoln once said that
1 you can fool
2 some of the people
3 all of the time and
4 you can fool
5 all of the people
6 some of the time,
7 but you cannot fool
8 all of the people
9 all of the time.

Please enter a line:
$Done

Here is the final text:
   Lincoln once said that
   you can fool
   some of the people
   all of the time and
   you can fool
   all of the people
   some of the time,
   but you cannot fool
>all of the people
   all of the time.

Please press the Enter key to close this output window.

System Test 1   Sample input is in boldface.

Please enter a line:
$Insert

Please enter a line:
Life is full of

Please enter a line:
successes and lessons.

Please enter a line:
$Delete 1 1

(continued on next page)

(continued from previous page)

Please enter a line:
$Insert

Please enter a line:
wondrous oppurtunities disguised as

Please enter a line:
hopeless situations.

Please enter a line:
$Last

2

Please enter a line:
$Print 0 2

0 Life is full of
1 wondrous oppurtunities disguised as
2 hopeless situations.

Please enter a line:
$Line 1

Please enter a line:
$Change %ur%or%

Please enter a line:
$Print 0 2

0 Life is full of
1 wondrous opportunities disguised as
2 hopeless situations.

Please enter a line:
$Done

  Here is the final text:
  Life is full of
>wondrous opportunities disguised as
  hopeless situations.

Please press the Enter key to close this output window.

An Alternate Design and Implementation of the list Class

Implement the doubly linked, head-and-tail design of the list class described in Section 6.1.6. The only list methods you need to implement for this project are the first thirteen methods given in Section 6.1.1. Set up a driver to validate your implementation. You will also need to implement at least a few iterator operators: *, !=, and ++ (either preincrement or postincrement).

CHAPTER 7

Queues and Stacks

In this chapter we introduce two more data structures in the Standard Template Library: the queue class and the stack class. Queues and stacks can be accessed or modified in only a limited way, so each has very few method interfaces: fewer than 10, versus at least 40 for each of the vector, deque, and list classes. And the implementations of these classes are straightforward. In fact, these classes "adapt" the implementations of some underlying container class. For example, any container class that has push_back, pop_back, back, empty, and size methods can serve as the underlying class for the stack class. Best of all, queues and stacks have a wide variety of applications. We'll start with the queue class because most of its applications are general-purpose, whereas stacks are utilized mainly within a computer system. ∎

CHAPTER OBJECTIVES

1. Be able to define the properties of queues and stacks.

2. Understand why the queue and stack classes are called "container adaptors."

3. Examine the role of queues in computer simulation.

4. Examine the role of stacks in the implementation of recursion and in converting from infix notation to postfix notation.

7.1 | QUEUES

A *queue* is a finite sequence of items in which

1. Insertions are allowed only at the back
2. Deletions, retrievals, and modifications are allowed only at the front

The items in a queue are stored in chronological order: first in, first out.

    The items in a queue are stored in chronological order: The first item inserted—at the back—will eventually be the first item to be deleted, retrieved, or modified—from the front. The second item inserted will be the second item to be deleted, retrieved, or modified, and so on. This defining property of queues is sometimes referred to as "first come, first served," "first in, first out," or simply FIFO. Figure 7.1 shows a queue through several stages of insertions and deletions.

    Examples of queues are numerous:

> Cars in line at a drive-up window
> Fans waiting to buy tickets to a ball game
> Customers in a checkout line at a supermarket
> Airplanes waiting to take off from an airport.

Figure 7.1 | A queue through several stages of insertions and deletions.

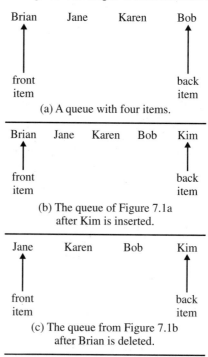

(a) A queue with four items.

(b) The queue of Figure 7.1a
after Kim is inserted.

(c) The queue from Figure 7.1b
after Brian is deleted.

We could continue listing queue examples almost indefinitely. In Section 7.3 we will present an application of queues in the field of computer simulation.

7.1.1 Method Interfaces of the queue Class

As with the other container classes in the Standard Template Library, the queue class is a template class:

template <**class** T, **class** Container = deque<T> >

In addition to the item type T, each instance of a queue also has a container template, with deque<T> as the default. The implicit idea behind this is that a deque can handle, in constant time on average, the defining attributes of a queue: back insertions, front deletions, and front accesses. We'll look at this aspect of queues when we consider implementations.

Unlike the sequential container classes from Chapters 5 and 6, the queue container class has a minimal interface. Here are the interfaces for *all* the methods:

1. // Precondition: this queue has been initialized with a copy of this Container.
    explicit queue (**const** Container& = Container( ));

> *Note* The reserved word **explicit**—used only with constructors—indicates to the compiler that no automatic type conversion[1] should be performed on the constructor's argument. That is, the constructor's argument—if one is supplied—must be a container object in the Container class specified in the second template argument. For example, here are some legal queue definitions:
>
> **a.** queue<string> q1;
> **b.** queue<string, deque<string> >q2 (q1);
> **c.** queue<string> q3 (q1);
> **d.** queue<**double,** list<**double**> > q4;
> **e.** queue<**double,** list<**double**> > q5 (q4);
>
> The definitions of q1, q2, and q3 are equivalent, as are the definitions of q4 and q5. On the other hand, the following two definitions are illegal:
>
> **f.** queue<string, list<string> > q6 (q1);
>   // constructor argument should be a list
>
> **g.** queue<**double**> > q7 (q4);
>   //constructor argument should be a deque

---

[1]Recall that in the list class's iterator class in Chapter 6, an automatic type conversion converted a pointer to an iterator.

2. // Postcondition: true has been returned if this queue is empty. Otherwise, false
    //   has been returned.
    bool empty( ) **const**;

3. // Postcondition: the number of items in this queue object has been returned.
    unsigned size( ) **const**;

4. // Postcondition: the item x has been inserted at the back of this queue. The
    //   averageTime(n) is constant. The worstTime(n) is O(n), but for
    //   n consecutive pushes, worstTime(n) for all n pushes is only
    //   O(n). That is, amortizedTime(n) is constant.
    void push (**const** value_type& x);

> *Note 1*   This method is often referred to as "enqueue".

> *Note 2*   A **typedef** declares value_type to be a synonym for T.

5. // Precondition: this queue is not empty.
    // Postcondition: a reference to the item at the front of this queue has been
    //   returned.
    T& front( );

> *Note*   Because the value returned is a reference, this method can be
> used to modify the front item in a queue. For example, if my_queue is a
> nonempty queue of strings,

> my_queue.front( ) = "Courtney";

> replaces the front item in my_queue with "Courtney".

6. // Precondition: this queue is not empty.
    // Postcondition: a constant reference to the item at the front of this queue has
    //   been returned.
    const T& front( );

> *Note*   Because the value returned is a constant reference, this method
> *cannot* be used to modify the front item in a queue. But we can use this
> method to retrieve that front item. For example, if my_queue is a non-
> empty queue,

> cout << my_queue.front( );

> will print out the front item in my_queue.

7.   // Precondition: this queue is not empty.
　　　// Postcondition: the item that had been at the front of this queue before this
　　　//　　　　　　call has been deleted from this queue.
　　　void pop( );

> *Note 1*   The pop method does not return the item popped. To retrieve
> that item, call front( ) before calling pop( ).

> *Note 2*   This method is often referred to as "dequeue" (not "deque").

8.   // Precondition: this queue is not empty.
　　　// Postcondition: a reference to the item at the back of this queue has been
　　　//　　　　　　returned.
　　　T& back( );

> *Note 1*   The definition of a queue does not require a back method, but
> the Standard Template Library includes that method.

> *Note 2*   This method can be used to modify the last item inserted in a
> queue.

9.   // Precondition: this queue is not empty.
　　　// Postcondition: a constant reference to the item at the back of this queue has
　　　//　　　　　　been returned.
　　　const T& back( );

Recall our convention that when no time estimates are given, the method's worst
Time(n) is constant. So for all methods except push, worstTime(n) is constant. For
the push method, worstTime(n) is $O(n)$, but amortizedTime(n) is constant. For all the
methods in the queue class, averageTime(n) is constant.

The queue class does not have an associated iterator class. Why not? According
to the definition of a queue, the only accessible item in a queue object is the item at
the front of the queue. So it would violate the definition of a queue if we could retrieve
each one of the items. (In fact, the back methods violate the definition of a queue.)

In Section 7.1.2, you'll see how easy it is to use the queue class.

7.1.2   Using the queue Class

The queue class has few methods, and *no iterators*. That does not mean you cannot
print out a queue, for example, but it requires a little extra work. For example, here
is a program that generates the queue in Figure 7.1. By making the queue a value

formal parameter, the printQueue function allows us to print out a copy of a queue without destroying the queue.

```cpp
#include <iostream>
#include <string>
#include <queue>
using namespace std;

void printQueue (queue<string> names)
{
    cout << endl << endl << "Here is the current queue:" << endl;
    while (!names.empty( ))
    {
        cout << names.front( ) << endl;
        names.pop( );
    } // while
} // function printQueue

int main( )
{
    const string CLOSE_WINDOW_PROMPT =
        "Please press the Enter key to close this output window.";

    queue<string> names;

    names.push ("Brian");
    names.push ("Jane");
    names.push ("Karen");
    names.push ("Bob");
    printQueue (names);

    names.push ("Kim");
    printQueue (names);

    names.pop( );
    printQueue (names);

    cout << endl << endl << CLOSE_WINDOW_PROMPT;
    cin.get( );
    return 0;
} // main
```

In the main function, the argument names in the call to printQueue is unchanged, but the trade-off is that the printQueue method has to make a copy of that argument.

As you might guess, the implementation of the queue class is fairly simple—just how simple might surprise you! Section 7.1.3 shows that the work is already done.

7.1.3   Container Adaptors

From what you know already about the Standard Template Library, you may well conclude that a compiler writer is free to design and implement the queue class in any way that satisfies the given method interfaces. That is not the case. In fact, the design and implementation of the queue class are part of the Standard Template Library, not the option of a compiler writer.

The queue class is an example of a container adaptor. A ***container adaptor*** C transforms some underlying container into a container of class C. The container adaptors—queue, stack, and priority_queue—are handled differently from the rest of the Standard Template Library. Their method definitions *must* invoke the underlying container's methods.

*A **container adaptor** C uses some underlying container object to define C's methods.*

In the case of the queue class, all that is required of the underlying class Container is that it supports the empty, size, front, push_back, and pop_front methods (and the back method). For example, here is part of the definition of the queue class in the Standard Template Library:

```
template <class T, class Container = deque<T>>
class queue
{
    protected:
        Container c;
    public:
        void pop( ) { c.pop_front( ); }
        const T& front( ) const { return c.front( ); }
```

As a user or implementer of the queue class, the only choice you have is what to use for the underlying class. The list class can serve as the underlying class. Recall that the list class has size, empty, push_back. pop_front, front, and back methods.

Also the deque class can serve as the underlying class; in fact, the deque class is the default. In the Hewlett-Packard implementation of the deque class, the size, empty, pop_front, front, and back methods take constant time. For the push_back method, averageTime(n) is constant. The worstTime(n)—which occurs when the map array must be resized—is linear in n, but then the next n back insertions will each take constant time. That is, for the push_back method in the deque class, amoritizedTime(n) is constant.

The vector class will not suffice as the underlying class: there is no pop_front method. This was not an oversight on the part of the Standard Template Library creators. Rather, this intentional omission was meant as a warning to users that for removing the front item in a vector, worstTime(n) is linear in n (for all implementations based on the Hewlett-Packard implementation).

If you have some other container class lying around that has these methods, you could define a queue object in terms of that other class. For example, with a little work on your part, the Linked class could be expanded enough to serve as the adapted class; see Exercise 7.7. Section 7.1.4 develops another adapted class for the queue container adaptor.

7.1.4 A Contiguous Design

We have noted that the vector class could not serve as the underlying class for a queue because the vector class lacks a pop_front method. Another option, also array-based, directly manipulates an array field to achieve constant time, on average, for calls to push_back and pop_front. For the design of this underlying class, queueArray, there are five fields:

T[ ] data;

unsigned size;

int head,
    tail,
    max_size;   // maximum number of items that can be stored in data

The data array holds the items, size holds the number of items, and max_size holds the maximum number of items (before a resizing must be done). The front item is always at index head, but head does not always have the value 0. Basically, the queue "slides down" the array data as calls to push_back and pop_front occur. The head field contains the index, in data, of the queue's front item, and the tail field contains the index of the queue's back item. We initialize tail to -1 to indicate that the queue is empty. Figure 7.2 shows the effect on these fields of two calls to push_back and a call to pop_front. A question mark indicates an unknown or irrelevant value.

Figure 7.2 has several interesting features. First, notice that tail is incremented during each call to push_back. During a call to pop_front, items are not physically removed. In Figure 7.2d, "Kay" is still at data[0]. All that happens during a pop_front is that head is incremented to indicate that the front item of the queue is at the next higher index. But if we increment tail during each call to push_back and increment head during each call to pop_front, we could eventually arrive at the four-item queue shown in Figure 7.3.

What happens if we now use the push_back method to enqueue "Jason"? The size of the container object queueArray is only 4, so there is no need to increase the length of the array data. We could move the four items to indices 0 through 3 and then insert "Jason" at index 4. But we should avoid moving items if we can. Do you see an alternative? The slot at index 0 is available, so let's put "Jason" there. Figure 7.4 shows the result.

The container object queueArray shown in Figure 7.4 is *circular:* the item at index 0 follows the item at index 99 in the array data. This arrangement takes some getting used to because we can have tail < head. But the beauty of it is that such calls to push_back take constant time. And with the same idea—and allowing head to advance to 0 after 99—calls to pop_front also take constant time. The only noncon-

Figure 7.2 | An array-based underlying container for a queue: (**a**) initially, (**b**) after push_back ("Kay"), (**c**) after push_back ("Bob"), (**d**) after pop_front( ).

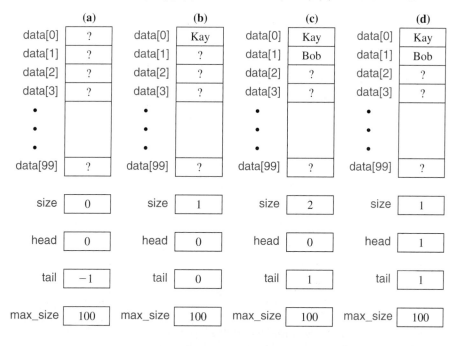

stant operation is the expansion of the array when size = max_size and push_back is called. In that case, we create an array with twice the room and copy the old items to the new array. This takes linear time, but occurs only once per n calls to push_back, so amoritizedTime(n) is constant, and therefore averageTime(n) is constant.

The implementation details are left to Project 7.4. Now let's look at an area in which many applications of queues are found: computer simulation.

7.2 | COMPUTER SIMULATION

A *system* is a collection of interacting parts. We are often interested in studying the behavior of a system, for example, an economic system, a political system, an ecological system, or even a computer system. Because systems are usually complicated, we may utilize a model to make our task manageable. A *model,* that is, a simplification of a system, is designed so that we may study the behavior of the system.

A *physical model* is similar to the system it represents, except in scale or intensity. For example, we might create a physical model of tidal movements in the Chesapeake Bay or of a proposed shopping center. War games, spring training, and scrimmages are also examples of physical models. Unfortunately, some systems cannot be modeled physically with currently available technology—there is, as yet, no

*A **model**—a simplification of a system—allows us to study the behavior of the system.*

Figure 7.3 I The four items in the queue are at indices 96 through 99.

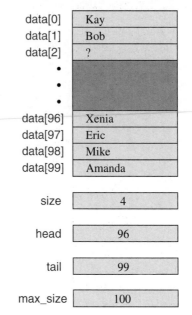

Figure 7.4 I The container object queueArray has five items stored in the array data: the first four items are at indices 96 through 99, and the last item is at index 0.

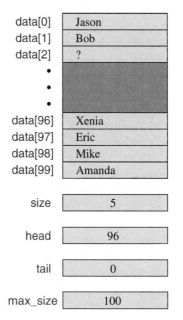

physical substance that could be expected to behave like the weather. Often, as with pilot training, a physical model may be too expensive, too dangerous, or simply inconvenient.

Sometimes we may be able to represent the system with a ***mathematical model:*** a set of assumptions, variables, constants, and equations pertaining to the system. A mathematical model is certainly more tractable than a physical model. In many cases, such as distance = rate * time and the Pythagorean Theorem, the equations can be solved analytically in a reasonable amount of time. But sometimes this is not the case. For example, most differential equations cannot be solved analytically, and an economic model with thousands of equations cannot be solved by hand in a reasonable period of time.

In such cases the mathematical model is usually represented by a computer program. Computer models are essential in studying complex systems such as weather forecasting, space flight, and urban planning. The use of computer models is called "computer simulation." There are several advantages to working with a computer model rather than the original system:

Computer models permit the efficient simulation of complex systems.

1. *Safety.* Flight simulators can assail pilot trainees with a welter of dangerous situations such as hurricanes and hijackings, but no one gets hurt.[2]

2. *Economy.* Simulation games in business policy courses enable students to run a hypothetical company in competition with other students. If the company goes "belly up," the only recrimination is a lower grade for the students.

3. *Speed.* The computer usually makes predictions soon enough for you to act on them. This feature is essential in almost every simulation, from the stock market to national defense.

4. *Flexibility.* If the results you get do not conform to the system you are studying, you can change your model. This is an example of ***feedback:*** a process in which the factors that produce a result are themselves affected by that result. See Figure 7.5.

These benefits are so compelling that computer simulation has become the accepted method for studying complex systems. This is not to say that computer simulation is a panacea for all systems problems. The simplification required to model a system necessarily introduces a disparity between the model and the system. For example, suppose you had developed a computer simulation of the Earth's ecosystem 30 years ago. You probably would have disregarded the effects of CFCs (chlorofluorocarbons). Virtually all environmental scientists now believe that CFCs seriously damage the ozone layer.

---

[2]Except once, when a trainee panicked because one of his engines failed during a simulated blizzard. He "bailed out" of his simulated cockpit and broke his ankle when he hit the unsimulated floor.

Figure 7.5 | Feedback in computer simulation.

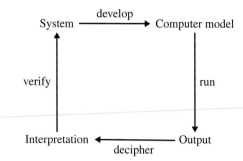

Another disadvantage of computer simulation is that its results are often interpreted as predictions, and prediction is always a risky business. For this reason, a disclaimer such as the following usually precedes the results of a computer simulation: "If the relationships among the variables are as described and if the initial conditions are as described, then the consequences will probably be as follows. . . ."

7.3 | QUEUE APPLICATION: A SIMULATED CAR WASH

Queues are employed in many simulations. For example, we now illustrate the use of a queue in simulating traffic flow at Speedo's Car Wash.

Problem

Given the arrival times at the car wash, calculate the average waiting time per car.

Analysis

We assume that there is one station in the car wash; that is, there is one "server." Each car takes exactly 10 minutes to get washed. At any time there can be at most five cars waiting—in the queue—to be washed. If an arrival occurs when there is a car being washed and there are five cars in the queue, that arrival is turned away as an "overflow" and not counted.

The average waiting time is determined by adding up the waiting times for each car and dividing by the number of cars. The sentinel is 999. Here are the details regarding arrivals and departures:

1. If an arrival and departure occur during the same minute, the departure is processed first.
2. If a car arrives when the queue is empty and no cars are being washed, the car starts getting washed immediately; it is not put on the queue.
3. A car leaves the queue, and stops waiting, once the car starts through the 10-minute wash cycle.

System Test 1   Input is in boldface.

Please enter the next arrival time. The sentinel is 999.
1

Please enter the next arrival time. The sentinel is 999.
3

Please enter the next arrival time. The sentinel is 999.
5

Please enter the next arrival time. The sentinel is 999
8

Please enter the next arrival time. The sentinel is 999
8

Please enter the next arrival time. The sentinel is 999
15

departure time = 11

Please enter the next arrival time. The sentinel is 999
999

departure time = 21
departure time = 31
departure time = 41
departure time = 51
departure time = 61

The average waiting time, in minutes, was 19.3333.

Please press the Enter key to close this output window.

System Test 2   Input is in boldface.

Please enter the next arrival time. The sentinel is 999.
5

Please enter the next arrival time. The sentinel is 999.
5

Please enter the next arrival time. The sentinel is 999.
7

Please enter the next arrival time. The sentinel is 999.
12

Please enter the next arrival time. The sentinel is 999.
12

Please enter the next arrival time. The sentinel is 999.
13

Please enter the next arrival time. The sentinel is 999.
14
Overflow

Please enter the next arrival time. The sentinel is 999.
18
departure time = 15
Please enter the next arrival time. The sentinel is 999.
19
overflow
Please enter the next arrival time. The sentinel is 999.
25
departure time = 25
Please enter the next arrival time. The sentinel is 999.
999
departure time = 35
departure time = 45
departure time = 55
departure time = 65
departure time = 75
departure time = 85
The average waiting time, in minutes, was 27.875.
Please press the Enter key to close this output window.

7.3.1 PROGRAM DESIGN

The major class we will work with is CarWash. The simulation will be *event driven,* that is, the pivotal decision in processing is whether the next event will be an arrival or a departure.

For now, three methods can be identified. Their interfaces are as follows:

```
// Postcondition: the car wash is empty.
CarWash( );
```

```
// Postcondition: all of the arrivals and departures have been processed.
void runSimulation( );
```

```
// Postcondition: the average waiting time, or an error message, has been
//                printed.
void printResult( );
```

The next step in the design of the CarWash class is to choose its fields. We'll start with some variables needed to solve the problem and then select the fields from those variables. The cars waiting to be washed should be saved in chronological order, so one of the variables needed will be the queue carQueue. Each item in car Queue is a Car object, so we temporarily suspend development of the CarWash class in order to determine the methods the Car class should have.

When a car leaves the queue to enter the wash station, we can calculate that car's waiting time by subtracting the car's arrival time from the current time. So the Car class will provide, at least, a getArrivalTime( ) method that returns the arrival time of the car that was just popped (that is, dequeued).

We now continue with the task of determining needed variables in the CarWash class. As indicated in the previous paragraph, we should have waitingTime and current Time variables. To calculate the average waiting time, we need the variables number OfCars and sumOfWaitingTimes. How do we decide whether the next event is an arrival or a departure? We can make this decision based on the variables next ArrivalTime (which is read in) and nextDepartureTime. When there is no car being washed, we want to process an arrival, so we will set the nextDepartureTime variable to a large number—say 10,000—in that case.

At this point, we have amassed seven variables. Which of these should be fields? A simple heuristic (rule of thumb) is that most of a class's public methods should use most of the class's fields; see Riel (1996) for more details. Clearly, the printResult method uses only the variables sumOfWaitingTimes and numberOfCars. And the run Simulation method uses all the variables. So the decision on fields comes down to this: Which variables must be initialized in the constructor?

Because carQueue is an object, it will automatically be initialized when it is defined, so it need not be a field. Nonobjects that must be initialized are sumOfWaiting Times, numberOfCars, currentTime, and nextDepartureTime; these will be fields. There is no need to initialize waitingTime (the difference between currentTime and the value returned by getArrivalTime( )), and nextArrivalTime (its value is read in).

Here is CarWash.h so far:

```
#ifndef CAR_WASH
#define CAR_WASH

#include <string>
#include <queue>
#include <iostream>

#include "car.h"

using namespace std;

class CarWash
{
    public:
            // Postcondition: this CarWash has been initialized.
            CarWash( );

            // Postcondition:  all of the arrivals and departures for this
            //                 CarWash have been processed.
            void runSimulation( );
```

```
        // Postcondition: the average waiting time, or an error message,
        //                  has been printed.
        void printResult( );


    protected:

        const static int INFINITY; // indicates no car being washed

        const static int MAX_SIZE; // maximum cars allowed in
                                    // carQueue

        const static int WASH_TIME; // minutes to wash one car

        int currentTime,
            nextDepartureTime,
            numberOfCars,
            sumOfWaitingTimes;
}; // class CarWash
#endif
```

There is no dependency diagram because the **CarWash** class has no fields that are objects.

7.3.2　IMPLEMENTATION OF THE CarWash CLASS

We can start on the method definitions since we have finished, at least for now, the selection of fields. The definition of the constructor is straightforward:

```
CarWash::CarWash( )
{
    currentTime = 0;
    numberOfCars = 0;
    sumOfWaitingTimes = 0;
    nextDepartureTime = INFINITY;
} // default constructor
```

Before we go any further, here are the constant definitions:

```
const int CarWash::INFINITY = 10000;
const int CarWash::MAX_SIZE = 5;
const int CarWash::WASH_TIME = 10;
```

The definition of the runSimulation method illustrates that this is an event-based simulation. For each nextArrivalTime value read in, if that time is less than the next DepartureTime value, we process an arrival and read in another nextArrivalTime value. Otherwise, we process a departure. When the sentinel is reached, we need to wash the car in the wash station and all the cars that are still in the queue.

The method definition is fairly simple because we postpone the work of processing an arrival or departure:

```
void CarWash::runSimulation( )
{
      const string PROMPT =
            "\nPlease enter the next arrival time. The sentinel is ";

      const int SENTINEL = 999;
      queue <Car> carQueue;

      int nextArrivalTime;

      cout << PROMPT << SENTINEL << endl;
      cin >> nextArrivalTime;
      while (nextArrivalTime != SENTINEL)
      {
            if (nextArrivalTime < nextDepartureTime)
            {
                  processArrival (nextArrivalTime, carQueue);
                  cout << PROMPT << SENTINEL << endl;
                  cin >> nextArrivalTime;
            } // if
            else
                  processDeparture (carQueue);
      } // while SENTINEL not reached

      // Wash any cars remaining on the carQueue.
      while (nextDepartureTime < INFINITY)
            processDeparture (carQueue);
} // runSimulation
```

Here are the interfaces for the **protected** methods processArrival and process
Departure:

```
// Postcondition: the car that arrived at nextArrivalTime has either been
//                turned away—if carQueue was full before this message was
//                sent—or has entered this CarWash.
void processArrival (int nextArrivalTime, queue<Car>& carQueue);

// Postcondition: a car has finished getting washed and carQueue, if non-
//                empty, has been popped.
void processDeparture (queue<Car>& carQueue);
```

To process an arrival, we first update the currentTime field and check for an
overflow. If this arrival is not an overflow, the numberOfCars field is incremented
and the car either starts getting washed (if the server is empty) or is enqueued on the
carQueue object. Here is the code:

```
void processArrival (int nextArrivalTime, queue <Car>& carQueue)
{
```

```
                const string OVERFLOW = "Overflow";
                currentTime = nextArrivalTime;
                if (carQueue.size( ) == MAX_SIZE)
                        cout << OVERFLOW << endl;
                else
                {
                        numberOfCars++;
                        if (nextDepartureTime == INFINITY)
                                nextDepartureTime = currentTime + WASH_TIME;
                        else
                                carQueue.push (Car (nextArrivalTime));
                } // not an overflow
        } // method processArrival
```

This method reveals how the Car class gets involved: there is a constructor with nextArrivalTime as its argument. Here are the header and source files for the Car class:

```
// Car.h
#ifndef CAR
#define CAR
class Car
{
        public:
                // Postcondition: this Car has been initialized.
                Car ( );
                // Postcondition: this Car has been initialized by nextArrivalTime.
                Car (int nextArrivalTime);

                // Postcondition: this Car's arrival time has been returned
                int getArrivalTime( );

        protected:
                int arrivalTime;
}; // class Car
#endif

// Car.cpp

#include "car.h"
Car::Car( ) { }
Car::Car (int nextArrivalTime)
{
        arrivalTime = nextArrivalTime;
} // constructor

int Car::getArrivalTime( )
{
```

```
    return arrivalTime;
} // method getArrivalTime
```

For this project, we could easily have avoided the Car class, but a subsequent extension of the project might require more knowledge about a car—its perimeter, whether it is a convertible, the number of axles, and so on.

To process a departure, we first update the currentTime field and then check to see if there are any cars in the carQueue object. If so, we dequeue the front car, calculate its waiting time, add that to the sumOfWaitingTimes value, and begin washing that car. Otherwise, we set the nextDepartureTime field to a large number to indicate that no car is now being washed. Here is the definition:

```
void CarWash::processDeparture (queue <Car >& carQueue)
{
    int waitingTime;

    cout << "departure time = " << nextDepartureTime << endl;
    currentTime = nextDepartureTime;
    if (!carQueue.empty( ))
    {
        Car car = carQueue.front( );
        carQueue.pop( );
        waitingTime = currentTime − car.getArrivalTime( );
        sumOfWaitingTimes += waitingTime;
        nextDepartureTime = currentTime + WASH_TIME;
    } // carQueue was not empty
    else
        nextDepartureTime = INFINITY;
} // method processDeparture
```

The final **CarWash** method, and easiest of all, is the printResult method:

```
void CarWash::printResult( )
{
    const string NO_CARS_MESSAGE = "There were no cars in the car
            wash.";
    const string AVERAGE_WAITING_TIME_MESSAGE =
        "\nThe average waiting time, in minutes, was ";
    if (numberOfCars == 0)
        cout << NO_CARS_MESSAGE << endl;
    else
        cout << AVERAGE_WAITING_TIME_MESSAGE
            << ((double)sumOfWaitingTimes / numberOfCars)
            << endl;
} // method printResult
```

The main function does little more than invoke the three public methods in the CarWash class:

```
#include <iostream>
#include <string>

#include "CarWash.h"

using namespace std;
int main( )
{
    const string CLOSE_WINDOW_PROMPT =
            "Please press the Enter key to close this output window.";

    CarWash carWash;

    carWash.runSimulation( );
    carWash.printResult( );
    cout << endl << endl << CLOSE_WINDOW_PROMPT;
    cin.get( );
    cin.get( );

    return 0;
} // main
```

7.3.3   ANALYSIS OF THE CarWash METHODS

How much time does each CarWash method take? With the default underlying deque class, all the queue methods take constant time in the worst case, except for the push method, which has constant average time but a worstTime(n) linear in n. Even in the worst case, n consecutive pushes take only linear time. So all we need to consider are the loops in the runSimulation method, specifically, the read-and-process loop and process-remaining-cars loop. If there are n cars that arrive, the read-and-process loop will be executed n times, and the process-remaining-cars loop will be executed at most six times: one car being washed and five on the queue. We conclude that for the runSimulation method, worstTime(n) is linear in n. For all the other methods, worstTime(n) is constant.

7.3.4   RANDOMIZING THE ARRIVAL TIMES

It is not necessary that the arrival times be read in. They can be generated by your simulation program provided the input includes the ***mean arrival time,*** that is, the average time between arrivals for the population. In order to generate the list of arrival times from the mean arrival time, we need to know the distribution of arrival times. We now define a function that calculates the distribution, known as the ***Poisson distribution,*** of times between arrivals. The mathematical justification for the following discussion is beyond the scope of this book—the interested reader may consult a text on mathematical statistics.

Let x be any time between arrivals. Then $F(x)$, the probability that the time until the next arrival will be at least x minutes from now, is given by

$$F(x) = \exp(-x\ /\ \text{meanArrivalTime})$$

For example, $F(0) = \exp(0) = 1$; that is, it is certain that the next arrival will occur at least 0 minutes from now. Similarly, $F(\text{meanArrivalTime}) = \exp(-1) \approx 0.4$. $F(10{,}000 * \text{meanArrivalTime})$ is approximately 0. The graph of the function F is shown in Figure 7.6.

To generate the arrival times randomly, we introduce an integer variable called timeTillNext, which will contain the number of minutes from the current time until the next arrival. We determine the value for timeTillNext as follows. According to the distribution function F, the probability that the next arrival will take at least timeTill Next minutes is given by

$$\exp(-\ \text{timeTillNext}\ /\ \text{meanArrivalTime})$$

This expression represents a probability, specifically, a floating-point number that is greater than 0 and less than or equal to 1. To randomize this probability, we associate the expression with a random value, randomDouble, in the same range. The function call to rand( ) returns an integer value between 0 and RAND_MAX, inclusive, where RAND_MAX is an implementation defined variable whose value is at least 32,767. So we set

```
randomDouble = rand ( ) / double (RAND_MAX + 1);
```

The cast ensures that the quotient is a **double**. Then the randomDouble variable contains a **double** value that is greater than or equal to 0.0 and less than 1.0. So 1 − randomDouble will contain a value that is greater than 0.0 and less than or equal to 1.0. This is what we want, so we equate 1 − randomDouble with exp(− timeTillNext / meanArrivalTime). The appropriate value for timeTillNext is found by solving this equation for timeTillNext:

Figure 7.6 | Graph of the Poisson distribution of interarrival times.

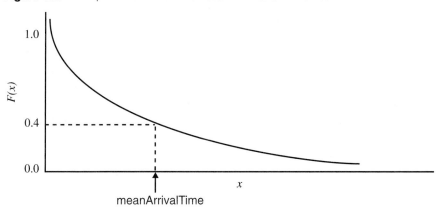

timeTillNext = −meanArrivalTime * log (1 − randomDouble);

The function log returns the natural logarithm of its argument. Finally, we add 0.5 to the expression on the right-hand side to round the result to the nearest integer:

timeTillNext = −meanArrivalTime * log (1 − randomDouble) + 0.5;

To illustrate how the values would be calculated, suppose that the mean arrival time is 3 minutes and the list of values of 1 − randomDouble starts with 0.71582, 0.280151, and 0.409576. Then the first three values of timeTillNext will be

1, that is, −3 * log(0.71582) + 0.5
4, that is, −3 * log(0.280151) + 0.5
3, that is, −3 * log(0.409576) + 0.5

Thus the first car will arrive 1 minute after the car wash opens and the second car will arrive 4 minutes later, at minute 5. The third car will arrive 3 minutes later, at minute 8.

LAB   **Lab 18: Randomizing the arrival times.**

(All Labs Are Optional.)   **LAB**

In Section 7.4, we introduce another container adaptor class, the stack class, most of whose applications are internal to a computer system.

7.4 | STACKS

A *stack* is a finite sequence of items such that the only item that can be deleted, retrieved, or modified is the item that was most recently inserted into the sequence. That item is referred to as the "top" item on the stack.

The items in a stack are stored in reverse-chronological order: last in, first out.

For example, a tray-holder in a cafeteria holds a stack of trays. Insertions and deletions are made only at the top. To put it another way, the tray that was most recently put on the holder will be the next one to be removed. This defining property of stacks is sometimes abbreviated "last in, first out," or LIFO. In keeping with this view, an insertion is referred to as a "push," and a deletion as a "pop." Figure 7.7a shows a stack with three items and Figure 7.7b, c, and d shows the effect of two pops and then a push.

In Section 7.4.1, we look at the method interfaces of the stack class. The stack class has even fewer interfaces than the queue class because in a stack, there is only one position where an item can be inserted, deleted, retrieved, or modified.

7.4.1   Method Interfaces for the Stack Class

The stack class is templated, with deque as the default container class:

```
template <class T, class Container = deque <T> >
class stack
{
```

Figure 7.7 | A stack through several stages of pops and pushes: 17 and 13 are
popped and then 21 is pushed.

```
17
13    13                    21
28    28        28          28
(a)   (b) pop   (c) pop     (d) push 21
```

Here are the interfaces for all the methods in the **stack** class. Note the similarity with
the **queue** class.

1. // Postcondition: this stack is empty, that is, it contains no items.
    explicit stack (**const** Container& = Container( ));

2. // Postcondition: true has been returned if this stack is empty. Otherwise, false
    //   has been returned.
    bool empty( );

3. // Postcondition: The number of items in this stack has been returned.
    unsigned size( );

4. // Postcondition: x has been inserted at the top of this stack. The averageTime
    //   (n) is constant. The worstTime(n) is O(n), but for n
    //   consecutive pushes, worstTime(n) for all n pushes is only
    //   O(n). That is, amortizedTime(n) is constant.
    void push (**const** T& x);

5. // Precondition: this stack is not empty.
    // Postcondition: a reference to the top item on this stack has been returned.
    T& top( );

6. // Precondition: this stack is not empty.
    // Postcondition: a constant reference to the top item on this stack has been
    //   returned.
    const T& top( ) **const**;

7. // Precondition: this stack is not empty.
    // Postcondition: the item that had been at the top of this stack before this
    //   method was called has been removed.
    void pop( );

> *Note* The popped item is not returned by this method. If you want to
> access the popped item, call the top( ) method before calling pop( ).

7.4.2   Using the stack **Class**

There are no iterators available for stacks because the only accessible item is the
item at the top of the stack. That does not mean that a stack cannot be printed, for
example. But the printing could not use any stack details beyond the method interfaces. We saw a similar situation in Section 7.1.2 when we wanted to print out the
contents of a **queue** container. Here is a small program that generates the stack from
Figure 7.7:

```
#include <iostream>
#include <vector>
#include <string>
#include <stack>

using namespace std;

void printStack (stack< int, vector<int> > ages)
{
        cout << endl << endl << "Here is the current stack:" << endl;
        while (!ages.empty( ))
        {
            cout << ages.top( ) << endl;
            ages.pop( );
        } // while
} // function printStack

int main( )
{
        const string CLOSE_WINDOW_PROMPT =
            "Please press the Enter key to close this output window.";
        stack<int, vector< int> > ages;
        ages.push (28);
        ages.push (13);
        ages.push (17);
        printStack (ages);

        ages.pop ( );
        printStack (ages);

        ages.pop( );
        printStack (ages);

        ages.push (21);
        printStack (ages);

        cout << endl << endl << CLOSE_WINDOW_PROMPT;
        cin.get( );
        return 0;
} // main
```

7.4.3   The stack **Class is a Container Adaptor**

As with the queue class, the stack class is a container adaptor: that is, the stack class methods are defined in terms of methods from some underlying container class. The adapted container class must have the following methods: empty, size, push_back, pop_back, and back. Notice what this implies:

> The top of a stack is at the back of the underlying container!

For vectors, lists, and deques, push_back and pop_back take only constant time, on average, and amortizedTime(n) is constant. So either the vector class, the deque class, or the list class can be adapted by the stack class, with the deque class the default.

For all container adaptors in the Standard Template Library, the design has a single field:

    Container c;

And just as with the implementation of the queue class, all the stack method definitions are one-liners in which c invokes the appropriate method. For example, here are two of the method definitions in the stack class:

```
void pop( )
{
      c.pop_back( );
} // method pop

T& top
{
      return c.back( );
} // method top
```

In Section 7.1.4, we considered adapting a user-developed container for the queue class. The queueArray class satisfied the requirements of a container to be adapted and had an interesting feature: a circular array in which no resizing would be needed as long as the number of items in the queue was no larger than the array size. We could develop a stackArray class that satisfied the requirements of a container to be adapted for the stack class. But that class would have no redeeming features: it would mimic, clumsily, the vector class. Since any C++ compiler is required to supply a vector class, we will bypass the development of a stackArray class.

We now turn our attention to a couple of important applications.

7.5 | STACK APPLICATION 1: HOW RECURSION IS IMPLEMENTED

APPLICATION

You have already seen several examples of recursive methods in Chapter 4. In obedience to the Principle of Abstraction, we focused on what recursion did and ignored the question of how recursion is implemented by a compiler or interpreter. It turns out that the visual aids—execution frames—are closely related to this implementation. We now outline how a stack is utilized in implementing recursion and the time-space implications for functions, especially recursive functions, in that utilization.

Each time a function call occurs, whether it is a recursive function or not, the return address in the calling function is saved. This information is saved so the computer will know where to resume execution in the calling function after the execution of the function has been completed. Also, a substantial amount of information about the function's local variables must be saved. This is done to prevent the destruction of that information in the event that the function is—directly or indirectly—recursive. As we noted in Section 4.9, the compiler saves this information for all functions, not just the recursive ones. This information is collectively referred to as an ***activation record*** or ***stack frame.***

Each activation record includes

1. A variable that contains the return address in the calling function
2. For each reference formal parameter, a variable that contains the *address* of the corresponding argument
3. For each value formal parameter, a variable that initially contains a *copy* of the value of the corresponding argument
4. Each variable declared in the function's block

Recursion can be implemented with a run-time stack.

Part of main memory—the ***stack***—is allocated for a run-time stack onto which an activation record is pushed when a function is called and from which an activation record is popped when the execution of the function has been completed. During the execution of that function, the top activation record contains the current state of the function.

For a simple example, let us trace the execution of a small program that includes the writeBinary function from Chapter 4. The return addresses have been commented as RA1 and RA2.

```
#include <iostream>
#include <string>
int main( )
{
        const string PROMPT = "Please enter a nonnegative integer";

        const string CLOSE_WINDOW_PROMPT =
                "Please press the Enter key to close this output window.";

        int n;
        cout << PROMPT;
        cin >> n;
        if (n < 0)
                cout << "Error: You entered a negative integer.";
        else
                writeBinary (n); // RA1

        cout << endl << endl << CLOSE_WINDOW_PROMPT;
        cin.get( );

        return 0;
} // function main
```

```
// Precondition: n is a nonnegative integer, in decimal notation.
// Postcondition: The binary representation of n has been printed. The
//                 worstTime(n) is O(log n).
void writeBinary (int n)
{
    if (n == 0 || n == 1)
        cout << n;
    else
    {
        writeBinary (n / 2); // RA2
        cout (n % 2);
    } // else
} // writeBinary
```

The writeBinary function has the value formal parameter n as its only local variable, and so each activation record will have two fields:

1. One for the return address
2. One for the value of the value formal parameter n

Assume that the integer 6 is read in. When writeBinary is called from the main function, an activation record is created and pushed onto the stack, as shown in Figure 7.8. Since n > 1, writeBinary is called recursively with 3 (that is, 6 / 2) as the value of the actual parameter. A second activation record is created and pushed onto the stack. See Figure 7.9.

Figure 7.8 | The activation stack just prior to the first activation of the writeBinary method. RA1 is the return address.

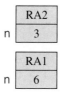

	RA1
n	6

Activation stack

Figure 7.9 | The activation stack just prior to the second activation of the writeBinary method.

	RA2
n	3

	RA1
n	6

Activation stack

(two records)

Since the value of n is still greater than 1, writeBinary is called again, this time with 1 (that is, 3 / 2) as the value of the actual parameter. A third activation record is created and pushed. See Figure 7.10.

Since n = 1, the value of n is written. The output is

1

This completes the third activation of the writeBinary method, and so the stack is popped and a return is made to the address RA2. The resulting stack is shown in Figure 7.11. The output statement at RA2 in the writeBinary method is executed, and the value output is 3 % 2, namely,

1

The stack is popped again and another return to RA2 is made, as shown in Figure 7.12. The output from the output statement at RA2 is the value of 6 % 2, namely,

0

Figure 7.10 I The activation stack just prior to the third activation of the writeBinary method.

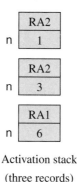

Activation stack
(three records)

Figure 7.11 I The activation stack just after the completion of the third activation of the writeBinary method.

Activation stack
(two records)

That completes the original activation of the writeBinary method. The stack is popped once more, leaving it empty, and a return to RA1—at the end of the main function—is made. The entire output was

110

which is the binary equivalent of 6, the value input.

For a reference formal parameter, the address of the corresponding argument is pushed onto the stack. When the machine code is being generated, the compiler treats each occurrence of the reference formal parameter as a pointer to the corresponding argument. For example, consider the following main function:

```
int main( )
{
        string s = "maybe ";
        int i = 3;

        sample (s, i); // RA1
        cout << s << " " << i;

        return 0;
} // function main
```

The definition of the sample function is

```
void sample (string& x, int y)
{
        x.insert (0, "$");
        y--;
        if (y > 0)
                sample (x, y); // RA2
} // sample
```

The code generated is the same as if the body of the sample function were

```
x->insert (0, "$");
y--;
if (y > 0)
        sample (*x, y);
```

Figure 7.12 | The activation stack just after the completion of the second activation of the writeBinary method.

Activation stack

At the start of the second recursive call to sample, the stack reaches its maximum height of 3:

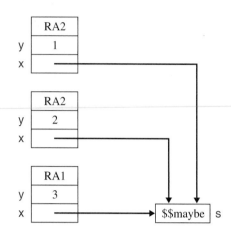

At this point, another "$" is prepended to x, and y is decremented. Since y is no longer greater than 0, no further recursive calls are made. After three pops, the output is

   $$$maybe 3

The argument s is affected by the calls to the sample function because the corresponding formal parameter x is a reference parameter. On the other hand, the argument i was unaffected by the calls to the sample function because the formal parameter corresponding to i, namely y, is a value parameter.

   This discussion should give you a general idea of how recursion is implemented by the compiler. There is a single stack of activation records to handle all function calls, and so each record must include a field that holds the size of the record. That way, the correct number of bytes can be popped. For the sake of simplicity, we ignored that detail in our discussion. Another technicality involves what to do with the value returned by a (non-**void**) function. The details can vary from one compiler to the next. One common technique is for the value to be pushed on top of the stack just before the return is made. It is then the job of the calling function to take appropriate action, which would include, at least, popping the stack.

   The compiler must generate code for the creation and maintenance, at run-time, of the activation stack. Each time a call—even a nonrecursive call—is made, the entire local environment must be saved. This can be inefficient, in terms of both time and space if, for example, a large container object is passed to a value formal parameter. In that case, a copy of the entire container would be stacked whenever a call is made.

   If you have designed a recursive function, you should assess the potential impact of the time-space overhead of recursion on your program. If you decide that the overhead is excessive, you will need to convert the recursive function to an iterative one. This can *always* be done.

If you have trouble coming up with an iterative function, you can simulate the recursive function with an iterative function that creates and maintains its own stack of information to be saved. For example, Project 7.3 requires an iterative version of the (recursive) tryToSolve method in the backtracking application from Chapter 4. When you create your own stack, you get to decide what each item will consist of. For example, if the recursive version of the function contains a single recursive call, you need not save the return address. Here is an iterative, stack-based version of the writeBinary function (see Exercise 4.2 for an iterative version of the writeBinary function that is not stack-based).

```
// Precondition: n is a nonnegative integer, in decimal notation.
// Postcondition: The binary representation of n has been printed. The
//                worstTime(n) is O(log n).
void writeBinary (int n)
{
        stack<int> myStack;

        myStack.push (n);
        while (n > 1)
        {
                n = n/2;
                myStack.push (n);
        } // pushing
        while (!myStack.empty( ))
        {
                n = myStack.top( );
                myStack.pop( );
                cout << (n % 2);
        } // popping
        cout << endl << endl;

} // method writeBinary
```

Do not overlook the cost, in terms of your time, of making the conversion from a recursive function to an iterative one. Some recursive functions, such as the factorial and Fibonacci functions, can easily be converted to iterative functions. Sometimes the conversion is nontrivial, such as for the move, tryToSolve, and permute functions of Chapter 4. Furthermore, the iterative version may well lack the simple elegance of the recursive version, and this may complicate verification and maintenance.

As noted in Chapter 4, if an iterative function is readily available and acceptably efficient, go for it. If not, you certainly should consider a recursive function if circumstances warrant. That is, try recursion whenever the problem is such that complex instances of the problem can be reduced to simpler instances of the same form as the original, and the simplest instance(s) can be solved directly. This discussion on the activation stack enables you to make better-informed trade-off decisions.

Section 7.6 presents another compiler-related application: converting expressions into machine code. One important aspect of the conversion is to make sure that the parentheses are matched. As a warm-up to that application, here is a short program to test for matching parentheses. The input is a string of left and right parentheses, and the output indicates whether the parentheses are matched. For example, the following strings consist of matched parentheses:

(( )( ))
( )((( )))

And the following two strings have unmatched parentheses:

( ))(
(( ))

The basic strategy is this: When a '(' is encountered, push it onto a stack; when a ')' is encountered, pop the stack unless it is already empty. When the end of the input string has been reached, the parentheses are matched if the stack is empty.

```cpp
#include <vector>
#include <stack>
#include <iostream>
#include <string>

using namespace std;

int main( )
{
        const string PROMPT = "Please enter a string of parentheses: ";

        const char LEFT = '(';

        const char RIGHT = ')';

        const string SUCCESS = "The parentheses are matching.";

        const string FAILURE = "The parentheses are NOT matching.";

        const string CLOSE_WINDOW_PROMPT =
                "Please press the Enter key to close this output window.";

        stack< char, vector<char> > parenStack;

        string parens;

        bool matching = true;

        cout << PROMPT;
        cin >> parens;
        for (unsigned i = 0; i < parens.length( ) && matching; i++)
                if (parens [i] == LEFT)
                        parenStack.push (LEFT);
```

```
        else if (parens [i] == RIGHT)
                if (parenStack.empty( ))
                        matching = false;
                else
                        parenStack.pop( );

    if (matching && parenStack.empty( ))
            cout << endl << SUCCESS << endl;
    else
            cout << endl << FAILURE << endl;
    cout << endl << endl << CLOSE_WINDOW_PROMPT;
    cin.get( );

        return 0;
} // main
```

Note that the loop is exited if the stack is empty when a right parenthesis is encountered. All characters except left and right parentheses are ignored. This program is available from the Source Code link on the book's website.

7.6 | STACK APPLICATION 2: CONVERTING INFIX TO POSTFIX

APPLICATION

In Section 7.5 we saw how a compiler or interpreter could implement recursion. In this section we present another "internal" application: the translation of arithmetic expressions from infix notation into postfix notation. This can be one of the key tasks performed by a compiler as it creates machine-level code or by an interpreter as it evaluates an arithmetic expression.

In infix notation, a binary operator is placed between its operands. For example, Figure 7.13 shows several arithmetic expressions in infix notation. For the sake of simplicity, we initially restrict our attention to expressions with single-letter identifiers, parentheses, and the binary operators $+$, $-$, $*$, and $/$.

The usual rules of arithmetic apply:

1. Operations are normally carried out from left to right. For example, if we have

   $a + b - c$

   then the addition will be performed first.

Figure 7.13 | Several arithmetic expressions in infix notation.

```
a + b
b - c * d
(b - c) * d
a - c - h / b * c
a - (c - h) / (b * c)
```

2. If the current operator is + or − and the next operator is * or /, then the next operator is applied before the current operator. For example, if we have

b + c * d

then the multiplication will be carried out before the addition. For

a − b + c * d

the subtraction is performed first, then the multiplication and, finally, the addition. We can interpret this rule as saying that multiplication and division have "higher precedence" than addition and subtraction.

3. Parentheses may be used to alter the order indicated by rules 1 and 2. For example, if we have

a − (b + c)

then the addition is performed first. Similarly, with

(a − b) * c

the subtraction is performed first.

Figure 7.14 shows the order of evaluation for the last two expressions in Figure 7.13.

The first widely used programming language was FORTRAN (from FORmula TRANslator), so named because its compiler could translate arithmetic formulas into machine-level code. In early (pre-1960) compilers, the translation was performed directly. But direct translation is awkward because the machine-level code for an operator cannot be generated until both of its operands are known. This requirement leads to difficulties when either operand is a parenthesized subexpression.

7.6.1 POSTFIX NOTATION

In postfix *notation, an operator is placed immediately after its operands.*

Modern compilers do not translate arithmetic expressions directly into machine-level code. Instead, they can utilize an intermediate form known as ***postfix notation.*** In postfix notation, an operator is placed immediately after its operands. For exam-

Figure 7.14 | The order of evaluation for the last two expressions in Figure 7.13.

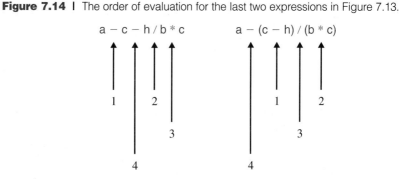

ple, given the infix expression a + b, the postfix form is a b +. For a + b * c, the postfix form is a b c * + because the operands for + are a and the product of b and c. For

(a + b) * c

the postfix form is

a b + c *

Since an operator immediately follows its operands in postfix notation, parentheses are unnecessary and therefore not used. Figure 7.15 shows several arithmetic expressions in both infix and postfix notation.

How can we convert an arithmetic expression from infix notation into postfix notation? Let's view the infix notation as a string of characters and try to produce the corresponding postfix string. The identifiers in the postfix string will be in the same order as they are in the infix string, so each identifier can be appended to the postfix string as soon as it is encountered. But in postfix notation, operators must be placed after their operands. So when an operator is encountered in the infix string, it must be saved somewhere temporarily.

For example, suppose we want to translate the infix string

a − b + c * d

into postfix notation. (The blanks are for readability only—they are not, for now, considered part of the infix expression.) We would go through the following steps:

'a' is appended to postfix, which is now "a"
'−' is stored temporarily
'b' is appended to postfix, which is now "ab"

When '+' is encountered, we note that since it has the same precedence as '−', the subtraction should be performed first by the left-to-right rule (rule 1). So the '−' is appended to the postfix string, which is now "ab−" and '+' is saved temporarily. Then 'c' is appended to postfix, which now is "ab−c".

Figure 7.15 I Several arithmetic expressions in both infix and postfix notation.

Infix	Postfix
a − b + c * d	ab − cd *+
a + c − h / b * r	ac + hb / r * −
a + (c − h) / (b * r)	ach − br */+

Multiplication has higher precedence than addition, so '*' should be moved to postfix before '+'. But '*' must also be stored somewhere temporarily because one of its operands (namely 'd') has not yet been appended to postfix.

When 'd' is appended to postfix, the postfix string is "ab−cd". Then '*' is appended, making the postfix string "ab−cd*". Finally, '+' is appended, and the final postfix representation is "ab−cd*+".

The temporary storage facility is handled conveniently with a stack. The rules governing this operatorStack object are

R1.   Initially, the operatorStack object is empty.

R2.   For each operator in the infix string, loop until the operator has been pushed onto the operatorStack object:

        If the operatorStack object is empty or the infix operator has higher precedence than the operator on the top of the operatorStack object, then

            Push the operator onto the operatorStack object.

     else

        Pop the operatorStack object and append that popped operator to the postfix string.

R3.   Once the end of the input string is encountered,

        Loop until the operatorStack object is empty:

            Pop the operatorStack object and append that popped operator to the postfix string.

The essential fact from these rules can be summarized as follows:

INFIX HIGHER, PUSH

For example, Figure 7.16 shows the history of the operator stack during the conversion of

    a + c − h / b * r

to its postfix equivalent. How are parentheses handled? When a left parenthesis is encountered in the infix string, it is immediately pushed onto the operatorStack object, but its precedence is defined to be *lower* than the precedence of any binary operator. When a right parenthesis is encountered in the infix string, the operator Stack object is repeatedly popped, and the popped item appended to the postfix string, until the "operator" on the top of the stack is a left parenthesis. Then that left parenthesis is popped but not appended to postfix, and the scan of the infix string is resumed.

For example, when we translate a * (b + c) into postfix, the items *, (, and + would be pushed and then '+' and '(' would be popped (last in, first out) when the right parenthesis is encountered. The final postfix form is

    a b c + *

For a more complex example, Figure 7.17 illustrates the conversion of

Figure 7.16 | The conversion of a + c − h / b * r to postfix notation. At each stage, the top of the operatorStack object is shown as the *rightmost* item.

Infix	operatorStack	Postfix
— Infix expression: a + c − h / b * r		
a	(empty)	a
+	+	a
c	+	ac
−	−	ac+
h	−	ac+h
/	−/	ac+h
b	−/	ac+hb
*	−*	ac+hb/
r	−*	ac+hb/r
	−	ac+hb/r*
	(empty)	ac+hb/r*−

$$x - (y * a / b - (z + d * e) + c) / f$$

to its postfix form.

7.6.2 TRANSITION MATRIX

At each step in the conversion process, we know what action to take as long as we know the current character in the infix string and the top character on the operator stack. We can therefore create a matrix to summarize the conversion. The row indices represent the possible values of the current infix character. The column indices represent the possible values of the top character on the operator stack. The matrix entries represent the action to be taken. Such a matrix is called a ***transition matrix*** because it directs the transition of information from one form to another. Figure 7.18 shows the transition matrix for converting a simple expression from infix notation to postfix notation.

The graphical nature of the transition matrix in Figure 7.18 enables us to see at a glance how to convert simple expressions from infix to postfix. We could now design and implement a program to do just that. The program may well incorporate the transition matrix in Figure 7.18 for the sake of extensibility: more complex expressions can be accommodated by expanding the matrix.

Figure 7.17 I The conversion of x − (y * a / b − (z + d * e) + c) / f from infix to postfix. At each stage, the top of the operatorStack object is shown as the *rightmost* item.

Infix expression: x − (y * a / b − (z + d * e) + c) / f		
Infix	*operatorStack*	Postfix
x	(empty)	x
−	−	x
(	−(	x
y	−(	xy
*	−(*	xy
a	−(*	xya
/	−(/	xya*
b	−(/	xya*b
−	−(−	xya*b/
(	−(−(	xya*b/
z	−(−(	xya*b/z
+	−(−(+	xya*b/z
d	−(−(+	xya*b/zd
*	−(−(+*	xya*b/zd
e	−(−(+*	xya*b/zde
)	−(−(+	xya*b/zde*
	−(−(	xya*b/zde*+
	−(−	xya*b/zde*+
+	−(+	xya*b/zde*+−
c	−(+	xya*b/zde*+−c
)	−(	xya*b/zde*+−c+
	−	xya*b/zde*+−c+
/	−/	xya*b/zde*+−c+
f	−/	xya*b/zde*+−c+f
	−	xya*b/zde*+−c+f/
	(empty)	xya*b/zde*+−c+f/−

Postfix expression: x y a * b / z d e * + − c + f / −		

7.6.3   TOKENS

A program that utilized a transition matrix would probably not work with the characters themselves because there are too many possible (legal) values for each character. For example, a transition matrix that used a row for each legal infix character would need 52 rows just for an identifier. And if we changed the specifications to allow multi-character identifiers, we would need millions of rows!

Instead, the legal characters would usually be grouped together into "tokens." A *token* is the smallest meaningful unit in a program. Each token has two parts: a generic part that holds its category and a specific part that enables us to recapture the character(s) tokenized. For converting simple infix expressions to postfix, the token

*When a program is **tokenized**, it is split up into small, meaningful units.*

Figure 7.18 I The transition matrix for converting simple expressions from infix notation to postfix notation.

Action taken		Top character on operator stack			
		(	+,−	*,/	(empty)
Infix character	Identifier	Append to postfix	Append to postfix	Append to postfix	Append to postfix
	)	Pop; pitch '('	Pop to postfix	Pop to postfix	Error
	(	Push	Push	Push	Push
	+,−	Push	Pop to postfix	Pop to postfix	Push
	*,/	Push	Push	Pop to postfix	Push
	(empty)	Error	Pop to postfix	Pop to postfix	Done

categories would be: identifier, rightPar, leftPar, addOp (for + and −), multOp (for * and /), and empty (for a dummy value). The specific part would contain the index, in the infix string, of the character tokenized. For example, given the infix string

    a+b*c

to tokenize 'b', we would set its category to identifier and its index to 2.

The structure of tokens varies widely among compilers. Typically, the specific part of a variable identifier's token contains an address into a table, called a *symbol table.* At that address would be stored the identifier, an indication that it is a variable identifier, its type, initial value, the block it is declared in, and other information helpful to the compiler.

In Lab 19, a complete infix-to-postfix project is developed, with tokens and massive input-editing.

LAB   **Lab 19: Converting from Infix to Postfix.**

(All Labs Are Optional.)   **LAB**

7.6.4   Prefix Notation

In Section 7.6.1 we described how to convert an infix expression into postfix notation. Another possibility is to convert from infix into ***prefix*** notation, in which each operator immediately precedes its operands.[3] Figure 7.19 shows several expressions in both infix and prefix notation.

How can we convert a simple arithmetic expression from infix to prefix notation? As in converting from infix to postfix notation, we will need to save each operator until both of its operands have been obtained. But we cannot simply append each identifier to the prefix string as soon as it is encountered. Instead, we will need to save each identifier, in fact, each operand, until its operator has been obtained.

The saving of operands and operators is easily accomplished with the help of two stack objects, operandStack and operatorStack. Initially, both stacks are empty. When an identifier is encountered in the infix string, that identifier is pushed onto the operandStack object. The rules governing the operatorStack object are exactly the same as they were for converting from infix to postfix.

What about the operandStack object? Suppose we have just popped the top operator, opt, from the operatorStack object. Then we also pop the top two operands, opnd1 and opnd2, from the operandStack object. Concatenate (join together) opt, opnd2, and opnd1 and push the result onto the operandStack object. Important: opnd2 comes *before* opnd1 in the concatenation because opnd2 was pushed onto the operandStack object before opnd1.

This continues until we reach the end of the infix expression. We then repeat the following until the operatorStack object is empty:

> Pop opt from the operatorStack object.
>
> Pop opnd1 from the operandStack object.

Figure 7.19 | Several arithmetic expressions in both infix and prefix notation.

Infix	Prefix
a − b	− a b
a − b * c	− a * b c
(a − b) * c	* − a b c
a − b + c * d	+ − a b * c d
a + c − h / b * d	− + a c * / h b d
a + (c − h) / (b * d)	+ a / − c h * b d

---

[3]Prefix notation was invented by Jan Lucasiewicz, a Polish logician. It is sometimes referred to as ***Polish notation,*** and postfix as ***reverse Polish notation.***

Pop opnd2 from the operandStack object.

Concatenate opt, opnd2, and opnd1 together and push the result onto the operandStack object.

When the operatorStack object is finally empty, the top (and only) operand on the operatorStack object will be the prefix string corresponding to the original infix expression.

For example, if we start with

a + b * c

then the history of the two stacks would be as follows:

1.
a	a	
infix	operandStack	operatorStack

2.
+	a	+
infix	operandStack	operatorStack

3.
| | b | |
b	a	+
infix	operandStack	operatorStack

4.
| | b | * |
*	a	+
infix	operandStack	operatorStack

5.
| | c | |
| | b | * |
c	a	+
infix	operandStack	operatorStack

6.
| | *bc | |
	a	+
infix	operandStack	operatorStack

7.
	+a*bc	
infix	operandStack	operatorStack

The prefix string corresponding to the original string is

+ a * b c

294   **CHAPTER 7**   Queues and Stacks

For a more complex example, suppose the infix string is

    a + (c − h) / (b * d)

Then the items on the two stacks during the processing of the first right parenthesis would be as follows:

		h	−
		c	(
1.	)	a	+
	infix	operandStack	operatorStack

		−ch	(
		a	+
2.		operandStack	operatorStack

		−ch	
		a	+
3.		operandStack	operatorStack

During the processing of the second right parenthesis in the infix string, we would have

		d	*
		b	(
		−ch	/
1.	)	a	+
	infix	operandStack	operatorStack

		*bd	(
		−ch	/
		a	+
2.		operandStack	operatorStack

		*bd	
		−ch	/
		a	+
3.		operandStack	operatorStack

The end of the infix expression has been reached, so the **operatorStack** object is repeatedly popped.

	/−ch*bd a	+
4.	_____	_____
	operandStack	operatorStack

	+a/−ch*bd	
5.	_____	_____
	operandStack	operatorStack

The prefix string is + a / − c h * b d.

SUMMARY

A *queue* is a finite sequence of items in which retrievals, deletions, and modifications can take place only at the front, and insertions can take place only at the back. The inherent fairness of the *first-come–first-served* restriction has made the queue class an important component of many systems. Specifically, the queue class plays a key role in the development of computer models to study the behavior of those systems.

A *stack* is a finite sequence of items in which the only item that can be deleted, retrieved, or modified is the item that was most recently inserted into the sequence. That item is referred to as the *top* item on the stack. Compilers implement recursion by generating code for creating and maintaining an *activation stack:* a run-time stack that holds the state of each active function. Another stack application occurs in the translation of infix expressions into machine code. With the help of an operator stack, an infix expression can easily be converted into postfix notation, which is an intermediate form between infix notation and machine language.

EXERCISES

7.1   Suppose we define

queue <**int**> x;

Show what the queue will look like after each of the following messages is sent:

a.   x.push (2000):

b.   x.push (1215):

c.   x.push (1035):

d.   x.push (2117):

e.   x.pop( );

f.   x.push (1999);

g.   x.pop( );

7.2 Repeat Exercise 7.1 if x is defined as

stack<**int**> x;

7.3 Expand the Linked class from Lab 7 so that it could serve as the underlying class for the queue container adaptor.

7.4 Can the expanded Linked class from Exercise 7.3 also serve as the underlying class for the stack container adaptor? Explain.

7.5 Recall that "deque" stands for "double-ended queue," that is, a queue in which insertions, deletions, and retrievals are allowed at both the front and the back (and require only constant time). What other significant feature does a deque have? Why would it have been inconsistent with the Standard Template Library if we had defined the queue class before the deque class?

7.6 Suppose that items a, b, c, d, e are pushed, in that order, onto an initially empty stack. That stack is then popped four times, and as each item is popped off the stack, it is inserted into an initially empty queue. If one item is then deleted from the queue, what is the *next* item to be deleted?

7.7 Could the queue class serve as the underlying class for the stack class? Explain.

Hint What methods must the underlying class provide?

7.8 Use a stack of activation records to trace the execution of the recursive factorial method after an initial call of factorial (4).

7.9 Translate the following expressions into postfix notation:

a. x + y * z
b. (x + y) * z
c. x − y − z * (a + b)
d. (a + b) * c − (d + e * f / ((g / h + i − j) * k)) / r

7.10 Translate each of the expressions in Exercise 7.9 into prefix notation.

7.11 An expression in postfix notation can be evaluated at run-time by means of a stack. For simplicity, assume that the postfix expression consists of integer values and binary operators only. For example, we might have the following postfix expression:

8 5 4 + * 7 −

The evaluation proceeds as follows: When a value is encountered, it is pushed onto the stack. When an operator is encountered, the first and second items on the stack are retrieved and popped, the operator is applied (the second item is the left operand, the first item is the right operand), and the result is pushed onto the stack. When the postfix expression has been processed, the value of that expression is the top (and only) item on the stack.

For example, for the given expression, the contents of the stack would be as follows:

```
                          4
                  5       5
          8       8       8
____     ____    ____    ____

  9               7
  8       72      72      65
____     ____    ____    ____
```

Convert the following expression into postfix notation and then use a stack to evaluate the expression:

5 + 2 * (30 − 10 / 5)

7.12 Neither the queue class nor the stack class defines a destructor. Could these omissions lead to memory leaks? Explain.

PROGRAMMING PROJECT 7.1

Extending the Car Wash Simulation

Make the Speedo's Car Wash simulation more realistic.

Analysis

The arrival times—with a Poisson distribution—should be generated randomly from the mean arrival time. Speedo has added a new feature: The service time is not necessarily 10 minutes, but depends on what the customer wants done, such as wash only, wash and wax, and wash and vacuum. The service time for a car should be calculated just before the car begins to get washed—that's when the customer knows how much time will be taken until the customer leaves the car wash. The service times, also with a Poisson distribution, should be generated randomly from the mean service time.

Calculate the average waiting time and the average queue length, both to one fractional digit. The average waiting time is the sum of the waiting times divided by the number of customers.

The average queue length is the sum of the queue lengths for each minute of the simulation divided by the number of minutes until the last customer departs. To calculate the sum of the queue lengths, we add, for each minute of the simulation, the total number of customers on the queue during that minute. We can calculate this sum another way: We add, for each customer, the total number of minutes that customer was on the queue. But this is the sum of the waiting times! So we can calculate the average queue length as the sum of the waiting times divided by the number of minutes of the simulation until the last customer departs. And we already calculated the sum of the waiting times for the average waiting time.

Also calculate the number of overflows. Use a seed of 500 for the random-number generator.

System Test 1   The input is in boldface.

Please enter the mean arrival time: **3**
Please enter the mean service time: **5**
Please enter the maximum arrival time: **25**

Time	Event	Waiting time
1	Arrival	
4	Arrival	
6	Arrival	
7	Departure	0
7	Arrival	
7	Arrival	
8	Departure	3
11	Departure	2
14	Departure	4
15	Arrival	
15	Arrival	
17	Departure	7
20	Arrival	
24	Departure	2
24	Arrival	
25	Departure	9
27	Departure	5
36	Departure	3

The average waiting time was 3.9 minutes.

The average queue length was 1.0 cars.

The number of overflows was 0.

System Test 2   Input is in boldface.

Please enter the mean arrival time: **8**
Please enter the mean service time: **5**
Please enter the maximum arrival time: **20**

Time	Event	Waiting time
3	Arrival	
9	Departure	0
10	Arrival	
12	Arrival	
13	Departure	0
13	Arrival	
14	Departure	1
17	Departure	1

The average waiting time was 0.5 minutes.

The average queue length was 0.1 cars.

The number of overflows was 0.

PROGRAMMING PROJECT 7.2

Evaluating a Condition

Develop a program to evaluate a condition.

Analysis

The input will consist of a condition (that is, a Boolean expression) followed by the values—one per line—of the variables as they are first encountered in the condition. For example:

```
b * a > a + c
6
2
7
```

The variable b gets the value 6, a gets 2, and c gets 7. The operator * has precedence over >, and + has precedence over >, so the value of the expression is **true** (12 is greater than 9).

Each variable will be given as an identifier, consisting of lowercase letters only. All variables will be integer-valued. There will be no constant literals. The legal operators and precedence levels—high to low—are

> *, /, %
>
> +, − (that is, integer addition and subtraction)
>
> >, >=, <=, <
>
> ==, !=
>
> **&&**
>
> ||

Parenthesized subexpressions are legal. *You need not do any input editing.*

System Test 1

```
Please enter a condition, or $ to quit.
b * a > a + c
Please enter a value.
6
Please enter a value.
2
Please enter a value.
7
The value of the condition is true.
Please enter a condition, or $ to quit.
b * a < a + c
Please enter a value.
6
Please enter a value.
2
```

Please enter a value.
7
The value of the condition is false.
Please enter a condition, or $ to quit.
first + last * next == current * (next − previous)
Please enter a value.
6
Please enter a value.
2
Please enter a value.
7
Please enter a value.
5
Please enter a value.
3
The value of the condition is true.
Please enter a condition, or $ to quit.
first + last * next != current * (next − previous)
Please enter a value.
6
Please enter a value.
2
Please enter a value.
7
Please enter a value.
5
Please enter a value.
3
The value of the condition is false.
Please enter a condition, or $ to quit.
a * (b + c / (d − b) * e) >= a + b + c + d + e
Please enter a value.
6
Please enter a value.
2
Please enter a value.
7
Please enter a value.
5
Please enter a value.
3
The value of the condition is true.
Please enter a condition, or $ to quit.
a * (b + c / (d − b) * e) <= a + b + c + d + e

(continued on next page)

(continued from previous page)

Please enter a value.
6
Please enter a value.
2
Please enter a value.
7
Please enter a value.
5
Please enter a value.
3
The value of the condition is false.
Please enter a condition, or $ to quit.
$

System Test 2

Please enter a condition, or $ to quit.
b < c && c < a
Please enter a value.
10
Please enter a value.
20
Please enter a value.
30
The value of the condition is true.
Please enter a condition, or $ to quit.
b < c && a < c
Please enter a value.
10
Please enter a value.
20
Please enter a value.
30
The value of the condition is false.
Please enter a condition, or $ to quit.
b < c ll a < c
Please enter a value.
10
Please enter a value.
20
Please enter a value.
30

The value of the condition is true.
Please enter a condition, or $ to quit.
c < b || c > a
Please enter a value.
10
Please enter a value.
20
Please enter a value.
30
The value of the condition is true.
Please enter a condition, or $ to quit.
b != a || b <= c && a >= c
Please enter a value.
10
Please enter a value.
20
Please enter a value.
30
The value of the condition is true.
Please enter a condition, or $ to quit.
(b != a || b <= c) && a >= c
Please enter a value.
10
Please enter a value.
20
Please enter a value.
30
The value of the condition is false.
Please enter a condition, or $ to quit.
a / b * b + a % b == a
Please enter a value.
17
Please enter a value.
5
The value of the condition is true.
Please enter a condition, or $ to quit.
$

> *Hint* See Lab 19 on converting infix to postfix, and Exercise 7.11. After con-
> structing the postfix queue, create values, a vector of **int** items corresponding to
> symbolTable, a vector of identifiers. Also, create runtimeStack, a stack of **int** items,
> for pushing and popping **int** and **bool** values (recall that **false** is a synonym for 0
> and **true** is a synonym for 1).

PROGRAMMING PROJECT 7.3

An Iterative Maze Search

Redo the maze-search project in Chapter 4 by replacing the tryToSolve method with an iterative method that simulates recursion.

Hint   Use a stack to simulate the recursive calls to tryToSolve.

The original version of the project is accessible from the Source Code link on the book's website.

PROGRAMMING PROJECT 7.4

Alternate Design of the queue Class

Implement the queueArray class described in Section 7.1.4. Include a driver to validate the class.

> *Hint*   The only complication arises if the push_back method is called and queue Array occupies the entire data array, that is, size = max_size, or equivalently, (tail + 1) % max_size = head. You should then create an array twice as large as data is, and copy the old array to this new array. First, copy the items between index head and the end of the old array to the new array, starting at index 0. If head = 0, there is nothing more to be copied. Otherwise, copy the remaining items in the old array (at indices 0 ... tail) to the new array, starting just after where the previous copy finished.

The generic algorithm copy will simplify your work. Remember that generic algorithms work with arrays as well as with container objects. For example, to copy each item from oldData [head . . . max_size − 1] to data [0 . . . max_size − head]:

```
copy (oldData + head, oldData + max_size, data);
```

For the push_back and pop_front methods, use modular arithmetic. For example, instead of

```
if (head == max_size)
        head = 0;
else
        head++;
```

write, equivalently,

```
head = (head + 1) % max_size;
```

CHAPTER 8

Binary Trees and Binary Search Trees

I n this chapter we "branch" out from the linear structures of Chapters 2, 5, 6, and 7 to introduce what is essentially a two-dimensional construct: the binary tree. After spending some time on the definition and properties of binary trees, we will turn our attention to a special type of binary tree—the binary search tree—that imposes an ordering on its items.

Binary search trees are interesting data structures because they require only logarithmic time, on average, for inserting, removing, and searching (but linear time in the worst case). This performance is far better than the linear average-case time for insertions, removals, and searches in an array, vector, or list. For example, when $n = 1,000,000$, $\log_2 n < 20$.

We implement the binary-search-tree data structure with the BinSearchTree class, which is not included in the Standard Template Library. The main reason for studying the BinSearchTree class is that it is a simplified version of the AVLTree and rb_tree classes of Chapters 9 and 10. These are "balanced" binary search trees, whose height is always logarithmic in n. It follows that for insertions, deletions, and searches, worstTime(n) is logarithmic in n. Two other kinds of binary tree, the heap and the Huffman tree, are investigated in Chapter 11, and decision trees are studied in Chapter 12. The material in the current chapter will help you to better understand the trees in Chapters 9 through 12. ■

CHAPTER OBJECTIVES

1. Understand binary-tree concepts and important properties, such as the Binary Tree Theorem and the External Path Length Theorem.

2. Be able to perform various traversals of a binary tree.

3. Compare the time efficiency of the BinSearchTree class's insert and erase methods to that of the corresponding methods in the vector, deque, and list classes.

4. Discuss the similarities and differences of the BinSearchTree class's find method and the generic algorithms find and binary_search.

8.1 | DEFINITION AND PROPERTIES

The following definition sets the tone for the whole chapter:

A recursive definition

> A **binary tree** *t* is either empty or consists of an item, called the **root item,** and two disjoint binary trees, called the **left subtree** and **right subtree** of *t*.

We denote those subtrees as leftTree(*t*) and rightTree(*t*), respectively. Functional notation, such as leftTree(*t*), is utilized instead of object notation, such as t.leftTree( ), because there is no binary-tree data structure. Why not? Widely differing methods—even different parameters lists—for such operations as inserting and removing are used for different types of binary trees. Note that the definition of a binary tree is recursive, and many of the definitions associated with binary trees are naturally recursive.

In depicting a binary tree, the root item is shown at the top, by convention. To suggest the association between the root item and the left and right subtrees, we draw a southwesterly line from the root item to the left subtree and a southeasterly line from the root item to the right subtree. Figure 8.1 shows several binary trees.

The binary tree in Figure 8.1a is different from the binary tree in Figure 8.1b because *B* is in the left subtree of Figure 8.1a but *B* is not in the left subtree of Figure 8.1b. As we will see in Chapter 14, those two binary trees *are* equivalent when viewed as general trees.

A subtree of a binary tree is itself a binary tree, and so Figure 8.1a has seven binary trees: the whole binary tree, the binary tree whose root item is *B*, the binary tree whose root item is *C,* and four empty binary trees. Try to calculate the total number of subtrees for the tree in Figure 8.1d.

Botanical terminology: root, branch, leaf

The line from a root item to a subtree is called a **branch.** An item whose associated left and right subtrees are both empty is called a **leaf.** A leaf has no branches going down from it. In the binary tree shown in Figure 8.1e, there are four leaves: 15, 28, 36, and 68. We can determine the number of leaves in a binary tree recursively. Let *t* be a binary tree. The number of leaves in *t*, written **leaves(t),** can be defined recursively as follows:

if *t* is empty
    leaves(*t*) = 0
else if *t* consists of a root item only
    leaves(*t*) = 1
else
    leaves(*t*) = leaves(leftTree(*t*)) + leaves(rightTree(*t*))

Figure 8.1 | Several binary trees.

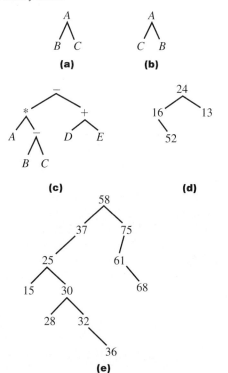

This is a mathematical definition, not a C++ method. The last line in the definition states that the number of leaves in *t* is equal to the number of leaves in *t*'s left subtree plus the number of leaves in *t*'s right subtree. Just for practice, try to use this definition to calculate the number of leaves in Figure 8.1a. Of course, you can simply look at the whole tree and count the number of leaves, but the definition is atomic rather than holistic.

Each item in a binary tree is uniquely determined by its location in the tree. For example, let *t* be the binary tree shown in Figure 8.1c. There are two items in *t* with the value '−'. We can distinguish between them by referring to one of them as "the item whose value is '−' and whose location is at the root of *t*" and the other one as "the item whose value is '−' and whose location is at the root of the right subtree of the left subtree of *t*." We loosely refer to "an item" in a binary tree when, strictly speaking, we should say "the item" at such and such a location.

Let *t* be the following binary tree:

We say that x is the **parent** of y and that y is the **left child** of x. Similarly, we say that x is the **parent** of z and that z is the **right child** of x. In a binary tree, each item has zero, one, or two children. For example, in Figure 8.1d, 24 has two children, 16 and 13; 16 has 52 as its only child; 13 and 52 are childless, that is, they are leaves. For any item w in a tree, we write parent(w) for the parent of w, left(w) for the left child of w and right(w) for the right child of w.

In a binary tree, the root item does not have a parent, and every other item has exactly one parent. Continuing with the terminology of a family tree, we could define sibling, grandparent, grandchild, first cousin, ancestor, and descendant. For example, an item A is an **ancestor** of an item B if B is an item in the subtree whose root item is A. To put it recursively, A is an ancestor of B if parent(A) = B or if A is an ancestor of parent(B).

If A is an ancestor of B, the **path** from A to B is the sequence of items, starting with A and ending with B, in which each item in the sequence (except the last) is the parent of the next item. For example, in Figure 8.1e, the sequence 37, 25, 30, 32 is the path from 37 to 32.

Informally, the height of a binary tree is the number of branches between the root and the farthest leaf, that is, the leaf with the most ancestors. For example, here is a binary tree of height 3:

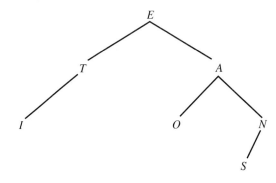

The height of this tree is 3 because the path from E to S has three branches. Suppose for some binary tree, the left subtree has a height of 12 and the right subtree has a height of 20. What is the height of the whole tree? The answer is 21.

In general, the height of a binary tree is one more than the maximum of the heights of the left and right subtrees. This leads us to a recursive definition of the height of a binary tree. But first, we need to know what the base case is, namely, the height of an empty tree. We want the height of a single-item tree to be 0: there are no branches from the root item; that is, the left and right subtrees are empty. But if 0 is one more than the height of an empty subtree, we need to define the height of an empty subtree to be, strangely enough, -1.

Let t be a binary tree. We define height(t), the **height** of t, as follows:

if t is empty,
    height(t) $= -1$
else
    height(t) $= 1 +$ maximum of {height(leftTree(t)), height(rightTree(t))}

It follows from this definition that a binary tree with a single item has height 0 because each of its empty subtrees has a height of -1. Also, the height of the binary tree in Figure 8.1a is 1. And the height of the binary tree in Figure 8.1e is 5.

Height is a property of an entire binary tree. For each item in a binary tree, we can define a similar concept: the level of the item. Informally, the level of a given item is the number of branches between the root item and the given item. For example, here is a binary tree, with the levels shown:

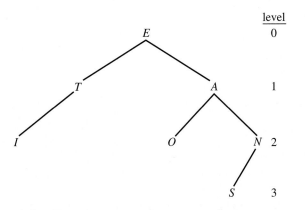

Notice that the level of the root item is 0, and the height of a tree is equal to the highest level in the tree. Here is a formal definition. Let t be a nonempty binary tree; for any item x in t, we define **level(x)**, the level of item x, as follows:

if x is the root item,
$\quad$ level$(x) = 0$
else
$\quad$ level$(x) = 1 +$ level(parent(x))

An item's level is also referred to as that item's **depth.** Strangely, the *height* of a non-empty binary tree is the *depth* of the farthest leaf!

A **two-tree** is a binary tree that either is empty or in which each nonleaf has two branches going down from it. For example, Figure 8.2a is a two-tree and Figure 8.2b is not a two-tree. Recursively speaking, a binary tree t is a **two-tree** if

$\quad$ t is empty

or

$\quad$ both subtrees of t are empty or both subtrees of t are nonempty two-trees.

A binary tree t is **full** if t is a two-tree with all its leaves on the same level. For example, Figure 8.3a is full and Figure 8.3b is not full. Recursively speaking, a binary tree t is **full** if

$\quad$ t is empty

or

$\quad$ t's left and right subtrees have the same height and both are full.

Figure 8.2 | (**a**) A two-tree; (**b**) a binary tree that is not a two-tree.

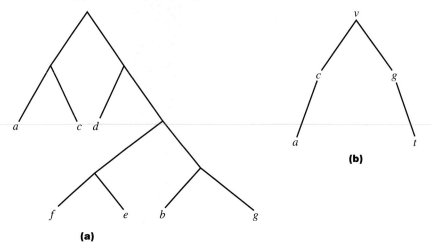

(**a**)

(**b**)

Of course, every full binary tree is a two-tree, but the converse is not necessarily true. For example, the tree in Figure 8.3b is a two-tree but is not full. For full binary trees, there is a relationship between the height and number of items in the tree. For example, if a full binary tree has a height of 2, the tree must have exactly 7 items:

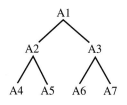

How many items must there be in a full binary tree of height 3? Of height 4? For a full binary tree t, can you conjecture the formula for the number of items in t as a function of height(t)?

A slightly weaker notion than fullness is completeness. A binary tree t is **complete** if t is full through level height(t) − 1, and all the leaves at the lowest level are as far to the left as possible. By "lowest level," we mean the level farthest from the root.

Any full binary tree is complete, but not every complete binary tree is full. Figure 8.4 shows several binary trees. For example, Figure 8.4a has a complete binary tree that is not full. The tree in Figure 8.4b is not complete because C has only one child. The tree in Figure 8.4c is not complete because leaves I and J are not as far to the left as they could be.

In a complete binary tree, we can associate an "index" with each item. The root item is assigned an index of 0. For any positive integer i, if the item at index i has children, the index of its left child is $2i + 1$ and the index of its right child is $2i +$

Figure 8.3 | (**a**) A full binary tree; (**b**) a binary tree that is not full.

(a)   (b)

Figure 8.4 | Three binary trees, of which only (**a**) is complete.

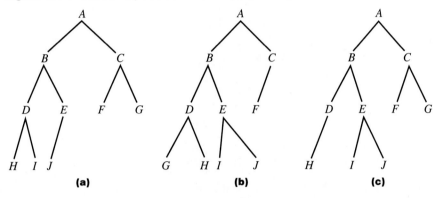

(a)   (b)   (c)

2. For example, if a complete binary tree has 10 items, the indices of those items are as follows:

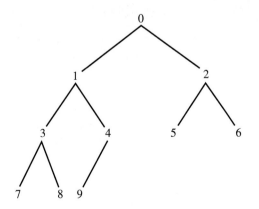

The parent of the item at index 8 is at index 3, and the parent of the item at index 5 is at index 2. In general, if i is a positive integer, the parent of the item at index i is at index $(i - 1) / 2$.

The index of an item is important in that we can store the items of a complete binary tree in an array. Specifically, we will store the item that is in index i in the tree at index i in the array. For example, here is an array with the items from Figure 8.4a:

A	B	C	D	E	F	G	H	I	J

Actually, what we will do (in Chapter 11) is store items in an array and then access the items as if they were in a complete binary tree. So the complete binary tree is an abstraction that can be implemented as an array. Most of the accessing will be of a child's index from the parent's index or of the parent's index from a child's index. Not only can these indices be calculated quickly,[1] the corresponding items can be quickly retrieved, thanks to the random-access property of arrays.

We have shown how we can recursively calculate leaves(t), the number of leaves in a binary tree t, and height(t), the height of the binary tree t. We can also recursively calculate the number of items, $n(t)$, in t:

> if t is empty
> > $n(t) = 0$
> else
> > $n(t) = 1 + n(\text{leftTree}(t)) + n(\text{rightTree}(t))$

8.1.1   The Binary Tree Theorem

For any binary tree t, leaves(t) $\leq n(t)$, and leaves(t) $= n(t)$ if and only if t consists of one item only. The following theorem characterizes the relationships between leaves(t), height(t), and $n(t)$.

Binary Tree Theorem   For any nonempty binary tree t,

1. leaves(t) $\leq \dfrac{n(t) + 1}{2.0}$

2. $\dfrac{n(t) + 1}{2.0} \leq 2^{\text{height}(t)}$

3. If t is a two-tree, then leaves(t) $= \dfrac{n(t) + 1}{2.0}$

4. If leaves(t) $= \dfrac{n(t) + 1}{2.0}$, t is a two-tree.

5. If t is full, $\dfrac{n(t) + 1}{2.0} = 2^{\text{height}(t)}$

6. If $\dfrac{n(t) + 1}{2.0} = 2^{\text{height}(t)}$, t is full.

---

[1] At the bit level, the value of $2i + 1$, for example, can be obtained from i with a left shift and an increment, and these are very fast, machine-level operations.

Note Because 2.0 is the denominator in the equations in the Binary Tree Theorem, the quotient is a floating point value. For example, 7/2.0 = 3.5. We cannot use integer division because of part 4 of the theorem. Let t be the following binary tree:

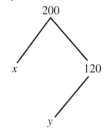

For this tree t, leaves(t) = $(n(t) + 1) / 2$, but t is not a two-tree.

All six parts of the theorem can be proved by induction on the height of t. Some of the details are given in Appendix 1. As it turns out, most theorems about binary trees can be proved by induction on the *height* of the tree. The reason for this is that if t is a binary tree, then both leftTree(t) and rightTree(t) have height less than height(t), and so the Principle of Mathematical Induction often applies. For example, here is a proof of part 2 of the Binary Tree Theorem (Example 5 of Appendix 1 has a proof of part 1):

Proof For $k = 0, 1, 2, \ldots$, let S_k be the statement:

If t is a binary tree of height k,

$$\frac{n(t) + 1}{2.0} \leq 2^{\text{height}(t)}$$

1. *Base case.* If $k = 0$, t has only one item, so

$$\frac{n(t) + 1}{2.0} = \frac{1 + 1}{2.0} = 1 = 2^0 = 2^{\text{height}(t)}$$

That is, S_0 is true.

2. *Inductive case.* Let k be any nonnegative integer, and assume S_0, $S_1, \ldots, S_k$ are true. Let t be a binary tree of height $k + 1$. Any item in t is either the root or in the left or right subtree. That is,

$$n(t) = 1 + n(\text{leftTree}(t)) + n(\text{rightTree}(t))$$

We have

$$\frac{n(t) + 1}{2.0} = \frac{1 + n(\text{leftTree } (t)) + n(\text{rightTree}(t)) + 1}{2.0}$$

$$= \frac{n(\text{leftTree}(t)) + 1}{2.0} + \frac{n(\text{rightTree}(t)) + 1}{2.0}$$

The heights of leftTree(t) and rightTree(t) are less than height(t), so the heights of leftTree(t) and rightTree(t) are $\leq k$, and the induction hypothesis applies. That is,

$$\frac{n(\text{leftTree}(t)) + 1}{2.0} + \frac{n(\text{rightTree}(t)) + 1}{2.0} \leq 2^{\text{height}(\text{leftTree}(t))} + 2^{\text{height}(\text{rightTree}(t))}$$

Let hmax be the maximum of height(leftTree(t)) and height(right Tree(t)). Then

$$2^{\text{height}(\text{leftTree}(t))} + 2^{\text{height}(\text{rightTree}(t))} \leq 2^{\text{hmax}} + 2^{\text{hmax}}$$
$$= 2^{1 + \text{hmax}}$$
$$= 2^{\text{height}(t)}$$

Following the trail of equalities and inequalities, we get

$$\frac{n(t) + 1}{2.0} \leq 2^{\text{height}(t)}$$

This proves that the inductive case is true. We conclude, by the Principle of Mathematical Induction, that part 2 of the Binary Tree Theorem is true for any nonempty binary tree t.

End of Proof

The height of a full binary tree is logarithmic in n, *the number of items in the tree.*

If t is a full binary tree, then from the Binary Tree Theorem, and the fact that any empty tree has height of -1, we conclude that

$$\text{height}(t) = \log_2 ((n(t) + 1) / 2.0)$$
$$= \log_2 (n(t) + 1) - 1$$

So we can say that the height of a full tree is logarithmic in n, where n is the number of items in the tree (we often use n instead of $n(t)$ when it is clear which tree we are referring to). Even if t is merely complete, its height is still logarithmic in n. See Exercise 8.7. On the other hand, t could be a chain. A ***chain*** is a binary tree in which each nonleaf has exactly one child. For example, here is an example of a chain:

The height of a chain is linear in n, *the number of items in the tree.*

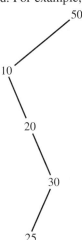

If t is a chain, then height(t) = $n(t) - 1$, so for chains the height is linear in n. Much of our work with trees in Chapters 9 and 10 will be concerned with maintaining logarithmic height and avoiding linear height. Basically, for inserting into or deleting from a binary tree whose height is logarithmic in n, worstTime(n) is logarithmic in n. That is why, in many applications, trees are preferable to sequential containers. For example, suppose we want the items stored in order in the container. Then with vectors, deques, and lists, for inserting or removing a specific item, worstTime(n) is linear in n.

8.1.2   External Path Length

You may wonder why we would be interested in adding up all the root-to-leaf path lengths, but the following definition turns out to be of great practical value. Let t be a nonempty binary tree. $E(t)$, the ***external path length*** of t, is the sum of the depths of all the leaves in t. For example, in Figure 8.5, the sum of the depths of the leaves is $2 + 4 + 4 + 4 + 5 + 5 + 1 = 25$.

The following lower bound on external path lengths yields an important result in the study of sorting algorithms (see Chapter 12).

External Path Length Theorem   Let t be a binary tree with $k > 0$ leaves. Then
$$E(t) \geq (k/2) \, \text{floor}(\log_2 k)$$

Figure 8.5 I A binary tree whose external path length is 25.

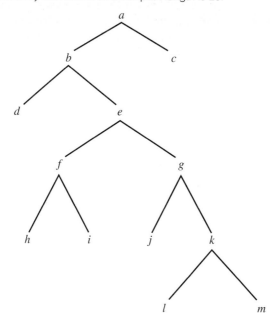

Proof   Let t be a binary tree with $k > 0$ leaves. For any level L, the maximum number of leaves possible at level L is 2^L—this can easily be shown by induction—and this occurs only if t is full. So the maximum number of leaves possible at *all* levels $\leq L$ is still 2^L because any leaf at a level less than L would prevent a full tree. When we substitute floor($\log_2 k$) $-$ 1 for L, we see that the maximum number of leaves at all levels less than or equal to floor($\log_2 k$) $-$ 1 is

$$2^{\text{floor}(\log_2 k) - 1} \leq 2^{\log_2 k - 1} = k/2$$

because $2^{\log_2 k} = k$. Therefore the *minimum* number of leaves at all levels greater than floor($\log_2 k$) $-$ 1 must be at least $k/2$. That is, the minimum number of leaves at all levels greater than or equal to floor($\log_2 k$) must be at least $k/2$. Each such leaf contributes at least floor($\log_2 k$) to the external path length, so we must have

$$E(t) \geq (k/2) \text{ floor}(\log_2 k)$$

End of Proof

Note   This result is all we will need in Chapter 12, but at a cost of a somewhat more complicated proof, we could show that $E(t) \geq k \log_2 k$ for any nonempty *two-tree* with k leaves. See Kruse (1987, pp. 177–178) for details.

8.1.3   Traversals of a Binary Tree

A *traversal* of a binary tree t is an algorithm that accesses each item in t exactly once. There is no BinaryTree class: It would not be flexible enough to support the variety of insert and delete methods already in the binary tree–related data structures in the Standard Template Library. So the following algorithms are not methods. We identify four different kinds of traversal.

Traversal 1. inOrder traversal: Left-Root-Right   Here is the algorithm—assume that t is a binary tree:

```
inOrder(t)
{
    if (t is not empty)
    {
        inOrder(leftTree(t));
        access the root item of t;
        inOrder(rightTree(t));
    } // if
} // inOrder traversal
```

During each recursive call, one item is accessed. If n represents the number of items in the tree, worstTime(n) is linear in n. We can use this recursive description to list the items in an inOrder traversal of the following binary tree t:

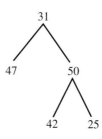

The tree *t* is not empty, so we start by performing an inOrder traversal of leftTree(*t*), namely,

47

This one-item tree becomes the current version of *t*. Since its left subtree is empty, we access the root item of this *t*, namely, 47. That completes the traversal of this version of *t* since rightTree(*t*) is empty. So now *t* again refers to the original tree. We next access *t*'s root item, namely,

31

After that, we perform an inOrder traversal of rightTree(*t*), namely,

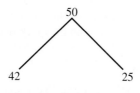

This becomes the current version of *t*. We start by performing an inOrder traversal of leftTree(*t*), namely,

42

Now this tree with one item becomes the current version of *t*. Since its left subtree is empty, we access *t*'s root item, 42. The right subtree of this *t* is empty. So we have completed the inOrder traversal of the tree with the single item 42, and now, once again, *t* refers to the binary tree with three items:

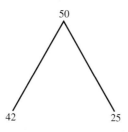

We next access the root item of this version of *t*, namely,

50

Finally, we perform an inOrder traversal of rightTree(t), namely,

25

Since the left subtree of this single-item tree t is empty, we access the root item of t, namely 25. We are now done since t's right subtree is also empty.

The complete listing is

47 31 42 50 25

The inOrder traversal gets its name from the fact that, for a special kind of binary tree—a binary search tree—an inOrder traversal will access the items in order. For example, here is a binary search tree:

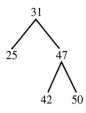

An inOrder traversal accesses the items as follows:

25 31 42 47 50

In a binary search tree, all the items in the left subtree are less than or equal to the root item, which is less than or equal to all the items in the right subtree. What other property do you think a binary search tree must have so that an inOrder traversal accesses the items in order?

Hint   The following is not a binary search tree:

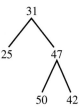

We will devote most of the rest of this chapter and all of Chapters 9 and 10 to the study of binary search trees.

Traversal 2. postOrder Traversal: Left-Right-Root   The algorithm, with t a binary tree, is

```
postOrder(t)
{
    if (t is not empty)
    {
            postOrder(leftTree(t));
            postOrder(rightTree(t));
```

    access the root item of *t*;
      } // if
   } // postOrder traversal

The worstTime(*n*) is linear in *n* because one item is accessed during each recursive call.
    Suppose we conduct a postOrder traversal of the following tree:

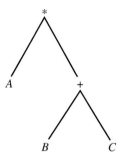

The items will be accessed in the following order:

$$A \; B \; C + *$$

We can view this binary tree as an "expression tree": each nonleaf is a binary operator whose operands are the associated left and right subtrees. With this interpretation, a postOrder traversal produces postfix notation!

Traversal 3. preOrder Traversal: Root-Left-Right The algorithm, with *t* a binary tree, is

```
preOrder(t)
{
    if (t is not empty)
    {
        access the root item of t;
        preOrder(leftTree(t));
        preOrder(rightTree(t));
    } // if
} // preOrder traversal
```

As with the inOrder and postOrder algorithms, worstTime(*n*) is linear in *n*.
    A preOrder traversal of

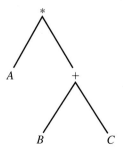

accesses the items in the following order:

$$* A + B\ C$$

For an expression tree, a preOrder traversal produces prefix notation.

A search of a binary tree that employs a preOrder traversal is called a ***depth-first search*** because the search goes to the left as deeply as possible before searching to the right. For example, suppose we make a depth-first search of

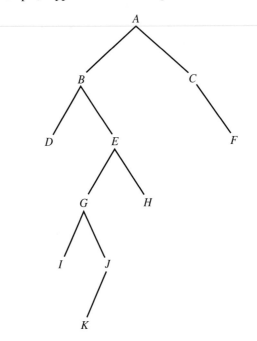

If the goal is *H,* then the order in which the items will be accessed is

$$A\ B\ D\ E\ G\ I\ J\ K\ H$$

The ***backtracking*** strategy from Chapter 4 includes a depth-first search, but at each stage there may be more than two choices. For example, in the maze-search, the choices are to move north, east, south, or west. Because moving north is the first option, that option will be repeatedly applied until either the goal is reached or moving north is not possible. Then a move east will be taken, if possible, and then as many moves north as possible or necessary. In Chapter 14, we will revisit backtracking for a generalization of binary trees.

Traversal 4. breadthFirst Traversal: Level-by-Level   To perform a breadth-first traversal of a nonempty binary tree *t,* first access the root item; then the children of the root, from left to right; then the grandchildren of the root, from left to right; and so on.

For example, suppose we perform a breadth-first traversal of the following binary tree:

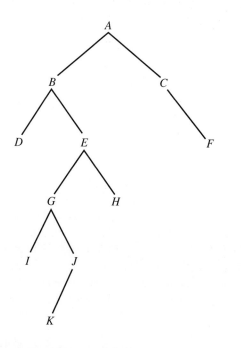

The order in which items would be accessed is

$$A\ B\ C\ D\ E\ F\ G\ H\ I\ J\ K$$

One way to accomplish this traversal is to generate, level by level, a list of (pointers to) nonempty subtrees. We need to retrieve these subtrees in the same order they were generated so the items can be accessed level by level. What kind of container allows retrievals in the same order as insertions? A queue! Here is the algorithm, with t a binary tree:

```
breadthFirst(t)
{
        // my_queue is a queue of binary trees
        // tree is a binary tree

        if (t is not empty)
        {
                my_queue.push(t);
                while (my_queue is not empty)
                {
                        tree = my_queue.front( );
                        my_queue.pop( );
                        access tree's root;
                        if (leftTree(tree) is not empty)
                                my_queue.push (leftTree(tree));
                        if (rightTree(tree) is not empty)
                                my_queue.push(rightTree(tree));

                } // while
```

} // if *t* not empty

} // breadthFirst traversal

During each loop iteration, one item is accessed, so worstTime(n) is linear in n.

We used a queue for a breadth-first traversal because we wanted the subtrees retrieved in the same order they were saved (first in, first out). With inOrder, postOrder, and preOrder traversals, the subtrees are retrieved in the reverse of the order they were saved in (last in, first out). For each of those three traversals, we utilized recursion, which, as we saw in Chapter 7, is equivalent to an iterative, stack-based algorithm.

We will encounter this type of traversal again in Chapter 14 when we study breadth-first traversals of structures less restrictive than binary trees. Incidentally, if we are willing to be more restrictive, specifically, if we require a complete binary tree, then the tree can be stored in an array, and a breadth-first traversal is simply an iteration through the array. The root is at index 0, the root's left child at index 1, the root's right child at index 2, the root's leftmost grandchild at index 3, and so on.

After all of this theoretical treatment of binary trees, you are probably ready to study a real-live class. In Section 8.2, we explore the BinSearchTree class, first as a data structure, that is, from the user's point of view. In a BinSearchTree, the average Time(n) for inserting and deleting is logarithmic in n. This represents a marked improvement over ordered vectors, deques, and lists, for which the corresponding insertion and deletion methods have averageTime(n) that is linear in n. But in the worst case, a BinSearchTree is no better than the sequential container classes: For inserting or deleting in a BinSearchTree, worstTime(n) is linear in n.

If you prefer a class whose worstTime(n) for inserting and deleting is logarithmic in n, you will have to wait until Chapter 9, when we study AVL trees. The AVL Tree class, and the rb_tree (for red-black tree) class in Chapter 10, attain logarithmic worst time for inserting and deleting. But the method definitions—for example, in the Hewlett-Packard implementation of the rb_tree class—are quite a bit more complicated than those for binary search trees. From a practical standpoint, the main reason for studying the BinSearchTree class is that it will prepare you for the AVLTree class and the rb_tree class.

8.2 | BINARY SEARCH TREES

We start with a recursive definition of a binary search tree:

Another recursive definition

A **binary search tree** *t* is a binary tree such that either *t* is empty or

1. Each item in leftTree(*t*) is less than or equal the root item of *t*.
2. Each item in rightTree(*t*) is greater than or equal to the root item of *t*.
3. Both leftTree(*t*) and rightTree(*t*) are binary search trees.

Figure 8.6 shows a binary search tree.

Figure 8.6 | A binary search tree.

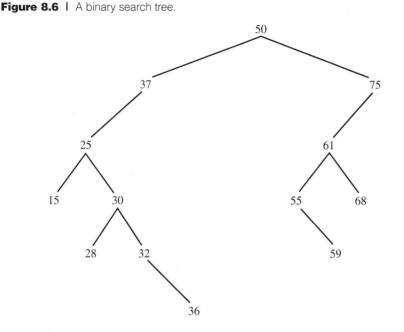

An inOrder traversal of a binary search tree accesses the items in increasing order. For example, with the binary search tree in Figure 8.6, an inOrder traversal accesses, in order,

15 25 28 30 32 36 37 50 55 59 61 68 75

As we have defined a binary search tree, duplicate items are permitted. Some authors have "less than" and "greater than" in the binary search tree definition. For the sake of consistency with what follows in Chapter 10, we opt for using "less than or equal to" and "greater than or equal to."

A binary search tree is an example of an associative container. In an ***associative container,*** the location of an item in the container is determined by comparing the item with other items in the container. Each item has a ***key:*** that part of an item used in comparisons. In Chapters 9 and 10, we will study several other associative containers.

Section 8.2.1 describes the binary-search-tree data structure as a user's view of a BinSearchTree class.

8.2.1   The BinSearchTree **Class**

We will study the binary-search-tree data structure through the method interfaces of the BinSearchTree class. For the BinSearchTree class, we assume that each user will supply an instantiated version of the item class T, with **operator**< for comparing items. Equality, **operator**==, need not be explicitly defined in the template argument corresponding to T because a == b is equivalent to !(a < b) && !(b < a).

The item class corresponding to the template parameter T must define operator< for comparing items.

The BinSearchTree class is intended to provide a simple introduction to binary search trees. For production work—programs that will be run repeatedly—the associative containers of the Standard Template Library (see Chapter 10) are recommended. So rather than endowing the BinSearchTree class with a large number of methods, we take the opposite approach. Here are the eight method interfaces in a minimal binary-search-tree class (for the sake of validation, Lab 20 adds a height method):

1. // Postcondition: this BinSearchTree is empty.
    BinSearchTree( );

2. // Postcondition: the number of items in this BinSearchTree has been returned.
    unsigned size( ) **const;**

3. // Postcondition: if there is an item in this BinSearchTree that equals item, the
    //   value returned is an iterator pointing to that item. Otherwise,
    //   the value returned is an iterator with the same value as the
    //   iterator returned by the end( ) method. The averageTime(n) is
    //   O(log n) and worstTime(n) is O(n).
    Iterator find (**const** T& item) **const;**

    > *Note*   This is a method in the BinSearchTree class. This is not the generic algorithm find, whose averageTime(*n*) is *O*(*n*), not *O*(log *n*).

4. // Postcondition: item has been inserted into this BinSearchTree. An iterator
    //   positioned at the inserted item has been returned. The
    //   averageTime(n) is O(log n) and worstTime(n) is O(n).
    Iterator insert (**const** T& item);

    > *Note 1*   There is no parameter that specifies *where* the item is to be inserted. That is because the item must be inserted where it belongs according to the ordering. If a user were allowed to specify where an item was to be inserted, the insertion could destroy the ordering. Then we would no longer have a binary search tree.

    > *Note 2*   A user can preclude the insertion of duplicate items into a binary search tree. Suppose dictionary is an object in the BinSearchTree class. To insert item in dictionary only if item is not already in dictionary:

    > **if** (dictionary.find (item) == dictionary.end( ))
    >   dictionary.insert (item);

5. // Precondition: itr is positioned at an item in this BinSearchTree.
    // Postcondition: the item that itr is positioned at has been deleted from this
    //   BinSearchTree. Any iterator that was, before this call,

```
//            positioned at the successor of *itr has been invalidated. The
//            worstTime(n) is O(n). The amoritizedTime(n) is constant, and
//            so averageTime(n) is constant.
void erase (iterator itr);
```

> *Note*   To delete an arbitrary item from a binary search tree, we combine the find and erase methods. For example, to remove one copy of word from the BinSearchTree object dictionary:
>
> dictionary.erase (dictionary.find (word));
>
> A loop can be used to delete *all* copies of an item from a BinSearchTree object.

6.
```
//  Postcondition: if this BinSearchTree is nonempty, an iterator positioned at
//                 the smallest item in the tree has been returned. Otherwise,
//                 the iterator returned has the same value as the iterator
//                 returned by the end( ) method.
Iterator begin( );
```
7.
```
//  Postcondition: the value returned is an iterator that can be used in a
//                 comparison for ending the traversal of this BinSearchTree. If
//                 this BinSearchTree is nonempty, the largest item is in the
//                 position just before the position of the iterator returned.
Iterator end( );
```
8.
```
//  Postcondition: The space allocated for this BinSearchTree has been
//                 deallocated. The worstTime(n) is O(n).
~BinSearchTree( );
```

What's missing from this listing of method interfaces? Binary search trees lack the mainstays of the sequential containers: push_back, pop_back, push_front, and pop_front. The pushes would be illegal because, as explained in note 1 of the insert method (method 4), a user is not allowed to specify where an item is to be inserted. The pops would be legal, but are not included because users would seldom want to delete the smallest or largest item unless they knew what that item happened to be. And in those cases, the erase method could be used; we will show how to do this after we specify the method interfaces for the Iterator class.

8.2.2   The Iterator **Class for the** BinSearchTree **Class**

Binary-search-tree iterators are bidirectional, so the iterator methods are the same as those for the list class iterators: both prefix and postfix versions of $++$ and $--$, * (for dereferencing), $==$, and $!=$. So if itr is an Iterator object, we can iterate through a BinSearchTree object my_tree in the following loop:

```
for (itr = my_tree.begin( ); itr != my_tree.end( ); itr++)
    *itr . . . // accesses item that itr is positioned at
```

As you may expect, the code needed to increment or decrement a BinSearchTree iterator is quite a bit more complex than an iterator for a vector, a list, or even a deque.

Here is a small program that illustrates the use of the BinSearchTree class and its associated Iterator class:

```cpp
#include <string>
#include <iostream>
#include "bst.h" // defines BinSearchTree class

// This program validates searches, insertions and deletions in a binary
// search tree.

using namespace std;

int main ( )
{
    const string CLOSE_WINDOW_PROMPT =
        "Please press the Enter key to close this output window.";

    BinSearchTree<int> tree;
    BinSearchTree<int>:Iterator itr;

    tree.insert (85);
    tree.insert (70);
    tree.insert (91);
    tree.insert (70);

    cout << "Here is the tree:" << endl;
    for (itr = tree.begin( ); itr != tree.end( ); itr++)
        cout << *itr << " ";

    if (tree.find (72) == tree.end( ))
        cout << endl << endl << "72 was not found in the tree"
             << endl;;

    itr = tree.find (85);
    if (itr != tree.end( ))
        cout << endl << endl << "85 was found in the tree" << endl;
    tree.erase (itr);
    cout << endl << endl << "Here is the tree after 85 was deleted:"
         << endl;
    for (itr = tree.begin( ); itr != tree.end( ); itr++)
        cout << *itr << " ";

    cout << endl << endl << "The largest item in the tree is "
                 << *--tree.end( );

    cout << endl << endl << "size = " << tree.size ( );
```

```
          cout << endl << endl << CLOSE_WINDOW_PROMPT;
          cin.get( );
      } // binsearchtreeexample
```

The output is as follows:

```
Here is the tree:
70 70 85 91

72 was not found in the tree

85 was found in the tree

Here is the tree after 85 was deleted:
70 70 91

The largest item in the tree is 91

size = 3

Please press the Enter key to close this output window.
```

Notice how the largest item in the tree is accessed: since tree.end( ) returns an iterator positioned just beyond the largest item, −−tree.end( ) returns an iterator positioned *at* the largest item. How would you access the smallest item in the tree?

We now turn our attention to one possible implementation of the BinSearchTree class. Project 8.1 considers another implementation.

8.2.3   Fields and Implementation of the BinSearchTree **Class**

The fields in the BinSearchTree class are similar to the fields in the list class in Chapter 6. The major field is header, a pointer to the **struct** tree_node:

```
struct tree_node
{
    T item;
    tree_node* parent,
             * left,
             * right;
    bool isHeader;    // indicates whether this node is the header node
}; // tree_node

tree_node* header;
```

The only other field in the BinSearchTree class is

```
unsigned node_count;
```

The node_count field keeps track of the size of the tree. When a tree is created, node_count gets the value 0, and in header's tree_node, the parent link gets the value NULL, the left and right links point back to header, and isHeader gets the value **true**. The item field is undefined; in fact, the item field of the header's tree_node remains undefined, just as with data field in the list class. Figure 8.7 shows the configuration for an empty BinSearchTree object.

When an item is added to an empty tree, that item's value is copied into the item field of a root node, the root node's parent field points back to the header node, and the root node's left and right fields get NULL values. All the pointer fields in header now point to this root node. The purpose of the isHeader field is to distinguish the header node from the root node. For example, after the item 17 is inserted into an empty tree, we have the tree shown in Figure 8.8.

Notice a weird feature of this representation: The parent of the root node is the header node, and the parent of the header node is the root node! So the root node is the grandparent of itself. There once was a hit song, "I'm My Own Grandpa."[2]

Figure 8.7 | The representation of an empty BinSearchTree object.

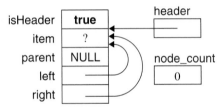

Figure 8.8 | The internal representation of a BinSearchTree object with a single item, 17.

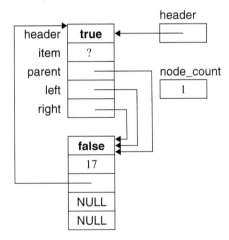

---

[2]A man *M* married a widow *W* who had a grown daughter *D*. *D* married *M*'s father and they had a son *S*. That made *S* the "brother" of *M* (because they had the same father) and also the "grandson" of *M* (because *M*'s wife was the grandmother of *S*). But the "grandfather" of *S* is also the grandfather of *S*'s brother. So *M* was his own grandfather.

As items are added to this tree, the left and right fields of the root node will be adjusted, as you would expect. What you might not expect is that the left and right fields of the node referenced by header are also adjusted. They point to the nodes containing the *smallest* and *largest* items, respectively. For example, Figure 8.9 shows the internal representation of a BinSearchTree object with five items.

By having header's left field point to the smallest item, the design of the begin( ) method becomes simple and fast: return an iterator positioned at the node pointed to by header's left field. What about the largest item? The end( ) method returns an iterator positioned at the header's node, that is, just beyond the last node. So a user can—as we saw in the program in Section 8.2.2—access the largest item in a BinSearchTree by retreating from the end. The effect is to access the item in the node pointed to by the header's right field.

We will implement the Iterator class after we finish up the BinSearchTree class, but for now, all we need to know about the Iterator class's fields and implementation is that there is a pointer field and a one-parameter constructor:

> *In the header node, the* left *and* right *fields point to the nodes with the smallest and largest items, respectively, in the tree.*

typedef tree_node* Link;

protected:

Figure 8.9 | The internal representation of a **BinSearchTree** object with five items.

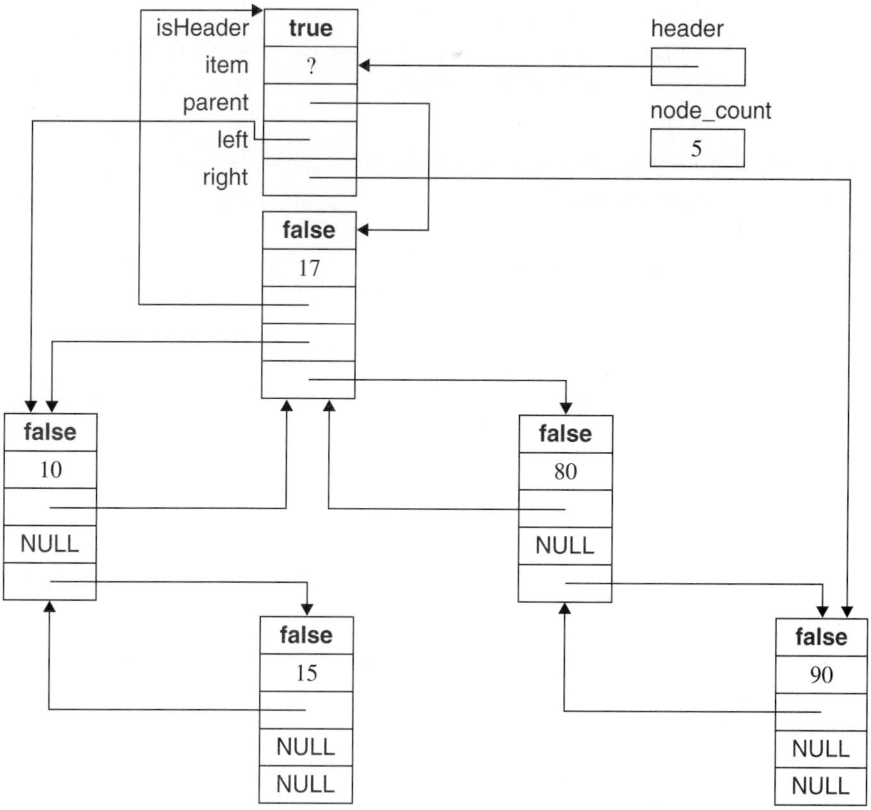

```
    Link link;

    Iterator (Link new_link) : link (new_link) { }
```

Recall that the iterator class associated with the list class had a similar pointer field and one-parameter constructor, and both were **protected**.

Getting back to the BinSearchTree class, let's focus on the definitions of the three essential methods: find, insert, and erase. For the find method, we start a child pointed at the root and descend the tree, replacing child with its left or right child based on the comparison between child -> item and the item sought. The method definition is

```
    Iterator find( const T& item)
    {
        Link parent = header;
        Link child = header -> parent;

        while (child != NULL)
        {
            if (! (child -> item < item) )
            {
                parent = child;
                child = child -> left;
            } // if <
            else
                child = child -> right;
        } // while

        if (parent == header || item < parent -> item)
            return end( );
        else
            return parent;
    } // find
```

For example, suppose we start with the following binary search tree:

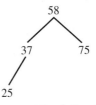

If we search for 30 in this tree, we get the following sequence of values for parent and child (dereferenced items are given when the pointer is non-NULL):

parent	child
NULL	58
58	37
37	25
	NULL

The loop is now terminated because child has the value NULL. And since item is less than parent -> item, the value returned is an iterator positioned beyond the last item in the tree.

One of the unusual features of this method is that it does not stop as soon as the item sought is accessed in the tree! (This is similar to the binary_search algorithm in Lab 11.) Suppose, for example, that the tree were searched for 37. We would have the following sequence of values for parent and child (dereferenced if non-NULL):

parent	child
NULL	58
58	37
37	25
	NULL

During the second loop iteration, child -> item will be equal to the item sought, namely, 37. Then child is saved in parent and child is replaced with child -> left. From that point on, the child item can never be greater than the item sought. That is, the child item will, from then on, be less than or equal to the item sought. So parent ->item, from then on, will be less than or equal to the item sought. At the conclusion of the loop, parent is not equal to header and item is not less than parent -> item, so (an iterator positioned at) parent will be returned, as is appropriate. Why was this loop designed not to stop when the item is found? For the sake of efficiency: Each loop iteration has only one comparison instead of two.

How long does this method take? For this method, indeed, for all the noneasy methods in the BinSearchTree class, the essential feature for estimating worst Time(n) or averageTime(n) is the *height* of the tree. Suppose the search is successful; a similar analysis can be used for the unsuccessful case. In the worst case, we will have a chain, and be seeking the leaf. For example, suppose we are seeking 25 in the following binary search tree:

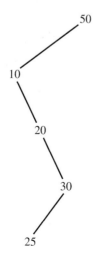

In such a case, the number of loop iterations is equal to the height of the tree. In general, if n is the number of items in the tree, the height of the tree is $n - 1$, so worstTime(n) is linear in n.

We now determine averageTime(n) for a successful search. Again, the key is the height of the tree. For binary search trees constructed through random insertions and removals, the average height H is logarithmic in n (see Cormen, 1992). This claim is tested in Lab 20. The find method starts searching at level 0, and each loop iteration descends to the next lower level in the tree. Since averageTime(n) requires no more than H iterations, we immediately conclude that averageTime(n) is O(log n).

To establish that averageTime(n) is logarithmic in n, we need to show that $O(\log n)$ is the smallest upper bound of averageTime(n). The average—over all binary search trees—number of iterations is greater than or equal to the average number of iterations for a complete binary search tree. In a complete binary tree t, at least half of the items are leaves (see Exercise 8.13), so the average number of iterations by the find method must be at least (height(t) $-$ 1)/2, which is, by Exercise 8.7, (ceil($\log_2(n(t) + 1)$) $-$ 2)/2. That is, the average number of iterations for the find method is greater than or equal to a function of log n. So averageTime(n) cannot be any better than $O(\log n)$.

For the find *method in the* BinSearchTree *class, averageTime(*n*) is logarithmic in* n.

We conclude from the two previous paragraphs that averageTime(n) is logarithmic in n. Incidentally, that is why we defined the find method instead of using the generic algorithm find. For that version, averageTime(n) is linear in n.

If the binary search tree is full, the height of the tree is logarithmic in n. And it is this situation that gives the binary search tree its name. For then the find method accesses the same items, in the same order, as the binary_search generic algorithm applied to an array with the same items. For example, the root item in a full binary search tree corresponds to the middle item in the array.

8.2.4   Recursive Methods?

One curiosity with the definition of the find method is that it is not recursive. Up to this point in the chapter, most of the concepts—including the binary search tree itself—were defined recursively. But when it comes to method definitions, looping is the rule rather than the exception. Why is that? The glib answer is that left and right are of type tree_node*, not of type BinSearchTree, so we cannot call

```
left.find (item) // illegal
```

But we could make find a wrapper method for a recursive findItem method:

```
bool find (const T& item)
{
        return findItem (header -> parent, item);
} // method find
```

The findItem method is quite simple:

```
Iterator findItem (Link link, const T& item)
{
```

```
        if (link == NULL)
                return end( );
        if (link -> item < item)
                return findItem (link -> right, item);
        if (item < link -> item)
                return findItem (link -> left, item);
        return link; // automatic type conversion to Iterator
}
```

This recursive version is slightly less efficient—in both time and space—than the iterative version (although the Big-O time estimates are identical). And it is this slight difference that sinks the recursive version. For the iterative version is virtually identical to one we will see in Chapter 10 in the Hewlett-Packard implementation of the rb_tree class, where efficiency is prized above elegance. Besides, some of the luster of recursion is diminished by the necessity of having a wrapper method.

The insert method is similar to the find method in that there is a loop in which we descend the tree and save the parent of the adjusted node pointer. Special care must be taken in case the inserted item becomes the leftmost or rightmost item in the tree. Here is the definition:

```
Iterator insert (const T& item)
{
        if (header -> parent == NULL)
        {
                insertLeaf (item, header, header -> parent);
                header -> left = header -> parent;
                header -> right = header -> parent;
                return header -> parent;
        } // inserting at tree's root
        else
        {
                Link parent = header,
                        child = header -> parent;

                while (child != NULL)
                {
                        parent = child;
                        if (item < child -> item)
                                child = child -> left;
                        else
                                child = child -> right;
                } // while
                if (item < parent -> item)
                {
                        insertLeaf (item, parent, parent -> left);
```

```
                         if (header -> left == parent) // parent -> item was smallest
                                               // item
                            header -> left = parent -> left;
                         return parent -> left;
                      } // insert at left of parent
                   else
                   {
                         insertLeaf (item, parent, parent -> right);
                         if (header -> right == parent) // parent -> item was
                                               // largest item
                            header -> right = parent -> right;
                         return parent -> right;
                      } // insert at right of parent
                } // tree not empty
             } // insert
```

The insert *method inserts an item as a leaf in the* BinSearch Tree *object.*

The insertLeaf method actually inserts the item as a leaf, adjusts the links, and increments node_count:

```
    void insertLeaf (const T& item, Link parent, Link& child)
    {
          child = new tree_node;
          child -> item = item;
          child -> parent = parent;
          child -> left = NULL;
          child -> right = NULL;
          child -> isHeader = false;
          node_count++;
    } // insertLeaf
```

For example, suppose we insert 30 into the following binary search tree:

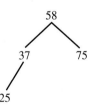

We would have the following sequence of values for parent and child (dereferenced if non-NULL):

parent	child
NULL	58
58	37
37	25
25	NULL

The execution of the **while** statement would now terminate because child has the value NULL. Then, with 30 >= parent -> item, 30 would be inserted—as a leaf—to the right of parent. In fact, *each inserted item in a binary search tree becomes a leaf.*

The analysis of insert is the same as for find: averageTime(*n*) is logarithmic in *n* but worstTime(*n*) is linear in *n*. A recursive version of insert is somewhat more elegant (and nominally slower) than the iterative version. As with the recursive find method, we start with a wrapper method:

```
Iterator insert (const T& item)
{
     if (header -> parent == NULL)
     {
          insertLeaf (item, header, header -> parent);
          header -> left = header -> parent;
          header -> right = header -> parent;
          return header -> parent;
     } // inserting at tree's root
     return insertItem (item, header, header -> parent);
} // insert
```

The recursive method insertItem is as follows:

```
Iterator insertItem (const T& item, Link parent, Link& child)
{
     if (child == NULL)
     {
          insertLeaf (item, parent, child);
          if (item < header -> left -> item)
               header -> left = child;
          if (item > header -> right -> item)
               header -> right = child;
          return child;
     }
     if (item < child -> item)
               return insertItem (item, child, child -> left);
     return insertItem (item, child, child -> right);
} // method insertItem
```

We now tackle the erase (Iterator itr) method. Given the Iterator parameter itr, we need to access the field in itr's parent node that points to itr's node. This field will be the parent field if itr is positioned at the root node, and otherwise the left or right field of itr's parent. We then alter that pointer field to accomplish the deletion of itr's node. So the method that accomplishes the deletion—deleteLink—will have a pointer as a reference parameter. See Exercise 8.15.

We have mentioned that the Iterator class has a pointer field, link, that points to the node the iterator is positioned at. That's all we need to know about the Iterator class in order to define the erase method. Here is the definition of erase:

```
void erase (Iterator itr)
{
        if (itr.link -> parent -> parent == itr.link) // itr positioned at root node
                deleteLink (itr.link -> parent -> parent);
        else if (itr.link -> parent -> left == itr.link) // itr positioned at a left child
                deleteLink (itr.link -> parent -> left);
        else
                deleteLink (itr.link -> parent -> right);
} // erase
```

The deleteLink method removes the node pointed to by the parameter link. If that node's left or right subtree is empty, we simply prune that node. That is, we replace the node with its right subtree's node (if the left subtree is empty) or with the left subtree's node. Figure 8.10 shows before and after examples of this case. The deletion is somewhat more difficult if both subtrees are nonempty. To get an idea of how to proceed in this case, suppose we want to delete the root of the tree in Figure 8.11.

For an item with two children, the erase *method replaces the item with its immediate successor, and then prunes that successor from the tree.*

We want to accomplish the deletion without restructuring the tree. So before 28 can be removed, we need to find an item to substitute for 28. The only items suitable in this regard are the immediate predecessor, 26, and the immediate successor, 37. For example, if in Figure 8.11, we substitute 37 for 28 and then delete the root from the tree whose root item is the "old" 37, we would get the tree shown in Figure 8.12. Because the immediate successor of the to-be-deleted item is the leftmost item in the right subtree, that item has no left child, and so deleting that item is covered by pruning—see Figure 8.10.

Figure 8.10 | (**a**) A binary search tree, from which 30 is to be deleted and in which the left subtree is empty. (**b**) The same binary search tree after 30 has been deleted.

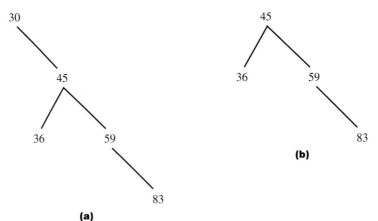

The deleteLink method so far is shown here. The prune method replaces link with its left or right subtree, whichever is appropriate. The hard work, finding and deleting the successor in the right subtree, is postponed.

```
// Postcondition: The item pointed to by link has been deleted.
void deleteLink (Link& link) {
```

Figure 8.11 I A binary search tree from which 28 is to be deleted.

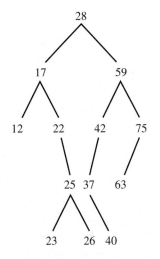

Figure 8.12 I The binary search tree obtained from the binary search tree in Figure 8.11 when 28 is deleted by substituting its immediate successor, 37, for 28 and then deleting the "old" 37.

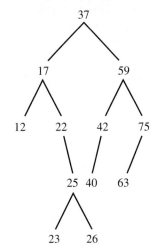

> **if** (link->left == NULL || link->right == NULL) // the item has no
>   // children
>   prune (link);
> **else**
>   // Delete the successor of link from link's right subtree.
> } // deleteLink

The definition of the prune method would be easy except that the deleted node might have contained the smallest or largest item. For example, suppose we prune the root of the following tree:

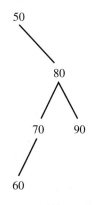

Before the deletion, 50 was the smallest item. To get the smallest item after the deletion, we need to start at the new root, whose item is 80, and go left as far as possible, to the node whose item is 60. We then store a pointer to this node in header's left field; recall that header's left field points to the node with the smallest item.

Here is the definition of the prune method:

```
// Precondition: the subtree pointed to by link has at most one child.
// Postcondition: The item pointed to by link has been deleted from this
// BinSearchTree.
void prune (Link& link)
{
        Link linkCopy = link,
              newLink;

        node_count--;
        if ((link -> left == NULL) && (link -> right == NULL))
        {
                if (link == header -> left)
                        header -> left = link -> parent; // new leftmost
                if (link == header -> right)
                        header -> right = link -> parent; // new rightmost
                link = NULL;
```

```
    } // link's item is a leaf
    else if (link -> left == NULL)
    {
        link = link -> right;
        link -> parent = linkCopy -> parent;
        if (linkCopy == header -> left)
        {
            newLink = link;
            while ((newLink -> left) != NULL)
                newLink = newLink -> left;
            header -> left = newLink; // new leftmost
        } // recalculate leftmost
    } // link -> left nonempty
    else
    {
        link = link -> left;
        link -> parent = linkCopy -> parent;
        if (linkCopy == header -> right)
        {
            newLink = link;
            while ((newLink -> right) != NULL)
                newLink = newLink -> right;
            header -> right = newLink; // new rightmost
        } // recalculate rightmost
    } // root -> right nonempty
    delete linkCopy;
} // prune
```

Finally, we develop the code to delete link's successor from the right subtree of link. The basic idea is that we want to get to the leftmost node in this right subtree. When we finally reach a node whose left subtree is empty, then the node's item is the successor of the item to be deleted. So we replace link's item with that successor item and then prune that successor node from the tree.

Here is the definition of deleteLink:

```
// Postcondition: The item that had been the link item has been deleted.
void deleteLink (Link& link)
{
    if (link -> left == NULL || link -> right == NULL)
        prune (link);
    else if (link -> right -> left == NULL)
    {
        link -> item = link -> right -> item;
        prune (link -> right);
```

```
        } // empty left subtree of right subtree of link
        else
        {
                Link temp = link -> right -> left;
                while (temp -> left != NULL)
                        temp = temp -> left;
                link -> item = temp -> item;
                prune (temp -> parent -> left);
        } // nonempty left subtree of right subtree of link
} // deleteLink
```

Let's start the analysis of the erase method and its subordinates by considering the worst case: when the Iterator parameter is positioned at the root of a tree and the tree is a chain whose only leaf is the root item's successor. Then the number of loop iterations in deleteLink will be $n - 1$. So worstTime(n) is linear in n. For the average time, the number of loop iterations to find the successor is equal to the number of iterations made by **operator**++ in the Iterator class. In Section 8.2.5, we will show that for **operator**++, averageTime(n) is constant; in fact, amortizedTime(n) is constant. So for the erase method, averageTime(n) is constant.

Finally, we develop the destructor. The recursive version, with a wrapper, is short and sweet. The method destroy, called by the wrapper, recursively destroys the left and right subtrees of a node, and then deallocates the space for the node:

```
~BinSearchTree( )
{
        destroy (header -> parent);
} // destructor

void destroy (Link link)
{
        if (link != NULL)
        {
                destroy (link -> left);
                destroy (link -> right);
                delete (link);
        } // if
} // destroy method
```

For each pair of recursive calls, one node is deallocated, so the total number of recursive calls is $2n$, and worstTime(n) is linear in n. An iterative version of the destructor is somewhat cumbersome because once a node has been deallocated, its parent is no longer accessible. For a hint in developing an iterative version, see Exercise 8.8.

8.2.5 BinSearchTree **Iterators**

Before we leave our discussion of binary search trees, we need to say a few words about the design of the associated Iterator class. As we saw, the class Iterator has a single field, link, which points to a node, and a constructor that creates an iterator from a node pointer.

The dereferencing operator, that is, **operator*,** and **operator**== have one-line definitions. But ++ and -- are nontrivial. To see why, suppose we have an iterator itr positioned at the node with item 50 in the following tree. How do we increment itr?

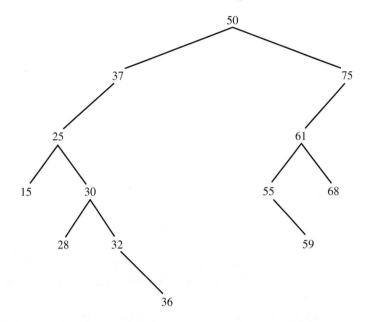

The successor of 50 is 55. To get to this successor from 50, we move right (to 75) and then move left as far as possible. Will this always work? Only for those nodes that have a nonnull right child. What if a node—for example, the one whose item is 36—has a null right child? If the right child of a node link is NULL, we get to link's successor by going back up the tree to the left as far as possible; the successor of link is the parent of that leftmost ancestor of link. For example, the successor of 36 is 37. Similarly, the successor of 68 is 75. Also, the successor of 28 is 30; since 28 is a left child, we go up the tree to the left zero times—remaining at 28—and then get that node's parent, whose item is 30. Finally, the successor of 75 is NULL because its leftmost ancestor is 50, which has no parent.

Here is the definition of the preincrement version of ++:

```
Iterator& Iterator:operator++ ( )
{
      Link tempLink;

      if ((link -> right) != NULL)
      {
            link = link -> right;
            while ((link -> left) != NULL)
                  link = link -> left;
```

```
          } // node has right child
          else
          {
                  tempLink = link -> parent;
                  while (link == tempLink -> right)
                  {
                          link = tempLink;
                          tempLink = tempLink -> parent;
                  } // moving up and leftward as far as possible
                  if ((link -> right) != tempLink)
                          link = tempLink;
          } // node has no right child
          return *this;
     } // prefix ++
```

The time for **operator++( )** is not necessarily constant. For example, if we insert the sequence $n, 1, 2, 3, \ldots, n - 1$ into an initially empty tree, $O(n)$ iterations will be required to advance from $n - 1$ to n. So worstTime(n) is linear in n. But in a traversal of the tree, each node is pointed to at least once and at most three times: once to get to its left subtree, once for itself, and once to get to the successor of its right subtree. Then traversing the n items in the tree requires between n and $3n$ iterations. This implies not only that averageTime(n) is constant, but that for n consecutive calls to **operator++( )**, worstTime(n) is only linear in n. In other words, amortizedTime(n) is constant for **operator++( )**.

The only place where the isHeader field is needed is in the decrement operator, which starts as follows:

```
     Iterator& operator--( )

     {
          if (link -> isHeader)
                  link = link -> right; // Return rightmost

          . . .
```

This if statement makes it possible to iterate through a BinSearchTree container in reverse order. We could not replace the condition with

```
     link == header
```

because a BinSearchTree field, such as header, cannot be used in the Iterator class unless that field is associated with a specific BinSearchTree object (for example, myTree.header). And we could not replace the condition with

```
     link -> parent -> parent == link
```

because this condition is also true for the root. The complete BinSearchTree class, including the embedded Iterator class, is available from the Source Code link on the book's website.

Lab 20 provides run-time support for the claim made earlier that the average height of a BinSearchTree object is logarithmic in *n*.

LAB **Lab 20:** **The average height of a** BinSearchTree.

(All Labs Are Optional.) **LAB**

We do not include any applications of the BinSearchTree class because any application would be superseded by redefining the tree instance from one of the classes in Chapters 9 and 10: AVLTree, tree, set, multiset, map, or multimap. For any of those classes, insertions, removals, and searches take logarithmic time, even in the worst case, and all the other methods are identical in performance to those in the BinSearchTree class.

SUMMARY

A *binary tree* *t* is either empty or consists of an item, called the *root item,* and two disjoint binary trees, called the *left subtree* and *right subtree* of *t*. This is a recursive definition, and there are recursive definitions for many of the related terms: height, number of leaves, number of items, two-tree, full, and so on. The interrelationships among some of these terms is given by the

---

Binary Tree Theorem   For any nonempty binary tree *t*,

$$\text{leaves}(t) \leq \frac{n(t) + 1}{2.0} \leq 2^{\text{height}(t)}$$

Equality holds for the first relation if and only if *t* is a two-tree.
Equality holds for the second relation if and only if *t* is full.

For a binary tree *t*, the *external path length* of *t*, *E(t)*, is the sum of the distances from the root to the leaves. A lower bound for comparison-based sorting algorithms can be obtained from the

---

External Path Length Theorem   Let *t* be a binary tree with $k > 0$ leaves. Then

$$E(t) \geq (k/2)\ \text{floor}(\log_2 k)$$

A *binary search tree* *t* is a binary tree such that either *t* is empty or

1. Each item in leftTree(*t*) is less than or equal to the root item of *t*.
2. Each item in rightTree(*t*) is greater or equal to than the root item of *t*.
3. Both leftTree(*t*) and rightTree(*t*) are binary search trees.

The BinSearchTree class maintains a binary search tree of items. For the find, insert, and erase methods, worstTime(*n*) is $O(n)$, where *n* is the number of items in the tree. But averageTime(*n*) is $O(\log n)$ for those three methods.

EXERCISES

8.1 Answer the questions about the following binary tree:

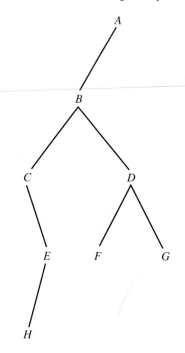

a. What is the root item?

b. How many items are in the tree?

c. How many leaves are in the tree?

d. What is the height of the tree?

e. What is the height of the left subtree?

f. What is the height of the right subtree?

g. What is the level of *F?*

h. What is the depth of *C?*

i. How many children does *C* have?

j. What is the parent of *F?*

k. What are the descendants of *B?*

l. What are the ancestors of *F?*

m. What would the output be if the items were written out during an inOrder traversal?

n. What would the output be if the items were written out during a post-Order traversal?

o. What would the output be if the items were written out during a pre-Order traversal?

p. What would the output be if the items were written out during a breadth-first traversal?

8.2 a. Construct a binary tree of height 3 that has eight items.

b. Can you construct a binary tree of height 2 that has eight items?

c. For n going from 1 to 20, determine the minimum height possible for a binary tree with n items.

d. Based on your calculations in part c, try to develop a formula for the minimum height possible for a binary tree with n items, where n can be any positive integer.

e. Let n be any positive integer. Use induction on n to show that for binary trees with n items, the minimum height possible is floor ($\log_2 n$).

8.3 a. What is the maximum number of leaves possible in a binary tree with 10 items? Construct such a tree.

b. What is the minimum number of leaves possible in a binary tree with 10 items? Construct such a tree.

8.4 a. Construct a two-tree that is not complete.

b. Construct a complete tree that is not a two-tree.

c. Construct a complete two-tree that is not full.

d. How many leaves are there in a two-tree with 17 items?

e. How many leaves are there in a two-tree with 731 items?

f. A two-tree must always have an odd number of items. Why?

> *Hint*   Use the Binary Tree Theorem and the fact that the number of leaves must be an integer.

g. How many items are there in a full binary tree of height 4?

h. How many items are there in a full binary tree of height 12?

i. Use the Binary Tree Theorem and the fact that every full tree is a two-tree to determine the number of leaves in a full binary tree with 63 items.

8.5 For the following binary tree, show the order in which items would be visited for an inOrder, postOrder, preOrder, and breadthFirst traversal.

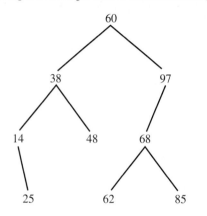

8.6 Show that a binary tree with n items has $2n + 1$ subtrees (including the entire tree). How many of these subtrees are empty?

8.7 Show that if t is a complete binary tree, then

$$\text{height}(t) = \text{ceil}(\log_2(n(t) + 1)) - 1$$

The ceil function returns the smallest integer greater than or equal to its argument. For example, ceil(35.3) = 36.

> **Hint**   Let t be a complete binary tree and let t1 be a full binary tree whose height is one less than t's. Let t2 be a full binary tree whose height is the same as t's. So $n(t1) < n(t) \le n(t2)$. Because the log function is strictly increasing:
>
> $$\log_2(n(t1) + 1) - 1 < \log_2(n(t) + 1) - 1 \le \log_2(n(t2) + 1) - 1$$
>
> The value of the left-hand side of the first inequality is an integer (why?) that is one less than the value of the right-hand side of the second inequality (why?). So
>
> $$\text{ceil}(\log_2(n(t) + 1)) - 1 = \log_2(n(t2) + 1) - 1$$
>
> Also,
>
> $$\log_2(n(t2) + 1) - 1 = \text{height}(t2) \quad \text{(Why?)}$$

8.8 The Binary Tree Theorem is stated for nonempty binary trees. Which of the six parts of the theorem fails for an empty binary tree?

> **Hint** $(0 + 1) / 2.0 \mathrel{!=} 0$.

8.9 Give an example of a nonempty binary tree that is not a two-tree but where

$$\text{leaves}(t) = (n(t) + 1)/2$$

8.10 Prove part 3 of the Binary Tree Theorem.

> **Hint**   Use the Principle of Mathematical Induction (general form) on the height of the tree.

8.11 a. Show the effect of making the following insertions into an initially empty BinSearchTree object:

$$30 \ 40 \ 20 \ 90 \ 10 \ 50 \ 70 \ 60 \ 80$$

   b. Find a different ordering of the items in part a whose insertions would generate the same BinSearchTree object as in part a.

8.12 Describe in English how to remove each of the following from a binary search tree:

    a.   An item with no children

    b.   An item with one child

    c.   An item with two children

8.13 Show that in any complete binary tree t, at least half of the items are leaves.

> *Hint*   If t is empty, there are no items, so the claim is vacuously true. If the leaf at the highest index is a right child, then t is a two-tree, and the claim follows from part 3 of the Binary Tree Theorem. Otherwise, t was formed by adding a left child to *the* complete two-tree with $n(t) -$ 1 items.

8.14 Develop a recursive version of the deleteLink method in the BinSearchTree class.

> *Hint*   Have deleteLink call the recursive method deleteSuccessor, which has the following interface:
>
> // Postcondition: successor contains the item that, before it was deleted
> //   during this call, was the successor of the tree's link
> //   item.
> **void** deleteSuccessor (T& successor, Link& link);

8.15 The first two lines in the body of the erase method are

itr(itr.link-> parent -> parent == itr.link)   //itr positioned at root node
    deleteLink (itr.link -> parent -> (parent);

Even though itr.link -> parent -> parent is equal to itr.link, it would be incorrect if the call to deleteLink were

deleteLink (itr.link);

Explain.

> *Hint*   What field in what tree node points to the root node (and therefore must be modified if the root node is to be deleted)?

8.16 Develop an iterative version of the destructor in the BinSearchTree class.

> *Hint*   Implement the breadth-first-traversal algorithm in Section 8.1.2. Instead of a queue of binary trees, use a queue of links. Start by enqueuing the root, that is header -> parent. As each link is dequeued, enqueue its left and right subtree links unless those links are NULL. Finally, deallocate the node pointed to by link.

PROGRAMMING PROJECT 8.1

Alternative Implementation of the BinSearchTree Class

This project illustrates that the binary-search-tree data structure has more than one implementation. You can also use the technique we will describe to save a binary search tree (in fact, any binary tree) to disk so that it can be subsequently retrieved with its original structure.

Develop an array-based design and implementation of the binary-search-tree data structure. Your class, BinSearchTreeArray, will have the same method descriptions as the BinSearchTree class but will use indices to simulate the parent, left link, and right link. For example, tree_node might be declared as follows

```
struct tree_node
{
    T item;
    int parent,
        left,
        right;
}; // tree_node
```

Similarly, the BinSearchTreeArray class might have the following three fields:

```
tree_node[ ] tree;
int header;
unsigned nodeCount;
```

The header node is stored in tree [0], and the root node in tree [1], so there is no need for an isHeader field in tree_node. A NULL pointer is represented by the index −1. For example, suppose we create a binary search tree by entering the strings "dog", "turtle", "wombat", "cat", and "ferret" in that order. The binary search tree would be as follows:

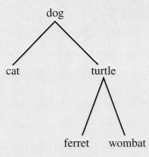

The items would be stored, starting at index 1, in the tree array in the order in which they were inserted. The array representation is

	item	parent	left	right
0	?	1	4	3
1	dog	0	4	2
2	turtle	1	5	3
3	wombat	2	−1	−1
4	cat	1	−1	−1
5	ferret	2	−1	−1

The method definitions are very similar to those in the BinSearchTree class, except that an expression such as

    header -> left

is replaced with

    tree [HEADER].left   // const int HEADER = 0;

For example, here is a possible definition of the find method:

```
Iterator find (const T& item)
{
        int parent = HEADER;   // const int HEADER = 0;
        int child = tree [HEADER].parent;
        while (child != −1)
        {
            if (!(tree [child].item < item))
            {
                    parent = child;
                    child = tree [child].left;
            } // item <= tree [child].item
            else
                    child = tree [child].right;
        } // while

        if (parent == HEADER || item < tree [parent].item)
            return end( );
        else
            return parent;
} // find
```

You will also need an embedded Iterator class.

AVL Trees

A s we noted in Chapter 8, one of the serious problems with binary search trees is that they can become badly unbalanced. In particular, worstTime(n) is linear in n for the find, insert, and erase methods in the BinSearchTree class. We would like to avoid linear-in-n worstTime for these methods. The overall strategy is to keep the height of the tree logarithmic in n. This chapter introduces a data structure that improves on the binary search tree. AVL trees are binary search trees in which the height is always logarithmic in n.

AVL trees are not included in the Standard Template Library. But the algorithms for inserting and removing in an AVL tree are somewhat simpler than those for a red-black tree, which we will study in Chapter 10. The Standard Template Library has four associative-container classes—set, multiset, map, and multimap—that are commonly implemented with red-black trees. ■

CHAPTER OBJECTIVES

1. Understand how balanced binary search trees are an improvement over ordinary binary search trees.

2. Show that AVL trees are balanced binary search trees.

3. Explain what a function object is and how function objects are used.

4. Be able to follow the methods for inserting in an AVL tree.

9.1 | BALANCED BINARY SEARCH TREES

From the analyses of the find, insert, and erase methods in Chapter 8, it is clear that binary search trees are efficient on average, but in the worst case—a chain—are no better than vectors, deques, or lists. There are several data structures that are based on binary search trees but are always balanced. A binary search tree is ***balanced*** if its height is logarithmic in n, the number of items in the tree.

Three widely known data structures in this category of balanced binary search trees are AVL trees, red-black trees, and splay trees. AVL trees are investigated in Section 9.2 and explored further in Project 9.1. Red-black trees are investigated in Chapter 10. For information on splay trees, the interested reader may consult Sahni (2000). None of these data structures is part of the Standard Template Library. But in the Hewlett-Packard implementation of the Standard Template Library, the rb_tree (for red-black tree) class is used in a **private** field in defining the Standard Template Library's four associative-container classes.

In Section 9.2, we describe how to achieve logarithmic-in-n height in a binary search tree.

9.2 | ROTATIONS

The basic mechanism that keeps a binary search tree balanced is the ***rotation:*** an adjustment to the tree, around an item, that maintains the required ordering of items. We'll explore the nuts and bolts of rotations here; you will see how they are used in Sections 9.3.4, 10.1.3, 10.1.4, and in Project 9.1.

There are two basic kinds of rotation. In a ***left rotation,*** an item is moved to where its left child is, and the item's right child is moved to where the item was. For example, Figure 9.1 shows a left rotation around the item 50. *Before and after the rotation, the tree is a binary search tree.*

Figure 9.2 has another example of a left rotation, around item 80, that reduces the height of the tree from 3 to 2. An interesting feature of Figure 9.2 is that 85, which was the left child of 90 before the rotation, ends up the right child of 80. This phenomenon is common to all left rotations around an item x: the left subtree of x's right child becomes the right subtree of x. This also happened in Figure 9.1, but the left subtree of 50's right child was empty.

Figure 9.3 shows the rotation of Figure 9.2 in a broader context: the item rotated around is not the root item of the tree. Figure 9.3 illustrates another aspect of all rotations: all the items not in the subtree of the rotated item are unaffected by the rotation. That is, in both trees, we still have

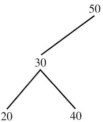

Figure 9.1 | A left rotation around 50.

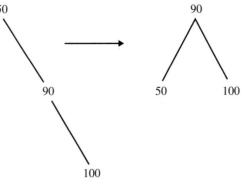

Figure 9.2 | A left rotation around 80.

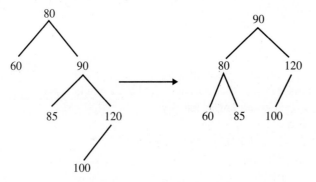

Figure 9.3 | The left rotation around 80 from Figure 9.2, but here 80 is not the root item.

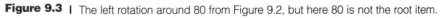

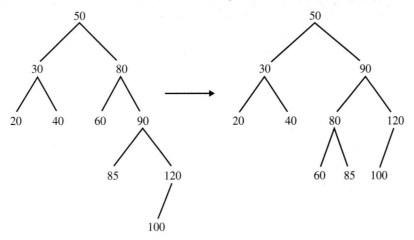

The code for a rotation does not involve any movement of items; only the pointers to nodes are manipulated. Suppose that x is a pointer to a node and y is a pointer to x's right child. Basically, a left rotation around x can be accomplished in just two steps:

```
x -> right = y -> left; // for example, look at 85 in Figure 9.2
y -> left = x;
```

Unfortunately, we also have to adjust the parent fields, and that adds quite a bit of code. Here is the complete definition of a rotate_left method in the BinSearchTree class—recall from Chapter 8 that the header node's parent field points to the root node:

```
// From Cormen (1990)
// Postcondition: a left rotation around x has been performed.
void rotateLeft (tree_node* x)
{
        tree_node* y = x -> right;
        x -> right = y -> left;
        if (y -> left != NULL)
                y -> left -> parent = x;
        y -> parent = x -> parent;
        if (x == header -> parent) // if x is the root
                header -> parent = y;
        else if (x == x -> parent -> left) // if x is a left child
                x -> parent -> left = y;
        else
                x -> parent -> right = y;
        y -> left = x;
        x -> parent = y;

}
```

Most of the code for a rotation entails adjustments to the parent of the item rotated about.

This indicates how much of a bother parents can be! But on the bright side, no items get moved, and the time is constant.

What about a right rotation? Figure 9.4 shows a simple example: a right rotation around the item 100. Let x be a pointer to a tree node, and let y be a pointer to the tree node that is the left child of x. Basically, a right rotation around x can be accomplished in just two steps:

```
x -> left = y -> right;
y -> right = x;
```

Of course, once we include the parent adjustments, we get a considerably longer—but still constant time—method. In fact, if you interchange left with right in the definition of the rotate_left method, you get the definition of rotate_right! And, as with left rotations, the tree after a right rotation is still a binary search tree.

In all the rotations shown so far, the height of the tree was reduced by 1. That is not surprising; in fact, reducing height is the motivation for rotating. But it is not necessary that every rotation reduce the height of the tree. For example, Figure 9.5

Figure 9.4 I A right rotation around 100.

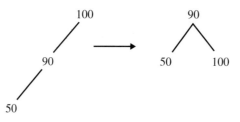

Figure 9.5 I A left rotation around 50. The height of the tree is still 3 after the rotation.

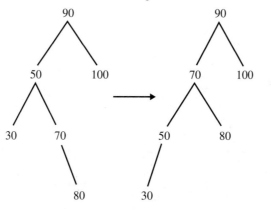

shows a left rotation—around the tree node whose item is 50—that does not affect the height of the tree.

It is true that the left rotation in Figure 9.5 did not reduce the height of the tree. But a few minutes of experimenting should convince you that no single rotation can reduce the height of the tree on the left side of Figure 9.5. Now look at the tree on the right side of Figure 9.5. Can you figure out a rotation that will reduce the height of *that* tree? Not a right rotation around 70; that would just get us back where we started. How about a right rotation around 90? Bingo! Figure 9.6 shows the effect.

The rotations in Figures 9.5 and 9.6 should be viewed as a package: a left rotation around 90's left child, followed by a right rotation around 90. This is referred to as a ***double rotation.*** Figure 9.7 shows another kind of double rotation: a right rotation around the right child of 50, followed by a left rotation around 50.

Before we go any further, let's list the major features of rotations:

1. There are four kinds of rotation:
   a. Left rotation
   b. Right rotation
   c. Left rotation around the left child of an item, followed by a right rotation around the item itself

Here are the major properties of rotations.

Figure 9.6 I A right rotation around 90. The height of the tree has been reduced from 3 to 2.

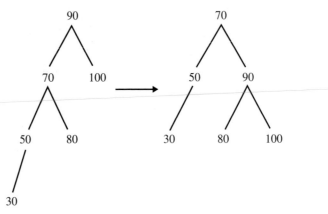

Figure 9.7 I A double rotation: a right rotation around 50's right child, followed by a left rotation around 50.

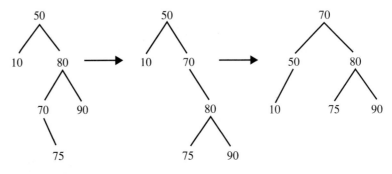

    d.   Right rotation around the right child of an item, followed by a left rotation around the item itself

2.   Nodes not in the subtree of the item rotated about are unaffected by the rotation.

3.   A rotation takes constant time.

4.   Before and after a rotation, the tree is still a binary search tree.

5.   The code for a left rotation is symmetric to the code for a right rotation (and vice versa): simply swap the words left and right.

Section 9.3 introduces a data structure, the AVL tree, that is based on a binary search tree but employs rotations to maintain balance.

9.3   AVL TREES

An *AVL tree* is a binary search tree that either is empty or has the following two properties:

Figure 9.8 I Three AVL trees.

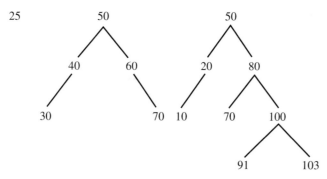

Figure 9.9 I Three binary search trees that are not AVL trees.

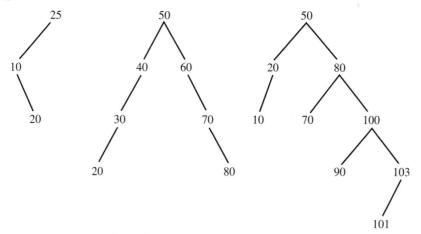

1. The heights of the left and right subtrees differ by at most 1.
2. The left and right subtrees are AVL trees.

A recursive definition of AVL tree.

AVL trees are named after the two Russian mathematicians, Adel'son-Vel'skii and Landis, who invented them (see Adel'son-Vel'skii and Landis, 1962). Figure 9.8 shows three AVL trees, and Figure 9.9 shows three binary search trees that are not AVL trees.

The first tree in Figure 9.9 is not an AVL tree because its left subtree has a height of 1 and its right subtree has a height of -1. The second tree is not an AVL tree because its left subtree is not an AVL tree, and neither is its right subtree. The third tree is not an AVL tree because its left subtree has a height of 1 and its right subtree has a height of 3.

In Section 9.3.1, we show that an AVL tree is a balanced binary search tree, that is, that the height of an AVL tree is always logarithmic in n. This compares favorably to binary search trees in general, whose height is linear in n in the worst case (for example, a chain). The difference between linear and logarithmic can be huge. For example, suppose $n = 1,000,000,000,000$. Then $\log_2 n$ is less than 40.

9.3.1   The Height of an AVL Tree

We can prove that the height of an AVL tree is logarithmic in n, and the proof relates AVL trees back to, of all things, Fibonacci numbers!

The height of an AVL tree is logarithmic in n, the number of items in the tree.

Claim   If t is a nonempty AVL tree, height(t) is logarithmic in n, where n is the number of items in t.

Proof   We will show that, even if an AVL tree t has the maximum height possible for its n elements, its height will still be logarithmic in n. How can we determine the maximum height possible for an AVL tree with n items? As Kruse (1987) suggests, rephrasing the question can help us get the answer. Given a height h, what is the minimum number of items in any AVL tree of that height?

For $h = 0, 1, 2, \ldots$, let $\min_h$ be the minimum number of items in an AVL tree of height h. Clearly, $\min_0 = 1$ and $\min_1 = 2$. The values of $\min_2$ and $\min_3$ can be seen from the following AVL trees:

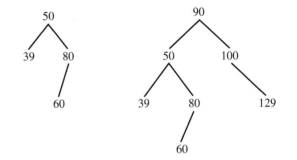

In general, if $h1 > h2$, then $\min_{h1}$ is greater than the number of items needed to construct an AVL tree of height $h2$. That is, if $h1 > h2$, then $\min_{h1} > \min_{h2}$. In other words, $\min_h$ is an increasing function.

Suppose that t is an AVL tree with height h and $\min_h$ items, for some value of $h > 1$. What can we say about the heights of the left and right subtrees of t? By the definition of height, one of those subtrees must have a height of $h - 1$. And by the definition of an AVL tree, the other subtree must have a height of $h - 1$ or $h - 2$. If fact, because t has the minimum number of items for its height, one of its subtrees must have height $h - 1$ and $\min_{h-1}$ items, and the other subtree must have height $h - 2$ and $\min_{h-2}$ items.

A tree always has one more item than the number of items in its left and right subtrees. So we have

$$\min_h = \min_{h-1} + \min_{h-2} + 1 \qquad \text{for any integer } h > 1$$

This recurrence relation looks a lot like the formula for generating Fibonacci numbers. The term ***Fibonacci tree*** refers to an AVL tree with the minimum number of items for its height. From the recurrence relation and the values of min_0 and min_1, we can show, by induction on h, that

$$min_h = \text{fib}(h + 3) - 1 \qquad \text{for any nonnegative integer } h.$$

For example, because $min_6 = 33$ and $min_7 = 54$, the maximum height of an AVL tree with 50 items is 6.

We can further show, by induction on h (see Exercise 9.5),

$$\text{fib}(h + 3) - 1 \geq (3/2)^h \qquad \text{for any nonnegative integer } h$$

Combining these results,

$$min_h \geq (3/2)^h \qquad \text{for any nonnegative integer } h$$

Taking logs in base 2 (but any base will do), we get

$$\log_2 min_h \geq h \log_2(3/2) \qquad \text{for any nonnegative integer } h$$

Rewriting this in a form suitable for a Big-O claim, with $1/\log_2(1.5) <$ 1.75:

$$h \leq 1.75 \log_2 min_h \qquad \text{for any nonnegative integer } h$$

If t is an AVL tree with height h and n items, we must have $min_h \leq n$, so for any such AVL tree,

$$h \leq 1.75 \log_2 n$$

That is, any AVL tree with n items has a height of $O(\log n)$, even in the worst case.

This implies that the height of any AVL tree is $O(\log n)$. Is $O(\log n)$ the smallest upper bound? Yes, and here's why. For any binary tree of height h with n items,

$$h \geq \log_2(n + 1) - 1$$

by part 2 of the Binary Tree Theorem. We conclude that any AVL tree with n items has a height that is logarithmic in n, even in the worst case.

To give you a better idea of how AVL trees relate to binary search trees, we will design and implement an AVLTree class in Sections 9.3.3 and 9.3.4.

9.3.2   Function Objects

Before we can get to the design and implementation of the AVLTree class, there is an important concept to be introduced: the function object. A *function object*—also called a *functor*—is an object in a class in which the function-call operator,

A function object is an object in a class in which the function-call operator, **operator( ),** *has been overloaded.*

operator( ), has been overloaded. The class in which **operator( )** is overloaded is called a *function class* or *functor class.* For an example, suppose the function class MyClass overloads **operator( )** as follows:

```
int operator( ) (int i)
{
      return 5 * i;
} // operator( )
```

We can write

```
MyClass d;

cout << d (15);
```

In the output statement, the object d appears to be a function, and that is where the term "function object" comes from.

But of what value are function objects? Recall how important templates are. We have already seen examples where templates provide item-type flexibility, so that a container class can be used with a variety of item types. Templates also provide operator-type flexibility, so that a container class can be used with a variety of operators. The next few paragraphs illustrate exactly how function objects work, and the role that templates play.

One of the shortcomings of the BinSearchTree class is that comparisons between items must use **operator**<. This is fine for many but not all applications. For example, suppose the items in the tree are test scores, and you want them stored in decreasing order. Or perhaps each item in the tree consists of an employee's name, salary, and division. For one application, you might want the employees stored in the tree by division, and in alphabetical order within each division. For another application, you might want the employees stored in the tree by decreasing order of salaries. You cannot overload **operator**< in the item class to provide for both applications.

C++ allows users of a class to tailor comparisons for a specific application. The mechanism for this flexibility is a template parameter; the definition of the AVL Tree class starts with

```
template<class T, class Compare>
class AVLTree
{
      protected:

            Compare compare;
```

The field compare is an example of a function object. When a user defines an AVL Tree container, the definition includes a template argument for the class that overloads **operator( )**. For example, here are the definitions corresponding to the two employee applications cited in the previous paragraph:

```
AVLTree< Employee, ByDivision< Employee > > avl1;

AVLTree< Employee, ByDecreasingSalary< Employee > > avl2;
```

For the avl1 object, employees will be compared by division; within a division, the comparison will be alphabetical. Here is the definition of the class ByDivision:

```
template<class T>
class ByDivision
{
        bool operator( ) (const T& x, const T& y) const
        {
                if (x.division < y.division)
                        return true;
                if (x.division == y.division && x.name < y.name)
                        return true;
                return false;
        } // overloading ( )
} // class ByDivision
```

This is a strange class: no fields, and only one method! Of course, the compiler will provide a default constructor, but that constructor will do nothing because there are no fields. Within the class AVLTree, the function object compare will appear in place of **operator<**. For example, in the insert method of the BinSearchTree class, we had

```
if (item < child -> item)
```

The corresponding line in the AVLTree class is

```
if (compare (item, child -> item))
```

Here the function object compare is invoking its function-call operator, **operator( )**. The result depends on which AVLTree object called the insert method. If it was avl1, then **true** will be returned if item's division is less than child -> item's division, or if the divisions are the same and item's name is lexicographically less than child -> item's name.

Now that you have seen the ByDivision class, the ByDecreasingSalary class should come as no surprise:

```
template<class T>
class ByDecreasingSalary
{
        bool operator( ) (const T& x, const T& y) const
        {
                return x.salary > y.salary;
        } // overloading ( )
} // class ByDecreasingSalary
```

At this point, you may grudgingly agree that function objects can, at times, be worthwhile. But what if all you need is a simple comparison, such as would be provided by **operator<**? No problem. In the file <function>, there are several predefined classes in which **operator( )** has been overloaded for simple comparisons. For example, the function class less overloads **operator( )** as follows:

bool operator( ) (const T& x, **const** T& y) **const { return** x < y; }

So if all you want is an AVLTree object in which **int** items are compared by **operator**<, you can define

AVLTree< **int**, less<**int**> > myTree;

Function objects are essential in the Standard Template Library's associative-container classes, and not merely for specializing comparisons. Lab 21 provides more details on function objects, especially on how they are more powerful than mere functions.

9.3.3   The AVLTree **Class**

Other than the function-object feature noted in Section 9.3.2, the AVLTree class is quite similar to the BinSearchTree class. For the essential methods—size, find, insert, and erase—the method headings are identical. The only difference in the method interfaces is that for the find, insert, and erase methods, worstTime(n) is logarithmic in n. The reason for this is that the height of an AVL tree is always logarithmic in n.

The AVLTree class will have the same fields as we saw in the BinSearchTree class, plus the function object compare:

protected:

Compare compare;

tree_node* header;

unsigned node_count;

The tree_node class has been expanded. In addition to the five fields (item, parent, left, right, isHeader) in the tree_node **struct** of the BinSearchTree class, the AVLTree class's tree_node **struct** has an additional field:

char balanceFactor;

If a node's balance Factor field has the value 'L', the height of the node's left subtree is one greater than the height of the node's right subtree.

If a node's balanceFactor field has the value '=', the node's left subtree has the same height as the node's right subtree. If the balanceFactor field's value is 'L', the left subtree's height is one greater than the right subtree's height. And a balanceFactor field's value of 'R' means that the right subtree's height is one greater than the left subtree's height.

Except for find, insert, and erase, the AVLTree class's method definitions are the same as those in the BinSearchTree class. The AVLTree class's find method utilizes the function object compare instead of **operator**<. Here is the definition:

```
Iterator find (const T& item)
{
      Link parent = header;
      Link child = header -> parent;
      while (child != NULL)
      {
            if (!compare (child -> item, item))
            {
                  parent = child;
                  child = child -> left;
            } // item "<=" child -> item
            else
                  child = child -> right;
      } // while

      if (parent == header || compare (item, parent -> item))
            return end( );
      else
            return parent;
} // find
```

This definition of find is equivalent to the definition in the BinSearchTree class if the instantiation of the AVLTree class has less in the second template argument. For example,

```
AVLTree <string, less< string > > words;
```

The definition of the insert method is somewhat more complex than that of the BinSearchTree class. The considerable details illustrate that the guarantee of logarithmic height comes at a price. The definition of the erase method is left for Project 9.1.

Here is the method interface for the insert method:

```
// Postcondition: item has been inserted into this AVLTree, and an iterator
//                 positioned at the newly inserted item has been returned. The
//                 worstTime(n) is O(log n).
Iterator insert (const T& item);
```

The following implementation of the insert method is based on Horowitz et al. (1995). The insert method in the AVLTree class resembles the insert method in the Bin SearchTree class. But as we work our way down the tree from the root to the insertion point, we keep track of the inserted node's closest ancestor whose balanceFactor field's value is 'L' or 'R'. We refer to this node as ancestor. For example, if we insert 60 into the AVLTree in Figure 9.10, ancestor is the node whose item is 80.

When an insertion is made, the variable ancestor *holds (a pointer to) the nearest ancestor—of the inserted item—whose balance factor is 'L' or 'R'.*

Figure 9.10 | An AVL tree, with associated balance factors for each node.

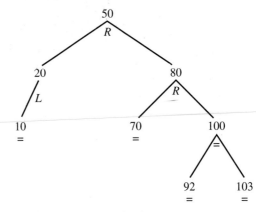

After the item has been inserted, BinSearchTree-style, into the AVLTree object, we call a fix-up method to handle rotations and balanceFactor field adjustments. Here is the definition of the insert method:

```
Iterator insert (const T& item)
{
    if (header -> parent == NULL)
    {
        insertItem (item, header, header -> parent);
        header -> left = header -> parent;
        header -> right = header -> parent;
        return header -> parent;
    } // inserting at tree's root
    else
    {
        Link parent = header,
             child = header -> parent,
             ancestor = NULL;

        while (child != NULL)
        {
            parent = child;
            if (child -> balanceFactor != '=')
                ancestor = child;
            if (compare (item, child -> item))
                child = child -> left;
            else
                child = child -> right;
```

```
        } // while
        if (compare (item, parent -> item))
        {
                insertItem (item, parent, parent -> left);
                fixAfterInsertion (ancestor, parent -> left);
                if (header -> left == parent)
                        header -> left = parent -> left; // child is leftmost
                return parent -> left;
        } // insert at left of parent
        else
        {
                insertItem (item, parent, parent -> right);
                fixAfterInsertion (ancestor, parent -> right);
                if (header -> right == parent)
                        header -> right = parent -> right; // child is rightmost
                return parent -> right;
        } // insert at right of parent
    } // tree not empty
} // insert
```

The definition of the insertItem method differs from the BinSearchTree class's insertItem method only in that the balanceFactor field's value is set to '='. The fix AfterInsertion method is sufficiently complex that it deserves a section of its own.

9.3.4   The fixAfterInsertion Method

Here is the method interface for the fixAfterInsertion method (recall that Link is just an abbreviation for tree_node*):

```
// Postcondition:  the AVL property has been restored, if necessary, by
//                 rotations and balance-factor adjustments between the
//                 inserted tree_node and its nearest ancestor with a
//                 balanceFactor of 'L' or 'R'.
void fixAfterInsertion (Link ancestor, Link inserted);
```

The definition of the fixAfterInsertion method starts with the definition of root and item:

```
Link root = header -> parent;

T item = inserted -> item;
```

The rest of the method consists of six cases. The case chosen to complete the method depends on the ancestor node's balanceFactor value and where the item was inserted.

ancestor is **NULL**; that is, each ancestor of the inserted node has a **balanceFactor** of '='. We adjust the **balanceFactor** values of those ancestors and we are done. For example, Figure 9.11 shows the before and after trees for this case. In Figure 9.11, and in all the figures for other cases, we assume that the function object **compare** is an instance of the class **less**, so **compare (a, b)** can be interpreted as **a** < **b**.

It turns out that each of the six cases includes an adjustment of balance factors in a path from the inserted node's parent up to *but not including* some ancestor of the inserted node. So the action taken in this case is to adjust the root's balance factor and then call **adjustPath (root, inserted)**. Here is that method's interface:

    // Postcondition: the balanceFactors of all nodes between the inserted node
    //   (exclusive) and the to node (exclusive) have been adjusted,
    //   if necessary.
    void adjustPath (Link to, Link inserted);

The adjustPath method adjusts the balance factors, if needed, of each node in the path between two given nodes (exclusive).

The **adjustPath** method works its way back up the tree from the inserted node. Each balance factor along the path must currently have a value of '='. The balance factor of any given node on the path can be determined by comparing the inserted item with the given node's item. In particular, the new balance factor should be 'L' if the inserted item is less than the given item, and 'R' otherwise. Here is the definition:

Figure 9.11 I On the left-hand side, an AVLTree object just before the call to fixAfter Insertion; the item inserted was 55, and all its ancestors have a balance Factor value of '='. On the right-hand side, the AVLTree object with adjusted balance factors.

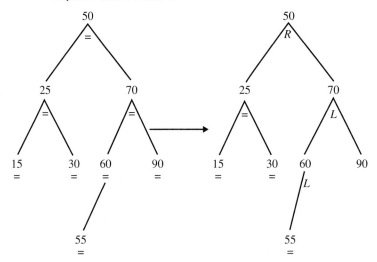

```
void adjustPath (Link to, Link inserted)
{
        T item = inserted -> item;

        Link temp = inserted -> parent;
        while (temp != to)
        {
                if (compare (item, temp -> item))
                    temp -> balanceFactor = 'L';
                else
                    temp -> balanceFactor = 'R';
                temp = temp -> parent;
        } // while
} // method adjustPath
```

For this method, the number of loop iterations, and therefore worstTime(n), is logarithmic in n because the height of an AVL tree is always logarithmic in n.

The complete action for case 1 simply adjusts the root's balance factor and then calls the **adjustPath** method:

```
if (ancestor == NULL)
{
        if (compare (item, root -> item))
                root -> balanceFactor = 'L';
        else
                root -> balanceFactor = 'R';
        adjustPath (root, inserted);
} // Case 1: all ancestors' balance factors are '='
```

CASE 2

The value of **ancestor -> balanceFactor** is 'L' and the insertion was made in the **ancestor** node's right subtree, or the value of **ancestor -> balanceFactor** is 'R' and the insertion was made in the **ancestor** node's left subtree. This case applies, for example, if 28 is inserted into the AVL tree on the right-hand side of Figure 9.11. In this case, which follows case 1's **if** statement, we set the **ancestor** node's balance factor to '=' and then make the usual adjustments to the nodes between **inserted** and **ancestor**:

```
else if ((ancestor -> balanceFactor == 'L' &&
                !compare (item, ancestor -> item)) ||
                (ancestor -> balanceFactor == 'R' &&
                compare (item, ancestor -> item)))
{
```

Figure 9.12 | On the left-hand side, an AVL tree into which 28 has just been inserted. The balance factors of the other nodes are *pre-insertion*. On the right-hand side, the same AVL tree after the balance factors have been adjusted. The only balance factors adjusted are those in the path between 28 and 50.

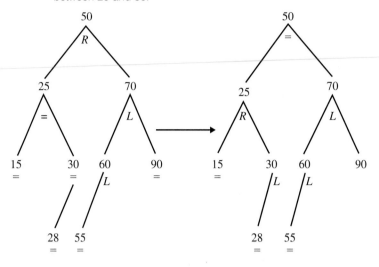

```
        ancestor -> balanceFactor = '=';
        adjustPath (ancestor, inserted);
    } // Case 2: insertion in opposite subtree of ancestor's balance factor
```

Figure 9.12 shows an example of the before and after trees in this case.

The remaining four cases entail rebalancing, accomplished through rotations: left, right, left-right, and right-left. After each such rotation, the balance factors are adjusted, chiefly through a call to the **adjustPath** method.

CASE 3

The value of **ancestor -> balanceFactor** is 'R' and the inserted node is in the right subtree of the right subtree of the **ancestor** node. In this case, a left rotation is performed around the **ancestor** node. Here is the code:

```
    else if (ancestor -> balanceFactor == 'R' &&
            !compare (item, ancestor -> right -> item))
    {
            ancestor -> balanceFactor = '=';
            rotate_left (ancestor);
            adjustPath (ancestor -> parent, inserted);
    } // Case 3: insertion in right subtree of ancestor's right subtree
```

Figure 9.13 illustrates this case.

Figure 9.13 | On the left side, what was an AVL tree has become imbalanced by the insertion of 93. The balance factors of the other nodes are *pre-insertion*. In this case, ancestor is the node whose item is 70. A left rotation around 70 is required. On the right side, the restructured AVL tree with adjusted balance factors.

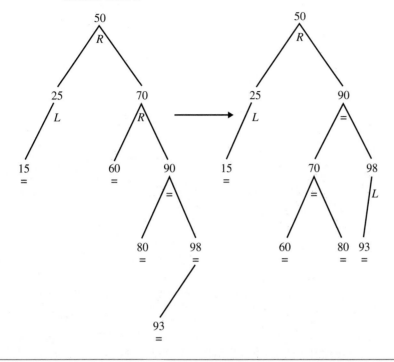

CASE 4

The value of **ancestor -> balanceFactor** is 'L' and the inserted node is in the left subtree of the left subtree of the **ancestor** node. In this case, a right rotation is performed around the **ancestor** node:

```
else if (ancestor -> balanceFactor == 'L' &&
        compare (item, ancestor -> left -> item))
{
        ancestor -> balanceFactor = '=';
        rotate_right (ancestor);
        adjustPath (ancestor -> parent, inserted);
} // insertion in left subtree of ancestor's left subtree
```

Figure 9.14 illustrates this case.

Figure 9.14 | On the left side, what was an AVL tree has become imbalanced by the insertion of 13. The balance factors of the other nodes are *pre-insertion*. In this case, **ancestor** is the node whose item is 50. A right rotation around 50 is required. On the right side, the restructured AVL tree with adjusted balance factors.

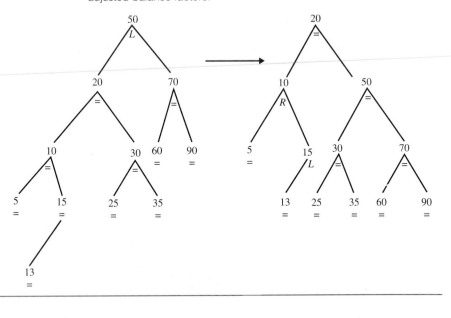

CASE 5

The value of **ancestor -> balanceFactor** is 'L' and the inserted node is in the right subtree of the left subtree of the **ancestor** node. In this case, a left rotation is performed around the **ancestor** node's left child, and then a right rotation is performed around the **ancestor** node. The **balanceFactor** adjustments are handled in the **adjustLeftRight** method, which we will discuss right after the case 5 code.
   Here is the code for Case 5:

```
else if (ancestor -> balanceFactor == 'L' &&
            !compare (item, ancestor -> left -> item))
     {
         rotate_left (ancestor -> left);
         rotate_right (ancestor);
         adjustLeftRight (ancestor, inserted);
     } // Case 5: insertion in right subtree of ancestor's left subtree
```

The method interface for **adjustLeftRight** is as follows:

```
// Postcondition:  all the balance factors in the path from inserted (exclusive)
//                       to ancestor's sibling (inclusive) have been adjusted after a
//                       left-right rotation.
void adjustLeftRight (Link ancestor, Link inserted);
```

Figure 9.15 | On the left side, what was an AVL tree has become imbalanced by the insertion of 40. The balance factors of the other nodes are *pre-insertion*. In this case, ancestor is the node whose item is 50. A left rotation around 30 is followed by a right rotation around 50. On the right side, the restructured AVL tree with adjusted balance factors.

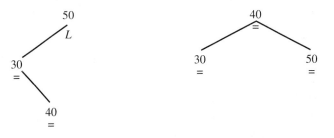

Figure 9.16 | On the left side, what was an AVL tree has become imbalanced by the insertion of 35. The balance factors of the other nodes are *pre-insertion*. In this case, ancestor is the node whose item is 50. A left rotation around 20 is performed, followed by a right rotation around 50. On the right side, the restructred AVL tree with adjusted balance factors.

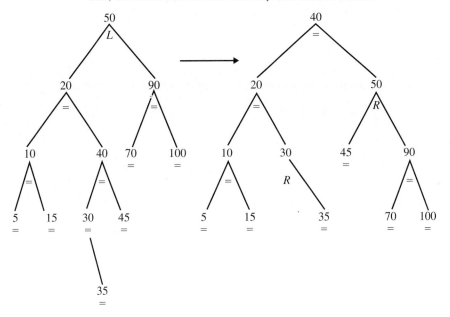

This method entails three subcases for case 5. The simplest subcase (case 5a) occurs for the simplest left-right rotation, as shown in Figure 9.15. In this subcase, the only change is to set the value of the **ancestor** node's **balance Factor** field to '='.

The other two subcases are determined by comparing the inserted item to the **ancestor** node's postrotation parent. Figure 9.16 illustrates the former (case 5b) of these two subcases. Because 35 is less than the **ancestor** node's parent (40), 35 ends up in the left subtree instead of the right subtree, so the value of the **ancestor** node's **balanceFactor** field is 'R'. The path for rebalancing goes from the inserted item up to the **ancestor** node's sibling, exclusive:

```
else if (compare (item, ancestor -> parent -> item))
{
        ancestor -> balanceFactor = 'R';
        adjustPath (ancestor -> parent -> left, inserted);
} // case 5b: item "<" ancestor's parent's item
```

Figure 9.17 illustrates the last subcase (case 5c), when the inserted item ends up in the right subtree of the **ancestor** node's parent. In this subcase, 42 ends up in the right subtree of the **ancestor** node's parent (40), so the value of the **ancestor** node's **balanceFactor** is '=' and the balance factor of the ancestor node's sibling (20) is 'L'.

The code for this subcase is

```
else
{
        ancestor -> balanceFactor = '=';
        ancestor -> parent -> left -> balanceFactor = 'L';
```

Figure 9.17 | On the left side, what was an AVL tree has become imbalanced by the insertion of 42. The balance factors of the other nodes are *pre-insertion*. In this case, ancestor is the node whose item is 50. A left rotation around 20 is performed, followed by a right rotation around 50. On the right side, the restructured AVL tree with adjusted balance factors.

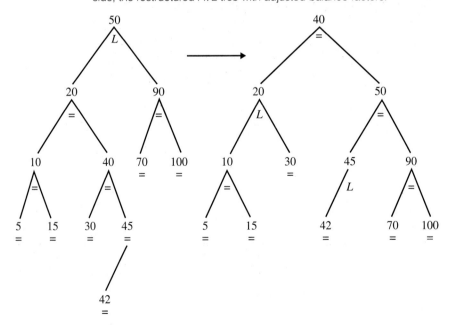

```
        adjustPath (ancestor, inserted);
    } // case 5c: item "<" ancestor's parent's item
```

The value of **ancestor** -> **balanceFactor** is 'R' and the inserted node is in the left sub-tree of the right subtree of the **ancestor** node. In this case, a right rotation is performed around the **ancestor** node's right child, and then a left rotation is performed around the **ancestor** node. Just as with case 5, case 6 has three subcases. Fortunately, they are symmetric with respect to the three subcases of case 5. For example, Figure 9.18 illustrates case 6b, where the inserted item ends up in the right sub-tree of the **ancestor** node's (postrotation) parent.

Because 75 ends up in 70's right subtree, the value of the **balanceFactor** field of 50 (that is, of the **ancestor** node) is set to 'L'. Here is the complete definition of the **adjustRightLeft** method:

```
    void adjustRightLeft (Link ancestor, Link inserted)
    {
        T item = inserted -> item;

        if (ancestor -> parent == inserted) // case 6a
            ancestor -> balanceFactor = '=';
        else if (!compare (item, ancestor -> parent -> item))
```

Figure 9.18 | On the left side, what was an AVL tree has become imbalanced by the insertion of 75. The balance factors of the other nodes are *pre-insertion*. In this case, ancestor is the node whose item is 50. A right rotation around 80 is performed, followed by a left rotation around 50. On the right side, the restructured AVL tree with adjusted balance factors.

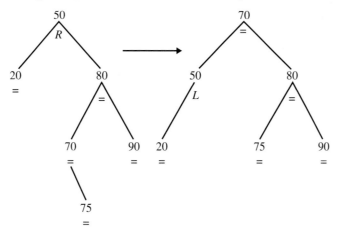

```
        {
                ancestor -> balanceFactor = 'L';
                adjustPath (ancestor -> parent -> right, inserted);
        } // case 6b: item ">=" ancestor's parent's item
        else
        {
                ancestor -> balanceFactor = '=';
                ancestor -> parent -> right -> balanceFactor = 'R';
                adjustPath (ancestor, inserted);
        } // case 6c: item "<" ancestor's parent's item
} // method adjustRightLeft
```

Here, finally, is the **fixAfterInsertion** method, with all six cases:

```
void fixAfterInsertion (Link ancestor, Link inserted)
{
        Link root = header -> parent;

        T item = inserted -> item;

        if (ancestor == NULL)
        {
                if (compare (item, root -> item))
                        root -> balanceFactor = 'L';
                else
                        root -> balanceFactor = 'R';
                adjustPath (root, inserted);
        } // Case 1: all ancestor's balance factors are '='
        else if ((ancestor -> balanceFactor == 'L' &&
                        !compare (item, ancestor -> item)) ||
                        (ancestor -> balanceFactor == 'R' &&
                        compare (item, ancestor -> item)))
        {
                ancestor -> balanceFactor = '=';
                adjustPath (ancestor, inserted);
        } // Case 2: insertion in opposite subtree of ancestor's balance factor
        else if (ancestor -> balanceFactor == 'R' &&
                        !compare (item, ancestor -> right -> item))
        {
                ancestor -> balanceFactor = '=';
                rotate_left (ancestor);
                adjustPath (ancestor -> parent, inserted);
        } // Case 3: insertion in right subtree of ancestor's right subtree
        else if (ancestor -> balanceFactor == 'L' &&
```

```
                   compare (item, ancestor -> left -> item))
        {
              ancestor -> balanceFactor = '=';
              rotate_right (ancestor);
              adjustPath (ancestor -> parent, inserted);
        } // Case 4: insertion in left subtree of ancestor's left subtree
        else if (ancestor -> balanceFactor == 'L' &&
                    !compare (item, ancestor -> left -> item))
        {
              rotate_left (ancestor -> left);
              rotate_right (ancestor);
              adjustLeftRight (ancestor, inserted);
        } // Case 5: insertion in right subtree of ancestor's left subtree
        else
        {
              rotate_right (ancestor -> right);
              rotate_left (ancestor);
              adjustRightLeft (ancestor, inserted);
        } // Case 6: insertion in left subtree of ancestor's right subtree
   } // method fixAfterInsertion
```

We still need to establish that the insert method is correct and efficient. First, we tackle correctness.

9.3.5   Correctness of the insert Method

We need to show that, if an AVLTree object really is an AVL tree before a call to the insert method, then that calling object is still an AVL tree after the call. Rotations preserve the binary-search-tree properties, so all that remains is to verify that the heights of the left and right subtrees differ by at most one, and that those two sub-trees are AVL trees. Instead of calculating height directly, the insert method utilizes balance factors. We need to show that the balance factors accurately reflect height; that is, we need to show that if the balance factors were correct before the call, then the balance factors are also correct after the call.

In fact, of the six cases in the fixAfterInsertion method, the only case that increases the height of the whole tree is case 1, the case in which the value of ancestor is NULL. In that case, the only heights increased are those of subtrees in the path from the inserted item (exclusive) to the root item (inclusive). All those subtrees had a balance factor of '=' before the call, and each balance factor was adjusted to 'L' or 'R' depending on whether the inserted item was "less than" or "greater than or equal to" the root item of the subtree.

In case 2, assume that the ancestor node's balance factor was 'L' and that the insertion was made in the ancestor node's right subtree. Then the only heights increased are those in the path from the inserted item (exclusive) to ancestor's item (exclusive), and those balance factors are adjusted accordingly. And the ancestor node's balance factor is set to '='.

Figure 9.19 illustrates the effect of case 3, the left-rotation case. The height of the subtree that was rooted at the ancestor node before the call to insert is unaffected by the rotation. Outside of that subtree, all heights and balance factors are unaffected. The correctness of the case 4 action follows by symmetry with case 3.

The general situation for case 5c is shown in Figure 9.20. The correctness of the case 5a action is easily established because of the simplicity of the tree. The correctness of the case 5b action can be shown with a figure similar to Figure 9.20, and the correctness of the case 6 actions follows from case 5 by symmetry.

Figure 9.19 | A left rotation in an AVLTree container. The item x represents the ancestor node, the insertion was made in z2's subtree, and the relative heights are in boldface. The height h may be as small as 1, so y, z1, and (before the insertion) z2 may be NULL. The height of the subtree shown—and therefore the height of the whole tree—is unaffected by the rotation.

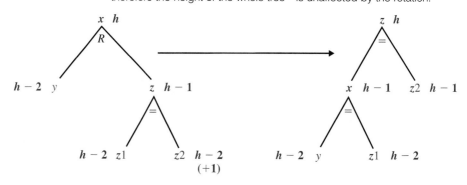

Figure 9.20 | The general situation for case 5c: the insertion is made in the right subtree of z. On the left-hand side, the ancestor node's item is v. A left rotation is performed around w, followed by a right rotation around v. The height h may be as small as 2, or z1 and (before the insertion) z2 may be NULL. The height of the subtree shown—and therefore the height of the whole tree—is unaffected by the rotation.

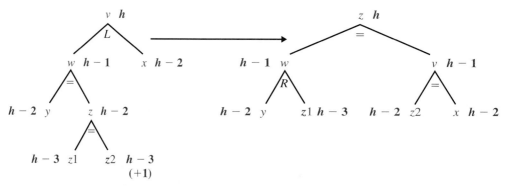

A run-time test can further increase confidence in the correctness of the insert method. An AVL tree of size *n* is constructed, where the value of *n* is entered by the end-user. Each item in the tree is randomly generated and is of type **int**. First, here is a wrapper method to make sure a binary search tree is an AVL tree:

```
// Postcondition: true has been returned if this tree really is an AVLTree.
//                Otherwise, false has been returned.
bool isAVLTree( )
{
        return checkAVLTree( header -> parent );
} // method isAVLTree
```

And here is the method wrapped:

```
// Postcondition: The tree has been checked to make sure that the heights of
//                the left and right subtrees (if they exist) are within 1 of each
//                other, and that those subtrees are AVL trees.
bool checkAVLTree (Link root)
{
        if (root == NULL)
                return true;
        else
                if ((abs (height (root -> left) − height (root -> right)) <= 1)
                        && (checkAVLTree (root -> left))
                        && (checkAVLTree (root -> right)))
                        return true;
        return false;
} // checkAVLTree
```

Finally, here is the essential code for the main function:

```
for (i = 0; i < n; i++)
        tree.insert (rand( ));

if (tree.isAVLTree( ))
        cout << "success" << endl;
else
        cout << "failure" << endl;
cout << "height = " << tree.height( ) << endl;
```

When 10000 was entered for *n*, the result was successful, that is, the tree was indeed an AVL tree.

This test also helps us to analyze the performance of the insert method. The height of this tree was 15, not far from 12.29 ($= \log_2 10001 − 1$), the minimum height of an AVL tree of 10,000 items. And 15 is less than half the average height—see Lab 20—of a randomly generated BinSearchTree object of 10,000 items. But BinSearchTree insertions, on average, take only slightly more time than AVLTree insertions! Why?

Because BinSearchTree objects are low-maintenance containers. With each AVLTree object, there is an insurance policy that guarantees the height of the tree will always be logarithmic in n. That policy gives you peace of mind that for insertions, removals, and searches, worstTime(n) is logarithmic in n. The price of the policy is the extra time, for insertions and removals, to maintain the AVL tree properties.

The definition of the erase method, with cases and subcases galore, is the goal of Project 9.1. Section 9.4 provides an application of AVL trees: checking words in a document to see if they appear in a dictionary.

9.4 I AVL TREE APPLICATION: A SIMPLE SPELL-CHECKER

One of the most helpful features of modern word processors is the spell-checker, which scans a document for possible misspellings. We say "possible" misspellings because the document may contain words that are legal but not found in a dictionary. For example, the words "iterator" and "postorder" were cited as *not found* by the word processor used in typing this chapter.

The overall problem is this: Given a dictionary, in dictionaryFile, and a document, in a file whose name is provided by the user, print out all words in the document that are not found in the dictionary. We make some simplifying assumptions:

1. The dictionary consists of lowercase words only.
2. Each word in the document consists of letters only—some or all may be in uppercase.
3. Each word in the document is followed by zero or more punctuation symbols followed by any number of blanks and end-of-line markers.
4. The dictionary file is in alphabetical order and will fit in memory. The document file, not necessarily in alphabetical order, will fit in memory if duplicates are excluded.

Here are the contents of a small dictionary file, a small document file, and the words in the latter that are not in the former.

```
// the dictionary file:
a
all
and
be
done
is
more
said
than
when
where
```

// the document file:

When all is sed and done,
more is said than done.

// the possibly misspelled words:

sed

To solve the problem, we create a **SpellCheck** class with the following methods:

```
// Postcondition: The words in the dictionary file have been read in. The
//                worstTime(n) is O(n log n), where n is the number of words
//                in the dictionary file.
void readDictionaryFile( );
```

```
// Postcondition: The words in the document file have been read in. The
//                worstTime(k) is O(k log k), where k is the number of words
//                in the document file.
void readDocumentFile( );
```

```
// Postcondition: Each word that is in the document but not in the dictionary
//                has been printed. The worstTime(k, n) is O(k log n), where k
//                is the number of words in the document file and n is the
//                number of words in the dictionary file.
void compare( );
```

The only fields are dictionary, to hold the words in the dictionary file, and words, to hold each unique word in the document file—there is no purpose in storing multiple copies of any word. Both of these fields are AVLTree objects in which each item is a string, and the string comparisons are alphabetical:

protected:

```
AVLTree<string, less<string> > dictionary,
                               words;
```

The dependency diagram is as follows:

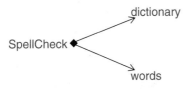

Here is the straightforward definition of the readDictionaryFile( ) method:

```
void readDictionaryFile( ) {

    const string DICTIONARY_FILE = "dictfile.dat";

    fstream dictionaryFile;
    string word;
```

```
        dictionaryFile.open (DICTIONARY_FILE.c_str( ), ios::in);
        while (dictionaryFile >> word)
                dictionary.insert (word);
    } // readDictionaryFile
```

How long will this method take? Assume that there are *n* words in dictionary File. Then the **while** loop will be executed *n* times. During each iteration, there is an insertion into dictionary. For each insertion in the AVLTree object dictionary, worst Time(n) is logarithmic in *n*, so for the readDictionaryFile method, worstTime(n) is $O(n \log n)$, and this is the smallest upper bound.

The definition of readDocumentFile is only slightly more complicated. The name of the document file is read in, and then the file is read. For each word read from the file, the word is converted to lowercase, stripped of the ending punctuation symbols if there are any, and inserted into words unless the word is already in words. Here is the complete definition:

```
    void readDocumentFile( )
    {
        const string DOCUMENT_FILE_PROMPT =
            "Please enter the name of the document file: ";
        fstream documentFile;
        string documentFileName,
            word;

        cout << endl << DOCUMENT_FILE_PROMPT;
        cin >> documentFileName;
        documentFile.open (documentFileName.c_str( ), ios::in);
        while (documentFile >> word)
        {
            // Make word lower case:
            string temp;
            for (unsigned i = 0; i < word.length( ); i++)
                    temp += (char)tolower(word [i]);
            word = temp;

            // Eliminate punctuation at end of word:
            while (!isalpha (word [word.length( ) −1]))
                    word.erase(word.length( ) − 1);

            // Insert word into words unless already there:
            if (words.find (word) == words.end( ))
                    words.insert (word);
        } // while more words in documentFile
    } // readDocumentFile
```

The time it takes for the readDocumentFile method to complete is easily estimated. To read in the k words from the file, worstTime(k) is linear in k. For inserting each word into the AVLTree object words, worstTime(k) is logarithmic in k. So for the readDocumentFile method, worstTime(k) is $O(k \log k)$, and this is the smallest upper bound.

Finally, and easiest of all, here is the definition of the compare method:

```
void compare( )
{
        const string MISSPELLED =
            "Here are the possibly misspelled words:";

        AVLTree< string, less< string > >::Iterator itr;

        cout << endl << MISSPELLED << endl;
        for (itr = words.begin( ); itr != words.end( ); itr++)
            if (dictionary.find (*itr) == dictionary.end( ))
                cout << *itr << endl;
} // compare
```

For iterating through the k words in words, worstTime(k) is linear in k, and for each search of the n words in dictionary by the find method, worstTime(n) is logarithmic in n. So for the compare, worstTime(k, n) is $O(k \log n)$, and this is the smallest upper bound. Project 9.2 is an enhancement of this application.

In Chapter 13, we will encounter another container class, the hash_set class, that is not yet in the Standard Template Library. In this class, the average time for insertions, deletions, and searches is, basically, constant. So we can redo this problem with hash_set objects for the dictionary and words fields. No other changes need be made! For that version of the spell-check project, averageTime(n) would be linear in n for the readDictionaryFile method, and averageTime(k) would be linear in k for the readDocumentFile method. For the compare method, averageTime(k, n) would be linear in k. But don't sell your stock in AVLTrees-R-Us. For the hash_set version of spell-check, worstTime(k, n) for the compare method, for example, would be $O(kn)$.

SUMMARY

This chapter looked at improving on the BinSearchTree class by making sure that the tree was **balanced**—that is, had a height that was logarithmic in n—after each insertion or removal. The rebalancing is accomplished with rotations. A **rotation** is an adjustment to the tree, around an item, that maintains the required ordering of items.

An **AVL tree** is a binary search tree that either is empty or has the following two properties:

1.   The heights of the left and right subtrees differ by at most 1.
2.   The left and right subtrees are AVL trees.

The height of an AVL tree is always logarithmic in *n,* the number of items in the tree.

EXERCISES

9.1   In each of the following binary search trees, perform a left rotation around 50.

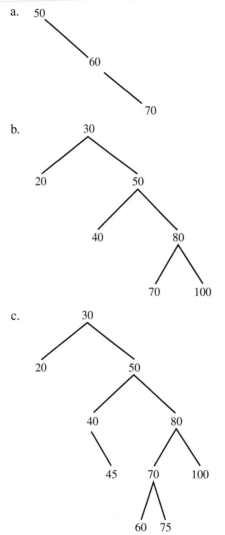

9.2   In each of the following binary search trees, perform a right rotation around 50.

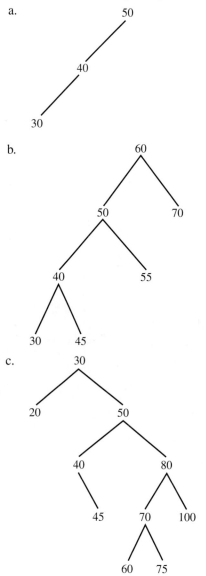

9.3 In the following binary search tree, perform a double rotation (a left rotation around 20 and then a right rotation around 50) to reduce the height to 2.

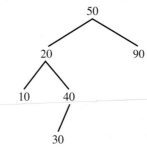

9.4 In the following binary search tree, perform a double rotation to reduce the height to 2:

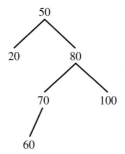

9.5 Show that for any nonnegative integer h,

$$\text{fib}(h + 3) - 1 \geq (3/2)^h$$

  Hint   For $h > 1$,

$$(3/2)^{h-1} + (3/2)^{h-2} = (3/2)^{h-2}(3/2 + 1) > (3/2)^{h-2}(9/4)$$

9.6 Suppose we define max_h to be the maximum number of items in an AVL tree of height h.

  a.   Calculate max_3.

  b.   Determine the formula for max_h for any $h \geq 0$.

  Hint   Use part 2 of the Binary Tree Theorem from Chapter 8.

  c.   What is the maximum height of an AVL tree with 100 items?

9.7 Show that the height of any AVL tree with 32 items must be exactly 5.

  Hint   Calculate max_4 and min_6.

9.8   In the AVLTree class, develop a height( ) method for which worstTime(n) is $O(\log n)$.

Hint   The balance factor of a tree node indicates which subtree's height is greater.

9.9   For the find method in the AVLTree class, worstTime(n) is logarithmic in n. For the find method in the BinSearchTree class, worstTime(n) is linear in n. But the definitions of the two methods are identical (except that the function object compare replaces **operator**<) ! Explain.

PROGRAMMING PROJECT 9.1

The erase **Method in the** AVLTree **Class**

Define the erase method in the AVLTree class. Here is the method interface:

```
// Precondition: itr is positioned at an item in this AVLTree.
// Postcondition: the item that itr was positioned at has been removed from this
//                AVLTree. The worstTime is O(log n). (Any iterator that was, before
//                this call, positioned at the successor of *itr has been invalidated.)
//                The amortizedTime(n) is constant, and so averageTime(n) is
//                constant.
void erase (Iterator itr)
```

Hint After performing a BinSearchTree-style removal, let ancestor be the parent of the node actually removed. (If *itr has two children, the node actually removed holds the successor of *itr, so the ancestor node will be the parent of that successor.) Loop until the tree is an AVL tree with appropriate balance factors. Within the loop, suppose that the item removed was in the right subtree of the ancestor node (a symmetric analysis handles the left-subtree case). Then there are three subcases, depending on whether the ancestor node's balance factor was '=', 'L', or 'R'. In all three cases, the ancestor node's balance factor must be adjusted. For the '=' subcase, the loop then terminates. For the 'R' subcase, the ancestor node is replaced with the (*ancestor).parent node and the loop continues. For the 'L' subcase, there are three sub-subcases depending on whether the (*ancestor).left node's balance factor is '=', 'L', or 'R'. And the 'R' sub-subcase has three sub-sub-subcases!

PROGRAMMING PROJECT 9.2

Enhancing the SpellChecker Project

Modify the spell-checker project. If document word x is not in the dictionary but word y is in the dictionary and x differs from y either by an adjacent transposition or by a single letter, then y should be proposed as an alternative for x. For example, suppose the document word is "asteriks" and the dictionary contains "asterisk". By transposing the adjacent letters "s" and "k" in "asteriks", we get "asterisk". So "asterisk" should be proposed as an alternative. Similarly, if the document word is "seperate" or "seprate" and the dictionary word is "separate", then "separate" should be offered as an alternative in either case.

Here are the dictionary words for both system tests:

a
algorithms
asterisk
coat
equals
he
pied
pile
plus
programs
separate
structures
wore

Here is document file doc1.dat:

She woar a pide coat.

And here is document file doc2.dat:

Alogrithms plus Data Structures equals Pograms

System Test 1   Input is in boldface.

In the Input line, please enter the name of the document file.
doc1.dat

Possible misspellings	Possible alternatives
pide	pied, pile
she	he
woar	

(continued on next page)

(continued from previous page)

System Test 2 Input is in boldface.

In the Input line, please enter the name of the document file.
doc2.dat

Possible misspellings	Possible alternatives
alogrithms	algorithms
data	
pograms	programs

CHAPTER 10

Red-Black Trees

T his chapter introduces another kind of balanced binary search tree: the red-black tree. Red-black trees have a less stringent—but still logarithmic in n—height restriction than AVL trees. The algorithms for inserting and erasing in a red-black tree are somewhat harder to follow than the algorithms for inserting and erasing in an AVL tree. The main advantage to studying red-black trees is that they are the basis, in the Hewlett-Packard implementation, for the associative-container classes in the Standard Template Library: set, multiset, map, and multimap. These associative-container classes are also investigated in this chapter. ■

CHAPTER OBJECTIVES

1. Explain why red-black trees are balanced binary search trees.

2. Be able to follow the methods for inserting or erasing in a red-black tree.

3. Understand the distinction between sets, multisets, maps, and multimaps.

4. Compare an associative array with an ordinary array.

10.1 I RED-BLACK TREES

Basically, a red-black tree is a binary search tree in which we adopt a coloring convention for each item in the tree. Specifically, with each item we associate a color of either red or black, according to rules we will give shortly. One of the rules involves paths. Recall, from Chapter 8, that if item *A* is an ancestor of item *B*, the ***path*** from *A* to *B* is the sequence of items, starting with *A* and ending with *B*, in which each item in the sequence (except the last) is the parent of the next item.

Specifically, we will be interested in paths from the root to items with no children *or with one child.*[1] For example, in the following tree, there are five paths from the root to an item (boxed) with no children or with one child.

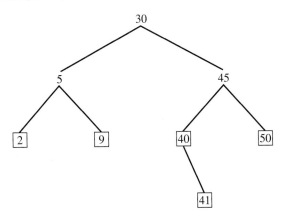

Note that one of the paths is to the item 40, which has one child. So the paths described are not necessarily to a leaf.

A ***red-black tree*** is a binary search tree that is empty or in which the root item is colored black, every other item is colored red or black, and the following properties are satisfied:

Every red-black tree must satisfy the Red Rule and the Path Rule.

> *Red Rule:* If an item is red, its parent must be black.
>
> *Path Rule:* The number of black items must be the same in all paths from the root item to an item with no children ***or with one child.***

For example, Figure 10.1 shows a red-black tree in which the items are integers. Observe that this is a binary search tree with a black root. Since no red item has a red parent, the Red Rule is satisfied. Also, there are two black items in each of the five paths from the root to an item with no children or one child, so the Path Rule is satisfied. In other words the tree is a red-black tree.

---

[1]Equivalently, we could consider paths from the root item to an empty subtree, because an item with one child also has an empty subtree, and a leaf has two empty subtrees. When this approach is taken, the binary search tree is expanded to include a special kind of item, a stub leaf, for each such empty subtree.

Figure 10.1 | A red-black tree with eight items.

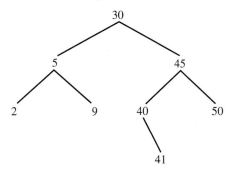

Figure 10.2 | A binary search tree that is *not* a red-black tree.

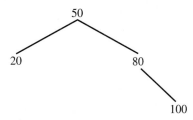

The tree in Figure 10.2 is *not* a red-black tree even though the Red Rule is satisfied and every path from the root to a leaf has the same number of black items. The Path Rule is violated because the path from 50 to 80 (an item with one child) has only one black item, whereas the path from 50 to 20 has two black items, as does the path from 50 to 100.

Similarly, the tree in Figure 10.3 is not a red-black tree. The Path Rule is violated because, for example, the path from 70 to 40 (an item with one child) has three black items, but the path from 70 to 110 has four black items. That tree is badly unbalanced: The height of any tree with just two leaves must be linear in *n*.

The red-black tree in Figure 10.1 is fairly evenly balanced, but not every red-black tree has that characteristic. For example, Figure 10.4 shows one that droops to the left. You can easily verify that this is a black-rooted binary search tree and that the Red Rule is satisfied. For the Path Rule, there are exactly two black items in any path from the root to an item with no children or with one child. That is, the tree is a red-black tree. But there are limits to how unbalanced a red-black tree can be. For example, we could not hang another item under item 10 in Figure 10.4. For if we tried to add a red item, the Red Rule would no longer be satisfied. And if we tried to add a black item, the Path Rule would fail.

If a red-black tree is complete, with all black items except for red leaves at the lowest level, the height of that tree will be minimal, approximately $\log_2 n$. To get the maximum height for a given *n*, we would have to have as many red items as possible

Even if every path from the root to a leaf has the same number of black items, the Path Rule might not be satisfied!

Figure 10.3 | A binary search tree that is *not* a red-black tree.

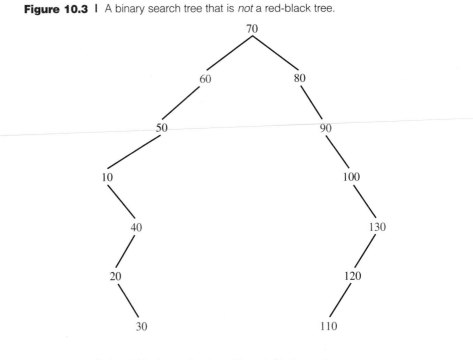

Figure 10.4 | A red-black tree that is not "evenly" balanced.

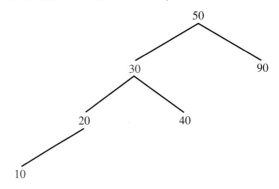

on one path, and all other items black. For example, Figure 10.4 contains one such tree, and Figure 10.5 contains another. The path with all the red items will be about twice as long as the path(s) with no red items. These trees lead us to hypothesize that the maximum height a red-black tree is less than $2 \log_2 n$. We prove this conjecture in Section 10.1.1.

10.1.1   The Height of a Red-Black Tree

Red-black trees are fairly bushy in the sense that almost all nonleaves have two children. In fact, if an item has only one child, that item must be black and the child must be a red leaf. This bushiness leads us to believe that a red-black tree is balanced, that

Figure 10.5 | A red-black tree of 14 elements with maximum height, 5.

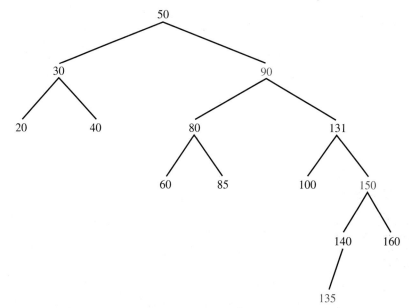

is, has a height that is logarithmic in n, even in the worst case. Compare that with the worst-case height that is linear in n for a binary search tree! In order to establish that red-black trees always have height that is logarithmic in n, we need a couple of preliminary results.

CLAIM 1

Let y be the root of a subtree of a red-black tree. The number of black items is the same in a path from y to any one of its descendants with no children or one child.

To prove this claim, suppose x is the root of a red-black tree, and y is the root of a subtree. Let $b0$ be the number of black items from x (inclusive) to y (exclusive); let $b1$ be the number of black items from y (inclusive) to any one of its descendants (inclusive) with no children or one child, and let $b2$ be the number of black items from y (inclusive) to any other one of its descendants (inclusive) with no children or one child. Figure 10.6 depicts this situation.

For example, back in Figure 10.5, suppose x is 50, y is 131, and the two descendants of y are 100 and 135. Then $b0 = 1$, the number of black items in the path from 50 through 90; 131 is not counted in $b0$. The value of $b1$ is 2, as is the value of $b2$.

In general, by the Path Rule for the whole tree, we must have $b0 + b1 = b0 + b2$. This implies that $b1 = b2$. In other words, the number of black items is the same in any path from y to any of its descendants that have no children or one child.

Figure 10.6 | Part of a red-black tree rooted at *x*; *y* is a descendant of *x*, and z1 and z2 are two arbitrarily chosen descendants of *y* that have no children or one child. Then b0 represents the number of black items in the path from *x* (inclusive) to *y* (exclusive); b1 and b2 represent the number of black items in the path from *y* (inclusive) to z1 and z2 (inclusive), respectively.

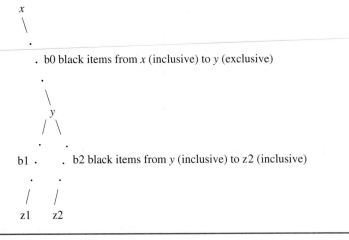

. b0 black items from *x* (inclusive) to *y* (exclusive)

b1 .   . b2 black items from *y* (inclusive) to z2 (inclusive)

Figure 10.7 | A red-black tree whose root has a black-height of 3.

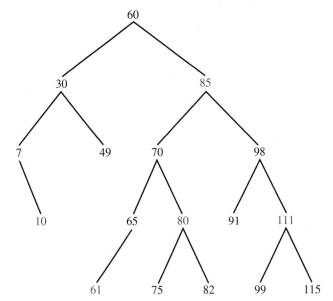

Now that claim 1 has been verified, we can make the following definition. Let y be an item in a red-black tree; we define the ***black-height*** of y, written $\mathrm{bh}(y)$, as follows:

$\mathrm{bh}(y)$ = number of black elements in any path from y to any descendant of y that has no children or one child

By claim 1, the number of black items must be the same in any path from an item to any of its descendants with no children or one child. So black-height is well defined. For example, in Figure 10.4, the black-height of 50 is 2; the black height of 20, 30, 40, and 90 is 1; and the black-height of 10 is 0. Figure 10.7 shows a red-black tree in which 60 has a black-height of 3 and 85 has a black-height of 2.

CLAIM 2

For any nonempty subtree t of a red-black tree,

$$n(t) \geq 2^{\mathrm{bh}(\mathrm{root}(t))} - 1$$

(In the claim, $n(t)$ is the number of items in t, and $\mathrm{root}(t)$ is the root item of t.) The proof of this claim is, as usual, by induction on the height of t.

Base case

Assume that $\mathrm{height}(t) = 0$. Then $n(t) = 1$, and $\mathrm{bh}(\mathrm{root}(t)) = 1$ if the root is black and 0 if the subtree rooted at t is red. In either case, $1 \geq \mathrm{bh}(\mathrm{root}(t))$. So

$$n(t) = 1 = 2^1 - 1 \geq 2^{\mathrm{bh}(\mathrm{root}(t))} - 1$$

This proves claim 2 for the base case.

Inductive case

Let k be any nonnegative integer, and assume claim 2 is true for any subtree whose height is less than or equal to k. Let t be a subtree of height $k + 1$. If the root of t has one child, we must have $\mathrm{bh}(\mathrm{root}(t)) = 1$, and so

$$n(t) = 1 = 2^1 - 1 = 2^{\mathrm{bh}(\mathrm{root}(t))} - 1$$

This completes the proof of the inductive case if the root of t has only one child. Otherwise, the root of t must have a left child, $v1$, and a right child, $v2$. If the root of t is red, $\mathrm{bh}(\mathrm{root}(t)) = \mathrm{bh}(v1) = \mathrm{bh}(v2)$. If the root of t is black, $\mathrm{bh}(\mathrm{root}(t)) = \mathrm{bh}(v1) + 1 = \mathrm{bh}(v2) + 1$. In either case,

$$\mathrm{bh}(v1) \geq \mathrm{bh}(\mathrm{root}(t)) - 1$$

and

$$\mathrm{bh}(v2) \geq \mathrm{bh}(\mathrm{root}(t)) - 1$$

The left and right subtrees of t have height less than or equal to k, and so the induction hypothesis applies and we have

$$n(\text{leftTree}(t)) \geq 2^{bh(v1)} - 1$$

and

$$n(\text{rightTree}(t)) \geq 2^{bh(v2)} - 1$$

The number of items in t is one more than the number of items in left Tree(t) and rightTree(t).

Putting all this together, we get

$$
\begin{aligned}
n(t) &= n(\text{leftTree}(t)) + n(\text{rightTree}(t)) + 1 \\
&\geq 2^{bh(v1)} - 1 + 2^{bh(v2)} - 1 + 1 \\
&\geq 2^{bh(root(t))-1} - 1 + 2^{bh(root(t))-1} - 1 + 1 \\
&= 2 * 2^{bh(root(t))-1} - 1 \\
&= 2^{bh(root(t))} - 1
\end{aligned}
$$

This completes the proof of the inductive case when the root of t has two children.

Therefore, by the Principle of Mathematical Induction, claim 2 is true for all non-empty subtrees of red-black trees.

Finally, we get to show the important result that the height of a red-black tree is logarithmic in n, where n represents the number of items in the tree.

CLAIM 3

The height of a red-black tree is logarithmic in n, *even in the worst case.*

For any red-black tree t with n items, height(t) is logarithmic in n.

To prove claim 3, let t be a red-black tree. By the Red Rule, at most half of the items in the path from the root to the farthest leaf can be red, so at least half of those items must be black. That is,

$$bh(\text{root}(t)) \geq \text{height}(t)/2$$

From Claim 2,

$$
\begin{aligned}
n(t) &\geq 2^{bh(root(t))} - 1 \\
&\geq 2^{height(t)/2} - 1
\end{aligned}
$$

From this we obtain

$$\text{height}(t) \leq 2 \log_2(n(t) + 1)$$

This implies that height(t) is $O(\log n)$. By part 2 of the Binary Tree Theorem,

$$\text{height}(t) \geq \log_2(n(t) + 1) - 1$$

We conclude the $O(\log n)$ is the smallest upper bound of height(t). In other words, height(t) is logarithmic in n.

Claim 3 states that red-black trees never get far out of balance. For binary search trees, on the other hand, the height can be linear in the worst case—for example, if the tree is a chain.

We outline Hewlett-Packard's rb_tree class in Section 10.1.2. The payoff is that the find, insert, and erase methods take only $O(\log n)$ time, even in the worst case. There is no red-black tree class of any kind in the Standard Template Library. But any implementation of that library will most likely have an instance of a red-black tree class, modeled after the rb_tree class, that is a field in the definition of the set, multiset, map, and multimap classes.

10.1.2   Hewlett-Packard's rb_tree **Class**

The essential concept in understanding the rb_tree class is the *key.* Recall from Chapter 8 that an item's key consists of that part of the item used in comparisons with other items. For example, a social security number may be used as a key for an employee item, and a student identification number may be used as a key for a student item.

Here is the start of the definition of the rb_tree class:

```
template <class Key, class Value, class KeyOfValue, class Compare>
class rb_tree
{
```

Let's spend some time to make sure you understand the line that specifies the template parameters. The **class** Key represents the type of the keys. When an rb_tree object is instantiated, an actual class is substituted for the dummy type Key. For example, if the keys are of type string, the instantiation would start with

```
rb_tree<string, . . . > my_tree;
```

The template argument corresponding to the Value template parameter is the type of the items to be inserted into the tree. Often, the keys and values will be the same. For example, each value might be an automobile manufacturer, such as "Ford", and each key is the same thing. So what will be stored in the tree will be "Ford", for example, and to compare that item with other items, the key "Ford" will be compared with other keys. Big deal!

The next template parameter, KeyOfValue, is a function-class type. Function classes and function objects were introduced in Chapter 9, and investigated in Lab 21. The KeyOfValue parameter will be replaced by a function class in which **operator( )** returns the key from the value. Suppose that key is a function object in that function class and item v is of type Value. There are only two cases of interest:

1.   The key and value are the same: In this case, key (v) simply returns v. This case applies for the set and multiset classes in the Standard Template Library.

2. v is a pair[2] whose first component is a key: In this case key (v) returns the first component of v. This case applies for the map and multimap classes in the Standard Template Library. For example, suppose each value consists of the following pair: auto manufacturer and gross sales in billions of dollars. Then the key is the auto manufacturer, and the second component of each pair contains the gross sales of that auto manufacturer. For example, two of the pairs might be

> "Ford", 14
>
> "Honda", 22

The final template parameter is Compare, another function-class type. An rb_tree object will often be instantiated with the built-in function class less as the fourth template argument. Why? Keys are usually compared by **operator**<. Recall from Chapter 9 that the function class less, defined in <function>, overloads **operator( )** as follows:

> **bool operator( ) (const** T& x, **const** T& y) **const { return** x < y; }

In other words, if less is the fourth template argument in instantiating an rb_tree object, the keys will be compared according to **operator**<. To make comparisons within an rb_tree object, a function object is defined:

> Compare key_compare;

So if less is the fourth template argument in instantiating an rb_tree object, a message within the rb_tree object such as

> key_compare (x, y)

can be interpreted as

> x < y

The fields in the rb_tree class are quite similar to the fields in the list class.

The basic organization of the rb_tree class is similar to that of the list class: There are nodes, and fields header, free_list, buffer_list, next_avail, and last. Also, the rb_tree class handles its own memory management, with the get_node and put_node methods (instead of **new** and **delete**). The structure of each node reflects a red-black tree. Here is the definition of rb_tree_node:

> **enum** color_type = {red, black};
>
> **struct** rb_tree_node

---

[2]The file <utility> has a template **struct**, pair, with a two-parameter constructor:

```
template<class T1, class T2>
struct pair {
    T1 first;
    T2 second;
    pair (cont T1& x, const T2& y);
    . . .
```

```
{
        color_type color_field;
        rb_tree_node* parent_link;
        rb_tree_node* left_link;
        rb_tree_node* right_link;
        Value value_field;
};
```

There are two coloring conventions:

1. header's node is colored red.
2. When a node is originally inserted, it is colored red; a recoloring may be needed to satisfy the Red Rule.

For the most part, fields are accessed with functions—such as parent, color, and left—rather than directly. So parent (header) is used instead of (*header).parent_link to return a reference to header's parent_link field. One reason for using these accessor functions is that their definitions encapsulate any allocation-model details. Another simplification allows a NULL pointer to be treated as a pointer to an ordinary rb_tree_node: There is a special node, NIL, whose color is black, whose left and right fields are NULL, and whose parent field is, at least initially, NULL. And this demonstrates another advantage of using accessor functions: We can test to see if color (y) returns the color black without making a special case for y being NULL.

Compared to the find method in the AVLTree class, the definition of the find method in the rb_tree class is slightly more abstract (a function object is used for obtaining the key from the value) and slightly more abstruse (with the comma operator and the conditional operator). But the basic algorithm is the same, and worst Time(n) is still logarithmic in n:

```
iterator find(const Key& k)
{
        rb_tree_node* y = header;
        rb_tree_node* x = root( );
        while (x != NIL)
                if (!key_compare(key(x), k))
                        y = x, x = left(x);
                else
                        x = right(x);

        iterator j = iterator(y);
        return (j == end( ) || key_compare(k, key(j.node))) ? end( ) : j;
}
```

The method definitions for insert and erase are somewhat shorter but more complicated than their AVLTree counterparts. Before we go any further, you need to know that the definitions of the insert and erase methods are not intuitively obvious.

Red-black trees were originally developed in the paper "Symmetric binary B-trees: Data structure and maintenance algorithms," by R. Bayer (1972). The algorithms for inserting and removing in these trees, called "2-3-4 trees," were lengthy but the over-all strategies for inserting and removing were easy to understand. Shorter but harder to follow methods were supplied when the red-black coloring was imposed on these structures in "A diochromatic framework for balanced trees" by L. Guibas and R. Sedgewick (1978).

10.1.3   The insert **Method in the** rb_tree **Class**

The heading of the insert method is

pair<iterator,**bool**> insert (**const** value_type& v)

The Hewlett-Packard implementation of the Standard Template Library's associative container classes is based on a red-black tree class.

Before we get into the details of inserting, we have to explain the return type: pair<iterator, **bool**>. In the Hewlett-Packard implementation of the Standard Tem-plate Library, the rb_tree class serves as the underpinning for the four associative-container classes: set, multiset, map, and multimap. In the set and map classes, it is illegal to insert a value whose key is the same as the key of some value already in the container. But in the multiset and multimap classes, duplicate keys are allowed. To distinguish between these choices, the rb_tree class has a field:

bool insert_always;

Each rb_tree constructor has a **bool** parameter always that initializes the insert_always field. So the set and map classes construct their rb_tree field with **false** for the argument corresponding to the always parameter, thereby disallowing duplicate keys. In the multiset and multimap classes, the argument is **true,** and duplicate keys are permitted.

When the insert method in the rb_tree class is called, if the value of the insert_always field is **true** or if v's key *does not* duplicate a key already in the tree, v is inserted. Then the pair returned consists of an iterator positioned at the inserted value and the value **true**. But if the value of the insert_always field is **false** and v's key *does* duplicate a key already in the tree, v is not inserted, and the pair returned consists of an iterator positioned at the original value with the given key and the value **false**.

Now we can look at how the inserting is performed. There are five steps to accomplish the insertion of v:

1. Create a node pointed to by x.
2. Store the item, v, in the value_field field of the node (pointed to by) x.
3. Insert that node as a leaf using a BinSearchTree-style insertion, and set x's color to red.
4. Fix up the tree by recoloring and restructuring, if necessary.
5. Set the root's color to black.

The insert method actually accomplishes only steps 1 and 2 before calling the real workhorse, __insert, which has as arguments x, x's parent, and the item to be inserted. The only step that requires some thought is step 4. You may first want to see why step 4 is needed. Suppose we have just inserted 20 into a red-black tree, and after completing step 3, the tree is as follows:

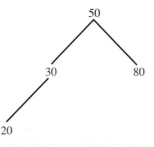

The Red Rule has been violated, so something must be done. In this case, there is a simple solution: change the color of both 30's node and 80's node from red to black. That gives us the following red-black tree:

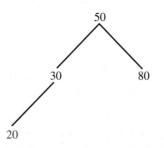

Sometimes a mere recoloring is not enough. For example, suppose 25 has just been inserted into a red-black tree, and the tree is as follows:

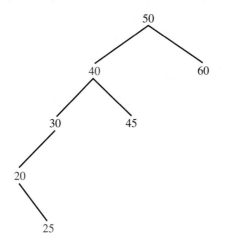

This tree violates the Red Rule, so something must be done. Can recoloring alone restore this to a red-black tree? Try to see if you can do it.

In fact, it is impossible to restore the above tree to a red-black tree by recoloring alone, and here is why. Since the black-height of this tree is 2, the path with items 50, 40, 30, 20, and 25 must have exactly two black nodes. But because the root, 50, must be black, the path of items 40, 30, 20, and 25 must have exactly one black item. The Red Rule requires that a path of four items have at most two red nodes. But a path of four items cannot have only one black item and at most two red items.

The restructuring that must be done in such cases is to rotate part of the tree. Rather than considering this example in isolation, let's develop a general framework for restructuring.

Suppose we have just made an insertion of x's node. To simplify the following discussion, we will refer to this node as x rather than as the node pointed to by x. Do we need to rotate? The answer is "no" if x is the root because the root's color will be set to black in step 5 of the insertion. Similarly, no restructuring is done if the color of x's parent is black, because then the Red Rule is not violated. So we will keep looping until one of those conditions is satisfied:

> **while** (x != root( ) && color(parent(x)) == red)

In fact, the critical factor is the color of the *sibling* of x's parent. Here is an outline of what happens when x's parent is a left child—by flipping "left" and "right", you will get an outline of what happens when x's parent is a right child. Let y point to the (right) sibling of x's parent. We refer to this sibling node as y rather than the node pointed to by y. There are three cases to consider.

CASE 1   color (y) = red

For example, suppose 40 has just been inserted into a red-black tree, part of which is shown here:

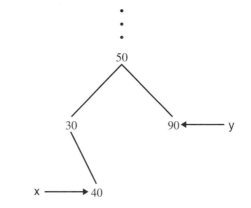

Here is the action to take in this case:

```
color (y) = black;
color (parent (x)) = black;
```

color (parent (parent (x))) = red;
x = parent (parent (x));

The resulting partial tree is

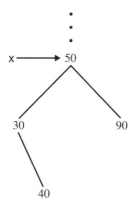

After this case, and only after this case, we continue looping. But now **x** is two levels farther up the tree, so the maximum number of loop iterations will be one-half the height of the tree. That is why, for the **insert** method in the **rb_tree** class, worstTime(*n*) is logarithmic in *n,* the number of items in the tree.

color (y) = black and x Is a Right Child ▮ CASE 2

For example, suppose 40 has just been inserted into a red-black tree, and here is the resulting tree:

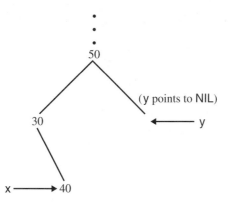

Note that when **y** is NULL, **y** becomes a pointer to NIL, whose color is **black**. The action taken in this case is

x = parent (x);
rotate_left (x);

Here is the tree after this left rotation:

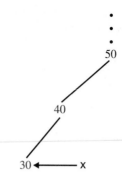

We are not done yet because **x** and its parent are both red, and that leads us to case 3.

CASE 3	color (y) = black, and x Is a Left Child

For example, suppose 30 has just been inserted into a red-black tree, part of which is shown here:

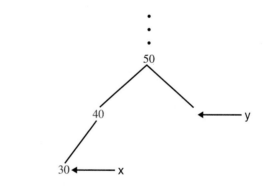

The action taken in this case is

        color (parent (x)) = black;
        color (parent (parent (x))) = red;
        rotate_right (parent (parent (x)));

Here is the partial tree after this right rotation:

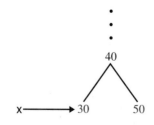

Notice that after the prescribed action is taken for case 3, the color of **x**'s parent will always be **black**, and that will terminate the execution of the **while** loop.

The basic idea is that if case 1 does not apply, we first check for case 2 and then, whether or not case 2 applied, we apply case 3. Note that case 3 always applies after case 2. Here is the overall structure (when x's parent is a left child):

if (y is red) { // Case 1

     ...

}
else { // y must be black

    if (x is a right child) { // Case 2

        ...

    }
    // Case 3
    ...

}

If, during any loop iteration, case 1 does not apply, case 3 must apply (possibly preceded by case 2), and x's parent's color will be set to black. So the execution of the loop will terminate after that iteration.

Here is the complete **while** loop:

```
while (x != root( ) && color(parent(x)) == red)
    if (parent(x) == left(parent(parent(x)))) // if parent(x) is a left child
    {
        y = right(parent(parent(x)));
        if (color(y) == red) // Case 1
        {
            color(parent(x)) = black;
            color(y) = black;
            color(parent(parent(x))) = red;
            x = parent(parent(x));
        }
        else // color of y must be black
        {
            if (x == right(parent(x))) // Case 2
            {
                x = parent(x); rotate_left(x);
            }
            // Case 3
            color(parent(x)) = black;
            color(parent(parent(x))) = red;
```

```
                    rotate_right(parent(parent(x)));
            }
        }
        else // parent (x) is a right child
        {
            y = left(parent(parent(x)));
            if (color(y) == RED) // Case 1
            {
                color(parent(x)) = black;
                color(y) = black;
                color(parent(parent(x))) = red;
                x = parent(parent(x));
            }
            else // color of y must be black
            {
                if (x == left(parent(x))) // Case 2
                {
                    x = parent(x); rotate_right(x);
                }
                // Case 3
                color(parent(x)) = black;
                color(parent(parent(x))) = red;
                rotate_left(parent(parent(x)));
            }
        }
    }
```

And right after that loop:

```
    color(root( )) = black;
```

Lab 22 includes an example in which all three cases apply for inserting an item.

LAB   **Lab 22: A red-black tree insertion with all three cases.**

(All Labs Are Optional.)   **LAB**

The bottom line, as proved in Section 10.1.1, is that the height of any red-black tree is logarithmic in n, the number of items in the tree. So for the part of inserting that adds an item as a leaf, worstTime(n) is logarithmic in n. Then the **while** loop is executed, for which worstTime(n) is also logarithmic in n. We conclude that, for the entire insert method, worstTime(n) is logarithmic in n.

10.1.4   The erase **Method**

To finish up our study of the rb_tree class, we now look at the details of the erase method. Here is its heading:

void erase (iterator position)

This method deletes from the tree the node that position is positioned at. There are cases, just as with inserting, but now there are four cases instead of three, and before we get down to cases, there is some preliminary work.

The code starts innocently enough. We delete the node as we would delete a node using the BinSearchTree version of the erase method. Make sure you understand how the BinSearchTree class's erase method works. For example, if the deleted node had only one child, then that child replaces the deleted node. And if the deleted node had two children, the immediate successor of the deleted node replaced the deleted node in the tree.[3] The height of a red-black tree is $O(\log n)$, so this part of the rb_tree class's erase method takes logarithmic time in the worst case. We cannot simply stop after the deletion, because the Red Rule or the Path Rule may now be violated.

If the deleted node had only one child, then there is little more to do. That's because, as noted in Section 10.1.1, the deleted node must have been black, and the replacement node must have been red. So we set the color of the replacement node to black, and we still have a red-black tree.

If the Deleted Node Was a Leaf   So we have more work to do only if the deleted node was a leaf or had two children. Suppose that the deleted node was a leaf. If that leaf was the root or red, there is nothing more to do. Otherwise, let x be (a pointer to) the NIL node that replaced the deleted black leaf, and let w be (a pointer to) the sibling of x. For example, suppose we want to delete 50 from the following red-black tree:

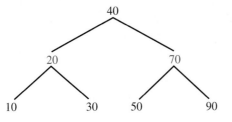

Then 50 is replaced with a NIL node, and we have

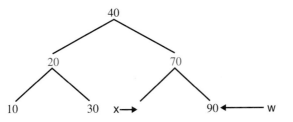

---

[3]Because of the possibility that another iterator may be positioned at that successor, the code is more complicated than that for simply replacing the deleted node.

By the Path Rule, since the deleted node was not NIL, w cannot be (a pointer to) NIL. We will keep looping through the four cases until x—which starts out black— is the root or red.

If the Deleted Node Had Two Children   Now consider the situation if the deleted node had two children. If the deleted node was red and the replacement node is red, then we still have a red-black tree. For example, if 80 is deleted from the red-black tree in Figure 10.8, we get the red-black tree in Figure 10.9.

Figure 10.8 | A red-black tree from which 80 is to be removed.

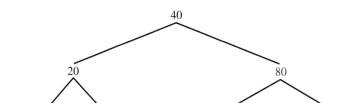

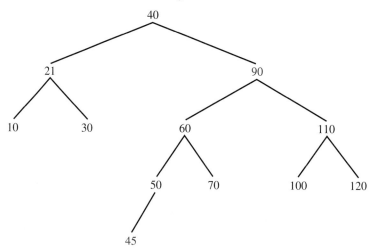

Figure 10.9 | The red-black tree from Figure 10.8 after the removal of 80.

Furthermore, if the deleted node was black and the replacement node is red, then we simply change the replacement node's color to black and we still have a red-black tree. For example, if we delete 40 from the red-black tree in Figure 10.9, we get the red-black tree in Figure 10.10. So if the deleted node had two children and the replacement node is red, then there is very little that we need to do to make sure the Red Rule and Path Rule are still satisfied.

So let's assume that the deleted node had two children and the replacement node is black. We start by giving the replacement node the color of the deleted node. If the replacement node had a nonempty right child, that child must be red because the replacement node could not have a left child. When the deletion occurred, the right child of the replacement node replaced the replacement node. Then we color that right child black and we have a red-black tree.

So assume that the replacement node has an empty right child. Let x be (a pointer to) the NIL node that replaced the replacement node. Let w be (a pointer to) the sibling of x. That is, w is what had been the sibling of the replacement node. For example, after deleting 40 from the red-black tree in Figure 10.11, we would be working with the tree in Figure 10.12. Note that, because the replacement node was black, the Path Rule requires that w cannot be NIL.

If x ever gets to be red, then all we need to do is make x black and both rules will be satisfied. Similarly, if x ever gets to be the root, we make x black and we are done. The only situation that requires more work occurs when x is a black nonroot, so we will loop until x is red or x is the root node.

If the Deleted Node Was a Leaf or Had Two Children   If the deleted node was a leaf, x is (a pointer to) the NIL node that replaced the deleted node. If the deleted node had two children, x is (a pointer to) the right child of the replacement node. In both situations, w is the sibling of x after the deleted node was removed. We will keep looping until x is red or x is the root. There are four cases that arise when x is a left child, and four symmetric cases (simply switch "left" and "right") when x

Figure 10.10 | The red-black tree from Figure 10.9 after the removal of 40.

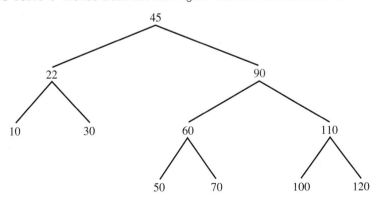

Figure 10.11 | A red-black tree from which 40 is to be removed. The replacement item is 50.

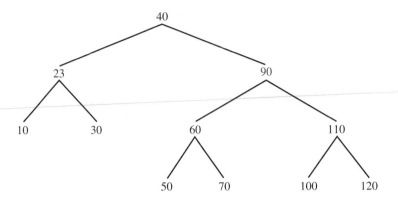

Figure 10.12 | The tree from Figure 10.11 after the removal of 40.

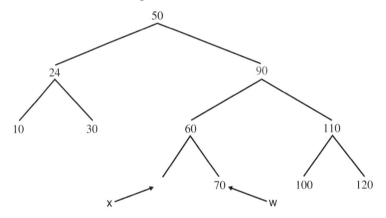

is a right child. As we did with insertions, we will present the cases in which x is a left child. All eight cases are shown at the end of this section.

All the following cases apply whether the deleted node was a leaf or had two children.

CASE 1	color (w) = red

The action taken in this case is

```
color (w) = black;
color (parent (x)) = red;
rotate_left( parent (x));
w = right (parent (x));
```

For example, suppose we delete 65 from the following tree:

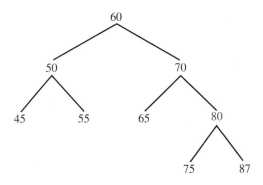

After 65 is removed, **x** and **w** are as shown:

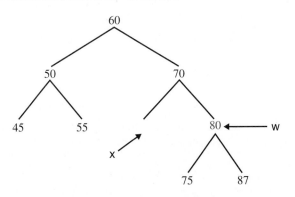

In this tree, **x** is (a pointer to) **NIL.** Because **w** is **red,** case 1 applies, with **x** a left child. So we set **w**'s color to **black, x**'s parent's color to **red,** left rotate at **x**'s parent, and set **w** to **x**'s parent's right child:

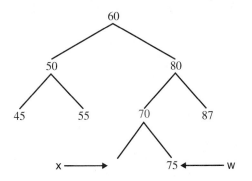

The Path Rule is still violated, but we have a new **w,** and it is **black!**

So case 1 devolves into one of the other three cases.

| CASE 2 | w's children are black |

Recall that **w** cannot be **NIL**. One or both of **w**'s children may be **NIL**, but **NIL**'s color is **black**, so we need not make a special case for **w**'s children being **NIL**. The action in case 2—whether **x** is a right child or a left child—is

$$color\ (w) = red;$$
$$x = parent\ (x);$$

For example, we can apply case 2 to the binary search tree we had at the end of the case 1 example. At the end of that example we had

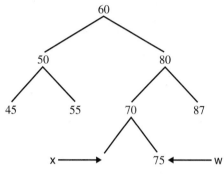

Because both of **w**'s children are **black** (recall that **NIL** nodes are **black**), case 2 applies, and we get

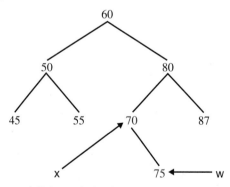

Now **x** is **red**, so we fall through the loop, set **x**'s color to **black**, and we end up with the following red-black tree:

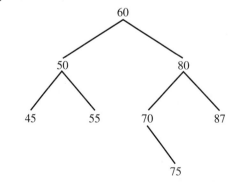

The outline of the **erase** method's loop so far is

```
while (x is not the root and x's color is black)
{
        if (x == x's parent's left)
        {
                w = x's parent's right;
                if (w's color is red)
                {
                        . . . Case 1 . . .
                }
                if (w's children are both black)
                {
                        . . . Case 2 . . .
                }
                else
                {
                        . . . Cases 3 and 4 . . .
                }
        else // x is a right child
        {
                . . .
        }
} // while
color (x) = black;
```

Fortunately, the loop always terminates after either case 3 or case 4. The loop always terminates after a single iteration if case 1 applies unless, after case 1 has been handled, case 2 applies. Case 2 is the only case that allows for additional loop iterations, and when that happens, **x** is closer to the root, so the **while** loop will be executed at most $O(\log n)$ times.

w's right child is black

From the just given outline of the **erase** method, it is clear that to get to this case, it is impossible for both of **w**'s children to be **black**. So **w**'s left child must be red. In this case, we do the following:

```
color (left (w)) = black;
color (w) = red;
rotate_right (w);
w = right (parent (x));
```

For example, suppose we delete 45 from the following red-black tree:

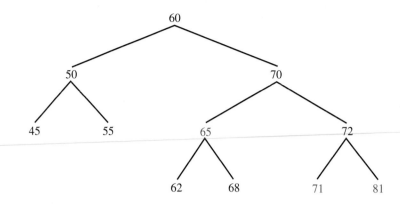

At the beginning of the **while** loop, we have

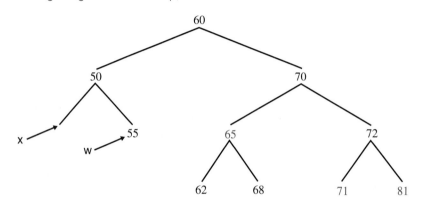

Since **w** is **black** and both of **w**'s children are **black** (**NIL** nodes are colored **black**), case 2 applies. After applying case 2, in the next loop iteration we get

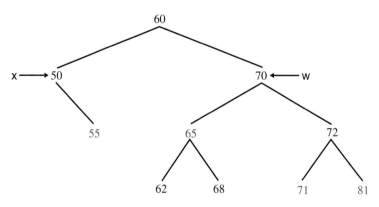

Case 3 applies because **w** is **black** and **w**'s left child is **red** and **w**'s right child is **black**. After recoloring, right-rotating, and resetting **w**, we get

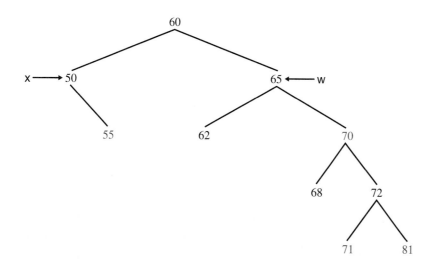

At first glance, this does not seem to be an improvement. But notice that **w**'s right child is now **red,** and that brings us to case 4.

w's right child is red

CASE 4

Here is the action taken:

```
color (w) = color (parent (x));
color (parent (x)) = black;
color (right (w)) = black;
left_rotate (parent (x));
break; // to end the loop
```

For example, suppose we start with the following red-black tree:

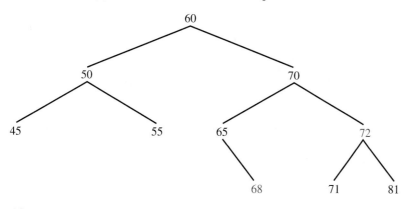

After deleting 50, we have

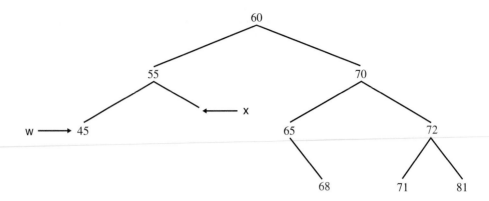

Case 2 applies, and the same action is taken when **x** is a right child as when **x** is a left child. So we set **color (w)** to **red** and set **x** to **parent (x)**. During the next iteration of the loop, we have

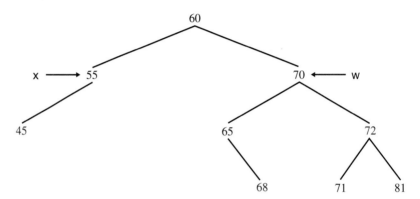

Now case 4 applies, so we recolor and rotate left around the parent of **x**:

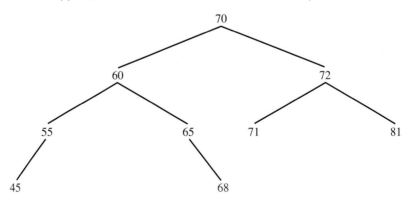

This tree satisfies both the Red Rule and the Path Rule, so we are done.

For an example in which case 4 is preceded by case 3, suppose we start with the tree at the end of the case 3 example:

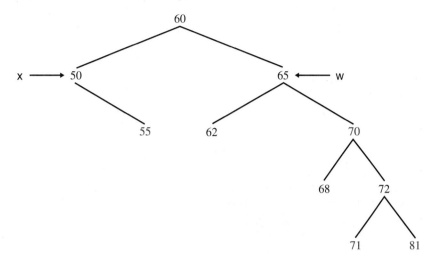

The right child of w is red, so case 4 applies. After recoloring and left-rotating at x's parent, we get

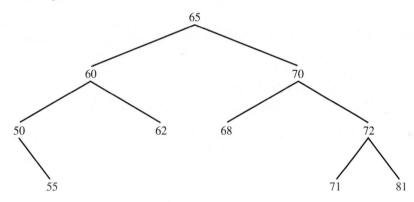

Both the Red Rule and the Path Rule are now satisfied, so we are done.

Whenever case 3 is applied, w's right child will become red, so case 4 will always apply after case 3. Rather than repeat the code for case 4, we place that code after the case 3 code. The outline for cases 3 and 4, when x is a left child, is

```
if(w's right child is black)
{
. . . Case 3 . . .
}
. . . Case 4 . . .
```

At the beginning of this section, we noted that the first part of the erase method—using a BinSearchTree-style erase—took logarithmic-in-n time in the worst case. In the **while** loop that constitutes the second part of the erase method, the loop continues only if case 2 applies, and then x is moved closer to the root, for a maximum of $O(\log n)$ iterations. Putting the two parts together, the time for the erase method is logarithmic in n in the worst case. On average, each of the two parts takes only constant time, so averageTime(n) is constant. In fact, amortizedTime(n) is constant.

Here is the complete **while** loop with the four cases when x is a left child, and the symmetric four cases when x is a right child.

```
while (x != root( ) && color(x) == black)
    if (x == left(parent(x)))
    {
        link_type w = right(parent(x));
        if (color(w) == red) // Case 1
        {
            color(w) = black;
            color(parent(x)) = red;
            rotate_left(parent(x));
            w = right(parent(x));
        }
            if (color(left(w)) == black && color(right(w)) == black)//
                            Case2
            {
            color(w) = red;
            x = parent(x);
            }
            else
            {
            if (color(right(w)) = black) // Case 3
            {
                color(left(w)) = black;
                color(w) = red;
                rotate_right(w);
                w = right(parent(x));
            }
            // Case 4
            color(w) = color(parent(x));
            color(parent(x)) = black;
            color(right(w)) = black;
            rotate_left(parent(x));
            break;
            }
```

```
          }
      else
      {
            //
            // symmetric with above; swap "left" and "right"
            //
            link_type w = left(parent(x));
            if (color(w) == red) // Case 1
            {
                  color(w) = black;
                  color(parent(x)) = red;
                  rotate_right(parent(x));
                  w = left(parent(x));
            }
            if (color(right(w)) == black && color(left(w)) ==black)// Case 2
            {
                  color(w) = red; x = parent(x);
            }
            else
            {
            if (color(left(w)) == black) // Case 3
            {
                  color(right(w)) = black;
                  color(w) = red;
                  rotate_left(w);
                  w = left(parent(x));
            }
            // Case 4
            color(w) = color(parent(x));
            color(parent(x)) = black;
            color(left(w)) = black;
            rotate_right(parent(x));
            break;
            }
      }
} // end of while loop
color(x) = black;
```

Lab 23 illustrates how all four cases can apply from a single call to the erase method.

LAB   **Lab 23: A call to erase in which all four cases apply.**

(All Labs Are Optional.)   **LAB**

10.2 I THE STANDARD TEMPLATE LIBRARY'S ASSOCIATIVE CONTAINERS

We are now ready to investigate the four associative-container classes in the Standard Template Library. Recall, from Chapter 8, that an *associative container* is one in which the location of an item is determined by comparing that item's key to the keys of other items in the container.

The rb_tree class is not intended for direct use, but rather as the foundation for the typical implementation of the four associative container classes in the Standard Template Library. The four corresponding data structures are categorized according to the four possible answers to the following two questions:

Does an item consist of a key only?

Does the container allow multiple items with the same key?

The following table shows how the answers to these questions determine the four data structures.

	Duplicate items?	
Key only?	**Yes**	**No**
Yes	multiset	set
No	multimap	map

For example, we define a *set* to be an associative container in which each item consists of a key only and no duplicate items are permitted; and for inserting, deleting, and searching, worstTime(n) is logarithmic in n. From here on, our main interest will be in the possible implementations of those four data structures. We start with the set and multiset classes, and then move onto the map and multimap classes.

10.2.1   The set Class

In Standard C++, the declaration of the set class starts as follows:

```
template <class Key, class Compare = less<Key>,
          class Allocator = allocator<Key>>
class set
{
```

As always, we ignore anything to do with allocators. In the set class, the key is the entire item, and the keys are unique. For example, here is the definition of a set object with string items in lexicographical order:

```
set< string > names;
```

Because a set is an associative container, where an item is stored in a set depends on a comparison of that item with other items. The comparison uses the template argument corresponding to the template parameter Compare. That template argument, by default, is the function class less, defined as follows in <function> in the Standard Template Library:

```
template <class T>
struct less : binary_function<T, T, bool> {
        bool operator( )(const T& x, const T& y) const { return x < y; }
};
```

So if the function object comp is an instance of the function class less, then comp (x, y) returns the value of the expression x < y. Of course, instead of the default, you can specify function classes other than less—you can even specify a function class you have declared. For example, you can define a set object with **double** items in decreasing order:

```
set<double, greater <double> > salaries;
```

In the Hewlett-Packard implementation, there is a **private** field of type rb_tree:

```
        typedef Key key_type;
        typedef Key value_type;
        typedef Compare key_compare;
        typedef Compare value_compare;
private:
        typedef rb_tree<key_type, value_type,
                ident<value_type, key_type>, key_compare> rep_type;
        rep_type t; // red-black tree representing set
```

In the ident function class, **operator( )** takes an argument of type value_type and simply returns the argument. So t is an instance of an rb_tree in which the key is the entire value.

The set class has the usual assortment of container methods: constructors, a destructor, begin, end, size, empty, find, insert, and erase. Most of the method definitions involve little more than having t invoke the corresponding rb_tree method. For example, the definitions of find and erase are as follows:

```
iterator find(const key_type& x) const { return t.find(x); }

void erase(iterator position) { t.erase((rep_type::iterator&)position);}
```

The insert method is unusual because an item will not be inserted if it matches an item already in the set container. So, as explained in Section 10.1.3, the insert method in the rb_tree class has to return a pair: an iterator and a **bool.** Here is the definition, including the method interface:

```
//Postcondition:  If the item x already occurs in the set, the pair returned
//                         consists of an iterator positioned at the previously inserted
//                         item, and false. Otherwise, the pair returned consists of an
//                         iterator positioned at the newly inserted item, and true.
```

```
pair<iterator, bool> insert(const value_type& x)
{
       pair<iterator, bool> p = t.insert(x);
       return pair<iterator, bool>(p.first, p.second);
}
```

For example, if my_company is a set of employees, we could have

```
pair<iterator, bool> p = my_company.insert (employee);
if (!p.second)
       cout << "duplicate item; insertion not made." << endl;
```

Since the find, erase, and insert methods simply call their rb_tree counterparts, worstTime(n) is logarithmic in n for all three of those set methods.

The following program inserts integers into a set in decreasing order; duplicate integers are rejected:

```
#include <iostream>
#include <string>
#include <set>

using namespace std;

int main( )
{
       typedef set< int, greater< int > > my_set;

       const int SIZE = 8;

       const string HEADING = "Here are the items in the set:";

       const string REPEAT = " is already in the set. Insertion rejected.";

       const string CLOSE_WINDOW_PROMPT =
              "Please press the Enter key to close this output window.";

       my_set s;
       my_set::iterator itr;
       int data [SIZE] = { 5, 3, 9, 3, 7, 2, 9, 3 };

       for( int i = 0; i < SIZE; i++ )
       {
              pair< my_set::iterator, bool > p = s.insert (data [i]);
              if( !p.second)
                     cout << data[ i ] << REPEAT << endl;
       } // for

       cout << endl << HEADING << endl;
       for( itr = s.begin( ); itr != s.end( ); itr++ )
              cout << *itr << endl;
```

```
        cout << endl << CLOSE_WINDOW_PROMPT;
        cin.get( );
        return 0;
} // main
```

The output is

```
3 is already in the set. Insertion rejected.
9 is already in the set. Insertion rejected.
3 is already in the set. Insertion rejected.

Here are the items in the set:

9
7
5
3
2
Please press the Enter key to close this output window.
```

Of course, if we were certain that all the items in the array data were unique in this program, we could simply ignore the return value and write

```
s.insert (data [i]);
```

10.3 | SET APPLICATION: SPELL-CHECKER, REVISITED

APPLICATION

In Section 9.4, we developed a spell-checker as an application of the AVLTree class. With very minor changes, the spell-checker program becomes an application of the set class. Here is what has to be done:

1. In spellcheck.h, replace #include "avl.h" with #include <set>.
2. In spellcheck.h, replace AVLTree with set in the definitions of dictionary and words.
3. In spellcheck.cpp, replace AVLTree and Iterator with set and iterator, respectively, in the definition of itr in the method compare( ).

The time estimates, as a set application, are identical to those as an AVLTree application.

10.3.1 THE multiset CLASS

In a multiset container, each item consists of a key only, and duplicate items are allowed. To permit duplicates, each multiset constructor passes **true** to always for the call to the rb_tree constructor. Then the insert_always field in the rb_tree object will get the value **true.**

Since duplicate items are allowed in a multiset object, the insert method simply returns an iterator positioned at the newly inserted item. Because there may be several copies of an item, there is a multiset method that returns an iterator positioned at the first location that the item could be inserted without disordering the multiset:

    iterator lower_bound (**const** T& x) **const**;

Similarly, the upper_bound method returns an iterator positioned at the last location the item could be inserted without disordering the multiset object. The equal_range method returns a pair of iterators positioned at the first and last such locations for the given item. For example, the following program creates a multiset container of integers, with duplicates allowed:

```
#include <iostream>

#include <string>

#include <set> // declares set and multiset

using namespace std;

int main( )
{
        typedef multiset< int, less< int > > my_set;

        typedef pair<my_set::iterator, my_set::iterator > Range;

        const int SIZE = 8;

        const string HEADING = "Here are the items in the multiset:";

        const string THREES = "Here are the threes: " ;

        const string CLOSE_PROMPT =
                "Please press the Enter key to close this output window.";

        my_set s;
        int data [SIZE] = { 5, 3, 9, 3, 7, 2, 9, 3 };
        my_set::iterator itr;

        for(int i = 0; i < SIZE; i++ )
                s.insert (data [i]);

        cout << endl << HEADING << endl;
        for (itr = s.begin( ); itr != s.end( ); itr++)
                cout << *itr << endl;

        cout << endl << THREES << endl;
        Range result = s.equal_range (3);
        for ( itr = result.first; itr != result.second; itr++ )
                cout << *itr << endl;

        cout << endl << CLOSE_PROMPT;
```

```
        cin.get( );
        return 0;
    } // main
```

The result variable contains a pair of iterators: result.first is positioned at the first instance of 3 in the multiset; result.last is positioned just beyond the last instance of 3 in the multiset.

Lab 24 gives you the opportunity to experiment with the set and multiset classes.

LAB   **Lab 24: More on the** set **and** multiset **classes.**
                                                    (All Labs Are Optional.)   LAB

We'll finish up this chapter with a look at the map and multimap classes. Of special significance is the map class's associative-array operator, **operator**[ ]. What's special is that the index need not be an integer: the index can be a string, an Employee, or whatever!

10.3.2 **THE** map **CLASS**

In Standard C++, the declaration of the map class begins with

```
template<class Key, class T, class Compare = less<Key>,
        < Allocator = allocator<T> >
class map
{
```

In a map, each value is a pair<Key, T> and duplicate keys are disallowed. For example, to define a map container called students in which the key is the student's name (a string), T represents the type of the student's current grade point average, and the names are stored in alphabetical order, we would write

```
map< string, float, less< string > > students;
```

Because a given student can have only one grade point average at a given time, the map container students defines a unique association between a student and that student's grade point average. In effect, students "maps" each student to her grade point average. Within the map container students, there will be no pairs with the same key, that is, no values with the same student name.

As with the other associative classes, the expected methods are available: constructors, size, empty, insert, erase, find, begin, end, ... The insert method takes a value—that is, a pair—as its argument; recall that the pair class constructor is used to initialize a pair object. So we can write

```
pair<string, float>student ("Stamp, Lisa", 3.96);

students.insert (student);
```

The map class has one glorious feature: the associative array. In an ordinary array, the index is an integer. In an *associative array,* the index is a key, and the key type can be any type: string, **double, int,** or even some user-defined class. An assignment such as

```
a [x] = m;
```

inserts the pair <x, m> into the map a. What if the map already had a pair with key x? Then the effect of the assignment would be to replace the second component in that pair with m. For example, the above insertion into the map container students could be replaced with

```
students ["Stamp, Lisa"] = 3.6;
```

To see how convenient associative arrays can be, consider the problem of counting the frequency of each word in a text file. Each word may be followed by punctuation symbols, which are not part of the word. We will create a map in which each item is a pair: a unique word—the key—and the number of times that word occurs in the file. Here is the program:

```cpp
#include <string>

#include <ctype.h> // declares tolower, isalpha

#include <fstream>

#include <map>

using namespace std;

typedef map< string, int, less< string >>  FrequencyMap;

int main( )
{
        const string INPUT_PROMPT =
            "Please enter the name of the input file:";

        const string OUTPUT_PROMPT =
            "Please enter the name of the output file:";

        const string CLOSE_WINDOW_PROMPT =
            "Please press the Enter key to close this output window.";

    FrequencyMap frequencies;
    FrequencyMap::iterator itr;

    string in_file_name,
            out_file_name,
            word;
    ifstream in_file;
    ofstream out_file;
```

```
        cout << INPUT_PROMPT << endl;
        cin >> in_file_name;
        in_file.open (in_file_name.c_str( ), ios::in);

        cout << endl << OUTPUT_PROMPT << endl;
        cin >> out_file_name;
        out_file.open (out_file_name.c_str( ), ios::out);

        while (in_file >> word)
        {
                // Make word lower case:
                string temp;
                for (unsigned i = 0; i < word.length( ); i++)
                        temp += (char)tolower (word [i]);
                word = temp;

                while (!isalpha (word [word.length( ) − 1]) )
                        word.erase (word.length( ) − 1);
                if (frequencies.find (word ) == frequencies.end( ))
                        frequencies [word] = 1;
                else
                        frequencies [word]++;
        } // while

        for (itr = frequencies.begin( ); itr != frequencies.end( ); itr++)
                out_file << (*itr).first << ", " << (*itr).second << endl;

        cout << endl << endl << CLOSE_WINDOW_PROMPT;
        cin.get( );
        return 0;
} // main
```

The output file consists of pairs of the form <word, frequency>, and the words are listed in alphabetical order. For example, suppose the input file is

> This program counts the
> number of occurrences of words in a text.
> The text may have many words
> in it, including big words.

Then the output file will be

> a, 1
> big, 1
> counts, 1
> have, 1
> in, 2
> including, 1

it, 1
many, 1
may, 1
number, 1
occurrences, 1
of, 2
program, 1
text, 2
the, 2
this, 1
words, 3

Any implementation of the map class will probably be based on a balanced binary search tree. For example, the following is from the Hewlett-Packard implementation:

```
private:

    typedef rb_tree<key_type, value_type,
        select1st<value_type, key_type>, key_compare> rep_type;

    rep_type t; // red-black tree representing map
```

In the select1st function class, the function-call operator, **operator**( ), takes a parameter of type value_type, that is, pair<**const** Key, T>. The first component—the key—in the pair is returned. So t is an rb_tree object in which each value is a pair, and comparisons of pairs are made using the first component in each pair.

From that point on, all the method definitions in the map class become one-liners in which t invokes a corresponding rb_tree method. Even the definition of the associative-array operator, **operator**[ ], is a one-liner:

```
T& operator[ ](const key_type& k)
{
    return (*((insert(value_type(k, T( )))).first)).second;
}
```

Deciphering this one-liner takes a paragraph. Because value_type is of type pair, the pair constructor is applied to the parameter k and the default constructor for T; a pair object is constructed. This pair object, call it p, is inserted into the map. In effect, the map's insert method invokes t.insert (p), which returns an iterator-**bool** pair. If there was already a value in the tree that had k as its key, then the iterator is positioned at this value. Otherwise, the iterator is positioned at the newly inserted <k, T( )> pair. In either case, that iterator is dereferenced, which yields a value, that is, a pair of type <Key, T>. A reference to the second component—of type T—in this pair is returned. One reason the **return** statement is hard to understand is that first refers to the first component in an iterator-**bool** pair, and second refers to the second component in a Key-T pair.

Project 10.1 is an application of the map class, and Chapters 13 and 14 have several examples of associative arrays. The multimap class is included here for the sake of completeness: it has few applications.

10.3.3   THE MULTIMAP CLASS

As you would expect, a multimap allows multiple items with identical key values, and each item is a pair <Key, T>. Associative arrays are *disallowed* to avoid ambiguity: If a multimap container myMulti had pairs <"Mark", 3> and <"Mark", 5>, the expression

    myMulti ["Mark"]

could refer to the second component of either pair.

Here is an example of a multimap definition:

    multimap< **int,** string, greater< **int**> > most_wins;

The multimap container most_wins will consist of the most wins in one year in Major League Baseball over the last 100 years, and the pitchers who got those wins. A multi map is needed because there may be duplicates for games won. The multimap will be in decreasing order of wins. Here is a sample insertion:

    most_wins.insert (pair< **int,** string> (31, "Denny McLain"));

One curious feature of the multimap class is the version of the insert method that includes a *hint* iterator:

    iterator insert (iterator position, **const** value_type& x);

As with the other versions of insert, the tree will be searched to find where x belongs. The iterator position *suggests* where to begin the search. For example, suppose we want to insert into the multimap multi the n items in an array data, and suppose those items in data are already in the right order—increasing order, to be specific. We can proceed as follows:

    itr = multi.begin( );
    for (**int** i = 0; i < n; i++)
            itr = multi.insert (itr, data [i]);

During each iteration of the **for** loop, the insert method is called, with itr providing the starting point for the search. And because the items are inserted in order, itr will always be positioned at the largest item. Then the new item will be inserted in constant, rather than logarithmic, time. The total time for inserting n items will be only $O(n)$, rather than $O(n \log n)$ if we did not use a hint iterator.

In fact, the insert-with-hint method is also available for the set, multiset, and map classes, but they had other interesting features as well.

LAB	**Lab 25: More on the** map and multimap **classes.**	
	(All Labs Are Optional.)	LAB

SUMMARY

A *red-black tree* is a binary search tree that is empty or in which the root item is colored black, every other item is colored red or black, and the following properties are satisfied:

> *Red Rule:* If an item is red, its parent must be black.
>
> *Path Rule:* The number of black items must be the same in all paths from the root item to an item with no children **or with one child.**

The height of a red-black tree is always logarithmic in *n*.

This chapter also introduced the four container classes in the Standard Template Library whose implementations are, typically, based on red-black trees. Those four classes are

1. set: value_type = key_type; no duplicates allowed
2. multiset: value_type = key_type; duplicates allowed
3. map: value_type = pair<key_type, T>; no duplicates allowed
4. multimap: value_type = pair<key_type, T>; duplicates allowed

EXERCISES

10.1 Show the effect of making the following insertions into an initially empty red-black tree:

30, 40, 20, 90, 10, 50, 70, 60, 80

10.2 Delete 20 and 40 from the red-black tree in Exercise 10.1. Show the complete tree after each deletion.

10.3 It is impossible to construct a red-black tree of size 20 with no red items. Explain.

10.4 Pick any integer $h \geq 1$, and create a red-black tree as follows: Insert 1, 2, 3, ..., 2^{h+1}. Remove 2^{h+1}, $2^{h+1} - 1$, $2^{h+1} - 2$, ..., 2^h. Try this with $h = 1, 2,$ and 3. What is unusual about the red-black trees that you end up with? Alexandru Balan helped to develop this formula.

10.5 Suppose v is an item with one leaf in a red-black tree. Explain why v must be black and v's child must be a red leaf.

10.6 Construct a red-black tree that (when the colors are ignored) is not an AVL tree.

10.7 Guibas and Sedgewick (1978) provide a simple algorithm for coloring any AVL tree into a red-black tree: For each item in the AVL tree, if the height of the subtree rooted at that item is an even integer and the height of its parent's subtree is odd, color the item red; otherwise, color the item black.

For example, consider the following AVL tree:

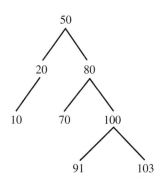

In this tree, 20's subtree has a height of 1, 80's subtree has a height of 2, 10's subtree has a height of 0 and 70's subtree has a height of 0. Note that since the root of the entire tree has no parent, this algorithm guarantees that the root will be colored black. Here is that AVL tree, colorized to a red-black tree:

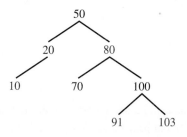

Create an AVL tree of height 4 with min_4 items, and then colorize that tree to a red-black tree.

10.8 Suppose, in the definition of red-black tree, we replace the Path Rule with the following:

> Path-etic Rule: The number of black items must be the same in all paths from the root item to a leaf.

a. Give an example of a red-black tree (with this new definition) of n items whose height is linear in n.

b. Give an example of a binary search tree that cannot be colored to make it a red-black tree (even with this new definition).

10.9 In the BinSearchTree class, the tree_node **struct** had an isHeader field that was needed in the Iterator class's decrement method, **operator--( )**:

```
Iterator& operator-- ( )
{
    if (link -> isHeader)
        link = link -> right; // Return rightmost
    . . .
```

In the rb_tree class, the rb_tree_node **struct** does not have an isHeader field. What code replaces the condition link -> isHeader?

10.10 Suppose we are given the name and division number for each employee in a company. There are no duplicate names. We would like to store this information alphabetically, by name. For example, part of the input might be the following:

Misino,John	8
Nguyen,Viet	14
Panchenko,Eric	6
Dunn,Michael	6
Deusenbery,Amanda	14
Taoubina,Xenia	6

We want these items stored in the following order:

Deusenbery,Amanda	14
Dunn,Michael	6
Misino,John	8
Nguyen,Viet	14
Panchenko,Eric	6
Taoubina,Xenia	6

Should we do this using a set, multiset, map, or multimap?

10.11 Redo Exercise 10.10, but now the ordering should be by increasing division numbers, and within each division number, by alphabetical order of names. For example, part of the input might be the following:

Misino,John	8
Nguyen,Viet	14
Panchenko,Eric	6
Dunn,Michael	6
Deusenbery,Amanda	14
Taoubina,Xenia	6

We want these items stored in the following order:

Dunn,Michael	6
Panchenko,Eric	6
Taoubina,Xenia	6
Misino,John	8
Deusenbery,Amanda	14
Nguyen,Viet	14

Should we do this using a set, multiset, map, or multimap?

10.12 Suppose we have

map<string, **int**> my_map;

Explain the difference between

    my_map.insert ("Ford", 20000);

and

    my_map ["Ford"] = 20000;

Hint   What if "Ford" already occurs as the key component of a value in my_map?

10.13 For each of the following types, make up an appropriate object of that type and explain why the type is appropriate for the object.

    set< **double,** greater< **double**> >
    multiset<string>
    map< **double,** string>
    multimap< **int, double,** greater<**int**>>

PROGRAMMING PROJECT 10.1

A Simple Thesaurus

A *thesaurus* is a dictionary of synonyms. For example, here is a small thesaurus, with each word followed by its synonyms:

```
close near confined
confined cramped
correct true
cramped confined
near close
one singular unique
singular one unique
true correct
unique singular one
```

The problem we want to solve is this: Given a thesaurus file and words entered from the keyboard, print the synonym of each word entered.

Analysis

The thesaurus file will be in alphabetical order. For each word entered from the keyboard, the synonyms of that word should be printed if the word's synonyms are in the thesaurus file. Otherwise, an error message should be printed.

System Test Input is boldfaced. The thesaurus file is as has been given.

Please enter a word; the sentinel is ***
one
Here are the synonyms:
singular unique

In the Input line, please enter a word; the sentinel is ***
two
The word is not in the thesaurus.

Please enter a word; the sentinel is ***
close
Here are the synonyms:
near
confined

Please enter a word; the sentinel is ***
***

PROGRAMMING PROJECT 10.2

Building a Concordance

Given a text, develop a concordance for the words in the text. A *concordance* consists of each word in the text and, for each word, each line number that the word occurs in. Include Big-O time estimates of all methods.

Analysis

1. The first line of input will contain the path to the text file. The second line of input will contain the path to the output file.

2. Each word in the text consists of letters only—some or all may be in uppercase.

3. Each word in the text is followed by zero or more punctuation symbols followed by any number of blanks and end-of-line markers.

4. The output should consist of the words, lowercased and in alphabetical order; each word is followed by each line number that the word occurs in. The line numbers should be separated by commas.

5. The text will fit in memory.

6. The line numbers in the text start at 1.

7. For this project, you must use a map to build the concordance. In Lab 25, a multi-map was used.

Assume that doc1.in contains the following file:

> This program counts the
> number of words in a text.
> The text may have many words
> in it, including big words.

Also, assume that doc2.in contains the following file:

> Fuzzy Wuzzy was a bear.
> Fuzzy Wuzzy had no hair.
> Fuzzy Wuzzy was not fuzzy.
> Was he?

System Test 1

> In the Input line, please enter the path to the text file.
> **doc1.in**
> In the Input line, please enter the path to the output file.
> **doc1.out**

Here are the contents of doc1.out after the completion of the program.

(continued on next page)

(continued from previous page)

Here is the concordance:

a: 2
big: 4
counts: 1
have: 3
in: 2, 4
including: 4
it: 4
many: 3
may: 3
number: 2
of: 2
program: 1
text: 2, 3
the: 1, 3
this: 1
words: 2, 3, 4

System Test 2

In the Input line, please enter the path to the text file.
doc2.in
In the Input line, please enter the path to the output file.
doc2.out

Here are the contents of doc2.out after the completion of the program.

Here is the concordance:

a: 1
bear: 1
fuzzy: 1, 2, 3
had: 2
hair: 2
he: 4
no: 2
not: 3
was: 1, 3, 4
wuzzy: 1, 2, 3

CHAPTER 11

Priority Queues and Heaps

The primary focus of this chapter is the priority queue data structure. A ***priority queue*** is a container in which the only item that can be accessed or deleted is the item with highest priority, according to some way of assigning priorities to items. And interestingly, that restricted focus of a priority queue allows an implementation in which insertions take only constant time, on average, and deletions take only logarithmic time, even in the worst case. After providing the method interfaces for the priority_queue class, we present the Standard C++ implementation.

Because the priority_queue class is a container adaptor, it might seem that the implementation of the class will be quite simple, as were the implementations of the queue and stack classes in Chapter 7. But that is not the case. We will need the services of a couple of generic algorithms, push_heap and pop_heap, which lead us into a discussion of heaps. A ***heap*** is a complete binary tree in which each item is greater than or equal to its children. Finally, we develop an application of priority queues in the area of data compression. Specifically, a ***Huffman Tree*** encodes information in a condensed form to save time transmitting the information. ■

CHAPTER OBJECTIVES

1. Define what a priority queue is.

2. Understand the heap operations of push_heap, pop_heap, and make_heap.

3. Compare the trade-offs with various implementations of the priority queue data structure.

4. Be able to follow the Huffman algorithm for data compression.

5. Determine the characteristic of a greedy algorithm.

11.1 | INTRODUCTION

A variation of the queue, the priority queue, is a commonplace structure. The basic idea is that we have items waiting in line for service. Selection is not strictly on a first-come–first-served basis. For example, patients in an emergency room are treated based on the severity of their injuries, not on when they arrived. Similarly, in air-traffic control, there is a queue of planes waiting to land, but the controller can move a plane to the front of the queue if the plane is low on fuel or has a sick passenger.

A shared printer in a network is another example of a resource suited for a priority queue. Normally, jobs are printed based on arrival time, but while one job is printing, several others may enter the service queue. The highest priority could be given to the job with the fewest pages to print. This would optimize the average time for job completion. The same idea of prioritized service can be applied to any shared resource: a central processing unit, a family car, the courses offered next semester, and so on.

Here is the definition:

A *priority queue* is a container in which access or deletion is of the item in the container with highest priority, according to some way of assigning priorities to items.

For example, suppose the items are integers, and integer i has a higher priority than integer j if $i > j$. Then the largest item is the one with the highest priority. This definition does not specify *where* insertions are to be made. Keeping track of where items are inserted is the responsibility of the developer of the priority queue, not a responsibility of the user of the priority queue.

A priority queue is fair if, for any two items of equal priority on the priority queue, the first one removed is the one that had been on the priority queue the longest.

You might be wondering what happens if two or more items are tied for highest priority. In the interest of fairness, the tie should be broken in favor of the item that has been in the priority queue for the longest time. This appeal to fairness is not part of the definition, and is not part of the priority_queue class. In fact, as will be seen in Lab 26, ties are not handled fairly in the standard implementation of the priority_queue class. Lab 26 provides a solution to this problem.

Most of this chapter is devoted to a premier application of priority queues: Huffman encoding. In Chapter 14, priority queues are used in two graph algorithms: Prim's minimum-spanning-tree algorithm and Dijkstra's shortest-path algorithm. For a lively discussion of the versatility of priority queues, see Dale (1990).

In Section 11.1.1, we begin the definition of the priority_queue class by supplying method interfaces for the methods in that class.

11.1.1 The priority_queue **Class**

The declaration of the priority_queue class starts as follows:

```
template<class T, class Container = vector<T>,
      class Compare = less<Container::value_type> >
class priority_queue
{
```

The first template parameter, T, is for the type of the items stored in the priority queue. The Container template parameter refers to the underlying container class whose method interfaces are *adapted* by the priority_queue class. The requirements for the corresponding template argument class are that it has methods front, push_back, and pop_back and supports random-access iterators. Either the vector or deque class satisfies these requirements, and the vector class is the default. (Why would the list class be unacceptable?) The template argument corresponding to the Compare parameter must be a function class for which **operator( )** compares value_types, which will almost always be the same as T. The default is the built-in function class less, so the item with the *largest* value will be at the front of a priority_queue object.

The priority_queue *class is a container adaptor.*

There are only seven methods in the priority_queue class. Here are the method interfaces:

By default, the highest-priority item is the one with the largest value.

1. // Postcondition: this priority queue has been initialized with x and a copy of a
   //   Container object.
   explicit priority_queue (**const** Compare& x = Compare( ),
                      const Container& = Container( ));

   Example   We can define two priority queues as follows:

   pq<employee> e_pq1 ( );

   pq<employee> e_pq2 (e_pq1); // e_pq2 contains a copy of e_pq1.

2. // Postcondition: this priority_queue has been initialized to a copy of the items
   //   at positions from first (inclusive) to last (exclusive), with
   //   Compare object x and underlying Container object y.
   template<**class** InputIterator>
   priority_queue (InputIterator first, InputIterator last,
              const Compare& x = Compare( ),
              const Container& y = Container( ));

3. // Postcondition: The number of items in this priority_queue has been returned.
   size_type size( ) **const**;

4. // Postcondition: if this priority_queue has no items in it, true has been
   //   returned. Otherwise, false has been returned.
   bool empty( ) **const**;

5. // Postcondition: x has been inserted into this priority_queue. The
   //   averageTime(n) is constant, and worstTime(n) is O(n).
   void push (**const** value_type& x);

6. // Precondition: this priority_queue is not empty.
   // Postcondition: the item on this priority_queue that had, before this message
   //   was sent, the highest priority has been deleted. The

```
//                          worstTime(n) is O(log n).
void pop( );
```

7.
```
// Precondition: this priority_queue is not empty.
// Postcondition: a constant reference to the item with highest priority in this
//                          priority_queue has been returned.
const value_type& top ( ) const;
```

> *Note*   Because **const** is part of the return-type specification, it is illegal to modify the top item in a priority_queue object. Such a modification could alter the top item's priority.

Here is a small program that creates and maintains two priority queues, one of string items in alphabetical order, and one of **int** items in descending order:

```
#include <vector>
#include <queue> // defines priority_queue class
#include <iostream>
#include <string>

using namespace std;

int main( )
{
     const string WORDS = "Here are the words in alphabetical order:";

     const string SCORES = "Here are the scores in descending order:";

     const string CLOSE_WINDOW_PROMPT =
          "Please press the Enter key to close this output window.";

     priority_queue<string, vector<string>, greater<string> > words;
     priority_queue<int> scores; // uses defaults for 2nd and 3rd
                                      // template arguments

     words.push ("yes");
     words.push ("no");
     words.push ("maybe");
     words.push ("wow");

     cout <<WORDS <<endl;
     while (!words.empty( ))
     {
          cout <<words.top( ) <<endl;
          words.pop( );
     } // printing and popping words

     scores.push (50);
     scores.push (71);
     scores.push (65);
```

```
        scores.push (57);
        scores.push (60);

        cout <<endl <<endl <<SCORES <<endl;
        while (!scores.empty( ))
        {
            cout <<scores.top( ) <<endl;
            scores.pop( );
        } // printing and popping scores

        cout <<endl <<endl <<CLOSE_WINDOW_PROMPT;
        cin.get( );

        return 0;
    } // main
```

The output is

```
Here are the words in alphabetical order:
maybe
no
wow
yes

Here are the scores in descending order:
71
65
60
57
50


Please press the Enter key to close this output window.
```

We now turn our attention to the fields and implementation of the priority_queue class. The task is apparently simplified by adapting another container class's method interfaces. But the hard work involves imposing a new kind of tree structure—called a heap—on an array-based container such as a vector or deque.

11.1.2 Fields and Implementation of the priority_queue **Class**

Just as with the queue and stack classes, the method definitions of the priority_queue class are part of Standard C++. According to Standard C++, the definition of the priority_queue class is in (the file denoted by) <queue>, but in the Hewlett-Packard implementation, it is in (the file denoted by) <stack>.

The two fields in the priority_queue class are a container object c and a function object comp:

protected:
   Container c;
   Compare comp;

The container c will, by default, be an instantiation of the vector class. The function object comp will instantiate some built-in or user-defined function class, with the less class being the default.

As you might expect, the top( ) method returns the reference returned by c.front( ), but you may be perplexed to learn that the pop( ) method calls c.pop_back( ) to delete the highest-priority item. Where is the item, at the front or the back? The mystery deepens when we see the definition[1] of the pop( ) method:

```
void pop( )
{
       pop_heap (c.begin( ), c.end( ), comp);
       c.pop_back( );
} // pop
```

So behind the scenes there is a pop_heap generic algorithm[2] that manipulates the container c. The subsequent call to the pop_back method is just finishing up. The hard work of the pop method is done in the pop_heap method. Similarly, the code for the push method is

```
void push (const value_type& x)
{
       c.push_back(x);
       push_heap(c.begin( ), c.end( ), comp);
} // push
```

You may have surmised that the generic algorithms push_heap and pop_heap use a heap, but what is a heap? All will be revealed in Section 11.1.3.

11.1.3 Heaps

A *heap* t is a complete binary tree such that either t is empty or

1.   The root item is the largest item in t, according to some method for comparing items.

*A recursive definition of **heap**.*

2.   leftTree(t) and rightTree(t) are heaps.

   Figure 11.1 shows a heap with 10 **int** items.

   The ordering in a heap is top-down, but not left-to-right: Each root item is greater than or equal to each of its children, but some left siblings may be greater than their right siblings and some may be less. In Figure 11.1, for example, 85 is greater than its right sibling, 48, but 30 is less than its right sibling, 36.

The ordering in a heap is top-down, but not left-to-right.

---

[1]Technically, the Standard specifies only that the *effect* of the definition must be the same as the effect of the definition shown.

[2]This algorithm is defined in <heap> for the Hewlett-Packard implementation, but is required to be in <algorithm> for Standard C++.

Figure 11.1 | A heap with 10 **int** items.

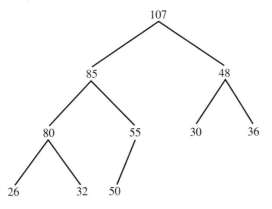

A heap is a curious structure, but it turns out to be useful in a variety of applications. One of them, of course, is in the implementation of the priority_queue class. We will focus on the two major heap operations, push_heap and pop_heap. We will touch on another operation, make_heap, which creates a heap from scratch and which is invoked in the priority_queue constructor calls. In Chapter 12, we will see the fourth and final heap operation, sort_heap, used to create a sorted container from a heap.

A heap is a complete binary tree. As we saw in Chapter 8, with each item in a complete binary tree t, we can associate a position in the range $0 \ldots n(t) - 1$. If we think of these positions as indices, we see that the items in a heap can be stored in an array. For example, here is an array representation of the heap shown in Figure 11.1:

107	85	48	80	55	30	36	26	32	50	...

The random-access feature of arrays is convenient for heap processing: given the index of an item, we can quickly access that item's children. For example, the children of the item at index i are at indices $2i + 1$ and $2i + 2$. And the parent of the item at index j is at index $(j - 1) / 2$. As we will see shortly, the ability to quickly move a parent into its child's slot and vice versa makes a heap an efficient storage structure for implementing a priority queue. The interface for the push_heap method is

```
// Precondition: the range of items from first (inclusive) to last − 1
//                (exclusive) is a heap.
// Postcondition: the value at last − 1 has been inserted into the heap.
template <class RandomAccessIterator, class Compare>
inline void push_heap (RandomAccessIterator first,
                       RandomAccessIterator last, Compare comp);
```

Any container—such as an array, vector, or deque—that supports random-access iterators can serve as a heap.

The item to be inserted, which last − 1 is positioned at, is stored in a temporary variable value, and the vacated slot (which still contains the item to be inserted) is referred to as the *hole*. Technically, the variable holeIndex is used; it contains the index in the container of the current hole. For example, Figure 11.2 shows the heap in Figure 11.1 when the push_heap method has been called to insert 90.

To see if the heap will be maintained if 90 is stored at the hole, we compare 90 to the item stored at the hole's parent, 55, whose index is (hole_index − 1) / 2. Since 90 > 55, we move 55 into the hole and move holeIndex to where 55 had been. See Figure 11.3. We continue looping until we get to the top of the heap or find a slot where 90 ≤ the item at the hole's parent. Then 90 is inserted at the slot whose index is the hole. The final heap is shown in Figure 11.4.

Figure 11.2 | The heap from Figure 11.1 at the start of the push_heap method. The item to be inserted is 90.

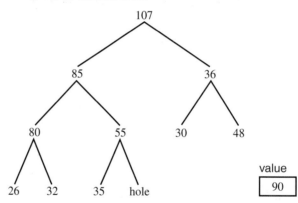

Figure 11.3 | The heap from Figure 11.2 after 90 was compared to 55 during the push_heap method.

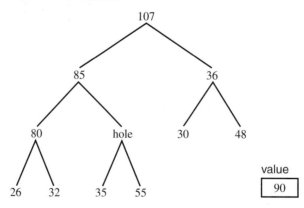

Figure 11.4 | The heap from Figure 11.1 after 90 was inserted by a call to the push_heap method.

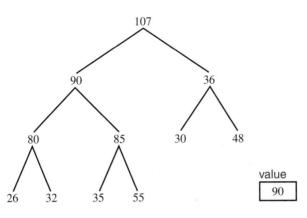

Here, from the definition of the __push_heap method, is the essential code (think of Distance as a synonym for **int**):

```
Distance parent = (holeIndex − 1) / 2;
while (holeIndex > topIndex && comp (*(first + parent), value))
{
       *(first + holeIndex) = *(first + parent);
       holeIndex = parent;
       parent = (holeIndex − 1) / 2;
} // while
*(first + holeIndex) = value;
```

In the worst case, the item to be inserted is larger than the item first is positioned at. Then the number of iterations of the **while** loop is proportional to the height of the tree. The height of a complete binary tree is logarithmic in *n* (see Exercise 8.7). That is, worstTime(*n*) is logarithmic in *n*.

In the average case, about half of the items in the heap will have a smaller value than the item inserted, and about half will have a larger value. But heaps are very bushy: at least half of the items are leaves. And because of the heap properties, most of the smaller-valued items will be at or near the leaf level. In fact, the average number of loop iterations is less than three (see Schaffer and Sedgewick, 1993), which satisfies the postcondition requirement that averageTime(*n*) be constant.

Now we can analyze the push method. The worst case occurs when the heap is full. The action taken at this point depends on the underlying container class—for example, a vector or a deque. In any case, there will be a linear-in-*n* copying, so worstTime(*n*) is linear in *n*. But this copying occurs infrequently—once in every *n* insertions—so averageTime(*n*) is constant (in fact, amortizedTime(*n*) is constant), just as for the push_heap method.

For the definition of the push *method in the* priority_queue *class, averageTime(n) is constant.*

The method interface for the pop_heap method is as follows:

```
// Precondition: the heap is not empty.
// Postcondition: the item that last − 1 was positioned at has been removed
//                from the heap.
template <class RandomAccessIterator, class Compare>
inline void pop_heap (RandomAccessIterator first,
                      RandomAccessIterator last, Compare comp);
```

The iterator last is positioned just beyond the item at the bottom of the heap. The pop_heap algorithm is just the opposite of push_heap: pop_heap works from the top of the heap downward. The item at the top is the item to be deleted, and this will be stored at the index that last − 1 is positioned at. (The purpose of saving the item to be deleted is to simplify the sort_heap method.) So we temporarily move the item at last − 1 to the variable value. The hole is, initially, the slot at the top of the heap. Figure 11.5 shows the initial setting for the pop_heap method applied to the heap in Figure 11.4.

The item 107 has been stored beyond the bottom of the heap, but we still need to find where 55, now stored in value, can go. Instead of comparing 55 to other items, we first move the hole down by comparing the children of the hole item to each other. The larger child gets moved to the spot the hole occupies, and the hole is set to the slot that held that larger child. Figure 11.6 shows the heap after the hole has been moved down to the slot previously occupied by 90. After two more loop iterations, the hole has settled to the leaf level, as shown in Figure 11.7. Note that 107 is not included in the comparisons because 107 is no longer considered part of the heap.

We are not quite done, because 55 cannot be inserted at the hole's slot. So we now call the push_heap method to insert 55. Figure 11.8 shows the final tree, but 107—the popped value—is not part of the heap.

Figure 11.5 I The heap from Figure 11.4 at the start of a call to the pop_heap method.

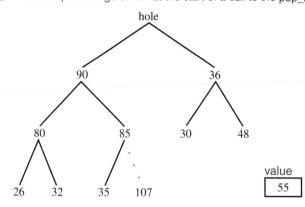

Figure 11.6 I The heap from Figure 11.5 after the hole has been moved to the slot that was occupied by 90.

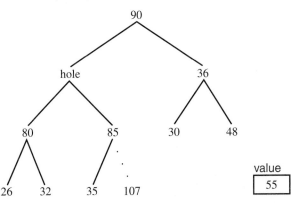

Figure 11.7 I The heap from Figure 11.6 after the hole has been moved to the slot that was occupied by 35.

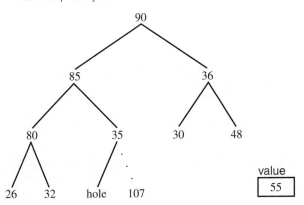

Figure 11.8 I The heap from Figure 11.4 after the call to the pop_heap method. Note that 107 is not part of the heap.

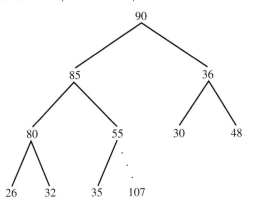

The real work of the pop_heap method is done in the auxiliary method, __adjust_heap. Here is the definition of __adjust_heap:

```
template <class RandomAccessIterator, class Distance, class T,
          class Compare>

void __adjust_heap (RandomAccessIterator first, Distance holeIndex,
                    Distance len, T value, Compare comp)
{
    Distance topIndex = holeIndex;
    Distance secondChild = 2 * holeIndex + 2;
    while (secondChild < len)
    {
        if (comp(*(first + secondChild), *(first + (secondChild − 1))))
            secondChild--;
        *(first + holeIndex) = *(first + secondChild);
        holeIndex = secondChild;
        secondChild = 2 * (secondChild + 1);
    }
    if (secondChild == len)
    {
        *(first + holeIndex) = *(first + (secondChild − 1));
        holeIndex = secondChild − 1;
    }
    __push_heap(first, holeIndex, topIndex, value, comp);
}
```

How long does pop_heap take? The loop to move the hole down to the leaf level takes time proportional to the height of the tree. A heap is a complete binary tree, so its height is always logarithmic in n. The additional call to push_heap takes anywhere from constant time (on average) to logarithmic time (worst case because no resizing is necessary). So for the pop_heap method, worstTime(n) is logarithmic in n, and so is averageTime(n).

We needed to move easily between parent and child. This is easily accomplished with random-access iterators (equivalent to array indices). Red-black trees also move easily between parent and child, but the overhead is extra space: each item is stored in a node with parent, color, left, and right fields. Heaps are sleek by comparison: no extra space with each item.

Finally, we consider the make_heap algorithm, which creates a heap from a container that supports random-access iterators. The method interface is

```
// Postcondition: the items from iterator position first (inclusive) to last
//                  (exclusive) form a heap.
template <class RandomAccessIterator, class Compare>
inline void make_heap (RandomAccessIterator first,
                       RandomAccessIterator last, Compare comp);
```

The first item is a heap by itself, so we *could* simply loop through the rest of the container and call push_heap during each iteration:

```
itr = first++;
while (itr != last)
        push_heap (first, itr++, comp);
```

But in a heap, half of the items are leaves, and a leaf is automatically a heap. So half of the calls to push_heap would be wasted.

Instead, the heap building will start with the highest index whose item is not a leaf. For example, in Figure 11.9, we start at the index whose item is 30. The adjustment is similar to the one we made with pop_heap, except that the item at the hole index, namely 30, will be temporarily stored in the variable value. After 35 gets moved up to the hole, and the hole gets moved down to where 35 was, push_heap is called to insert 30 in the hole. Figure 11.10 shows what the tree looks like after 30

Figure 11.9 I A complete binary tree that will become a heap after a call to the make_heap method.

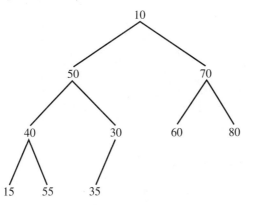

Figure 11.10 I The complete binary tree of Figure 11.9 after the subtree that was rooted at 30 got heapified.

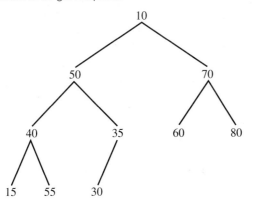

is successfully inserted. Moving to lower indices in the container, we next adjust the subtree rooted at 40 and then adjust the subtree rooted at 70. At this point we have the tree shown in Figure 11.11.

To heapify the subtree rooted at 50, the hole is the index of the slot occupied by 50, and 50 is stored in the variable value. After 55 is moved into the hole, the hole is moved to the slot 55 had occupied, which gets 40 during the next iteration. After push_heap is applied to insert 50 into the path starting at this new hole, the final heapification takes place, starting with the root of the whole tree. After adjusting, we end up with the heap shown in Figure 11.12.

Here is the essential code (__adjust_heap is called by pop_heap; the second argument to __adjust_heap is the initial hole index):

```
if (last − first < 2)
    return;
```

Figure 11.11 I The complete binary tree of Figure 11.10 after the heapification of the subtrees rooted at 40 and 70.

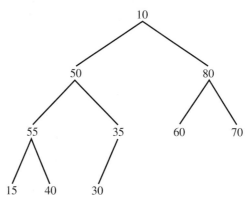

Figure 11.12 I The complete binary tree of Figure 11.11 after the heapification of the subtrees rooted at 50 and 10.

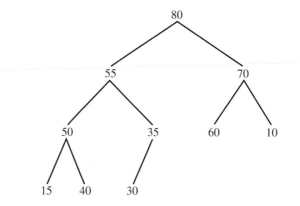

```
Distance len = last − first;
Distance parent = (len − 2) / 2;

while (true)
{
        __adjust_heap (first, parent, len, T(*(first + parent)), comp);
        if (parent == 0)
                return;
        parent--;
} // while
```

The analysis of the make_heap method is somewhat difficult, but the result is that worstTime(n) is always linear in n no matter how the items are arranged in the container originally. Here are the gory details. There are about $n/2$ heaps to adjust, and each adjustment takes time proportional to the distance from that heap's root to its farthest leaf. For root index i going from $n/2$ down to 0, that distance is, approximately, $\log_2(n/(i + 1))$. Paradoxically, the worst case occurs when the container is already a heap. Because then each adjustment requires following a path down the tree to find a leaf hole, and then following the same path up the tree when push_heap is called. So the total number of iterations in the worst case is, approximately,

$$\sum_{i=1}^{n/2} 2 \log_2(n/i)$$

Let $m = n/2$. Then—recall that the log of a quotient is the difference of the logs—the sum is equal to

$$2\left(m \log_2 n - \sum_{i=1}^{m} \log_2 i \right)$$

which is equal to

$$2\left(m \log_2 n - \log_2\left(\prod_{i=1}^{m} i \right) \right) = 2(m \log_2 n - \log_2(m!))$$

The sum of logs is the log of the product. (See Section A1.3 for an explanation of product notation.)

By the logarithmic form of Stirling's approximation of factorials,

$$\log_2(m!) \approx \log_2((m/e)^m)$$
$$= m \log_2 m - m \log_2 e$$
$$\approx m \log_2 m - 1.5m$$

Since $\log_2 m = \log_2(n/2) = \log_2 n - \log_2 2 = \log_2 n - 1$,

$$2(m \log_2 n - \log_2 m!) \approx 2(m \log_2 n - (m \log_2 m - 1.5m))$$
$$= 2 (m \log_2 n - m(\log_2 n - 1) + 1.5m)$$
$$= 2(m + 1.5m)$$
$$= 5m$$
$$= 2.5n$$

So worstTime(n) is linear in n. The average case requires about half as many iterations, so averageTime(n) is also linear in n.

Now that we have, by a roundabout route, covered the implementation details of the priority_queue class, we can study the "fairness" issue in more detail. Recall that a priority queue is *fair* if, when two items have the same priority, the item inserted first is accessed or removed first.

LAB **Lab 26: Fairness in priority queues.**

(All Labs Are Optional.) **LAB**

11.1.4 Alternative Designs and Implementations of the priority_queue Class

Before we leave the topic of design and implementation of the priority_queue class, let's spend a few moments considering alternatives to the heap. As discussed, Standard C++ virtually requires that the priority_queue class be implemented with a heap. But there are some other implementations that are easily attainable and offer some interesting trade-offs with respect to heaps.

One alternative implementation is list-based. The only field is

    list<value_type> c;

The idea is that the items in the priority queue are stored, in descending order, in the container c. So the front of c holds the highest-priority item. The top and pop methods simply invoke c.front( ) and c.pop_front( ), respectively, so worstTime(n) for those methods is constant. This is better than the heap versions, which take constant and logarithmic time, respectively.

The push method is also a one-liner, but is more complicated. Recall, from Lab 11, that the upper_bound generic algorithm returns an iterator that is the last position in a container where an item can be inserted without violating the ordering relation. That tells us where in c the item should be inserted: the push method inserts the item in the last position in c where the item can be inserted by its relative value:

    void push (**const** value_type& x)
    {
        c.insert (upper_bound (c.begin( ), c.end( ), x, greater<value_type>), x);
    } // method push

The upper_bound method, when applied to a class that supports only bi-directional (not random-access) iterators, takes linear-in-n time. The list class's insert method takes only constant time, so for push, worstTime(n) is linear in n, the same as for the heap version of push. But averageTime(n) is also linear in n for this version of push, versus constant for the heap version. And because the inserted item is stored after items with the same priority, this version is fair.

Another worthwhile implementation uses a set container in which items are stored in descending order:

```
set<value_type, greater< value_type>> c;
```

Again, the top, push, and pop methods are one-liners:

```
const value_type& top ( ) const
{
      return *(c.begin( ));
} // method top

void push (const value_type& x)
{
      c.insert (x);
} // method push

void pop( )
{
      c.erase (c.begin( ));
} // method pop
```

According to the analysis of the set methods in Chapter 10, this implementation of the priority_queue class requires constant time for the top method. For the push and pop methods, worstTime(n) is logarithmic in n.

Table 11.1 summarizes the time estimates. Of course, the only legitimate implementation in Standard C++ is the heap-based implementation, but the others have their advantages.

Section 11.2 introduces an important application of priority queues: data compression.

Table 11.1 | A comparison of averageTime(n) and worstTime(n) (separated by semicolons) for the top, push, and pop methods under three implementations of the priority_queue class.

Implementations	top	push	pop
heap	$O(1)$; $O(1)$	$O(1)$; $O(n)$	$O(\log n)$; $O(\log n)$
list	$O(1)$; $O(1)$	$O(n)$; $O(n)$	$O(1)$; $O(1)$
set	$O(1)$; $O(1)$	$O(\log n)$; $O(\log n)$	$O(\log n)$; $O(\log n)$

11.2 | APPLICATION OF PRIORITY QUEUES: HUFFMAN CODES

Suppose we have a large file of information. It would be advantageous if we could save space by compressing the file without losing any of the information. What is even more important is that the time to transmit the information might be significantly reduced if we could send the compressed version instead of the original.

For the sake of simplicity and specificity, assume the message file M contains 100,000 characters, and each character is either "a", "b", "c", "d", "e", "f", or "g". Since there are seven characters, if we want to use the same number of bits for each character, we can encode each character uniquely with $ceil(\log_2 7)$ bits, which is 3 bits.[2] For example, we could use 000 for "a", 001 for "b", 010 for "c", and so on. A word such as "cad" would be encoded as 010000011. Then the encoded file E need take up only 300,000 bits, plus an extra few bits for the encoding itself: "a" = 000, and so on.

We can save space by reducing the number of bits for some characters. For example, we could use the following encoding:

a = 0

b = 1

c = 00

d = 01

e = 10

f = 11

g = 000

This would reduce the size of the encoded file E by about one-third (unless the character "g" occurred very frequently). But this encoding leads to ambiguities. For example, the bit sequence 001 could be interpreted as "ad" or as "cb" or as "aab" depending on whether we grouped the first two bits together or the last two bits together, or treated each bit individually.

The reason this encoding scheme is ambiguous is that some of the encodings are prefixes of other encodings. For example, 0 is a prefix of 00, so it is impossible to determine whether 00 should be interpreted as "aa" or "c". We can avoid ambiguities by requiring that the encoding be *prefix-free,* that is, no encoding can be a prefix of any other encoding.

A prefix-free encoding is unambiguous.

One way to guarantee prefix-free bit encodings is to create a binary tree in which a left branch is interpreted as a 0 and a right branch is interpreted as a 1. If each encoded character is a leaf in the tree, then the encoding for that character could not be the prefix of any other character's encoding. In other words, the path to each character provides a prefix-free encoding. For example, Figure 11.13 has a binary tree that illustrates a prefix-free encoding of the characters "a" through "g":

---

[2]$ceil(x)$ returns the smallest integer that is greater than or equal to x. For example, $ceil(17.2) = 18$.

To get the encoding for a character, start with an empty encoding at the root of the binary tree, and continue until the leaf to be encoded is reached. Within the loop, append 0 to the encoding when turning left and append 1 to the encoding when turning right. For example, "b" is encoded as 01 and "f" is encoded as 1110. Because each encoded character is a leaf, the encoding is prefix-free and therefore unambiguous. But it is not certain that this will save space or transmission time. It all depends on the frequency of each character. Since three of the encodings take up 2 bits and four encodings take up 4 bits, this encoding scheme may actually take up more space than the simple, 3-bits-per-character encoding.

This suggests that if we start by determining the frequency of each character and then make up the encoding tree *based* on those frequencies, we may be able to save a considerable amount of space. The idea of using character frequencies to determine the encoding is the basis for a ***Huffman encoding*** (Huffman, 1952). Huffman encoding is a prefix-free encoding strategy that is guaranteed to be optimal—among prefix-free encodings. Huffman encoding is the basis for the Unix compress utility, and also part of the Joint Photographic Experts Group (JPEG) encoding process.

Huffman encoding uses the frequency of each character in a message.

We begin by calculating the frequency of each character in a given message M. Note that the time for these calculations is linear in the length of M. For example, suppose that the characters in M are the letters "a" through "g" and their frequencies are as follows:

a: 5000
b: 2000
c: 10,000
d: 8000
e: 22,000
f: 49,000
g: 4000

The size of M is 100,000 characters. If we ignored frequencies and encoded each character into a unique 3-bit sequence, we would need 300,000 bits to encode the message M. We'll soon see how far this is from an optimal encoding.

Figure 11.13 I A binary tree that generates a prefix-free encoding of the letters "a" through "g".

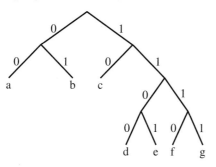

Once we have calculated the frequency of each character, we will insert each character-frequency pair into a priority queue ordered by increasing frequencies. So the top character-frequency pair in the priority queue will have the *least* frequently occurring character. Initially we have the priority queue:

(b:2000) (g:4000) (a:5000) (d:8000) (c:10000) (e:22000) (f:49000)

Actually, all we know about this priority queue is that an access or deletion would be of the pair (b:2000). As users of the priority_queue class, we should not assume this is a heap (even though this is the current implementation in Standard C++). The pairs are shown in increasing order just for simplicity.

We will create the binary tree, called a ***Huffman tree,*** from the bottom up. We start by popping the priority queue twice to get the two characters with lowest frequencies (that is, highest priorities). The first character popped, "b", becomes the left leaf in the binary tree, and "g" becomes the right leaf. The sum of their frequencies becomes the root of the tree and is inserted into the priority queue. We now have the Huffman tree:

The priority queue contains

(a:5000) (:6000) (d:8000) (c:10000) (e:22000) (f:49000)

Technically, the priority queue and the Huffman tree consist of character-frequency pairs. But the character can be ignored when two frequencies are summed, and the frequencies can be ignored in showing the leaves of the Huffman tree. Actually, the algorithm works with references to the pairs rather than with the pairs themselves. This allows references to represent the typical binary-tree constructs—left, right, root, parent—that are needed for navigating through the Huffman tree.

When the pairs (a:5000) and (:6000) are popped from the priority queue, they become the left and right branches of the extended tree whose root is the sum of their frequencies. That sum is inserted into the priority queue. We now have the Huffman tree:

The priority queue now contains

(d:8000) (c:10000) (:11000) (e:22000) (f:49000)

Notice the significance of popping the *least* frequently occurring characters during each iteration. They will end up at the bottom of the Huffman tree, with the longest encoding. The most frequently occurring characters, such as "f", will end up near the root of the Huffman tree and have the shortest encoding. That's why the Huffman encoding is minimal.

When "d" and "c" are popped, they cannot yet be connected to the main tree, so they become the left and right branches of another tree, whose root—their sum—is inserted into the priority queue. We temporarily have two Huffman trees:

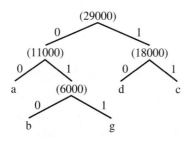

The priority queue now contains

    (:11000) (:18000) (e:22000) (f:49000)

When the pair (:11000) is popped, it becomes the left branch of the binary tree whose right branch is the next pair popped, (:18000). The sum becomes the root of this binary tree, and that sum is inserted into the priority queue, so we have the Huffman tree:

(29000)
   0   1
(11000)   (18000)
 0   1   0   1
a   (6000)   d   c
    0   1
    b   g

The priority queue now contains

    (e:22000) (:29000) (f:49000)

When the next two pairs are popped, "e" becomes the left branch and (:29000) becomes the right branch of the Huffman tree whose root, (:51000), is inserted into the priority queue. Finally the last two pairs, (f:49000) and (:51000) are popped and become the left and right branches of the final Huffman tree. The sum of those two frequencies is the frequency of the root, (:100000), which is inserted as the sole item into the priority queue. The final Huffman tree is shown in Figure 11.14. The Huffman encoding is

    a: 1100
    b: 11010
    c: 1111
    d: 1110
    e: 10
    f: 0
    g: 11011

Figure 11.14 I The final Huffman tree.

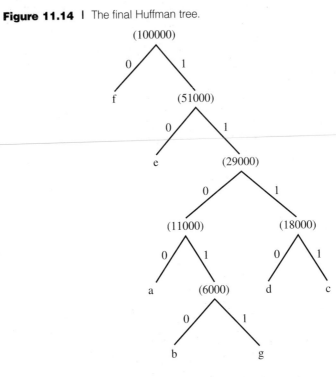

It is now an easy matter to translate the message M into an encoded message E. What about on the receiving end? How easy is it to decode E to get the original message M? Start at the root of the tree and the beginning of E, take a left branch in the tree for a 0 in E, and take a right branch for a 1. Continue until a leaf is reached. That is the first character in M. Start back at the top of the tree and continue reading E. For example, if M is "cede", then E is 111110111010. Starting at the root of the tree, the four 1s at the beginning of E lead us to the leaf "c". Then we go back to the root, and continue reading E with the fifth 1. We take a right branch for that 1 and then a left branch for the 0, and we are at "e". And so on.

The size of the message E is equal to the sum, over all characters, of the number of bits in the encoding of the character times the frequency of that character in M. So to get the size of E in this example, we take the product of the 4 bits in the encoding of "a" and the 5000 occurrences of "a", add to that the product of the 5 bits in the encoding of "b" and the 2000 occurrences of "b", and so on. We get

$$(4 * 5000) + (5 * 2000) + (4 * 10{,}000) + (4 * 8000) + (2 * 21{,}000)$$
$$+ (1 * 49{,}000) + (5 * 4000) = 213{,}000$$

This is about 30 percent less than the 300,000 bits required with the fixed-length, 3-bits-per-character encoding. So the savings in space required and transmission time is significant. But it should be noted that a fixed-length encoding can usually be decoded more quickly than a Huffman encoding; for example, the encoded bits can be interpreted as an array index—the entry at that index is the character encoded.

11.2.1 DESIGN OF THE huffman CLASS

To add substance to our discussion of the Huffman tree, let's develop a huffman class that handles the encoding of a message. The message will be in an input file, and the encoded message will be sent to an output file. The constructor initializes the huffman object (including the input and output files), given the path names:

```
// Postcondition: This huffman object has been initialized from in_file_name
//                 and out_file_name.
huffman (string in_file_name, string out_file_name);
```

The other tasks to be performed are easily identified: we need to create the priority queue and Huffman tree, calculate the Huffman codes, and, finally, save the Huffman codes and encoded message to the output file. The method interfaces are

```
// Postcondition: the priority queue has been created. The worstTime(n) is O(n).
void create_pq( );
```

```
// Postcondition: the Huffman tree has been created.
void create_huffman_tree( );
```

```
// Postcondition: the Huffman codes have been calculated.
void calculate_huffman_codes( );
```

```
// Postcondition: the Huffman codes and encoded message have been
//                 saved to the output file. The worstTime(n) is O(n).
void save_to_file( );
```

Each node in a Huffman tree will have some coding information (the character, its frequency, and its encoding) and some binary-tree information (pointers to the left subtree, right subtree, and parent). The huffman_node class will not be embedded in the huffman class so that other classes—for example, a class to decode an encoded message—can also access the huffman_node class.

Here is the huffman_node class, with all public fields and no methods:

```
struct huffman_node;

typedef huffman_node* node_ptr;

struct huffman_node
{
        char id;
        int freq;
        string code;
        node_ptr left,
                 right,
```

```
                    parent;
}; // huffman_node
```

The huffman class has an embedded function class, compare. The compare class has no fields and a single method: **operator( )**, of course.

```
class compare
{
      public:

            bool operator( ) (const node_ptr& c1,
                              const node_ptr& c2) const
            {
                  return (*c1).freq > (*c2).freq;
            } // overloaded operator( )
} // class compare
```

Because **operator>** is used in the comparison, the item with the lowest frequency will have the highest priority in the priority queue.

What other fields should we have in the huffman class? Given a character in the input, we want to be able to access its huffman_node quickly. By creating an array whose indices are the characters themselves, we utilize the random-access property of arrays to provide *constant-time* access:

```
static const int MAX_SIZE = 256; // legal only for static integer constants

node_ptr node_array [MAX_SIZE];
```

This gives us one array slot for each character in the (extended) ASCII character set. For example, in the Huffman encoding example, the frequency for "d" was 8000 and the code for "d" was "1110". The information for that character is stored in a **struct** pointed to by a pointer at index (**int**)'d', which is 99. So part of node_array will have

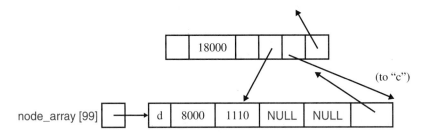

We also need a priority queue, an input file, an output file, and an input-file name. The input-file name allows us to open the input file twice: once to calculate the frequencies, and later to encode the message. So we have the following fields in huffman:

```
priority_queue< node_ptr, vector<node_ptr>, compare > pq;
```

```
fstream in_file,
          out_file;

string in_file_name;
```

In the dependency diagram,

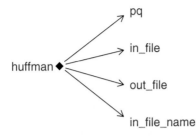

all the fields represent composition, even in_file and out_file, because there are no references to these files outside of the huffman class.

That completes the design—roughly, the header file huffman.h—of the huffman class. In Section 11.2.2, we turn our attention to the source file, huffman.cpp.

11.2.2 IMPLEMENTATION OF THE huffman CLASS

The constructor, as promised, opens the files:

```
huffman::huffman (string in_file_name, string out_file_name)
{
      (*this).in_file_name = in_file_name;
      in_file.open (in_file_name.c_str( ), ios::in);

      out_file.open (out_file_name.c_str( ), ios::out);
} // constructor
```

The create_pq method first fills in node_array and, from that, the priority queue pq:

```
void huffman::create_pq( )
{
      const string DEFAULT_TOTAL =
      "With a fixed number of bits per character, the message size in bits is ";
      node_ptr entry;

      int sum = 0,
          n_chars = 0,
          n_bits_per_char;

      for (int i = 0; i < MAX_SIZE; i++)
      {
```

```
                node_array [i] = new huffman_node;
                (*node_array [i]).freq = 0;
        } // initializing array

        create_node_array( );

        for (int i = 0; i < MAX_SIZE; i++)
        {
                entry = node_array [i];
                if ((*entry).freq > 0)
                {
                        pq.push (entry);
                        sum += (*entry).freq;
                        n_chars++;
                } // if
        } // counting chars and frequencies
        n_bits_per_char = ceil(log (n_chars) / log(2));
        cout <<endl <<DEFAULT_TOTAL
                        <<(sum * n_bits_per_char)<<endl;
} // create_pq
```

The calculation of n_bits_per_char deserves an explanation. In C++, the log function returns the natural logarithm (that is, base e of its argument. We apply a property of logarithms from Appendix 1 to convert from base e into base 2.

The create_node_array method addresses an interesting problem. After each line is read from the input file named in_file, an entry for a new-line marker is created in node_array. So a blank line in the input file will not be ignored. But how should a line be read in? Certainly not with

```
    in_file >> line;
```

The extraction operator, **operator**>>, starts by skipping over all white space (including blanks and new-line markers), and then reads up to the next white space. So blank lines would not be counted—and neither would blank spaces, for that matter. Fortunately, the function getline reads an entire line and does not skip over initial white space. Here is the create_node_array method:

```
    void huffman::create_node_array( )
    {
        node_ptr entry;
        string line;

        while (getline (in_file, line))
        {
                for (unsigned j = 0; j < line.length( ); j++)
                {
                        entry = node_array [(int)(line [j])];
```

```
                (*entry).freq++;
                if ((*entry).freq == 1)
                {
                        (*entry).left = NULL;
                        (*entry).right = NULL;
                        (*entry).parent = NULL;
                } // first time character occurred
        } // for
        entry = node_array [(int)'\n'];
        (*entry).freq++;
        (*entry).left = NULL;
        (*entry).right = NULL;
        (*entry).parent = NULL;
    } // while
} // create_node_array
```

The create_huffman_tree method is just as described in Section 11.2:

```
void huffman::create_huffman_tree( )
{
    node_ptr left,
            right,
            sum;

    while( pq.size( ) > 1 )
    {
        left = pq.top( );
        pq.pop( );
        (*left).code = string ("0");

        right = pq.top( );
        pq.pop( );
        (*right).code = string ("1");

        sum = new huffman_node;
        (*sum).parent = NULL;
        (*sum).freq = (*left).freq + (*right).freq ;
        (*sum).left = left;
        (*sum).right = right;
        (*left).parent = sum;
        (*right).parent = sum;

        pq.push( sum );
    } // while
} // create_huffman_tree
```

The calculate_huffman_codes method iterates through node_array. For each entry whose character frequency is nonzero, we create the code for that entry as follows: starting with an empty string variable code, we *prepend* the entry's code field to code, and then replace the entry with the entry's parent. The final value of code is then inserted as the code field for that entry in node_array.

For example, suppose part of the Huffman tree is as follows:

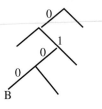

Then the code for 'B' would be calculated in four iterations, with the following values for the code after each iteration:

    0

    00

    100

    0100

This string, "0100", is stored in the code field of the node at index 66 of nodeArray—recall that (**int**)'B' = 66 in the ASCII collating sequence.

Here is the method definition:

```
void huffman::calculate_huffman_codes( )
{
    const string HUFFMAN_CODES = "Here are the Huffman codes: ";

    const string ENCODED_SIZE_MESSAGE =
        "\n\nThe size of the encoded message, in bits, is ";

    int total = 0;

    string code;
    node_ptr entry;

    cout <<endl <<HUFFMAN_CODES <<endl;
    for (int i = 0; i < MAX_SIZE; i++)
    {
        code = "";
        entry = node_array [i];
        if ((*entry).freq > 0)
        {
            cout <<(char)i <<" ";
            do
```

```
        {
            code = (*entry).code + code;
            entry = (*entry).parent;
        } // do
        while ((*entry).parent != NULL);

        cout <<code <<endl;
        (*node_array [i]).code = code;
        total += code.length( ) * (*node_array [i]).freq ;
    } // if
} // for
cout <<ENCODED_SIZE_MESSAGE <<total <<endl;
} // calculate_huffman_codes
```

Now that node_array includes the Huffman code for each character, we can create the output file. This file contains both the encodings—for example, 'a' 0100—and the encoded message. So first the Huffman codes are written to the output file, then the input file is reread, each character is encoded, and the encoded message is sent to the output file. Here is the definition:

```
void huffman::save_to_file( )
{
    node_ptr entry;

    string line;

    in_file.close( );
    in_file.open (in_file_name.c_str( ), ios::in);

    for (int i = 0; i < MAX_SIZE; i++)
    {
        entry = node_array [i];
        if ((*entry).freq > 0)
            out_file <<(char)i <<" " <<(*entry).code <<endl;
    } // for
    out_file <<"**" <<endl;

    while (getline (in_file, line))
    {
        for (unsigned j = 0; j < line.length( ); j++)
        {
            entry = node_array [(int)(line [j])];
            out_file <<(*entry).code;
        } // for
        entry = node_array [(int)'\n'];
        out_file <<(*entry).code;
    } // while
```

```
        out_file.close( );
   } // save_to_file
```

How long does all this take? Let n be the number of characters in the input message. Both the create_node_array and save_to_file methods iterate through the message, so for those two methods, worstTime(n) is linear in n. The create_pq method takes linear time, only because it calls create_node_array to calculate the frequency of each character: the rest of create_pq takes only constant time because at most 256 items can be inserted into the priority queue. Similarly, the create_huffman_tree and calculate_huffman_codes methods take only constant time. The save_to_file method reads the input file, so worstTime(n) is linear in n.

These methods would be invoked by a user who wanted to encode a message. For example, if the input file contained

more money needed

then the output file would be

```
        0000
         100
    d  1011
    e   11
    m  001
    n  011
    o  010
    r  0001
    y  1010
    **
    0010100001111000010100111110101010001111111101111110110000
```

In this encoding, the new-line character is a nonprinting character, so it appears as a blank when printed. But printing that character causes a new line to be printed, so we get a blank line and on the next line a blank space and the code 0000.

Later, another user may want to decode the message. This is done in two steps. First, we must read in the encoding to recreate the Huffman tree. Second, we read in the encoded message and output the decoded message, which should be identical to the original message. Project 11.1 entails the decoding of the encoded message. All the relevant files are available from the Source Code link on the book's website.

A greedy algorithm makes locally optimal choices in seeking a globally optimal solution.

A Huffman encoding is an example of a ***greedy algorithm:*** when a choice is to be made, the most economical candidate is chosen. In the context of a Huffman encoding, the next item added to the Huffman tree is the character-frequency pair with lowest frequency. That pair will always be at the top of the priority queue. In the case of a Huffman encoding, greed succeeds: the resulting encoding uses the minimum number of bits. There are two more examples of a greedy algorithm—also using a priority queue—in Chapter 14, and Exercise 14.6 shows that greed does not always succeed.

SUMMARY

This chapter introduced the ***priority queue:*** a container in which access and removal are allowed only for the highest-priority item in the container, according to some method for assigning priorities to items. For accessing, worstTime(n) is constant, whereas for removing, worstTime(n) is $O(\log n)$. There is no stipulation about *where* an item is to be inserted in a priority queue, but worstTime(n) must be $O(n)$, and averageTime(n) must be constant.

In the design of the priority_queue class, the items are stored in a heap. A ***heap*** t is a complete binary tree such that either t is empty or

1. The root item of t is the largest item in t, according to some method for comparing items.
2. The left and right subtrees of t are heaps.

Because complete binary trees allow calculation of a parent's index from a child's index, and vice versa, the heap is represented as an array. This utilizes an array's ability to randomly access the item at a given index.

The application of priority queues was in the area of data compression. Given a message, it is possible to encode each character, unambiguously, into a minimum number of bits. One way to achieve such a minimum encoding is with a Huffman tree. A ***Huffman tree*** is a two-tree in which each leaf represents a distinct character in the original message, each left branch is labeled with a 0, and each right branch is labeled with a 1. The Huffman code for each character is constructed by tracing the path from that leaf character back to the root and prepending each branch label in the path.

EXERCISES

11.1 Show the steps involved in making the following alterations, consecutively, to the heap in Figure 11.12, repeated here:

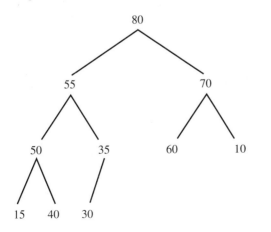

      a.   push (83);

      b.   push (61);

      c.   pop( );

11.2 Illustrate the unfairness of the Hewlett-Packard implementation of the priority-queue class. That is, give an example of two items in a priority queue that are tied for highest priority, but the one inserted first is not the one removed first.

11.3 Suppose a vector container c1 has the following sequence of items: 10, 20, 30, 40, 50, 60, 70, 80, 90, 100. Show what will happen if we call

make_heap (c1.begin( ), c1.end( ), less<int>);

11.4 Suppose a vector container c2 has the same items as c1 in Exercise 11.3, but in reverse order. Show what will happen if we call

make_heap (c2.begin( ), c2.end( ), less <int>);

11.5 Estimate the time for the call to make_heap in Exercise 11.3 relative to the time for the call to make_heap in Exercise 11.4.

11.6 For the following character frequencies, create the heap of character-frequency pairs (highest priority = lowest frequency):

a: 5,000

b: 2,000

c: 10,000

d: 8,000

e: 22,000

f: 49,000

g: 4,000

11.7 Use the following Huffman code to translate the word "faced" into a bit sequence:

a: 1100

b: 11010

c: 1111

d: 1110

e: 10

f: 0

11.8 Use the following Huffman tree to translate the bit sequence 11101011111100111010 back into letters 'a' through 'g':

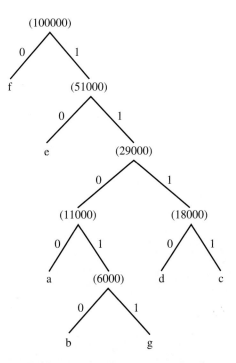

11.9 For the following Huffman code, give an example of a sequence of 5 bits that could not be the start of any encoded message:

a: 1100
b: 11010
c: 1111
d: 1110
e: 10
f: 0

Can you find another such 5-bit sequence? Explain.

11.10 Must a Huffman tree be a two-tree? Explain.

11.11 Describe how to create a message with the alphabet 'a' through 'h' in which two of the letters have a Huffman code of 7 bits. Create a message with the alphabet 'a' through 'h' in which all the letters have a Huffman code of 3 bits.

11.12 In the Huffman tree for Exercise 11.8, the sum of the frequencies of all the nonleaves is 215,000. This is also the size of the encoded message E. Explain why in any Huffman tree, the sum of the frequencies of all non-leaves is equal to the size of the encoded message.

11.13 How many loop iterations are required when the pop_heap method is called for the following heap? Can you think of another heap with the same number of items for which pop_heap would require more iterations?

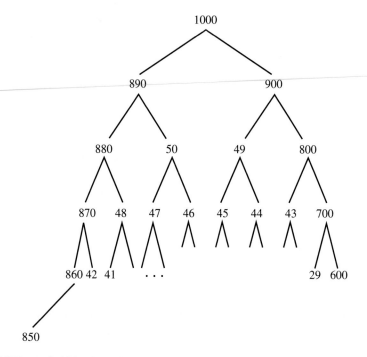

11.14 The id field in the huffman_node class is not used in the huffman class. Why not omit that field?

PROGRAMMING PROJECT 11.1

Decoding a Message

Suppose a message has been encoded by a Huffman encoding. Develop a project to decode the encoded message and thus retrieve the original message.

Analysis

As shown in the output file in the Huffman application of this chapter, the input file will consist of two parts:

Each character and its encoding

The encoded message

Suppose the file huffman.ou1 contains the following (the encoded message has been split between three lines to fit on this page):

```
 0010
  0111
a 000
b 1
c 0011
d 010
e 0110
**
1000010011100110110010011001110011000101110100001001001001100000100111010
000010011100110000100010111111111111111111111111111110010
```

System Test 1

In the Input line, please enter the name of the input file.

huffman.ou1

In the Input line, please enter the name of the output file.
decode.ou1

Please press the Enter key to close this output window.

The file **decode.ou1** will contain

bad cede cab dab
dead dad cad
bbbbbbbbbbbbbbbbbbbbbbbbbbbbbbb

Suppose the file huffman.ou2 contains the following (the message is from Coleridge's "Rubiyat of Omar Khayam"):

```
 10000
  101
, 001110
```

(continued on next page)

(continued from previous page)

```
.   0011010
A   001100
D   0010100
I   0010101
K   001111
T   0010010
W   0010110
X   0010111
a   1111
b   011000
c   00000
d   11011
e   010
g   0010011
h   11100
i   100011
l   0001
m   00001
n   0111
o   11010
p   011001
r   1001
s   1100
t   01101
u   11101
v   100010
w   001000
y   0011011
**
```

```
0010101011110100101111111011111111011111011011101110
0011110111010011111110101100000011111000111010011111
1100111101111000000110010111000110111101101010000100
1101110101100100010101111110011101100101010111011101
0000010101011101101000000100101001000111010000001011000
1110001010010101010011000001011001111001010110111100
10101110011110000010010101101111011001100011110000100101
00110110011111011110000000100101110010011101011101000
0111110010100000111110001001010010111110010101111101
0000010110000101001000101011001100101011011101010010000
1111101111001110100000001010011010001000011110101101110
1010111111011100111010111000101011001100101110001011
1001101010000
```

System Test 2

In the Input line, please enter the name of the input file.

huffman.ou2

In the Input line, please enter the name of the output file.
decode.ou2

Please press the Enter key to close this output window.

The file decode.ou2 will contain

In Xanadu did Kubla Khan
A stately pleasure dome decree,
Where Alph the sacred river ran
Through caverns numberless to man,
Down to a sunless sea.

Sorting

One of the most common computer operations is *sorting,* that is, putting a container of items in order. From simple, one-time sorts for small containers to highly efficient sorts for frequently used mailing lists and dictionaries, the ability to choose among various sort algorithms is an important skill in every programmer's repertoire. Most of the sort algorithms discussed in this chapter are included in the Standard Template Library, but their implementations are left to developers. For specificity, we will study the Hewlett-Packard implementations. Several additional sort algorithms, such as Selection Sort, Bubble Sort, and Radix Sort, are investigated in the exercises. ∎

CHAPTER OBJECTIVES

1. Be able to decide which sort algorithm is appropriate for a given application.

2. Understand the limitations of each sort algorithm.

3. Explain the criteria for a divide-and-conquer algorithm.

12.1 | INTRODUCTION

We consider comparison-based sorts only; that is, the sorting entails comparing items to other items. Comparisons are not necessary if we know, in advance, the final position of each item. For example, if we start with an unsorted list of 100 distinct integers in the range 0 . . . 99, we know without any comparisons that the integer 0 must end up in position 0, and so on. The best-known sort algorithm that is not comparison-based is Radix Sort: see Exercise 12.14.

For each sorting algorithm, the user can choose the default comparison operator, **operator**<, or provide a function object that will be used in comparing items. If the default is chosen, the result of sorting will be a collection in ascending order. For the sake of simplicity, we will use the default of **operator**< throughout this chapter.

In analyzing a sorting method, both averageTime(n) and worstTime(n) are important. In some applications, such as national defense and life-support systems, the worst-case performance of a sort method can be critical. We will see several sort algorithms that provide a kind of insurance policy against unacceptably bad worst-case performance.

We will illustrate the effect of each method on the following 10 integers:

59 46 32 80 46 55 87 43 70 81

The space requirements of the sort algorithms are worth mentioning. Most have minimal needs: a few iterators and indices, and a temporary variable to hold one item. For one sort algorithm, Quick Sort, averageSpace(n) is logarithmic in n and worst Space(n) is linear in n. And for Tree Sort, both averageSpace(n) and worstSpace(n) are linear in n.

The other criterion we'll use for measuring a sort algorithm is stability. A ***stable*** sort method preserves the relative order of equal items. For example, suppose we have a vector container of students in which each entry consists of a student's last name and the total quality points for that student, and we want to sort by total quality points. If the sort method is stable and ("Balan", 28) appears at an earlier index than ("Wang", 28) before sorting, then ("Balan" 28) will still appear at an earlier index than ("Wang" 28) after sorting. Stability can simplify project development. For example, assume that the above vector container is already in order by name, and the application calls for sorting by quality points; for students with the same quality points the ordering should be alphabetical. A stable sort will accomplish this without any additional work needed to make sure students with the same quality points are ordered alphabetically.

We'll start with a sort algorithm whose stand-alone performance is poor, but when combined with another sort, produces the fastest—on average—run-time.

12.1.1 Insertion Sort

We assume that the items to be sorted are in a container that supports ***random-access*** iterators. We loop through the container with an iterator i. During each loop iteration, we have another loop to insert *i where it belongs relative to items at positions less than i. For example, suppose that i is positioned at the rightmost item in the following:

32 45 59 80 91 46

Then after that iteration, we will have

32 45 46 59 80 91

The __insertion_sort algorithm is

```
template <class RandomAccessIterator>
void __insertion_sort(RandomAccessIterator first,
                       RandomAccessIterator last)
{
    if (first == last)
        return;
    for (RandomAccessIterator i = first + 1; i != last; ++i)
        __linear_insert(first, i, value_type(first));
}
```

In the call to __linear_insert, the third argument allows us to determine the type of the items. To accomplish the insertion of *i with maximum efficiency, the code for __linear_insert is more complicated than you would expect. Corresponding to the arguments first and i are the parameters first and last, respectively. We save *last in a local variable, value. If value < *first, we copy (backward) everything in the range between first and last − 1 to the range between first + 1 and last; then we store value at position first. For example, suppose i is positioned at index 4 in the following:

46 59 85 91 32

We save 32 in value, move 91 to where 32 was, move 85 to where 91 was, move 59 to where 85 was, and move 46 to where 59 was. Finally, we move value to where 46 was:

32 46 59 85 91

Otherwise, value is not less than *first, and the __unguarded_linear_insert method is called. This method starts at position last − 1 and keeps moving items up until the slot where value belongs has been found. Here is the code for both the __linear_insert and __unguarded_linear_insert methods:

```
template <class RandomAccessIterator, class T>
inline void __linear_insert(RandomAccessIterator first,
                             RandomAccessIterator last, T*)
{
    T value = *last;
    if (value < *first) {
        copy_backward(first, last, last + 1);
        *first = value;
```

```
        }
        else
                __unguarded_linear_insert(last, value);
    }

    template <class RandomAccessIterator, class T>
    void __unguarded_linear_insert(RandomAccessIterator last, T value)
    {
        RandomAccessIterator next = last;
        --next;
        while (value < *next)
        {
            *last = *next;
            last = next--;
        }
        *last = value;
    }
```

"Unguarded" means that no attempt is made to make sure the **while** loop eventually terminates. Termination is guaranteed because of the **if** statement in __linear_ insert. So the purpose of that **if** statement was to allow the **while** condition to avoid the additional test of next != first − 1. This kind of complicated but hyperefficient code is a hallmark of the Hewlett-Packard implementation and others based on that implementation.

Example of Insertion Sort Here is a trace of the first five iterations of the **for** loop in __insertion_sort, including the **while** loop iterations. The item where i is positioned is in boldface, and the items in the range from first through i are underlined after each iteration:

for loop, iteration 1

59 **46** 32 80 46 55 87 43 70 81
59 59 32 80 46 55 87 43 70 81
46 59 32 80 46 55 87 43 70 81

for loop, iteration 2

46 59 **32** 80 46 55 87 43 70 81
46 59 59 80 46 55 87 43 70 81
46 46 59 80 46 55 87 43 70 81
32 46 59 80 46 55 87 43 70 81

for loop, iteration 3

32 46 59 **80** 46 55 87 43 70 81
32 46 59 80 46 55 87 43 70 81

for loop, iteration 4

32 46 59 80 **46** 55 87 43 70 81
32 46 59 80 80 55 87 43 70 81
32 46 59 59 80 55 87 43 70 81
32 46 46 59 80 55 87 43 70 81

for loop, iteration 5

32 46 46 59 80 **55** 87 43 70 81
32 46 46 59 80 80 87 43 70 81
32 46 46 59 59 80 87 43 70 81
32 46 46 55 59 80 87 43 70 81

Analysis of Insertion Sort Let n be the number of items in the range from first (inclusive) to last (exclusive). The **for** loop in __insertion_sort will always be executed exactly $n - 1$ times. If the container starts out in increasing order, the number of iterations of the **while** loop in __linear_insert will be zero. And so the total number of iterations will be $n - 1$, which is linear in n. Speaking loosely, we can say that if the container starts out to be "almost" in increasing order, there will not be many inner-loop iterations. Then the total number of iterations will still be linear in n.

On the other hand, suppose the container starts out in decreasing order, such as

92 85 71 55 42 23

Then during the first iteration of the **for** loop, there will be one iteration of the **while** loop—to open up the slot for 85. During the second iteration of the **for** loop, there will be two iterations of the **while** loop—to open up the slot for 71. During the third, fourth, and fifth iterations of the **for** loop, there will be three, four, and five iterations of the **while** loop, respectively. In general, if the container is in decreasing order, the number of iterations of the **while** loop will be

$$1 + 2 + 3 + \cdots + (n - 2) + (n - 1) = \sum_{k=1}^{n-1} k = n(n - 1)/2$$

That is, worstTime(n) is quadratic in n. In the average case (see Exercise 12.7) there will be approximately $n^2/4$ iterations of the **while** loop, and so averageTime(n) is also quadratic in n.

Insertion Sort is stable because the **while** loop stops if value = *next, and then value is inserted at position next + 1. By "sifting down" from i rather than sifting up from first, we obtain the best time when the container is already in order, and very good time when the container is almost in order. We will take advantage of this behavior in Section 12.3.4.

For Insertion Sort, averageTime(n) is quadratic in n.

12.2 | HOW FAST CAN WE SORT?

For using Insertion Sort to sort a container that supports random-access iterators, worstTime(n) is quadratic in n. Before we look at some faster sorts, let's spend a few moments to see how much of an improvement is possible. The tool we will use for this analysis is the decision tree. A ***decision tree*** is a binary tree in which each non-leaf represents a comparison between two items and each leaf represents a sorted sequence of those items. For example, Figure 12.1 shows a decision tree for applying Insertion Sort in which the items to be sorted are stored in the variables a_1, a_2, and a_3.

A decision tree must have one leaf for each permutation of the items to be sorted.[1] The total number of permutations of n items is $n!$, so if we are sorting n items, then the corresponding decision tree must have $n!$ leaves. According to the Binary Tree Theorem, the number of leaves in any nonempty binary tree t is $\leq$ $2^{\text{height}(t)}$. Thus, for a decision tree t that sorts n items,

$$n! \leq 2^{\text{height}(t)}$$

Taking logs, we get

$$\text{height}(t) \geq \log_2 n!$$

In other words, for any comparison-based sort, there must be a leaf whose depth is at least $\log_2 n!$. In the context of decision trees, that means that there must be an arrangement of items whose sorting requires at least $\log_2 n!$ comparisons. So for comparison-based sorts, $\text{worstTime}(n) \geq \log_2 n!$. According to Exercise 12.8, $O(\log n!) = O(n \log n)$. This allows us to say, loosely, that

> For comparison-based sorts, $\text{worstTime}(n)$ cannot be less than $O(n \log n)$.

We can go even further: For any comparison-based sort, $\text{averageTime}(n)$ can be no less than $O(n \log n)$. To obtain this result, suppose t is a decision tree for sorting n items. Then t has $n!$ leaves. The average—over all $n!$ permutations—number of

Figure 12.1 ∣ A decision tree for sorting three items by Insertion Sort.

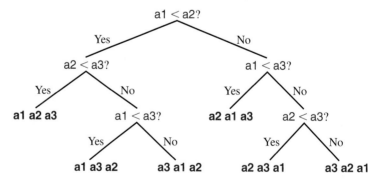

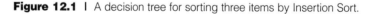

———————

[1] For the sake of simplicity, we assume the sort method does not make any redundant comparisons.

comparisons to sort the n items is the total number of comparisons divided by $n!$, that is, $E(t)/n!$. By the External Path Length Theorem in Chapter 8, $E(t) \geq (n!/2)$ floor($\log_2 n!$). So we get

averageTime(n) ≥ average number of comparisons
$$= E(t)/n!$$
$$\geq (n!/2) \text{ floor}(\log_2 n!)/n!$$
$$= (1/2) \text{ floor}(\log_2 n!)$$

Since floor($\log_2 n!$) $\leq \log_2 n!$, floor($\log_2 n!$) is $O(\log n!)$. By Exercise 12.8, $O(\log n!) = O(n \log n)$. We conclude that floor($\log_2 n!$) is $O(n \log n)$. Putting this in the context of averageTime, we get

> For comparison-based sorts, averageTime(n) cannot be less than $O(n \log n)$.

Fortunately, this is not some lofty, unattainable goal. For each of the remaining algorithms in this chapter, averageTime(n) is $O(n \log n)$. In fact, for the next three sort algorithms, worstTime(n) is only $O(n \log n)$. And we can use that fact to show that averageTime(n) must also be $O(n \log n)$. Why? Suppose we have a sort algorithm for which worstTime(n) is $O(n \log n)$. Then averageTime(n) is certainly no worse than $O(n \log n)$. But according to our estimate on average times, average Time(n) cannot be faster than $O(n \log n)$ either. So we conclude that if a sort algorithm's worstTime(n) is $O(n \log n)$, then its averageTime(n) must also be $O(n \log n)$.

For any comparison-based sort, if worst Time(n) is O($n \log n$), then averageTime(n) is also O($n \log n$).

12.3 | FAST SORTS

In Sections 12.3.1 to 12.3.4, we will look at four sort methods whose average Time(n) is only $O(n \log n)$. For three of them, worstTime(n) is also $O(n \log n)$, while for the other, worstTime(n) is $O(n^2)$. Strangely enough, this last algorithm, called Quick Sort, is generally considered the most efficient all-around sort! Quick Sort's worst-case performance is bad, but for average-case, run-time speed, Quick Sort is the best of the lot. You will have the opportunity to witness that performance in Lab 27. We start with a sort algorithm based on the multiset class from Chapter 10.

12.3.1 Tree Sort

The items to be sorted are inserted, one by one, into an initially empty multiset container. That's all there is to Tree Sort because the hard work is done in the insert method of the multiset class, or more likely, in the insert method of the rb_tree class. The generic algorithm tree_sort, which is not part of the Standard Template Library, is a wrapper for a function that does the real work.

```
template<class ForwardIterator>
void tree_sort (ForwardIterator first, ForwardIterator last)
{
```

```
        if (first != last)
               tree_sort_aux (first, last, *first);
   } // algorithm tree_sort
```

The third parameter to the auxiliary function tree_sort_aux is the type of the items to be sorted. This type is necessary for the construction of the set container. Here is the definition of tree_sort_aux:

```
template<class ForwardIterator, class T>
void tree_sort_aux (ForwardIterator first, ForwardIterator last, T)
{
       multiset< T, less< T > > tree_set;

       ForwardIterator itr;

       for (itr = first; itr != last; itr++)
              tree_set.insert (*itr);
       copy (tree_set.begin( ), tree_set.end( ), first);

}
```

For example, to apply Tree Sort to a vector container v use

```
tree_sort (v.begin( ), v.end( ));
```

Example of Tree Sort   We show the initial collection of items, and then the red-black tree formed by inserting those items, one at a time, into an initially empty multiset container (assuming the multiset class is implemented with a red-black tree). The items in their original order are

59 46 32 80 46 55 87 43 70 81

The resulting red-black tree is

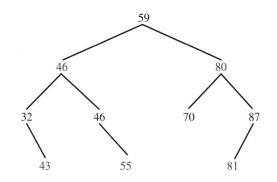

The items are then copied to the original container.

Analysis of Tree Sort For $i = 1, 2, \ldots, n - 1$, inserting the ith item requires, at most, $\log_2 i$ iterations. If restructuring the red-black tree is required after the insertion of the ith item, another $(\log_2 i)/2$ iterations, at most, are needed (recall, from Chapter 10, that in case 2 for inserting in a red-black tree, x is replaced with the grandparent of x). The total number of iterations in this worst case is

$$1.5 \sum_{i=1}^{n} \log_2 i \leq 1.5 \sum_{i=1}^{n} \log_2 n = 1.5n \log_2 n$$

So for Tree Sort, worstTime(n) is $O(n \log n)$ and, from the discussion in Section 12.2, $O(n \log n)$ must be the smallest upper bound of worstTime(n). What about averageTime(n)? Because averageTime(n) $\leq$ worstTime(n), averageTime(n) is $O(n \log n)$. And, also by the results in Section 12.2, $O(n \log n)$ must be the smallest upper bound of averageTime(n).

Tree Sort is fast and stable, but requires linear-in-n space.

Tree Sort requires a multiset of n items to be created, so worstSpace(n) is linear in n. Tree Sort is stable because if an item y to be inserted is equal to an item x already in a red-black tree, y will be inserted in x's *right* subtree. From then on, for all rotations, y will be treated just as if x were less than y, so x will come before y in any forward iteration.

12.3.2 Heap Sort

The Heap Sort method was invented by J. W. J. Williams (1964). Given a container c that supports random-access iterators, Heap Sort is a two-step process:

```
make_heap (c.begin( ), c.end( )); // comparisons use operator<
sort_heap (c.begin( ), c.end( ));
```

We saw the make_heap algorithm in Chapter 11. The sort_heap algorithm is quite simple, because the hard work is done by the pop_heap method:

```
// Precondition: the items in the container, from the range first (inclusive) to
//               last (exclusive), form a heap.
// Postcondition: the items in the container, from the range first (inclusive) to
//               last (exclusive), are in ascending order. The worstTime(n) is
//               O(n log n).
void sort_heap (RandomAccessIterator first, RandomAccessIterator last)
{
        while (last − first > 1)
                pop_heap (first, last--); // comparisons use operator<
} // sort_heap
```

Example of Heap Sort If we start with our usual collection of 10 items, then after the execution of the make_heap algorithm, we will have the following heap:

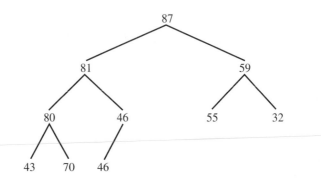

In the call to sort_heap, we repeatedly pop the root item and insert it at the end of the container, so after 10 iterations we get the following complete binary tree, no longer a heap:

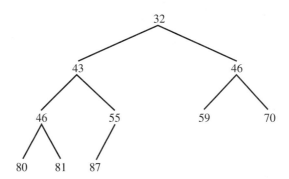

Within the container, the sequence of items will be in ascending order.

Analysis of Heap Sort   The analysis of Heap Sort depends on the analyses of the algorithms make_heap and pop_heap. We saw at the end of Chapter 11 that worst Time(n) for make_heap is only $O(n)$. Within sort_heap, we make n calls to pop_heap. The first such call requires no more than 2 log$_2$ n iterations. The factor of 2 is used because we have to go all the way down to the leaf level to open up a space, and then we might have to go all the way back to the root level to insert what had been the last item. The second call requires no more than 2 log$_2(n - 1)$ iterations, ... , and the next-to-last call no more than two iterations. The last call to pop_heap requires no iterations. That is, in the worst case, the total number of iterations is

$$2 \sum_{i=1}^{n} \log_2 i$$

Heap Sort is a fast, in-place sort that is not stable.

The rest of the analysis is the same as for Tree Sort: worstTime(n) is $O(n \log n)$ and averageTime(n) is $O(n \log n)$, and these are the smallest upper bounds. Because Heap Sort is an in-place sort, worstSpace(n) is constant.

Heap Sort is not a stable sort. For example, suppose the vector object vec consists of the following names and test scores, with highest priority for the highest test score:

"Jones", 85   "Smith", 85

The call to make_heap will leave vec unchanged because Smith's priority is not greater than Jones's priority. Then sort_heap will store "Jones" at index 1 and "Smith" at index 0:

"Smith", 85   "Jones", 85

12.3.3 Merge Sort

The Merge Sort algorithm is provided as the sort method in the list class. Here is the method interface:

```
// Postcondition: This list is in ascending order according to operator<. The
//                 worstTime(n) is O(n log n).
void sort( );
```

Recall that, in the Hewlett-Packard implementation of the list class, each item in a list is stored as a field in a node that also has pointer fields prev and next. Almost all the work of sorting is done by manipulating these pointer fields; *the items themselves are not moved.* Before we study the design of this sort method, we need to develop an auxiliary method, merge. The **protected** method merge has the following heading:

```
// Precondition: Both this list and x are sorted lists, ordered by operator<.
// Postcondition: This list is a sorted list which contains all of the items that
//                 were, before this call, either in this list or in x. And x is now
//                 empty. The worstTime(n) is O(n), where n is the (pre-call)
//                 size of the calling list object.
void merge (list<T>& x);
```

> *Note* If, for example, an item appeared once in the calling object and twice in x, then after the call to merge, that item would appear three times in the calling object.

The Hewlett-Packard definition of the merge method uses a couple of iterators, first1 and first2. Initially, first1 is positioned at the first node in the calling object, and first2 is positioned at the first node in x. We loop until we exhaust one of the lists. During each iteration, if first2's item is less than first1's item, we transfer—by adjusting pointers—first2's node to just before first1's node and bump first2. Otherwise, we bump first1. After looping, if x has not been exhausted, we transfer all the remaining items from x to the end of the calling object. And finally, we increase the calling object's length by x's length and set x's length to 0.

For example, suppose the call is lis1.merge(lis2), and those lists contain the following items:

lis1: 50, 60, 100, 110

↑

first1

lis2: 30, 40, 60, 80, 90, 150, 160, 180

↑

first2

Because first2's item, 30, is less than first1's item, 50, we transfer (by pointer adjustments) first2's node to just before first1's node and bump first2. We now have

lis1: 30, 50, 60, 100, 110

↑

first1

lis2: 40, 60, 80, 90, 150, 160, 180

↑

first2

Since first2's item is still less than first1's item, we transfer first2's node and bump first2:

lis1: 30, 40, 50, 60, 100, 110

↑

first1

lis2: 60, 80, 90, 150, 160, 180

↑

first2

Now first2's item is not less than first1's item, so we simply bump first1:

lis1: 30, 40, 50, 60, 100, 110

↑

first1

lis2: 60, 80, 90, 150, 160, 180

↑

first2

We bump first1 again because first2's item, 60, is not less than first1's item, also 60:

lis1: 30, 40, 50, 60, 100, 110

↑

first1

lis2: 60,   80,   90, 150, 160, 180

↑

first2

For the next three loop iterations, first2's item is less than first1's item, so we transfer and bump first2:

lis1: 30,   40,   50,   60,   60,   80,   90, 100, 110

↑

first1

lis2: 150, 160, 180

↑

first2

During the next two iterations, first2's item is not less than first1's item, so we bump first1:

lis1: 30,   40,   50,   60,   60,   80,   90, 100, 110

↑

first1

lis2: 150, 160, 180

↑

first2

We have now exhausted lis1, so we transfer (by pointer adjustments) all the remaining nodes from the list object lis2 to the end of the list object lis1:

lis1: 30,   40,   50,   60,   60,   80,   90, 100, 110, 150, 160, 180

↑

first1

lis2:

↑

first2

Here is the Hewlett-Packard definition:

```
template <class T>
void list<T>::merge(list<T>& x)
{
        iterator first1 = begin( );
```

```
        iterator last1 = end( );
        iterator first2 = x.begin( );
        iterator last2 = x.end( );
        while (first1 != last1 && first2 != last2)
            if (*first2 < *first1) {
                iterator next = first2;
                transfer(first1, first2, ++next);
                first2 = next;
            }
        else
                ++first1;
        if (first2 != last2) transfer(last1, first2, last2);
            length += x.length;
        x.length = 0;
    }
```

For future reference, let's see how bad merge can be if both lists have the same number of items. Suppose the items from the two lists are interleaved, for example,

> lis1: 10, 30, 50, 70
>
> lis2: 20, 40, 60, 80

In this case, seven loop iterations are required: (10 20), (20 30), (30 40), (40 50), (50 60), (60 70), (70 80). In general, if each sublist is of size k, the total number of loop iterations in the worst case is $2k - 1$.

With the merge method handling the merging of sublists, the list class's sort method starts at the beginning of the calling object and repeatedly merges sublists into double-sized sublists. Sublists of size 1 (which are automatically sorted) are merged into sorted sublists of size 2; sorted sublists of size 2 are merged into sorted sublists of size 4, and so on. The merged sublists are stored in an array of lists called counter. For each value of i from 0 to 63, counter [i] will initially be empty and thereafter may hold 0, 2^i or 2^{i+1} items. Whenever counter [i] has 2^{i+1} items, they are transferred to counter [i+1] if counter [i+1] is empty and otherwise merged with counter [i+1].

Example of Merge Sort Suppose that the message is lis.sort( ) and that lis contains the following items:

> lis: 30, 10, 20, 50, 40, 90, 25, 35, 15, 85, 60

The first node in lis is transferred to a temporary list called carry, and then swapped with counter [0]. We now have

> lis: 10, 50, 20, 40, 90, 25, 35, 15, 85, 60
>
> carry:
>
> counter [0]: 30

When the next item from lis is transferred to carry, that list is merged with counter [0] and then transferred to counter [1]:

lis: 50, 20, 40, 90, 25, 35, 15, 85, 60

carry:

counter [0]:

counter [1]: 10, 30

When 50 is transferred to carry, that item is transferred to counter [0] since counter [0] was empty. When 20 is transferred to carry, that item is merged with 50, and that makes counter [0] full. So counter [0] is merged with counter [1]:

lis: 40, 90, 25, 35, 15, 85, 60

carry:

counter [0]:

counter [1]: 10, 20, 30, 50

But now counter [1] is full, so its items are transferred to counter [2]:

lis: 40, 90, 25, 35, 15, 85, 60

carry:

counter [0]:

counter [1]:

counter [2]: 10, 20, 30, 50

After the next four items from lis have been merged, counter [3] contains the first eight items in the original list, in increasing order. When the final three items in lis have been merged, we have the following:

lis:

carry:

counter [0]: 60

counter [1]: 15, 85

counter [2]:

counter [3]: 10, 20, 25, 30, 35, 40, 50, 90

Finally, starting at counter [2] and moving down to counter [0], all the counter lists are merged into counter [3], which is then swapped with (the empty) lis. So we end up with

lis: 10, 15, 20, 25, 30, 35, 40, 50, 60, 85, 90

The carry list plays an important role in the algorithm, even though carry is empty at the beginning and end of each iteration. Each item from the list is stored in carry before being merged or swapped with one of the counter lists. And when for some i, counter [i] fills up, counter [i] is swapped with an empty carry. Then, if counter [i+1] is empty, carry is simply swapped with counter [i+1]; otherwise, carry is merged with counter [i+1]. In both cases, carry and counter [i] are empty.

Here is the Hewlett-Packard definition:

template <**class** T>

```
void list<T>::sort( )
{
     if (size( ) < 2)
          return;
     list<T> carry;
     list<T> counter[64];
     int fill = 0;
     while (!empty( ))
     {
          carry.splice(carry.begin( ), *this, begin( ));
          int i = 0;
          while(i < fill && !counter[i].empty( ))
          {
               counter[i].merge(carry);
               carry.swap(counter[i++]);
          }
          carry.swap(counter[i]);
          if (i == fill)
               ++fill;
     }
     for (int i = 1; i < fill; ++i)
          counter[i].merge(counter[i−1]);
     swap(counter[fill−1]);
}
```

Analysis of Merge Sort   How long does the list class's sort method take? As we did with Tree Sort and Heap Sort, we consider a worst-case analysis to get both worstTime(n) and averageTime(n). For each consecutive pair of items in the list, the second item in the pair gets merged with the first item from the pair in counter [0]. Each of these $n/2$ mergers requires a single loop iteration in the merge method, so the total number of iterations for pair mergers is $n/2$. For each consecutive quadruple of items in the list, the second pair in each quadruple gets merged with the first pair from the quadruple in counter [1], and each of those $n/4$ mergers requires, at most, three loop iterations in the merge method. Continuing in this fashion, we are led to the following chart, in which $k = \text{floor}(\log_2 n)$:

From carry to:	Number of mergers	Iterations per merger
counter [0]	$n/2$	1
counter [1]	$n/4$	3
counter [2]	$n/8$	7
counter [3]	$n/16$	15
•	•	•
•	•	•
•	•	•
counter [k − 1]	n/k	$2^k - 1$

At each row in the table, the total number of iterations is less than n. The number of rows is k, that is, floor($\log_2 n$). So the total number of iterations through all rows is less than n(floor($\log_2 n$)), which is $O(n \log n)$. But any comparison-based sort must take at least $O(n \log n)$ iterations. We conclude that for the sort method in the list class, worstTime(n) is $O(n \log n)$, and therefore averageTime(n) is $O(n \log n)$, and these are the smallest upper bounds.

What are the space requirements? We start with a list of n items, and those items are *never moved:* all "transfers" use pointer manipulation rather than copying. So we can say that worstSpace(n) is constant. Strictly speaking, it is inappropriate to even discuss the Big-O behavior of Merge Sort because the method fails for large n. In particular, the counter array holds at most 64 lists and at most $2^{64} - 1$ items. Practically speaking, this flaw is unlikely to have any unfortunate consequences since 2^{64} is larger than a quadrillion.

To establish that Merge Sort is stable, we first consider the merge method. Suppose there is a message of the form

Merge Sort is a fast, in-place sort that is stable.

    lis1.merge (lis2)

with x1 in lis1 equal to x2 in lis2. Because x2 is not less than x1, the comparison of x2 to x1 will result in the incrementing of the iterator first1 in the merge method. This has the effect of ensuring that x1 will *precede* x2 in lis1 when the merging is complete.

Now suppose that in the original list, x is closer to the front of the list than y, and x is equal to y. By the time y is transferred to the temporary list carry, x will already be in counter [k] for some $k \geq 0$. If $k = 0$, then the comparison of x and y will take place when

    counter [0].merge (carry);

is called, and x will precede y by our analysis of merge. Otherwise, the comparison of x to y will take place with the call

    counter [k].merge (counter [k − 1]);

Again, by our analysis of merge, x will precede y. We conclude that Merge Sort is stable.

12.3.4 Quick Sort

One of the most efficient and, therefore, widely used sorting algorithms is Quick Sort, developed by C. A. R. Hoare (1962). The generic algorithm sort, in <algorithm> of the Standard Template Library, has the following interface:

```
// Postcondition: the items in the container, in the range from first through last
//                 − 1, are in ascending order. The averageTime(n) is
//                 O(n log n) and worstTime(n) is O(n * n).
template <class RandomAccessIterator>
void sort (RandomAccessIterator first, RandomAccessIterator last);
```

This version of sort assumes that comparisons between items use **operator**<. There is another version whose third parameter is a function object for comparing items.

The container could be an array, a vector, a deque, or some user-defined container that supports random-access iterators. Basically, the Hewlett-Packard sort method starts by partitioning the items in the range from first through last − 1 into a left subsection and a right subsection such that each item in the left subsection is less than or equal to each item in the right subsection. Finally, the left and right subsections are sorted using Quick Sort. This last statement is easily accomplished with two recursive calls, so we will concentrate on the partitioning phase.

First, we identify a *pivot* item: the item that we will compare with the items in the container in order to partition the container into two segments. The pivot is chosen as the median[2] of the three items: *first, *(first + (last − first) / 2), and *(last − 1).

Example of Quick Sort's Partitioning Suppose we want to partition the following container:

72   56   28   101   47   16   34   19   27   18   92   45   61   39

        ↑   ↑
      first   last

Note that since last − first is 14, the item 19 is *(first + (last − first) / 2). The pivot is 39; that is the median of 72, 19, and 39. We now want to move to the left subsection all the items that are less than or equal to 39 and move to the right subsection all the items that are greater than or equal to 39. Items with a value of 39 may end up in either subsection, and the two subsections need not have the same size.

To accomplish this partitioning, there is a **while** loop that continues until a **return** is made. Within this loop there are two **while** loops. The first of these inner loops increments first until *first is ≥ pivot. Then last is decremented once, and a second inner loop decrements last until *last ≤ pivot. If first ≥ last, first is returned. Otherwise, the items at first and last are swapped, first is incremented, and the outer loop is executed again.

In this example, the first inner loop terminates immediately, with 72 being first's item, because 72 ≥ 39. Then last is decremented once and the second inner loop is entered. This loop also terminates immediately, with 39 being last's item, because 39 ≤ 39. When 72 and 39 are swapped and first is incremented, we have

39   56   28   101   47   16   34   19   27   18   92   45   61   72

          ↑   ↑
        first   last

---

[2]The *median* of three values is the middle value, that is, the value that would be in the middle position if the three values were sorted.

Again, the first inner loop terminates immediately because 56 ≥ 39. Then last is decremented once, and the second inner loop is entered. This loop iterates three times, and ends with *last = 18. After swapping and incrementing first, we have:

During the next two iterations of the outer loop, 101 is swapped with 27 and 47 is swapped with 19. We now have

39 18 28 27 19 16 34 47 101 56 92 45 61 72

first last

During the next iteration of the outer loop, the first inner loop iterates twice, last is decremented, and the second inner loop terminates immediately. Because first ≥ last, the outer loop terminates, and first is returned. The segment is as follows:

39 18 28 27 19 16 34 47 101 56 92 45 61 72

last first

The left subsection consists of the items 39, 18, . . . , 34. The right subsection consists of the items 47, 101, . . . , 72. Notice that every item before first is ≤ 39 and every item at or after first is ≥ 39. Sorting the left subsection using Quick Sort, we have new values for first and last:

39 18 28 27 19 16 34 47

first   last

Note that last is positioned one past the last item in the subsection. The pivot is 34, the median of (39, 27, 34). For the right subsection of the original container, the setup is

47 101 56 92 45 61 72

first   last

Here the pivot is 72, the median of (47, 92, 72). You are asked to complete the second level of partitioning in Exercise 12.10.

The algorithm just described is called __unguarded_partition. Here is the definition of __unguarded_partition:

```
// Precondition: first < last. There is at least one item x and one item y in the
//                range from first through last − 1 such that (pivot < x) is false
//                and (y < pivot) is false.
// Postcondition: for any iterators itr1 and itr2 such that the original value of
//                first <= itr1 and itr2 < the original value of last, if itr1 < final
//                value of first then (pivot < *itr1) is false, and if itr2 >= final
//                value of first then (*itr2 < pivot) is false. The worstTime(n) is
//                O(n).
template <class RandomAccessIterator, class T>
RandomAccessIterator __unguarded_partition(RandomAccessIterator first,
                                            RandomAccessIterator last,
                                                T pivot)

{
    while (1)
    {
        while (*first < pivot)
            ++first;
        --last;
        while (pivot < *last)
            --last;
        if (!(first < last))
            return first;
        iter_swap(first, last);
            ++first;

    }

}
```

Now that we have seen how partitioning works, we can develop the high-level Quick Sort algorithm. The __quick_sort_loop_aux function first determines the pivot and then calls __unguarded_partition. The return value from __unguarded_partition is stored in the RandomAccessIterator cut. The smaller of the two segments (first through cut − 1, cut to last − 1) and then the larger are sorted by Quick Sort. The reason for choosing the smaller segment first is that it can be partitioned fewer times than the larger segment, so the number of activation records on the stack at any time is reduced.

The choosing of the pivot, the call to __unguarded_partition, and the sorting by Quick Sort of the smaller segments take place in a **while** loop that continues until last − first is less than or equal to some threshold. The purpose of the threshold is explained in the section "The Threshold." For now, pretend the threshold is 1, so the loop continues as long as the segment from first to last − 1 has at least two items. Here is the complete __quick_sort_loop_aux algorithm:

```
template <class RandomAccessIterator, class T>
void __quick_sort_loop_aux(RandomAccessIterator first,
```

```
                          RandomAccessIterator last, T*)
{
     while (last − first > __stl_threshold)
     {
          RandomAccessIterator cut = __unguarded_partition (first, last,
                    T(__median(*first, *(first + (last − first)/2), *(last − 1))));
          if (cut − first >= last − cut)
          {
               __quick_sort_loop(cut, last);
               last = cut;
          }
          else
          {
               __quick_sort_loop(first, cut);
               first = cut;
          }
     }
}
```

The __quick_sort_loop algorithm, with parameters first and last, simply gets the type T of the item *first, and then calls __quick_sort_loop_aux, which is templated on T. Here is the definition of __quick_sort_loop:

```
template <class RandomAccessIterator>
inline void __quick_sort_loop(RandomAccessIterator first,
                              RandomAccessIterator last) {
     __quick_sort_loop_aux(first, last, value_type(first));
}
```

Analysis of Quick Sort To analyze the performance of Quick Sort, let's start with the simplifying assumption that a constant, _stl_threshold has the value 1. That is, each segment will be partitioned unless that segment's size is 0 (that is, if first = last) or 1 (if first = last − 1). But that means approximately n partitions are required to sort a container of size n. When we partition a segment into two parts, the number of iterations of the two innermost **while** loops is, approximately, equal to the size of the segment, since each item is compared to the pivot. So the total number of iterations depends on the sizes of the segments that are partitioned.

We can view the effect of a Quick Sort as if it created an imaginary binary search tree, whose root item is the pivot and whose left and right subtrees are the left and right segments. For example, Figure 12.2 shows an example of the full binary search tree induced when Quick Sort is most efficient, that is, when each partition splits its segment into two subsegments that have the same size. We would get such a tree if the items were originally *in order or in reverse order,* because then the pivot of *first, *(first + (last − first)/2), and *(last − 1) would always be *(first + (last − first) / 2).

Since each partition splits its segment into two equal parts, the number of partitioning levels in the tree of Figure 12.2 is equal to its height, floor($\log_2 7$), namely 2. The total number of iterations is, approximately, 14 (that is, $n *$ floor($\log_2 n$), where $n = 7$). For a container size of n, if we get equal-sized subsections for each partition, the number of partitioning levels is approximately $\log_2 n$, and so the total number of iterations is, approximately, $n \log_2 n$.

Contrast the tree in Figure 12.2 with the tree shown in Figure 12.3. The tree in Figure 12.3 represents the partitioning generated, for example, by the following sequence of items:

20 30 40 10 80 50 60 70

The worst case will occur when, during each partition, the pivot is either the next-to-smallest or next-to-largest item. That is what happened for the sequence that generated the tree in Figure 12.3.

In the worst case, the first partition requires about n iterations and produces a segment of size $n - 1$ (and another segment of size 1). When this segment of size $n - 1$ is partitioned, about $n - 1$ iterations are required, and a segment of size $n - 2$

Figure 12.2 I The imaginary binary search tree created by repeated partitions, into equal-sized segments, of a random-access container with seven items.

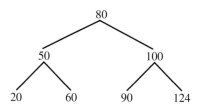

Figure 12.3 I Worst-case partitioning: Each partition reduces by only 1 the size of the segment to be sorted by Quick Sort. The corresponding (imaginary) binary search tree has a leaf at every nonroot level.

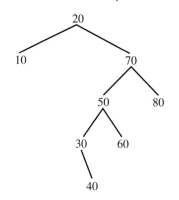

is produced. This process continues until, finally, the larger subsection produced has a size of 1. The total number of iterations is approximately $n + (n - 1) + (n - 2) + \ldots + 1$, which sums to $n(n + 1) / 2$. We conclude that worstTime(n) is quadratic in n. Incidentally, this worst-case behavior is not something that you are likely to run across every day. In Exercise 12.5 you are asked to develop an algorithm to produce the worst case.

We now estimate the average time for Quick Sort. The average is taken over all $n!$ initial arrangements of items in the container. At each level in the imaginary binary search tree that represents the partitioning, about n iterations are required. The number of levels is the average height of that binary search tree. Since the average height of a binary search tree is logarithmic in n, we conclude that the total number of iterations is $O(n \log n)$. That is, averageTime(n) is $O(n \log n)$. By the results in Section 12.2 about how fast we can sort, this must be the smallest upper bound.

The Threshold The machinery of partitioning a segment of two or three items is more time-consuming than sorting them directly. Because of this, Quick Sort is performed on a segment only if its size is greater than some constant, __stl_threshold. In the Hewlett-Packard implementation, the value of this constant is 16, but the appropriate value is machine-dependent.

When the execution of __quick_sort_loop_aux has been completed, the segment of the container from first to last − 1 will not be fully sorted, but will be "semi-sorted." That is, the items in the range from first through last − 1 will consist of k segments for some positive integer k:

first through $itr_1 - 1$, itr1 through $itr_2 - 1$, itr_2 through $itr_3 - 1$, . . . , itr_{k-1} through last − 1

For any j between 1 and $k - 1$, all the items in segment j are less than or equal to all the items in segment j + 1. The size of each segment is at most __stl_threshold.

To achieve these semisorted segments takes $O(n \log n)$ time, on average, because there are approximately $\log_2(n/\_\_stl\_threshold)$ levels of partitioning with about n iterations per level.

"But," you may exclaim, "we're still taking $O(n \log n)$ time on average and we don't even get a sorted list? What's the point?" The point, as we will see when we look at run-times, is that using a threshold is quite a bit faster than not using one, because the Quick Sort machinery is avoided for small segments.

To complete the sorting, we apply Insertion Sort to all the items in the range from first through last − 1. Recall that the time for that algorithm is linear in n for a container that is sorted or nearly so. Specifically, since each semisorted segment has a size less than or equal to __stl_threshold, the number of loop iterations executed by Insertion Sort in sorting such a segment is, approximately, __stl_threshold^2/4. There are at most n segments, and so to sort the items in the range from first through last − 1 this way takes, at most, $n *$ __stl_threshold^2/4 loop iterations, which is linear in n because __stl_threshold is a constant.

Thus averageTime(n) for this improved version of Quick Sort is still $O(n \log n)$, but the actual run-time performance is somewhat faster than if we set __stl_threshold to 1. Note that worstTime(n) will still be quadratic in n.

The space requirements for Quick Sort depend on the number of recursive calls. In the worst case, the number of recursive calls is linear in n, so worstSpace(n) is linear in n. On average, the number of recursive calls is logarithmic in n, so average Space(n) is logarithmic in n.

Quick Sort is not stable. For example, suppose we start with the following:

0 10 10 2 3 4 5 6 7 8 9 10 11 12 13 14 5 6 15

The pivot is 8. During the first partitioning, the 10 at index 1 is swapped with the 6 at index 17 and the 10 at index 2 is swapped with the 5 at index 16. These two 10s are now not in the same relative position that they were originally, and this will remain the case (recall that Insertion Sort *is* stable).

Quick Sort is very fast on average, slow in the worst case, unstable, and not an in-place sort.

To summarize, Quick Sort's worst time is terrible, its space needs are not constant, and it is not a stable sort. All that Quick Sort has going for it, on average, is blazing speed; you will get to witness this in Lab 27.

12.3.5 Divide-and-Conquer Algorithms

Quick Sort is a divide-and-conquer algorithm. Every ***divide-and-conquer*** algorithm has the following characteristics:

- The function consists of at least two recursive calls to the function itself.
- The recursive calls are independent and can be executed in parallel.
- The original task is accomplished by combining the effects of the recursive calls.

Quick Sort is a divide-and-conquer algorithm.

In the case of Quick Sort, the partitioning of the left and right subsections can be done separately, and then the left and right subsections are sorted by Quick Sort. When all subsections have been sorted by Quick Sort, Insertion Sort is called to put the original container in order. So the requirements of a divide-and-conquer algorithm are met.

How does a divide-and-conquer algorithm differ from an arbitrary recursive algorithm that includes two recursive calls? The difference is that, for an arbitrary recursive algorithm, the recursive calls need not be independent. For example, in the Towers of Hanoi problem, $n - 1$ disks had to be moved from the source to the temporary pole *before* the same $n - 1$ disks could be moved from the temporary pole to the destination. Note that the original Fibonacci function from Lab 9 was a divide-and-conquer algorithm, but the fact that the two function calls were independent was an indication of the function's gross inefficiency.

Lab 27 has run-time experiments for all the fast sort algorithms in this chapter.

LAB **Lab 27: Run-times for sorting algorithms.**

(All Labs Are Optional.) **LAB**

SUMMARY

This chapter covered five comparison-based sort methods. Insertion Sort can be used only for containers that support random-access iterators (such as arrays, vectors, and deques) and takes only linear in n time for a container that is in increasing order, or nearly so. Insertion Sort is not directly available (and its averageTime(n) is quadratic in n), but it is part of the generic sort algorithm.

For comparison-based sorts, worstTime(n) can be no faster than $O(n \log n)$, and averageTime(n) can be no faster than $O(n \log n)$.

The Tree Sort algorithm repeatedly inserts items into a multiset container; worstTime(n) is $O(n \log n)$. For the sort_heap algorithm, worstTime(n) is also $O(n \log n)$. Merge Sort, the sort method for the list class, also takes $O(n \log n)$ time in the worst case. For all three of these sort algorithms, averageTime(n) is therefore $O(n \log n)$, and all these upper bounds are minimal.

Quick Sort, the generic sort algorithm, can be applied only to containers—such as arrays, vectors, and deques—that support random-access iterators. The algorithm starts by partitioning the segment first through last − 1 into a left segment and a right segment such that each item in the left segment is less than or equal to each item in the right segment. The left and right segments are themselves partitioned, and this process continues as long as the size of a segment is at least 16. Finally, a version of Insertion Sort is called to complete the sorting. Although the sort takes quadratic time in the worst case, averageTime(n) is only $O(n \log n)$.

Table 12.1 provides a thumbnail sketch of the sort algorithms presented in this chapter.

EXERCISES

12.1 Trace the execution of each of the sort methods given in Table 12.1 with the following sequence of values:

10 90 45 82 71 96 82 50 33 43 67

Use a threshold of 1 for Quick Sort.

Table 12.1 | Important features of the sort algorithms

Sort algorithm	averageTime(n)	worstTime(n)	Run-time rank	Stable?
Insertion sort	$O(n^2)$	$O(n^2)$	5	Yes
Tree sort	$O(n \log n)$	$O(n \log n)$	3	Yes
Heap sort	$O(n \log n)$	$O(n \log n)$	2	No
Merge sort	$O(n \log n)$	$O(n \log n)$	4	Yes
Quick sort	$O(n \log n)$	$O(n^2)$	1	No

*Run-time rank is based on the time to sort n randomly generated integers. See Lab 27 for details.

12.2 a. For each sort method, rearrange the list of values in Exercise 12.1 so that the minimum number of item comparisons would be required to sort the container.

   b. For each sort method, rearrange the list of values in Exercise 12.1 so that the maximum number of item comparisons would be required to sort the container.

12.3 Suppose we sort a collection of items by inserting them into an initially empty BinSearchTree container. Estimate worstTime(n) and average Time(n).

12.4 For which sort algorithms from this chapter do the averageTime(n) and worstTime(n) have the same Big-O estimate?

12.5 Develop an algorithm to arrange the integers $0 \ldots n - 1$ in a container so that Quick Sort will require quadratic time to sort the container.

Hint   In order to get the worst time, each partition should produce a segment with just one item, either the smallest or largest item in the segment. One way to get this is to put the items in order except that the middle two items will be the smallest and largest items. For example, if the numbers are $0 \ldots 9$, we start with

$$1, 2, 3, 4, 0, 9, 5, 6, 7, 8$$

Note that when each partition is performed, the pivot is either the next-to-smallest item or the next-to-largest item. So each partition will produce a segment of size 1.

12.6 a. Suppose we have a sort algorithm whose averageTime(n) is $O(n \log n)$, and assume that this is the smallest upper bound. For example, any of the fast sorts in this chapter would qualify as such an algorithm. Recall from Lab 16 that runTime(n) then represents the time for the implementation of the algorithm to sort n random integers on a particular computer system. So we can write:

$$\text{runTime}(n) \approx k(c) \, n \log_c n \quad \text{seconds}$$

where c is an integer variable and k is a function whose value depends on c. Show that runTime(cn) $\approx$ runTime(n)$(c + c / \log_c n)$.

   b. Use the technique in Exercise 12.6a to estimate runTime(200,000) if runTime(100,000) = 10 seconds.

12.7 Show that the average number of **while**-loop iterations needed in Insertion Sort is

$$n(n - 1)/4$$

Hint First show that for k in $[1 \ldots n]$, the average number of **while**-loop iterations needed to insert the kth item is $(k-1)/2$. (The first item inserted corresponds to $k = 1$; there is no "zeroth" item.)

12.8 Show that $O(\log n!) = O(n \log n)$.

Hint

$$n! = \prod_{i=1}^{n} i \le \prod_{i=1}^{n} n = n^n$$

(Product notation is explained in Section A1.3.) Also,

$$n! = \prod_{i=1}^{n} i \ge \prod_{i=1}^{n/2} (n/2) = (n/2)^{n/2}$$

So $(n/2)^{n/2} \le n! \le n^n$
    Now take logs.

12.9 Show how seven comparisons are sufficient to sort any list of five items.

Hint Compare the first and second items. Compare the third and fourth items. Compare the two larger items from the earlier comparisons. With three comparisons, we have an ordered chain of three items, with the fourth item less than (or equal to) one of the items in the chain. Now compare the fifth item to the middle item in the chain. Complete the sorting in three more comparisons. Note that $\log_2(5!) > 6$, so six comparisons are not sufficient to sort every list of five items.

12.10 For Quick Sort, complete the second level of partitioning of the following container; after the first level of partitioning, we have

39 18 28 27 19 16 34 47 101 56 92 45 61 72

↑ ↑

last first

Assume that the threshold is 1.

12.11 Given a container (such as an array, vector, or deque) that supports random-access iterators, the generic algorithm nth_element will partition the items in the range from iterators first through last − 1. The algorithm's interface is

```
// Postcondition: for any iterators itr1 and itr2 such that first <= itr1, itr2 <
//                last, if itr1 <= position, then !(*position < *itr1) and if
//                position <= itr2, then !(*itr2 < *position).
```

```
template<class RandomAccessIterator>
void nth_element (RandomAccessIterator first,
                  RandomAccessIterator position,
                  RandomAccessIterator last);
```

For example, suppose v is a vector container of **int** items. We can print out the median of all the items in v as follows:

```
vector<int>::iterator mid_itr = v.begin( ) + (v.end( ) − v.begin( )) / 2;
nth_element (v.begin( ), mid_itr, v.end( ));
cout << *mid_itr << endl;
```

The Hewlett-Packard implementation is a wrapper function that starts by calling a helper algorithm to identify the type of the item *first. Here is the definition of nth_element and the helper algorithm:

```
template <class RandomAccessIterator>
inline void nth_element(RandomAccessIterator first,
                        RandomAccessIterator nth,
                        RandomAccessIterator last)
{
      __nth_element(first, nth, last, value_type(first));
}


template <class RandomAccessIterator, class T>
void __nth_element(RandomAccessIterator first,
                   RandomAccessIterator nth,
                   RandomAccessIterator last, T*)
{
      while (last − first > 3)
      {
            RandomAccessIterator cut = __unguarded_partition
                  (first, last,
                      T(__median(*first, *(first + (last − first)/2), *(last − 1))));
            if (cut <= nth)
                  first = cut;
            else
                  last = cut;
      }
      __insertion_sort(first, last);
}
```

Estimate averageTime(n) and worstTime(n). Develop run-time tests to support your estimates.

12.12 The simplest of all sort algorithms is Selection Sort. We assume the container that supports random-access iterators—we could get by with just bidirectional iterators. To sort the items from positions first (inclusive) to last (exclusive), swap the smallest item with the item at position first, swap the second smallest item with the item at position first + 1, and so on. Here is the method interface:

```
// Postcondition: the items from first (inclusive) to last (exclusive) are in
//                 ascending order. The worstTime(n) is O(n * n).
template<class RandomAccessIterator>
void selection_sort (RandomAccessIterator first, RandomAccessIterator last);
```

Example   Suppose the container consists of the following values:

> 59 46 32 80 46 55 87 43 70 81

First, loop from first through last − 1 to find the position of the smallest item, 32, at position first + 2. We swap 32 with 59; the container is now

> 32 46 59 80 46 55 87 43 70 81

Second, loop from first + 1 through last − 1 to find the position of the next smallest item, 43, at position first + 7. We swap 43 with *(first + 1). The container is now

> 32 43 59 80 46 55 87 46 70 81

During the next loop, the item at position first + 2 (namely, 59) is swapped with the item at position first + 4 (namely, 46). The container is now

> 32 43 46 80 59 55 87 46 70 81

And so on.

Implement Selection Sort, and provide estimates of worstTime(*n*) and averageTime(*n*).

12.13 One of the well-known, but terribly inefficient, sort algorithms is Bubble Sort. We start with a container that supports random-access iterators—we could get by with just bidirectional iterators. For the first loop iteration, there is a nested loop that compares each item to the item in the next higher position, swapping where necessary. The second (outer-loop) iteration starts back at the beginning, and the inner loop compares and swaps items. Continue until the container is sorted. To avoid needless comparisons, the inner loop goes only as far as the last interchange from the previous iteration of the outer loop. Here is the method interface:

// Postcondition: the items from first (inclusive) to last (exclusive) are in
//   ascending order. The worstTime(n) is O(n * n).
template<**class** RandomAccessIterator>
void bubble_sort (RandomAccessIterator first, RandomAccessIterator last);

Example   Suppose the container consists of the following:

$$59\ 46\ 32\ 80\ 46\ 55\ 87\ 43\ 70\ 81$$

After the first iteration of the outer loop, we have

$$46\ 32\ 59\ 46\ 55\ 80\ 43\ 70\ 81\ 87$$

At this point, all that is guaranteed is that the largest item is at the last index in the container. In the second iteration of the outer loop, the comparing and swapping continues only until 80 is swapped with 70:

$$32\ 46\ 46\ 55\ 59\ 43\ 70\ 80\ 81\ 87$$

In the third iteration of the outer loop, the only swap is of 43 and 59, and the inner loop stops when 59 is found to be less than 70.

$$32\ 46\ 46\ 55\ 43\ 59\ 70\ 80\ 81\ 87$$

After three more outer-loop iterations, the array is sorted:

$$32\ 43\ 46\ 46\ 55\ 59\ 70\ 80\ 81\ 87$$

Implement Bubble Sort. Incidentally, the average number of inner-loop iterations, as you probably would have guessed, is

$$\frac{n^2 - n}{2} - \frac{(n+1)\ln(n+1)}{2} + \frac{n+1}{2}\left(\ln 2 + \lim_{k \to \infty}\left(\sum_{i=1}^{k}\frac{1}{i} - \ln k\right)\right)$$
$$+ (2/3)\sqrt{2\pi(n+1)} + 31/36 + \text{some terms in } O(n^{-1/2})$$

As Knuth (1973) says, "In short, the bubble sort seems to have nothing going for it, except a catchy name and the fact that it leads to some interesting theoretical problems."

12.14 Radix Sort is "radically" different from the other sorts presented in this chapter. The sorting is based on the internal representation of the items to be sorted, not on comparisons between items. For this reason, the restriction that worstTime(n) can be no better than $O(n \log n)$ no longer applies. And in fact, Radix Sort is the basis for an algorithm whose worstTime(n) is $O(n \log \log n)$ (see Andersson, 1995).

   Radix Sort was widely used on electromechanical punched-card sorters that appear in old FBI movies. The interested reader may consult Shaffer (1998).

Suppose we want to sort a container, from the positions of iterators first to last − 1, that supports random-access iterators. For the sake of simplicity, we start with each item being a nonnegative integer of at most two decimal digits. The representation is in base 10, also referred to as radix 10, and this is how Radix Sort gets its name. In addition to the container to be sorted, we also have an array, lists, of 10 list containers, with one linked list for each of the ten possible digit values.

During the first outer-loop iteration, each item in the container is appended to the linked list corresponding to the item's one's digit (the least-significant digit). Then, starting at the beginning of each list, the items in lists [0], lists [1], and so on are stored back in the original container. This overwrites the original container. In the second outer-loop iteration, each item in the container is appended to the linked list corresponding to the item's ten's digit. Then, starting at the beginning of each list, the items in lists [0], lists [1], and so on are stored back in the original container. Here is the method interface:

```
// Precondition: the items are integers.
// Postcondition: the items from first (inclusive) to last (exclusive) are in
//                ascending order. For worstTime(n), see note below.
template<class RandomAccessIterator>
void radix_sort (RandomAccessIterator first, RandomAccessIterator last);
```

Example Suppose we start with the following container:

85 3 19 43 20 55 42 21 91 85 73 29

Each of these is appended to the linked list corresponding to its rightmost digit. (Conceptually, it is simpler to view each linked list as singly linked and NULL terminated, instead of doubly linked with a header.) The array of linked lists will be as follows:

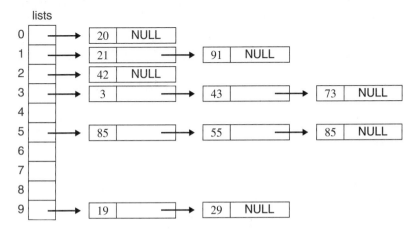

Then, starting at the beginning of each list, the items in lists [0], lists [1], and so on are stored back in the container:

20 21 91 42 3 43 73 85 55 85 19 29

In the next outer-loop iteration, each item in the container is appended to the list that corresponds to the item's ten's digit:

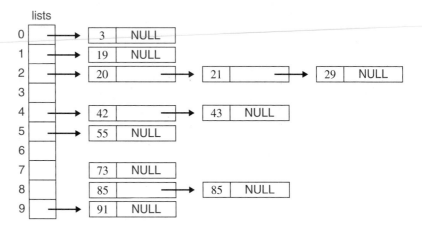

Finally (because the integers had at most two digits), starting at the beginning of each list, the integers in lists [0], lists [1], and so on are stored back in the container, which is now sorted:

3 19 20 21 29 42 43 55 73 85 85 91

Implement Radix Sort for any container of nonnegative **int** items. Suppose N is the largest integer in the container. The number of outer-loop iterations is at least ceil($\log_{10} N$), so worstTime(n, N) is $O(n \log N)$.

Note   The items in Radix Sort are integers, but with a slight change, the item type could instead be string, for example. Then there would be one list for each character in the string class.

PROGRAMMING PROJECT 12.1

Sorting a File

Sort a file into ascending order.

ANALYSIS

The input line will contain the path to the file to be sorted. Each item in the file will consist of a name—last name followed by a blank followed by first name followed by a blank followed by middle name—and social security number. The file is to be sorted by name; equal names should be ordered by social security number. For example, after sorting, part of the file might be as follows:

> Jones Jennifer Mary 222222222
>
> Jones Jennifer Mary 644644644

For convenience, you may assume that each name will have a middle name. Suppose the file persons.dat consists of the following:

Kiriyeva Marina Alice	333333333
Johnson Kevin Michael	555555555
Misino John Michael	444444444
Panchenko Eric Sam	888888888
Taoubina Xenia Barbara	111111111
Johnson Kevin Michael	222222222
Deusenbery Amanda May	777777777
Dunn Michael Holmes	999999999
Reiley Timothy Patrick	666666666

System Test 1

Please enter the path for the file to be sorted.
persons.dat
The file persons.dat has been sorted. Please close this output window when you are
ready.
The file persons.dat will now consist of

Deusenbery Amanda May	777777777
Dunn Michael Holmes	999999999
Johnson Kevin Michael	222222222
Johnson Kevin Michael	555555555
Kiriyeva Marina Alice	333333333
Misino John Michael	444444444
Panchenko Eric Sam	888888888
Reiley Timothy Patrick	666666666
Taoubina Xenia Barbara	111111111

(continued on next page)

(continued from previous page)

For a larger system test, randomly generated, use the same name for each person. The social security numbers will be randomly generated **int** items in the range 0 . . . 32,767. For example, part of the file might have

a a a 9736
a a a 5917
a a a 8476

Hint   This would be a fairly simple problem if we could be certain that the entire file would fit in main memory. Unfortunately, this is not the case. Suppose we want to sort a large file of objects from the class Person. For specificity, we assume that an object in the Person class occupies 50 bytes and that the maximum storage for an array is 500,000 bytes. So the maximum size of an array of Persons is 10,000.

We start by reading the file of persons, in blocks of 10,000 persons each, into an array (or vector). Each block is sorted by Heap Sort and stored, in an alternating fashion, on one of two temporary files: leftTop and leftBottom. Figure 12.4 illustrates the effect of this first stage in file sorting.

We then go through an alternating process that continues until all the items are sorted and in a single file. The temporary files used are leftTop, leftBottom, and right Bottom; personsFile itself plays the role of rightTop. At each stage, we merge two blocks from a top and bottom pair of files, with the resulting double-sized blocks stored alternately on the other top and bottom pair. The code for merging sorted blocks in two files into sorted, double-sized blocks in another file is essentially what was done—using lists instead of file blocks—in the merge method. Figure 12.5 illustrates the first merge pass.

Figure 12.4 | The first stage in file sorting: each of the unsorted blocks in personsFile is inserted into an array, sorted by Heap Sort, and stored in leftTop or leftBottom.

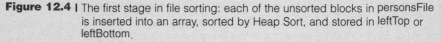
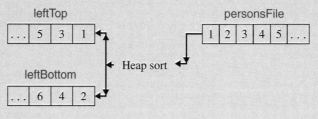

If rightBottom is still empty after a left-to-right merge, then the sort is complete and personsFile holds the sorted file. Otherwise a right-to-left merge is performed, after which we check to see if leftBottom is still empty. If so, leftTop is copied onto persons File and the sort is complete.

How much time will this take? Suppose that we have n items in n/k blocks, each of size k. In the Heap Sort phase, creating each of the n/k sorted blocks takes, roughly, $k \log_2 k$ time, on average. Each merge phase takes about n iterations, and there are about $\log_2 (n/k)$ merge phases. The total time is the sum of the times for all phases: roughly,

$$
\begin{aligned}
(n/k)\, k \log_2 k + n \log_2(n/k) &= n \log_2 k + n \log_2(n/k) \\
&= n \log_2 k + n \log_2 n - n \log_2 k \\
&= n \log_2 n
\end{aligned}
$$

Because the averageTime(n) is optimal, namely $O(n \log n)$, a sorting method such as this is often used for a system sort utility.

Figure 12.5 | The first merge pass in file sorting. The files leftTop and leftBottom contain sorted blocks, and personsFile and rightBottom contain double-sized sorted blocks.

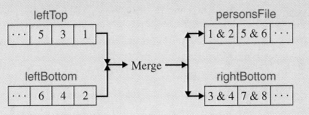
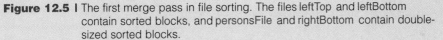

CHAPTER 13

Searching and
the Hash Classes

In Chapter 12 we designed several sorting algorithms. We now present a parallel
study of searching. We will start by summarizing some simple search algorithms
as a prelude to the introduction of a new class: hash_map. This class is not yet
included in the Standard Template Library. But hash maps are extremely useful in
certain applications, such as creating a symbol table. Basically, for the insert, find,
and erase methods, the average time is constant! This remarkable performance is
due to a special technique called *hashing*. ■

CHAPTER OBJECTIVES

1. Understand how hashing works, when it should be used, and when it should
   not be used.

2. Explain the significance of the Uniform Hashing Assumption.

3. Compare the various collision handlers: chaining, offset-of-1, quotient-offset.

13.1 | A FRAMEWORK TO ANALYZE SEARCHING

Before we start looking at search methods, we need a framework for analyzing them. Because the search may be successful or unsuccessful, the analysis of search methods should include both possibilities. For each search method we estimate average $\text{Time}_S(n)$, the average time—over all n items in the collection—of a successful search. We make the simplifying assumption that each item in the container is equally likely to be sought.

We will also be interested in $\text{worstTime}_S(n)$, the largest number of statements needed to successfully search for an item. That is, for a given value of n, we look at all permutations of the n items and all possible choices of the item to be successfully sought. For each permutation and item, we determine the number of iterations (or recursive calls) to find that item. Then $\text{worstTime}_S(n)$ corresponds to the largest number of iterations attained.

We also estimate $\text{averageTime}_U(n)$, the average time of an unsuccessful search, and $\text{worstTime}_U(n)$. For an unsuccessful search, we assume that on average, every possible failure is equally likely. For example, in an unsuccessful search of an ordered container of n items, there are $n + 1$ possibilities for where the given item can occur:

> Before the first item in the container
> Between the first and second items
> Between the second and third items
> .
> .
> .
> Between the $(n - 1)$st and nth items
> After the nth item

Section 13.2 reviews the search methods employed up to this point.

13.2 | REVIEW OF SEARCHING

Up to this point, we have seen three different kinds of searches: sequential search, binary search, and tree-oriented search. Let's look at each one in turn.

13.2.1 Sequential Search

The generic search algorithm find has the following interface:

```
// Postcondition: if there is an item in the range of iterators from first
//                 (inclusive) through last (exclusive) that is equal to value, the
//                 iterator returned is the first iterator i in that range such that *i
//                 = value. Otherwise, last is returned. worstTime(n) is O(n).
template <class InputIterator, class T>
InputIterator find(InputIterator first, InputIterator last, const T& value);
```

And here is the Hewlett-Packard implementation:

```
template <class InputIterator, class T>
InputIterator find(InputIterator first, InputIterator last, const T& value)
{
       while (first != last && *first != value)
              ++first;
       return first;

}
```

The find algorithm conducts a ***sequential search*** over a range of iterators, from first (inclusive) to last (exclusive). The items *first, *++first, and so on are compared to the value sought until either the value has been found or it is certain that no iterator in the range is positioned at the value. Because the items are accessed linearly, find can be used with any container class that supports forward iterators, that is, with any container class we have seen so far except for the container adaptors.

In searching a container, we assume that each item is equally likely to be sought. So the average number of loop iterations (or recursive calls) is approximately $n / 2$. Thus averageTime$_S(n)$ is linear in n. In the worst case, the last item in the container is the one sought, so n iterations are made, and worstTime$_S(n)$ is still linear in n.

For an unsuccessful search, find must access all n items before concluding that the given item is not in the container, so averageTime$_U(n)$ and worstTime$_U(n)$ are both linear in n.

For a sequential search, whether successful or unsuccessful, the average and worst times are linear in n.

13.2.2 Binary Search

Sometimes we know beforehand that the container is sorted. For sorted items, we can call the generic algorithm binary_search, so called because the size of the segment searched is repeatedly divided by 2. Here, repeated from Lab 10, is the Hewlett-Packard implementation of that algorithm (items sorted by **operator<**):

```
template <class ForwardIterator, class T>
inline bool binary_search (ForwardIterator first,
                           ForwardIterator last,
                           const T& value)
{
       ForwardIterator i = lower_bound(first, last, value);
       return i != last && !(value < *i);
}
```

Recall that generic algorithm lower_bound returns an iterator positioned at the first location in the container where item could be stored without disordering the sequence. The lower_bound algorithm calls one of two auxiliary algorithms, both named __lower_bound, but with a different parameter depending on whether the iterators are random-access iterators or merely forward iterators. Here is the version with random-access iterators:

```
template <class RandomAccessIterator, class T, class Distance>
RandomAccessIterator __lower_bound (RandomAccessIterator first,
                                    RandomAccessIterator last,
                                    const T& value,
                                    Distance*,
                                    random_access_iterator_tag)
{
        Distance len = last − first;
        Distance half;
        RandomAccessIterator middle;

        while (len > 0)
        {
                half = len / 2;
                middle = first + half;
                if (*middle < value)
                {
                        first = middle + 1;
                        len = len − half − 1;
                }
                else
                        len = half;
        }
        return first;
}
```

Before we analyze the binary_search algorithm, note that it returns a **bool** value, not an iterator, so binary_search should be used if all you want to know is *whether* the item is in the sequence. If you want to know *where* the item is or could be inserted, you should call lower_bound directly.

For a binary search, whether successful or unsuccessful, the average and worst times are logarithmic in n.

For a container that supports random-access iterators (such as an array, vector, or deque), binary_search is much faster than the generic algorithm find. For either a successful or unsuccessful search, the **while** loop in __lower_bound will continue until len = 0. Let n represent the distance between first and last. Since len starts out with the value of n, the number of loop iterations will be the number of times n can be divided by 2 until $n = 0$, and that number is, approximately, $\log_2 n$. So we get averageTime$_S(n)$ = worstTime$_S(n)$ = averageTime$_U(n)$ = worstTime$_U(n)$, which is logarithmic in n.

Recall, from Lab 10, why the **while** loop in __lower_bound was not designed to stop if a match is found. The reason is efficiency. To put in an extra comparison to test for a match would take longer unless the search is successful and the sought item is found in an early iteration.

The version of the __lower_bound algorithm that assumes the iterators are merely forward iterators is virtually identical to the version with random-access iterators, except that the line middle = first + half;

is replaced with

middle = first;
advance(middle, half);

The advance algorithm, in iterator.h, has a loop executed half times in which middle is incremented (by one) during each iteration. This version of __lower_bound takes linear time in both successful and unsuccessful, average and worst cases.

13.2.3 Red-Black Trees

Red-black trees were introduced in Chapter 10. The find method (as opposed to the find generic algorithm) in the rb_tree class is quite similar to the __lower_bound generic algorithm. Here is the find *method:*

```
iterator find(const Key& k)
{
        link_type y = header; /* Last node that is not less than k. */
        link_type x = root( ); /* Current node. */

        while (x != NIL)
                if (!key_compare(key(x), k))
                        y = x, x = left(x); // legal: the comma operator
                else
                        x = right(x);
        iterator j = iterator(y);
        return (j == end( ) || key_compare(k, key(j.node))) ? end( ) : j;
}
```

As with the __lower_bound generic algorithm, not having a special test for a match is more efficient. The height of a red-black tree *t* is logarithmic in *n,* and the find method always iterates from the root to a leaf. The distance from the root to any leaf in *t* is at least height(*t*) / 2. So for the find method in the rb_tree class, we get averageTime$_S$(*n*) = worstTime$_S$(*n*) = averageTime$_U$(*n*) = worstTime$_U$(*n*), which is logarithmic in *n*.

For a red-black-tree search, whether successful or unsuccessful, the average and worst times are logarithmic in n.

We will devote the rest of this chapter to the hash_map class. Except for the time estimates in the postconditions, the method interfaces of the hash_map class are virtually indistinguishable from those of the map class in Chapter 10.

13.3 I THE hash_map CLASS

In this section we outline the user interface for the hash_map class, which is not yet part of the Standard Template Library. Recall that a *key* is that part of an item by which the item can be accessed. The hash_map class is templated and, just as in the map class, two of the template parameters are Key and T. Each value is a pair whose first component is of type Key and whose second component is of type T. No two values in a hash_map container can have the same key, and keys are compared according to the equality operator, **operator**==.

   Instead of providing a production-strength version of the hash_map class, we will settle for a bare-bones version (augmented only by the beautiful associative-array operator, **operator**[ ]). That will allow more discussion of the essential features. From a user's point of view, a hash_map is indistinguishable from a map except for the time estimates. Basically, for searching, inserting, and deleting in a hash_map, averageTime(*n*) is constant!

   Here are the method interfaces:

1. // Postcondition: this hash_map is empty.
    hash_map( );

2. // Postcondition: the number of items in this hash_map has been returned.
    int size( );

3. // Postcondition: If an item with x's key had already been inserted into this
    //   hash_map, the pair returned consists of an iterator positioned
    //   at the previously inserted item, and false. Otherwise, the pair
    //   returned consists of an iterator positioned at the newly
    //   inserted item, and true. Timing estimates are discussed in
    //   Section 13.3.6.
    pair<iterator, **bool**> insert (**const** value_type<**const** key_type, T>& x);

4. // Postcondition: if this hash_map already contains a value whose key part is
    //   key, a reference to that value's second component has been
    //   returned. Otherwise, a new value, <key T( )>. is inserted into
    //   this map. Timing estimates are discussed in Section 13.3.6.
    T& **operator**[ ] (**const** key_type& key);

5. // Postcondition: if this hash_map contains a value whose key component is
    //   key, an iterator positioned at that value has been returned.
    //   Otherwise, an iterator with the same value as end( ) has
    //   been returned. Timing estimates are discussed in Section
    //   13.3.6.
    iterator find (**const** key_type& key);

6. // Precondition: itr is positioned at value in this hash_map.
    // Postcondition: the value that itr is positioned at has been deleted from
    //   this hash_map. Timing estimates are discussed in Section
    /   13.3.6.
    void erase (iterator itr);

7. // Postcondition: an iterator positioned at the beginning of this hash_map has
    //   been returned. Timing estimates are discussed in Section
    //   13.3.6.
    iterator begin( );

8. // Postcondition: an iterator has been returned that can be used in comparisons
    //   to terminate iterating through this hash_map.
    iterator end( );

9. // Postcondition: the space for this hash_map object has been deallocated.
~hash_map( );

For the sake of simplicity, the associated iterators are forward iterators. The only operators are (postincrement) **operator++ (int)**, **operator***, **operator==**, and **operator!=**. Those are all we need to iterate through a container.

13.3.1 Fields in the hash_map Class

In trying to determine the fields for the hash_map class, you might at first be tempted to bring back a linked or contiguous representation from a previous chapter. But if the items are unordered, we will need sequential searches, and these take linear time, on average. Even if the items are ordered and we utilize that ordering, the best we can get is logarithmic average time for searches.

The rest of this chapter is devoted to showing how, through the miracle of hashing, we can achieve searches—and insertions and deletions—in constant average time. Once we have defined what hashing is and how it works, the definitions of the hash_map methods will be relatively easy.

13.3.2 Hashing

For starters, let's look at a contiguous implementation with the following two fields:

buckets: an array of values

count: the number of values in the hash_map container

We first present a hypersimple example and then move on to something more realistic. Suppose that the array is initialized to hold 1000 items—that is, values—and each item consists of a three-digit key component that holds an identification (ID) number and a string component that holds a name. If the constructor for the hash_map class is called, we would have the state shown in Figure 13.1.

Figure 13.1 I The design representation of an empty hash_map container.

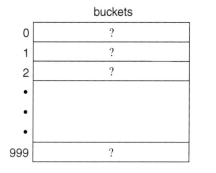

At what index should we store the value whose key component is 251? An obvious choice is index 251. There are several advantages:

1. The value can be directly inserted into the array without accessing any other values.
2. Subsequent searches for the value can be made by accessing only location 251.
3. The value can be deleted directly, without first accessing other values.

Figure 13.2 shows what the hash_map container might look like after three values, with keys 251, 118, and 335, have been inserted; we ignore the string components for now because they are irrelevant to this discussion.

So far, this is no big deal. Now, for a slightly different application, suppose that the array buckets will still hold up to 1000 items, but each item has a social security number as the key. We need to transform the key into an index in the array, and we want this transformation to be accomplished quickly, that is, with few loop iterations.

Figure 13.2 I The hash_map container of Figure 13.1 after three items have been inserted. Only the key fields are shown.

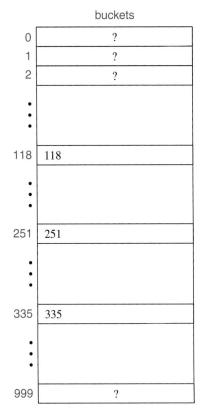

To allow fast access, we take the rightmost three digits of a social security number and store the item at the location whose index is that three-digit number. For example, the item with a key of 214-30-3261 (the hyphens are for readability only) would be stored at index 261. Similarly, the item with a key value of 033-51-8000 would be stored at location 0. Figure 13.3 shows the resulting hash_map container after these two insertions.

You might already have noticed a potential pitfall with this scheme: Two distinct keys might have the same rightmost three digits, for example, 214-30-3261 and 814-02-9261. When two distinct keys yield the same table index, this is called a **collision,** and the colliding keys are called **synonyms.** We will deal with collisions shortly. For now we simply acknowledge that the possibility of collisions always exists when the size of the key space, that is, the number of legal key values, is larger than the size of the index space, the number of locations available.

A **collision** *occurs when two distinct keys generate the same index.*

Hashing is the process of transforming a key into a table index. The transformation starts with a **hash function:** some easily computable operation on the key that returns an **unsigned long,** which is then converted into an index in the array buckets. The other ingredient in hashing is the collision handler.

Hashing *is the process of transforming a key into a table index.*

Figure 13.3 I A hash_map container with two items. The key is a social security number. The string component representing a name is omitted.

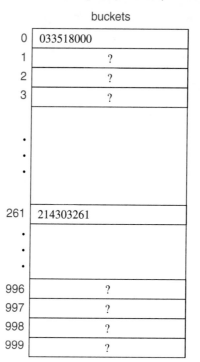

The term *hashing* suggests that we scramble up the key in some way; in other words, that we *make hash* out of the key. No matter how successfully we hash the keys, collisions may still occur, so we must deal with them as part of our hashing algorithm. We will investigate a simple but effective and quite efficient collision handler: chaining.

13.3.3 Chaining

One way to resolve collisions is to store at each bucket entry the *linked list* of all items whose keys hashed to that index in the array buckets. The declaration of the hash_map class starts out as follows:

```
template<class Key, class T, class HashFunc>
class hash_map
{
        typedef Key key_type;
        typedef HashFunc hash_func;
```

The template argument corresponding to the third template parameter is a function class, that is, a class in which the function-call operator, **operator( )**, is overloaded. The heading for this overloaded operator is

unsigned long operator( ) (const key_type& key)

For example, if each key is an **int,** we can define the following, simple function class:

```
class hash_func
{
        public:
                unsigned long operator( ) (const int& key)
                {
                        return (unsigned long)key;
                } // overloaded operator( )
} // class hash_func
```

Before we go any further, here is a simple program that uses a hash_map container to store some students' six-digit ID numbers and first names.

```
#include <iostream>
#include <string>
#include "hash_map1.h"

class hash_func
{
        public:
                unsigned long operator( ) (const int& key)
                {
```

```
                    return (unsigned long)key;
            } // operator( )
}; // class hash_func

int main( ) {

        typedef hash_map <int, string, hash_func> hash_map_class;

        const string CLOSE_WINDOW_PROMPT =
                "Please press the Enter key to close this output window.";

        hash_map_class students;
        hash_map_class::iterator itr;

        value_type<const int, string> student(555555, "Mike");
        students.insert (student);

        students.insert (value_type<const int, string> (333333, "Alan"));

        students [111111] = "Bob";

        cout << "size = " << students.size( ) << endl;
        for (itr = students.begin( ); itr != students.end( ); itr++)
            cout << (*itr).first << " " << (*itr).second << endl;
        cout << "looking for " << 333333 << endl;
        itr = students.find (333333);
        if (itr == students.end( ))
            cout << "not found " << endl;
        else
            cout << "found " << (*itr).first << endl;

        cout << "looking for " << 222222 << endl;
        itr = students.find (222222);
        if (itr == students.end( ))
            cout << "not found " << endl;
        else
            cout << "found " << (*itr).first << endl;

        for (int i = 0; i < 500; i++) // ids: 000000, 000001, 000002, . . .
            students [i] = "";

        cout << "size = " << students.size( ) << endl;

        cout << "removing 111111" << endl;
        students.erase (students.find (111111));

        cout << "size = " << students.size( ) << endl;
        if (students.find (111111) == students.end( ))
            cout << "111111 not in map" << endl;
        else
            cout << "oops, 111111 found in map" << endl;
```

```
    if (students.find (444444) == students.end( ))
          cout << "444444 not in map" << endl;
    else
          cout << "oops, 444444 found in map" << endl;
    cout << endl << CLOSE_WINDOW_PROMPT;
    cin.get( );

    return 0;
}
```

The output from this program is

```
size = 3
555555 Mike
111111 Bob
333333 Alan
looking for 333333
found 333333 Alan
looking for 222222
not found
size = 503
removing 111111
size = 502
111111 not in map
444444 not in map
Please press the Enter key to close this output window.
```

We now resume the design of the hash_map class. We will store at each index in the array buckets the list of all items whose keys hash to that index. The fields for this design—known as *chained hashing*—are

```
list <value_type<const key_type, T> >*  buckets; // at each index in the
                                                 // array buckets, we will
                                                 // store the list of all items
                                                 // whose keys hashed
                                                 // to that index
int count,       // number of items in this hash_map
    length;      // number of buckets in this hash_map
hash_func hash;  // hash is a function object
```

The items in each list form a chain, and that is where the term *chaining* comes from. Each list object is referred to as a *bucket,* and each item is stored in a list-class node. Recall, from Chapter 6, that each node has data (that is, item), prev, and next fields. The prev field is irrelevant in the hash_map class, so we will pretend that each node consists of an item field and a next field.

To see how chained hashing works, consider the problem of storing up to 1000 items with social security numbers as keys. Each item—that is, value—consists of a key plus a name. Since each key is an **int,** the message hash (key) simply returns the key itself, so the index is key % 1000. Initially, each location would contain an empty list. Figure 13.4 shows what we would have after applying

buckets [hash (key) % 1000].push_back (value);

to insert the values with the following keys:

    214-30-3261
    033-51-8000
    214-19-9528
    819-02-9528
    819-02-9261
    033-30-8262
    215-09-1766
    214-17-0261

  To avoid cluttering up Figure 13.4, the contents of each bucket are abbreviated. Strictly speaking, each bucket contains a list object, so each bucket includes the fields in the list class, such as __node, __length, __last, and __next_avail. All that is shown in each bucket of Figure 13.4 is __node-> next, which points to the first node in the list. And we pretend that each list is NULL-terminated.

Figure 13.4 I A chained hash_map container to which eight items have been posted. Each item is a <key, name> pair. The name field is omitted from this figure.

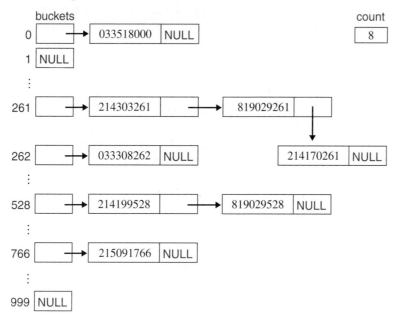

To gain a better insight into some implementation issues, we consider the situation when key_type is not an integer type. For example, suppose each key is a string object of up to 20 characters. Here is a first attempt at a hash_func class:

```
// Warning: this function class is for illustrative purposes only. Do not use!!
class hash_func
{
    public:
        unsigned long operator( ) (const string& key)
        {
            unsigned long total = 0;

            for (unsigned i = 0; i < key.length( ); i++)
                total += key [i];
            return total;
        } // operator( )
}; // class hash_func
```

This class meets the minimum requirement of converting a string key to an **unsigned long,** but it has several drawbacks. For one thing, strings that have the same letters but in a different order would yield the same number. For example, for both "sewn" and "news" the number returned would be 445 (since **int** ('n') = 110, **int** ('e') = 101, **int** ('w') = 119 and **int** ('s') = 115).

A more serious problem is that this class may severely limit the number of usable buckets. For example, suppose that each key consists of lowercase letters only. Then the largest total generated is less than 2500 (with 20 z's), and many smaller numbers cannot be generated (for example, 123 to 193). If we are working with a lot of strings, we will have a lot of collisions, and list searches are sequential.

In general, we would like each key to generate a different number. This is not possible for strings of up to 20 lowercase letters because there are, approximately, 26^{21} such strings. That number is much larger than the largest possible **unsigned long** $(= 2^{32}$ if **long** values are stored in 4 bytes). What we will settle for is the following: if L is the number of **unsigned long**s, the probability that two keys will generate the same **unsigned long** is $1 / L$.

The following program has a hash_func class that also totals up the characters in the string, but each partial total is multiplied by 13. The final total is multiplied by a large prime number to ensure that, even if key.length( ) is small, a large number can be generated:

```
#include <iostream>
#include <string>
#include "hash_map1.h"

class hash_func
{
```

```
public:

        unsigned long operator( ) (const string& key)
        {
                const unsigned long BIG_PRIME = 4294967291;
                unsigned long total = 0;

                for (unsigned i = 0; i < key.length( ); i++)
                        total = total * 13 + key [i];
                return total * BIG_PRIME;
        } // operator( )
}; // class hash_func
```

The following main function creates a hash_map container of student names and grade point averages. Each student name is hashed to an index in the hash_map container.

```
int main( ) {

        typedef hash_map <string, float, hash_func> hash_map_class;

        const string CLOSE_WINDOW_PROMPT =
                "Please press the Enter key to close this output window.";

        hash_map_class students;
        hash_map_class::iterator itr;

        value_type<const string, float> student("Mike", 3.2);
        value_type<hash_map_class::iterator, bool>p = students.insert (student);

        students.insert (value_type<const string, float> ("Alan", 3.6));
        students ["Bob"] = 3.1;
        for (itr = students.begin( ); itr != students.end( ); itr++)
                cout << (*itr).first << " " << (*itr).second << endl;

        (*(p.first)).second = 1.7;
        students ["Bob"] = 3.04;
        cout << "size = " << students.size( ) << endl;
        for (itr = students.begin( ); itr != students.end( ); itr++)
                cout << (*itr).first << " " << (*itr).second << endl;

        cout << "looking for " << "Alan" << endl;
        itr = students.find ("Alan");
        if (itr == students.end( ))
                cout << "not found " << endl;
        else
                cout << "found " << (*itr).first << endl;

        cout << "looking for " << "Jack" << endl;
        itr = students.find ("Jack");
```

```
        if (itr == students.end( ))
               cout << "not found " << endl;
        else
               cout << "found " << (*itr).first << endl;

        for (int i = 0; i < 500; i++)
        {
               string temp = "";
               students [temp + char (i)] = 2.0;
        } // for

        cout << "size = " << students.size( ) << endl;

        cout << "removing Bob" << endl;
        students.erase (students.find ("Bob"));

        cout << "size = " << students.size( ) << endl;
        if (students.find ("Bob") == students.end( ))
               cout << "no Bob" << endl;
        else
               cout << "oops" << endl;
        if (students.find ("Mike") == students.end( ))
               cout << "no Mike--oops" << endl;
        else
               cout << "Mike found" << endl;

               cout << endl << CLOSE_WINDOW_PROMPT;
               cin.get( );

               return 0;
} // main
```

The output is

```
Bob 3.1
Mike 3.2
Alan 3.6
size = 3
Bob 3.04
Mike 1.7
Alan 3.6
looking for Alan
found Alan
looking for Jack
not found
size = 259
removing Bob
```

size = 258
no Bob
Mike found

Please press the Enter key to close this output window.

(Can you figure out why the next-to-last size printed is only 259?

Hint There are only 256 distinct ASCII characters.)

It is vitally important to the success of hashing for the hash_func class to generates **int**s for which the resulting indices are spread throughout the table. This notion is referred to as the ***Uniform Hashing Assumption.*** Probabilistically speaking, the Uniform Hashing Assumption states that the set of all possible keys is uniformly distributed over the set of all table indices. That is, each key is equally likely to hash to any one of the array indices.

The Uniform Hashing Assumption states that the index a key hashes to is independent of the indices that other keys have hashed to.

There is no hash_func class that will satisfy the Uniform Hashing Assumption for all applications. Even the hash_func class whose function-call operator returns the **unsigned long** parameter can be a bad choice. For example, suppose the key is a nine-digit employee number in which the rightmost four digits hold the division the employee works in. If the table size is 10,000 and all the employees in the current application are from the same division, all the keys will hash to the same index!

One important point is that the hash_func class is determined by the *user* of the hash_map class, not by the developer of the hash_map class. The user knows the key type and, presumably, the best way to convert the key into an **unsigned long**. In the hash_map class, this **unsigned long** is converted into an index in the array buckets as follows (recall that the length field holds the number of buckets):

The hash_func *class is determined by the* user *of the* hash_map *class, not by the developer of the* hash_map *class.*

```
int index = hash_func (key) % length;
```

Let's talk about how large the array buckets should be. If the hash_map class starts with a large number of buckets, this will waste space for a lot of applications. Instead, a conservative approach is taken: the original number of buckets is fairly small—namely, 211—and can be increased as conditions warrant. When will that be? Because the individual lists can get arbitrarily large, we can store more than count (= size( )) items in the array-of-lists buckets, so we need not resize even when count gets close to length. But if we never resize, the average size of each list will get bigger and bigger. Since list searches are sequential, the averageTime(n) will be linear in n, but our goal is for constant time, on average.

We will resize whenever the ***load factor,*** that is, the ratio of count to length, exceeds some fixed number. This fixed number is defined as

```
const static float MAX_RATIO;
```

That is, MAX_RATIO is the maximum ratio of count to length before expansion of the array buckets will take place. MAX_RATIO has the value 0.75, so expansion will take place if (**float**)count / length $>$ 0.75. This ensures that the average size of the lists will be small, in fact, less than 1.0.

When we resize, each item in the array must be hashed to the new array; the index of the item in the new array will almost always be different from its index in the old array. Incidentally, the reason an array was chosen over a vector was to enable expansion without copying. With a vector, expansion always entails copying the old underlying array to the same indices in the new underlying array, and this extra, fruitless work would diminish the speed of hashing

The definitions of the hash_map methods are simplified because a lot of the work was already done during the definition of the list class methods. For example, the definition of the insert method in the hash_map class includes a call to the push_back method in the list class. But even with this simplification, the definition of the insert method has to deal with the complication of resizing.

The hash_map iterators allow us to access list iterators, which are needed for the definitions of several hash_map methods. So we start with the fields and implementation of the hash_map class's embedded iterator class.

13.3.4 Fields and Implementation of the iterator Class

In order to iterate through all the items in a hash_map container, a hash-map iterator must be able to iterate through each of the lists. So a hash_map iterator must include a list iterator to be able to iterate through a list. But a hash_map iterator cannot simply *be* a list iterator. Why not? Because when a hash_map iterator gets to the end of one list, it needs to be able to get to the beginning of the next list. To overcome this problem, a hash_map iterator class will have information about the current list iterator, as well as where that list is—that is, the index in the array buckets. So the iterator class has these two fields:

```
unsigned index;
list<value_type<const key_type, T> > ::iterator list_itr;
```

We need a little more because an iterator needs some way of determining which hash_map container—in particular, which array buckets—is currently being iterated over. So each iterator will have a buckets field that points to the same array as the current hash_map container's buckets field:

```
list <value_type<const key_type, T> >* buckets;
```

Finally, we need to determine when an iterator has reached the end of the array buckets, so the iterator class will have

```
unsigned length;
```

All four fields will get their initial values in the hash_map container's begin method, which we will see in Section 13.3.5.

All the iterator method-definitions, except for **operator++**, are straight-forward. For example:

```
bool operator== (const iterator& other) const
{
     return (index == other.index) &&
            (list_itr == other.list_itr) &&
            (buckets == other.buckets) &&
            (length = other.length)
} // ==

value_type<const key_type, T>& operator* ( )
{
     return *list_itr;
} // operator*
```

The postincrement operator starts by saving the calling object, ***this,** and then incrementing the list_itr field. If we are not at the end of this bucket, we return the saved iterator. Otherwise, we advance through the remaining buckets until (unless) we find a nonempty bucket. If we *do* find a nonempty bucket, we set the list_itr field to the beginning of that bucket and return the saved iterator. Otherwise, we set the list_itr field to the end of the last bucket and return the saved iterator.

Here is the definition:

```
iterator operator++ (int)
{
     iterator old_itr = *this;
     if (++list_itr != buckets [index].end( ))
           return old_itr;
     while (index < length − 1)
     {
           index++;
           if (!buckets [index].empty( ))
           {
                list_itr = buckets [index].begin( );
                return old_itr;
           } // bucket entry not empty
     }// while
     list_itr = buckets [index].end( );
     return old_itr;
} // postincrement operator++
```

The time needed for this method is estimated after we have implemented the hash_map class.

13.3.5 Implementation of the hash_map Class

We can now complete method definitions for the hash_map class. Let's start with the constructor:

```
hash_map( )
{
        count = 0;
        length = DEFAULT_SIZE; // = 211
        buckets = new list<value_type<const key_type, T> > [DEFAULT_SIZE];
} // default constructor
```

The begin method searches through the array buckets looking for a nonempty slot:

```
iterator begin( )
{
        int i = 0;
        iterator itr;

        itr.buckets = buckets;
        while (i < length − 1)
        {
                if (!buckets [i].empty( ))
                {
                        itr.list_itr = buckets [i].begin( );
                        itr.index = i;
                        itr.length = length;
                        return itr;
                } // buckets [i] not empty
                i++;
        } // while
        itr.list_itr = buckets [i].end( );
        itr.index = i;
        itr.length = length;
        return itr;
} // begin
```

The end method has a simpler definition: return an iterator positioned beyond the last position in the last bucket:

```
iterator end( )
{
        int i = length − 1;
        iterator itr;

        itr.buckets = buckets;
```

```
        itr.list_itr = buckets [i].end( );
        itr.index = i;
        itr.length = length;
        return itr;
    } // end
```

Now let's try the tough one: insert. Under normal circumstances, inserting is straightforward. To insert the value_type<**const** key_type, T> x, first find out if x is already in the hash_map:

```
    iterator old_itr;
    key_type key = x.first;
    old_itr = find (key);
    if (old_itr != end( ))
```

In that case, we simply return the pair <old_itr, **false**>. Otherwise, we hash key to a buckets index, append x to that list and increment count. The only remaining task is to check to see if the array buckets has to be resized, that is, if count > **int** (MAX_RATIO * length). For the sake of modularity, this subtask is handled in the auxiliary method check_for_expansion.

Here is the definition of insert:

```
    pair<iterator, bool> insert (const value_type<const key_type, T>& x)
    {
        iterator old_itr;
        key_type key = x.first;

        old_itr = find (key);
        if (old_itr != end( ))
                return pair <iterator, bool> (old_itr, false);
        int index = hash (key) % length;
        buckets [index].push_back (x);
        count++;
        check_for_expansion( );
        return pair<iterator, bool> (find (key), true);
    } // insert
```

If expansion is needed, a new array of one more than double the current length is created. Each item from the current array is rehashed and added to a linked list in the new array, which then replaces the old array. Finally, each item in each linked list in the old array is erased.

Here is the definition of check_for_expansion:

```
    void check_for_expansion( )
    {
                list<value_type <const key_type, T> >::iterator list_itr;
```

```
int index;

if (count > int (MAX_RATIO * length))
{
        list< value_type<const key_type, T> >* temp_buckets = buckets;
        length = 2 * length + 1;
        buckets = new list< value_type <const key_type, T> > [length];
        Key new_key;
        for (int i = 0; i < length / 2; i++) // rehash old values
                if (!temp_buckets [i].empty( ))
                        for (list_itr = temp_buckets [i].begin( );
                                        list_itr != temp_buckets [i].end( );
                                        list_itr++)
                        {
                                new_key = (*list_itr).first;
                                index = hash (new_key) % length;
                                buckets [index].push_back (*list_itr);
                        } // storing temp_buckets [i] back into buckets
        // destroy the old linked lists
        for (int i = 0; i < length / 2; i++)
                if (!temp_buckets [i].empty( ))
                        temp_buckets [i].erase (temp_buckets [i].begin( ),
                                        temp_buckets [i].end( ));
        delete[ ] temp_buckets;
        } // doubling buckets size
        } // method check_for_expansion
```

If an expansion takes place, the length of the array buckets changes, and so the index corresponding to each key will have to be recalculated. As a result, items that were in the same linked list before resizing may be in different linked lists afterwards. For example, suppose the length of the array is 48 before resizing. Then items with keys of 63 and 111 will be in the linked list at buckets [15]. After resizing, length = 97; the item whose key is 63 will be in the linked list at buckets [63], but the item whose key is 111 will be in the linked list at buckets [14].

We postpone an analysis of the insert method (and check_for_expansion method) until we have developed the find and erase methods.

By comparison with the insert method, the find method is a no-brainer: we utilize the generic algorithm find to search the list (that is, bucket) to which the key hashed. If the list iterator returned is not the same as the iterator returned by the end( ) method, we fill in the buckets_ptr and index fields in a newly created iterator and return that iterator.

Here is the code:

```
iterator find (const key_type& key)
{
        int index = hash (key) % length;
```

```
        iterator itr;
        itr.list_itr = std::find (buckets [index].begin( ), buckets [index].end( ),
                            value_type <const key_type, T> (key, T( )));
    if (itr.list_itr == buckets [index].end( ))
            return end( );
        itr.buckets = buckets;
        itr.index = index;
        itr.length = length;
        return itr;
    } // find
```

We specified std::find to emphasize that the call is to the generic algorithm find, not the hash_map method find.

The erase method's definition is even easier:

```
    void erase (iterator itr)
    {
            buckets [itr.index].erase (itr.list_itr);
            count--;
    } // erase
```

The definition of the associative-array operator, **operator**[ ], in the hash_map class is the same one-liner used by its map cousin in Chapter 10 (except that value_type is not an abbreviation for pair<**const** key_type, T>):

```
    T& operator[ ] (const key_type& key)
    {
            return (*((insert(value_type<const key_type, T> (key, T( )))).first)).second;
    } // operator[ ]
```

The complete hash_map class is available from the Source Code link on the book's website.

13.3.6 Analysis of Chained Hashing

For now, let's make the Uniform Hashing Assumption. That is, we assume that each key is equally likely to hash to any one of the array indices, independently of where other keys have hashed.

Let n = count and let m = length = number of buckets = number of lists. If the Uniform Hashing Assumption holds, the n items will be fairly evenly distributed over m lists, with an average list size of n/m. Then the time estimates will depend on both n and m. If MAX_RATIO = 0.75, we always have

$$n/m \leq 0.75$$

The average size of each list will be at most 0.75. Then searching a list, on average, will require at most 0.75 iterations. That is, for the find method, averageTime$_S(n, m)$ and averageTime$_U(n, m)$ are both constant.

If chained hashing is used and the Uniform Hashing Assumption holds, the average time for both successful and unsuccessful searches is constant.

Figure 13.5 summarizes the search-time estimates for chained hashing. In each approximation, the time depends, not on n, but on the ratio n/m. Figure 13.6 estimates the number of loop iterations for successful and unsuccessful searches with various values of the ratio n/m. In the two charts of Figures 13.5 and 13.6, we assume that the Uniform Hashing Assumption holds. For the erase method, the analysis is the same, with constant average time—for each item removed—in both the successful and unsuccessful cases.

What about the insert method? For inserting, we have the possibility of expanding to contend with, but you have heard that song before. Whenever we expand the array buckets, its length is doubled (plus one), so buckets will not be expanded until n has again doubled in size. That is, we expand only once for every $2n$ insertions, so averageTime(n, m) is still constant, and in fact, amortizedTime(n, m) is constant. Practically speaking, that constant will seem very large when expanding does occur. Alternate techniques, such as gradual expanding and extendible expanding, increase the array by only a small amount at a time and avoid large-scale rehashing and reinserting. For a discussion of extendible hashing, see Heileman (1996, pp. 232–233).

For **operator++** in the iterator class, we first calculate the total number of iterations and divide this total by n. To traverse the entire array buckets, there will be a total of n iterations to access each item, and a total of m iterations to access each of the m linked lists, for $n + m$ iterations altogether. Assuming MAX_RATIO = 0.75, we resize buckets whenever $n \geq 3m/4$, and after a resizing, the new value of m is twice the old value (approximately). Equivalently, after a resizing, the old value of m is one-half the new value. Then after the first resizing, we will always have $3(m/2)/4 \leq n$. So $n + m \leq n + 8n/3 < 4n$. The average number of iterations is the total num-

Figure 13.5 | A summary of the average-time estimates for successful and unsuccessful searches with chained hashing. We make the Uniform Hashing Assumption. In the figure, n = number of values inserted; m = length = number of buckets = number of lists.

Chaining:

$$\text{averageTime}_S(n, m) \approx \frac{n}{2m} \text{ iterations}$$

$$\text{averageTime}_U(n, m) \approx \frac{n}{m} \text{ iterations}$$

Figure 13.6 | Search-time (approximately, the number of loop iterations) estimates for various ratios of n to m, with chained hashing. This figure does not assume that MAX_RATIO = 0.75. In fact, MAX_RATIO could even be greater than 1!

$\frac{n}{m}$	0.25	0.5	0.75	0.90	0.99
Successful	0.13	0.25	0.38	0.45	0.50
Unsuccessful	0.25	0.50	0.75	0.90	0.99

ber divided by *n,* so the average number of iterations for **operator**++ is less than 4. That is, averageTime(*n, m*) is constant.

Worst Time? So far we have blithely ignored any discussion of the worst time. This is the Achilles' heel of hashing, just as worst time was the vulnerable aspect of Quick Sort. Whether the Uniform Hashing Assumption holds or not, we can still have a data set in which an inordinate number of keys hash to the same index, leading to searches for which the number of iterations is linear in *n.* So worstTime(*n, m*), for both successful and unsuccessful searches, is linear in *n.* By the same line of reasoning, we can show that worstTime(*n, m*) is linear in *n* for the insert and erase methods as well as for the find method.

If chained hashing is used, the worst time for both successful and unsuccessful searches is linear in n, whether or not the uniform hashing assumption holds.

In the worst case for **operator**++, we would have *n* − 1 items in buckets [0] and one item in buckets [*m* − 1]. To advance to this last item would require *m* − 1 iterations of the **while** loop, and so worstTime(*n, m*) is linear in *m* for **operator**++ **(int)**.

The bottom line is this: unless you are confident that the Uniform Hashing Assumption is reasonable for the key space in the application, and average-case performance is your overriding concern, use a map container, with its guarantee of logarithmic worst-time performance.

13.3.7 The value_type **Class**

The items in each list are of type value_type, and up until now, you have probably assumed that value_type was defined by

> **typedef** pair<**const** key_type, T> value_type;

That is how value_type was defined for the map class in Chapter 10. Why should there be any difference for the hash_map class? The reason there is a difference is that the hash_map class invokes methods from the list class. For example, one of the statements in the hash_map class's find method is

> itr.list_itr = std::find (buckets [index].begin( ), buckets [index].end( ),
>   value_type <**const** key_type, T> (key, T( )));

This statement searches a list, but the pair class has no **operator**== as the basis for comparing items in a list. Note that the comparisons should use only the first component, that is, the key.

A solution to this problem is to make value_type a templated **struct**; value_type will overload **operator**==. Here is the value_type **struct**:

```
template<class key, class T>
struct value_type
{
    public:
        value_type (const value_type& p): first (p.first)
        {
            second = p.second;
        }
```

```
value_type (const key& key, const T& t): first(key)
{
        second = t;
}
bool operator == (const value_type& x)
{
        return first == x.first;
} // operator ==
key first;
T second;
}; // struct value_type
```

In the constructors, a constructor-initializer section (see Chapter 6, Section 6.1.4) avoids the problem of assigning a value to a **const** field. A **const** field must be initialized before the body of the constructor is entered, and that's why we need a constructor-initializer section.

13.3.8 Applications

We need not look far to find applications of hashing. In Chapter 10, we developed a program to count the frequency of each word in a text. The program relied on a map container to save pairs of the form <word, frequency>. We can substantially speed up the average time by replacing the map container with a hash_map container:

```
#include "hash_map1.h"

typedef hash_map< string, int, hash_func > FrequencyMap;

FrequencyMap frequencies;
```

And the third template argument is now a hash-function class. Because a hash_map container is used, the output file is not in alphabetical order:

```
program 1
of 2
a 1
text 2
words 3
big 1
many 1
counts 1
this 1
in 2
occurrences 1
number 1
the 2
it 1
may 1
have 1
including 1
```

This order is based on the array indices the words hashed to. To get the output file alphabetically ordered by the words, we iterate through frequencies and insert each <string, **int**> pair into a map container:

```
map<string, int>s_frequencies;
map<string, int>::iterator s_itr;

for (itr = frequencies.begin( ); itr != frequencies.end( ); itr++)
    s_frequencies.insert (pair <string, int> ((*itr).first, (*itr).second));
for( s_itr = s_frequencies.begin( ); s_itr != s_frequencies.end( ); s_itr++ )
    out_file << (*s_itr).first << " " << (*s_itr).second << endl;
```

Curiously, printing the word-frequency pairs in alphabetical order takes longer (averageTime(n) is $O(n \log n)$) than creating the pairs in the first place—average Time(n) is only $O(n)$.

For a very important example, let's reconsider the infix-to-postfix program developed in Lab 19. In the Compiler class, we defined

```
vector<string> symbolTable;
```

Later, in the Token class (a **friend** of Compiler), we had:

```
index = find (symbolTable.begin( ), symbolTable.end( ), referent)
            - symbolTable.begin( );
if (index == symbolTable.size( ))
    symbolTable.push_back (referent);
```

This search of symbolTable took $O(n)$ time in both the worst and average cases because symbolTable was a vector container. We could have sped that up to $O(\log n)$ time in the average and worst cases by replacing the vector container with a map container. If we replace the vector container with a hash_map container, the average time is reduced to $O(1)$, but worstTime is $O(n)$. This indicates a trade-off between a map container and a hash_map container. In this application, average time is considered crucial, so hash_map containers are invariably chosen. A similar trade-off of average-time to worst-time makes Quick Sort preferred over other sorts for system sort utilities.

Hashing is also useful for the direct accessing of disk files. When a key hashes to a file position, the entire bucket is brought into main memory with only one cylinder access. Keeping cylinder accesses to a minimum is a primary goal of file processing because each cylinder access requires movement of the electromechanical arm on the disk.

In Lab 28, you will get a chance to compare the run-time speed of hash_map containers versus map containers.

LAB **Lab 28: Timing a** hash_map.

(All Labs Are Optional.) **LAB**

13.4 | THE hash_set CLASS

With hashing, all the work involves the key-to-index relationship. It doesn't matter if the value consists of the key only or has another component. In the former case, we have a hash_set, and in the latter case, we have a hash_map. Developing the hash_set class is fairly straightforward. In fact, we can view a hash_set as a hash_map in which the nonkey component is ignored. For this perspective, the hash_set class has a hash_map field. Here is a glimpse of the implementation:

```
template<class Key, class HashFunc >
class hash_set
{
       class T{ };

       hash_map<Key, T, HashFunc> my_hash_map;

       . . .

       iterator find(const key_type& x) const { return my_hash_map.find(x); }
       . . .
} // class hash_set
```

We could now redo the spell-checker application from Chapter 9 but substitute hash_set containers for the AVLTree containers. Assume that the Uniform Hashing Assumption holds, let n represent the size of the dictionary file, and let k represent the size of the document file. Each search of the dictionary file for a given word takes only constant time on average. So for the compare method, averageTime(k, n) is linear in k for the hash_set version. Recall that this method's averageTime(k, n) was $O(k \log n)$ for the AVLTree version. The trade-off is that the worstTime(k, n) for the hash_set version of the compare method is $O(kn)$, versus $O(k \log n)$ for the AVLTree version.

Section 13.5 explores another collision handler, one that avoids linked lists.

13.5 | OPEN-ADDRESS HASHING

To handle collisions with chaining, the basic idea is this: When a key hashes to a given index in the array buckets, that key's value is inserted at the back of the linked list at buckets [index].

With open addressing, collisions are handled by searching the table for an empty (that is, "open") location.

Open addressing provides another approach to collision handling. With **open addressing,** each table location contains a single value; there are no linked lists. To insert a value, if the value's key hashes to an index whose value contains a different key, the rest of the table is searched systematically until an empty, that is, "open" location is found.

The simplest open-addressing strategy is to use an offset of 1. That is, to insert a value whose key hashes to index j, if buckets [j] is empty, the value is inserted there. Otherwise, index j + 1 is investigated, then index j + 2, and so on until an open slot is found. Figure 13.7 shows the table created when values with the following keys are inserted:

214-30-3261

033-51-8000

214-19-9528

819-02-9528

819-02-9261

033-30-8262

215-09-1766

214-17-0261

Figure 13.7 I A table to which eight values have been inserted. Open addressing, with an offset of 1, handles collisions.

0	033-51-8000
1	?
	• • •
260	?
261	214-30-3261
262	819-02-9261
263	033-30-8262
264	214-17-0261
265	?
	• • •
527	?
528	214-19-9528
529	819-02-9528
530	?
	• • •
765	?
766	215-09-1766
767	?
	• • •
999	?

To determine if a location is occupied, the value_type class will have a **bool** field, occupied. When a hash map is constructed, the occupied field in every value of the table will be set to **false.** When the insert method inserts a value in the table, that value's occupied field is set to **true.** Figure 13.8 shows the effect of having this field on the table in Figure 13.7.

There are a couple of minor details with open addressing:

Figure 13.8 | The effect of inserting several values into a table: the occupied field for each value inserted is set to true.

	key	occupied
0	033-51-8000	**true**
1	?	**false**
⋮		
260	?	**false**
261	214-30-3261	**true**
262	819-02-9261	**true**
263	033-30-8262	**true**
264	214-17-0261	**true**
265	?	**false**
⋮		
527	?	**false**
528	214-19-9528	**true**
529	819-02-9528	**true**
530	?	**false**
⋮		
766	215-09-1766	**true**
⋮		
999	?	**false**

1. To ensure that an open location will be found if one is available, the table must wrap around: if the location at index length − 1 is not open, the next index tried is 0.

2. The number of entries cannot exceed the array length, so the load factor cannot exceed 1.0. It will simplify the implementation and efficiency of the find, insert, and erase methods if the array always has at least one open (that is, empty) location. So we require that the load factor be strictly less than 1.0. Recall that with chaining, the load factor can exceed 1.0.

Let's see what is involved in the design and implementation of a hash_map class with open addressing and an offset of 1. We'll include all of the fields from the chained-hashing design: buckets, count, length, and hash, but buckets will be an array of values, not an array of lists of values. Similarly, the embedded iterator class will have index, length, and buckets fields, but no list_itr field. The value_type class will have the same first and second fields as with chained hashing, and an occupied field as well. The find, insert, and erase methods will have to be redefined because the chained version of those methods accessed linked lists.

13.5.1 The erase Method

We need to define the erase method before the find and insert methods because the details of removing values have a subtle impact on searches and insertions. To see what this is all about, suppose we want to remove the value with key 214-30-3261 from the table in Figure 13.8. If we simply set that value's occupied field to **false**, we will get the table in Figure 13.9.

Do you see the pitfall with this removal strategy? The path taken by synonyms of 214303261 has been blocked. A search for the value with key 819029261 would be unsuccessful, because the find method would stop as soon as a value with occupied = **false** is encountered. To avoid this problem, we will add another field to the value_type class:

    bool marked_for_removal;

This field is initialized to **false** when a value is inserted into the table buckets. The erase method sets this field to **true.** The marked_for_removal field, when **true,** indicates that its value is no longer part of the hash map, but allows the offset-of-1 collision handler to continue along its path. Figure 13.10 shows a table after eight insertions, and Figure 13.11 shows the subsequent effect of "erasing" the item whose key is 214303261.

A search for the value with the key 819029261 would now be successful. Because the parameter of the erase method is an iterator, that iterator's index field provides access to the value to be deleted. Here is the definition:

    void erase (iterator itr)
    {

Figure 13.9 I The effect of removing the value with key 214-30-3261 from the table in Figure 13.8 by setting that value's occupied field to false.

	key	occupied
0	033-51-8000	true
1	?	false
	• • •	
260	?	false
261	214-30-3261	false
262	819-02-9261	true
263	033-30-8262	true
264	214-17-0261	true
265	?	false
	• • •	
527	?	false
528	214-19-9528	true
529	819-02-9528	true
530	?	false
	• • •	
766	215-09-1766	true
	• • •	
999	?	false

```
        buckets [itr.index].occupied = false;
        buckets [itr.index].marked_for_removal = true;
        count--;
    } // erase
```

We postpone an analysis of the erase method until we complete the developments of the find and insert methods.

Figure 13.10 | A table to which eight values have been inserted. Open addressing, with an offset of 1, handles collisions. In each value, only the key (that is, first) occupied, and marked_for_removal fields are shown.

	key	occupied	marked_for_removal
0	033-51-8000	true	false
1	?	false	false
	• • •		
260	?	false	false
261	214-30-3261	true	false
262	819-02-9261	true	false
263	033-30-8262	true	false
264	214-17-0261	true	false
265	?	false	false
	• • •		
527	?	false	false
528	214-19-9528	true	false
529	819-02-9528	true	false
530	?	false	false
	• • •		
766	215-09-1766	true	false
	• • •		
999	?	false	false

The find method loops until an unoccupied or matching key is found. A value's key is checked only if that value is not marked for removal. Here is the definition:

```
iterator find (const key_type& key)
{
        unsigned long hash_int = hash (key);
        int index = hash_int % length;
```

Figure 13.11 | The contents of the table from Figure 13.10 after the message erase
(214303261) was sent.

	key	occupied	marked_for_removal
0	033-51-8000	true	false
1	?	false	false
	⋮		
260	?	false	false
261	214-30-3261	false	true
262	819-02-9261	true	false
263	033-30-8262	true	false
264	214-17-0261	true	false
265	?	false	false
	⋮		
527	?	false	false
528	214-19-9528	true	false
529	819-02-9528	true	false
530	?	false	false
	⋮		
766	215-09-1766	true	false
	⋮		
999	?	false	false

iterator itr;

while (buckets [index].marked_for_removal
         || (buckets [index].occupied && buckets [index].first != key))
     index = (index + 1) % length;
if (!buckets [index].occupied && !buckets [index].marked_for_removal)
     return end( );
itr.buckets = buckets;

```
        itr.index = index;
        itr.length = length;
        return itr;
} // find
```

The marked_for_removal "solution" to removing a value without breaking the offset-of-1 path creates a problem for the check_for_expansion method. The problem is to determine the appropriate condition for rehashing. Let's start with the condition used with chained hashing:

```
count > int (MAX_RATIO * length)
```

To see what's wrong with using this condition for deciding whether to rehash with open addressing, suppose the length field is 1000 and there have been a large number of interleaved insertions and removals. For example, let's say there have been 980 insertions and 780 removals. Then the count field would have the value 200, so there would apparently be plenty of room left in the table. But there would be only 20 unoccupied locations. Then the average unsuccessful search using the find method would require more than 15 loop iterations! That is unacceptable.

The solution is to rehash whenever the value of count plus the number of recent removals exceeds the value of MAX_RATIO * length. By "recent" removal we mean one that occurred since the value of length was last changed. This solution requires that we add a count_plus field to the hash_map class:

```
int count_plus; // the value of count + the number of removals since length
                // was last changed
```

We will rehash when the value of count_plus exceeds the threshold of MAX_RATIO * length. We need not insert the marked_for_removal values into the new table because we will be creating new paths for the inserted values; that is, we will be starting afresh. So after rehashing, the value of count will be assigned to count_plus. From that point until the next rehash, the count and count_plus fields are incremented when a value is inserted, but the count field is decremented when a value is removed. (Exercise 13.7 considers a possible improvement: rehash and double the table size when the value of count exceeds the value of MAX_RATIO * length; rehash but do not change the table size when the value of count_plus exceeds the value of MAX_RATIO * length.)

Here is the definition of the check_for_expansion method:

```
void check_for_expansion( )
{
    unsigned long hash_int;
    int index,
        offset,
        old_length;

    if (count_plus > int (MAX_RATIO * length))
```

```
        {
                value_type<key_type, T>*temp_buckets = buckets;

                old_length = length;
                length = next_prime (old_length);
                buckets = new value_type<key_type, T> [length];
                for (int i = 0; i < old_length; i++)
                        if (temp_buckets [i].occupied)
                        {
                                hash_int = hash (temp_buckets [i].first);
                                index = hash_int % length;
                                while (buckets [index].occupied)
                                        index = (index + 1) % length;
                                buckets [index] = temp_buckets [i];
                        } // posting temp_buckets [i] back into buckets
                        delete[ ] temp_buckets;
                count_plus = count;
        } // doubling buckets size
    } // method check_for_expansion
```

And here is the definition of the insert method:

```
pair<iterator, bool> insert (const value_type<const key_type, T>& x)
{
        key_type key = x.first;
        unsigned long hash_int = hash (key);
        int index = hash_int % length;
        while ((buckets [index].marked_for_removal)||
                        buckets [index].occupied && key != buckets [index].first)
                index = (index + 1) % length;
        if (buckets [index].occupied && key == buckets [index].first)
                return pair <iterator, bool> (find (key), false);
        buckets [index].first = x.first;
        buckets [index].second = x.second;
        buckets [index].occupied = true;
        buckets [index].marked_for_removal = false;
        count++;
        count_plus++;

        check_for_expansion( );
        return pair<iterator, bool> (find (key), true);
    } // insert
```

Because we rehash when the value of count_plus exceeds the value of MAX_
RATIO * length, and the value of MAX_RATIO is required to be strictly less than 1.0,
there will always be at least one slot in the table that is unoccupied and not marked
for removal. As a result, the **while** loop in the find method is guaranteed to eventually terminate.

13.5.2 Primary Clustering

There is still a disturbing feature of the offset-of-1 collision handler: all the keys that hash to a given index will probe the same path: index, index + 1, index + 2, and so on. What's worse, all keys that hash to any index in that path will follow the same path from that index on. For example, Figure 13.12 shows part of the table from Figure 13.10. In Figure 13.12, the path traced by keys that hash to 261 is 261, 262, 263, 264, ... And the path traced by keys that hash to 262 is 262, 263, 264, 265, ... A *cluster* is a sequence of nonempty locations. With the offset-of-1 collision handler, clusters are formed by synonyms, including synonyms from different collisions. In Figure 13.12, the locations at indices 261, 262, 263, and 264 form a cluster. As each entry is added to a cluster, the cluster not only gets bigger, but also grows faster, because any keys that hash to that new index will follow the same path as keys already stored in the cluster. *Primary clustering* is the phenomenon that occurs when the collision handler allows the growth of clusters to accelerate.

Primary clustering occurs when the open-addressing collision handler allows the growth of clusters to accelerate.

Clearly, the offset-of-1 collision handler is susceptible to primary clustering. The problem with primary clustering is that we get ever-longer paths that are sequentially traversed during searches, insertions, and removals. Long sequential traversals are the bane of hashing, so we should try to avoid this problem.

What if we choose an offset of, say, 20 instead of 1? We would still have primary clustering: keys that hashed to index would overlap the path traced by keys that hashed to index + 20, index + 40, and so on. In fact, this could create an even bigger problem than primary clustering! For example, suppose the table size is 100 and the offset is 20. If a key hashes to index 33, the only locations that would be allowed in that cluster have the following indices:

33 53 73 93 13

Once those locations fill up, there would be no way to insert any value whose key hashed to any one of those indices. The reason we have this additional problem is that the offset and table size have a common factor. We can avoid this problem by making the table size a prime number, but we would still have primary clustering.

Figure 13.12 | The path traced by keys that hash to 261 overlaps the paths traced by keys that hash to 262, 263, or 264.

	key	occupied	marked_for_removal
260	?	false	false
261	214-30-3261	true	false
262	819-02-9261	true	false
263	033-30-8262	true	false
264	214-17-0261	true	false
265	?	false	false

The reason that the offset-of-1 (or any linear offset) collision handler leads to primary clustering is that the offset is the same for any key. In Section 13.5.3, we solve the problem of primary clustering by making each key determine, not only the index, but also the offset.

13.5.3 Double Hashing

We can avoid primary clustering if, instead of using the same offset for all keys, we make the offset dependent on the key. For example, we can set

offset = hash_int / length;

To see how this works in a simple setting, let's insert the following keys into a table of size 19:

    33
    72
    71
    55
    112
    109

These keys were created, not randomly, but to indicate that keys from different collisions, even from the same collision, do not follow the same path. Here are the relevant remainders and quotients:

key	key % 19	key / 19
33	14	1
72	15	3
71	14	3
112	17	5
55	17	2
109	14	5

The first key, 33, is stored at index 14, and the second key, 72, is stored at index 15. The third key, 71, hashes to 14, but that location is occupied, so the index 14 is incremented by the offset 3 to yield index 17; 71 is stored at that location. The fourth key, 112, hashes to 17 (occupied); the index 17 is incremented by the offset 5. Since 22 is beyond the range of the table, we try index 22 % 19, that is, 3, an unoccupied location. The key 112 is stored at index 3. The fifth key, 55, hashes to 17 (occupied) and then to (17 + 2) % 19, that is, 0, an empty location. The sixth key, 109, hashes to 14 (occupied) and then to (14 + 5) % 19, that is 0 (occupied), and then to (0 + 5) % 19, that is, 5, an unoccupied location. Figure 13.13 shows the effect of these insertions.

This collision handler is known as *double hashing* (because both indices and offsets are obtained from hashing the keys), or the *quotient-offset* collision handler. There is one last problem we need to address before we get to the code and analysis: What happens if the offset is a multiple of the table size? For example, suppose we try to add the entry whose key is 736 to the table in Figure 13.13. We have

$$736 \% 19 = 14$$
$$736 / 19 = 38$$

Because location 14 is occupied, the next location tried is $(14 + 38) \% 19$, which is 14 again! To avoid this impasse, we use 1 as the offset whenever key / length is a multiple of length. This is an infrequent occurrence: It happens, on average, once in every m keys, where m = length. Exercise 13.8 shows that if this collision handler is used and the table size is a prime number, the sequence of offsets from any key covers the whole table.

Here, little changed from the offset-of-1 version, is the insert method for double hashing:

```
pair<iterator, bool> insert (const value_type<const key_type, T>& x)
{
```

Figure 13.13 I The effect of inserting six values into a table; the collision handler uses the hash value divided by the table size as the offset.

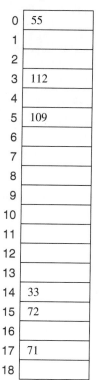

```
key_type key = x.first;
unsigned long hash_int = hash (key);
int index = hash_int % length,
    offset = hash_int / length;
if (offset % length == 0)
        offset = 1;
while ((buckets [index].marked_for_removal)||
            buckets [index].occupied && key != buckets [index].first)
    index = (index + offset) % length;
if (buckets [index].occupied && key == buckets [index].first)
        return pair <iterator, bool> (find (key), false);
buckets [index].first = x.first;
buckets [index].second = x.second;
buckets [index].occupied = true;
buckets [index].marked_for_removal = false;
count++;
count_plus++;

check_for_expansion( );
return pair<iterator, bool> (find (key), true);
} // insert
```

The check_for_expansion method incorporates both the quotient offsets and the need for a prime table size:

```
void check_for_expansion( )
{
    unsigned long hash_int;
    int index,
        offset,
        old_length;

    if (count_plus > int (MAX_RATIO * length))
    {
        value_type<key_type, T> * temp_buckets = buckets;

        old_length = length;
        length = next_prime (old_length);
        buckets = new value_type<key_type, T> [length];
        for (int i = 0; i < old_length; i++)
            if (temp_buckets [i].occupied)
            {
                hash_int = hash (temp_buckets [i].first);
                index = hash_int % length;
                offset = hash_int / length;
                if (offset % length == 0)
```

```
                      offset = 1;
              while (buckets [index].occupied)
                    index = (index + offset) % length;
              buckets [index] = temp_buckets [i];
          } // posting temp_buckets [i] back into buckets
       delete[ ] temp_buckets;
       count_plus = count;
    } // doubling buckets size
  } // method check_for_expansion
```

The method **next_prime** returns the smallest prime at least twice as large as the argument.

```
// Postcondition: the smallest prime at least twice as large as p has been
//                returned.
int next_prime (int p) {

    int i;

    bool factorFound;

    p = 2 * p + 1;
    while (true)
    {
        i = 3;
        factorFound = false;

        // Check 3, 5, 7, 9, . . . , sqrt (p) for a factor of p
        while (i * i < p && !factorFound)
            if (p % i == 0)
                factorFound = true;
            else
                i += 2;
        if (!factorFound)
            return p;
        p += 2; // get the next candidate for primality
    } // while prime not found
} // method next_prime
```

The only changes to the find method—from the offset-of-1 version—are that the offset is calculated from hash (key) / length, and within the **while** loop, index is incremented by offset instead of by 1:

```
iterator find (const key_type& key)
{
    unsigned long hash_int = hash (key);
    int index = hash_int % length,
```

```
                    offset = hash_int / length;
                if (offset % length == 0)
                        offset = 1;
                iterator itr;
                while (buckets [index].marked_for_removal
                            || (buckets [index].occupied
                                && buckets [index].first != key))
                    index = (index + offset) % length;
                if (!buckets [index].occupied && !buckets [index].marked_for_removal)
                        return end( );
                itr.buckets = buckets;
                itr.index = index;
                itr.length = length;
                return itr;
            } // find
```

Section 13.5.4 shows that open addressing, with quotient-offsets and a prime table size, delivers the expected performance. If we make the Uniform Hashing Assumption, the average time for insertions, removals and searches is constant.

13.5.4 Analysis of Open-Address Hashing

We now estimate the times for successful and unsuccessful searches—calls to the find method—with open-address hashing. Specifically, we assume that quotient offsets are used, that the table size is a prime number, and that the Uniform Hashing Assumption holds.

As we did in the analysis of chained hashing, we use m for the value of length and n for the value of count. We take the number of loop iterations as an estimate of the average and worst times for successful and unsuccessful searches. The number of iterations needed for an unsuccessful search for a value with $k \geq 0$ values already in the table is exactly the same as the number of iterations needed to insert the $(k + 1)$st value. And that is also the number of iterations needed for a successful search of that $(k + 1)$st value.

For any k such that $0 \leq k < m$, we define

$$E(k, m)$$

to be the expected number of iterations needed to insert the $(k + 1)$st value.

By what was just noted about the relationship between inserting the $(k + 1)$st value and an unsuccessful search for the kth value, the following estimate holds for the find method:

$$\text{averageTime}_U(n, m) \approx E(n, m) \text{ iterations}$$

So we will calculate $E(n, m)$ to estimate $\text{averageTime}_U(n, m)$ for the find method. Clearly,

$$E(0, m) = 1 \quad \text{for any } m > 1$$

For any $k > 0$, $E(k, m) = 1$ if the $(k + 1)$st value initially hashes to an open address; by the Uniform Hashing Assumption, the probability of this is $(m - k)/m$. Otherwise, with probability k/m, the $(k + 1)$st value will initially hash to an occupied address, and so the number of iterations required is 1 plus the number of iterations required in the rest of the table. But the number of iterations needed in the rest of the table is exactly the number of iterations needed to insert the kth value in a table of size $m - 1$, namely, $E(k - 1, m - 1)$.

Writing this last paragraph as an equation, we get

$$E(k, m) = \frac{m - k}{m} * 1 + \frac{k}{m} (1 + E(k - 1, m - 1)) \qquad \text{where } 1 \le k < m$$

When we combine this recurrence relation with the initial condition (namely, $E(0,m) = 1$ for all $m \ge 1$), we get a recursive definition for the function E. Simplifying the recurrence relation, we get

$$E(k, m) = 1 + \frac{k}{m} E(k - 1, m - 1) \qquad \text{where } 1 \le k < m$$

In Example A1.6, we develop a closed form for this equation; that is, the calculation of the result requires neither loops (such as summations) or recursive calls. The solution is

$$E(k, m) = (m + 1)/(m + 1 - k) \qquad \text{for all } m \text{ and } k \text{ such that } 0 \le k < m.$$

This conjecture can be proved by induction (on either k or m).

We now relate this back to averageTime$_U(n, m)$ for the find method:

$$averageTime_U(n, m) = E(n, m) = (m + 1) / (m + 1 - n)$$
$$\approx 1/(1 - n/m)$$

All that remains is to estimate averageTime$_S(n, m)$. This is, approximately, the average number of iterations needed to insert each of the n values into the table. That is,

$$averageTime_S(n, m) \approx \frac{E(0, m) + E(1, m) + \cdots + E(n - 1, m)}{n}$$
$$= \frac{1}{n} \frac{m + 1}{m + 1} + \frac{m + 1}{m} + \frac{m + 1}{m - 1} + \cdots + \frac{m + 1}{m - n + 2}$$
$$= \frac{m + 1}{n} \left(\frac{1}{m + 1} + \frac{1}{m} + \frac{1}{m - 1} + \cdots + \frac{1}{m - n + 2} \right)$$

An important, calculus-based property of natural logarithms is that

$$\sum_{j=1}^{k} 1/j \approx \ln k \qquad \text{for any integer } k > 1$$

This approximation is better as k gets larger. Then

$$\frac{1}{m+1} + \frac{1}{m} + \frac{1}{m-1} + \cdots + \frac{1}{m-n+2} \approx \sum_{j=1}^{m+1} 1/j - \sum_{j=1}^{m-n+1} 1/j$$

$$\approx \ln(m+1) - \ln(m-n+1)$$

We conclude that for the find method,

$$\text{averageTime}_S(n, m) \approx \frac{m+1}{n} (\ln(m+1) - \ln(m-n+1))$$

$$= \frac{m+1}{n} \ln\left(\frac{m+1}{m-n+1}\right)$$

$$\approx \frac{m}{n} \ln\left(\frac{1}{1-n/m}\right)$$

The significance of these estimates is that the time for successful and unsuccessful searches depends only on the ratio n/m. For example, if n/m is 0.5,

$$\text{averageTime}_S(n, m) \approx 2 \ln\left(1 - \frac{1}{2}\right) = 2 \ln 2 \approx 1.39 \text{ iterations}$$

$$\text{averageTime}_U(n, m) \approx (1/\left(1 - \frac{1}{2}\right) = 2 \text{ iterations}$$

Figure 13.14 summarizes the time estimates for successful and unsuccessful searches (that is, invocations of the find method). For purposes of comparison, the information in Figure 13.5 on chained hashing is included. Figure 13.15 provides some specifics: the expected number of loop iterations for various ratios of n to m. For purposes of comparison, the information in Figure 13.6 on chained hashing is included.

A cursory look at Figure 13.15 suggests that chained hashing is much faster than double hashing. But the figures given are mere estimates of the number of loop iterations. Run-time testing may, or may not, give a different picture. Run-time comparisons are the subject of Project 13.1.

Figure 13.14 I Estimates of average times for successful and unsuccessful calls to find, under both chaining and double hashing. In the figure, $n =$ number of values inserted; $m =$ length of table = number of buckets.

Chaining:

$$\text{averageTime}_S(n, m) \approx \frac{n}{2m} \text{ iterations}$$
$$\text{averageTime}_U(n, m) \approx \frac{n}{m} \text{ iterations}$$

Double hashing:

$$\text{averageTime}_S(n, m) \approx \frac{m}{n} \ln\left(\frac{1}{1 - \frac{n}{m}}\right) \text{ iterations}$$

$$\text{averageTime}_U(n, m) \approx \frac{1}{1 - \frac{n}{m}} \text{ iterations}$$

Figure 13.15 | Estimated average number of loop iterations for successful and unsuccessful calls to find, under both chained hashing and double hashing. In the figure, n = number of values inserted; m = length of table = number of buckets.

$\frac{n}{m}$	0.25	0.50	0.75	0.90	0.99
Chained hashing:					
Successful	0.13	0.25	0.38	0.45	0.50
Unsuccessful	0.25	0.50	0.75	0.90	0.99
Double hashing:					
Successful	1.14	1.39	1.85	2.56	4.65
Unsuccessful	1.33	2.00	4.00	10.00	100.00

Even if the Uniform Hashing Assumption applies, we could still, in the worst case, get every key to hash to the same index and yield the same offset. So for the find method under double hashing, worstTime$_S$(n, m) and worstTime$_U$(n, m) are linear in n.

All the relevant files, both for chained hashing as well as double hashing, are available from the Source Code link on the book's website.

SUMMARY

In this chapter, we developed the hash_map class, for which insertions, searches, and deletions take only constant time, on average. This exceptional performance is due to **hashing,** the process of transforming a key into a table index. A hashing algorithm must include a collision handler for the possibility that two keys might hash to the same index. A widely used collision handler is chaining. With **chaining,** the hash_map container is represented as an array of lists. Each list contains the items whose keys hashed to that index in the array. Another collision handler is **open-addressing:** when the table location whose index the key hashed to contains an item with another key, the rest of the table is searched until an unoccupied location or matching key is found.

The **Uniform Hashing Assumption** states that an arbitrary key is equally likely to hash to any of the table's indices. With respect to chaining, the Uniform Hashing Assumption implies that the average size of each list in the table is less than some constant. For open-address hashing, the same assumption implies that the ratio of items in the table to the table's length is bounded above by some constant.

The **load factor** is the ratio of the number of items in the table to the size of the table. If the Uniform Hashing Assumption holds, the time for successful and unsuccessful searches depends only on the load factor. The same is true for insertions and removals. If we double the table size whenever the load factor reaches some fixed ratio, then the average time to insert, erase, or search is constant.

EXERCISES

13.1 Construct a hash_map container of the 25,000 students at Moo University. Each student's key will be that student's unique six-digit ID number. The second component in a student pair is the student's grade point average. Insert a few items into the hash_map container.

13.2 Construct a hash_map container of the 25,000 students at Moo University. Each student's key will be that student's unique six-digit ID number. The second component in a student pair will be that student's grade point average and class rank. Insert a few values into the hash_map container. Note that the second component does not consist of a single datum.

13.3 Suppose you have a hash_map container, and you want to insert an item unless it is already there. How could you accomplish this?

13.4 As a programmer who uses the hash_map class, develop a print_sorted function:

```
// Precondition: The class of keys includes operator<.
// Postcondition: The items in the range from first (inclusive) to last
//                (exclusive) have been printed in order of increasing keys.
template <class ForwardIterator>
void print_sorted (ForwardIterator first, ForwardIterator last);
```

> *Hint* The basic idea is to copy the hash map to a map, and then print out the map. But in order to construct a map object, the definition must include the first two template arguments (the precondition allows the function class less to be the default third template argument). We saw this situation before in the definition of the tree_sort method in Chapter 12. In order to determine the template arguments for a map definition, print_sorted calls
>
> print_sorted_aux (first, last, (*first).first, (*first).second);
>
> The definition of print_sorted_aux starts with
>
> ```
> template <class ForwardIterator, class Key, class T>
> void print_sorted_aux (ForwardIterator first, ForwardIterator last, Key, T)
> {
>         map<Key, T> my_map;
> ```

13.5 For each of the following methods, find functions g and h in the order hierarchy such that averageTime(n) is $O(g)$ and worstTime(n) is $O(h)$, and these are the smallest upper bounds. The functions g and h may be the same for some methods.

    a.   Making a successful call—that is, the item was found—to the generic algorithm find to search for an item in a sequential container (array, vector, deque, or list).

    b.   Calling the generic algorithm binary_search; assume the items in the container are in order, and the container supports random-access iterators.

    c.   Making a successful call to the find method in the BinSearchTree class.

    d.   Making a successful call to the find method in the map class.

    e.   Making a successful call to the find method in the hash_map class—you should make the Uniform Hashing Assumption.

13.6. In the implementation of chained hashing, why was an array used instead of a vector?

13.7 With the open-address strategy discussed in this chapter, we rehash and double the table size whenever the value of count_plus reaches the threshold, even though the value of count may be far below the threshold. Suppose we do the following instead: rehash and double the table size whenever the value of count reaches the threshold, and rehash without doubling the table size when the value of count_plus reaches the threshold. Under what circumstance would this "improvement" be inefficient?

    Hint   What if the value of count is close to the value of count_plus?

13.8 Assume that p is a prime number. Use modular algebra to show that for any positive integers *index* and *offset* (with *offset* not a multiple of p), the following container has exactly p elements:

$$(index + k * offset) \ \% \ p \quad \text{for } k = 0, 1, 2, \ldots, p - 1$$

13.9 Given the following program fragment, add the code to print out all the keys, and then add the code to print out all the values:

```
hash_map<string, int, hash_func>age_map;

age_map.insert (value_type<const string, int> ("dog", 15));
age_map.insert (value_type<const string, int> ("cat", 20));
age_map.insert (value_type<const string, int> ("turtle", 15));
age_map.insert (value_type<const string, int> ("human", 15));
```

13.10 Compare the space requirements for chained hashing and open-address hashing with quotient offsets. Assume that a pointer or **int** value occupies 4 bytes and a **bool** value occupies 1 byte. Specifically, suppose table.length = 100003, loadFactor is 0.75, and count = count_plus = 75000.

13.11 We noted in Chapter 10 that the term *dictionary,* viewed as an arbitrary collection of key-value pairs, is a synonym for *map.* If you were going to create a real dictionary, would you prefer to store the elements in a map container or in a hash_map container?

13.12 In open-addressing, with the quotient-offset collision handler, insert the following keys into a table of size 13:

> 20
>
> 33
>
> 49
>
> 22
>
> 26
>
> 202
>
> 508
>
> 38
>
> 9

Here are the relevant remainders and quotients:

key	key % 13	key / 13
20	7	1
33	7	2
49	10	3
22	9	1
26	0	2
202	7	15
508	1	39
38	12	2
9	9	0

PROGRAMMING PROJECT 13.1

A Run-Time Comparison of Chaining and Double Hashing in Building a Symbol Table

Perform a run-time experiment to compare chained hashing, open addressing with an offset of 1, and open addressing with a quotient offset. In each case, use 0.75 as the maximum load factor and a prime table size (the next_prime method will enable you to generate a prime number large enough to avoid rehashing the table). The hash_map1.h (for chaining), hash_map2.h (for offset-of-1), and hash_map3.h (for quotient-offset) files are available from the Source Code link on the book's website.

The experiment will simulate part of a compiler, specifically, hashing identifiers into a symbol table. Symbol tables were discussed in the infix-to-postfix application of Chapter 7, and implemented in Lab 17. For the sake of simplicity, the value part of each element will be the empty string.

CHAPTER 14

Graphs, Trees, and Networks

There are many situations in which we want to study the relationships between objects. For example, in a curriculum, the objects are courses and the relationship is based on prerequisites. In airline travel, the objects are cities; two cities are related if there is a flight between them. It is visually appealing to describe such situations graphically, with points (called *vertices*) representing the objects and lines (called *edges*) representing the relationships. In this chapter, we will introduce several containers based on vertices and edges. Finally, we will define, design, and implement one of those containers in a class from which the other structures can be defined as subclasses. Neither the class nor the subclasses are currently part of the Standard Template Library. ■

CHAPTER OBJECTIVES

1. Define the terms *graph, tree,* and *network,* for both directed and undirected containers.

2. Compare breadth-first iteration and depth-first iteration.

3. Understand Prim's greedy algorithm for finding a minimum-cost spanning tree and Dijkstra's greedy algorithm for finding the minimum-cost path between vertices.

4. In the network class, compare the adjacency-list design with the adjacency-matrix design.

5. Be able to solve problems that include backtracking through a graph, tree, or network.

14.1 I UNDIRECTED GRAPHS

An undirected graph consists of vertices and unordered vertex-pairs called edges.

An **undirected graph** consists of items called **vertices** and distinct, unordered vertex-pairs called **edges.** Here is an example of an undirected graph:

Vertices: A, B, C, D, E

Edges: (A, B), (A, C), (B, D), (C, D), (C, E)

The vertex pair in an edge is enclosed in parentheses to indicate the pair of vertices is unordered. For example, to say there is an edge from *A* to *B* is the same as saying there is an edge from *B* to *A*. That's why "undirected" is used. Figure 14.1 depicts this undirected graph, with each edge represented as a line connecting its vertex pair.

From the illustration in Figure 14.1 we could obtain the original formulation of the undirected graph as a container of vertices and edges. And furthermore, Figure 14.1 gives us a better grasp of the undirected graph than the original formulation. So from now on we will often use illustrations such as Figure 14.1 instead of the formulations.

Figure 14.2 contains several additional undirected graphs. Notice that the number of edges can be fewer than the number of vertices (Figure 14.2a and b), equal to the number of vertices (Figure 14.1), or greater than the number of vertices (Figure 14.2c).

An undirected graph is **complete** if it has as many edges as possible. What is the number of edges in a complete undirected graph? Let *n* represent the number of vertices. Figure 14.3 shows that when $n = 6$, the maximum number of edges is 15.

Can you determine a formula that determines the number of edges in a complete undirected graph of *n* vertices for any positive integer *n*? In general, start with any one of the *n* vertices, and construct an edge to each of the remaining $n - 1$ vertices. Then from any one of those $n - 1$ vertices, construct an edge to each of the remaining $n - 2$ vertices (the edge to the first vertex was constructed in the previous step). Then from any one of those $n - 2$ vertices, construct an edge to each of the remaining $n - 3$ vertices. This process continues until, at step $n - 1$, a final edge is constructed. The total number of edges constructed is

$$(n - 1) + (n - 2) + (n - 3) + \cdots + 2 + 1 = \sum_{i=1}^{n-1} i = n(n - 1)/2$$

This last equality can either be proved directly by induction on *n* or can be derived from the proof—in Example A1.1—that the sum of the first *n* positive integers is equal to $n(n+1) / 2$.

Figure 14.1 I A visual representation of an undirected graph.

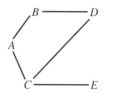

Figure 14.2 | **(a)** An undirected graph with six vertices and five edges. **(b)** An undirected graph with eight vertices and seven edges. **(c)** An undirected graph with eight vertices and eleven edges.

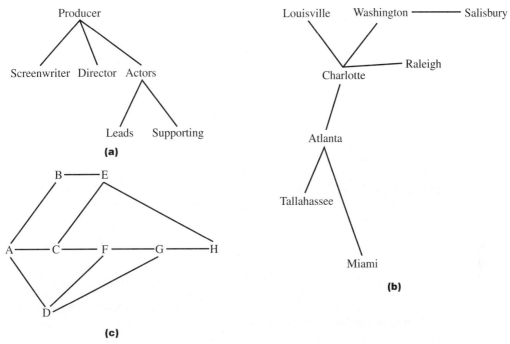

(a)

(b)

(c)

Figure 14.3 | An undirected graph with six vertices and the maximum number (15) of edges for any undirected graph with six vertices.

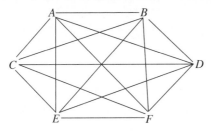

Two vertices are ***adjacent*** if they form an edge. For example, in Figure 14.2b, Charlotte and Atlanta are adjacent, but Atlanta and Raleigh are not adjacent. Adjacent vertices are called ***neighbors.***

A ***path*** is a sequence of vertices in which each successive pair is an edge. For example, in Figure 14.2c,

A, B, E, H

*A **path** is a sequence of vertices in which each successive pair is an edge.*

is a path from *A* to *H* because (*A, B*), (*B, E*), and (*E, H*) are edges. Another path from *A* to *H* is

A, C, F, D, G, H

For a path of *k* vertices, the ***length*** of the path is $k - 1$. In other words, the path length is the number of *edges* in the path. For example, in Figure 14.2c the following path from *C* to *A* has a length of 3:

C, F, D, A

There is, in fact, a shorter path from *C* to *A*, namely,

C, A

In general, there may be several shortest paths between two vertices. For example, in Figure 14.2c,

A, B, E

and

A, C, E

are both shortest paths from *A* to *E*.

A ***cycle*** is a path in which the first and last vertices are the same and there are no repeated edges. For example, in Figure 14.2b,

Atlanta, Tallahassee, Miami, Atlanta

is a cycle. In Figure 14.2c,

B, E, C, A, B

is a cycle, as is

E, C, A, B, E

The undirected graph in Figure 14.2a is ***acyclic,*** that is, it does not contain any cycles. In that undirected graph,

producer, director, producer

is *not* a cycle since the edge (producer, director) is repeated—recall that an edge in an undirected graph is an unordered pair.

An undirected graph is ***connected*** if there is a path between any two distinct vertices in the graph. Informally, an undirected graph is connected if it is "all one piece." For example, all the graphs in Figures 14.1 to 14.3 are connected. The following undirected graph, with six vertices and five edges, is not connected:

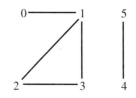

14.2 I DIRECTED GRAPHS

Up to now we have not concerned ourselves with the direction of edges. If we could go from vertex V to vertex W, we assumed that we could also go from vertex W to vertex V. In many situations this assumption may be unrealistic. For example, suppose the edges represent streets and the vertices represent intersections. If the street connecting vertex V to vertex W is one way going from V to W, there would be no edge connecting W to V.

A *directed graph*—sometimes called a *digraph*—consists of vertices and edges in which the edges are *ordered* pairs of vertices. For example, here is a directed graph, with edges in angle brackets to indicate ordered pairs:

In a directed graph, *an edge is an ordered pair of vertices.*

> *Vertices: A, T, V, W, Z*
> *Edges: <A, T>, <A, V>, <T, A>, <V, A>, <V, W>, <W, Z>,*
>   *<Z, W>, <Z, T>*

Pictorially, these edges are represented by arrows, with an arrow's direction going from the first vertex in the ordered pair to the second vertex. For example, Figure 14.4 contains the directed graph just defined.

A path in a directed graph must follow the direction of the arrows. Formally a *path* in a directed graph is a sequence of $k > 1$ vertices $V_0, V_1, \ldots, V_{k-1}$ such that $<V_0, V_1>, <V_1, V_2>, \ldots, <V_{k-2}, V_{k-1}>$ are edges in the directed graph. For example, in Figure 14.4,

> *A, V, W, Z*

is a path from A to Z because $<A, V>$, $<V, W>$ and $<W, Z>$ are edges in the directed graph. But

> *A, T, Z, W*

is not a path because there is no edge from T to Z. A few minutes checking should convince you that for any two vertices in Figure 14.4, there is a path from the first vertex to the second.

A digraph D is *connected* if, for any pair of distinct vertices x and y, there is a path from x to y. Figure 14.4 is a connected digraph, but the following connected digraph is not connected (try to figure out why):

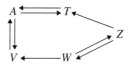

Figure 14.4 I A directed graph.

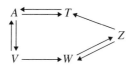

From these examples, you can see that we actually could have defined the term "undirected graph" from "directed graph": an ***undirected graph*** is a directed graph in which, for any two vertices *V* and *W*, if there is an edge from *V* to *W*, there is also an edge from *W* to *V*. This observation will come in handy when we get to developing C++ classes.

In Sections 14.3 and 14.4 we will look at specializations of graphs: trees and networks. When the term "graph," "tree," or "network" appears by itself, you may assume the word "directed" is an implicit prefix. Undirected structures will be explicitly named "undirected graph," "undirected tree," or "undirected network".

14.3 | TREES

An ***undirected tree*** is a connected, acyclic, undirected graph with one item designated as the ***root item.*** For example, here is the undirected tree from Figure 14.2a; "producer" is the root item.

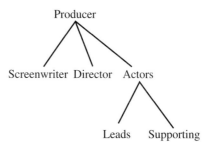

On most occasions, we are interested in directed trees, that is, trees that have arrows from a parent to its children. A ***tree,*** sometimes called a ***directed tree,*** is a directed graph that either is empty or has an item, called the ***root item*** such that

1. There are no edges coming into the root item.
2. Every nonroot item has exactly one edge coming into it.
3. There is a path from the root item to every other item.

For example, Figure 14.5 shows that we can easily redraw the undirected tree from Figure 4.2a as a directed tree: Normally, we do not bother to draw the arrows in a tree, because the direction is always from the top down (except when drawing a hierarchy of classes and subclasses).

Many of the binary tree terms from Chapter 8—such as "child," "leaf," and "branch"—can be extended to apply to arbitrary trees. For example, the tree in Figure 14.5 has four leaves and height 2. But "full" does not apply to trees in general because there is no limit to the number of children a parent can have. In fact, we cannot simply define a binary tree to be a tree in which each item has at most two children. Why not? Figure 14.6 has two distinct binary trees that are equivalent as trees.

We can define a binary tree to be a (directed) tree in which each vertex has at most two children, labeled the "left" child and the "right" child. Trees allow us to

Figure 14.5 I A (directed) tree.

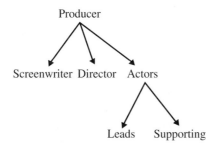

Figure 14.6 I Two distinct binary trees, one with an empty right subtree and one with an empty left subtree.

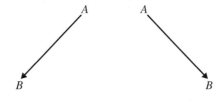

study hierarchical relationships such as parent-child and supervisor-supervisee. And with arbitrary trees, we are not subject to the at-most-two-children restriction of binary trees.

14.4 I NETWORKS

Sometimes we associate a nonnegative number with each edge in a graph (which can be directed or undirected). The nonnegative numbers are called *weights,* and the resulting structure is called a *network* or *weighted graph.* For example, Figure 14.7 has an undirected network in which each weight represents the distance between cities for the graph of Figure 14.2b.

Of what value is a (directed) network, that is, why might the direction of a weighted edge be significant? Even if one can travel in either direction on an edge, the weight for going in one direction may be different from the weight for going in the other direction. For example, suppose the weights represent the time for a plane flight between two cities. Because of the prevailing westerly winds, the time to fly from New York to Los Angeles is usually longer than the time to fly from Los Angeles to New York. Figure 14.8 shows a network in which the weight of the edge from vertex D to vertex F is different from the weight of the edge going in the other direction.

With each path between two vertices in a network, we can calculate the total weight of the path. For example, in Figure 14.8, the path A, C, D, E has a total weight

*A **network,** or **weighted graph,** is a graph in which each edge has an associated nonnegative number, called the **weight** of the edge. A network can be directed or undirected.*

Figure 14.7 | An undirected network in which vertices represent cities, and each edge's weight represents the distance between the two cities in the edge.

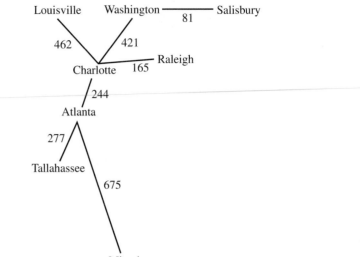

Figure 14.8 | A network with eight vertices and eleven edges.

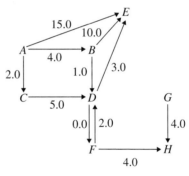

of 10.0. Can you find a shorter path from *A* to *E*, that is, a path with smaller total weight?[1] The shortest path from *A* to *E* is *A, B, D, E* with total weight 8.0. In Section 14.5.4, we will develop an algorithm to find a shortest path (there may be several of them) between two vertices in a network.

The network in Figure 14.8 is not connected because, for example, there is no path from *B* to *C*. Recall that a path in a directed network must follow the direction of the arrows.

Now that we have seen how to define a graph, tree, or network, we can outline some well-known algorithms. The implementation of those algorithms will be developed in Sections 14.7.4 to 14.7.6.

---

[1]This is different from the meaning of "shorter" in the graph sense, namely, having fewer edges in the path.

14.5 I GRAPH ALGORITHMS

A prerequisite to other graph algorithms is being able to iterate through a graph, so we start by looking at iterators in general. We focus on two kinds of iterators: breadth-first and depth-first. These terms may ring a bell; in Chapter 8, we studied breadth-first and depth-first (also known as preorder) traversals of a binary tree.

Two common graph algorithms are breadth-first iteration and depth-first iteration.

14.5.1 Iterators

There are several kinds of iterators associated with directed or undirected graphs, and these iterators can also be applied to trees and networks (directed or undirected). First, we can simply iterate over all the vertices in the graph. The iteration need not be in any particular order. For example, here is an iteration over the vertices in the network of Figure 14.8:

A, B, D, F, G, C, E, H

In addition to iterating over all the vertices in a graph, we are sometimes interested in iterating over all vertices reachable from a given vertex. For example, in the network of Figure 14.8, we might want to iterate over all vertices *reachable* from A, that is, over all vertices that are in some path that starts at A. Here is one such iteration:

A, B, C, D, E, F, H

The vertex G is not reachable from A, so G will not be in any such iteration from A.

Breadth-First Iterators A *breadth-first iterator,* similar to a breadth-first traversal in Chapter 8, visits the start vertex, then the not-yet-reached neighbors of the start vertex, then the not-yet-reached neighbors of those neighbors, and so on. For example, assume that the vertices in the following graph—from Figure 14.2b—were entered in alphabetical order:

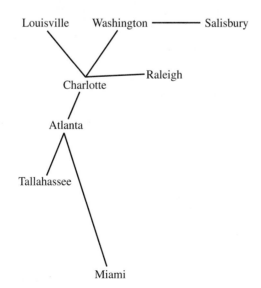

We will perform a breadth-first iteration starting at Atlanta and visit neighbors in alphabetical order. So we start with

Atlanta

The neighbors of Atlanta can now be reached. When we visit those neighbors, in alphabetical order, we get

Charlotte, Miami, Tallahassee

We then visit the not-yet-reached neighbors of Charlotte, in alphabetical order, and then the not-yet-reached neighbors of Miami and Tallahassee. The first neighbor of Charlotte, Atlanta, is ignored because we have already accessed Atlanta. The three not-yet-reached neighbors of Charlotte are

Louisville, Raleigh, Washington

Now that all of Charlotte's neighbors have been visited, we advance to the next city, Miami. We visit the not-yet-reached neighbors of Miami (there are none), Tallahassee (there are none), Louisville (there are none), Raleigh (there are none), and Washington, whose not-yet-reached neighbor is

Salisbury

Now we are done because Salisbury has no not-yet-reached neighbors. In other words, we have iterated through all cities reachable from Atlanta, starting at Atlanta:

Atlanta, Charlotte, Miami, Tallahassee, Louisville, Raleigh, Washington, Salisbury

The order of visiting cities would be different if we started a breadth-first iteration at Louisville:

Louisville, Charlotte, Atlanta, Raleigh, Washington, Miami, Tallahassee, Salisbury

Try to determine the order of visiting the cities if we started a breadth-first iteration at Charlotte.

Let's do some preliminary work on the design of the breadth_first_iterator class. We will need to keep track of which vertices have already been reached. To do this, we will store the reached vertices in some kind of container. To be specific, let's say we want to visit the neighbors of the current vertex in the order in which those neighbors were initially stored in the container. Because we want the vertices removed from the container in the order in which they were added to the container, a *queue* is the appropriate container. And we will also want to keep track of the *current* vertex.

We can now develop high-level algorithms for the breadth_first_iterator methods—the details will have to be postponed until we create a class, such as network, in which the breadth_first_iterator class will be embedded. The constructor enqueues the start vertex and marks all other vertices as not-yet-reached:

```
breadth_first_iterator (vertex start)
{
      for every vertex in the network:
            mark that vertex as not reached.
      mark start as reached.
```

```
        vertex_queue.push (start);
    } // algorithm for constructor
```

The postincrement operator, **operator++ (int)**, dequeues the front vertex in vertex_
queue and then iterates over the neighbors of that vertex. Each neighbor that has not
yet been reached is marked as reached and enqueued.

```
breadth_first_iterator operator++ (int)
{
    breadth_first_iterator temp = *this;
    current = vertex_queue.front( );
    vertex_queue.pop( );

    for each vertex that is a neighbor of current:
            if that vertex has not yet been reached
            {
                    mark that vertex as reached;
                    enqueue that vertex onto vertex_queue
        } // if
    return temp;
} // algorithm for operator++ (int)
```

For an example of how a breadth-first iteration proceeds, suppose we create a
network by entering the sequence of edges and weights in Figure 14.9. The network
created is the same one shown in Figure 14.8:

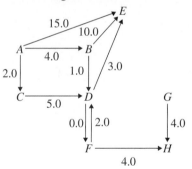

Figure 14.9 | A sequence of edges and weights to generate the network in Figure 14.8.

```
A B  4.0
A C  2.0
A E 15.0
B D  1.0
B E 10.0
C D  5.0
D E  3.0
D F  0.0
F D  2.0
F H  4.0
G H  4.0
```

To conduct a breadth-first iteration starting at, say *A*, we first enqueue *A* in the constructor. The first call to ++ dequeues *A;* enqueues *B, C,* and *E;* and returns a breadth_first_iterator positioned at *A*. The second call to ++ dequeues *B*, enqueues *D*, and returns a breadth_first_iterator positioned at *B*. Figure 14.10 shows the entire queue generated by a breadth-first iteration starting at *A*.

Notice that vertex *G* is missing from Figure 14.10. The reason is that *G* is not reachable from *A*. If we performed a breadth-first iteration from any other vertex, there would be even fewer vertices visited than in Figure 14.10. For example, a breadth-first iteration starting at vertex *B* would visit

B, D, E, F, H

in that order.

Breadth-first iterators are especially useful in iterating over a tree. The start vertex is the root and, as we saw in Chapter 8, the vertices are visited level by level: the root, the root's children, the root's grandchildren, and so on.

Depth-First Iterators The other specialized iterator is a ***depth-first iterator.*** A depth-first iterator is a generalization of the preorder traversal of Chapter 8. Recall, from Chapter 8, the algorithm for a preorder traversal:

```
preOrder(t)
{
    if (t is not empty)
    {
        access the root item of t;
        preOrder(leftTree(t));
        preOrder(rightTree(t));
    } // if
} // preOrder traversal
```

Figure 14.10 ⏐ A breadth-first iteration of the vertices starting at *A*. The vertices are enqueued—and therefore dequeued—in the same order in which they were entered in Figure 14.9.

vertex_queue	Vertex where the iterator returned by ++ is positioned
A	
B, C, E	A
C, E, D	B
E, D	C
D	E
F	D
H	F
	H

To help you remember how a preorder traversal works, Figure 14.11 shows a binary tree and a preorder traversal of its items. We can describe a preorder traversal of a binary tree as follows: start with a leftward path from the root. Once the end of a path is reached, the algorithm *backtracks* to an item that has an as-yet-unreached right child. Another leftward path is begun, starting with that right child.

A depth-first iteration of a graph is slightly more complicated because there is no notion of "left" or "right" in a graph. First, mark the start vertex as reached, and every other vertex as not reached. Then, as long as there are reached vertices that have not been visited, visit the most recently reached, unvisited vertex, and mark its unreached neighbors as reached.

Figure 14.11 | A binary tree and the order in which its items would be visited during a preorder traversal.

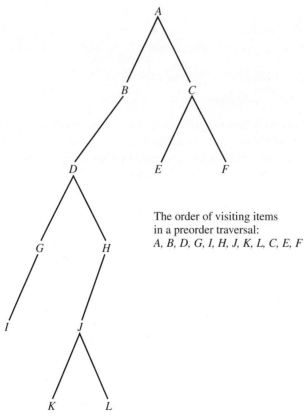

The order of visiting items in a preorder traversal:
A, B, D, G, I, H, J, K, L, C, E, F

For example, let's perform a depth-first iteration of the following graph, starting at Atlanta—we assume that the vertices were initially entered in alphabetical order:

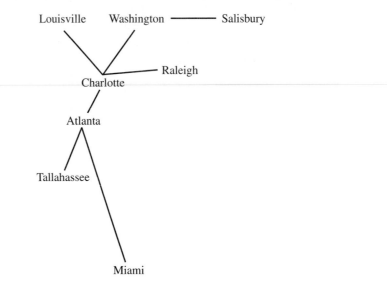

We first visit the start vertex:

Atlanta

Then we mark as reached the neighbors of Atlanta:

Charlotte, Miami, Tallahassee

We then visit the most recently reached vertex, namely Tallahassee, *not* Charlotte. Tallahassee has no unreached neighbors, so we visit the next most recently reached vertex: Miami. Miami also has no unreached neighbors, so we visit Charlotte, and mark as reached Charlotte's unreached neighbors:

Louisville, Raleigh, Washington

Washington, the most recently reached vertex, is visited, and its only unreached neighbor,

Salisbury

is marked as reached. Now Salisbury is the most recently reached vertex, so Salisbury is visited. Finally, Raleigh and then Louisville are visited. The order in which the vertices are visited is as follows:

Atlanta, Tallahassee, Miami, Charlotte, Washington, Salisbury, Raleigh, Louisville

For a depth-first iteration starting at Charlotte, the order in which vertices are visited is

Charlotte, Washington, Salisbury, Raleigh, Louisville, Atlanta, Tallahassee, Miami

With a breadth-first iteration, we saved vertices in a queue so that the vertices were visited in the order in which they were saved. With a depth-first iteration, the next vertex to be visited is the *most recently reached* vertex. So the vertices will be *stacked* instead of queued. Other than that, the basic strategy of a depth-first iterator is exactly the same as the basic strategy of a breadth-first iterator. Here is the high-level algorithm for **operator++ (int)**:

```
depth_first_iterator operator++ (int)
{
        depth_first_iterator temp = *this;
        current = vertex_stack.top( );
        vertex_stack.pop( );

        for each vertex that is a neighbor of current:
                if that vertex has not yet been reached
                {
                        mark that vertex as reached;
                        push that vertex onto vertex_stack
                } // if
        return temp;

} // algorithm for operator++ (int) in a depth-first iteration
```

Suppose, as we did for a breadth-first iteration, we create a network from the following input, in the order given:

A B 4.0
A C 2.0
A E 15.0
B D 1.0
B E 10.0
C D 5.0
D E 3.0
D F 0.0
F D 2.0
F H 4.0
G H 4.0

The network created is the same one shown in Figure 14.8:

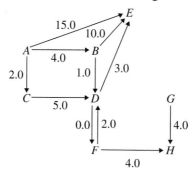

Figure 14.12 shows the sequence of stack states for a depth-first iteration of the network in Figure 14.8, as generated from the input in Figure 14.9. We could also develop a backtrack version of a depth-first iteration. The backtrack version is equivalent, but may utilize recursion instead of an explicit stack.

14.5.2 Connectedness

In Section 14.1, we defined an undirected graph to be **_connected_** if there was a path between any two distinct vertices in the graph. For example, the following is a connected undirected graph:

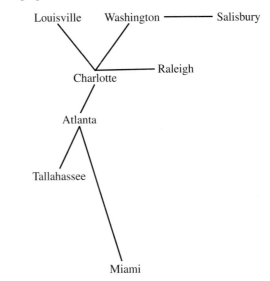

Figure 14.12 | A depth-first iteration of the vertices reachable from *A*. We assume the vertices were entered as in Figure 14.9.

Stack (top vertex is shown leftmost)	Vertex where iterator returned by ++ is positioned
A	
E, C, B	A
C, B	E
D, B	C
F, B	D
H, B	F
B	H
	B

A breadth-first or depth-first iteration over all vertices in a network (or undirected network) can be performed only if the network is connected. In fact, we can
use the ability to iterate between any two vertices as a test for connectedness. Suppose itr is an iterator over *all* the vertices in a network. Let vertex be the class in
which vertices are items. For each vertex v where the iterator returned by itr++ is
positioned, let b_itr be a breadth-first iterator starting at v. We check to make sure
that the number of vertices reachable from v (including v itself) is equal to the number of vertices in the network.

Here is a high-level algorithm to determine connectedness in a network:

```
// Postcondition: true has been returned if this network is connected.
//                Otherwise, false has been returned.
bool is_connected( )
{
        let itr be an iterator over the network;

        // For each vertex v, see if the number of vertices reachable from v
        // is equal to the total number of vertices in this network.
        for (itr = beginning of network; itr != end of network; itr ++)
        {
                vertex v = *itr;
                // Count the vertices reachable from v.
                unsigned int count = 0;
                breadth_first_iterator b_itr;
                for (b_itr = breadth_first_begin (v); b_itr != breadth_first_end( );
                            b_itr++)
                        count++;
                if (count < size of network)
                        return false;
        } // while itr not finished iterating
        return true;
} // algorithm for method is_connected
```

We cannot yet estimate the time and space requirements for this algorithm because
they depend, for example, on the analysis of the iterator methods.

In Sections 14.5.3 and 14.5.4, we outline the development of two important network algorithms. Each algorithm is sufficiently complex that it is named after the
person (Prim, Dijkstra) who invented the algorithm.

14.5.3 Generating a Minimum Spanning Tree

Suppose a cable company has to connect a number of houses in a community. Given
the costs, in hundreds of dollars, to lay cable between the houses, determine the minimum cost of connecting the houses to the cable system. This can be cast as a connected, undirected network problem; each weight represents the cost to lay cable
between two neighbors. Figure 14.13 gives a sample layout. Some house-to-house
distances are not given because they represent infeasible connections (over a moun-
tain, for example).

Figure 14.13 ❙ A connected, undirected network in which the vertices represent houses and the weights represent the cost, in hundreds of dollars, to connect the two houses.

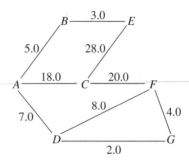

Figure 14.14 ❙ A spanning tree for the undirected network in Figure 14.13.

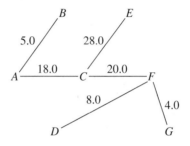

Figure 14.15 ❙ Another spanning tree for the undirected network in Figure 14.13.

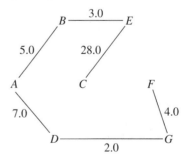

*A **spanning tree** for a network consists of all the vertices and some of the edges and their weights. A spanning tree is **minimum** if no other spanning tree for the network has weights with a smaller total value.*

In a connected, undirected network, a **spanning tree** is a tree that consists of all the vertices and some of the edges (and their weights) from the network. For example, Figures 14.14 and 14.15 show two spanning trees for the network in Figure 14.13. For the sake of specificity, we designate vertex *A* as the root of each tree.

A **minimum spanning tree** is a spanning tree in which the sum of all the weights is no greater than the sum of all the weights in any other spanning tree. The original problem about laying cable can be restated in the form of constructing a minimum spanning tree for a connected, undirected network. To give you an idea of how difficult it is to solve this problem, try to construct a minimum spanning tree for the network in Figure 14.13. How difficult would it be to "scale up" your solution to a community with 1000 houses?

An algorithm to construct a minimum spanning tree is due to R. C. Prim (1957). Here is the basic strategy. Start with an empty tree T and pick any vertex v in the network. Add v to T. For each vertex w such that (v, w) is an edge with weight *wweight*, save the ordered triple $<v, w, wweight>$ in a container—we'll see what kind of container shortly. Then loop until T has as many vertices as the original network. During each loop iteration, remove from the container the triple $<x, y, yweight>$ for which *yweight* is the smallest weight of all triples in the container. If y is not already in T, add y and the edge (x, y) to T and save in the container every triple $<y, z, zweight>$ such that z is not already in T and (y, z) is an edge with weight *zweight*.

Prim's algorithm constructs a minimum spanning tree.

What kind of container should we have? The container should be ordered by weights; we need to be able to add an item, that is, a triple, to the container and to remove the triple with lowest weight. A *priority queue* will perform these tasks quickly: with a heap-based implementation, averageTime(n) for the push method is constant, and averageTime(n) for pop is logarithmic in n. At any time, the triple with *lowest* weight will be on top of the priority queue.

To see how Prim's algorithm works, let's start with the undirected network in Figure 14.13, repeated here:

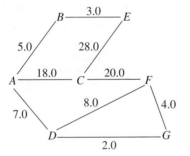

Initially, the tree T and the priority_queue object pq are both empty. Pick A (we could just as well have picked any other vertex), add A to T, and add to pq each triple of the form $<A, w, wweight>$ where (A, w) is an edge with weight *wweight*. Figure 14.16 shows the contents of T and pq at this point. For ease of readability, the triples in pq are shown in increasing order of weights; strictly speaking, all we know for sure is that the top method returns the triple with smallest weight, and the pop method removes that triple from pq.

When the lowest-weighted triple, $<A, B, 5.0>$ is removed from pq, the vertex B and the edge (A, B) and its weight are added to T, and the triple $<B, E, 3.0>$ is added to (the top of) pq. See Figure 14.17.

During the next iteration, the triple $<B, E, 3.0>$ is removed from pq, the vertex E and edge (B, E) are added to T, and the triple $<E, C, 28.0>$ is added to pq. See Figure 14.18.

Figure 14.16 | The contents of T and pq at the start of Prim's algorithm as applied to the undirected network in Figure 14.13.

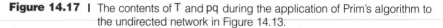

T	pq
A	<A, B, 5.0>
	<A, D, 7.0>
	<A, C, 18.0>

Figure 14.17 | The contents of T and pq during the application of Prim's algorithm to the undirected network in Figure 14.13.

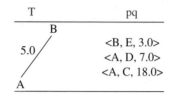

pq: <B, E, 3.0> <A, D, 7.0> <A, C, 18.0>

Figure 14.18 | The contents of T and pq during the application of Prim's algorithm to the undirected network in Figure 14.13.

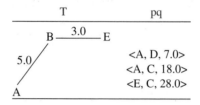

pq: <A, D, 7.0> <A, C, 18.0> <E, C, 28.0>

Figure 14.19 | The contents of T and pq during the application of Prim's algorithm to the undirected network in Figure 14.13.

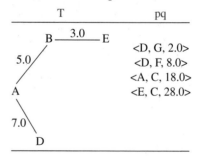

pq: <D, G, 2.0> <D, F, 8.0> <A, C, 18.0> <E, C, 28.0>

During the next iteration, the triple <A, D, 7.0> is removed from pq, the vertex D and the edge (A, D) and its weight are added to T, and the triples <D, F, 8.0> and <D, G, 2.0> are added to pq. See Figure 14.19.

During the next iteration, the triple <D, G, 2.0> is removed from pq, the vertex G and the edge (D, G) and its weight are added to T, and the triple <G, F, 4.0> is added to pq. See Figure 14.20.

During the next iteration, the triple <G, F, 4.0> is removed from pq, the vertex F and the edge (G, F) and its weight are added to T, and the triple <F, C, 20.0> is added to pq. See Figure 14.21.

Figure 14.20 I The contents of T and pq during the application of Prim's algorithm to the undirected network in Figure 14.13.

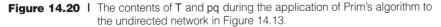
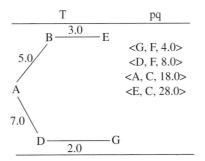

Figure 14.21 I The contents of T and pq during the application of Prim's algorithm to the undirected network in Figure 14.13.

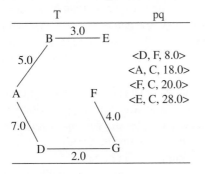

During the next iteration, the triple <*D, F,* 8.0> is removed from pq. But *nothing* is added to T or pq because *F* is already in T!

During the next iteration, the triple <*A, C,* 18.0> is removed from pq, the vertex C and the edge (*A, C*) and its weight are added to T, and nothing is added to pq. The reason nothing is added to pq is that, for all of *C*'s edges, (*C, A*), (*C, E*) and (*C, F*), the second item in the pair is already in T. See Figure 14.22. Even though pq is not empty, we are finished because every vertex in the original network is also in T.

From the way T is constructed, we know that T is a spanning tree. We can show, by contradiction, that T is a minimum spanning tree. Assume that T is not a minimum spanning tree. Then during some iteration, a triple <*x, y, yweight*> is removed from pq and the edge (*x, y*) is added to T, but there is some other vertex *v,* already in T, such that edge (*v, y*) has lower weight than edge (*x, y*). We can show this pictorially:

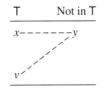

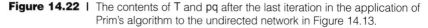

Figure 14.22 | The contents of T and pq after the last iteration in the application of Prim's algorithm to the undirected network in Figure 14.13.

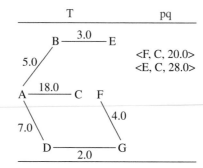

Note that since v was already in T, the triple starting with $<v, y, ?>$ must have been added to pq earlier. But the edge (v, y) could not have a lower weight than the edge (x, y) because the triple $<x, y, yweight>$ was removed from pq, not the triple starting with $<v, y, ?>$. This contradicts the claim that (v, y) had lower edge weight than (x, y). So T, with edge (x, y) added, must still be minimum. The get_minimum_ spanning_tree method is defined in Section 14.7.5.

Prim's algorithm is another example of a greedy algorithm (the Huffman encoding algorithm in Chapter 11 was also a greedy algorithm). During each loop iteration, the locally optimal choice is made: the edge with lowest weight is added to T. This sequence of locally optimal—that is, greedy—choices leads to a globally optimal solution: T is a minimum spanning tree.

Another greedy algorithm appears in Section 14.5.4. Exercise 14.6 and Lab 29 show that greed does not always succeed.

14.5.4 Finding the Shortest Path through a Network

The strategy for constructing a minimum spanning tree is similar to the following strategy for finding a shortest path in a network (or undirected network) from some vertex v1 to some other vertex v2. In this context, "shortest" means having the lowest total weight. Both algorithms are greedy, and both use a priority queue. The shortest-path algorithm, due to Edsgar Dijkstra (1959), is essentially a breadth-first iteration that starts at v1 and stops as soon as v2's pair is removed from the priority queue pq. Each pair consists of a vertex w and the sum of the weights of all edges on the shortest path so far from v1 to w.

Given two vertices in a network, Dijkstra's algorithm constructs a shortest path, that is, a path with lowest total weight.

The priority queue is ordered by *lowest* total weights. To keep track of total weights, we have a map container, weight_sum, in which each key is a vertex w that maps to the sum of the weights of all the edges on the shortest path so far from v1 to w. To enable us to reconstruct the shortest path when we are through, there is another map container, predecessor, in which each key is a vertex w that maps to the vertex that is the immediate predecessor of w on the shortest path so far from v1 to w.

Basically, weight_sum keeps track of the minimum weight, so far, of the path from v1 to every other vertex. Initially, pq consists of the vertices (and their weights) adjacent to v1. On each iteration we greedily choose the vertex-weight pair < from, weight> in pq that has the minimum total weight among all vertex-weight pairs in pq. If there is a neighbor to of from whose total weight can be reduced by the path < v1, . . . , from, to>, then to's path and minimum weight are altered, and to (and its new total weight) is added to pq. For example, we might have

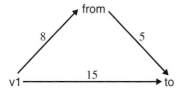

Then the total weight between v1 and to is reduced to 13, the pair < to, 13> is added to pq, and to's predecessor becomes from. Eventually, this yields the shortest possible path from v1 to v2, if there is a path between those vertices.

To start, weight_sum associates with each vertex a very large total weight (say, 10,000.0), and predecessor associates with each vertex an empty vertex. We then refine those initializations by iterating over v1's neighbors. For each neighbor w, where the weight of edge (v1, w) is weight, weight_sum maps w to weight, predecessor maps w to v1, and we add to pq the vertex-weight pair <w, weight>. For v1 itself, weight_sum maps v1 to 0.0 and predecessor maps v1 to v1. This completes the initialization phase.

Suppose we want to find the shortest path from *A* to *E* in the network from Figure 14.8, repeated here:

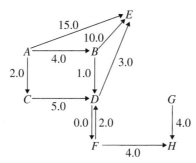

The effect of the initializations is shown in Figure 14.23. Note that vertex G is ignored because *G* is not reachable from *A*.

Now we find the shortest path, if there is one, from *A* to *E*. We keep looping until that path is found or pq is empty. After the initializations shown in Figure 14.23, this outer loop is executed for the first time: the pair <*C, 2.0*> is removed from pq and we iterate (the inner loop) over the neighbors of *C*. The only vertex on an edge from *C* is *D*, and the weight of that edge is 5.0. This weight plus 2.0 (*C*'s weight sum) is

Figure 14.23 | The initialization phase of Dijkstra's shortest-path algorithm.

weight_sum	predecessor	pq
A, 0.0	A	<C, 2.0>
B, 4.0	A	<B, 4.0>
C, 2.0	A	<E, 15.0>
D, 10000.0		
E, 15.0	A	
F, 10000.0		
H, 10000.0		

Figure 14.24 | The state of the application of Dijkstra's shortest-path algorithm after the first iteration of the outer loop.

weight_sum	predecessor	pq
A, 0.0	A	<B, 4.0>
B, 4.0	A	<D, 7.0>
C, 2.0	A	<E, 15.0>
D, 7.0	C	
E, 15.0	A	
F, 10000.0		
H, 10000.0		

Figure 14.25 | The state of the application of Dijkstra's shortest-path algorithm after the second iteration of the outer loop.

weight_sum	predecessor	pq
A, 0.0	A	<D, 5.0>
B, 4.0	A	<D, 7.0>
C, 2.0	A	<E, 14.0>
D, 5.0	B	<E, 15.0>
E, 14.0	B	
F, 10000.0		
H, 10000.0		

7.0, which is less than D's weight sum. So in weight_sum, D's weight sum is upgraded to 7.0. Figure 14.24 shows the effect on weight_sum, predecessor, and pq.

Figure 14.24 indicates that at this point, the lowest-weight path from A to D has a total weight of 7.0. During the second iteration of the outer loop, <B, 4.0> is removed from pq and we iterate over neighbors of B, namely, D and E. The effects are shown in Figure 14.25.

At this point, the lowest-weight path to D has a total weight of 5.0 and the lowest-weight path to E has a total weight of 14.0. During the third iteration of the outer loop, <D, 5.0> is removed from pq, and we iterate over the neighbors of D, namely, F and E. Figure 14.26 shows the effects of this iteration.

Figure 14.26 | The state of the application of Dijkstra's shortest-path algorithm after the third iteration of the outer loop.

weight_sum	predecessor	pq
A, 0.0	A	<F, 5.0>
B, 4.0	A	<D, 7.0>
C, 2.0	A	<E, 8.0>
D, 5.0	B	<E, 14.0>
E, 8.0	D	<E, 15.0>
F, 5.0	D	
H, 10000.0		

Figure 14.27 | The state of the application of Dijkstra's shortest-path algorithm after the fourth iteration of the outer loop.

weight_sum	predecessor	pq
A, 0.0	A	<D, 7.0>
B, 4.0	A	<E, 8.0>
C, 2.0	A	<H, 9.0>
D, 5.0	B	<E, 14.0>
E, 8.0	D	<E, 15.0>
F, 5.0	D	
H, 9.0	F	

During the fourth outer-loop iteration, $<F, 5.0>$ is removed from pq; the neighbors of F, namely D and H are examined; and the containers are updated. See Figure 14.27.

At the start of the fifth outer-loop iteration, $<D, 7.0>$ is removed from pq. The minimum total weight, so far, from A to D is recorded in weight_sum as 5.0. So during the inner-loop iteration, neither weight_sum, predecessor, nor pq is changed.

During the sixth iteration of the outer loop, $<E, 8.0>$ is removed from pq. Because E is the vertex we want to find the shortest path to, we are done. How can we be sure there are no shorter paths to E? If there were another path to E with total weight t less than 8.0, then the pair $<E, t>$ would have been removed from pq before the pair $<E, 8.0>$.

We construct the shortest path, as a list of vertices, from predecessor by *prepending E, E's* predecessor *D, D's* predecessor *B,* and *B's* predecessor *A.* The list will then be in the correct order:

A, B, D, E

There are a few details that are missing in this description of Dijkstra's algorithm. For example, how will the vertices, edges, and neighbors be stored? In Section 14.6 we develop a class to fill in the missing details, not only of Dijkstra's algorithm, but of all our graph-related work.

14.6 | DEVELOPING A NETWORK CLASS

In this chapter, we have introduced six data structures: undirected graph, (directed) graph, undirected tree, (directed) tree, undirected network, and (directed) network. We would like to develop classes for these structures with a maximum amount of code sharing. The object-oriented solution is to utilize inheritance, but exactly how should this be done? If we make the directed_graph class a subclass of undirected_ graph, then virtually all the code relating to edges will have to be overridden. That's because in an undirected graph, each edge (A, B) represents two links: from A to B and from B to A. Similarly, code written for graphs would have to be rewritten for networks.

For the sake of code reuse, we define a (directed) network class, and define other graph classes as sub-classes of network.

A better approach is to define the (directed) network class, and make the other classes subclasses of that class. For example, we can view an undirected_ network container as a directed_network container in which all edges are two-way. So to add an edge (A, B) to an undirected_network container the method definition is

```
// Postcondition: if the edge <v1, v2> is already in this undirected network,
//                 false has been returned. Otherwise, that edge with the given
//                 weight has been inserted in this undirected network and true
//                 has been returned.
bool insert_edge (const vertex& v1, const vertex v2, double& weight)
{
        if (contains_edge (v1, v2))
                return false;
        network::insert_edge (v1, v2, weight);
        network::insert_edge (v2, v1, weight);
        return true;
} // method insert_edge in undirected_network class, a subclass of network
```

(In this method definition, the scope-resolution operator, that is, **operator**::, is necessary to indicate that the method invoked is the network class's insert_edge method, not the undirected_network class's insert_edge method.)

Furthermore, we can view a directed graph as a network in which all weights have the value of 1.0. The directed_graph class will have the following method:

```
// Postcondition: if <v1, v2> was not an edge in this directed_graph before
//                 this call, that edge has been added to this directed_graph
//                 and true has been returned. Otherwise, false has been
//                 returned.
boolean insert_edge (const vertex& v1, const vertex& v2)
{
        network::insert_edge (v1, v2, 1.0);
} // method insertEdge in directed_graph class, a subclass of network
```

In Section 14.7 we develop a (directed) network class. The development of the subclasses—undirected_graph, directed_graph, undirected_tree, directed_tree, and undirected_network—is left as an exercise.

14.7 | THE network CLASS

The first issue in developing a class is to decide what public methods the class should have: These constitute the user's view of the class. For the network class, we have vertex-related methods, edge-related methods, and network-as-a-whole methods. We start with the vertex-related method interfaces (timing estimates are given in Section 14.7.7):

```
// Postcondition: true has been returned if this network contains v;
//                otherwise, false has been returned.
bool contains_vertex (const vertex& v);

// Postcondition: if v is already in this network, false has been returned.
//                Otherwise, v has been added to this network and true
//                has been returned.
bool insert_vertex (const vertex& v);

// Postcondition: if v is a vertex in this network, v and all of its edges have
//                been deleted from this network and true has been returned.
//                Otherwise, false has been returned.
bool erase_vertex (const vertex& v);
```

Here are the edge-related method interfaces:

```
// Postcondition: the number of edges in this network has been returned.
unsigned int get_edge_count( );

// Postcondition: if <v1, v2> forms an edge in this network, the weight of that
//                edge has been returned. Otherwise, −1.0 has been returned.
double get_edge_weight (const vertex& v1, const vertex& v2);

// Postcondition: true has been returned if this network contains the edge
//                <v1, v2>. Otherwise, false has been returned.
bool contains_edge (const vertex& v1, const vertex& v2);

// Postcondition: if the edge <v1, v2> is already in this network false has
//                been returned. Otherwise, that edge with the given weight
//                has been inserted in this network and true has been
//                returned.
bool insert_edge (const vertex& v1, const vertex& v2, const double& weight);

// Postcondition: if <v1, v2> is an edge in this network, that edge has been
//                removed and true has been returned. Otherwise, false has
//                been returned.
bool erase_edge (const vertex& v1, const vertex& v2);
```

Finally, we have the method interfaces for those methods that apply to the network as a whole, including three flavors of iterators:

```
// Postcondition: this network is empty.
network( );

// Postcondition: this network contains a copy of other.
network (const network& other);

// Postcondition: the number of vertices in this network has been returned.
unsigned int size( );

// Postcondition: true has been returned if this network contains no vertices.
//               Otherwise, false has been returned.
bool empty( );

// Precondition: v is in this network.
// Postcondition: the list of neighbors of v has been returned.
list< vertex > get_neighbor_list (const vertex& v);

// Postcondition: true has been returned if this network is connected.
//               Otherwise, false has been returned.
bool is_connected( );

// Precondition: this network is connected.
// Postcondition: a minimum spanning tree for this network has been
//               returned.
network<vertex> get_minimum_spanning_tree( );

// Postcondition: the shortest path from v1 to v2 and its total weight have
//               been returned.
pair<list<vertex>, double> get_shortest_path (const vertex& v1,
                                              const vertex& v2);

// Postcondition: an iterator positioned at the beginning of this network has
//               been returned.
iterator begin( );

// Postcondition: the iterator returned can be used in comparisons to
//               terminate an iteration of this network.
iterator end( );

// Precondition: vertex v is in this network.
// Postcondition: a breadth_first_iterator over all vertices reachable from v
//               has been returned.
breadth_first_iterator breadth_first_begin (const vertex& v);
```

```
// Postcondition: the breadth_first_iterator returned can be used in
//                 comparisons to terminate this iteration of this network.
breadth_first_iterator breadth_first_end( );


// Precondition: vertex v is in this network.
// Postcondition: a depth_first_iterator over all vertices reachable from v has
/                 been returned.
depth_first_iterator depth_first_begin (const vertex& v);


// Postcondition: the depth_first_iterator returned can be used in comparisons
//                 to terminate this iteration of this network.
depth_first_iterator depth_first_end( );
```

In the heading of the get_minimum_spanning_tree method, the return type is network instead of tree. The reason for this is that in a tree, as a subclass of directed_ graph, each edge would have a weight of 1.0. So the get_minimum_spanning_tree method returns a network in which there is a specially designated item, called the **root,** and

1. There are no edges coming into the root item.
2. Every nonroot item has exactly one edge coming into it.
3. There is a path from the root to every other item.
4. Every edge has a nonnegative weight.

14.7.1 **Fields in the** network **Class**

As usual, the fundamental decisions about designing a class involve selecting its fields. In the (directed) network class, we will associate with each vertex v all the vertices w such that <v, w> forms an edge. Because this is a network, if <v, w> forms an edge, we will include with each such vertex w the weight of the edge <v, w>.

We can rephrase our overall organization as follows: we will associate with each vertex v in the network all pairs of the form

> w, weight

where <v, w> forms an edge with the given weight. Two questions still remain: What container will be used to hold the associations, and what container will be used to hold "all the pairs" associated with a given vertex? To answer the second question, we do not know beforehand how many pairs there will be, and the order of the pairs is not important. We will probably want to iterate over all the pairs associated with a given vertex, so we choose a list container to hold the pairs.

Finally, we need a container to associate each vertex *v* with the list container of pairs <w, weight>, where <v, w> is an edge whose weight is weight. The crucial feature of this association is that, given a vertex v, we want to quickly access the associated list container. As the term "association" suggests, we will "map" each vertex to its list container. For speed on average, a hash_map container is indicated. Recall, from Chapter 13, that the average time for inserting in, removing from, or searching a hash_map container is constant—provided the Uniform Hashing Assumption holds.

Unfortunately, the hash_map class is not yet part of the Standard Template Library, so in the interests of portability, we will use the map class instead. Recall, from Chapter 10, that the *worst* time for inserting in, removing from, or searching a map container is logarithmic in n. That is not as fast as a hash_map class's average time, but pretty fast, and much faster than the hash_map class's worst time (linear in n).

The heading of the network class is

template <**class** vertex, **class** Compare = less<vertex> >
class network;

The second template parameter is required for the map class. That is, the user of the network class supplies a template argument to specify how vertices are to be compared. The comparisons determine where a vertex-list pair will be stored in the map container (probably a red-black tree).

The only field in the network class is

protected:

map_class adjacency_map;

where map_class is defined by

typedef map<vertex, list< vertex_weight_pair > , Compare> map_class;

In the **adjacency-list** *design of the* network *class, the only field is* adjacency_map, *a* map *object in which each key is a vertex and each value is the linked list of neighbors (and weights) of the key.*

Recall that in the map class, each value is a pair. In the adjacency_map container, each value will consist of a vertex-list pair, where the vertex is the key and the list contains each vertex adjacent from the key, along with the weight of the corresponding edge. This design is referred to as the ***adjacency-list*** design.

If itr is of type map_class::iterator, then *itr returns a pair. Specifically, (*itr).first is a vertex and (*itr).second is the adjacency list for that vertex. The items in the adjacency list are of type vertex_weight_pair, a **struct** with to and weight fields of type vertex and **double,** respectively. These fields will be easier to understand than the first and second fields in a pair **struct**, and so it is less likely that a reader will confuse a vertex_weight_pair item with the pair returned by dereferencing a map iterator. A further advantage of having a vertex_weight_pair **struct**[2] is that we can overload **operator**> for priority-queue comparisons.

Here is the definition of vertex_weight_pair:

struct vertex_weight_pair
{
        vertex to;

---

[2]Recall that a **struct** is a class with all **public** members.

```
        double weight;

        // Postcondition: this vertex_weight_pair has been initialized from x and y.
        vertex_weight_pair (const vertex& x, const double& y)
        {
            to = x;
            weight = y;
        } // two-parameter constructor

        // Postcondition: true has been returned if this vertex_weight_pair is
        //                 less than x. Otherwise, false has been returned.
        bool operator> (const vertex_weight_pair& p) const
        {
            return weight > p.weight; // smallest weight has highest priority.
        } // operator>
    }; // class vertex_weight_pair
```

14.7.2 **Implementation of the** network **Class**

Because the only field is a map, several of the method definitions are brief because the work is done in the corresponding map methods:

```
network( ) { }

network (const network& other)
{
    adjacency_map = other.adjacency_map;
} // copy constructor

unsigned size( )
{
    return adjacency_map.size( );
} // method size

bool empty( )
{
    return size( ) == 0;
} // method empty

bool contains_vertex (const vertex& v)
{
    return adjacency_map.find (v) != adjacency_map.end( );
} // method contains_vertex
```

The timing for these and other methods in the network class will be considered in Section 14.7.7.

Inserting a vertex v in a network container is straightforward. If v is not already in the network, the pair <v, empty list> is inserted in the adjacency_map container using the associative-array operator. Here is the definition of insert_vertex:

```
bool insert_vertex (const vertex& v)
{
        if (adjacency_map.find (v) != adjacency_map.end( ))
                return false;
        adjacency_map [v] = list< vertex_weight_pair >( );
        return true;
} // method insert_vertex
```

The definition of erase_vertex requires some work. It is easy to remove a vertex v from adjacency_map, and thus remove the associated list of edges going out from v. But each edge going *into* v must also be removed. Since the edge information is stored in a vertex-weight pair in a list, we must iterate over all vertices in the network container. For each vertex, we iterate over its list of pairs looking for v. Whenever v is found in one of those pairs, that pair is removed from that list. Here is the definition of erase_vertex:

```
bool erase_vertex (const vertex& v)
{
        map_class::iterator itr = adjacency_map.find (v);
        if (itr == adjacency_map.end( ))
                return false;
        adjacency_map.erase (itr);
        list<vertex_weight_pair>::iterator list_itr;
        for (itr = adjacency_map.begin( ); itr != adjacency_map.end( ); itr++)
                // In the list in (*itr).second, delete any pair <v, ?>
                for (list_itr = (*itr).second.begin( );list_itr != (*itr).second.end( );
                            list_itr++)
                        if ((*list_itr).to == v)
                        {
                                (*itr).second.erase (list_itr);
                                break; // to exit the inner for loop
                        } // v found in the list (*itr).second
        return true;
} // erase_vertex
```

14.7.3 Implementation of Edge-Related Methods

Now we move on to the edge-related methods. To count the number of edges in a network container, we use the fact that the size of any vertex's associated list container represents the number of edges going out from that vertex. So we iterate over all the vertices in the network, and accumulate the sizes of the associated list containers. Here is the definition:

```
unsigned get_edge_count( )
{
        int count = 0;

        map_class::iterator itr;

        for (itr = adjacency_map.begin( ); itr != adjacency_map.end( ); itr++)
                count += (*itr).second.size( );
        return count;
} // method get_edge_count
```

The calculation of an edge weight is similar. To determine the weight of <v1, v2>, we iterate over v1's associated list searching for a pair whose vertex is v2. If found, we return that pair's weight; otherwise, −1.0 is returned, which indicates <v1, v2> is not an edge in the network. Here is the definition:

```
double get_edge_weight (const vertex& v1, const vertex& v2)
{
        map_class::iterator itr = adjacency_map.find (v1);
        if (itr == adjacency_map.end( )
                        || adjacency_map.find (v2) == adjacency_map.end( ))
                return −1.0;
        // Iterate through the list of neighbors of v1:
        list<vertex_weight_pair >::iterator list_itr;
        for (list_itr = ((*itr).second).begin( ); list_itr != ((*itr).second).end( );
                        list_itr++)
                if ((*list_itr).to == v2)
                                return (*list_itr).weight; // return the weight of <v1, v2>
        return −1.0; // there is no edge <v1, v2>
} // get_edge_weight
```

A similar iteration determines if the network contains a given edge:

```
bool contains_edge (const vertex& v1, const vertex& v2)
{
        map_class::iterator itr = adjacency_map.find (v1);
        if (itr == adjacency_map.end( )
                        || adjacency_map.find (v2) == adjacency_map.end( ))
                return false;
        // See if v2 is in the list of vertices adjacent from v1:
        list<vertex_weight_pair >::iterator list_itr;
        for (list_itr = ((*itr).second).begin( ); list_itr != ((*itr).second).end( );
                        list_itr++)
                if ((*list_itr).to == v2)
                                return true;
        return false;
} // method contains_edge
```

The code for removing an edge is also similar:

```
bool erase_edge (const vertex& v1, const vertex& v2)
{
        map_class::iterator itr = adjacency_map.find (v1);
        if (itr == adjacency_map.end( )
                    || adjacency_map.find (v2) == adjacency_map.end( ))
              return false;
        // If <v1, v2> forms an edge, remove, from the list of edges adjacent
        // from v1, the edge <v1, v2> and the weight of that edge:
        list<vertex_weight_pair >::iterator list_itr;
        for (list_itr = (*itr).second.begin( ); list_itr != (*itr).second.end( );
                    list_itr++)
              if ((*list_itr).to == v2)
              {
                      (*itr).second.erase (list_itr);
                      return true;
              } // if
        return false;
} // method erase_edge
```

Adding an edge <v1, v2> entails appending the vertex_weight_pair <v2, weight> to the adjacency list associated with v1:

```
bool insert_edge (const vertex& v1, const vertex& v2, double weight)
{
        if (contains_edge (v1, v2))
              return false;
        insert_vertex (v1);
        insert_vertex (v2);
        (*(adjacency_map.find(v1))).second.push_back (vertex_weight_pair
                    (v2, weight));
        return true;
} // method insert_edge
```

14.7.4 Implementation of Global Methods

Finally, we tackle the methods that deal with the network as a whole. The list of neighbors of a vertex is obtained by iterating over the adjacency list associated with that vertex. The to vertex in each **vertex_weight_pair** item in the adjacency list is appended to an initially empty list. Here is the definition:

```
list<vertex > get_neighbor_list (const vertex& v)
{
        list<vertex_weight_pair>::iterator list_itr;
```

```
        list<vertex> vertex_list;

        for (list_itr = adjacency_map [v].begin( ); list_itr !=
                    adjacency_map[v].end( ); list_itr++)
            vertex_list.push_back (list_itr -> to);
        return vertex_list;
    } // method get_neighbor_list
```

To determine if the network is connected, we iterate over all vertices in the network. For each vertex v, we iterate over vertices reachable from v—with a breadth-first iterator. If, for any v, the number of vertices reachable from v is less than the number of vertices in the network, the network is not connected. Otherwise, the network is connected. Here is the definition:

```
    bool is_connected( )
    {
        map_class::iterator itr;

        // For each vertex v, see if the number of vertices reachable from v
        // is equal to the total number of vertices in this network.
        for (itr = adjacency_map.begin( ); itr != adjacency_map.end( );itr++)
        {
            vertex v = (*itr).first;

            // Count the vertices reachable from v.
            unsigned count = 0;
            breadth_first_iterator b_itr;
            for (b_itr = breadth_first_begin (v); b_itr != breadth_first_end( );
                    b_itr++)
                count++;
            if (count < adjacency_map.size( ))
                return false;
        } // iterating through all of the vertices in the network
        return true;
    } // method is_connected
```

In order to perform a breadth-first iteration of a network from a start vertex, we need to know not only the start vertex but also the network. The adjacency map would work for the second parameter, but we do not need a separate copy of that map. The breadth_first_begin method sends the start vertex and the *address* of adjacency_map to the constructor in the breadth_first_iterator class:

```
    // Precondition: vertex v is in this network.
    // Postcondition: a breadth_first_iterator over all vertices reachable from v
    //                has been returned.
    breadth_first_iterator breadth_first_begin (const vertex& v)
```

```
        {
            breadth_first_iterator b_itr (v, &adjacency_map);
            return b_itr;
        } // method breadth_first_begin
```

The breadth_first_iterator class follows the outline given in Section 14.5.1. To ensure a quick determination of whether a given vertex has been reached, we make reached a (pointer to a) map of pairs of the form <vertex, **bool**>. Another kind of pair! The heading and fields are

```
        class breadth_first_iterator
        {
            friend class network;

            protected:
                    queue<vertex>* vertex_queue;
                    map<vertex, bool, Compare>* reached;
                    map_class* map_ptr;
```

By making these fields pointers, we greatly simplify the test for equality of breadth-first iterators: instead of iterating through containers, we compare pointers. The breadth_first_iterator two-parameter constructor has a start vertex and a map pointer as its parameters. The map pointer parameter is assigned to the field map_ptr, and the fields reached and vertex_queue are initialized. For every vertex v, the pair <v, **false**> is inserted in *reached. The pair <start, **true**> is then inserted in *reached. And start is pushed onto *vertex_queue. Here is the code:

```
        // Postcondition: this breadth_first_iterator has been initialized at start.
        breadth_first_iterator (const vertex& start, map_class* ptr)
        {
            map_ptr = ptr;
            reached = new map<vertex, bool, Compare>( );
            vertex_queue = new queue <vertex>( );

            // Mark each vertex as not reached:
            map_class::iterator itr;
            for (itr = (*map_ptr).begin( ); itr != (*map_ptr).end( ); itr++)
                (*reached)[(*itr).first] = false;

            (*reached)[start] = true;
            (*vertex_queue).push (start);
        } // two-parameter constructor
```

The postincrement operator, **operator**++, dequeues the front of *vertex_queue, enqueues all vertices adjacent from that vertex that have not yet been reached, and nulls out the fields (for comparisons with method end( )) if *vertex_queue is empty. Here is the definition:

```
        // Precondition: this breadth_first_iterator has not yet reached all of the
        //                 reachable vertices in this network.
```

```
// Postcondition: this breadth_first_iterator has been advanced to the next
//                reachable vertex in this network; the pre-advanced iterator
//                has been returned.
breadth_first_iterator operator++ (int)
{
        breadth_first_iterator temp = *this;
        vertex current = (*vertex_queue).front( );
        (*vertex_queue).pop( );

        map_class::iterator itr = (*map_ptr).find (current);
        list<vertex_weight_pair>::iterator list_itr;

        // Iterate through the list of neighbors of current:
        for (list_itr = (*itr).second.begin( ); list_itr != (*itr).second.end( );
                 list_itr++)
        {
                vertex to = (*list_itr).to;

                // has vertex to been reached?
                if ((*reached) [to] == false)
                {
                        (*reached) [to] = true;
                        (*vertex_queue).push (to);
                } // if
        } // for
        if ((*vertex_queue).empty( ))
        {
                vertex_queue = NULL;
                reached = NULL;
                map_ptr = NULL;
        } // if queue empty
        return temp;
} // operator++
```

The **operator**== tests for field equality, and the dereference operator, **operator***, returns the front vertex on *vertex_queue. The only significant difference between the depth_first_iterator class and the breadth_first_iterator class is that a vertex_stack is used instead of a vertex_queue.

14.7.5 The get_minimum_spanning_tree **Method**

The definition of the get_minimum_spanning_tree method follows the outline given in Section 14.5.3. We start with some vertex as the root, and get the list of vertex_ weight pairs associated with that root. Each of those edge triples, <root, vertex, weight> is pushed onto a priority queue. Then, until the size of the spanning tree is equal to the size of the network, we pop the lowest-weight triple, <x, y, weight>

from the priority queue. If y is not in the spanning tree, we add y and the edge <x, y> and weight to the spanning tree and iterate over the neighbors of y; if a neighbor z is not in the spanning tree, we push the edge-triple <y, z, weight of edge <y, z>> onto the priority queue.

For convenience, we create the **struct** edge_triple, which allows easy access to an edge and its weight, and defines **operator**> needed by the priority queue of triples. Here is the definition of get_minimum_spanning_tree:

```
network<vertex> get_minimum_spanning_tree( ) {

    network min_spanning_tree; // the minimum spanning tree is a
                               // network so weights can be included
    priority_queue<edge_triple, vector<edge_triple>,
            greater<edge_triple> > pq;

    vertex root,
           x,
           y,
           z;

    iterator itr;

    list< vertex_weight_pair > adjacency_list;
    list< vertex_weight_pair >::iterator list_itr;
    double weight;

    if (empty( ))
            return min_spanning_tree;
    itr = begin( );
    root = (*itr).first;
    min_spanning_tree.insert_vertex (root);

    adjacency_list = adjacency_map [root];
    for (list_itr = adjacency_list.begin( ); list_itr != adjacency_list.end( );
            list_itr++)
            pq.push (edge_triple (root, list_itr -> to, list_itr -> weight));
    while (min_spanning_tree.size( ) < size( ))
    {
        x = pq.top( ).from;
        y = pq.top( ).to;
        weight = pq.top( ).weight;
        pq.pop( );
        if (!min_spanning_tree.contains_vertex (y))
        {
                min_spanning_tree.insert_vertex (y);
                min_spanning_tree.insert_edge (x, y, weight);

                adjacency_list = adjacency_map [y];
```

```
        for (list_itr = adjacency_list.begin( );
                        list_itr != adjacency_list.end( );
                        list_itr++)
        {
            z = list_itr -> to;
            if (!min_spanning_tree.contains_vertex (z))
            {
                weight = list_itr -> weight;
                pq.push (edge_triple (y, z, weight));
            } // z not already in tree
        } // iterating over y's neighbors
    } // y not already in tree
} // tree has fewer vertices than this network
return min_spanning_tree;
} // method get_minimum_spanningTree
```

14.7.6 The get_shortest_path Method

Finally, we define the get_shortest_path method, which returns the path from vertex v1 to vertex v2 that has lowest total weight. As indicated in the outline given in Section 14.5.4, Dijkstra's algorithm is a breadth-first iteration from v1. The priority_ queue container pq consists of pairs in the form <w, total_weight>, where total_ weight is the sum of the weights of all the edges on the shortest path, so far, between v1 and w. The priority queue is ordered by *smallest* total weights. To keep track of the total weights of all partial paths from v1, we have a map weight_sum that associates each vertex w with the sum of the weights of all the edges on the shortest path so far from v1 to w. To enable us to reconstruct the shortest path when we are through, there is another map container, predecessor, which associates each vertex w with the vertex that is the immediate predecessor of w on the shortest path so far from v1 to w.

Initially, list_itr iterates over the adjacency list of all vertex_weight pairs <w, wweight> where <v1, w> is an edge with weight wweight. For each pair *list_itr:

```
weight_sum [list_itr -> to] = list_itr -> weight;
predecessor [list_itr -> to] = v1;
pq.insert (*list_itr);
```

All other vertices have an initial weight sum of MAX_PATH_WEIGHT.

We then repeatedly pop the vertex from, with smallest total weight, from pq. Then list_itr iterates over the adjacency list of all pairs <to, weight> where <from, to> is an edge with weight weight. For each pair <to, weight>:

```
if (weight_sum [from] + weight < weight_sum [to])
{
    weight_sum [to] = weight_sum [from] + weight;
```

```
        predecessor [to] = from;
        pq.push (vertex_weight_pair (to, weight_sum [to]));
    }
```

When v2 is popped from pq, the predecessor vertices are prepended to a linked list and returned, along with the total weight of the shortest path. Here is the definition:

```
pair<list<vertex>, double> get_shortest_path (const vertex& v1,
                                              const vertex& v2)
{
    const double MAX_PATH_WEIGHT = 1000000.0;

    map<vertex, vertex, Compare> predecessor;
    map<vertex, double, Compare> weight_sum;
    priority_queue<vertex_weight_pair,
                   vector<vertex_weight_pair>,
                   greater<vertex_weight_pair> > pq;

    list<vertex_weight_pair >::iterator list_itr;

    breadth_first_iterator b_itr;

    vertex to,
           from;

    double weight;

    if (adjacency_map.find (v1) == adjacency_map.end( ) ||
                    adjacency_map.find (v2) == adjacency_map.end( ))
        return pair<list<vertex>, double> (list<vertex>( ), −1.0);

    bool found_v2 = false;
    for (b_itr = breadth_first_begin (v1); b_itr != breadth_first_end( );
            b_itr++)
        if (*b_itr == v2)
        {
            found_v2 = true;
            break;
        } // if
    if (!found_v2)
        return pair<list<vertex>, double> (list<vertex>( ), −1.0);

    weight_sum [v1] = 0.0;
    predecessor [v1] = v1;
    for (b_itr = breadth_first_begin (v1); b_itr != breadth_first_end( );
            b_itr++)
    {
        weight_sum [*b_itr] = MAX_PATH_WEIGHT;
        predecessor [*b_itr] = vertex( );
```

```
        } // initializing weight_sum and predecessor

    for (list_itr = adjacency_map [v1].begin( ); list_itr !=
                adjacency_map [v1].end( ); list_itr++)
    {
            weight_sum [list_itr -> to] = list_itr -> weight;
            predecessor [list_itr -> to] = v1;
            pq.push (vertex_weight_pair (*list_itr));
    } // adjusting weight_sum, predecessor, pq for vertices adjacent to v1

    bool path_found = false;
    while (!path_found)
    {
            from = pq.top( ).to; // get vertex in vertex_weight_pair
                              // with smallest weight sum
            pq.pop( );
            if (from == v2)
                path_found = true;
            else
            {
                for (list_itr = adjacency_map [from].begin( );
                        list_itr != adjacency_map [from].end( ); list_itr++)
                {
                        to = list_itr -> to;
                        weight = list_itr -> weight:
                        if (weight_sum [from] + weight < weight_sum [to])
                        {
                                weight_sum [to] = weight_sum [from] + weight;
                                predecessor [to] = from;
                                pq.push (vertex_weight_pair (to,
                                            weight_sum [to]));
                        } // if from_weight_sum + weight > to_weight_sum
                } // for iterating over from's list
            } // else path not yet found
    } // while path not found

    list<vertex> path;
    vertex current = v2;
    while (current != v1)
    {
            path.push_front (current);
            current = predecessor [current];
    } // while not yet back to v1
    path.push_front (v1);

    return pair<list<vertex>, double> (path, weight_sum [v2]);
} // method get_shortest_path
```

14.7.7 Time Estimates for the Network Methods

Let V be the number of vertices in a network and E the number of edges. For the sake of simplicity, we consider average times only. Basically, if a method entails iterating over all vertices and not over the associated lists, averageTime(V, E) is linear in V. That's because adjacency_map is stored in a red-black tree with vertex keys, and iterating through the vertices takes linear-in-V time. For iterating over a single vertex's adjacency list, the averageTime(V, E) is $O(\log V + E/V)$, since it takes $\log V$ time to access a vertex (that is, a key) in a red-black tree, and there are E edges among V lists.

The get_edge_count method iterates over all vertices, so averageTime(V, E) is linear in V. The get_edge_weight method, on the other hand, iterates over the list associated with its first vertex parameter, so averageTime(V, E) is $O(\log V + E/V)$, and this is the smallest upper bound.

The erase_vertex method first finds and erases its argument from the network, and for this, averageTime(V, E) is logarithmic in V. The method then iterates over all vertices and, for each vertex, iterates over the list of edges associated with that vertex, and for this, averageTime(V, E) is linear in $V * E/V$, which is equal to E. So for erase_vertex, averageTime(V, E) is $O(\log V + E)$, and this is minimal.

In analyzing a breadth-first or depth-first iteration, we make the simplifying assumption that the network is connected. Then the breadth-first iteration iterates through all V vertices, and for each vertex, its associated list is iterated over. So averageTime(V, E) is linear in E. Ditto for a depth-first iteration. The is_connected method iterates over all vertices and performs a breadth-first iteration for each vertex, so averageTime(V, E) is linear in VE.

In the get_minimum_spanning_tree method, the number of iterations of the outer loop is linear in V. During each outer-loop iteration, the priority queue is popped (which takes $\log E$ iterations) and the inner loop iterates over a list of neighbors (which takes E/V iterations), so the total number of iterations is $O(V(\log E + E/V))$. Then averageTime(V, E) is $O(V \log E + E)$. This may not be the smallest upper bound because we established only an upper bound for the number of iterations required to pop the priority queue.

To simplify the analysis of the get_shortest_path method, assume that the distance of the path between v1 and v2 is at least $V/2$. Then for each vertex in the path, the inner loop will iterate over its neighbors. So, as with the getMinimumSpanning Tree method, averageTime(V, E) is $O(V \log E + E)$.

The complete network class and a driver program are available from the Source Code link on the book's website. Lab 29 introduces the best-known network problem, further explores greedy algorithms, and touches on the topic of *very hard* problems.

LAB   **Lab 29: The traveling salesperson problem.**

(All Labs Are Optional.)   **LAB**

14.7.8 An Alternative Design and Implementation of the network Class

In the design of the network class in Section 14.7.1, vertices were stored as keys in a map container. The other component in each value was an *adjacency list* of vertex-weight pairs, that is, a linked list of the neighbors (and edge weights) of the vertex key. This structure works well for sparse networks, that is, networks in which the number of edges is not much larger than the number of vertices. In any connected network, we must have

$$V \leq E \leq V(V + 1)/2$$

There are E edges in V adjacency lists, so the average size of an adjacency list is E/V.

For the contains_edge method, it takes log V time to access to appropriate adjacency list, and E/V time to search that list. So, for the contains_edge method, the averageTime(V, E) is $O(\log V + E/V)$. We can refine this estimate if we know the relationship between E and V. Specifically, if the number of edges is linear in V, then the average size of each adjacency list will be constant, and we can quickly iterate through an adjacency list to determine if the network has a given edge. Then averageTime(V, E) is logarithmic in V for the contains_edge method.

On the other hand, if the number of edges is quadratic in V, the average size of an adjacency list will be linear in V. This implies that for an iteration, necessarily sequential, through an adjacency list, averageTime(V, E) is linear in V. Then average Time(V, E) is linear in V for the contains_edge method.

Another common representation of networks uses an adjacency matrix instead of adjacency lists. An *adjacency matrix* is a two-dimensional vector (or array) of **double** items, with V rows and V columns. At adjacency_matrix [i] [j] we store the weight of the edge from the ith vertex to the jth vertex. We need to be able to quickly associate a vertex with an array index, and to quickly associate an index with its vertex. For this last task, we create a vector or array of vertices; vertices [i] contains the vertex corresponding to adjacency_matrix [i]—the ith row in the matrix.

For the association of vertices to indices, we create vertex_map, a map container in which each key is a vertex and the other component in each value is the index corresponding to the vertex key. Figure 14.28 shows a network and the corresponding adjacency-matrix representation.

Figure 14.28 assumes the vertices were added to the network in the following order: "Karen", "Mark", "Don", "Courtney", "Tara". Each time a vertex is added to the network, the vertex is stored at the next unoccupied index in the vector vertices, and that vertex-index pair is added to the vertex_map container. There are four fields in this design:

*In the **adjacency-matrix** design of the network class, a matrix with V rows and V columns holds the weight of each edge.*

```
vector<vector<double>> adjacency_matrix; // holds the weight of each edge

vector<vertex> vertices;                 // holds the vertices
```

Figure 14.28 | An adjacency matrix representation of a network. An entry of −1.0 indicates no edge. For the sake of visibility, the weights of the edges are in boldface.

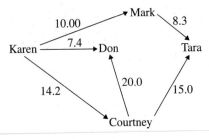

	0	1	2	3	4
0	−1.0	**10.0**	**7.4**	**14.2**	−1.0
1	−1.0	−1.0	−1.0	−1.0	**8.3**
2	−1.0	−1.0	−1.0	−1.0	−1.0
3	−1.0	−1.0	**20.0**	−1.0	**15.0**
4	−1.0	−1.0	−1.0	−1.0	−1.0

adjacency_matrix

0	Karen
1	Mark
2	Don
3	Courtney
4	Tara

vertices

vertex_map

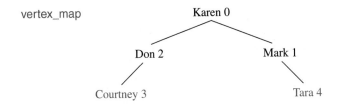

```
map<vertex, int> vertex_map; // associates each vertex with its index

int next;                     // the index in vertices where the next vertex
                              // will go
```

In the default constructor, a default value for the initial number of vertices is defined. Then, the adjacency_matrix field is initialized to all −1.0's; the vertices field is initialized to an empty vector, respectively; and next is initialized to 0.

The insert_vertex method returns **false** if vertex is already in the network. Otherwise, the four fields are adjusted and **true** is returned. The averageTime(V, E) is logarithmic in V (unless expansion occurs) because vertex_map must be searched to determine the index corresponding to the given vertex. Here is the definition:

```
// Postcondition: if vertex is already in this network or if this network is full,
//                false has been returned. Otherwise, vertex has been added
```

```
//                      to this network and true has been returned.
bool insert_vertex (vertex v)
{
    if (vertex_map.find (v) != vertex_map.end( ) || next ==
            vertices.size( ) − 1)
        return false;
    check_for_expansion( );
    vertices [next] = v;
    for (unsigned i = 0; i < vertices.size( ); i++)
        adjacency_matrix[next][i] = −1.0;
    vertex_map.insert (pair <vertex, int> (v, next));
    next++;
    return true;
} // method insertVertex
```

The rest of this implementation of the network class is the subject of Project 14.1.

The final topic in this chapter is backtracking. In Chapter 4, we saw how backtracking could be used to solve a variety of applications. Now we expand the application domain to include networks and therefore, graphs and trees.

14.8 | BACKTRACKING THROUGH A NETWORK

When backtracking was introduced in Chapter 4, we saw three applications in which the basic framework did not change. Specifically, the same BackTrack class and Application header were used for

1. Searching a maze
2. Placing eight queens—none under attack by another queen—on a chessboard
3. Illustrating that a knight could traverse every square in a chessboard without landing on any square more than once

A network (or graph or tree) is also suitable for backtracking. For example, suppose we have a network of cities; each edge weight represents the distance, in miles, between its two cities. Given a start city and a finish city, find a path in which *each edge's distance is less than the previous edge's distance*. Figure 14.29 has sample data; the start and finish cities are given first, followed by each edge. Figure 14.30 depicts the network generated by the data in Figure 14.29.

The backtracking framework from Chapter 4 can also be applied to backtracking through a network.

One solution to this problem is the following path:

$$\text{Boston} \xrightarrow{214} \text{New York} \xrightarrow{168} \text{Harrisburg} \xrightarrow{123} \text{Washington}$$

A shorter that is, smaller total weight, solution is

Figure 14.29 | A network: the first line contains the start and finish cities; each other line contains two cities and the distance from the first city to the second city.

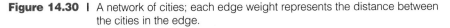

Boston	Washington	
Albany	Washington	371
Boston	Albany	166
Boston	Hartford	101
Boston	New York	214
Boston	Trenton	279
Harrisburg	Philadelphia	106
Harrisburg	Washington	123
New York	Harrisburg	168
New York	Washington	232
Trenton	Washington	178

Figure 14.30 | A network of cities; each edge weight represents the distance between the cities in the edge.

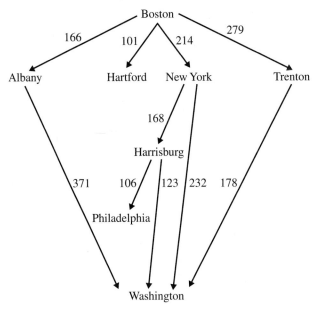

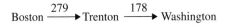

$$\text{Boston} \xrightarrow{279} \text{Trenton} \xrightarrow{178} \text{Washington}$$

The shortest path is illegal for this problem because the distances increase (from 214 to 232):

$$\text{Boston} \xrightarrow{214} \text{New York} \xrightarrow{232} \text{Washington}$$

When a dead end is reached, we can backtrack through the network. The basic strategy with backtracking is to utilize a depth-first search starting at the start position. At each position, we iterate through the neighbors of that position. The order in which neighboring positions are visited is the order in which the corresponding edges are initially inserted into the network. So we are guaranteed to find a solution path if one exists, but not necessarily the shortest solution path.

Here is the sequence of steps in the solution generated by backtracking:

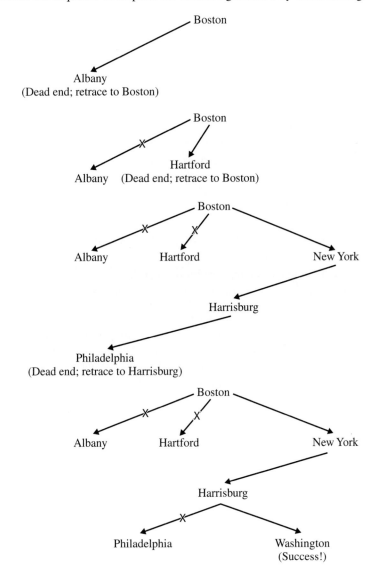

The framework introduced in Chapter 4 supplies the BackTrack class and Application header. What about the Position class? That class must be modified: The terms "row" and "column" have no meaning in a network. The details are left as Project 14.2.

SUMMARY

An ***undirected graph*** consists of items called ***vertices*** and distinct, unordered vertex-pairs called ***edges.*** If the pairs are ordered, we have a ***directed graph.*** A ***tree,*** sometimes called a ***directed tree,*** is a directed graph that either is empty or has an item, called the ***root item*** such that

1. There are no edges coming into the root item.
2. Every nonroot item has exactly one edge coming into it.
3. There is a path from the root to every other item.

A ***network*** (or undirected network) is a directed graph (or undirected graph) in which each edge has an associated nonnegative number called the ***weight*** of the edge. A network is also referred to as a ***weighted graph.***

Some of the important graph and network algorithms are

1. Breadth-first iteration of all vertices reachable from a given vertex
2. Depth-first iteration of all vertices reachable from a given vertex
3. Determining if a given graph is connected, that is, if for any two vertices, there is a path from the first vertex to the second
4. Finding a minimum spanning tree for a network
5. Finding the shortest path between two vertices in a network

One possible design and implementation of the network class is to associate, in a map container, each vertex with its neighbors. Specifically, adjacency_map is a map container in which each key is a vertex v that is mapped to the linked list of vertex-weight pairs, <w, weight>, where weight is the weight of edge <v, w>.

An alternative design and implementation stores the weights in a two-dimensional array with V rows and V columns, where V is the number of vertices. Specifically, the weight of the edge connecting vertices i and j is stored at adjacency_matrix [i] [j].

Some network problems can be solved through backtracking. The iteration around a given position corresponds to an iteration through the linked list of vertex-weight pairs that comprise the neighboring edges of a given vertex.

EXERCISES

14.1 a. Draw a picture of the following undirected graph:

Vertices: A, B, C, D, E

Edges: (A, B), (C, D), (D, A), (B, D), (B, E)

14.2 a.   Draw an undirected graph that has four vertices and as many edges as possible. How many edges does the graph have?

b.   Draw an undirected graph that has five vertices and as many edges as possible. How many edges does the graph have?

c.   What is the maximum number of edges for an undirected graph with V vertices?

d.   Prove the claim you made in part (c).

   Hint   Use induction on V.

e.   What is the maximum number of edges for a directed graph with V vertices?

14.3 Suppose we have the following undirected graph:

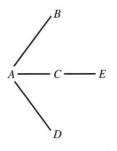

Assume the vertices were inserted into the graph in alphabetical order.

a.   Perform a breadth-first iteration of the undirected graph starting at A.

b.   Perform a depth-first iteration of the undirected graph starting at A.

14.4 For the given network, determine the shortest path from A to H by brute force; that is, list all paths and see which one has the lowest total weight.

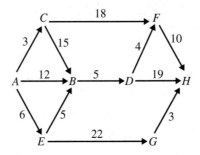

14.5 For the network given in Exercise 14.4, use Dijkstra's algorithm (in the get_shortest_path method) to find the shortest path from A to H.

14.6 Prim's algorithm (get_minimum_spanning_tree) and Dijkstra's algorithm (get_shortest_path) are ***greedy:*** the locally optimal choice has the highest priority. In these cases, greed succeeds in the sense that the locally optimal choice led to the globally optimal solution. Do all greedy algorithms succeed for all inputs? In this exercise we explore coin-changing algorithms. In one situation, the greedy algorithm succeeds for all inputs. In the other situation, the greedy algorithm succeeds for some inputs and fails for some other inputs.

Suppose you want to provide change for any amount under a dollar using as few coins as possible. Since fewest is best, the greedy (that is, locally optimal) choice at each step is the coin with the largest value whose addition will not surpass the original amount. Here is a greedy algorithm:

```
// Precondition: 0 <= amount <= 99.
// Postcondition: the change for amount, with as few coins as possible, has
//                been printed.
void print_fewest (int amount)
{
    int coin[ ] = {25, 10, 5, 1};

    const string RESULT =
        "With as few coins as possible, here is the change for ";

    cout << RESULT << amount << ":";
    for (int i = 0; i< 4; i++>
        while (coin [i] <= amount)
        {
            cout << coin [i] << endl;
            amount -= coin [i];
        } // while
} // print_fewest
```

For example, suppose that amount has the value 62. Then the output will be

```
25
25
10
1
1
```

Five is the minimum number of coins needed to make 62 cents from quarters, nickels, dimes, and pennies.

a. Show that this algorithm is optimal for any amount between 0 and 99 cents, inclusive.

b. Give an example to show that a greedy algorithm is not optimal for all inputs if nickels are not available. That is, if we have

```
int coins[ ] = {25, 10, 1};
```

. . .

```
for (int i = 0; i < 3; i++)
```
. . .

then the algorithm will not be optimal for some inputs.

14.7 Ignore the direction of arrows in the figure for Exercise 14.4. Then that figure depicts an undirected network. Use Prim's algorithm to find a minimum spanning tree for that undirected network.

14.8 Ignore the direction of arrows and assume all weights are 1.0 in the figure for Exercise 14.4. Use Dijkstra's algorithm to find a shortest path from *A* to *H*.

14.9 Modify Dijkstra's algorithm to find the shortest paths from a given vertex v to all other vertices in a network.

14.10 Starting with the adjacency-list design of the network class, define the erase_edge method in the undirected_network class.

14.11 If we design the undirected_network class with an adjacency matrix, what interesting property will that matrix possess?

14.12 Give specific examples of methods to show that the adjacency-list design of the network class is faster than the adjacency-matrix design if *E* is linear in *V*.

14.13 Give specific examples of methods to show that the adjacency-list design of the network class is slower than the adjacency-matrix design if *E* is quadratic in *V*.

14.14 If *V* is large—say, greater than 10,000—and *E* is linear in *V*, which design of the network class would you prefer?

14.15 What is the major drawback to the adjacency-matrix design of the network class?

14.16 Reorder the edges in Figure 14.29 so that the solution path generated by backtracking is different from the solution path provided.

14.17 There was no need to define a destructor for the adjacency-list design of the network class. Why? Is there a need to define a destructor for the adjacency-matrix design? Explain.

PROGRAMMING PROJECT 14.1

Completing the Adjacency-Matrix Implementation

Complete the implementation of the network class with the adjacency-matrix design. Here is a definition for the default constructor:

```
network( )
{
        const unsigned v = 100;
        vertices.resize (v);
        adjacency_matrix.resize (v);
        for (unsigned i = 0; i < v; i++)
        {
                adjacency_matrix[i].resize(v);
                for (unsigned j = 0; j < v; j++)
                        adjacency_matrix[i][j] = −1.0;
        } // initializing row i
        next = 0;
} // default constructor
```

In light of your implementation and Exercises 14.12 through 14.15, give an overall comparison of the adjacency-list design and the adjacency_matrix design of the network class.

PROGRAMMING PROJECT 14.2

Backtracking through a Network

Given a network in which each vertex is a city and each weight represents the distance between two cities, determine a path from a start city to a finish city in which each edge's distance is less than the previous edge's distance.

ANALYSIS

Each city will be given as a string of at most 14 characters, with no embedded blanks. The first line of input will contain the start city and finish city. Each subsequent line—until the sentinel of "***"—will consist of two cities and the distance in miles from the first of those two cities to the second.

There is no input editing to be done. The initial output will be the network. If there is no solution, the final output will be

There is no solution.

Otherwise the final output will be

There is a solution:

followed by the edges (from-city, to-city, distance) corresponding to the solution.

System Test 1   Input is in boldface.

In the Input line, please enter the start and finish cities, separated by a blank. Each city name should have no blanks and be at most 14 characters in length.
Boston Washington

In the Input line, please enter two cities and their distance; the sentinel is ***
Boston NewYork 214

In the Input line, please enter two cities and their distance; the sentinel is ***
Boston Trenton 279

In the Input line, please enter two cities and their distance; the sentinel is ***
Harrisburg Washington 123

In the Input line, please enter two cities and their distance; the sentinel is ***
NewYork Harrisburg 168

In the Input line, please enter two cities and their distance; the sentinel is ***
NewYork Washington 232

In the Input line, please enter two cities and their distance; the sentinel is ***
Trenton Washington 178

In the Input line, please enter two cities and their distance; the sentinel is ***
***

(continued on next page)

(continued from previous page)

The initial state is as follows:
Trenton Washington 178.0
NewYork Harrisburg 168.0
NewYork Washington 232.0
Harrisburg Washington 123.0
Boston NewYork 214.0
Boston Trenton 279.0

A solution has been found:

FROM CITY	TO CITY	DISTANCE
Boston	NewYork	214.0
NewYork	Harrisburg	168.0
Harrisburg	Washington	123.0

Please close this window when you are ready.

System Test 2   Input is in boldface.

In the Input line, please enter the start and finish cities, separated by a blank. Each city name should have no blanks and be at most 14 characters in length.
Boston Washington

In the Input line, please enter two cities and their distance; the sentinel is ***
Boston Trenton 279

In the Input line, please enter two cities and their distance; the sentinel is ***
Boston NewYork 214

In the Input line, please enter two cities and their distance; the sentinel is ***
Harrisburg Washington 123

In the Input line, please enter two cities and their distance; the sentinel is ***
NewYork Harrisburg 168

In the Input line, please enter two cities and their distance; the sentinel is ***
NewYork Washington 232

In the Input line, please enter two cities and their distance; the sentinel is ***
Trenton Washington 178

In the Input line, please enter two cities and a weight; the sentinel is ***
***

The initial state is as follows:
Trenton Washington 178.0
NewYork Harrisburg 168.0
NewYork Washington 232.0
Harrisburg Washington 123.0
Boston Trenton 279.0
Boston NewYork 214.0

A solution has been found:

FROM CITY	TO CITY	DISTANCE
Boston	Trenton	279.0
Trenton	Washington	178.0

Please close this window when you are ready.

Note The solution to system test 2 is different from the solution to system test 1 because in system test 2, the Boston–Trenton edge is entered before the Boston–New York edge.

APPENDIX 1

Mathematical Background

A1.1 | INTRODUCTION

Mathematics is one of the outstanding accomplishments of the human mind. Its abstract models of real-life phenomena have fostered advances in every field of science and engineering. Most of computer science is based on mathematics, and this book is no exception. This appendix provides an introduction to those mathematical concepts referred to in the chapters. Some exercises are given at the end of the appendix so that you can practice the skills while you are learning them.

A1.2 | FUNCTIONS AND SEQUENCES

An amazing aspect of mathematics, first revealed by Whitehead and Russell (1910), is that only two basic concepts are required. Every other mathematical term can be built up from the primitives *set* and *element*. For example, an ordered pair $<a, b>$ can be defined as a set with two elements:

$$<a, b> = \{a, \{a, b\}\}$$

The element a is called the *first component* of the ordered pair, and b is called the *second component.*

Given two sets A and B, we can define a *function* f from A to B, written

$$f: A \rightarrow B$$

as a set of ordered pairs $<a, b>$, where a is in A, b is in B, and each element in A is the first component of exactly one ordered pair in f. Thus no two ordered pairs in a function have the same first element. The sets A and B are called the *domain* and *codomain,* respectively.

For example,

$$f = \{<-2, 4>, <-1, 1>, <0, 0>, <1, 1>, <2, 4> \}$$

defines the "square" function with domain $\{-2, -1, 0, 1, 2\}$ and co-domain $\{0, 1, 2, 4\}$. No two ordered pairs in the function have the same first component, but it is legal for two ordered pairs to have the same second component. For example, the pairs

$$<-1, 1> \quad \text{and} \quad <1, 1>$$

have the same second component, namely, 1.

If $<a, b>$ is in f, we can write $f(a) = b$. This gives us a more familiar description of the function f: it is defined by

$$f(i) = i^2 \quad \text{for } i \text{ in } -2 \ldots 2$$

Another name for a function is a ***map.*** This is the term used in Chapter 10 to describe a container in which each value consists of a unique **key** component as well as a second component. There is, in effect, a function from the keys to the second components, and that is why the keys must be unique.

A ***finite sequence*** t is a function such that for some positive integer k, called the ***length*** of the sequence, the domain of t is the set $\{0, 1, 2, \ldots, k - 1\}$. For example, the following defines a finite sequence of length 4:

$$t(0) = \text{"Karen"}$$
$$t(1) = \text{"Don"}$$
$$t(2) = \text{"Mark"}$$
$$t(3) = \text{"Courtney"}$$

Because the domain of each finite sequence starts at 0, the domain is often left implicit, and we write

$$t = \text{"Karen"}, \text{"Don"}, \text{"Mark"}, \text{"Courtney"}$$

A1.3 | SUMS AND PRODUCTS

Mathematics entails quite a bit of symbol manipulation. For this reason, brevity is an important consideration. An example of abbreviated notation can be found in the way that sums are represented. Instead of writing

$$x_0 + x_1 + x_2 + \cdots + x_{n-1}$$

we can write

$$\sum_{i=0}^{n-1} x_i$$

This expression is read as "the sum, as i goes from 0 to $n - 1$, of x sub i." We say that i is the "count index." A count index corresponds to a loop-control variable in a **for** statement. For example, the following code will store in sum the sum of components 0 through $n - 1$ in the array x:

```
sum = 0.0;

for (int i = 0; i < n; i++)
    sum += x [i];
```

Of course, there is nothing special about the letter *i*. We can write, for example,

$$\sum_{j=1}^{10} (1/j)$$

as shorthand for

$$1 + 1/2 + 1/3 + \cdots + 1/10$$

Similarly, if $n \geq m$,

$$\sum_{k=m}^{n} (k\,2^{-k})$$

is shorthand for

$$m2^{-m} + (m + 1)2^{-(m+1)} + \cdots + n2^{-n}$$

Another abbreviation, less frequently seen than summation notation, is product notation. For example,

$$\prod_{k=0}^{4} a\,[k]$$

is shorthand for

$$a[0] * a[1] * a[2] * a[3] * a[4]$$

A1.4 | LOGARITHMS

John Napier, a Scottish baron and part-time mathematician, first described logarithms in a paper he published in 1614. From that time until the invention of computers, the principal value of logarithms was in number crunching: they enabled multiplication (and division) of large numbers to be accomplished through mere addition (and subtraction).

Nowadays, logarithms have only a few computational applications—for example, the Richter scale for measuring earthquakes. But logarithms provide a useful tool for analyzing algorithms, as you saw (or will see) in Chapters 3 through 14.

We define logarithms in terms of exponents, just as subtraction can be defined in terms of addition, and division can be defined in terms of multiplication. Given a real number $b > 1$, we refer to b as the ***base***. The ***logarithm***, base b, of any real number $x > 0$, written

$$\log_b x$$

is defined to be that real number y such that

$$b^y = x$$

For example, $\log_2 16 = 4$ because $2^4 = 16$. Similarly, $\log_{10} 100 = 2$ because $10^2 = 100$. What is $\log_2 64$? What is $\log_8 64$? Estimate $\log_{10} 64$.

The following relations can be proved from the given definition of logarithm and the corresponding properties of exponents: For any real value $b > 1$ and for any positive real numbers x and y,

1. $\log_b 1 = 0$
2. $\log_b b = 1$
3. $\log_b (xy) = \log_b x + \log_b y$
4. $\log_b (x/y) = \log_b x - \log_b y$
5. $\log_b b^x = x$
6. $b^{\log_b x} = x$
7. $\log_b x^y = y \log_b x$

From these equations, we can obtain the formula for converting from one base to another. For any bases a and $b > 1$ and for any $x > 0$,

$$\begin{aligned} \log_b x &= \log_b a^{\log_a x} &&\text{(by property 5)} \\ &= (\log_a x)(\log_b a) &&\text{(by property 7)} \end{aligned}$$

The base e (≈ 2.718) has special significance in calculus; for this reason logarithms with base e are called ***natural logarithms*** and are written *ln* instead of $\log_e$.

To convert from a natural logarithm to a base 2 logarithm, we apply the base-conversion formula. For any $x > 0$,

$$\ln x = (\log_2 x)(\ln 2)$$

Dividing by *ln* 2, we get

$$\log_2 x = \ln x\ /\ \ln 2$$

We assume the function *ln* is predefined, so this equation can be used to approximate $\log_2 x$.

The function *ln* and its inverse *exp* enable us to perform exponentiation. For example, suppose we want to calculate x^y where x and y are real numbers and $x > 0$. We first rewrite x^y:

$$\begin{aligned} x^y &= e^{\ln(x^y)} &&\text{(by property 6)} \\ &= e^{y \ln x} &&\text{(by property 7)} \end{aligned}$$

This last expression can be written in C++ as

```
exp (y * log (x))
```

where exp and log are defined in `<cmath>`.

A1.5 | MATHEMATICAL INDUCTION

Many of the claims in the analysis of algorithms can be stated as properties of integers. For example, for any positive integer n,

$$\sum_{i=1}^{n} i = n(n + 1)/2$$

In such situations, the claims can be proved by the Principle of Mathematical Induction.

Principle of Mathematical Induction   Let $S_1, S_2, \ldots$ be a sequence of statements. If both of the following cases hold,

1. S_1 is true.

2.   For any positive integer n, whenever S_n is true, S_{n+1} is true.

then the statement S_n is true for any positive integer n.

To help you to understand why this principle makes sense, suppose that $S_1, S_2, \ldots$ is a sequence of statements for which cases 1 and 2 are true. By case 1, S_1 must be true. By case 2, since S_1 is true, S_2 must be true. Applying case 2 again, since S_2 is true, S_3 must be true. Continually applying case 2 from this point, we conclude that S_4 is true, and then that S_5 is true, and so on. This indicates that the conclusion in the principle is reasonable.

To prove a claim by mathematical induction, we first state the claim in terms of a sequence of statements $S_1, S_2, \ldots$. We then show that S_1 is true—-this is called the "base case." Finally, we need to prove case 2, the "inductive case." The outline of this proof is as follows: Let n be any positive integer and assume that S_n is true. To show that S_{n+1} is true, relate S_{n+1} back to S_n, which is assumed to be true. The remainder of the proof often utilizes arithmetic or algebra.

EXAMPLE A1.1

We will use the Principle of Mathematical Induction to prove the following claim: For any positive integer n,

$$\sum_{i=1}^{n} i = n(n + 1)/2$$

Proof   We start by stating the claim in terms of a sequence of statements. For $n = 1, 2, \ldots$, let S_n be the statement

$$\sum_{i=1}^{n} i = n(n + 1)/2$$

1.   *Base case.*

$$\sum_{i=1}^{1} i = 1 = 1(2)/2$$

Therefore S_1 is true.

2. *Inductive case.* Let n be any positive integer and assume that S_n is true. That is,

$$\sum_{i=1}^{n} i = n(n + 1)/2$$

We need to show that S_{n+1} is true:

$$\sum_{i=1}^{n+1} i = (n + 1)(n + 2)/2$$

We relate S_{n+1} back to S_n by making the following observation: The sum of the first $(n + 1)$ integers is the sum of the first n integers plus $n + 1$. That is,

$$\sum_{i=1}^{n+1} i = \sum_{i=1}^{n} i + (n + 1)$$

$$= n(n + 1)/2 + (n + 1) \qquad \text{because } S_n \text{ is assumed true}$$

$$= n(n + 1)/2 + 2(n + 1)/2$$

$$= (n(n + 1) + 2(n + 1))/2$$

$$= (n + 2)(n + 1)/2$$

We conclude that S_{n+1} is true (whenever S_n is true). So, by the Principle of Mathematical Induction, the statement S_n is true for any positive integer n.

An important variant of the Principle of Mathematical Induction is the following:

Principle of Mathematical Induction—Strong Form   Let S_1, S_2, . . . be a sequence of statements. If both of the following cases hold,

1. S_1 is true.
2. For any positive integer n, whenever S_1, S_2, . . . , S_n are true, S_{n+1} is true.

then the statement S_n is true for any positive integer n.

The difference between this version and the previous version is in the inductive case. When we want to establish that S_{n+1} is true, we can now assume that S_1, S_2, . . . , S_n are true.

The Principle of Mathematical Induction is equivalent to the strong form of the Principle of Mathematical Induction.

Before you go any further, try to convince (or at least, persuade) yourself that this version of the principle is reasonable. At first glance, you might think that the *strong* form is more powerful than the original version. But, in fact, they are equivalent.

We now apply the strong form of the Principle of Mathematical Induction to obtain a simple but important result.

Show that for any positive integer n, the number of iterations of the following loop statement is floor($\log_2 n$):

$$\textbf{while } (n > 1)$$
$$n = n / 2;$$

For any positive integer n, the number of times that n can be divided by 2 until n = 1 is floor($\log_2$ n).

(Recall that the function floor(x) returns the largest integer $\leq x$. For example, floor(18) returns 18.)

Proof   For $n = 1, 2, \ldots$, let $t(n)$ be the number of loop iterations. For $n = 1, 2, \ldots$, let S_n be the statement:

$$t(n) = \text{floor}(\log_2 n)$$

1. *Base case.* When $n = 1$, the loop is not executed at all, and so $t(n) = 0 = $ floor($\log_2 n$), that is, S_1 is true.

2. *Inductive case.* Let n be any positive integer and assume that $S_1, S_2, \ldots, S_n$ are all true. We need to show that S_{n+1} is true. There are two cases to consider:

    a. $n + 1$ is even. Then the number of iterations after the first iteration is equal to $t((n + 1) / 2)$. Therefore, we have

    $$
    \begin{aligned}
    t(n + 1) &= 1 + t((n + 1) / 2) \\
    &= 1 + \text{floor}(\log_2((n + 1) / 2)) \quad \text{(by the induction hypothesis)} \\
    &= 1 + \text{floor}(\log_2(n + 1) - \log_2(2)) \quad \text{(because log of quotient} \\
    &\qquad\qquad\qquad\qquad\qquad\qquad\qquad\quad \text{equals difference of logs)} \\
    &= 1 + \text{floor}(\log_2(n + 1) - 1) \\
    &= 1 + \text{floor}(\log_2(n + 1)) - 1 \\
    &= \text{floor}(\log_2(n + 1))
    \end{aligned}
    $$

    Thus S_{n+1} is true.

    b. $n + 1$ is odd. Then the number of iterations after the first iteration is equal to $t(n / 2)$. Therefore, we have

    $$
    \begin{aligned}
    t(n + 1) &= 1 + t(n / 2) \\
    &= 1 + \text{floor}(\log_2(n / 2)) \quad \text{(by the induction hypothesis)} \\
    &= 1 + \text{floor}(\log_2 n - \log_2 2) \\
    &= 1 + \text{floor}(\log_2 n - 1) \\
    &= 1 + \text{floor}(\log_2 n) - 1 \\
    &= \text{floor}(\log_2 n) \\
    &= \text{floor}(\log_2(n + 1)) \quad \text{(since } \log_2(n + 1) \text{ cannot be an integer)}
    \end{aligned}
    $$

    Thus S_{n+1} is true.

Therefore, by the strong form of the Principle of Mathematical Induction, S_n is true for any positive integer n.

Before we leave this example, we note that an almost identical proof shows that in the worst case for a binary search, the number of iterations is

$$\text{floor}(\log_2 n) + 1$$

In the original and strong forms of the Principle of Mathematical Induction, the base case consists of a proof that S_1 is true. In some situations we may need to start at some integer other than 1. For example, suppose we want to show that

$$n! > 2^n$$

for any $n \geq 4$. (Notice that this statement is false for $n = 1, 2,$ and 3.) Then the sequence of statements is $S_4, S_5, \ldots$. For the base case we need to show that S_4 is true.

In still other situations, there may be several base cases. For example, suppose we want to show that

$$\text{fib}(n) < 2^n \quad \text{for any positive integer } n$$

(The method fib, defined in Lab 10, calculates Fibonacci numbers.) The base cases are

$$\text{fib}(1) < 2^1 \quad \text{and} \quad \text{fib}(2) < 2^2$$

These observations lead us to the following:

Principle of Mathematical Induction—General Form   Let K and L be any integers such that $K \leq L$ and let $S_K, S_{K+1}, \ldots$ be a sequence of statements. If both of the following cases hold,

1. $S_K, S_{K+1}, \ldots, S_L$ are true.

2.   For any integer $n \geq L$, if $S_K, S_{K+1}, \ldots, S_n$ are true, then S_{n+1} is true.

then the statement S_n is true for any integer $n \geq K$.

The general form extends the strong form by allowing the sequence of statements to start at any integer (K) and to have any number of base cases ($S_K, S_{K+1}, \ldots, S_L$). If $K = L = 1$, then the general form reduces to the strong form.

Examples A1.3 and A1.4 use the general form of the Principle of Mathematical Induction to prove claims about Fibonacci numbers.

EXAMPLE A1.3

Show that

$$\text{fib}(n) < 2^n$$

for any positive integer n.

Proof   For $n = 1, 2, \ldots$, let S_n be the statement

$$\text{fib}(n) < 2^n$$

In the terminology of the general form of the Principle of Mathematical Induction, $K = 1$ because the sequence starts at 1; $L = 2$ because there are two base cases.

1. $\text{fib}(1) = 1 < 2 = 2^1$, and so S_1 is true. $\text{fib}(2) = 1 < 4 = 2^2$, and so S_2 is true.

2.   Let n be any integer ≥ 2 and assume that $S_1, S_2, \ldots, S_n$ are true. We need to show that S_{n+1} is true (that is, that $\text{fib}(n + 1) < 2^{n+1}$). By the definition of Fibonacci numbers,

$$\text{fib}(n + 1) = \text{fib}(n) + \text{fib}(n - 1) \quad \text{for } n \geq 2$$

Since $S_1, S_2, \ldots, S_n$ are true, we must have that S_{n-1} and S_n are true. Thus

$$\text{fib}(n - 1) < 2^{n-1} \quad \text{and} \quad \text{fib}(n) < 2^n$$

We then get

$$
\begin{aligned}
\text{fib}(n + 1) &= \text{fib}(n) + \text{fib}(n - 1) \\
&< 2^n + 2^{n-1} \\
&< 2^n + 2^n \\
&= 2^{n+1}
\end{aligned}
$$

And so $\text{fib}(n + 1)$ is true.

We conclude, by the general form of the Principle of Mathematical Induction, that

$$\text{fib}(n) < 2^n$$

for any positive integer n.

You could now proceed, in a similar fashion, to develop the following lower bound for Fibonacci numbers:

$$\text{fib}(n) > (6/5)^n \quad \text{for } n \geq 3$$

    Hint   Use the general form of the Principle of Mathematical Induction, with $K = 3$ and $L = 4$.

Now that lower and upper bounds for Fibonacci numbers have been established, you might wonder if we can improve on those bounds. We will do even better! In Example A1.4 we verify an exact, closed formula for the nth Fibonacci number. A "closed" formula is one that is neither recursive nor iterative.

EXAMPLE A1.4

Show that for any positive integer n,

$$\text{fib}(n) = \frac{1}{\sqrt{5}}\left(\left(\frac{1+\sqrt{5}}{2}\right)^n - \left(\frac{1-\sqrt{5}}{2}\right)^n\right)$$

Before you look at the proof, calculate a few values to convince yourself that the formula actually does provide the correct values.

Proof   For $n = 1, 2, \ldots$, let S_n be the statement

$$\text{fib}(n) = \frac{1}{\sqrt{5}}\left(\left(\frac{1+\sqrt{5}}{2}\right)^n - \left(\frac{1-\sqrt{5}}{2}\right)^n\right)$$

Let $x = (1 + \sqrt{5})/2$ and let $y = (1 - \sqrt{5})/2$. Note that

$$x^2 = \frac{(1+\sqrt{5})^2}{4} = \frac{1 + 2\sqrt{5} + 5}{4} = \frac{3 + \sqrt{5}}{2} = x + 1$$

Similarly, $y^2 = y + 1$.

We now proceed with the proof.

1. $\dfrac{1}{\sqrt{5}}\left(\dfrac{1+\sqrt{5}}{2} - \dfrac{1-\sqrt{5}}{2}\right) = 1$, so S_1 is true. To show that S_2 is true, we proceed as follows:

$$\frac{1}{\sqrt{5}}\left(\left(\frac{1+\sqrt{5}}{2}\right)^2 - \left(\frac{1-\sqrt{5}}{2}\right)^2\right) = (1/\sqrt{5})(x^2 - y^2)$$

$$= (1/\sqrt{5})(x + 1 - (y + 1))$$

$$= (1/\sqrt{5})(x - y)$$

$$= \frac{1}{\sqrt{5}}\left(\frac{1+\sqrt{5}}{2} - \frac{1-\sqrt{5}}{2}\right)$$

$$= 1 \qquad = \text{fib}(2) \text{ (by definition)}$$

and so S_2 is also true.

2.   Let n be any positive integer greater than 1 and assume that $S_1, S_2, \ldots, S_n$ are true. We need to show that S_{n+1} is true; that is,

$$\text{fib}(n + 1) = \frac{1}{\sqrt{5}}\left(\left(\frac{1+\sqrt{5}}{2}\right)^{n+1} - \left(\frac{1-\sqrt{5}}{2}\right)^{n+1}\right)$$

By the definition of Fibonacci numbers,

$$\text{fib}(n + 1) = \text{fib}(n) + \text{fib}(n - 1)$$

Since S_n and S_{n-1} are true, we have (using x and y)

$$\text{fib}(n) = (1/\sqrt{5})(x^n - y^n)$$

and

$$\text{fib}(n - 1) = (1/\sqrt{5})(x^{n-1} - y^{n-1})$$

Substituting, we get

$$
\begin{aligned}
\text{fib}(n + 1) &= (1/\sqrt{5})(x^n + x^{n-1} - y^n - y^{n-1}) \\
&= (1/\sqrt{5})(x^{n-1}(x + 1) - y^{n-1}(y + 1)) \\
&= (1/\sqrt{5})(x^{n-1}x^2 - y^{n-1}y^2) \\
&= (1/\sqrt{5})(x^{n+1} - y^{n+1})
\end{aligned}
$$

Therefore S_{n+1} is true.

We conclude, by the general form of the Principle of Mathematical Induction, that S_n is true for any positive integer n.

The Example A1.5 establishes a result about nonempty binary trees: The number of leaves is at most the number of items in the tree plus 1, all divided by 2.0. The induction is on the height of the tree and so the base case is for a single-item tree, that is, a tree of height 0.

EXAMPLE A1.5

Let t be a nonempty binary tree, with leaves(t) leaves and $n(t)$ elements. We claim that

$$\text{leaves}(t) \leq \frac{n(t) + 1}{2.0}$$

Proof   For $k = 0, 1, 2, \ldots$, let S_k be the statement: For any nonempty binary tree t of height k,

$$\text{leaves}(t) \leq \frac{n(t) + 1}{2.0}$$

1.   If t has height 0, then leaves(t) = $n(t)$ = 1, and so

$$1 = \text{leaves}(t) \leq \frac{n(t) + 1}{2.0} = 1$$

Therefore S_0 is true.

2.   Let k be any integer ≥ 0, and assume that $S_0, S_1, \ldots, S_k$ are true. We need to show that S_{k+1} is true. Let t be a nonempty binary tree of height $k + 1$. Both leftTree(t) and rightTree(t) have height $\leq k$, so both satisfy the induction hypothesis. That is,

$$\text{leaves}(\text{leftTree}(t)) \leq \frac{n(\text{leftTree}(t)) + 1}{2.0}$$

and

$$\text{leaves}(\text{rightTree}(t)) \leq \frac{n(\text{rightTree}(t)) + 1}{2.0}$$

But each leaf in t is either in leftTree(t) or in rightTree(t). That is,

$$\text{leaves}(t) = \text{leaves}(\text{leftTree}(t)) + \text{leaves}(\text{rightTree}(t))$$

Then we have

$$\text{leaves}(t) \leq \frac{n(\text{leftTree}(t)) + 1}{2.0} + \frac{n(\text{rightTree}(t)) + 1}{2.0}$$
$$= \frac{n(\text{leftTree}(t)) + n(\text{rightTree}(t)) + 1 + 1}{2.0}$$

Except for the root item of t, each item in t is either in leftTree(t) or in rightTree(t), and so

$$n(t) = n(\text{leftTree}(t)) + n(\text{rightTree}(t)) + 1$$

Substituting the left-hand side of this equation for the right-hand side, in the previous inequality, we get

$$\text{leaves}(t) \leq \frac{n(t) + 1}{2.0}$$

That is, S_{k+1} is true.

Therefore, by the general form of the Principle of Mathematical Induction, S_k is true for any nonnegative integer k. This completes the proof of the claim.

A1.6 | INDUCTION AND RECURSION

Induction and recursion are similar, but the direction is different.

Induction is similar to recursion. Each has a number of base cases. Also, each has a general case that reduces to one or more simpler cases which, eventually, reduce to the base case(s). But the direction is different. With recursion, we start with the general case and, eventually, reduce it to the base case. With induction, we start with the base case and use it to develop the general case.

Example A1.6, referred to in the analysis of open-address hashing (Chapter 13), starts with a recursive definition and then conjectures a closed form.

EXAMPLE A1.6

Develop a closed form for the function E for any k and m such that $0 \leq k < m$:

$$E(0, m) = 1 \quad \text{for any } m > 1$$

$$E(k, m) = 1 + \frac{k}{m} E(k - 1, m - 1) \quad \text{where } 1 \le k < m$$

Solution First we note that

$$E(1, m) = 1 + \frac{1}{m} E(0, m - 1)$$

$$= 1 + \frac{1}{m} * 1$$

$$= \frac{m + 1}{m} \quad \text{for all } m > 1$$

Similarly,

$$E(2, m) = 1 + \frac{2}{m} E(1, m - 1)$$

$$= 1 + \frac{2}{m} \frac{m}{m - 1}$$

$$= \frac{m + 1}{m - 1} \quad \text{for all } m > 2$$

Furthermore,

$$E(3, m) = 1 + \frac{3}{m} E(2, m - 1)$$

$$= 1 + \frac{3}{m} \frac{m}{m - 2}$$

$$= \frac{m + 1}{m - 2} \quad \text{for all } m > 3$$

We therefore conjecture that

$$E(k, m) = \frac{m + 1}{m + 1 - k} \quad \text{for all } m \text{ and } k \text{ such that } 0 \le k < m$$

This conjecture can be proved by induction (on either k or m). For example, if the induction is on k, the sequence of statements S_k, for $k = 0, 1, 2, \ldots$, is

$$E(k, m) = \frac{m + 1}{m + 1 - k} \quad \text{for all } m \text{ such that } m > k$$

EXERCISES

A1.1 Use mathematical induction to show that, in the Towers of Hanoi game from Chapter 4, moving n disks from one pole to another pole requires a total of $2^n - 1$ moves for any positive integer n.

A1.2 Use mathematical induction to show that for any positive integer n,

$$\sum_{i=1}^{n} Af(i) = A \sum_{i=1}^{n} f(i)$$

where A is a constant and f is a function.

A1.3 Use mathematical induction to show that for any positive integer n,

$$\sum_{i=1}^{n} (i * 2^{i-1}) = (n - 1) * 2^n + 1$$

A1.4 Let n_0 be the smallest positive integer such that

$$\text{fib}(n_0) > n_0^2$$

a. Find n_0.

b. Use mathematical induction to show that, for all $n \geq n_0$,

$$\text{fib}(n) > n^2$$

A1.5 Show that fib is $O((1 + \sqrt{5})^n/2)$.

Hint   See the formula in Example A1.4. Note that

$$\text{abs}((1 - \sqrt{5})/2) < 1$$

and so $((1 - \sqrt{5})/2)^n$ becomes insignificant for "large" n.

A1.6 Show that

$$\sum_{i=0}^{n} 2^i = 2^{n+1} - 1$$

for any nonnegative integer n.

The string **Class**

A2.1 | INTRODUCTION

The purpose of this appendix is to familiarize you with the Standard C++ string class. Once you become aware of the power and elegance of this class, you will be glad you took the time to learn it—especially if you have spent any time suffering through C-style strings.

To use the string class in a file, you must have the following two lines:

#include <string>

using namespace std;

Both of these lines are directives to the compiler. The first line requests that the file—part of the Standard Template Library—declaring the string class be accessible in the current file. The second line states that identifiers from the Standard Template Library will appear in the current file without the qualifier std.

An individual character in a string can be referred to by its index, just as with an array. For example if a string object s contains "nevermore", then s [0] contains 'n', s [1] contains 'e', and so on. Don't forget that indices start at 0.

The string class has over 100 methods, so you are not expected to remember (or even recognize) all of them. Section A2.2 includes method interfaces and examples for the most widely used methods. Then a simple string-processing program is presented, followed by an outline of a typical implementation of the string class.

A2.2 | DECLARATION OF THE string **CLASS**

This section is divided into four parts: constructors, operators, nonmethod functions, and other methods. For the sake of readability, the following method interfaces deviate from the Standard C++ specifications by using **char** instead of charT and **unsigned int** instead of size_type.

A2.2.1 **Constructors**

1.   // Postcondition: this string is empty.
     string( );

> *Example*   We can initialize a string object to be empty as follows:
>
> string s1;

2.   // Postcondition: this string has been initialized to contain a string copy of s.
     string (**const** char* s);

> *Example*   We can define and initialize a string in a single statement:
>
> string s2 ("bed");
>
> Now s2 contains the characters 'b', 'e', and 'd' in that order.

> *Note*   An equivalent form of this constructor, one you are more likely to see, is
>
> string s2 = "bed";

3.   // Precondition: pos <= the number of characters in str.
     // Postcondition: this string has been initialized to a copy of the substring of str
     //   starting at index pos and of length the smaller of n and
     //   str.size( ) − pos. If the third argument is omitted, the largest
     //   unsigned int is assumed to be the third argument. If the
     //   second argument is also omitted, 0 is assumed to be the
     //   second argument.
     string (**const** string str, **unsigned int** pos = 0, **unsigned int** n = −1);

> *Example*   Suppose we define the following:
>
> string s3 = "jabberwocky";
> string s4 (s3),
>   s5 (s3, 5, 3);
>
> Then s4 contains "jabberwocky" and s5 contains "rwo", that is, the substring of s3 starting at index 5 and of length 3.

> *Note*   The binary representation of −1 consists of all 1s. When this is interpreted as an **unsigned int,** it represents the largest possible **unsigned int.** So when the heading has

unsigned int n = −1

That is just an efficient (and confusing) way to make n's default value the largest possible **unsigned int.**

A2.2.2 Operators

4. // Postcondition: this string contains a copy of str.
string& **operator** = (**const** string& str);

> *Example*   Suppose s2 has been defined as in the example of constructor 3. Then we can define
>
> string s3 = s2;
>
> Now s2 and s3 contain the same strings. If we change the value of s2, that will not affect s3's value (and the reverse is also true). For example, suppose we subsequently assign
>
> s2 = "flower"; // assignment operator
>
> Now s2 contains "flower" but s3 still contains "bed".
>
> *Note*   The right-hand side of a string assignment may consist of a string constant or a character, as well as a string. For example,
>
> s2 = "start-up";
> s3 = '?';

5. // Precondition: pos < the number of characters in this string.
// Postcondition: a reference to the character that is at index pos in this string
//   has been returned.
char& operator[ ] (**unsigned int** pos);

> *Example*   Suppose the string object s2 contains "flower", and we write
>
> s2 [0] = 'g';
>
> Because this operator, known as the index operator, returns a reference, this assignment statement replaces the 'f' with 'g' at index 0 of s2. So s2 now contains "glower".

A2.2.3 Nonmember Functions

These functions may be methods in another class.

6.   // Postcondition: str has been inserted in os, which has been returned.
ostream& **operator**<< (ostream& os, **const** string& str);

> *Example*   Suppose we have
>
> string s6 = "yes",
> s7 = "no";
> cout << s6 << " or " << s7 << endl;
>
> > The output will be

yes or no

7.   // Postcondition: any whitespace characters (blanks and end-of-line markers) in
    //   is have been skipped over, and then the sequence of
    //   characters up to, but not including, the next whitespace
    //   character, has been extracted from is and stored in str. Then is
    //   has been returned.
istream& **operator**>> (istream& is, string& str);

> *Example*   Suppose we have
>
> string s,
>   t;
>
> cin >> s;
> cin >> t;
>
> If the input stream contains a blank line followed by
>
> This was the next line.
>
> then s will contain "this" and t will contain "was".

8.   // Postcondition: the characters up to and including the end of this line have
    //   been extracted from is and (except for the delimiter '\n') have
    //   been inserted into str, and is has been returned.
ifstream getline (ifstream& is, string& str);

> *Example*   Suppose we have
>
> string line;
> getline (cin, line);
>
> Then the contents of the next line of input (not including the delimiter '\n') will be stored in line.
>
> *Note*   This function returns an ifstream object. When the end of the file is encountered, the value returned is NULL, which is equivalent to 0 and

false. So we can keep reading from a file, my_file, until the end of the file is reached as follows:

while (getline (my_file, line))
{
    . . .

9.   // Postcondition: the string returned is formed by joining (that is, concatenating)
     //   lhs and rhs.
     string **operator**+ (**const** string& lhs, **const** string& rhs);

        Example Suppose we have

        string s6 = "first",
             s7 = "last",
             s8 = s6 + s7;

        Then s8 will contain "firstlast", the string formed by joining the strings "first" and "last". If we wanted s8 to have s6 and s7 separated with a blank, we could write

        string s6 = "first",
             s7 = "last",
             s8 = s6 + " " + s7;

10. // Postcondition: true has been returned if lhs and rhs contain the same
     //   sequence of characters. Otherwise, false has been returned.
     bool operator ==(**const** string& lhs, **const** string& rhs);

        Example Suppose we have

        string sa = "nevermore",
             sb = "nevermore ";

        cout << (sa == sb) << endl;

        The output will be 0—that is, **false**—because sb has one more character than sa; the blank at the end of sb is a character.

11. // Postcondition: true has been returned if lhs is lexicographically less than rhs.
     //   Otherwise, false has been returned.
     bool operator ==(**const** string& lhs, **const** string& rhs);

        Example Suppose we have

        string s1 = "elephant",
             s2 = "mouse";

        if (s1 < s2)

cout << "\"elephant\" is less than \"mouse\".";

else

cout << "\"elephant\" is not less than \"mouse\".";

Because 'e' comes before 'm' in the ASCII collating sequence, "elephant" precedes "mouse" in a lexicographic ordering. So the output will be

"elephant" is less than "mouse".

A2.2.4 Methods That Are Neither Constructors nor Operators

The following methods are listed in alphabetical order.

12. // Postcondition: the value returned was a pointer to the first item of an array of
      //   size( ) + 1 items, whose first size ( ) items are equal to the
      //   corresponding items of this string and whose last item is a null
      //   character.
   const char* c_str( );

> *Example* In the open method of the ofstream (or ifstream) class, the first argument must be an array of characters representing the name of the file. So we can read in the file name as a string and open the file by using c_str:

> cout << "Enter the name of the file you want to create: ";
> string out_file_name;
> cin >> out_file_name;
> ofstream out_file;
> out_file.open(out_file_name.c_str( ), ios::out);

13. // Precondition: pos <= the number of characters in this string.
   // Postconditon: the substring of this string, starting at index pos and of length
      //   the smaller of n and str.size( ) − n, has been removed from
      //   this string. A reference to this string (after removal of the
      //   substring) has been returned.
   string& erase (**unsigned int** pos = 0, **unsigned int** n = −1);

> *Example* Suppose we have

> string s = "jabberwocky";

> s.erase (5, 3);
> cout << s << endl;

> Then the substring of s that starts at index 5 and is of length 3 is removed from s. So the output will be

"jabbecky"

Note   Regarding the assignment

unsigned int n = −1

in the heading, see the note for constructor 3.

14. // Precondition: The iterator position is positioned at an item in this string.
// Postcondition: The item that was, before this call, in the location where
//   position was positioned has been deleted from this string.
//   Each item that was, before the call, in a location with index >
//   position's index has been moved to the location at the next
//   lower index. The worstTime(n) is O(n).
void erase (iterator position);

>   *Note*   This is virtually the same interface as for the one-parameter
>   erase method in the vector class. In fact, the string class can be viewed
>   as a greatly expanded version of vector<**char**>. And, just as in the vector
>   class, the string class's erase method invalidates iterators beyond the
>   point of erasure.

15. // Postcondition: if, starting at index pos, str occurs as a substring of this string,
//   the index of the starting position of the first such occurrence of
//   str in this string has been returned. Otherwise, −1 has been
//   returned.
int find (**const** string& str, **unsigned int** pos = 0) **const**;

>   *Example*   Suppose we have
>
>   string message = "The snow is now on the ground.",
>   code = "now";
>
>   cout << message.find (code);
>
>   The first occurrence of "now" in the string message starts at index 5
>   (remember to start at index 0), so the output will be
>
>   5
>
>   Suppose we had instead written
>
>   cout << message.find (code, 6);
>
>   The string sought is still "now", but the search begins at index 6. The
>   first occurrence of "now" in the string message from that index is the
>   substring starting at index 12, so the output will be

12

Notice that this index is from the beginning of the string, even though the search started at index 6.

Finally, suppose we had instead written

cout << message.find (code, 14);

Because "now" does not appear in the string message from index 14 on, the output would be −1 interpreted as an **unsigned int** item (see note for constructor 3). For example, if **unsigned int** items occupy 32 bits, the output would be

4294967295

This is not exactly what you would expect! To remedy the situation, we cast to an int item the result returned by the find method:

cout << **int** (message.find (code, 14));

The output will be

−1

16. // Precondition: pos1 <= size( ).
    // Postcondition: the string str has been inserted into this string just before
    //   index pos1, and a reference to this string has been returned.
    string& insert (**unsigned int** pos1, **const** string& str);

Example   Suppose we have

string s = "bed",
       t = "and";

cout << s.insert (1, t) << endl;

Then string t is inserted into string s between the 'b' and the 'e' and s will contain "banded".

17. // Precondition: The iterator position is positioned at a location between the
    //   front and one-beyond-the-back of this string.
    // Postcondition: A copy of x is in the location where the iterator position is
    //   positioned. Each character that was, before the call, in a
    //   location with index > = position's index has been moved to
    //   the location at the next higher index. An iterator positioned at
    //   the newly inserted character has been returned. The
    //   worstTime(n) is O(n).
    iterator insert (iterator position, **const** char x);

Note   This method is virtually identical to the two-parameter insert method in the vector class. All iterators beyond the insertion point are invalidated.

18. // Postcondition: the number of characters in this string has been returned.
unsigned int length( ) **const**;

>*Example*   Suppose that the string objects s2 and s3 have the values
>given in the example for method 16, and we write
>
>cout << s2.length( ) << " " << s3.length( ) << endl;
>
>The output will be
>
>6   3
>
>*Note*   The string class also has a size( ) method, which is equivalent to
>the length( ) method.

19. // Postcondition: if, starting backward from index pos, str occurs as a substring
    //   of this string, the index of the starting position of the last such
    //   occurrence of str in this string has been returned. Otherwise,
    // -1 has been returned.
int rfind (**const** string& str, **unsigned int** pos = -1) **const**;

>*Example*   Suppose we have
>
>string code = "The snow is now on the ground, I know",
>   match = "now";
>
>cout << code.rfind (match) << "**"
>   << code.rfind (match, 22) << "**"
>   << code.rfind (match, 10) << "**"
>   << **int** (code.rfind (match, 3)) << endl;
>
>If we start all the way at the back of the string object code, "now" last
>appears at index 34. If we start from index 22 and work toward the front
>of code, the last occurrence of "now" is at index 12. If we start at index
>10 and work toward the front, the last occurrence of "now" is at index 5.
>If we start at index 3 and work toward the front of code, "now" does not
>appear. So the output is
>
>34**12**5**-1
>
>The reason for the cast to **int** in the last line of the code in this example
>is discussed in the note for the find method—method #15.

20. // Precondition: pos <= size( );
    // Postcondition: The value returned is the substring of this string, starting at
    //   index pos and of length the smaller of n and size( ) $-$ pos.
string substr (**unsigned int** pos = 0, **unsigned int** n = -1) **const**;

Example   Suppose we have

```
string s = "fruits and vegetables";
```

```
cout << s.substr ( ) << endl
     << s.substr (7) << endl
     << s.substr (7, 3);
```

The output will be

```
fuits and vegetables
and vegetables
and
```

Note   Please see the note for constructor 3 for the meaning of

unsigned int n = −1

in the heading of this method.

A2.2.5 A String Processing Program

The following program illustrates several string methods in concert. The program counts the number of occurrences of some target string in a file. The input consists of the name of the file and the target string.

```cpp
#include <string>
#include <fstream>

using namespace std;

int main( )
{
    const string INPUT_PROMPT =
        "Please enter the name of the input file: ";

    const string TARGET_PROMPT =
        "Please enter the target string: ";

    const string RESULT =
        "The number of occurrences of the target string is ";

    const string CLOSE_WINDOW_PROMPT =
        "Please press the Enter key to close this output window.";

    string in_file_name,
        target,
        line;
```

```
ifstream in_file;

int count = 0,
    pos;

cout << INPUT_PROMPT << endl;
cin >>in_file_name;
in_file.open( in_file_name.c_str( ), ios::in );

cout << endl << TARGET_PROMPT << endl;
cin >> target;

while (getline (in_file, line))
{
      pos = line.find (target);
      while (pos != -1)
      {
            count ++;
            line = line.substr (pos + target.length( ));
            pos = line.find (target);
      } // while line still holds a copy of target
} // while file still holds more lines
cout << endl << RESULT << count << endl;

cout << endl << endl << CLOSE_WINDOW_PROMPT;
cin.get( );
return 0;
} // main
```

Note 1   In this program, there is no need to cast to an **int** item the value returned by the find method because that value is immediately assigned to an **int** variable, pos.

Note 2   Could we have used >> to read in each word and then compared that word to the contents of the variable target?

```
string word;
  . . .
while (in_file >> word)
      if (word == target)
            count++;
```

This approach will not detect any occurrences of the target that appear *within* a word. For example, if the target is "count", that string would not be detected in "uncountable" or "accountant".

A2.3 | FIELDS AND IMPLEMENTATION OF THE string CLASS

The class that underlies the string class is basic_string. In effect, there is the following:

typedef basic_string<**char**> string;

The string class is similar to many of the container classes in the Standard Template Library. Here are the common methods:

empty, size, insert, erase, find, begin, end, = , == , !=

The string class and the vector class also have an index operator, **operator**[ ]. In fact, a typical—simplified—design of the string class has three fields that correlate with vector fields:

char* data; // compare to the vector field start

unsigned nchars; // compare to the vector field finish

unsigned capacity; // compare to the vector field end_of_storage

The data field is a pointer to an array whose items are of type **char.** The nchars field holds the number of characters currently in the string. The capacity field holds the current size of the array (pointed to by) data.

For example, suppose we start with

string s;

An array of some fixed size, say 256, is allocated. Figure A2.1 shows the relevant features of memory. If we then assign

s = "yes";

then the effect on the relevant memory locations is shown in Figure A2.2. It is fairly easy to see how most of the string class's method could be implemented with these fields. For example, here is a definition for the substr method, assuming a constructor that returns a string from a pointer (to an array of characters) and an **unsigned int**:

```
string substr (unsigned pos = 0, unsigned n = −1) const
{
        unsigned rlen = n < (length( ) − pos) ? n : (length( ) −pos);
        return string (data + pos, rlen);
} // method substr
```

Figure A2.1 | The design representation of an empty string.

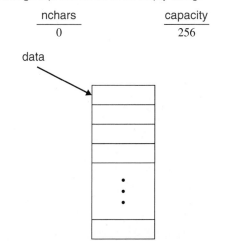

Figure A2.2 | The design representation of an three-character string.

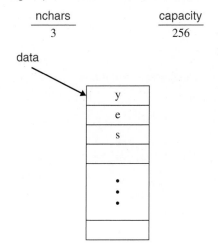

Polymorphism

A3.1 | INTRODUCTION

There are three essential features of object-oriented programming: the *encapsulation* of fields and methods into a single entity, the *inheritance* of a class's fields and methods by subclasses, and polymorphism. *Polymorphism*—from the Greek words for "many" and "shapes"—is the ability of a message to be interpreted differently depending on the run-time type of the object sending the message. For example, in Chapter 1, we created an Employee class with a readInto method and then created a subclass, HourlyEmployee, with a new version of readInto. C++ allows the following:

```
Employee* employeePtr;

employeePtr = new Employee;

// employeePtr points to an object in the Employee class.
. . .

employeePtr -> readInto( );
. . .

employeePtr = new HourlyEmployee;

// Now employeePtr points to an object in the HourlyEmployee class. . . .
employeePtr -> readInto( );
. . .
```

Initially, employeePtr points to an object in the Employee class, so the first message employeePtr -> readInto( ) will read in a name and gross pay. Later, employeePtr points to an object in the HourlyEmployee class, so the second message employeePtr -> readInto( ) will read in a name, hours worked, and pay rate.

This simple example illustrates an important aspect of polymorphism:

> When a message is sent, the version of the method invoked depends on the type of the object, not the type of the pointer.

Specifically, in our example, the version of readInto that is invoked depends on the type of the object—Employee or HourlyEmployee—not on the type of the pointer, which is pointer-to-Employee.

A3.2 | THE IMPORTANCE OF POLYMORPHISM

At this point, you are probably underwhelmed. The example given in Section A3.1 could easily be rewritten to avoid polymorphism, so you may wonder if polymorphism has practical value. The answer is definitely yes. Let's modify the example to illustrate how polymorphism allows code reuse for methods related by inheritance. We will revise the findBestPaid( ) method in the Company class so that the user can select whether to determine the best-paid employee or the best-paid hourly employee. Specifically, the user will be prompted to enter either "Employee" or "Hourly" to indicate what the subsequent input lines will consist of.

```
// Postcondition: The employee or hourly employee with the highest gross
//                pay has been determined. Ties have been ignored.
void Company::findBestPaid( )
{
       string CODE_PROMPT =
"Enter Employee for Employee input or Hourly for hourly employee: ";

       string EMPLOYEE_INPUT = "Employee";

       string HOURLY_EMPLOYEE_INPUT = "Hourly";

       Employee* employeePtr;

       string code;

       cout << endl << CODE_PROMPT;
       cin >> code;
       if (code == EMPLOYEE_INPUT)
             employeePtr = new Employee;
       else if (code == HOURLY_EMPLOYEE_INPUT)
             employeePtr = new HourlyEmployee;

       while (employeePtr -> readInto( ))
             if (employeePtr -> makesMoreThan (bestPaid))
                   bestPaid.getCopyOf (*employeePtr);
} // findBestPaid
```

The beauty of this code is that without rewriting the **while** loop, the findBest-Paid( ) method can now handle either employee input or hourly employee input.

A3.3 | DYNAMIC BINDING

The code in Section A3.2 raises a question: How can the C++ compiler generate the appropriate machine code for a message such as employeePtr -> readInto( )? Another way to ask the same question is this: How can the method identifier read Into be *bound* to the correct version—in Employee or HourlyEmployee—at compile time when the necessary information is not available until run-time? The answer is simple: The binding cannot be done at compile-time, but must be delayed until run-time! A method that is bound to its method identifier at run-time is called a *virtual method.* This delayed binding is also called *dynamic binding* or *late binding.*

Virtual methods exert a run-time cost on projects. At the very least, the compiler cannot *inline* a virtual method. With inlining, a function call is replaced with the code for the function body; this saves execution time because the save-call-restore-return mechanism of ordinary function calls is bypassed. Moreover, for each class with virtual methods, the compiler creates a special table, the VTABLE, to hold the addresses where the virtual-method code is stored. And each object in such a class is given a secret field, the vpointer, which points to the appropriate VTABLE address. The following picture illustrates what happens for the example at the end of Section A3.2:

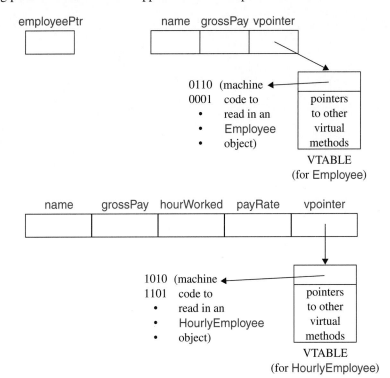

At run-time, employeePtr will point to either an Employee object or an Hourly Employee object, and the appropriate version of readInto will be invoked.

The extra work at run-time with vpointer is necessary for virtual methods, but would be a waste of time for other methods. For the sake of efficiency, each virtual method must be declared as such—with the keyword **virtual**—in the base class header file. So Employee.h would have

> **virtual bool** readInto( );

This single requirement allows the compiler to support late binding for virtual methods and slightly faster code for nonvirtual methods. The downside is that this imposes on the developer of the base class the responsibility for deciding if a method should be virtual without knowing anything about the applications or subclasses! As a consequence of the requirement that a method is virtual only if its base-class version has the keyword **virtual,** overloaded operators cannot be virtual. And so our application of polymorphism would not have worked if, instead of readInto, we had overloaded the insertion operator, **operator**>>.

REFERENCES

A

Accredited Standards Committee X3, INFORMATION PROCESSING SYSTEMS, *Draft Proposed International Standard for Information Systems—Programming Language C++,* Washington, DC, 1997.

ACM/IEEE-CS Joint Curriculum Task Force, *Computing Curricula 1991,* Association for Computing Machinery, New York, 1991.

Adel'son-Vel'skii, G. M., and E. M. Landis, "An Algorithm for the Organization of Information," *Soviet Mathematics,* vol. 3, 1962, pp. 1259–1263.

Albir, S. S., *UML in a Nutshell,* O'Reilly & Associates, Inc., Sebastopol, CA, 1998.

Andersson, A., T. Hagerup, S. Nilsson, and R. Raman, "Sorting in Linear Time?" *Proceedings of the 27th Annual ACM Symposium on the Theory of Computing,* 1995.

B

Bayer, R., "Symmetric Binary B-trees: Data Structure and Maintenance Algorithms," *Acta Informatica,* vol. 1, no. 4, 1972, pp. 290–306.

Bergin, J., *Data Structure Programming with the Standard Template Library in C++,* Springer-Verlag, New York, 1998.

Budd, T., *Data Structures in C++ Using the Standard Template Library,* Addison-Wesley Longman, Reading, MA, 1998.

C

Collins, W. J., *Data Structures and the Java Collections Framework,* McGraw-Hill, New York, 2002.

Cormen, T., C. Leierson, and R. Rivest, *Introduction to Algorithms,* McGraw-Hill, New York, 1992.

D

Dale, N., "If You Were Lost on a Desert Island, What One ADT Would You Like to Have with You?" *Proceedings of the Twenty-First SIGCSE Technical Symposium,* vol. 22, no. 1, 1990, pp. 139–142.

Dijkstra, E. W., "A Note on Two Problems in Connexion with Graphs," *Numerische Mathematick,* vol. 1, 1959, pp. 269–271.

Dijkstra, E. W., *A Discipline of Programming,* Prentice-Hall, Englewood Cliffs, NJ, 1976.

E

Eckel, B., *Thinking in C++,* Prentice-Hall, Englewood Cliffs, NJ, 1995.

G

Gries, D., *Science of Programming,* Springer-Verlag, New York, 1981.

Guibas, L., and R. Sedgewick, "A Diochromatic Framework for Balanced Trees", *Proceedings of the 19th Annual IEEE Symposium on Foundations of Computer Science,* 1978, pp. 8–21.

H

Heileman, G. L., *Data Structures, Algorithms, and Object-Oriented Programming,* McGraw-Hill, New York, 1996.

Hoare, C. A. R., "Quicksort," *Computer Journal,* vol. 5, no. 4, April 1962, pp. 10–15.

Horowitz, E., S. Sahni, and D. Mehta, *Fundamentals of Data Structures in C++,* W. H. Freeman, New York, 1995.

Huffman, D. A., "A Model for the Construction of Minimum Redundancy Codes," *Proceedings of the IRE,* vol. 40, 1952, pp. 1098–1101.

J

Jamsa, K., *Success with C++,* Boyd & Fraser, Danvers, MA, 1995.

K

Knuth, D. E., *The Art of Computer Programming,* vol. 1: Fundamental Algorithms, 2d ed., Addison-Wesley, Reading, MA, 1973. (1)

Knuth, D. E., *The Art of Computer Programming,* vol. 2: *Seminumerical Algorithms,* 2d ed., Addison-Wesley, Reading, MA, 1973. (2)

Knuth, D. E., *The Art of Computer Programming,* Vol. 3: *Sorting and Searching,* Addison-Wesley, Reading, MA, 1973. (3)

Kruse, R. L., *Data Structures and Program Design,* Prentice-Hall, Englewood Cliffs, NJ, 1987.

M

Meyer, B., *Object-oriented Software Construction,* Prentice-Hall International, London, 1988.

Meyers, S., *Effective STL,* Addison-Wesley, Boston, MA, 2001.

Musser, D., and A. Saini, *STL Tutorial and Reference Guide,* Addison-Wesley, Reading, MA, 1996.

N

Nelson, M., *C++ Programmer's Guide to the Standard Template Library,* IDG Books Worldwide, Foster City, CA, 1995.

Noonan, R. E., "An Object-Oriented View of Backtracking," *SIGCSE Bulletin,* vol. 32, no. 1, March 2000, pp. 362–366.

P

Pfleeger, S. L., *Software Engineering: Theory and Practice,* Prentice-Hall, Upper Saddle River, NJ, 1998.

Prim, R. C., "Shortest Connection Networks and Some Generalizations," *Bell System Technical Journal,* vol. 36, 1957, pp. 1389–1401.

R

Rawlins, G. J., *Compared to What? An Introduction to the Analysis of Algorithms,* Computer Science Press, New York, NY, 1992.

Riel, A. J., *Object-Oriented Design Heuristics,* Addison-Wesley, Reading, MA, 1996.

Roberts, S., *Thinking Recursively,* John Wiley & Sons, New York, 1986.

S

Sahni, S., *Data Structures, Algorithms, and Applications in Java,* McGraw-Hill, Burr Ridge, IL, 2000.

Savitch, W., *Problem Solving with C++: The Object of Programming,* 2d edition, Addison-Wesley Longman, Reading, MA, 1999.

Schaffer, R., and R. Sedgewick, "The Analysis of Heapsort," *Journal of Algorithms,* vol. 14, 1993, pp. 76–100.

Shaffer, C., *A Practical Introduction to Data Structures and Algorithm Analysis,* Prentice-Hall, Upper Saddle River, NJ, 1998.

Simmons, G. J., ed., *Contemporary Cryptology: The Science of Information Integrity,* IEEE Press, New York, 1992.

Sommerville, I., *Software Engineering,* 6th ed., Addison-Wesley, Reading, MA, 2001.

Stepanov, A. A., and M. Lee, *The Standard Template Library,* Technical Report HPL-94-34, April 1994, revised July 7, 1995.

W

Wallace, S. P., *Programming Web Graphics,* O'Reilly & Associates, Sebastopol, CA, 1999.

Weiss, M. A., *Data Structures and Problem Solving Using C++,* 2nd ed., Addison-Wesley Longman, Reading, MA, 2000.

Whitehead, A. N., and B. Russell, *Principia Mathematica,* Cambridge University Press, Cambridge, England, 1910 (volume 1), 1912 (volume 2), 1913 (volume 3).

Williams J. W., "Algorithm 232: Heapsort," *Communication of the ACM,* vol. 7, no. 6, 1964, pp. 347–348.

Wirth, N., *Algorithms + Data Structures = Programs,* Prentice-Hall, Englewood Cliffs, NJ, 1976.